THE GUINNESS BOOK
OF
EXPLORERS AND EXPLORATION

General Editor:

Michèle Gavet-Imbert

Editorial Director:

Perrine Cambournac

Preface:

Paul-Emile Victor

Early Voyages: Antiquity

Medieval Adventures

Assomption Vloebergh, historian; Jean-Michel Maman, historian and journalist.

Islamic Travellers

Yannick Yotte, sociologist, lecturer in Islamic art and civilization at the Sorbonne.

South America

Jacqueline Balcells, Chilean author and journalist, in collaboration with Gustavo Boldrini (La Conquista); Sophie Banet, historian and journalist (from the 17th century to the present).

North America

Philippe Jacquin, professor of history at the University of Lyons III, specialist in American Indians and the colonization of North America.

Oceans and the Antipodes

François Bellec, director of the French National Naval Museum, member of the Naval Academy of Portugal.

Asia

Guy Deleury, specialist in the mythology, religions, and literature of India.

Africa

Perrine Cambournac, author.

The Poles

Benjamin Lambert, author.

Mountains and Oceans, Caves and Volcanoes

Sophie Banet, historian and journalist; Benjamin Lambert

Space

Hubert Desrues, journalist and lecturer.

Translation

Sheila Mooney
Sogedicom Traductions

Editor for the English edition

Pia Clévenot

THE GUINNESS BOOK
OF
EXPLORERS AND EXPLORATION

General Editor

Michèle Gavet-Imbert

Published in Great Britain by
Guinness Publishing Ltd.,
33 London Road, Enfield, Middlesex

"Guinness" is a registered trademark of
Guinness Publishing Ltd.

First published 1991
Reprint 10 9 8 7 6 5 4 3 2 1 0
Copyright © 1991 by Compagnie 1212 SA

ISBN 0-85112-973-0

A catalogue record for this book is available
from the British Library.

This book was designed and produced by
Compagnie 1212 SA,
210 rue du Faubourg Saint-Antoine,
75012 Paris, France

Typeset in France by Optigraphic, Paris, France
Colour separation by Eurésys, Baisieux, France
Printed and bound in Italy by Amilcare Pizzi S.p.A.

EXPLORATION AND ADVENTURE

Exploration and adventure are not at all the same thing. While an explorer is invariably an adventurer (in the noblest sense of the word), an adventurer is an explorer only in certain instances.

Exploration is a profession; it is a vocation; it is an abiding passion. The search for adventure, though neither a profession nor a hobby, is also a vocation of sorts, and is certainly a passion.

Over time, the meaning of the word 'explorer' has naturally evolved. One dictionary defines it this way: 'a person who travels to or into an unknown or unfamiliar region'; now, does that mean that the hippies who some years ago swarmed into the valley of Katmandu deserve to be called 'explorers'? For Nepal was unknown to them, and, at the time, unfamiliar to the world at large…

According to another dictionary, an explorer is someone who 'investigates a far-off or unfamiliar land'. Perhaps that's a little closer. But what does the word 'explore' signify today? Does it mean to visit a land and study it closely? In that case, ought a modern-day ethnologist who sets out to study the Eskimos of Ammassalik, discovered in 1885, and whom my colleagues and I studied closely (and very carefully!), be considered an explorer? Not in my opinion.

Dictionaries state that to explore is to 'penetrate into and range over an unfamiliar area or region for purposes of scientific or geographical discovery'. That is a perfectly acceptable definition. But allow me to suggest the following nuance: in a historical context, to explore should mean 'to set out to discover an unknown or little-known region or country'; whereas today, to explore means 'to carry out scientific research by applying the techniques of exploration'.

Perhaps it would be useful to define a set of criteria that would give us a better grasp of these words and their meanings. A speleologist who leads a team for the first time into a previously unknown cave is performing an act of exploration. He is indeed an explorer. A glaciologist who takes ice samples on the Antarctic icecap at 3,000 metres above sea level, 1,000 miles from his base (where temperatures even in summer average around -50 °C, at Dome C Concorde), is also, in the true sense of the word, an explorer. But a biologist studying birds near a comfortable base (the Dumont d'Urville base in Adélie Land for example), is not, in my estimation, an explorer. Nor is a photographer who navigates up the Amazon River, even though he withstands considerable hardship in order to take his pictures. A film maker who travels to a remote region of the Marquesas Islands to shoot a film is not an explorer. Nor can a sportsman who descends the Nile in a kayak from the river's source to its delta (a course already covered, though never before in a kayak) claim to be an explorer.

And yet the distinction is less clear than these examples may make it seem. My friends who took part in the Transantarctica exploit, crossing the widest part of Antarctica (6,500 kilometres in seven months), deserve to be called explorers. An ethnologist who spends a year among New Guinea tribesmen briefly described by a passing traveller but otherwise unknown to the outside world, is indeed an explorer. And biologists who work in the canopy of the tropical forest, living on a 'raft' dropped into the treetops by a small dirigible, are rightly called explorers as well.

As for myself, I have twice made what I would call real explorations (forays, that is, into unknown regions). At the end of my second Arctic winter (1936-1937) I explored the hinterland of Ammassalik (the eastern coast of Greenland), a region as mountainous as the Alps, completely unknown at the time, for which there were virtually no maps.

A quarter of a century later, in January 1962, since ice conditions were favourable, I covered the entire coast of Adélie Land aboard the Magga Dan. *These shores were wholly unknown. And my companions on the early expeditions in Adélie Land (André F. Liotard 1949-1951; Mario Marret 1952-1953) who explored and first mapped part of the coastline can be considered real explorers too.*

To sum up, I've put together a list of the qualities that successful explorers—or adventurers, for that matter—must possess:

- *a bold, enterprising spirit*

- *a keen, inquiring mind*

- *the firm conviction that there are no problems, only solutions*

- *the self-control to remain calm in any and every situation*

- *a resilient sense of humour*

- *sufficient perspective never to take themselves too seriously, but to regard their work as serious business*

- *the ability to abandon personal pride, and even self-respect*

- *an inexhaustible supply of super-human patience*

- *the ability to tolerate vile smells, an iron stomach (and equally hardy intestines and liver), perfect teeth, a strong back, legs and feet*

- *a penetrating, eagle eye, always on the lookout*

- *unshakeable enthusiasm and optimism, and above all, the moral fortitude to hang on, and hang in: as my friends the high mountain guides in Chamonix say, Crapena!*

Paul-Émile Victor

CONTENTS

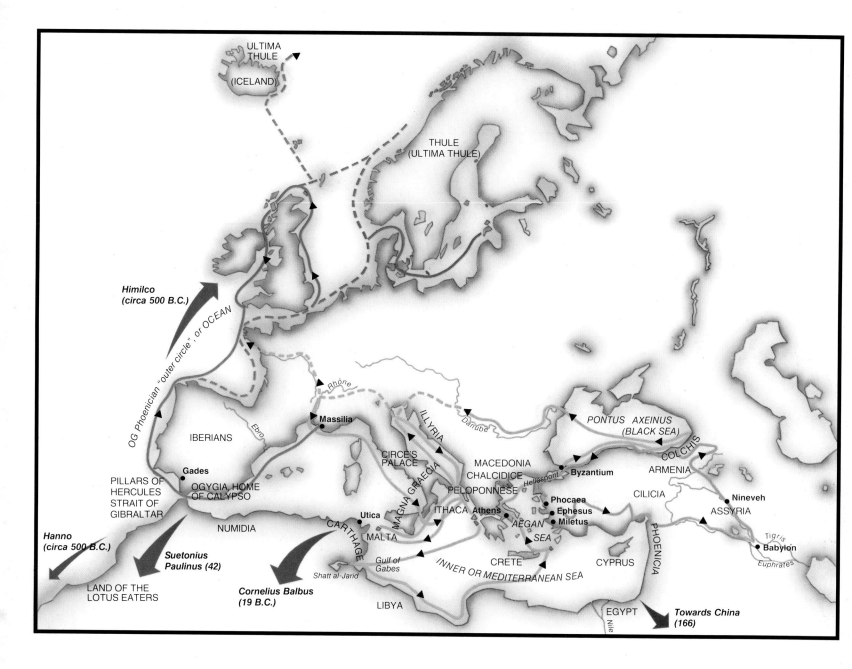

ULTIMA
THULE

(ICELAND)

THULE
(ULTIMA THULE)

Himilco
(circa 500 B.C.)

OG Phoenician "outer circle", or OCEAN

Rhône

Massilia

IBERIANS

Ebro

ILLYRIA

CIRCE'S
PALACE

Danube

PONTUS AXEINUS
(BLACK SEA)

COLCHIS

MACEDONIA
CHALCIDICE

Byzantium

ARMENIA

Gades

PILLARS OF
HERCULES
STRAIT OF
GIBRALTAR

OGYGIA, HOME
OF CALYPSO

MAGNA GRAECIA

PELOPONNESE

Hellespont

Phocaea
Ephesus
Miletus

CILICIA

Nineveh

ASSYRIA

ITHACA Athens

Hanno
(circa 500 B.C.)

NUMIDIA

Suetonius
Paulinus (42)

Utica

CARTHAGE

MALTA

AEGAN
SEA

PHOENICIA

Tigris

Babylon

Euphrates

CYPRUS

Cornelius Balbus
(19 B.C.)

Shatt al-Jarid

Gulf of
Gabes

INNER OR MEDITERRANEAN SEA

CRETE

LAND OF THE
LOTUS EATERS

LIBYA

EGYPT

Nile

Towards China
(166)

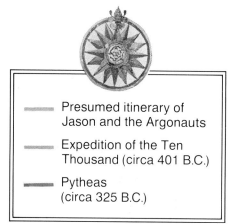

Presumed itinerary of
Jason and the Argonauts

Expedition of the Ten
Thousand (circa 401 B.C.)

Pytheas
(circa 325 B.C.)

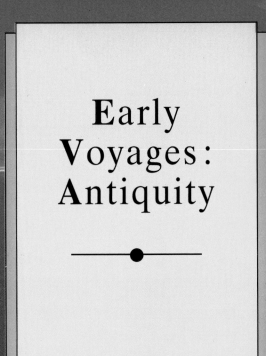

Early
Voyages:
Antiquity

Even in prehistory man was an explorer. What motivated him to seek new lands was not intellectual curiosity, but the far more basic needs for food and shelter. Primitive man migrated sporadically, and his wanderings had no particular order. But in Antiquity, with the development of civilizations in the Mediterranean, humanity passed from the migratory stage to the colonial stage; from random drifting to exploration.

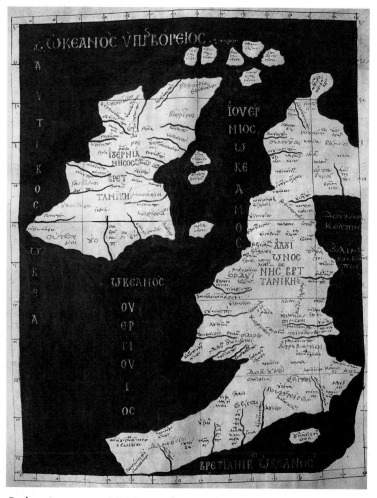

Ptolemy's maps—originating in the second century AD—were published in the fifteenth century by a group of German cartographers working in Lorraine. This particular map shows Great Britain and Ireland.

From migration to colonization

Of course any explorer is limited by the means of transport at his disposal. Before the third millennium BC, he could travel only so far as his feet would carry him. Then the domestication of horses—first accomplished in Asia—and the use of the wheel pushed back the frontiers of the unknown; once unfamiliar lands were made accessible thanks to roads and milestones that marked specific routes. Early seafarers in small, crude boats could not venture far from shore. But with time, sailors learned to use astronomy to guide them farther out to sea in larger, more reliable ships. By the second millennium BC Minoan and Mycenaean navigators plied the Mediterranean from Spain to Egypt. Still later, with the advance of navigational techniques, Phoenicians and Greeks turned their explorations to profit by opening up maritime trade routes.

The Greek *Oikoumene*: empirical knowledge

Greek colonization of foreign territories began around 800 BC. As sea routes became safer, commercial exchanges stabilized; trading posts grew into towns. Gradually the Mediterranean basin was settled and populated. The Greeks called it the *oikoumene*, or inhabited world, which they first equated with the earth itself. Approximately speaking, in the sixth century BC the *oikoumene* comprised the entire Mediterranean basin from Spain to the Pontus Euxinus or Black Sea. Still, some gaps remained. Part of the African coast between Cyrene and Carthage was unex-plored; Illyrian pirates discouraged mariners from venturing north of Epidamnus on the eastern Adriatic; and much of the eastern Italian mainland, locked behind the formidable barrier of the Apennines, was unfamiliar territory. Largely unexplored too were the often dangerous inland regions...

The first map of the world: Anaximander of Miletus

The systematic study of geography did not exist as such before the sixth century BC. Travellers and explorers only possessed disparate information gleaned from personal experiences. Few written vestiges remain: some Egyptian papyrus fragments dating from the thirteenth century BC display a crude map indicating important itineraries, such as one leading to the gold mines of Nubia. More often, in fact, information concerning maritime routes was transmitted orally, through vague stories that often included a dose of the fantastic—word-of-mouth accounts shared by navigators and traders, or reports of hazy, shifting landmarks. Nothing permanent, in any case, no systematic record of acquired knowledge.

The Ionian school, in Miletus, was home to the 'physicists', Greek philosophers essentially concerned with the observation of nature. It is to them we owe the first map, and indeed the science of geography. Anaximander of Miletus (610-547 BC) drew the first complete and coherent map of all the lands then known. It pictured the Mediterranean, surrounded by Europe, Libya (Africa), and Asia. But the Asian territories did not extend very far. They were merely narrow bands of land bounded by a great expanse of water: the River Oceanus (from the Phoenician word 'og', outer circle), believed to encircle the earth, and feed all rivers, lakes, and inland seas.

An eighteenth-century porcelain figurine of the giant Atlas who in Greek myth carried the Earth on his shoulders.

Explorers and geographers:
autopsia

Late in the fourth century BC, Alexander's expedition (see p. 20), the return of Nearchus (see p. 21), and the strange journey of Pytheas (see p. 15) widened still further the horizons of the known world. Explorers visited Ethiopia and India, progressing as far as the Ganges. It was a golden age for descriptive geography. Polybius (208-126 BC) gave the first accounts of Italy, Gaul, and Spain. Agatarchides (190-105 BC) roamed the Persian Gulf, pushed on to Nubia and the Sudan, and wrote a treatise *On the Red Sea*. Posidonius (135-50 BC) confined himself to Europe, endeavouring to define geographic zones according to races and climates. His history of the period 146-88 BC filled 52 volumes and was a storehouse of knowledge. One must remember that these 'descriptive geographers' were a conscientious lot, who scrupulously limited their 'autopsies' of the earth to places they had actually seen (from the Greek *autopsia*, 'seeing with one's own eyes'). They were not only scholars, therefore, but explorers in the truest sense.

Strabo: continuing
the tradition

Rome's conquest of the world provided an ever-widening field of study, yet the pursuit of geography as a branch of learning suffered a marked decline in the first centuries AD. Roman geographers reverted to a purely pragmatic conception of their discipline. They confined themselves to noting, without commentary, the names of cities, nations, regions, and to measuring distances and mentioning features of the terrain. Some simply compiled information from earlier works.

Under the Roman emperor Augustus, the Greek historian Strabo (58 BC-25 AD) renewed the tradition of descriptive geography. In his *Geographica* he attempted to create a universal geography. The first two books of his seventeen-volume work form a general outline of his methods and sources. The rest contain descriptions of the regions he visited. Strabo gave the earth's measurements, defined the limits of the *oikoumene* (Spain and India horizontally, Ireland and the southern Sudan vertically). Above all, he defined 'climates', which are in fact latitudinal bands or parallels. His was a first draft, so to speak, of Ptolemy's system.

Eratosthenes measures
the Earth

Eratosthenes (284-192 BC), a Greek scholar of the Alexandrian school, first measured the earth's circumference, using a simple and ingenious method. At Syene (present-day Aswan) the sun shone into a well, casting no shadow; it was therefore at its zenith. Eratosthenes measured at that same moment the shadow of an obelisk in Alexandria, and calculated the angle of the sun. It was a bit more than seven degrees, or one-fiftieth of the circumference. Now, the distance between Syene and Alexandria was known to be five thousand stadia (one stadium equals 607 feet). Eratosthenes reasoned that the circumference of the earth was fifty times five thousand, or 250,000 stadia, a figure less than ten percent off the actual mark!

Ptolemy: the sum of
geographical knowledge

Claudius Ptolemaeus, an Alexandrian astronomer of the second century AD, carried on the Greek scientific tradition, which he recapitulated in his comprehensive *Grand Collection (Almagest* in Arabic), and in his *Geography*. These works, considered authoritative until the Renaissance, expounded the geocentric theory in minute detail: the earth was well and truly the centre of the universe. Ptolemy's most important contribution was to have been the first to lay out the golden rules of cartography. He introduced latitudes and longitudes, and was thus able to calculate the position of nearly nine thousand sites. He was the first to orientate his maps with the north uppermost and the east on the right.

A flat world or a round one?

The general outline of Anaximander's map did not differ very much from the one Homer described as embossed on Achilles' shield. But in Homer's day, the world was thought to be flat—either rectangular or circular, depending on the mind imagining it. Anaximander was the first to attribute depth to the earth, which, he speculated, had the shape of a drum, and was freely suspended in space. Shortly after Anaximander's time, Parmenides of Elea (born 515 BC) affirmed that the earth was a sphere.

That theory did not convince the philosophers of the Ionian school. Not until Plato's era (428-348 BC) did the notion of the earth as a globe gain any acceptance. Plato considered the earth to be immobile, the pivot for the entire universe—a geocentric view that magnified humanity's importance in the scheme of things. Aristotle, Posidonius, Hipparchus and many other philosophers heartily approved this flattering conception. But some, like Herodotus, held to the 'flat earth' theory. The astronomer Aristarchus of Samos (310 BC) alone suggested that the earth might in fact orbit around the sun.

Hecataeus and Herodotus:
descriptive geography

The first geographical treatise was the work of Hecataeus of Miletus (520 BC). In his *Circuit of the World* he enumerated and briefly described cities, sites and regions with which he was familiar. A century later, in his *Histories*, Herodotus criticized his predecessor's work, and with it the school of Ionian geography. Herodotus held that the earth was flat, but he did not subscribe to the belief that the ocean surrounded it. On the contrary, he stated that Asia and Africa extended beyond the territories already explored. Yet Herodotus uncritically lent credence to such unlikely legends as the existence in Arabia of winged serpents, Cyclopes, and six-kneed camels.

A s the link between Europe, Asia, and Africa, the Mediterranean was the ancient world's most vital channel of communications. Its waters carried people and merchandise to foreign lands, and with them diverse customs, beliefs, and information. Commercial competition and the thirst for conquest incited navigators to venture forth from the Mediterranean to explore the wide, wild ocean beyond the Strait of Gibraltar and the Pillars of Hercules.

Reconstruction of a Greek trireme, a form of galley.

Triremes and Galleys

Heavy, bulky and slow, merchant vessels were propelled mostly by sail. In contrast, the galleys—long, slender, swift warships—were driven by oar. Their bows were armed with a sort of ram (an *embolon*), which could sink enemy ships. Late in the seventh century BC, Aminocles of Corinth invented the first trireme, a galley powered both by a sail and by three banks of oars. Galleys and triremes were quickly adopted throughout the Mediterranean, notably by the Romans.

14

Cargoes of ivory

A seafaring, trading nation, the Minoans of ancient Crete laid the foundations of their powerful maritime empire as early as the third millennium BC. In those remote times roving the seas was a hazardous business, for sailors had to fend off pirates, and steer their course without benefit of maps or navigational instruments. Thus most ships did not stray far from shore, for land remained the sole reliable means of ascertaining a position. These vessels—which, like the Egyptian boats on which they were modelled, had no decks—were unable to tack when strong gales arose; rudders were just heavy sculls unfit for delicate manoeuvring. Nev-

ertheless, the Minoans ventured out to sea to export their surplus produce—wine, grapes, oil, olives—as well as arms, bronzes, and the famous Kamares pottery. They returned to Crete with cargoes of ivory, alabaster and precious metals purchased in Egypt or Mesopotamia. Royal archives and paintings discovered at Mari (Syria), in the Palace of the Princes, attest to exchanges between that city and Crete.

Copper came from Cyprus, where deposits were so abundant that the island gave its name to that metal: *cyprium aes*, or Cypriot bronze. In 1550 BC the two island peoples initiated an important trade relationship: Minoans distributed Cypriot products all over the eastern Mediterranean, while Cypriots purchased Syrian and Egyptian jewellery and art objects from Crete.

Mycenaean expeditions

Although they lived for a long while under Minoan domination, the Mycenaeans of mainland Greece were ultimately able to seize Crete. The takeover followed the rapid decline of the Minoans, possibly hastened by the destruction wrought by tidal waves following the eruption around 1500 BC of the volcanic island of Santorini to the north. Once they were masters of Greece and Crete, the Mycenaeans set out to conquer the Mediterranean. In the fourteenth century BC they settled on Cyprus, creating commercial and political colonies called *achaies*, which gave the Mycenaeans access to Asia. To the west, their influence extended as far as the Iberian coast, as is indicated by the discovery of numerous Aegean objects in the western Mediterranean. It may be, however, that the goods were brought there from Sicily by local sailors. On the other hand, the Mycenaeans may have succeeded, well before the Phoenicians, in reaching the Pillars of Hercules.

Seafaring middlemen

Originating in cities such as Tyre, Sidon and Byblos on the Levantine coast, the Phoenicians enjoyed a period of great prosperity that began in the twelfth century BC. For these sea-loving traders the Mediterranean was a second home. They roved its waters in search of new merchandise to peddle from port to port along the eastern Mediterranean basin. As middlemen, the Phoenicians also exported their native goods: Tyrian purple (which they invented), dyed cloth, and especially the cedar and pine timber needed to build ships.

Late in the second millennium BC, hurt by Greek and Egyptian competition, the

Phoenicians undertook exploratory voyages to the western Mediterranean. Their wanderings brought them to the coasts of Africa, where they traded with Sudanese caravans. Ports sprang up at short intervals along the seacoast. Around 1100 BC the Phoenicians founded Utica in the Gulf of Tunis, followed by Carthage in 814 BC. Still later they reached Tarsis in southern Spain, with its rich mineral deposits, where the city of Gades (present-day Cadiz) grew up. Phoenician vessels still tended to navigate close to shore, but pilots had learned to observe the sky, and were thus guided by *Phoinike*, the Phoenician or Pole Star. Thanks to copper-lined hulls, their boats had acquired greater solidity. When swiftness was wanted, the sailors preferred galleys; equipped with a sail and a double bank of oars, these vessels were the forerunners of the trireme. The Phoenicians adorned their prows with a painted red horse, symbol of swiftness.

To the open ocean

In the sixth century BC Carthage shook off the yoke of Tyre, its Phoenician mother city, and grew into a powerful, independent city-state. Carthage jealously defended its commercial monopoly in the Mediterranean, which stretched from Libya to the Strait of Gibraltar. Aboard small vessels powered with oars and a trapezoidal sail, the Carthaginians launched their conquest of foreign lands, establishing trading posts in North Africa, Spain, and Sicily. In addition to their skill as seamen, which they inherited from the Phoenicians, the Carthaginians were also shrewd enough to keep their maritime routes secret. They did not hesitate, for example, to sink 'spy ships' on the spot. It is said that one of their vessels deliberately scuppered itself rather than reveal its itinerary to a Greek ship following it.

Having blocked the Strait of Gibraltar to foreign fleets, the Carthaginians were the first people to embark on the Atlantic Ocean. In the sixth century BC a general called Hanno sailed along the coast of West Africa, while another general, Himilco, was the first recorded voyager in the northern Atlantic. In the fifth century BC, he reached the Cassiterides Islands (probably the Scilly Isles), where tin was plentiful. Himilco was startled to observe that the inhabitants took to sea in small craft 'made simply from skins sewn together, a wonderful thing'. The Carthaginian general pursued his course as far as the Sacred Isle (Ireland), inhabited by Hibernians, before reaching the Isle of Albions (Britain).

Bas-relief of a Phoenician merchant ship from a second-century BC sarcophagus from Sidon.

East meets West

The Ionian cities of Asia Minor founded by Greek refugees between the twelfth and eleventh centuries BC were a crossroads for East and West. Miletus, a city thoroughly imbued with Oriental influence, as were Ephesus and Phocaea, contributed to the Hellenization of its neighbours. Two principal inland routes were opened up in Asia: the southern route, from Miletus, and the Royal Road, which linked the Gulf of Smyrna to Nineveh, on the River Tigris. Greek colonies were established along the shores of the Black Sea, and along the Adriatic. Once they reached Sicily and southern Italy, the Ionians laid the foundations of what would later be known as Magna Graecia. The Phocaeans explored the coasts of Spain and Gaul. In the sixth century BC they founded the little town of Massalia, the future Marseilles. As it prospered, the settlement formed offshoots of its own, creating new outposts in Arles and Nice, as well as on the Spanish littoral.

The voyage of Pytheas

The northern seas were discovered in the fourth century BC by a native of Marseilles, an astronomer called Pytheas. After he sailed up the coasts of Spain, Lusitania (modern-day Portugal) and Gaul, Pytheas steered out towards English and Scottish waters, and ultimately fetched up on the island of Thule. If we are to credit his account of the journey, *Description of the Ocean*, Thule may well have been Norway or Iceland. There Pytheas witnessed what may have been a thick fog or, more probably, ice forming on the sea; he described what he saw as 'jellyfish', for the notion of a frozen sea was utterly foreign to a man from the Mediterranean. On a second expedition, it appears he may have pushed as far as the Baltic Sea, to the mouth of a river that may have been the Vistula. Yet his exact itinerary remains unclear. A brilliant astronomer, Pytheas was also the first to note the relation between the tides and the phases of the moon.

The Pillars of Hercules

In Antiquity the Pillars of Hercules was the name given to the two promontories on either side of the Strait of Gibraltar: the Rock of Gibraltar in Europe, and the Jebel Musa in Africa. Legend has it that Hercules, journeying to the confines of the Occident to abduct the red cattle of Geryon, lifted up the ends of the earth at the close of his expedition. For a long time the Greeks considered the spot to be the farthest habitable place on earth. Horrible monsters were said to await any sailor foolhardy enough to cross the strait.

E *gyptians first explored the African interior in the third millennium BC. They launched expeditions on the Red Sea and across the desert that took them as far as Somalia and the Sudan. Later, intrepid sailors attempted to circumnavigate the African continent, while the Greeks, for their part, pushed ever farther into Asia, towards the Caspian Sea and India.*

The Ra II *on its transatlantic crossing, in 1970.*

Did the Egyptians discover America?

That at least is the theory put forward by Norwegian anthropologist Thor Heyerdahl. To prove that the ancient Egyptians could have crossed the Atlantic, Heyerdahl—who in 1947 sailed from Peru to Polynesia aboard the *Kon Tiki*—built a raft of papyrus reeds tied with rope, not unlike ancient Egyptian crafts. In 1969 he succeeded in covering five thousand kilometres on the *Ra I*, before running into trouble nine hundred kilometres east of Barbados. Heyerdahl set out the following year on the *Ra II*, and landed on Barbados after a fifty-seven-day voyage that covered 6,270 kilometres.   16

The land of incense

The mysterious country called Punt, 'land of incense', was already known to the Egyptians of the fifth dynasty (around 2500 BC). Rock inscriptions in the tomb of Pharaoh Sahure at Abū Sir (Cairo) represent Egyptian ships sailing on the Red Sea to a far-off shore—the modern Somalian coast. To reach Punt, Egyptian vessels—large, flat-bottomed craft with upturned prow and stern, powered by oars and a single sail—traversed canals connecting the Bitter Lakes, crossed the Gulf of Suez, and sailed along the Ethiopian coast. There Egyptian crews discovered a dark-skinned people who wore their hair in narrow braids and who lived in huts built on pilings. These natives welcomed the strangers cordially, and they exchanged offerings.

The Egyptians returned from this expedition with gold, ivory, fragrant balms, and incense destined for the gods. But before they sailed back home, the Egyptian vessels visited the Arabian coast that faces Somalia, to try to barter with the inhabitants. When the sailors finally returned to Egypt, triumphantly displaying their rich cargo, the pharaoh bestowed upon the fleet's captain the title of 'royal cousin'.

A story graven in stone

Much later, under the eighteenth dynasty, Queen Hatshepsut (1490-1468 BC) sent a fleet of five ships and 250 sailors to Punt with gifts for the inhabitants, and instructions to return with a full cargo of rich goods. In exchange for the glass beads and jewellery sent by the Egyptian queen, the Puntian chief, Parihou, offered elephant tusks, myrrh, panther skins, and thirty-one incense trees to be transplanted in Egypt. Every detail of this voyage is faithfully related on the wall of Hatshepsut's funerary temple at Dayr al-Bahrī, a veritable logbook of the expedition.

Across desert sands

An overland route had also been opened up around 2130 BC (during the eleventh dynasty) by Hannu, who had been commanded by the pharaoh to purchase incense and to 'spread fear of His Majesty'. Hannu set off, journeying sometimes on land, sometimes by sea. Accompanied by three thousand soldiers, Hannu departed from Coptos, a city situated on the Nile north of Thebes, and headed southeast. Scouts were sent ahead, and the expedition followed, crossing the desert where reservoirs had been dug. When the men finally reached the coast, Hannu had a ship built to take him to Punt. There he purchased the much-prized incense and many other exotic goods before returning by boat and on foot to Coptos.

Nearly a thousand years later, Ramses III (1184-1153 BC) put Hannu's route to good use; in his reign, travellers to the Land of Incense journeyed both by boat and by caravan. Ramses III probably exploited the gold mines of Nubia (Cush) and the copper mines at Sinai.

Pushing southward

Of all the African explorers, Hirkhouf is surely the most ancient on record. He lived under the sixth dynasty (circa 2420-2280), and inscriptions carved in Hirkhouf's tomb allude to three journeys into the land of Cush (Nubia). To carry out these distant explorations, all the supplies needed to survive in the wilderness—waterskins, bread, clothing and the barley beer favoured by the ancient Egyptians—were transported on the backs of men and donkeys. From his third expedition Hirkhouf brought back a Pygmy 'who could dance the dance of god' for the pharaoh, Pepi II.

Sinuhe, Man of the Desert

No Egyptian would venture into the fascinating, fearsome desert without taking ample precautions: it was, after all, the realm of serpents, wild animals, and mortal thirst—and woe to the traveller who wandered off beaten trails. And yet it was into these arid regions that Sinuhe, courtier of Amenemhet I (1991-1962 BC), fled upon the pharaoh's sudden death. Afraid he had been compromised in some murky intrigue surrounding the royal succession, Sinuhe quickly left Egypt. He intended to travel southward but was blown to the north while crossing the Nile. He then passed through the marshy lands of the Nile Delta, reached the Bitter Lakes, crossed the Isthmus of Suez, and forged on into the desert to escape the vengeance of the new pharaoh, Sesostris I. But another equally deadly enemy lay in wait: thirst. No source of water was in sight, yet Sinuhe had exhausted the meager supply he had brought with him in his precipitate flight. He owed his survival to a band of Bedouins who discovered him lying half-dead on the sand. The nomads carried him back to their camp, where the fugitive gradually recovered his strength. Sinuhe thenceforth shared his saviours' way of life; he fought and worked side by side with them. Soon the desert held no secrets for him; he had become a real Bedouin. He married and had children and ultimately rose to the rank of tribal chief. Yet homesickness gnawed at Sinuhe's heart. When he learned that Sesostris I had pardoned him, he abandoned his nomadic life and journeyed to the frontier outpost at the Roads of Horus. He completed the journey by boat, arriving at the royal residence of Itj-Tawi, south of Memphis. Still dressed as a Bedouin, Sinuhe made quite an impression when he entered the palace. No one recognized him, but after hearing the story of his remarkable adventures, and as a sign of his royal pardon, Sesostris covered him with honours and riches.

The voyage of Necho II

To make the passage from the Nile Delta to the Red Sea faster and easier, the pharaohs of the twelfth dynasty (1991-1786 BC) had already considered digging a canal along the lines of the Suez Canal, constructed some thirty-eight centuries later. Pharaoh Sesostris I initiated the project, which he may in fact have seen accomplished. Sesostris extended the Egyptian empire to Lybia,

Nubia and several oases in the Western Desert. It is known that between the sixteenth and thirteenth centuries BC the Nile and the Bitter Lakes were indeed linked by a canal. Around 600 BC Necho II decided to dredge and widen the waterway. But after 120,000 men had died at the task, an oracle advised that the project be abandoned.

Necho nevertheless harboured vast maritime and commercial ambitions. He commanded a Phoenician fleet (for Phoenicia was then under Egyptian rule) to circumnavigate Africa, starting from the Red Sea. Their voyage lasted three years. The navigators declared that they 'had seen the sun rise first on their left, then on their right', and that the fleet had sailed completely around the African continent. The Greek historian Herodotus faithfully reported what was by then a settled tradition; yet he voiced some doubts that such an exploit had actually been accomplished.

From Carthage to the Gulf of Guinea

A century later Hanno, a Carthaginian general, undertook to sail around Africa. He was instructed to explore the coastline and establish colonies along the way. Setting out from Carthage with a fleet of sixty ships and 30,000 colonists, he steered west and

crossed the Strait of Gibraltar. Hanno continued to follow the African coast to the Gulf of Guinea. A shortage of supplies compelled the Carthaginian to turn back, although he did succeed in founding several African colonies.

The enigma of the Caspian Sea

The first Greeks to have discovered the Caspian Sea were soldiers from the army of Alexander the Great (see p. 20). The men were convinced that the shores before them were simply an extension of the Sea of Azov, a bay of the Black Sea. Alexander ordered Heracleides to explore the region, to ascertain if the Caspian was a lake, or if it was part of the northern ocean.

Some years later, Alexander's lieutenant, Seleucus Nicator (354-280 BC), founder of the Greek Seleucid dynasty, revived the project. An energetic ruler, he instructed Patrocles to unravel the enigma of the Caspian Sea. He also hoped to discover new trade routes to northern India. After a reconnaissance expedition (and relying on more-or-less correctly interpreted information), Patrocles concluded that the mysterious sea was in fact a gulf of the northern ocean. Another officer, Meghastenes, explored the Ganges River.

(see p. 20)

On the brink of the Cape of Good Hope

Among the many voyages of discovery attempted under the Ptolemies—the Greek dynasty that ruled Egypt (305-31 BC)—the boldest was the expedition led by Eudoxus of Cyzicus. A merchant with a taste for exploration, Eudoxus travelled first to India, then undertook to sail unaccompanied along the coast of Africa. Not far beyond the Strait of Gibraltar, his ship foundered. Undaunted, Eudoxus built a raft and pursued his voyage to the continent's southern reaches. But the unfortunate Eudoxus made the mistake of turning back too soon, before he had reached the eastern coast of Africa.

Detail of the account of Hatshepsut's expedition to Punt. The queen is preceded by her husband.

F or generations Homer's Iliad *and* Odyssey *were regarded as mythical epics—until one day in 1868 when, owing to the unflagging efforts of German archaeologist Heinrich Schliemann, excavations were undertaken that ultimately revealed the ruins of ancient Troy. How much actual information lies hidden behind the mythical tales passed down to us from Antiquity?*

Odysseus lashed to the ship's mast, listening to the enchanting song of the Sirens.

'To the Sirens first shalt thou come, who beguile all men whosoever comes to them. Whoso in ignorance draws near to them and hears the Sirens' voice, he nevermore returns, that his wife and little children may stand at his side rejoicing, but the Sirens beguile him with their clear-toned song, as they sit in a meadow, and about them is a great heap of bones of mouldering men, and round the bones the skin is shrivelling. But do thou row past them...'
Odyssey, **XII 42-51.**

Real and present dangers

The Trojan War is generally admitted to be a matter of historical fact; but can the same be said of Odysseus' fabled voyages? Homer tells that after defeating the Trojans, the Greek hero wandered the seas for many years before returning to his native kingdom of Ithaca. These rovings over Mediterranean waters are related in minute detail in the *Odyssey*, the greatest sea adventure story ever told. First cast up on the beaches of Libya in the land of the Lotus Eaters, Odysseus and his comrades were later threatened by the Cyclops in Sicily, and subjugated by Circe's evil spells on the island of Aeaea. All but Odysseus finally perished in a tempest unleashed by an angry Zeus; the unfortunate hero ultimately landed on Ogygia, island home of the nymph Calypso, who held Odysseus prisoner for seven years. These epic adventures adroitly combine fact and sailors' lore. Inspired by the oral tradition, the epic dramatizes dangers that all seafaring men fear: storms, reefs, forbidding shores. The *Odyssey* probably incorporates a certain number of legends destined, in those times of intense maritime rivalry, to frighten off would-be competitors and warn them away from valued ports. The Phoenicians, then masters of the western Mediterranean, occupy an important place in Homer's story. Indeed, it would have suited their purpose to credit the poet's terrifying tales, and thus rid themselves of troublesome rivals.

On the trail of Odysseus

The Greeks situated the kingdom of Circe near the Tyrrhenian coast. The Romans identified her domain with present-day Monte Circello, south of Rome. As for Ogygia, the realm of Calypso, it is said to correspond to Ceuta, a Moroccan seaport facing Gibraltar. According to the Latin poet Ovid, the fearsome Sirens inhabited the small rocky islands scattered between Capri and the Italian mainland, the Sirenusi. The cries of seabirds that perch on these rocks, which are nearly covered by water, may explain how the legend took root. The birds' cries signalled the presence of reefs, a sailor's mortal enemy. Another tradition relates that the Sirens lived in the Strait of Messina, site of the perilous rock, Scylla, and the equally dangerous whirlpool, Charybdis. Greek mythology tells how Charybdis, daughter of the sea god Poseidon and the Earth, was transformed by Zeus's thunderbolt into a whirlpool: in Homer's words, 'thrice a day she belches it forth, and thrice she sucks it down terribly'. Nearby was Scylla, a nymph transformed into a hideous six-headed dog by a jealous Circe. Making a horrible yapping noise, she lay in wait for sailors, whom she would snatch from their ships and devour. Mediterranean sailors knew well to avoid the Strait of Messina, where so many ships had met destruction.

Jason and the Argonauts

The fabulous story of Jason, related by the Greek poet Apollonius of Rhodes (295-215 BC) in the *Argonautica*, is based on a far older oral tradition. Although it resembles in many respects the tale of an initiatory voyage, the story of Jason also alludes to the expansion of Greece.

Jason and his companions, already mentioned by Homer in the *Odyssey*, set sail on the *Argo*, 'the finest ship in the world', and headed for far-off Colchis (modern Georgia) to capture the Golden Fleece. Like Odysseus, Jason's voyage was long and eventful. He navigated from the Gulf of Paga-

Episode from the Golden Fleece cycle painted by Erasmus Quellinus (1607-1678).

The Quest for Atlantis

From north to south, from east to west, scholars searched for traces of Atlantis. Some believed it to be at the bottom of the ocean, others situated the lost continent in the depths of a volcano, or beneath desert sands, in Mongolia, in North Africa, in the Canaries or the Indies. The discovery of America led Francesco Lopez de Gamara and later Francis Bacon (1561-1626) to declare that the New World was a vestige of Atlantis. For the Swede Olof Rudbeck (1630-1702) there was no doubt: Atlantis, that 'insolent power', was none other than Scandinavia! In the eighteenth century a polemic raged between the astronomer Sylvain Bailly, who held that Siberia was the lost continent, and Voltaire, who argued that India was the legendary Atlantis. The true significance of the debate may lie elsewhere: in man's eternal pursuit of an inaccessible dream.

sae to Colchis on the eastern shore of the Black Sea, where he seized the Golden Fleece. Accompanied by Medea, daughter of the king of Colchis, Jason returned to his native Thessaly by a different route. Mythographers claimed that he sailed up the Ister (present-day Danube), reached the Po via the Adriatic Sea, then followed the course of the Rhone to the Mediterranean. But before mooring in the safe harbours of Thessaly, Jason and his crew had to resist the enchanting song of the Sirens, pass through the Strait of Messina, escape from storms...and from the wrath of the Colchidians, bent on avenging the theft of the Golden Fleece.

The tale of Jason's voyage very likely commemorated the settlement of the earliest Greek colonies in Asia Minor and on the shores of the Black Sea. The quest for the Golden Fleece may be a poetic transposition of the discovery of rich gold deposits in Georgia.

King Solomon's mines

It is in the Bible (I Kings 10:11) that Ophir—'the land of gold'—is first mentioned. Around 1000 BC Solomon, the king of the Hebrews, had ships built on the shores of the Red Sea in order to prospect the region's resources. His friend Hiram, King of Tyre, sent Solomon Phoenician 'sailors familiar with the sea', who brought back from Ophir 420 gold talents, precious stones and sandalwood from which Solomon had balustrades made for the 'House of the Eternal', the Temple of Jerusalem.

Where was this fabulous land of Ophir? Even for the ancient Greeks its exact location was a mystery. The gold mines of today's Zimbabwe are a possible site, for traces remain there of ancient gold mining. Some affirm that Ophir was the realm of the Queen of Sheba somewhere in southern Arabia. Impressed by King Solomon's renown, she travelled to Jerusalem 'with camels loaded with perfumes, great quantities of gold and precious stones'.

Another theory holds that the word 'Ophir' signified 'precious goods', particularly gold imported from trading posts established near the Strait of Bab el Mandeb. Situated at the junction of the Red Sea and the Gulf of Aden, it was a thriving commercial hub for north-south trade. That prosaic explanation would dispel the mystery surrounding the land of Ophir, Antiquity's El Dorado.

Atlantis, as seen by the Ancients

Atlantis, the mythical continent first described by Plato in the dialogue *Critias*, has long fired men's imaginations. In very ancient times, so the legend goes, an immense island 'larger than Libya and Asia put together' lay in the Atlantic; part of it nearly touched the Pillars of Hercules. The Atlantids allegedly attempted to invade Greece, but were fiercely resisted. A cataclysm destroyed the island, which sank to the bottom of the sea 'in the space of a terrible day and night'. According to Plato, the sinking of Atlantis occurred around 9600 BC.

Aristotle dismissed the story as a simple device used by Plato to expound his philosophy, politics and moral views. But others, Strabo for instance, believed in the existence of Atlantis, which they supposed lay at the bottom of the sea. It may be that the deluge recounted in Plato's *Critias* corresponds to a gigantic eruption on the volcanic island of Santorini in the Aegean. Knossos, in Crete, was shattered by the earthquakes that accompanied the eruption, around 1500 BC.

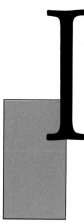

I n Antiquity, exploration and conquest went hand in hand. The search for new territories was fuelled by the need to find additional resources, to occupy strategic sites, or to find new land on which to settle a growing population. But when, as was the case with Alexander the Great, empire-building was backed up by a genuine desire to explore and discover new lands, conquest also became a tool to advance knowledge and spread civilization.

Alexander the Great and the 'savage' inhabitants of remote lands, as imagined in the Middle Ages.

The Long March of the Ten Thousand

In the fifth century BC the Persian leader Cyrus retreated with his army of ten thousand Greek mercenaries—there may in fact have been fewer—before the threat of Cyrus's brother, Artaxerxes II. This long march would be transformed into a heroic exploit thanks to the efforts of the Greek historian Xenophon, who participated in the expedition. It led them from Babylon to the Black Sea, an epic journey across Kurdistan and Armenia, territories which until that time were wholly unexplored.

A brief but brilliant career

The singular career of Alexander the Great, who reigned in the fourth century BC, marks an epoch in world history. By the breadth of his vision and the grandeur of his dream of uniting East and West, the young Macedonian prince appears to us as perhaps the greatest conqueror of all. He was born in 356 BC in Pella, the capital of Macedonia. His father, Philip II of Macedonia, appointed as Alexander's tutor Aristotle, who inspired in the young boy an interest in philosophy, medicine and science. The boy was introduced at an early age to the responsibilities of kingship when Philip, off to war with Byzantium, handed the reins of government over to his sixteen-year-old son. In 336 Philip was assassinated

by a Macedonian nobleman, Pausanias. Obliged to assume the crown at the age of twenty, Alexander lost no time consolidating his power. He had Pausanias executed, subjugated the aristocracy, and suppressed an uprising of Greek city-states. He spared Athens, but Thebes he burned to the ground 'as an example'. The League of Corinth (composed of delegates from Greek cities and states) made Alexander master of its armies in the struggle with Persia. The young general led this 'war of reprisals' as a true conqueror. After a relentless pursuit of Darius, the great Persian king, who was murdered by one of his own lieutenants in 330 BC, Alexander took possession of the immense Persian Achaemenid empire. He reached the Indus River in 326, and dreamed of pushing farther east to the Ganges. But his soldiers mutinied and

refused to advance. Alexander was compelled to abandon his project, and returned to Babylon, where he died in 323, probably a victim of swamp fever. He was thirty-three.

Beyond Samarkand

In April 334 Alexander crossed the Hellespont (now the Dardanelles) with an army of thirty-five thousand. Thus began one of the greatest exploits of history, and the conquest of a vast empire. From Egypt to India, from the Indian Ocean to the Caspian Sea, Alexander battled, vanquished, colonized, and built cities—Plutarch puts the number at seventy—fifteen of which were named Alexandria. The first among them was Alexandria in Egypt, founded in 331; the most remote was Alexandria-on-Jaxartes, dubbed 'Alexandria-at-earth's-end', located beyond Samarkand near the River Tanais (the present day Syr Darya) in 329 BC. To dominate this vast territory, the conqueror needed to discover its dangers as well as its riches. Alexander sent reconnaissance missions to the Upper Nile, the Persian Gulf, and the Caspian Sea (see p. 17). Like the excellent strategist he was, Alexander had a keen interest in topography. He had his geographers establish precise surveys of the regions he coveted.

Strictly speaking, Alexander did not discover any unknown lands. In the sixth century BC, the Persian Darius I already reigned over an empire that stretched from Egypt to India. He had opened access to the Indus, and established a direct sea route between Egypt and the Persian Gulf. But it was thanks to Alexander's conquests that the Greeks discovered Asia. Alexander was the first European to roam those vast territories, and to dream of 'merging' the Greeks and Persians into a single nation.

The return of Nearchus

Forced by his mutinous army to prepare for his return, Alexander had a fleet of two thousand boats built in record time on the Hydaspes (modern Jhelum) River. In November 326, he gave the signal to set sail. The army descended the Indus to the Indian Ocean. Alexander commanded the Cretan general Nearchus to return to Babylon by sea, while he himself journeyed back via the coast with a part of the army. For the Greek fleet, this expedition on the Indian Ocean was a first: the sight of a school of whales threw the crews into a panic. And to sailors familiar with Mediterranean waters, the ocean tides were something of a shock.

Nearchus navigated along the shores of Gedrosia (today's Baluchistan), passed through the Strait of Hormuz and entered the Persian Gulf. He followed the eastern shore of the Gulf to Babylon, where he finally rejoined Alexander. The voyage had lasted five months. If we can credit Nearchus's log, he used the long weeks to observe the coastline, make detailed notes on the inhabitants, and evaluate the local resources; thus he was able to give Alexander an exhaustive report on all he had seen.

Did Onesicritus reach Ceylon?

How much truth is there to the account of an expedition led by Nearchus's lieutenant, Onesicritus, who claimed to have landed on the island of Taprobane (Ceylon)? Alexander instructed him to visit that fascinating island, which was thought to open onto the Antipodes (see p. 29). Although there is evidence that Onesicritus was present on the voyage led by Nearchus in the Indian Ocean, his account of the excursion to Ceylon is a melange of convincing and totally extravagant details. Strabo calls him a 'master liar'; though that did not prevent the historian from cribbing some of Onesicritus's descriptions of Indian geography and customs.

A 'new Phoenicia'

Alexander's ambition was to snatch the control of the great maritime routes to India from the Arabs. His plan to colonize the Arabian coast and to make it, in the words

The Art of Gandhara

The Greek settlements in Bactria (today's Afghanistan) that sprung up in the wake of Alexander's conquests became independent kingdoms towards the middle of the third century BC. A hundred years later, they expanded militarily towards India, dominating Taxila, the Punjab, and Gandhara. The influence of Asian Greeks pervaded Indian artistic sensibility, giving rise at Gandhara to splendid sculptures of Greco-Buddhist inspiration.

The mainly Buddhist art of Gandhara produced this familiar image of the Master.

of the Greek historian Arrian, 'a new Phoenicia', would have assured him a monopoly on trade with India. Nearchus's voyage should be seen in this context. Other expeditions set out with a similar goal: in 325 Archias of Pella, Androsthenes of Thasos and Hieron navigated along the western shores of the Persian Gulf. Archias advanced as far as Tylos (modern Bahrain). Hieron did not complete his voyage around the Arabian peninsula, which was to conclude with the linking of Alexandria on the Tigris and Egyptian Alexandria. Alexander planned other expeditions to the western Mediterranean, towards Carthage and Italy, according to such reliable authorities as Arrian, Plutarch, and Diodorus Siculus. But the great conqueror met his death before these dreams could be realized.

Roman expeditions

The Romans persistently pushed back the frontiers of their empire. Concerned with the profit they could turn from these expeditions, they also sponsored explorations that advanced the geographical knowledge of their times.

The Romans made important inroads into Africa. At the request of the Roman general Scipio, Polybius—a Greek historian and geographer sent to Rome as a hostage after the Romans defeated Macedonia

in 168 BC—explored the Libyan coast and observed the Carthaginian trading posts there. Another notable prisoner, liberated by Julius Caesar, was the Numidian monarch, Juba II (52 BC-23 AD), an exceptionally intelligent and cultured individual with a passion for geography. He headed several expeditions, and explored the Canary Islands; these were familiar to the Phoenicians and Libyans, but virtually unknown to the Romans. The account of his expeditions was preserved by the writers Plutarch and Pliny the Elder. Juba also travelled to the Arabian coast, and sought—unsuccessfully—the sources of the Nile.

Eternal snows... and rhinoceroses

Roman soldiers sent on missions to far-off lands sometimes made rather startling discoveries. Paulinius Suetonius, for example, who set off in 37 AD to put down an uprising in Mauretania, was astonished to observe the snow-covered peaks of the Atlas Mountains—particularly in contrast to the torrid heat of the lowlands. In 86, two Roman generals, Julius Maternus and Septimus Flaccus, set out from Gamara in Fezzan (a province of Libya), and marched to the 'Land of Agisymba' (Ethiopia) where they stumbled upon some strange horned beasts—rhinoceroses.

The Silk Route

When silk appeared in Rome in the first century BC, the Romans had no clue as to the origins of the precious cloth, supplied to them by the powerful Parthian Empire which then controlled all caravan traffic from Central Asia. In fact silk is the first commodity we can actually track in its progress from China to the West. Near the end of the nineteenth century the caravan trail that led across Asia from the shores of the Mediterranean to central China, through Persia, Afghanistan, the Pamirs and Turkestan, was baptized 'The Silk Route'. Not just silk but ideas, religions, and artistic traditions also travelled along that long trail.

21

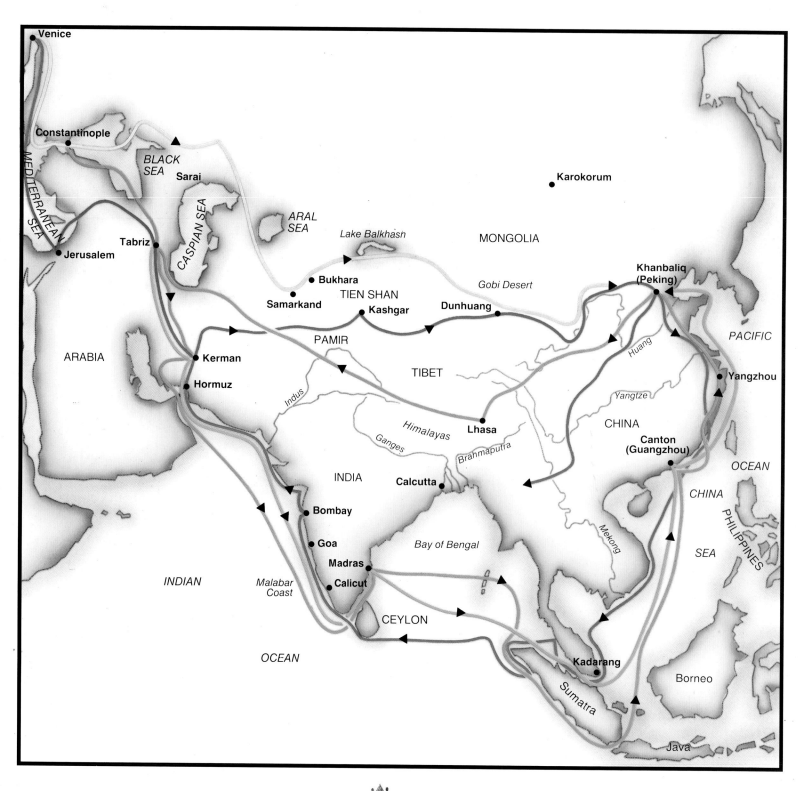

Venice

Constantinople

BLACK
SEA

MEDITERRANEAN SEA

Sarai

CASPIAN SEA

ARAL
SEA

Lake Balkhash

Karokorum

MONGOLIA

Tabriz

Jerusalem

Bukhara

Samarkand

TIEN SHAN

Kashgar

Dunhuang

Gobi Desert

Khanbaliq
(Peking)

Huang

ARABIA

Kerman

Hormuz

PAMIR

Indus

TIBET

Himalayas

Ganges

Lhasa

Brahmaputra

Yangtze

CHINA

PACIFIC

Yangzhou

INDIA

Calcutta

Canton
(Guangzhou)

OCEAN

CHINA

PHILIPPINES

Bombay

Goa

Madras

Calicut

INDIAN

Malabar
Coast

Bay of Bengal

Mekong

SEA

OCEAN

CEYLON

Kadarang

Borneo

Sumatra

Java

Nicolo & Maffeo Polo
(1255-1269)

Marco Polo (1271-1295)

Giovanni da Montecor-
vino (1289-1294)

Odoric of Pordenone
(1316-1330)

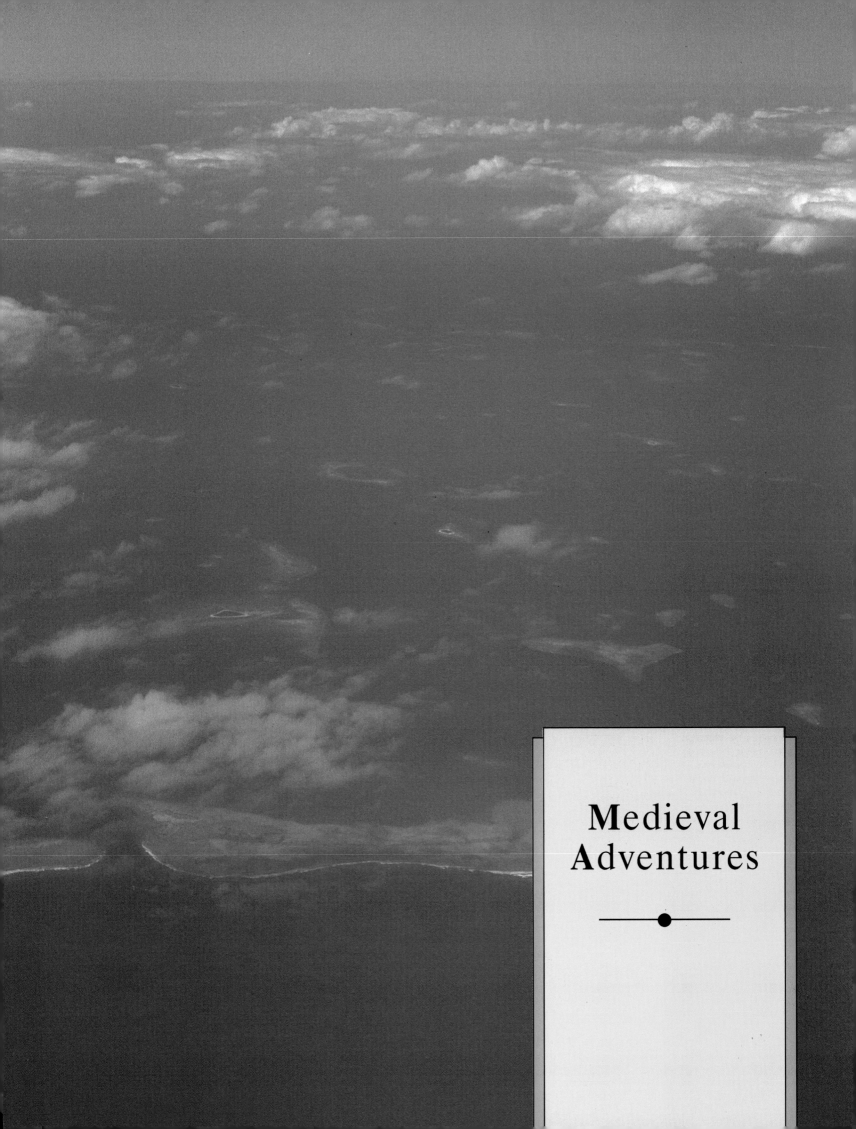

Medieval
Adventures

AN IMAGINARY GEOGRAPHY

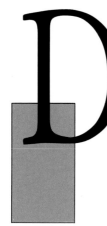

During the Christian Middle Ages, the science of geography took a giant step backwards. Information acquired in the classical era was cancelled out by religious dogma, which was regarded as the absolute source and reference point for all human knowledge. It was not until the thirteenth century that a new surge of interest brought the disciplines of geography and cartography into the modern age.

The Astrolabe

The astrolabe was invented by the Greek astronomer Hipparchus in the second century BC. Ptolemy's astrolabe, which resembled a kind of sphere, allowed the user to determine the position of the stars, and to measure their altitude above the horizon. In the fifteenth century, a group of mathematicians working for John II of Portugal discovered a way of calculating latitude by observing the altitude of the Pole Star above the horizon; in the southern hemisphere, the calculation was based on the height of the sun or the Southern Cross. Thanks to the efforts of the cosmographer Martin Behaim (1459-1507), the seaman's astrolabe became widely used for navigational purposes.

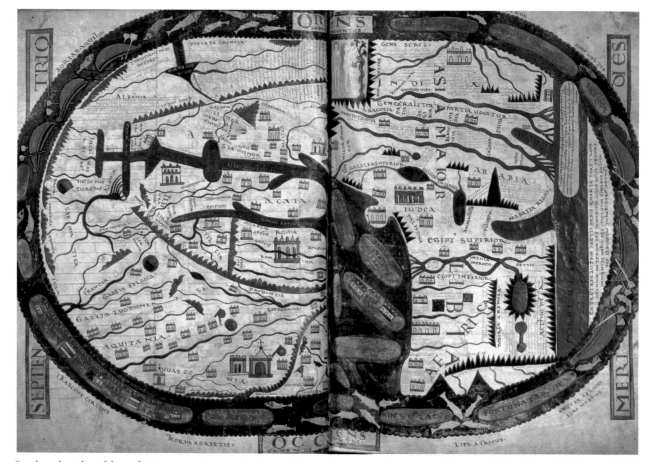

Produced at the Abbey of St Sever in Gascony in the mid-eleventh century, the oval world map of Friar Beatus Liebana (8ᵗʰ century) shows the three continents of the known world as equal in size, each portion the legacy of one of Noah's three sons.

Back to the flat-earth theory

———————————●———————————

In the sixth century a zealous Christian monk, an enthusiastic student of geography and theology, wrote the weighty *Topographia Christiana*, or *Christian Topography*, a view of the universe that broke completely with the Platonic conception. Cosmas of Alexandria, called the 'Indicopleustes' (navigator of India), entered the Church after having traded and travelled for many years in Abyssinia, Ceylon, the Red Sea, and the Indian Ocean. In his monumental work, which comprises no fewer than twelve volumes, Cosmas strove to demonstrate that the earth was not spherical, as certain Ancients had claimed, but flat and rectangular.

On each of the earth's four sides, he reasoned, was a gigantic wall; the tops of the walls curved inward, forming an immense dome above the earth: the vault of the heavens. The flat rectangle — its shape recalled the Tabernacle of Moses — was divided into three parts. In the centre was the inhabited world, surrounded by an ocean. The constantly moving ocean waters had hollowed out four gulfs, or bays. Beyond lay another, inaccessible continent, which supported the foundations of the four gigantic walls. It was there that men lived before the Great Flood. Careful always to base his claims on Scripture, Cosmas 'explained' the movement of the stars. North of the earth a colossal mountain served as a pivot for the revolutions of the sun and the moon. Cosmas utterly rejected the Ancients' more rational, scientific attempts at cosmography — the ideas of Plato or Eratosthenes had no currency in this world view.

The word according to Isidore

The transition from the classical tradition to medieval thought, which took place during the sixth and seventh centuries, was embodied in the work of a Spanish prelate. Isidore of Seville was destined to play a major role in the elaboration and spread of the new Christian culture. A close ally of Pope Gregory the Great, Isidore (560-636) was elected Bishop of Seville in 601. This learned theologian, lover of poetry and expert grammarian, was the author of several Latin works, most notably the *Etymologiae*, an encyclopaedia of universal knowledge. An inventory of the classical heritage, it is an early expression of the medieval mode of thought. Isidore views the works of the ancient Greek and Roman authors in a Christian perspective. His geography, for example, was directly inspired by Scripture. The inhabited world, he wrote, was divided among the three sons of Noah: Shem, Ham, and Japheth. One of Shem's descendants, Queen Asia, gave her name to that continent. The word 'Africa' derived from Afer, a descendant of Ham and Abraham. And Europe, named after the mythological nymph Europa, was peopled by the fifteen tribes of the sons of Japheth. Isidore faithfully noted the number and origins of the cities, nations and races that populated each continent.

Medieval thinkers in the Christian West were not concerned to describe the world empirically, but rather to portray it as a true reflection of Scripture. Thus Isidore of Seville did not hesitate to depict the earthly paradise in minute detail: 'Here grows the Tree of Life which gives immortality; there is the spring whose four streams flow through the world.'

While the Christian West was hampered by obscurantism, China pursued its geographical and astronomical investigations.

The Inventor of the 'Mediterranean'

The man who came up with the word 'mediterranean' (literally: 'situated in the middle of the land') was Caius Julius Solinus, a third-century Roman geographer. The word appears in a work entitled *Polyhistor*, an ethnographical treatise on the history of different countries, borrowing heavily from Pliny's *Natural History*.

Jerusalem, centre of the world

Until the late thirteenth century the most familiar representation of the world was the 'T-O map'. These maps were shaped like the letter T inscribed in a circle — the letter O, which represented the inhabited world, or *oikoumene*; hence the name 'oecumenical maps' often given to these documents. Each of the three known continents is situated in the circle outside of the T: Europe to the left, Africa to the right, and Asia above the T's horizontal bar. The East, therefore, occupies the uppermost portion of the map. The vertical bar of the T holds the Mediterranean, which separates Europe from Africa. In the horizontal bar are the Danube and the Nile rivers, which in medieval times were believed to be connected. Surrounding the circle is the ocean; and in the centre of the inhabited world stands Jerusalem. Working in a wholly Christian context, imbued with biblical stories and place names, geographers of that time could not do otherwise than make Jerusalem the centre of the world.

A Roman road map

The biblical maps produced by medieval Christian cartographers differed radically from maps drawn by the Romans, who viewed geography in a purely utilitarian light: it furthered their scheme of world domination. Romans drew maps of the lands they conquered, and military reports forwarded to Rome often included topographical documents as well. Road maps held a particular interest for the conquerors. One example, known as the Table of Peutinger, is drawn on a narrow, four-metre-long strip, and gives a stylized image of the Roman Empire. Provinces are indicated, as are nations, cities, roads, and distances. The map is probably a copy made by a monk in Colmar around 1265 from a third- or fourth-century original. Discovered in Speyer in 1494 by Konrad Celteis, librarian to Emperor Maximilian I, in 1507 the map became the property of the secretary of the Augsburg senate, Konrad Peutinger, by whose name the map is now known.

P'ei Hsiu, the Chinese Ptolemy

In contrast with the Western maps — which long retained their rudimentary appearance, noting neither latitude nor longitude — Chinese cartography by the third century had developed a sophisticated marking system that included graduated divisions. P'ei

Hsiu, appointed minister of public works in 267, produced an eighteen-page atlas of all China's territories. His method was analogous to that of Ptolemy (see p. 13), with parallels and meridians crossing at right angles. The use of rectangular grids permitted him to reproduce distances true to scale. As P'ei Hsiu himself explains in the preface to the atlas, 'when the principle of the rectangular grid is appropriately applied, the straight line and the curve, the near and the distant can hold no secret for us'. Research into the origins of this complex cartographical technique has led some to surmise that the warp and woof threads of the silk on which Chinese cartographers drew their maps may have inspired the use of coordinates to locate a given point. Others discern the influence of the squares of a Chinese chessboard.

Profit from Error

A map drawn by the Italian Toscanelli in 1474, and sent several years later to Christopher Columbus (see p. 54), probably helped push the Genoese captain towards the western route to the Indies — that is, to the discovery of America. On this map, ostensibly a representation of 'the entire space comprised between the West and the beginning of the Indies', the distance going westwards from Western Europe to the Far East was half as long as it is in reality. Toscanelli, however, only perpetuated errors rooted in a misinterpretation of Eratosthenes' measurement of the earth's circumference in the third century BC.

Mongol cartography

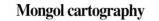

The procedure was progressively refined, and eventually geographical and astronomical coordinates were linked. In the Sung dynasty (960-1279) it became common practice to position the north on the upper portion of a map. In the thirteenth century the Mongol conquest of Asia provided a mass of new information for Chinese geographers, giving rise to the school of Mongol cartography. The contour of the earth finally disappeared from the map, leaving only a grid on which numerous inscriptions indicated the names and locations of sites and peoples.

The first marine maps

Not until the twelfth and thirteenth centuries did European cartography emerge from its long period of stagnation. Under the influence of such scholars as the German monk Albertus Magnus and the English friar Roger Bacon, the notion of a spherical earth regained lost ground. The Crusades, the first voyages of discovery, and the invention of the compass all fostered the development of map-making, and the production of marine charts in particular. Portolanos (or compass charts) — descriptive atlases comprising sailing directions and charts — allowed navigators on the high seas to determine the orientation of coastlines and the exact location of seaports.

The first portolanos were compiled by Genoese and Venetian navigators. They charted the coasts of the Mediterranean, the Black Sea and the Atlantic Ocean, indicating various coastal features, shoals, currents, lighthouses and harbours. The earliest examples, though quite detailed, were fairly primitive; they did not yet include gradations, and occasionally their geography was based more on legend than on scientific observation. Relative sizes of islands and bays are generally overestimated. There is also a constant drift from east to north.

In the fifteenth and sixteenth centuries, the era of the great discoveries, Spanish and Portuguese pilots greatly improved the accuracy of portolanos, while increasing the area they covered. Some of these charts, decorated with rich illuminations, include astronomical tables as well.

Portuguese exploration of the Atlantic

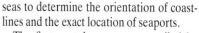

Prince Henry of Portugal (1394-1460) — Henry the Navigator — was the first great patron of discovery, and the driving force behind his country's maritime exploits. He was the third son of King John I and Philippa of Lancaster, the daughter of John of Gaunt. An austere, pious man with a rough manner and an uncertain temper, the prince's secretive nature concealed the mystical will of a Christian soldier. Henry was Grand Master of the Knights of Christ, an association that furnished the necessary funds for exploratory expeditions. In 1410 he established his royal residence at Sagres in the Algarve, not far from the port of Lagos, whence Portuguese caravels launched their expeditions, and in 1416 he founded a school of navigation. On 21 August 1425 Henry captured the Moroccan port of Ceuta, facing Gibraltar, the key to the Mediterranean and to Africa (see p. 53).

Urged on by their prince, the Portuguese explored Madeira, colonized the Azores, and rounded the African coast to the Gulf of Guinea. A scientist and scholar, Henry the Navigator surrounded himself with cartographers and astronomers, whose research contributed to the success of these voyages of discovery. Prince Henry himself wrote a learned treatise on astronomy. Among his collaborators was the cartographer Jaime of Majorca, son of Abraham Cresques, author of a celebrated atlas.

Portrayed side by side by artist Nuño de Gonçalves around 1460, Henry and his nephew, the future John II, launched the first great Atlantic explorations.

Equipped with the latest navigational instruments — compass, astrolabe, quadrant, and declination tables — mariners set sail aboard caravels, ships specially designed for the high seas.

The Caravel:
A New Kind of Ship

Advances in navigational techniques made the great voyages of discovery possible. One vital advance was a new type of sailing ship, the caravel. Tall, light and swift, the caravel was designed by Portuguese experts at Prince Henry's navigational school at Sagres. The innovative vessel could cover long distances into unknown waters and, if necessary, sail against the wind. With their lateen (triangular) sails rigged on a sloping yard, the caravels were far easier to manoeuvre than their predecessors, and were capable of sailing close to the wind. The rudder mounted on the sternpost gave the vessel improved stability.

Fra Mauro's map of the world

King Alfonso V of Portugal (1432-1481) know as 'The African' from his compaigns in Morocco, also showed a keen interest in cartography. At his behest an Italian monk, Fra Mauro, living in retirement at San Michele da Murano near Venice, constructed a planisphere destined for the monastery of Alcobaça. Fra Mauro also spent two years drawing a map of the world (1459), executed on a sheet of parchment four metres square. Embellished with legends and numerous details — the representation of Africa, for example, incorporated the most recent information — this monumental map, a masterpiece of cosmographical erudition, displayed the sum of the era's geographical knowledge. And naturally, reflecting the imperfect state of that knowledge, the map was flawed by imprecision and numerous inaccuracies. Yet Fra Mauro's map of the world marked a major step forward in cartography, particularly because of its greater respect for proportions in the rendering of physical features.

The first terrestrial globe

Like his uncle Henry the Navigator, John II of Portugal (1455-1495) gathered about him the most learned men of his day, and had them participate in the reconnaissance of the African coast. Thus the king instructed the German cosmographer Martin Behaim to accompany Captain Diogo Cão in 1483 on an expedition to the mouth of the River Congo (now the Zaïre). In 1491, back in Nuremberg, Behaim devised the first terrestrial globe. On a sphere fifty-seven centimetres in diameter, he inscribed the outline of the known world. The western coast of Africa is faithfully reproduced, but the continent's southern tip deviates towards the east. And despite Behaim's efforts to be 'scientific' in his approach, he remained tied to the beliefs of his time: thus the globe features the site of Saint Brendan's fabled isle (see p. 28), which Behaim situated near the equator, west of the Canaries. Behaim is also said to have introduced the brass version of the astrolabe — an instrument (previously made of wood) used in navigation to ascertain the altitude of the sun, moon and stars.

The sailor's companion

While advances in shipbuilding produced ever more seaworthy vessels, navigators acquired an invaluable aid for setting and following a course: the compass. Thanks to the magnetized needle that always pointed north, sailors could take to the high seas without fear of losing their way, so opening the way for long-haul voyages. Early Greeks and Romans had known of the lodestone, but they had not appreciated its navigational potential. It was the Chinese who first used the magnetized needle to determine direction: as early as the fourth century BC, the use of the lodestone compass is mentioned in the *Book of the Devil Valley Master*, and by the ninth century AD, all Chinese sailors knew how to use a compass. The Arabs inherited this knowledge, and passed it on to Western navigators during the Crusades. A French poet, Guyot de Provins, referred to an 'ugly, blackish stone' known as a *marinette*, or sailor's companion. The device was also called a 'calamite' (from the Latin *calamus*, reed): the needles of the earliest compasses were set upon a hollow reed that floated in a water-filled flask.

edieval geographers attached great importance to their representations of an imaginary world, whose boundaries were determined by myths, legends and folklore. This realm of marvels occupied a place in men's minds left vacant by the Church's condemnation of 'pagan' science. Medieval travellers' tales were a jumble of eye-witness accounts, hearsay, imaginary fancies, and biblical references.

Who was Prester John?

The legend of an immensely rich and powerful Christian Mongol king is not without a historical basis. Nestorianism, a schismatic Christian belief (see p. 32), was widely diffused through Asia towards India and China, and benefited from the support of Mongol sovereigns like Hulagu and Kublai Khan. Hulagu, though a Buddhist, married a Nestorian Christian girl.

A sixteenth-century picture of Prester John.

The legendary land of Prester John

The spread of the legend of Prester John coincided with the first Crusades, a time when Islam posed an ever-growing threat to Christendom. Events fanned European

hopes for the eventual conversion of the Tartars, who would then rally to the Christian cause.

In 1145 a Syrian bishop, Hugh of Jabala, announced to Rome the existence of a Nestorian Christian king, Prester (or 'Priest') John, who had defeated the infidel in Persia and who would soon join forces with the Crusader states in the Holy Land. The news

caused great rejoicing. So strong was the belief in an eastern ally that certain Christians identified Genghis Khan with Prester John. Twenty years later the pope received a letter from Prester John. It was in fact a fraud, but the rumour persisted to such a degree that in 1177 Pope Alexander III offered a Roman church to his mysterious ally. When John of Plano Carpini and William of Rubrouck travelled to Asia (see p. 31), they hoped to encounter the legendary Prester John, or his successors, and to ratify his alliance with Rome. For centuries this mythical character fired the medieval imagination. In the fifteenth century, travellers still sought traces of his kingdom in Christian Ethiopia. The desire to meet Prester John and join forces with him against the Muslims counted among the motives for Portugal's maritime expeditions to Africa.

The quest for Saint Brendan

Medieval tradition abounds with tales of heroes setting out to find the Garden of Eden, and who, to do so, must first overcome a multitude of obstacles and adventures, each more perilous than the last. The legend of the isle of Saint Brendan was so firmly anchored in the medieval mind that many contemporary navigators launched expeditions to find him. These quests lasted into the eighteenth century.

Brendan was born in Ireland in 484. He took holy orders and founded several monasteries in Ireland and England. Later, Brendan went off to sea in hopes of discovering the paradise which, he believed, was located somewhere in the Atlantic Ocean.

After years of roving the northern seas, and, as tradition says, having crossed a 'sea of darkness', Brendan finally reached a 'marvellous island' (perhaps the Azores), which he took for 'the promised land of the saints'. His story seemed so credible that medieval geographers did not hesitate to include Saint Brendan's isle on their maps — though its exact location varied. In 1492, on his terrestrial globe, Martin Behaim situated it east of the Canaries. Others believed the isle lay off the Irish coast; still others placed it near the West Indies.

The romance of Alexander the Great

In the Book of Genesis (2:8) it is written: 'and the Lord God planted a garden eastward of Eden'. Travellers thus journeyed east to seek the 'garden of earthly delights', as indicated in the *Romance of Alexander the Great (Historia Alexandri Magni)*. This fantastic chronicle, incorrectly attributed to the Greek philosopher Callisthenes, was hugely popular throughout Europe in the Middle Ages. The version that has come down to us was composed in Armenia in the fifth century AD. The legend cleverly entwines Alexander's actual exploits, fanciful Byzantine tales, and biblical references. It tells how Alexander, having conquered India, reached the banks of the Ganges and embarked on the river with five hundred soldiers. After four weeks the Macedonian and his comrades reached a town protected by high walls. Here dwelt the souls of the Just awaiting Judgement Day; Alexander had found the earthly paradise, which, as it had been written, lay 'eastward of Eden'.

Gog and Magog

In absolute contrast to Eden, site of every joy and delight, but equally vivid to the medieval mind, were Gog and Magog, the enemies of Israel, evoked on several occasions in Scripture. Geographers strove to situate the land of Magog, where, according to the prophet Ezekiel, reigned 'Gog, prince of Rosch, Meshech, and Tubal' (Ezekiel, 38:20).

The name Magog may have designated countries in northeastern Asia Minor, or the land of the Scythians, who lived between the Danube and Don rivers. These warlike, nomadic tribes, whose brutality and barbarous customs were described by the Greek historian Herodotus, surged through Mesopotamia to the edge of Egypt, sweeping aside all that lay in their path. Ezekiel prophesied against Gog, who attacked the people of God: 'I shall send fire upon Magog' and 'I shall give to Gog a place that will be his sepulchre in Israel' (Ezekiel, 39: 6, 11). Christians interpreted this prophecy as applying to the Syrian king Antiochus IV, who in the second century BC had marched on Jerusalem, massacring eighty thousand Jews before perishing himself in the battle.

Alter Orbis or the land of the Antipodes

Until the first Portuguese ships sailed along the west coast of Africa, the southern hemisphere was believed to be the *alter orbis*. Inaccessible to man, it was populated by Antipodes, creatures Sir John Mandeville (see below) defined as 'creatures whose feet are up against us, for they are at the opposite end of the earth'. This other world was a kind of 'negative' of our own; for every human there was a corresponding antipode who walked upside down.

The fifteenth-century voyages of discovery dealt a fatal blow to these mythical beings whose universe was a reverse image of the 'inhabited world'.

An inspired storyteller: Sir John Mandeville

Little is known about Sir John Mandeville. According to some sources, his real name was John of Burgundy and he was born in Liège in 1300. Others say he was born in Hertfordshire and began his travels on Michaelmas Day 1322. In any case, he was an unparalleled storyteller. His outlandish vision of the Orient was destined to influence the young Christopher Columbus.

According to his tales, Mandeville left his native city for the Holy Land. There, curiously enough, he waged war on the side of the infidels. Later he travelled all over Asia, and even lived for several years in Beijing (Peking). After an absence of thirty-three years he returned to Europe and related his adventures in his *Travels*, a work filled with the most extravagant details. Mandeville's widely read account in fact borrowed considerably from a work by Odoric of Pordenone, filling it out with passages lifted from tales of chivalry and historical chronicles. Although in his time he was famous as the greatest traveller of the Middle Ages, it is not even certain whether Mandeville ever travelled at all.

Eden in the East

Quests for the earthly paradise, so frequent in the Middle Ages, answered a need for harmonizing geographical reality and the teaching of Scripture. Travellers were guided by their faith. The Garden of Eden, believed to lie in the East, often appeared on the upper portion of maps (where medieval mapmakers usually placed the East). Adam, Eve and the serpent were illustrated as isolated from the rest of the world by a high mountain or wall. Paradise was thought to occupy a high place, which would explain how it survived the Flood.

In the Middle Ages the Romance of Alexander the Great, *embellished with fanciful anecdotes, enjoyed wide popularity.*

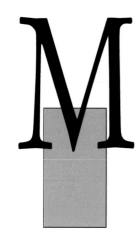

Medieval European society suffered from isolationism and lack of curiosity about the non-Christian world. It took the Muslim threat to make Europe look towards Asia, in the hope of finding new allies. But it was above all in the name of Christ that Crusaders and missionaries undertook expeditions to far-off lands.

Rabban Sauma in Europe

The Khans of Persia, traditionally Buddhists, sometimes married Nestorian Christian women. One such Khan was Arghun, who came to power in 1284. He was known for his great religious tolerance, yet he distrusted the Muslim Mamelukes, who then reigned over Egypt and Syria. In 1287 Arghun dispatched Rabban Sauma, a Nestorian monk of Turkish extraction, to Rome, France and England in the hope of convincing the pope and European sovereigns to launch a Crusade against the Mamelukes. But Rabban Sauma's mission was a failure.

En route to Jerusalem

Until the eleventh century, Christians and Arabs maintained friendly relations. In exchange for a certain sum, pilgrims could travel freely to Jerusalem to kneel and pray at the Holy Sepulchre. But the situation changed radically with the arrival of the Turks, who seized the Holy City in 1076. The Byzantine Empire, with its capital at Constantinople, was being threatened by the rising power of the Seljuk Turks, and the Marches of the Orient were closed to Europe. Pope Urban II, at the Council of Clermont in 1095, urged all Christians to take up arms against the infidels, to help the Byzantine Emperor Alexius and to liberate the Holy Sepulchre, the tomb of Christ. Men, women and children answered his call by the thousands. They took the Cross —

that is, wore a cross of red cloth on their right shoulders — and set off for Jerusalem on the First Crusade. The pope promised them the total remission of their sins, and vowed that anyone who attempted to seize their property in their absence would be excommunicated.

Christian nations of the Orient

The first expedition to the Holy Land, made up of peasants — many of them women and children ill-prepared for such a journey — was led by Peter the Hermit. Most of the motley company perished en route, or was massacred by the Turks. The main body of Crusaders, among whose leaders were Godfrey of Bouillon, assembled in and

around Constantinople. The Crusaders first captured Antioch, then laid siege to the Holy City. They attacked in 1099. The battle was fearsome: Jews and Muslims were savagely burned or put to the sword and the Christians plundered all they could find. Jerusalem was liberated, but the expedition had cost the lives of over ten thousand Crusaders.

Most survivors returned to Europe, though some preferred to remain in one of the four Christian principalities founded after the victory: Antioch, Edessa, Tripoli, and the kingdom of Jerusalem. To protect colonists and pilgrims from Saracen attacks, the military and religious orders of the Templars and Hospitallers were founded in the free states. Yet in 1187 Saladin's army recaptured Jerusalem for Islam.

Missionary geographers

In view of the menace hanging over the West, the pope and the king of France considered forging an alliance with the Mongols. Success would not only cancel the threat of a Mongol invasion, it would mean that Muslim armies could be attacked from the rear by the Great Khan's army. This motive, coupled with a desire to evangelize the heathen, spurred Europe's 'diplomatic missionaries' to undertake long, perilous expeditions to India and China.

Most of these pioneers belonged to the Franciscan order, founded in 1215 by Saint Francis of Assisi. John of Plano Carpini was the first monk to penetrate into Central Asia. But others followed: William of Rubrouck, John of Monte Corvino, Laurence of Portugal, and others. All of these travelling friars, when they returned from their missions, brought back precious information about the lands they had seen and the native customs they had observed.

In his History of the Mongols, *John of Plano Carpini displayed an ethnologist's precision; yet he was naïve enough to lend credence to certain fables he had heard, such as the existence of the dog-headed Cynocephalaes...*

The arrival of the Crusaders before the city of Antioch, which fell after a long siege in 1098. Painting by F. Schopin (1804-1880).

John of Plano Carpini in Mongolia

Pope Innocent IV dispatched a sixty-year-old Franciscan monk, John of Plano Carpini (1182-1251), as his personal envoy to the court of the Great Khan at Karakorum in Mongolia. The Council of Lyons in 1245 had decreed that everything possible should be done to keep the nomadic invaders out of Western Europe — since they had already overrun Poland, Silesia, and Hungary. If the papal ambassador could convert Guyuk, the Great Khan, to Christianity — or at least form an alliance with him — the threat to Europe would be erased.

Plano Carpini left Lyons on 16 April 1245. He was joined in Breslau by Brother Benedick of Poland. The pair set out on horseback for Kiev. On 23 February 1246 they encountered two Mongol horsemen who led the monks to their camp near the River Dnieper. On the advice of the Mongol commander, the friars journeyed to the banks of the Volga, where the court of Batu Khan, grandson of Genghis Khan, was established. The meeting took place on 4 April. Throughout the trip John carefully noted down information he was able to glean about the inhabitants of neighbouring regions. Among those he mentioned were the previously unknown Samoyeds, and more exotic characters such as the dog-headed Cynoscephalaes, and the Parossites with their minuscule mouths.

No conversion

Travelling on horseback, Plano Carpini and Friar Benedick crossed Russia and Turkestan. On 22 July, they finally reached their goal: the imperial camp stood at Sira Ordu, near Karakorum, capital of the empire, on the shores of Lake Baikal. Guyuk was preparing there for the ceremony that would invest him with supreme power as Great Khan of the Mongols. When he learned of the arrival of the papal ambassador, Guyuk agreed to receive him. But the Mongol leader rejected any suggestion that he convert to Christianity, and replied to the pope in a letter saying: 'We adore God, and with his help we shall cover the earth with ruins from East to West.'

On 13 November, Plano Carpini and his companion started back, retracing their steps all the way back to Kiev, then to Moscow and on through Poland and Germany. Eventually they arrived in Avignon, where John reported on his mission to Innocent IV late in 1247. Although it was a diplomatic failure, the mission and Plano Carpini's *Book of the Tartars* revealed to Europeans the existence of hitherto unknown lands and peoples.

The first and last Archbishop of Beijing

One of the most interesting of the Franciscan explorers was the Italian, John of Monte Corvino. Sent to Asia on a papal mission in 1289, he attempted to convert the Ilkhans, rulers of Persia, to Christianity. He preached the Gospel in Persia until 1291, then journeyed to India, where he stayed for just over a year. With his companions, Peter of Lucalonzo and Nicolas of Pistoia, he converted and baptized more than a hundred souls, before continuing on to China

31

— then known as Cathay. In 1294 John reached Khanbalik (Beijing), and gave the Great Khan messages from the pope. The Mongol emperor graciously permitted the Franciscan to establish China's first Christian mission, which soon flourished.

John of Monte Corvino took six years to build his first Chinese church in Khanbalik, of which he was declared archbishop by Pope Clement V. But the mission was short-lived. John's successor, it seems, never even took up his post.

The Nestorians: from Persia to China

Nestorianism is a doctrine that dates from the fifth century. Nestorius, patriarch of Constantinople, preached the existence of two distinct persons in Christ, the human and the divine. The Council of Ephesus, held in 431, condemned the teaching as heretical, yet it gained a fervent following in the East. Driven out of Syria, Nestorians won many converts in Persia, including the Sassanid kings, who propagated the doctrine in Arabia, India, Turkestan and China. In the thirteenth century, the Mongols' favourable attitude towards Nestorian Christians added credence to the legend of Prester John (see p. 28).

William of Rubrouck, the envoy of Saint Louis

King Louis IX of France (Saint Louis) was as eager as the pope to negotiate an alliance with the Mongols against the Muslims. In 1252 while in the Holy Land, he met William of Rubrouck, a Franciscan friar from Flanders. Louis sent William, together with a fellow-Franciscan, Bartholomew of Cremona, and a monk called Andrew, as envoys to the Great Khan, who was rumoured to have converted to Christianity.

The three ambassadors left Acre in 1253, journeyed to Constantinople, later reached Sudak, then crossed the Crimea. Their progress across the steppes was excruciatingly slow, for they were transported by oxcart. Not far from the River Volga, they finally

reached the camp of the Mongol prince Sartaq, son of Batu. William and his companions did not linger long; they set out on horseback for Mongolia. The party passed Lake Balkhash, travelled through Kazakhstan, and on 27 December reached the camp of the Great Khan Mongka, who accompanied the envoys to Karakorum.

At the court of the Great Khan

While at the Mongol court, William of Rubrouck met Nestorian priests and several Europeans. A woman from Metz called Pâquette had been kidnapped years before during a visit to Russia. A French jeweller, Guillaume Bouchier, had also settled in Karakorum, where his skill was much appreciated by the Great Khan. On behalf of Louis IX, William of Rubrouck presented the Mongol sovereign with relics of the True Cross; in exchange, Mongka gave William silken garments and messages for the king of France.

On 8 July 1254, William took leave of Mongka. A year later, he was in Tripoli, having crossed Anatolia and Armenia on his return journey. Prevented by his superiors from meeting with Louis IX, William resolved to write an account of his far-flung travels and Mongolian sojourn. The result — William's *Itinerarium* — is a mine of geographical, historical and ethnographical information on the Mongol Empire. William was the first, for example, to state clearly that the Caspian Sea was not connected to the Northern Ocean, as was then generally believed.

Among the Persian Mongols

Franciscans were not the only friars charged with embassies to Mongolia. The Dominican order also played a part in Europe's efforts to forge an alliance between East and West. In 1247 Pope Innocent IV appointed Nicolas Ascelin, a Dominican from Lombardy, as his emissary to the Mongols of Persia. After a long stay in Syria, Ascelin — joined by Simon de Saint-Quentin and later in the Crimea by Brother Viscardo of Cremona — travelled across Mesopotamia and Persia. In May he reached eastern Transcaucasia and the camp of the Mongol general Baichu. After two months of fruitless negotiations, Ascelin, with his companions and two Mongol envoys, left

the camp and headed west. They reached Lyons in September 1248, and were later granted an audience at the Vatican. Ascelin was a poor ambassador and a worse geographer; the account he left of his journey contributed no new information about the lands he had visited.

An insulting letter

Another Dominican, Andrew of Longjumeau (1200-1270) was dispatched in 1245 by Innocent IV to parley with the Great Khan Guyuk. On his way, Andrew travelled through Syria, where he met Muslim noblemen, who welcomed him graciously. His mission accomplished, Andrew headed back to Rome, and in 1247 he presented Guyuk's letters to the pope. Two years later, he journeyed again to Asia, this time as the emissary of Louis IX. After another eventful transcontinental expedition, Andrew reached the court of the Great Khan, where he discovered that Guyuk had died. His widow, the regent, dismissed Andrew with little ceremony, charging him with letters for Louis IX in which she replied with haughty curtness to the French king's diplomatic overtures. Andrew's return journey lasted an entire year. Back in France, the Dominican told far-fetched tales about the so-called kingdom of Prester John.

The first European in Lhasa: Odoric of Pordenone

The Franciscan friar Odoric of Pordenone, born in Friuli in 1286, devoted his energies to preaching the Gospel in Asia. He left Italy in 1316 to travel to Persia, and later India. He landed on the Coast of Southwest India, where he spent some considerable time. Later he sailed to Ceylon, Sumatra, Java and Borneo. Odoric then made his way to China, and stayed for three years in Canton. He journeyed north into Tibet and was the first European to penetrate the holy city of Lhasa. Odoric later crossed eastern Turkestan, and finally returned to Italy. He had travelled for sixteen years, and had baptized some twenty thousand Christians. Seriously ill, Odoric had to abandon plans to obtain money from the pope to continue his missionary work. The obedient Franciscan followed the bidding of his superior, and dictated his adventures to a fellow monk, William of Solagna, who faithfully recorded Odoric's extraordinary memoirs.

Map of the Mediterranean basin showing the itinerary of St Louis's Crusades. With Pope Innocent IV, the king sent emissaries to Central Asia to win the trust of the Mongols.

Facing page: In 1302 the khan of Ghazan requested the pope's aid against the Mamelukes.

Ever in search of rare and precious goods, the medieval merchant was also, in a way, an explorer and adventurer. Intrepidly he sailed the seas and travelled to the remotest lands. Marco Polo was one such merchant-adventurer. The Book of Ser Marco Polo Concerning the Kingdoms and Marvels of the East, *an account of his extraordinary travels, played a major part in the fascination that China has held for the Western imagination.*

Miniature from Marco Polo's Book of Marvels *representing the harvesting of pepper.*

Marco describes Ceylon

'Furthermore you must know that in the Island of Seilan there is an exceeding high mountain; it rises right up so steep and precipitous that no one could ascend it, were it not that they have taken and fixed to it several great and massive iron chains, so disposed that by help of these men are able to mount to the top.' He might be speaking of Adams Peak (2243 m) or of Pidurutalagala (2524 m), but nothing is certain.

Venetians at the court of the Great Khan

The adventures of Marco Polo began with those of his father, Niccolò, and his uncle, Maffeo, the first Europeans to gain an audience with the Great Khan. These two Venetian merchants had extensive commercial dealings with the East. In 1260, in possession of a superb collection of jewels, they set out from Constantinople for the Khanate of the Golden Horde, ruled in those days by Berke, successor of Batu and grandson of Genghis Khan. The pair reached Sarai on the Volga, where the khan was holding court, and showed him their sparkling wares. Niccolò and Maffeo cleared a comfortable profit on the sale, and began to think of going home to Venice. But they could not return by the route they had come: war was raging amongst the Tartar chiefs, making the territory too dangerous. So the Polo brothers resolved to head east, and visit the Great Khan, Kublai, who reigned over all of China. Kublai received the Polos graciously, and requested that they have the pope send him 'a hundred learned men versed in the seven liberal arts', and also some oil from the lamp burning at the Holy Sepulchre in Jerusalem.

With a promise to transmit the message, the brothers left China in 1266. Three years later, they reached Venice, where Niccolò finally met his fifteen-year-old son, Marco, born in his absence.

Four years to reach Peking

Niccolò and Maffeo did not forget their promise to the Great Khan. And when they decided to return to the khan's court, Marco, then seventeen, went along with them. Pope Gregory X received the Polos in Acre, north of Jerusalem, and gave them letters and jewels for Kublai. Two preaching friars reputed for their learning were to travel with them to Khanbalik (Beijing); but alarmed by the perils they had to face, the friars soon abandoned the trip.

In 1271 Marco, his father and his uncle set out from Lajazzo (now Yumurtalik in southeastern Turkey); it took them four years to reach the court of Kublai Khan. In the meantime, they crossed the khanate of the Persian Mongols, passed through Khorasan, 'Land of the Dry Tree' (in northeast Iran), before halting at Badakhshan, at the foot of the Pamir Mountains, to spend the winter of 1271-72. In the spring they traversed the high plateau, but it took them 'a good forty days, continually crossing tall mountains, deep valleys, and stretches of desert'. Beyond, they discovered an interminable desert of dunes, the Taklimakan (situated in Sinkiang, in western China), 'inhabited by spirits who call travellers by name', as Marco described it in his book. Amid such barrenness, each oasis seemed a godsend: in Kashgar, the Venetians were enraptured by the beautiful gardens; they admired Khotan, with its rich vineyards, jade and emerald deposits. Eventually they emerged from the desert, and reached the city of Kan-chou (Kansu), where the Polos waited for a year to be invited to visit the

Great Khan in his summer palace of Shang-tu (Ciandu). The meeting finally took place in 1275; Kublai was well pleased with the travellers, whom he offered to take into his service.

Kublai's China

Marco, appointed to an administrative post in the Mongol Empire, was sent by Kublai on numerous missions throughout China. He travelled from Khanbalik (Beijing) to the kingdom of Ta-li (in Yunnan province), which had only recently been conquered by the Mongols. There he visited districts 'most difficult of access, covered with vast forests and unscaleable mountains' and whose inhabitants 'had no knowledge of letters or writing'. A second journey took him across eastern China, from north to south. He visited the cities on the eastern coast, and was filled with admiration for 'Quinsay' (Hangzhou) which, with its many canals, reminded him of Venice. It was a prosperous city, a port of call for vessels transporting salt, sugar, spices and silk up and down the China Sea. Marco Polo found it luxurious with its paved streets and numerous fountains.

A tireless observer

As a member of many Mongol embassies, Marco Polo travelled as far as Ceylon. Upon his return from these voyages, he charmed Kublai with picturesque accounts of his expeditions. A tireless observer, he was struck by the contrast between northern China (Cathay), the seat of Mongol power, and the south (Manzi) with its prosperous towns. He saw the Chinese use paper money and asbestos, and he saw them burn coal, 'a kind of black stone which is mined in the mountainsides of Cathay, and which burns like charcoal, indeed better'. He studied the functioning of the Mongol Empire, in particular the organization of its postal and transport systems. He probably held for some time a responsibility in the administration of the salt monopoly. Polo was fascinated by the intense activity at Chinese seaports, and by the abundance of pearls, diamonds, and other precious merchandise. The Yangtze-Chang seemed so wide 'that it appears to be a sea rather than a river'. Marco Polo also mentioned (although he did not travel there) a far-off island, rich in gold, situated '1500 miles east of the continent', called Cipangu: Japan.

Return to Venice

Sixteen years passed, and the three Venetians dreamed of returning home. Kublai finally acquiesced to their requests to depart. But the Polos had one final duty to perform for Kublai: they were to escort a Mongol princess, Cocacin, to Persia, where she was to marry the widowed khan, Arghun. A fleet of fourteen vessels carried the party to Sumatra, where they were delayed for several months by adverse winds. They set sail again and reached Hormuz. From there they travelled to Persia, where they bid farewell to the princess, and pursued their journey to Trebizond on the Black Sea, where they embarked for Constantinople. The Polos eventually reached Venice in 1295; Marco was forty-two years old.

Il milione: the Book of Marvels

In Marco's time a bitter rivalry raged between Genoa and Venice. In 1298 all able-bodied Venetians were ordered to take up arms. On 7 September 1298 Marco Polo, in command of a galley, fought in the battle of Cuzola. The Genoese carried the day; Marco was taken prisoner. Locked in a tower in Genoa with another captive, the writer Rustichello, Marco Polo spent the three years of his imprisonment dictating the story of his Asian travels to his cellmate. Such is the origin of *Il Milione*, or *The Book of Ser Marco Polo the Venetian Concerning the Kingdoms and Marvels of the East*, the most extraordinary travel journal ever written.

The Golden Horde

Juji, son of Genghis Khan, was the first ruler of the Golden Horde, the westernmost territory of the Mongol Empire. Established in 1223, this immense state stretched north of the Caspian and the Black Sea. The kingdom was later divided among Juji's five sons. One of them, Batu, inherited the western Khanate of Kipchak; the Polo brothers visited its capital, Sarai. At his father's death, Batu ruled over Russia and Bulgaria, and he went on to conquer Moscow, Krakow, and Hungary. The Golden Horde was destroyed in 1502 by the Tartars of the Crimea.

Excerpt from the same book showing the second departure of the Polo brothers with Niccolò's son, the seventeen-year-old Marco.

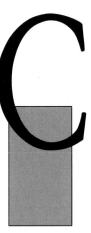

ommercial exchanges between Orient and Occident, encouraged by the Mongols in the thirteenth century, tapered off under Turkish domination. The fall of Constantinople (1453) signalled the closing of overland routes. Europeans then turned to the Atlantic and the coasts of Africa to discover a new route to the Indies.

Venetians in Constantinople

In 1203 the Venetian fleet helped the Crusaders capture Constantinople, capital of the Byzantine Empire. The city was sacked on 12 April 1204, and the Crusaders founded a Latin Empire. In exchange for its help, Venice received as its share of the spoils one quarter of the Byzantine Empire, notably the seaport of Candia (Herakleion) in Crete, and Morea (the Peloponnese). Fifty-seven years later, Michael VII Palaeologus captured the Byzantine throne, and with Genoa's help, expelled the Venetians from Constantinople.

The commercial revolution taking place in Europe between the 11th and 13th centuries was reflected in the extension of trading contacts to India and China. Above, ships unloading at Hormuz in the Persian Gulf.

In the footsteps of Marco Polo

Other Venetians, less celebrated than Marco Polo, had their share of strange adventures.

In his work *Delle Navigazione e Viaggi* ('Some Voyages and Travels') the Italian traveller and geographer Giovanni Battista Ramusio (1485-1557) records the astonishing story of a young aristocrat called Niccolò dei Conti. In 1419 Conti left Venice for Damascus, where he learned Arabic. Later,

having joined a caravan, he visited Babylon and Bassorah (Al-Basrah) before embarking on the Persian Gulf and sailing as far as the Malabar Coast of India. After exploring Ceylon and every corner of India, he pushed on to Sumatra, Java, and southern China. In 1444 Niccolò returned to Venice with his Indian wife and their children. A great worry gnawed at his conscience. His many adventures had placed him in drastic circumstances and at one point he had been compelled to renounce Christianity in order to save his life. He requested an audience from Pope Eugenius IV, to whom he confessed his crime. For his penance, the

pope required Conti to write an account of his travels, which has survived to this day.

The mysterious voyage of the Vivaldi brothers

Like Venice, the rival republic of Genoa was also a centre for merchants and navigators. Two wealthy Genoese businessmen, Ugolino and Vadino Vivaldi, were the first to attempt to reach the Indies by sailing

The Catalan Atlas was drawn up in 1375 after Marco Polo's travel reports.

southeast around Africa. In 1291, when the fall of Acre shut the Near East off to Christian traffic, the Vivaldi brothers departed from Genoa aboard two galleys. One of them, commanded by the Genoese captain Andrea Doria, was wrecked on the coast of Morocco. Doria gave up and returned to Italy. But the Vivaldis were not discouraged. They continued their voyage, but during a stopover in the Gambia they were captured by natives. Nothing was ever heard of them again.

The Canary Islands

———————●———————

In 1312 another Genoese, Lanzaroti Malocello, landed on a small volcanic island in the Atlantic off Morocco. Covered with craters and strangely shaped lava fields, the island belonged to the Canary archipelago, which had until then escaped colonization. The Italian did not linger long, but he left the island his name: Lanzarote.

The name of the islands comes from a text by the Roman writer Pliny the Elder who mentions 'Canaria, so called from the multitude of dogs [*canes*] of great size'.

Normans in the Canaries

———————●———————

A century later, Jean de Béthencourt and Gadifer de la Salle were the first to conquer a part of the Canary archipelago, helped by a handful of mercenaries. On 1 May 1402, Béthencourt, an impoverished Norman nobleman and former chamberlain of Charles VI, embarked with his companions at La Rochelle. After a brief halt in Spain, the crew reached the island of Lanzarote, which they quickly brought under their control. They resolved to bestow their prize on the King of Castile, who named Béthencourt 'Lord of the Canary Islands'. After returning to France several times to bring back contingents of colonists, Béthencourt left the Canaries for good, entrusting the government to his nephew, Maciot. He retired to Normandy, where he wrote *Le Canarien*, an account of his conquest of the archipelago. Béthencourt died in 1425.

Other islands were soon conquered, though with more difficulty, for the natives, the Guanches, fiercely fought off the invaders with their primitive weapons of stone and wood. Fuerteventura, Hierro ('the island of iron') and Gomera resisted for several years before they were subdued. Though he had bestowed his possessions on the King of Castile, some islands were conquered by Portuguese soldiers and the archipelago was disputed between Spain and Portugal until the Treaty of Alcaçovas in 1479, which allotted them to Spain.

Just as Jean de Béthencourt was setting off to conquer the Canary Islands, another Frenchman, a certain Anselme d'Ysalguier of Toulouse, commenced a long voyage to Africa. He may in fact have belonged to the force commanded by Béthencourt, for he landed in Gao (Mali) in 1405, when Béthencourt launched a raid on the African coast.

Anselme's story is known through the writings of a fifteenth-century scholar, Guillaume Bardin, and an eighteenth-century canon, Anthelme de Tricaud, who both affirm that they read Anselme's memoirs (now lost) in manuscript.

Anselme d'Ysalguier on the banks of the Niger

———————●———————

Anselme spent eight years in Gao, then part of the Mali empire. There he got married to Casaïs, a young Muslim noblewoman. She is probably responsible for preserving Anselme's life — as a Christian, he was a prime candidate to perish in the 'Holy War'. In Mali, he studied Arabic, Tuareg, and Songhaï. Finally, Anselme decided to return to Toulouse with his wife and daughter. It is not known how he made his way back to the Mediterranean, but it is likely he followed the trail linking the Niger to Tunis via the Ahaggar Mountains. At sea, the ship carrying Anselme and his family was attacked by pirates, then rescued by a band of Provençal corsairs. The voyagers eventually landed safely in Toulouse. They were accompanied by several black servants and a sorcerer, Aben Ali. Ali is credited with having cured the dauphin (the future Charles VII of France), who fell ill while visiting Toulouse in 1420. To the full account of his adventures in Africa, Anselme appended an Arab-Tuareg and African dictionary, the first of its kind.

The Portuguese displayed great thoroughness in charting the West African coast. Above, Bartholomeu Dias with Guinean leaders.

The Original Canary Islanders

When Spanish mariners discovered the Canary Islands, they stumbled upon a population that resembled Cro-Magnon man with an admixture of Berber traits. The Guanches lived in the Stone Age: they dwelt in caves, wore goat skins, and ate cheese and a kind of flour called *gofio*. They had no knowledge of metal. Yet armed with simple weapons of stone and hardened wood, they resisted the Spanish invaders for nearly a century. Decimated by the Spanish, by plague and famine, they left very few descendants.

Antonio Malfant at Tuat

Around 1446 a Genoese merchant, Centurione, sent his agent Antonio Malfant to North Africa to gather information on gold deposits in the Sahel, and to organize the transport of gold from Africa to Europe. In a letter written in 1447 to a Genoese friend, Malfant recounts his arrival and sojourn in Tuat, a group of oases in the northwest of the Sahara, twenty or thirty days' ride from the large commercial centres of the Maghreb: Fez, Tlemcen and Tunis. Antonio was the first Christian to enter the city of Tamentit. When they recovered from their surprise, the inhabitants grew accustomed to the European, and initiated him into the ways of the desert. Antonio admired the equestrian skill of the Tuaregs, praising them as 'incomparable horsemen'. Tuat was a great commercial crossroads, a central meeting place for caravans. Gold dust and vegetable butter from Timbuktu were exchanged there for wheat and barley brought in from the coast. Yet Malfant did no trading there, for 'the local inhabitants refuse to buy or sell or make any other transaction unless they receive a one-hundred-percent commission'. He foresaw that the future lay elsewhere: along the River Niger in the region of Timbuktu. His friend, the sheikh of Tamentit, spoke at length about Mali, where he had spent fourteen years and made a fortune. Unfortunately, Malfant could wrest no precise information about gold mines from his friend. But the sheikh regaled the Genoese with details about the inhabitants of Mali and their way of life. Malfant's letter relays all the information he could gather in the Niger basin.

Yet it roused no interest at all in Genoa, then involved in internecine rivalries, and no cartographer made use of his precious revelations. Malfant returned to Europe, and died in Majorca in 1450.

A new route to the Indies

In the fifteenth century, Western merchants keenly felt the need to discover a new route to the Indies. They had to meet the demands of clients accustomed since the Crusades to luxury goods from the Orient. But the Turks had effectively closed off traditional routes to the East, complicating the task of Genoese and Venetian traders, who could no longer procure their precious merchandise. Moreover, they needed huge quantities of gold and silver to conclude their transactions; hence the growing interest in sending expeditions to remote lands, which, the merchants hoped, would yield the gold they sorely lacked.

The Portuguese, for their part, were tempted by Africa, from which they hoped to derive a triple profit: control of the gold traffic, an alliance against Islam with the fabled Prester John, and the discovery of a new maritime route around Africa to the Indies. With such a new route, Portugal could break the commercial monopoly of Genoa and Venice in the Mediterranean.

Adventure on the high seas

Henry the Navigator and his nephew, King John II of Portugal, both motivated by intense scientific curiosity, were the driving forces behind Portugal's maritime explorations of the African coast (see p. 26). It was probably Bartholomeu Dias in 1487 who first rounded Cape Tormentoso, afterwards christened the Cape of Good Hope by King John II. But for several years before that, the Portuguese had profited from their African expeditions. Gold was discovered in the Gambia, and a lucrative slave trade added considerable sums to the kingdom's coffers.

Ca'Da Mosto reaches the Gambia

Adverse winds were responsible for starting the remarkable career of the Venetian adventurer Alvise da Ca'Da Mosto (1432-1477). He embarked in 1454 on a voyage to Flanders, but was compelled to land on the Portuguese coast, at Cape Saint Vincent. Not far from there, in Lagos, Prince Henry the Navigator had established the base for his maritime expeditions. A small town, La Villa do Infante, served both as an arsenal and a haven for passing seamen, and Henry, a skilled astronomer, had installed his observatory there. Ca'Da Mosto was introduced to the prince, who outlined to him his ambitious projects for exploring Africa. The Venetian listened with growing enthusiasm, and did not hesitate to accept Henry's offer to enter his service.

In 1434 the Portuguese succeeded in rounding the fearsome Cape Bojador (on the coast of Western Sahara) and returned without mishap despite the trade winds. Ca'Da Mosto set sail in 1455 on a reconnaissance expedition to the West African coast.

He passed Madeira (claimed for Portugal in 1420 by Zarco), the Canary Islands, Cap Blanc in Mauritania, Cape Verde in Senegal, and eventually reached the mouth of the River Gambia. The white men's arrival startled the natives, who thought the Europeans were 'sorcerers, not unlike devils'; the Africans rubbed the visitors' skin, to remove what they believed to be paint. However, Ca'Da Mosto lost no time concluding a pact with the king, Batimansa, to exchange gold and slaves for European goods.

The Cape Verde Islands

The following year, the Venetian undertook another expedition. He was accompanied by a Genoese, Uso di Mare, whom he had met on his previous voyage to Cape Verde. The two navigators set a southern course, and discovered the Cape Verde Islands, five hundred kilometres off the coast of Africa. They were uninhabited. A few years later, in 1460, the Genoese Antonio de Noli returned to explore these islands, and claimed them for Portugal. The first settlers from Portugal landed in 1462. The islands gained fame when King Louis XI of France sent there for sea turtles which, it was said, cured leprosy if one ate of their flesh and bathed in their blood. But the trade in sea turtles was soon supplanted by the more lucrative commerce in ebony. To his own memoirs Ca'Da Mosto appended the travels of Pietro di Cintra, a gentleman of the house of Alfonso V, who pursued the exploration of the African coast. Di Cintra set out in 1462 with two caravels, and eventually landed in Guinea.

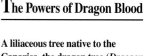

The Powers of Dragon Blood

A liliaceous tree native to the Canaries, the dragon tree (*Dracaena drago*), can grow to colossal heights and live for thousands of years. It secretes a resinous sap called dragon's blood, which, as it dries, turns crumbly and blood-red. The Guanches recognized the resin's medicinal properties — for example, it can stanch the flow of blood. Near Icod, a small village on the island of Tenerife, stands an immense dragon tree, probably the oldest in the Canaries.

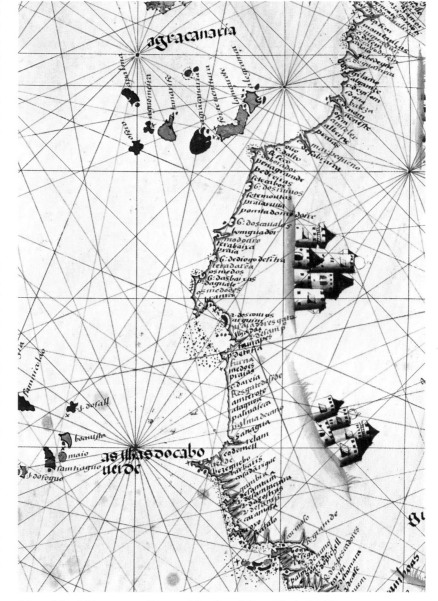

Map of the African coast, Canary Islands and Cape Verde (1514)

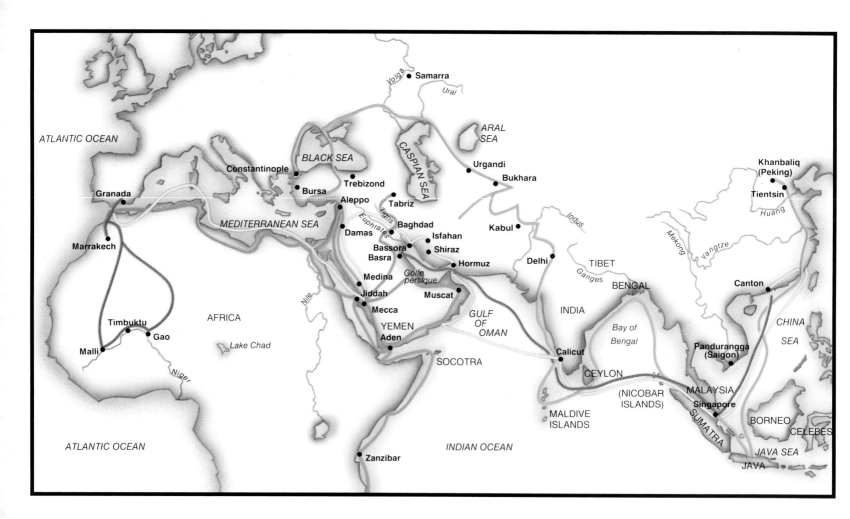

ATLANTIC OCEAN

Volga • Samarra
Ural

ARAL
SEA

BLACK SEA

CASPIAN SEA

Constantinople
Granada
Bursa
Trebizond
Aleppo
Tabriz
Urgandi
Bukhara
Khanbaliq
(Peking)

Tientsin
Huang

MEDITERRANEAN SEA
Euphrates
Tigris
Baghdad
Damas
Isfahan
Kabul
Indus
Marrakech
Bassora
Basra
Shiraz
Delhi
TIBET
Ganges
Mekong
Yangtze

Nile
Medina
Golfe
persique
Hormuz
Muscat
BENGAL
Canton

AFRICA
Jiddah
Mecca
INDIA
Bay of
Bengal
CHINA
SEA

Timbuktu
Gao
Lake Chad
YEMEN
Aden
GULF
OF
OMAN
Calicut
Pandurangga
(Saigon)

Malli
Niger
SOCOTRA
CEYLON
MALAYSIA
Singapore
SUMATRA
BORNEO
CELEBES

ATLANTIC OCEAN
(NICOBAR
ISLANDS)
JAVA SEA

MALDIVE
ISLANDS
JAVA

INDIAN OCEAN
Zanzibar

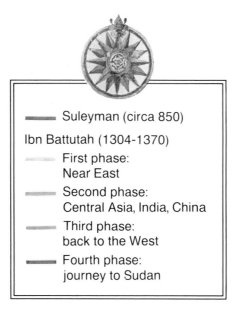

——— Suleyman (circa 850)

Ibn Battutah (1304-1370)

——— First phase:
Near East

——— Second phase:
Central Asia, India, China

——— Third phase:
back to the West

——— Fourth phase:
journey to Sudan

Islamic
Travellers

I slam and Jihad or 'Holy War' proclaimed by the Prophet Muhammad in the seventh century AD signalled the birth of a vast empire that stretched from the Iberian peninsula to India. A variety of expeditions funnelled back to Baghdad the information needed to administer the government and economy of a powerful empire. At the same time this wealth of data laid the foundations of a distinctively Arabic study of geography.

Arabic geography had both a mathematical aspect and a literary or descriptive aspect.

Geographers for the empire

The mosaic of peoples and languages that composed the Arab-Muslim Empire made it a highly diverse assemblage of nations. The unifying factors of the empire's ever-precarious political and cultural cohesion were the Muslim religion (founded by Muhammad who also lay behind the expansionism of the Arabian tribes) and the Arabic tongue. Two successive dynasties ruled over the Empire: the Omayyad caliphs (660-750) from Damascus, and the Abbasids (750-1253) of Baghdad. The Arab-Muslim Empire and civilization reached their peak in the ninth century. Thereafter a long decline set in, which culminated in the Mongols' destruction of Baghdad in 1253. Yet from the ninth century on, autonomous states had formed around new dynasties in Spain, Egypt, Iran, and Central Asia: these new states, whether Sunni or Shiite, concluded alliances with the Byzantine Empire against Baghdad. In these shifting circumstances the caliph needed a precise knowledge of his own domains, as well as of nations that were potential military allies or trading partners. The political value of such information explains why the regime provided support and assistance for geographers who were sometimes its agents, sometimes its censors.

All roads lead to Mecca

Geography was a learned discipline that encompassed the study of the earth and the heavens: geodesy, astronomy and astrology were all seen as closely interlinked fields of study. Rooted in the Greek Ptolemean tradition, Arab cosmology postulated that the Earth was the immobile centre of a system of concentric circles. This view was supplemented by a Persian-inspired geopolitical conception, which placed either Iraq or the Holy Cities of Arabia at the centre of the world.

The Arabs adapted Greek cartography to their own uses when it became necessary to provide travellers with geographical information. The Muslim faithful, for example, had to be able to find the direction of Mecca from any point at any time, if their prayers were to be valid. This religious imperative spurred cartographical research and the improvement of maps, which benefited not only scholars but the population at large: charts of seas, coastlines and rivers were naturally vital to navigators, while maps of mountains and deserts were invaluable to caravans. And in their turn travellers contributed their own knowledge and experience to make Arab maps ever more accurate and functional.

A new literary genre

The human and natural resources of every province in the empire were recorded in a centrally administered geographical survey, which proved to be of great political and economic value.

This information was eventually consigned to books, giving rise in the tenth century to monographs on the geography of Muslim kingdoms and descriptions of itineraries and routes within the empire. In this new literary genre the author's own commentary was combined with scientific and social information and enlivened by anecdotes drawn from other books. Although not professional geographers, the authors of these works had travelled widely for business or pleasure; it became fashionable for such men to recount what they had seen of the world for the instruction and amusement of their contemporaries.

The *Book of Roads and Kingdoms*

Ibn Khordadhbeh (meaning 'Blessing of the Sun') was typical of the senior civil servants whom the Abbassid Empire recruited from the Iranian aristocracy. Born in 820 in eastern Iran, Ibn Khordadhbeh was the son of a governor of Tabaristan, an Iranian province on the Caspian Sea. Educated in Baghdad, he was converted to Islam and named director of the Barid (intelligence service) of Jibal in western Iran. Later he was appointed to the Barid of Baghdad, and finally to the Barid of Samarra, where the court resided during the caliphate of al-Mutamid, a friend of Ibn Khordadhbeh. In his works, Ibn Khordadhbeh described the Turco-Mongol peoples of Central Asia—nomadic shepherds who served as mercenaries for the empire and the caliph's militia—as well as the itineraries of navigators who sailed to Asia and Africa. Though he described these routes in detail, it is not certain that he travelled them himself. More courtier than voyager, he wrote the first *Book of Roads and Kingdoms*, which won him fame as an author and geographer. Ibn Khordadhbeh was the founder of a scientific and literary genre, involving the minute description of roads, relays, watering places, caravanserais, rivers, deserts, peoples, and the location of seaports and maritime routes. The first *Book of Roads and Kingdoms*, written in 846, was an austere documentary work. In 885 Ibn Khordadhbeh published an annexe to the book, embellished with literary references, which considerably widened the work's appeal.

The merchant Suleyman in the Far East

The *Relation of China and India* has sometimes been attributed to Abu Zayd as Sirafi, but in fact the book was written in 851 by a merchant whose name (or pseudonym) was Suleyman. Abu Zayd as Sirafi, who lived a century later, was the author of *A Supplement to the Relation of China and India*. The two writers' accounts vary considerably.

The merchant Suleyman embarked on his voyage at Siraf on the Persian Gulf. He called at Suhar and Muscat, and then sailed on the open sea directly to Kerala in southern India. And a daring undertaking it was: a century later the itinerary described by Ibn Kordadhbeh closely hugged the coasts of Pakistan and India. After the cros-

sing Suleyman stopped awhile at Kulam-Mali in Kerala before setting off on another expedition. He skirted the southern tip of the Indian peninsula, and keeping to the high seas reached the present-day Nicobar Islands before calling at Kelang in Malaysia. He crossed the Strait of Malacca, keeping close to the coast of Sumatra, stopped at Singapore, and then sailed into the Gulf of Tonkin. He landed at Panduraga (Saigon) and then at Hainan, before finally putting in at Canton (Guangzhou) in southern China. Suleyman stayed for long periods at the Muslim trading posts in India and China; and like most travellers of his day he was a keen observer and commentator.

While the merchant Suleyman was a hardened traveller, Abu Zayd as Sirafi was 'a learned man interested in geography'. He brought the merchant's account up to date with technical information gleaned from sailors about the navigation and construction of ships. The sea stories that Sirafi collected were largely legend. He turned the true stories into a work of fiction in which he freely embroidered far-off lands, turning India and China into fabulous places where any flight of fancy was possible.

A ninth-century bestseller

The adventures of Sindbad were incorporated into the *Thousand and One Nights* in the eighteenth century by the copyist who transcribed the translation of Antoine Galland. Galland was a seventeenth-century French diplomat and translator of stories which he was the first to reveal to the West. *Sindbad the Sailor and Sindbad the Landsman* was a popular novel written in ninth-century Baghdad, in which two men of different personalities and social backgrounds confronted each other: Sindbad the Landsman, a porter of Baghdad who remained poor all his life, and Sindbad the Sailor who grew prosperous on his fabulous voyages. First rendered in English by Edward Lane in 1841, the tales were later translated by Sir Richard Burton (see p. 214).

Sindbad, the 'man of India' or the 'man lured by China', is the prototype of the boastful merchant seaman, ever on the lookout for profitable business. The character is not wholly fictional: his adventures are based on the exploits of the real-life Sindbad, who in the early ninth century was given a mission by Caliph Harun al-Rashid to visit the king of Ceylon. The novel, written around 840, is supposed to have inspired some of the descriptions of Ibn Khordadhbeh. Sindbad's seven voyages took him to

Sindbad being saved by an eagle of Diamond Valley, where he 'won for himself a great treasure of precious stones'.

sea for over sixty years. He always embarked from the Gulf of Oman with the January monsoon and returned in summer. His earlier voyages lasted from two to six years while the final one, which took him to Japan, lasted twenty-seven. Each voyage forms a chapter in the navigator's story, recapitulating the dreams of all the Arab sailors and merchants of the age. Sindbad chartered fine sailing ships: their wooden hulls formed deep holds to carry vast quantities of merchandise, while passengers remained above deck, on the bridge.

The fabulous voyages of Sindbad the Sailor

On his first voyage Sindbad shipped a cargo worth three thousand pieces of silver; two years later, upon his return, he had earned one hundred thousand pieces of gold in Sumatra and Celebes. His second voyage took him to Madagascar and Borneo, the third from Borneo to Java, the fourth through Indonesia, the fifth to the East African coast, Somalia and the Comoros, the sixth to India and Ceylon, the seventh to northern China (Tian Shan) and Japan (the island of Kyushu).

Whom did Sindbad encounter in these remote lands? Sailors and merchants from Basra, of course—a brotherhood bound

Sindbad's fright

'Presently we heard a terrible great cry like the loud-pealing thunder, whereat we were terror-struck and became as dead men, giving ourselves up for lost. Then behold, there came up to us a huge fish, as big as a tall mountain, at whose sight we became wild for affright and, weeping sore, made ready for death, marvelling at its vast size and gruesome semblance; when lo! a second fish made its appearance than which we had seen naught more monstrous. So we bemoaned ourselves of our lives and farewelled one another; but suddenly up came a third fish bigger than the two first; whereupon we lost the power of thought and reason and were stupefied for the excess of our fear and horror. Then the three fish began circling round about the ship and the third and biggest opened his mouth to swallow it, and we looked into its mouth and behold, it was wider than the gate of a city and its throat was like a long valley. So we besought the Almighty and called for succour upon His Apostle (on whom be blessing and peace!), when suddenly a violent squall of wind arose and smote the ship, which rose out of the water and settled upon a great reef, the haunt of sea-monsters, where it broke up and fell asunder into planks and all and everything on board were plunged into the sea.'
The Seventh Voyage of Sindbad the Sailor, translation by Sir Richard Burton, Benares: The Kamashastra Society, 1885.

Caravaneer and camel laden with merchandise — funerary statuettes of the T'ang dynasty (7 th — 8 th centuries).

The Abbasids of Baghdad

The Abbasid dynasty reigned from 750 to 1253. The Syrianization of Arab culture (in the Omayyad period) was succeeded by an era of Persianization. The Abbasids modelled their empire on the old Iranian state of the Sassanids; political and military functions were assumed by Persian dignitaries and Turkish mercenaries. As the dynasty declined, the caliphate was reduced to a mere fiction. Caliphs were little more than the hostages of their Persian viziers and their Turkish generals.

more by their shared life at sea than by common religious beliefs. Sindbad discovered cities and peoples with unfamiliar customs; he liked nothing better than to be surprised and astonished by their strangeness. Little concerned with religion—wealth was his true faith—less interested in culture than in fantastic legends, Sindbad told the tale of the fabulous roc, a bird widely known yet never seen, who saved Sindbad's life and made his fortune; we follow him in his stories from the pit of the dead to the isle of jewels, a fantastic journey filled with dangers and frights, insatiable curiosity, greed and generosity. His fabulous voyages take Sindbad on the wings of bird-men who show him the planet where Satan reigns, then return him finally, as a grizzled old man, to the land where his betrothed awaits him. The moral of Sindbad's travels is that courage will be rewarded by wealth and wisdom—a fitting ideal for a merchant society and a polished culture.

Among the Bulgarians of the Volga

All we really know of Ibn Fadlan is that he was not an Arab, though it was in the Arab language that he wrote of the secret mission despatched by Caliph Al-Muktadir (908-932) to the King of the Bulgars, in which Ibn Fadlan played an important part.

A close confidant of the sovereign, Ibn Fadlan probably belonged to the class of well-born adventurers whom the caliph took into his service because they were knowledgeable yet remote from court intrigues. The caliph's embassy sought an alliance with the Bulgars, in order to neutralize their common enemy, the Khazars, a Turco-Mongol nation whose rampages were disrupting international trade. In exchange for the caliph's support, the Bulgars—some of whom were already Muslims—would promise to renounce some of their ancient customs and become good Muslims and permanent allies on the borders of the empire. The embassy's caravan, led by a eunuch, left Baghdad on 21 June 921, crossed Iraq and northern Iran, rounded the Caspian Sea via present-day Turkmenistan, and arrived in Bulgaria on 12 May 922. On the way the caravan stopped in several cities—notably Bukhara and Gurgan—but the route followed on the return journey is not known.

Foreign lands, foreign customs

Ibn Fadlan described the lands he visited in minute detail. Everywhere he went he closely observed and noted the topography, climate, fauna and flora, inhabitants, political institutions, family structure and eating habits. Of the land of the Bulgars he wrote: 'I witnessed many a marvel there'. He was interested by the Bulgars' abodes: still half-nomadic, in summer they lived in yurts, round Turco-Mongol tents made of felt; in winter, they sheltered in wooden houses. Bulgar, the capital, and Suwar were the only towns of any consequence, but they boasted large mosques. The Bulgar king, a convert to Islam, was called Almus ("the Muslim"). Ibn Fadlan and the missionaries who accompanied him were shocked by the freedom of Bulgar women's manners. They were neither veiled nor sequestered; before marriage, young girls indulged in scandalously uninhibited behaviour and virginity was not an issue. 'Try as I might, all my efforts to make the women veil their faces in the presence of men were vain', the pious traveller lamented.

Ibn Fadlan also described the Petchenegs, the Bulgars' neighbours' and the Burtas, vassals of the Khazars. He was amazed by the Russians. These barbarians, their bodies covered with tattoos, bathed naked in the Volga and practised collective copulation. Their king had forty concubines, whom he enjoyed on his immense bed under the gaze of his guardsmen. Stranger still were the Russians' funeral rites, which incorporated animal sacrifice, immolation of slaves, and cremation of the corpse on a boat pushed out to drift along the Volga. The spectacle of such grandiose savagery fascinated the Muslim chronicler.

A Shiite encyclopedist and agitator

The biographical details of al-Masudi's life are hazy; it is known only that he was born in Baghdad and died in Cairo in 956. The descendant of a companion of the Prophet Abd Allah Massud, who joined the Shia sect of the Alides, al-Masudi was also a Shiite. He seems to have sympathized with

For coastal navigation, Arabs used simple boats, while out at sea they used decked ships.

the Ismailian sect and acted as their envoy. The Ismailis flourished in the tenth century, inspiring various political movements hostile to the caliphate. A Shiite missionary (or agitator) disguised as a simple traveller, al-Masudi was also a student of religions—Christianity, Judaism, Zoroastrianism—and of Greek philosophy. As a result of his controversial opinions he was forced out of Iraq into exile in Egypt, where he died.

Al-Masudi's tribulations on land and sea took him to the Persian city of Istakhr in 915, then to India. Descending the valley of the Indus, he reached India's western coast and landed in Ceylon, where he managed to join a merchant expedition to China. Al-Masudi's wanderings in Asia were followed by a voyage to the eastern coast of Africa. He stopped off on Zanzibar, an island near present-day Tanzania, before sailing towards Oman, the Persian Gulf and Iraq.

Later his traces can be picked up on the empire's caravan routes, in regions where Ismailian propaganda was widespread: in Iran on the southern shores of the Caspian from 922 to 924, at Antioch in Syria, at Tiberias in Palestine.

Back in Basra, threatened by the ruling dynasty, al-Masudi was obliged to flee first to Syria and later to Egypt. Al-Masudi is the author of some thirty works, of which only two have come down to us. Feverishly and in great haste, he wrote a thirty-volume *Universal History* in 932.

In the tradition of Muslim kingdoms

The great traveller and geographer al-Muqaddasi was born in Jerusalem early in the tenth century. As a merchant and a follower of Sufism, a mystical sect that had emerged in Iran and was rapidly spreading in the tenth century, he roamed the Muslim world both to trade and to win converts. Though al-Muqaddasi spoke of the island of Socotra in the Indian Ocean as a 'tower in the Sea of Darkness', he admitted himself that he had never ventured outside the borders of the Muslim world, for he had nothing but scorn for the 'infidel nations'. His considerable culture and travels inspired the book *The Best Distribution for Knowledge of the Provinces*. The original manuscript of this 'enlightening treatise', composed between 985 and 990, was found in India and is now in Berlin. The human and political geography described by al-Muqaddasi is in the eclectic tradition of 'Muslim roads and kingdoms'. Although he is interested in the sea, rivers and their legends are what really fascinate him: the Tigris and Euphrates, of course, but also 'the marvels of the Nile and the many gifts it bestowed on man'. To the map of climates, inhabited lands, zones of sunshine and the like, al-Muqaddasi added an imaginary

The Golden Prairies

This encyclopedic work, one of al-Masudi's most famous, reflected his era's intellectual ideal: a display of vast knowledge embellished with personal anecdotes. But al-Masudi's world view was considerably broader than that of medieval Islam, for he was familiar with and interested in non-Islamic religions and non-Arab peoples whom he had encountered in Africa and Asia.

map of holy places, marked by a 76 kilometre circle around Jerusalem. That city supplanted the holy places of Arabia, and reflected the author's Palestinian origins, as well as his religious convictions as a dissident missionary. What interested him most about large cities was their layout and their monuments, which al-Muqaddasi—thanks to his architectural knowledge—was able to reconstruct from memory. Rural and village life caught his attention too. This 'geography of mentalities' reflects both the author's reaction to the peoples he encountered, and the contemporary political tensions between Iraq and the caliphate on the one hand, and the dissident regions of Andalusia and Iran on the other.

What strange beasts are these?

A whale: 'A fish like a cow that bringeth forth its young and suckleth them like human beings; and of its skin bucklers are made.' *Sindbad the Sailor...*, trans. Sir Richard Burton.

The silver planisphere of al-Idrisi

Al-Idrisi takes us into the western Arab Empire. Born in Ceuta, Morocco, around 1100, he studied at the University of Cor-doba, the brilliant Muslim capital founded in the eighth century by a descendant of the Omayyads. In the twelfth century the Muslim West was in turmoil owing, among other setbacks, to the Norman reconquest of Sicily. The new Christian monarchs were charmed by the splendour of Oriental courts and harems; they also welcomed Muslim intellectuals together with Italian, Greek and Arab artists. Al-Idrisi lived and died in Sicily, considered a renegade by his fellow Muslims for having entered the service of a Christian ruler. Al-Idrisi's voyages in the Maghreb, in Spain, and in western Europe revealed Arabic geography to the West. For King Roger II of Sicily al-Idrisi-crafted a planisphere and map on a silver tablet, which demonstrated how his thorough knowledge of western Europe gave Arab geography a new dimension. Al-Idrisi's silver planisphere was both a splendid artifact and a valuable instrument, which encapsulated all the era's geographical knowledge in a readily understandable form. It was accompanied by a geographical treatise entitled the *Kitab Rudjar* or *Roger's Book*. Al-Idrisi also produced a map of the world, which was used as a model for several centuries, and a series of seventy maps of regions of the known world.

In 1154 al-Idrisi completed a book entitled *The Travellers' Recreation*, a work in the tradition of the Muslim 'Roads and Kingdoms', which had introduced Arabic geography to the West. He later composed a second cartographical work with a map of the world and eight coloured maps.

Break-up of the Muslim world

The Islamic Empire survived the Crusades but did not withstand the thirteenth-century Mongol invasions. Baghdad fell in 1257, putting an end to the empire and the caliphate. The descendants of Genghis Khan now ruled Asia and the Orient: the Persian Khanate (Ilkhans), the Golden Horde in Asia Minor where the Byzantine Empire had abandoned its possessions and Christian peoples, and the Mamelukes (1250-1517) in Egypt and Syria. In the West, the great Moorish dynasties of the twelfth century, the Almoravids and the Almohads, could not prevent the disintegration of Muslim Spain; Berber dynasties created new states in the Maghreb, while Muslim states eventually took form south of the Sahara (Mali, Niger and Ghana).

This new distribution of states and power in a turbulent political climate favoured the emergence of men with entrenched religious convictions. Such a man was Ibn Battutah, an Andalusian from Morocco, a Sunni Muslim and Malekite, who followed the strict rite that prevailed in the Muslim West.

The Traveller of Islam

Ibn Battutah preached the unity of Islam against the Ismaili sects—such as the Alamut sect in Syria headed by the Old Man of the Mountain—and Shiite extremists who were particularly active in the Near East and in Asia Minor. Born in Tangier (Morocco) in 1304, Ibn Battutah died in the same city in 1369 after a lifetime of travels that began in Arabia (where he made his first pilgrimage to Mecca in 1325). This contemporary of Marco Polo also spent several years in the Near East. He made three more pilgrimages to Mecca between 1327 and 1330, and visited Arabia, Yemen, and perhaps East Africa as well. After anoth-

Abu Zayd's manuscripts, written at the beginning of the 10th century, belong to the tradition of travellers' tales inspired by myth and fantasy.

er pilgrimage to Mecca in 1332, Ibn Battutah travelled to Egypt and Syria, then was rapidly initiated into Sufism in Jerusalem. He journeyed next to Asia Minor, Crimea, southern Russia and Afghanistan. In 1333 he roamed the valley of the Indus, and stayed in Delhi until 1342. He travelled twice to the Maldive Islands, visited Ceylon and Sumatra, and made numerous excursions into southern China. He may have reached Beijing, but there is no proof of it. He returned to India in 1347, and thence journeyed to Egypt and Morocco. From there Ibn Battutah travelled to the kingdom of Granada, the last Muslim bastion in Spain, and then made his way back to Morocco. After leaving Sijilmassa, an oasis in the Sahara, in 1352, he crossed the desert and spent one year in the Empire of Mali, then at the height of its power.

Back in Morocco once more, Ibn Battutah dictated his memoirs to a scribe appointed by the Sultan Abu Inan; certain distinctive features of the account, completed in 1357, are attributed to the scribe.

Sojourns in holy places

Why did the pious Ibn Battutah—a frequent guest in religious foundations—ceaselessly roam the Arab world? In the first place, to further his knowledge of Islam; but also to gain fame as a pilgrim, as a means to obtaining lucrative honorific positions. As a youth he carefully cultivated his image as a mystic and a holy man. This preoccupation crops up in each description Ibn Battutah gives of holy places, religious edifices and miracles. In his description of the Kaaba—the sacred black stone of the Great Mosque at Mecca, which pilgrims must walk round seven times—he compares it to a young bride: 'the mouth that embraces it feels great joy, and he who embraces it wishes never to cease embracing it ... It is the right hand of God on his earth.' Of Baghdad he says, citing an ancient poet: 'Baghdad is a vast dwelling place for the rich, but for the poor it is a place of discomfort and anxiety. I wandered lost in its streets like the Koran in the house of an unbeliever.'

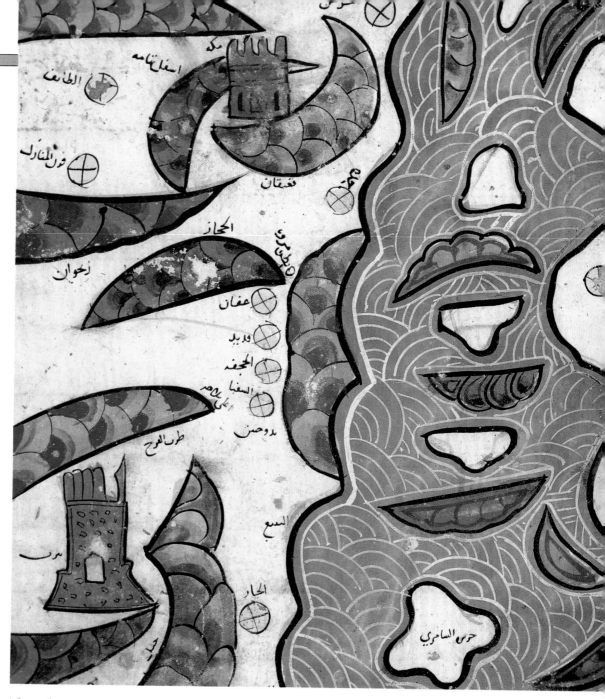

The Red Sea and holy cities. Excerpt from the treatise written by al-Idrisi for King Roger II of Sicily.

Festivals and epidemics

Ibn Battutah's description of India is more politically orientated, as he retraces the history and struggles of India's small Muslim states. The author embellishes his account with picturesque scenes such as an audience in the Sultan's court, with the ruler seated on a throne banked with white cushions, saluted by bowing elephants with iron-clad tusks. Plague epidemics and revolts alternate with festivals. Ibn Battutah recounts that he received entire villages as gifts, thus assuring him of a comfortable income. He was also given Indian women captured in war, slaves whom he nonchalantly offered to his friends: 'female captives have no value in India, for they are dirty and know nothing of urban life and manners'.

Porcelain and paper money

In China Ibn Battutah showed great interest in the manufacture of porcelain (then a very old Oriental art), and especially in the construction of large twelve-sail ships made of braided bamboo. Chinese cities and their Muslim quarters, religious customs, and funeral rites also fascinated the traveller. He noted the iron-weighted stick the Chinese carried, which they called their 'third leg', and the use of paper money, which made bartering and gold coins obsolete. Ibn Battutah's journey west gave him the chance to view and describe the Nile. He first mistook hippopotamuses for elephants. When he enquired about the strange beasts, he was informed that they were 'sea or river horses which grazed on land'.

At Timbuktu he saw men with veiled faces. Although Ibn Battutah found 'the blacks praiseworthy' for their justice, honesty and piety, he showed indignation at the nudity of their women: 'the servant girls, slave women and little girls appear before men entirely naked, with their private parts uncovered'.

An invitation to travel

'Let not exile affright you if you have means to live; let not separation afflict you if it procures for you a life of ease...'
'Travel afar, therefore, to seek your living; even if you do not make your fortune, you shall learn much...'
Ibn al-Faquih (d. after 903)

F rom time immemorial the merchant economy of Oriental societies made travel an important means of material and spiritual enrichment. Ships and caravans were fitted out to bring back rare merchandise but they were also sent out to win new believers for the Muslim faith. However diverse the motives for their journeys, Islam's tireless travellers, ambassadors, merchants, missionaries and mariners were major figures in the Oriental Middle Ages.

Pilgrims and merchants travelled on the main inland waterways in light boats.

48

Sewn skins and wooden hulls

True to their nomadic origins, Arab conquerors were more often caravaneers than seamen. They learned navigation from the peoples they conquered, and soon became as skilled at piloting ships as at driving camels through the desert.

The earliest Arab ships were light vessels made from animal skins sewn together. In the eighth century these craft were replaced by wooden-hulled ships held together by nails and coated with pitch. Large-scale shipbuilding resulted in the destruction of large areas of forest in the Maghreb, in the Near East and in Asia Minor. Hardwoods were also imported from Asia and, especially, Africa.

The Arab Empire eventually boasted large merchant fleets, as well as thriving ports on rivers and coasts. Seaborne expeditions to the West sailed from Alexandria in Egypt for Naples, Sicily, Sardinia, Venice or Narbonne. Coastal navigation in the Maghreb led to Gibraltar and beyond, to West Africa and the Canaries. From Basra, a river port in southern Iraq (now inland owing to the build-up of silt from the Tigris and Euphrates rivers), crews embarked for

The land of the *waq-waq*

Tales of adventure at sea told and retold in taverns and marketplaces portrayed a fictional world where anything could happen: violent death or undreamt-of good fortune and riches awaited the intrepid traveller. *Waq-waqs* (talking trees), fantastic beasts and tribes that inhabited fabulous islands and continents caused awestruck listeners to shiver with fear and delight.

the Persian Gulf and the Gulf of Oman, and thence to East Africa: Mozambique, the islands of the Indian Ocean, Socotra, the Maldive Islands, Zanzibar, Madagascar and Asia. Coastal navigation continued along India's shores, from Tanah (Bombay) to Kerala and Ceylon. The Indian Ocean was 'the great Oriental sea [which] produces excellent ambergris. She conceals in her depths a fish one hundred to two hundred cubits in length; fishermen fear it so they strike together pieces of wood and put it to flight...'

Caravan routes

In the ninth century great maritime expeditions took Arab navigators as far as China. In the following century piracy made sea routes and seaborne trade more dangerous, hence the development of relatively safer caravan routes. All of these started or ended in Baghdad, the political and economic centre of the empire. Eastern routes linked Baghdad to China via Iran and Central Asia, as well as to India and Tibet. To the south, the road from Baghdad to Basra joined the maritime routes to India, China, Socotra and Africa. The Arabian road led to the holy cities of Mecca and Medina, to which every good Muslim was obliged to make at least one pilgrimage in his lifetime. Syrian routes led via Damascus and Aleppo to the Byzantine Empire and the Christian world, to Trebizond on the Black Sea, and to the Danube. Syria was a stop on the road to Palestine (Jerusalem was another important destination for pilgrims), Egypt, the Maghreb and Spain. From North Africa and Egypt, Arabs travelled to the Sudan and Nubia.

Every major city was a market city, set at the junction of trade routes and equipped to receive, verify and tax passing caravans.

Caravanserais were fortified inns where men could find food and shelter for themselves and their animals; they could also exchange information about the prices of goods, indulge in political gossip, and pay their tolls and taxes. Caravans were composed of as many as a thousand camels (waggons came into use only in the thirteenth century, after the Mongol invasions). The heavily laden beasts crossed deserts and high plateaus, forded rivers or floated across on inflated goatskins.

Rich stuffs, precious ivory

Caravans supplied all sorts of goods, both commonplace and luxurious, for trade among the empire's various provinces; but they also provided rarer merchandise from far-off countries.

The farmlands of the high plateaus, oases, gardens and orchards furnished cities with everyday foodstuffs: vegetables, fruit, honey, wine, olives, oil, grain, wheat, rice, meat, and camel or buffalo milk. These same regions also produced a portion of the fibres (linen, cotton, silk) and dyes (indigo, madder, saffron, henna) used by artisans. Fragrant plants (flower essences, incense, benzoin) for perfumery, oils and soda for soap-making, and silver and semiprecious stones were adequate for local craftsmen. But the luxury trade—the one that made great fortunes and rich merchants—obtained supplies elsewhere. Urban aristocracies were a demanding, elegant clientele for whom the rarest goods were imported at great expense from China, India, Africa and the Baltic. From Europe and Central Asia merchants brought back furs, spices and precious weapons. From trading posts in faraway China, they procured paper, sumptuous silks and fragile porcelain. Indian traders supplied spices and perfumes, precious woods, ivory, and gems. The state held monopolies on the import of iron for the manufacture of arms, hardwoods for shipbuilding, and gold.

Slaves and eunuchs

Although the Koran recognized all men as equal before God, Arab-Muslim society was far from egalitarian. Slavery was practised in the Muslim world well into the twentieth century. In the Middle Ages the aristocratic cities of the Orient relied heavily upon the labour of slaves, some of

whom were Muslims. They were treated less rigorously in urban areas than in the country, where slave revolts sometimes occurred. So pervasive was slavery in urban life that many caliphs, Omayyads and Abbasids alike, were direct descendants of slaves. Traders imported their human merchandise from diverse sources and sold them for equally diverse purposes. Each city had its own slave market, where Africans, Asians (mostly Turks), and Europeans of every nationality were sold to the highest bidder. Blonds with pale complexions (Scandinavians, Slavs) were most highly prized. Beautiful young women were purchased for harems, bestowed as rewards for services rendered, or offered as payment for debts. Ill-favoured women or those whom youth had deserted were not used as concubines but as domestics, housekeepers and nurses. Still others were sold as singers or musicians, dancers or courtesans. Some male slaves, children and adults alike, were castrated and trained for service in harems, or as royal bodyguards (Turkish militia), as tutors, or guardians of mosques. Today as in the seventh century, the eunuchs who guard the Great Mosque at Mecca still come from the same village in Ethiopia.

A lucrative trade

Although slaves were not always mistreated, they were considered only as goods to be bought, sold, or traded like any other

merchandise. Strong demand in Arab-Muslim society made the slave trade one of the most lucrative businesses. Far more than the Mediterranean, Europe or Central Asia, the richest sources of black slaves were the Sudan and eastern Africa, and the Indian Ocean islands from Socotra to the Maldives. Arab merchants bought slaves cheaply from local agents who had captured and transported them to trading posts, or else bartered weapons for slaves. The perishable human merchandise was as precious as gold and ivory to the Arabs, just as the arms they needed to wage war were invaluable to African chiefs.

In the sixteenth century Arab merchants realized huge profits from the sale of African slaves to European dealers who supplied the New World. The role of these merchants in Africa, who had gained a near-monopoly in the slave trade, was sufficiently important to form an obstacle to European attempts to explore the 'Dark Continent'.

Muslims travelled mostly in caravans.

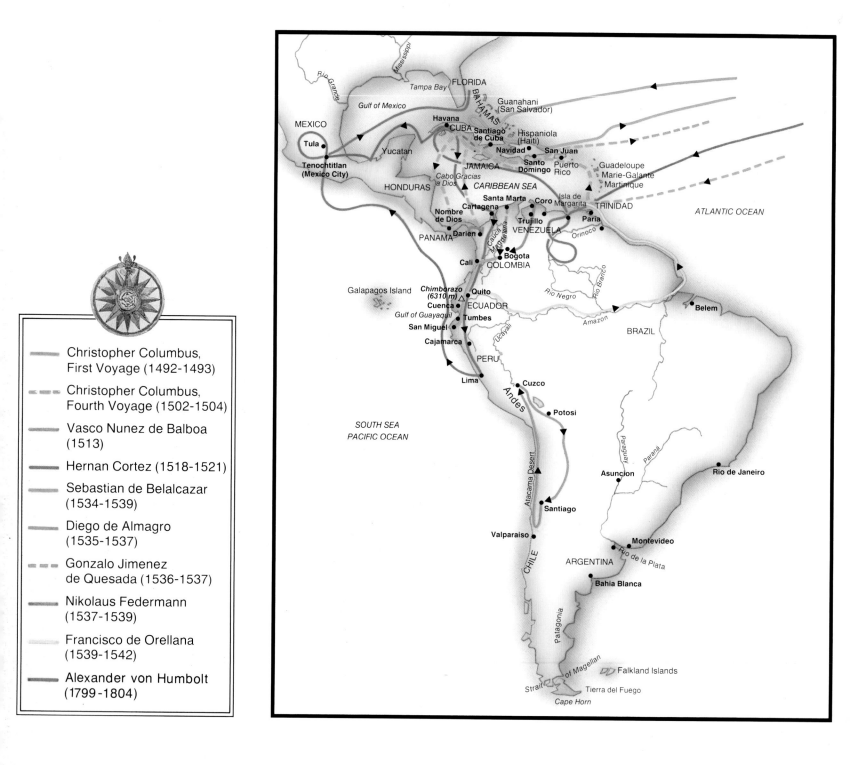

Legend:

Christopher Columbus,
First Voyage (1492-1493)

Christopher Columbus,
Fourth Voyage (1502-1504)

Vasco Nunez de Balboa
(1513)

Hernan Cortez (1518-1521)

Sebastian de Belalcazar
(1534-1539)

Diego de Almagro
(1535-1537)

Gonzalo Jimenez
de Quesada (1536-1537)

Nikolaus Federmann
(1537-1539)

Francisco de Orellana
(1539-1542)

Alexander von Humbolt
(1799-1804)

Map labels:

Rio Grande
Mississippi
Tampa Bay
FLORIDA
BAHAMAS
Gulf of Mexico
Guanahani (San Salvador)
MEXICO
Havana
CUBA
Hispaniola (Haiti)
Tula
Santiago de Cuba
Navidad
San Juan
Tenochtitlan (Mexico City)
Yucatan
JAMAICA
Santo Domingo
Puerto Rico
Guadeloupe
Marie-Galante
Martinique
HONDURAS
Cabo Gracias a Dios
CARIBBEAN SEA
Santa Marta
Coro
Isla de Margarita
TRINIDAD
ATLANTIC OCEAN
Nombre de Dios
Cartagena
Trujillo
Paria
PANAMA
Darien
Cauca
Magdalena
VENEZUELA
Orinoco
Cali
Bogota
COLOMBIA
Galapagos Island
Chimborazo (6310 m)
Quito
Rio Negro
Rio Branco
Cuenca
ECUADOR
Belem
Gulf of Guayaquil
Tumbes
Amazon
BRAZIL
San Miguel
Cajamarca
Ucayali
PERU
Andes
Lima
Cuzco
Potosi
SOUTH SEA
PACIFIC OCEAN
Paraguay
Parana
Atacama Desert
Asuncion
Rio de Janeiro
Santiago
Valparaiso
Montevideo
CHILE
ARGENTINA
Rio de la Plata
Bahia Blanca
Patagonia
Strait of Magellan
Falkland Islands
Tierra del Fuego
Cape Horn

South America

I n the second quarter of the fifteenth century, a wide-ranging intellectual, philosophical, scientific and technological movement revolutionized both the medieval view of the world, and the way Europeans regarded the Ocean. It was the dawn of the Age of Discovery. By circumnavigating Africa, discovering America and crossing the Pacific Ocean, Portuguese and Spanish navigators provided cartographers with the first true picture of the Earth.

The medieval world view

The cartographers of the Middle Ages, befogged by scholasticism, had lost sight of the geographical discoveries of Antiquity. Yet two centuries before the advent of Christianity, Eratosthenes had charted the inhabitable world, calculating the circumference of the earth to within several hundred metres. And around the year 150 AD, in his *Geography*, Ptolemy recorded the sum of the Greeks' knowledge of the Earth. But the classical tradition gave way to a Christian geography based on theology, rather than observation. Catholic theologians held that the Mediterranean was encompassed by a mythical river Ocean, which lay beyond the spiritual and material boundaries of Christendom.

The oldest maritime chart in existence dates from around 1290. It was the first global representation of the Mediterranean, a significant breakthrough for navigators who since ancient times had sailed close to the coastline, unwilling to risk their vessels in the open sea. Quite clearly, the invention of this invaluable aid to navigation coincided with the first practical use of the sea compass. The compass had been used in various forms in China and the Arab world since the eleventh century. From the moment the compass was introduced, the Christian West had the means to navigate out of sight of land, yet western sailors did not grasp the implications of the device.

The fabulous East

The fascination exerted by silks and spices provided the main impetus for the Age of Discovery. Combined with the desire to expand the commercial network was the avowed ,but ill-defined aim to convert heathen populations to Christianity. The ambivalence of these motivations is neatly summed up in the statement made by a companion of Vasco da Gama: 'We have come to make Christians and fetch spices.' Yet it is obvious that it took the lure of the vast and mythical riches of India to spur Renaissance explorers to overcome the prejudices, and the technological and scientific limitations that had discouraged them from exploring the open seas.

Marco Polo's *Book of Marvels* was published in several languages from 1477, at the very moment that Ptolemy's *Geography*, at last introduced into Europe, pushed back the limits of the theoretical world.

Overcoming fear

On 21 August 1415, the standard of Prince Henry the Navigator was unfurled in Ceuta. The Portuguese had gained a foothold in Africa, which they were to use as a storehouse for Indian goods. But they also had more ambitious plans—to sail around Africa in order to reach the source of spices and silks. However, Portuguese ambitions in this direction were not accompanied by

Navigational instruments and methods in the Age of Discovery

Navigators in the Age of Discovery used the compass and portulano charts to plot their position at sea. The newly felt need for universal references led to the principle—already familiar to the Arabs—of determining latitude in the northern hemisphere using quadrants to measure the altitude of the Pole Star. The mariner's astrolabe appeared in 1470, along with the first declination tables indicating the position of the sun, necessary for calculating longitude according to the altitude of the midday sun. The cross staff, invented around 1515, was easier to use. But an accurate means of measuring longitude was not perfected until the eighteenth century.

A Portuguese navigator using an crossbow to study the horizon.

innovations in navigational techniques. When the Portuguese set sail towards the south, they did not for a moment think of confronting the high seas, for they lacked the means of navigating in those dangerous waters. For them, circumnavigating Africa meant sailing along the continent's immense coastline, keeping close to the shore in the usual Mediterranean tradition. They did not dare venture into the mysterious Sea of Shadows beyond Cape Bojador, then the extreme limit of Portuguese navigation outside the Mediterranean.

Sailors from Northern Europe, Flanders and Dieppe had in fact established regular contacts with lands they called Mauritania and Guinea during the second half of the fourteenth century, but no Spaniard or Portuguese had ventured that for.

The Portuguese port adopted for this African venture was Lagos, not far from Sagres, where Prince Henry, governor of the Algarve, had set up his austere residence. Every year for fourteen years (1419-1433), a small ship left the port heading for Cape Bojador. Contemporary accounts describe how, in spite of their proven courage, the captains shrank from the dangers of this mental stumbling block. In 1434, Gil Eanes dared to sail beyond the Cape, thus breaking down the barrier of myth and opening the Atlantic to the Western world.

Used mainly in the Mediterranean, the tall Venetian carracks were made for windward navigation.

Sailing the high seas

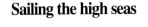

Year by year the Portuguese pushed farther along the coast of Africa towards Guinea. Finding their return to Lagos increasingly hampered by the northeast trade winds, they adopted the caravel, a ship whose lightweight lateen rigging made it possible to tack closer to the wind. Most importantly, however, they began to use the *volta*, a wide detour towards favourable winds in the vicinity of the Azores. This incursion into the open Atlantic confirmed the transition from a medieval mentality to a new outlook that would make the voyages of discovery possible.

It should not be forgotten, however, that the Maoris had elaborated a method for sailing in open seas some three thousand years earlier; and four or five centuries before the Iberian explorers, the Vikings and the Arabs had developed reliable techniques for navigating far from shore.

Through the united efforts of the finest intellects of Europe, Portugal perfected a system of navigating in open seas that was to remain virtually unchanged until the late eighteenth century. Progress in mathemat-

ics and astronomy counted less at this point in world history than the revolution in European attitudes towards the Atlantic Ocean. Europeans came to regard the Atlantic as something much grander than a mere network of coastal navigation routes. No longer encumbered by the mythical islands inherited from the Middle Ages, the Ocean became an area of manoeuvre open to every sort of initiative, in accordance with the new mental universe based on observation and experimentation. From then on, things advanced relatively quickly, given the necessarily slow pace of the period, particularly in Portugal. This tiny kingdom of one million souls, then in the throes of major political and economic difficulties was able to lead Christian Europe into an era of global expansion.

The natural route to India

The progress of the Portuguese was marked by *padroes*, stone pillars bearing the Portuguese coat of arms, which the nation's sea captains erected to indicate how far they had advanced. In 1474 Lopo Gonçalves crossed the Equator, thereby exploding the myth that any seaman who ventured into those waters would meet certain death by boiling. But as the Europeans sailed south, their traditional guide, the Pole Star, disap-

peared beneath the horizon. But a new star arose in its place, and sailors soon learned to navigate by the Southern Cross.

In December 1488, Bartolomeu Dias returned to Lisbon after a sixteen-month voyage. He confirmed that Ptolemy had been wrong to regard Africa as part of the hypothetical southern continent, which the Ancients had posited as a counterpart to the known continents of the northern hemisphere. The discovery of the Cape of Good Hope had at last opened a direct sea route to the Indian Ocean.

Eight years later, King Manoel of Portugal decided to consolidate the conquest of the sea route round Africa. The expedition led by Vasco da Gama reached Calicut in India on 20 May 1498, some seventy-nine years after Henry the Navigator first settled at Sagres to set the whole Atlantic venture in motion. This time lapse which appears incredibly long to us, testifies to the intellectual, scientific, technological and financial effort required to succeed in an undertaking whose novelty and boldness are difficult for modern minds to appreciate. Two years after Vasco da Gama's expedition, a Portuguese fleet reached the coast of Brazil while seeking favourable winds to carry them to India, where they wished to affirm their mastery (see p. 62). Thus did the Portuguese assert their dominance of the high seas—acquired through the efforts of an entire nation, and sustained for several generations.

(see p. 62)

The partition of the world

Bartolomeu Dias had reached the southernmost tip of Africa four years prior to the arrival of Christopher Columbus at what seemed to be a legitimate outpost of Cipango (Japan). The sovereigns of the Iberian Peninsula asked the Pope to establish a Christian order in the newly discovered territories and those yet to be discovered. In 1455, Calixtus III granted Castile and Portugal rights to the north and south (respectively) of the Canary Islands. But the newly opened Atlantic did not lend itself to the same type of arrangement, particularly since gold and precious stones were believed to proliferate in the regions below the Equator. Pope Alexander VI Borgia unambiguously divided the world between the two kingdoms, according to a meridian stretching from pole to pole and passing one hundred leagues to the west of Cape Verde. On 7 June 1494, the boundary was extended 270 leagues westward, in accordance with the Treaty of Tordesillas. And that is why, though Spanish is spoken everywhere else in South America, Portuguese is the language of Brazil.

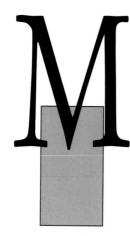

*M*ost legends have a certain factual basis. In the case of Columbus, the ascertained historic fact is that a man of uncertain origin demanded the title and rank of Admiral of the Atlantic and Viceroy of all the territory he might discover, in exchange for lands he was unable to situate with precision. Thus Columbus, borne on the wings of a dream, reached a continent whose existence he had never imagined.

A man of mystery

Genoese, Portuguese, Spanish, Christian or Jew? Very little is known about the origins of Christopher Columbus, and the hundreds of books written about him rarely agree on this point. Bartolomé de Las Casas, the son of one of Columbus's companions and his principal chronicler, referred to him as Crístobal Columbo de Terra Rubia. Bernaldez affirmed that he was Genoese, while Peter Martyr called him Colonus Ligur. Columbus himself appended the epithet 'The Foreigner' after his name, adding to the mystery surrounding his background.

Whether they are authentic or false, existing documents link Columbus with Genoa. Yet he did not even speak Italian, let alone write it. As for those determined to prove that he was Spanish, their argument is countered by the fact that Columbus spoke with a thick Portuguese accent. Most writers agree, however, that his father was a modest wool merchant of Genoa who later became a guardian of the Tower of Saint Andrew, one of the four towers guarding the city. This is where, towards the mid-fifteenth century, the future admiral is said to have been born. Until the age of twenty-two, he was referred to as a 'wool merchant', but other documents indicate that he was a navigator. Another known fact is that he emigrated to Portugal in the company of his brother Bartholomew, and while his brother produced and painted navigational charts, Columbus sailed aboard the ships of corsairs and Portuguese merchants.

Caravels

Caravels, sailing ships which first appeared in the fifteenth century, were a development of vital importance to the great voyages of the Age of Discovery. Their tall sides were a decisive factor in successfully weathering long voyages in stormy waters. Caravels were usually composed of a bridge, a ram on the prow, a broad poop deck and three masts (rigged with square and lateen sails), and were capable of carrying light artillery. In Columbus's fleet, the flagship *Santa María* was fully decked, of 100 tonnes burden and 39 metres length, while the *Pinta* was 17 metres long, and fitted with square sails. The *Pinta* proved her seaworthiness in March 1493, escaping undamaged from the worst storm ever seen in the seas around Portugal and Spain. Lastly, there was the *Niña*, a caravel of 40 tonnes burden.

The light, rapid and manoeuvrable caravel soon became the great vessel of discovery. Columbus's three ships were all caravels.

The apprentice navigator

'Very early on, I took to the sea,' wrote Columbus as an old man, giving rise to a storm of controversy. He tells how in 1475-6 he captained a pirate ship in the service of King René of Anjou: 'King René, now deceased, sent me to Paris to capture the galley *Ferdinanda*.' This statement has been challenged by historians. Later on in his writings, we find Columbus—under the name of Columbo Junior—in the service of a Frenchman fighting the Genoese, his own countrymen! We hear of his ship catching fire and of his being forced to land on the coast of Portugal. Chroniclers state that the Columbo referred to in this account was in fact a Frenchman named Georges Byssipat or George the Greek, and that in any case the dates are incompatible. Others maintain that Colombo (in Italian) or Colón (in Spanish) served under the banner of the French admiral Guillaume de Casenove-Coullon. 'I am not the first admiral in my family,' recalled Columbus in later years. The only facts that can be put forward with any certainty are these: Christopher Columbus went to sea, learned Latin and cosmography, and travelled to Lisbon at the age of about twenty-five.

First hopes, first refusals

In those days, Portugal was the centre of exploration and discovery. Its mariners were acquainted with the Mediterranean and the lengthy coasts of Africa. Geographers already knew that the Earth was round. While Bartholomew Colombus continued to plot new maps, Christopher immersed himself in books in the hope of finding information that would support his conviction that 'If one sails the seas, one will always find land.' Every source was grist to his mill: Marco Polo, Toscanelli—a Florentine astronomer and Columbus's teacher, the Bible and philosophy. Columbus claimed that 'by advancing towards the Orient', 'by sailing towards the West', 'towards Thule in the North', one would find Cipango (Japan) and continental lands, since the Earth was round! Unfortunately, when stating his case before the rulers of Portugal, Columbus did not express himself very well. The sovereigns were only able to form the vaguest picture of the reasons why this individual claimed that by crossing the Atlantic, he would reach India. Doubt also existed with regard to India itself: was this the same land that Marco Polo had spoken of with such eloquence? King John of Portugal was not impressed by the arguments of Christopher Columbus and refused to put up the money for his expedition.

Thule: 'the ends of the Earth'

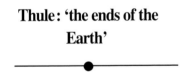

In his writings, Columbus refers to a voyage he made to Thule in the northern Atlantic, but historians have never been able to confirm the truth of this story. The navigator understood Latin and had probably read Polybius's account of the voyage of Pytheas, the Greek explorer and geographer who mentioned the island of Thule (see p. 15). This supposed voyage in the seas around Iceland is said to have provided Columbus with new evidence confirming what he had surmised: the existence of lands situated farther West. Colombus also listened attentively to seafarers in Madeira, Cape Verde and the Canaries. Some recounted tales of ships that sailed towards the setting sun, whose crews had found carved wood figures. Others related how they had discovered the remains of a boat made of an unknown wood. Far out to sea, on the same latitude as Cape Verde, sailors claimed they had seen the bodies of two drowned men

The great dream of Christopher Colombus was to find a westward route to the Indies.

with strange faces and complexions floating in the water.

A wedding and a king

Columbus has been described as far-sighted, intelligent, mystical and mendacious, but 'calculating' would surely be an appropriate addition to the list. This would explain the sudden piety which prompted Columbus to visit a convent frequented by the well-born bourgeoisie in 1479. It was here that he made the acquaintance of a noblewoman, Felipa Moniz Perestrello, whom he married and who bore him a son, Diego. The marriage enabled Columbus to forge links with influential courtiers. Columbus spent these years on Porto Santo, a small island off the coast of Madeira, where his father-in-law was governor, and passed the time navigating, reading, and studying geography, astronomy and mathematics. This period of retreat allowed Columbus to prepare and present a second plan for an expedition to King John II of Portugal in 1483-4; but the sovereign's response was again to be a resounding 'No'. Las Casas describes how the arguments put forward by Columbus were neither sufficiently convincing nor solid to persuade the king. Moreover, the privileges Columbus demanded in exchange seemed out of all proportion to the benefits to the king.

Disappointed, Columbus separated from

his wife and, taking his son Diego with him, fled to Spain. He settled in Palos, a port town north of Cadiz, with the intention of offering his services to the King of Spain.

A new world for Castile

On 20 January 1486, Columbus submitted a new plan to the Royal Chancellery of Castile a new project. An interminable wait preceded the royal refusal: 'I have spent seven years at your Royal Court and in all this time not a single person has said once and for all that my plans are absurd...'.

Following this latest defeat, Columbus turned up in Malaga; and also had a second son, Fernando. Rebuffed once more by the King of Portugal, he made another attempt to interest the Spanish crown, but Spain was then fighting the Moors. Columbus bided his time until 2 January 1492, when the fortress of Granada fell. After seven centuries Spain had banished the last Arab presence from her soil. Once they had reclaimed their own territories, the rulers of Spain were able to devote their energies to the extension of their kingdom. Queen Isabella the Catholic remembered the eloquent man who had promised much new land and inexhaustible riches for Spain. She summoned Columbus and the Capitulations of Santa Fé were signed on 17 April 1492. With this document preparations could begin in the port of Palos.

Was Columbus a Jew?

The most widely known theory concerning Columbus's nationality was put forward by the historian Salvador de Madariaga. It attempts to prove that Columbus was of Judeo-Catalan origin, thereby explaining why he never wrote or spoke Italian and always signed himself 'The Foreigner'. His Portuguese pronunciation of Spanish, his friendships with Moors and Jews, his continual changes of name, and his near-mystical faith in learning have all been cited as evidence to support this thesis. By a strange coincidence, the day Columbus set sail from Palos, the Jews were expelled from Spain.

To prove his good faith when he returned to Spain, Columbus took back with him Indians in their feather costumes as well as parrots and rare plants.

Somewhere in the Far East

'Land ahoy! Land ahoy!', shouted Rodrigo de Triana from aboard the *Pinta*. He had sighted on the horizon what looked like a grey-feathered bird whose open wings seemed to hover motionless in the far distance. It was in fact the crest of an island in the Bahamas.

The sailors hugged one another, and Columbus, offering up thanks to the Lord, baptized with the name of San Salvador ('Holy Saviour') the territories which the natives called Guanahani. Day had just broken on 12 October 1492. It was an emotional moment for Columbus, who had no doubt at all that they had arrived at one of the many islands in the Indian Ocean that lay off Cipango (Japan), which he believed to be the home of the Great Khan. Columbus had calculated that one thousand nautical leagues separated Gomera, their point of departure, from Cipango—a distance that could be covered in five weeks. And had they not taken five weeks to arrive at these territories! Columbus stuck to the belief that he had reached a region of the Far East of Asia until the day he died.

Columbus took possession of this beautiful island in the name of the Spanish monarchy, then set about plotting the exact positions of the many neighbouring islands, utterly unaware that he had discovered the New World.

Europe looks towards the sea

In 1492, following the expulsion of the Moors and Jews, the rulers of Spain fixed their sights on the sea. They were not alone: Portugal made no secret of its wish to build an overseas empire. The Pact of Alcazaba, a treaty containing the seeds of conflict, whereby the Canary Islands were ceded to Spain, while the coast of Africa—the Azores, Madeira and Cape Verde—went to Portugal, was signed between the two countries. More and more expeditions set sail; technical advances in cartography, compass design and ship-building opened the way for adventure on the high seas. Giovanni Caboto (known as John Cabot) in the service of England, and Giovanni da Verrazano on behalf of France (see p. 111), both led voyages of exploration across the Atlantic.

Sailing westward

Columbus now began to build the ships that were to carry him westward. The royal instructions—'the caravels must be fitted out by the townspeople'—were read by Columbus to the inhabitants of Palos on the morning of 23 May. Martín Alonso Pinzón, an influential sailor and merchant, took part in the commissionning of the ships. Three caravels—the *Pinta*, the *Niña* and the *Santa María*—were soon ready to sail. On the morning of 3 August 1492, captains and crews weighed anchor and set off for the unknown. At long last Columbus saw his dream become reality!

The first crossing

The three caravels headed towards the Canary Islands, manned by a crew some 120 strong. During the stopover in the Islands, repairs were made to the damaged rudder of the *Pinta*. Nearly one month later, on 6 September 1492, the ships left the island of Gomera, sailing into the unknown. Nothing much happened during the first days of the trip and the winds were favourable; but soon days turned into weeks without any sign of land. The voyage took longer than expected, and the atmosphere on board began to deteriorate as the sailors lost patience. Only Columbus remained confident as he looked towards the horizon from the *Santa María* and ordered everyone to remain calm. He was sufficiently well-versed in maritime lore to use an astrolabe and sextant, and had no doubt about the course he had charted. Nevertheless, time passed without the slightest trace of land on the horizon and Columbus remained tight-lipped in the face of a crew that showed little confidence in him. An attempted mutiny was firmly put down by Martín Alonso Pinzón, the captain of the *Pinta*, but feelings ran high and the crew clamoured to turn back. Confronted with the scepticism of his men, Columbus improvised a rousing speech full of confidence which soothed their troubled minds. But still there was no sign of land.

Eighty-seven days of euphoria

The island of Guanahani was far from uninhabited. Surprised but peaceful, the native Lucayas Indians watched with interest the arrival of these bearded men, clad in brilliant clothes—items they had never seen before. After nearly two and a half months at sea, the Spanish thought they were in paradise. Their fascination grew and grew for this green land, its splendid men and women who went naked, offered the Spaniards food and asked for nothing in return. The ship's logbook provides a complete inventory of new and marvellous discoveries: parrots of all colours, fish 'differently formed from those in Spain', fruit trees, giant trees, natives who were friendly and apparently worshipped no god, and who much to the sailors' glory, supposed that the white men had come from Heaven! Eighty-seven days thus slipped by in an atmosphere of general euphoria.

Greed is unleashed

Once the first wave of emotion had passed, several explorers who regarded themselves as something other than simple adventurers allowed their secret ambitions to come to the fore. Instead of offering gifts, they began to barter for items like the natives' labial and nasal rings, which were wrought of pure gold. Greed now raised its head, and the sailors avidly seized cotton, cinnamon and any stone that glittered. Although the natives had been docile and obedient, seven were captured by force and imprisoned aboard ship, as proof to be shown to Ferdinand and Isabella. Gold, obviously, was to be found somewhere in the region, but where? Locating its source became the Europeans' top priority. 'Somewhere, two days from here, lives a king who possesses great quantities of gold,' was the rumour in the islands. A desire to find him would spur the Spaniards' indefatigable wanderings for many years to come.

The search for the Great Khan

Columbus pursued his navigation, studying the depth of each bay and the best current for each route. He spent two weeks exploring the islands. Santa María de la Concepcion, Fernandina, Juana and Hispaniola (The Dominican Republic and Haiti) were all named at this time. Geographical landmarks such as mountains, rivers, and bays were also named, as were some birds.

Hispaniola, which Columbus reached on 6 December, seemed to hold out great promise. Following the coast of the island towards the west, Columbus was convinced by its size that it was 'terra firma'. Believing it to be the province of Cathay (China), he pushed onward, for he was the bearer of a letter from the Kings of Spain to the Great Khan. Since he encountered no further indication that he was in the land of the Khan, Columbus concluded that he had struck too far to the north. Winter had 'already come beating down', so he turned back to spend the stormy season in the south. Tales of hairless men, cannibals, and 'islands of women without men' spurred Columbus to continue his voyage.

But meanwhile violent quarrels had broken out between Columbus and Captain Martín Alonso Pinzón, their roots in questions of power and rivalry.

On 25 December 1492, the flagship *Santa María* ran aground, and the crews made the return voyage aboard the two remaining caravels. A garrison of 40 men was left behind at Navidad, on Hispaniola.

A hero's welcome

The voyage back to Spain was fraught with dangers. Bad weather drove the ships towards the island of Santa María, the southernmost island of the Azores, which was under Portuguese rule. Problems with the island authorities and the imprisonment of several sailors provided a foretaste of future relations between Spain and Portugal.

Columbus's return was celebrated as a landmark event; he was hailed as a conqueror. In Portugal he was received in Rastelo and in Lisbon by King John himself; and in Spain in Palos and Seville.... 'Word began to circulate in Castile that lands known as India had been discovered, inhabited by large numbers of men very different from ourselves, and new things, and that soon the person who had discovered them would arrive.' The navigator was at last received in pomp and with ceremony by Ferdinand and Isabella in Barcelona on 21 April 1493. At the close of the festivities, Columbus was named Captain of the Second Indian Fleet.

A key figure in the preparation of Columbus's great voyage, Martín Alonzo Pinzón claimed discoveries for his own advantage.

Where did Columbus land?

For many years, it was claimed that Guanahani—the island on which Columbus landed during his first voyage—corresponded to Watling Island (renamed San Salvador in 1926) in the Bahamas. However, according to a five-year study carried out by a team of American researchers and published in 1986, Columbus had reached the tiny island of Samana Cay, some 104 kilometres to the south of San Salvador. Several of the island's geological features answer to the description given by Columbus. In addition, archaeological evidence confirms the presence there five hundred years ago of the Lucayas, the very Indians encountered by Columbus.

The Pinzón Brothers

As a native of the port of Palos, north of Cadiz, Martín Alonso Pinzón obtained royal approval for his Atlantic voyage with the help of Father Antonio Marchena. Pinzón was a prosperous and highly influential merchant, as well as an experienced seafarer. He largely financed the building of the caravels for Columbus's first voyage. In spite of his friendship with the admiral, and for reasons which are obscure today, Pinzón's views were from the outset very different from those held by Columbus, and indeed cast doubt on his loyalty. Unlike Columbus, Pinzón did not live long enough to enjoy the status conferred by his exploits; he died just days after his return to Spain. His brother, Vicente Yañez, piloted the *Niña* on its first Atlantic voyage. In 1499-1500, he sailed southward, landing near Cape St Augustine on the coast of Brazil (see p. 63).

First the Catholics, then the Protestants

The discoveries made by Portugal and Spain in the Atlantic were by no means a matter of indifference to the other crowned heads of Europe. But except in a few rare cases, their own domestic wars left them little scope for sending exploratory expeditions. They were nevertheless kept closely informed: in 1488, Bartholomew Columbus is said to have personally presented his brother Christopher's project to Henry VII of England, and likewise to Charles VIII of France sometime after 1492. But it was not until the Reformation in the sixteenth century, which questioned papal omnipotence, that the English, Dutch and Germans launched their own expeditions. From that time onwards, the ocean became a vast battlefield.

Mermaids and cannibals

Columbus states that during his first return journey to Europe, he sighted three mermaids 'who rose high out of the depths of the sea, but were not as beautiful as they are said to be, and indeed even looked like men.' A more plausible account is given by the Spaniards of the inhabitants of the Caribbean islands, with whom they were in direct contact, and who 'cooked human beings in a cauldron'. The diary of Alvarez Chanca, the physician accompanying the expedition, contains amazing accounts of the life of the natives of the Caribbean, who were also known as the Cannibals. Chanca tells of the delicious flavour of human flesh, noting that the flesh of youngsters was less delicate, and that at certain banquets, the Cannibals served up the new-born offspring of women captives.

A French painting in the nineteenth-century exotic style showing the conquistadors' first Mass in the Bahamas archipelago.

The second voyage

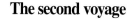

One thousand five hundred men, aboard seventeen caravels, set sail from Cadiz on 25 September 1493, heading for the West Indies. The purpose of Columbus's second voyage was mainly to affirm the rights of Castile over these recently discovered islands. On board were priests, peasants and artisans, as well as foot soldiers and cavalry. Two members of the expedition, Alonzo de Hojeda, commander of a caravel, and Juan de la Cosa, a geographer, subsequently made independent voyages to the New World. The holds of Columbus's ships were full of wheat, for what had begun as a voyage of discovery had turned into a process of colonization in which pride of place was given to trading and converting native populations to Christianity. But in fact, Columbus's particular genius was as a discoverer, not a colonial administrator. And that is why, once he had rediscovered Hispaniola on 22 November 1493, he entrusted the post of governor to his brother Diego and set out to seek new islands.

The division of the world

King John of Portugal was also looking for a western passage to India. Since rights to the sea routes and newly discovered lands were in question, and since Portuguese ambitions were growing ever more evident, it became urgent for the Spanish to consolidate their hold over the lands discovered by Columbus. Pope Alexander VI Borgia, of Spanish descent, agreed to hand down a law to settle the matter. Among several papal bulls issued in 1493, one of them, the *Inter Cetera*, designated which lands belonged to Spain and which to Portugal. An imaginary meridian was to divide the world, stretching from pole to pole and passing through a point located one hundred leagues to the west of the Cape Verde Islands and the Azores. Lands discovered to the west of the line would be the property of Spain, while everything east of the line would go to Portugal. However the Portuguese sovereign felt that he had been wronged by this so-called 'impartiality'. Thus on 7 June 1494, Ferdinand and Isabella of Spain were obliged to sign the Treaty of Tordesillas. This modified and moved the line of demarcation of Portuguese conquests further to the west, some 270 nautical leagues from Cape Verde. The Spanish had no inkling that they had thus delivered Brazil into the hands of Portuguese adventurers.

In the Caribbean sea

The southwestern course set by Columbus on his second expedition led directly to the Caribbean. After only twenty days at sea, a pilot on board Columbus's ship sighted two islands, subsequently named Dominica and Maria-Galante. He went on with reconnaissance expeditions. During one early expedition, Columbus and his men discovered an archipelago and six small islands. The next day, while searching for Hispaniola—where he had founded the garrison of Navidad during his first voyage—he discovered Santa María de Guadalupe and Puerto Rico. When he at last found Hispaniola, he was confronted with a garrison in ruins; all the Spaniards who had remained there were dead. Early in 1494 Columbus founded the town of Isabela in northwestern Hispaniola. He sent a detachment led by Hojeda towards the interior, and established the fort of Santo Tomas with a garrison of fifty men. He then embarked once again to explore southern Cuba and Jamaica.

Columbus was convinced that Cuba was the 'terra firma' he sought. So that there would be no doubt on the subject, he forced all of his men—including Juan de la Cosa, who complied though he was sure Columbus was wrong—to swear that such was the truth and that they would never retract. On his return to Isabela, after five months at sea, Columbus fell ill and remained bedridden for another five months. For the time being, his wanderings were at an end. Even though in 1493 the chronicler Peter Martyr had already spoken of a 'New World', Columbus's erroneous theory continued to circulate for many years. As far as he was concerned, Cuba was a continent, the Asiatic *Quersoneso Aureo*. Yet nothing proved that this supposed continent touched the Indian Ocean.

A difficult start

Diego Columbus had proved to be a totally incompetent administrator, and on his return, Columbus was obliged to cope with general discontent. On Hispaniola, people were desperate and dying of hunger. In the face of that disastrous situation, Columbus took drastic action—too drastic, some said. The hidalgos (minor nobility) and well-born gentlemen were forced to work the land, a humiliating task for men of their birth. Word went round that Columbus was using violence to impose his rule, and that the division of labour, property and even of

food was unjust. An attempted rebellion was put down, but these problems marked the beginning of the hostility between Columbus and Friar Bernardo Buíl, one of the monks who had remained faithful to Diego. This enmity would have serious repercussions, for Buíl later did his utmost to discredit Columbus in the eyes of Queen Isabella.

Enemies of Columbus

On Columbus's orders, Antonio de Torres led a fleet of twelve caravels back to Spain. He brought encouraging news, and apparently did not mention the heavy loss of life on Hispaniola. When Columbus's brother, Bartholomew, arrived at Isabela, Columbus appointed him as *adelantado*, the highest position of authority on the island. Pedro Margarite—governor of the fort of Santo Tomas—and Friar Buíl seized the opportunity afforded by Bartholomew's caravels to return to Spain and denounce the administrative ineptitude of Columbus and his brothers.

On another return voyage, Diego Columbus brought back to Madrid no fewer than five hundred slaves as 'prisoners of war'. This act shocked the Spanish and led to a long-lasting theological and ethical debate in which the legitimacy of capturing islanders and selling them as slaves was questioned. To decide between the conflicting reports presented by Buíl and Antonio de Torres, King Ferdinand sent Juan de Aguado to carry out an independent inquiry on Hispaniola in October 1495. Columbus himself travelled to Spain in order to defend himself personally against the accusations levelled at him. He arrived at Cadiz on 11 June 1496 and, to quote his biographer Las Casas, discovered that 'the admiral and his arguments were no longer given the same hearing as before.'

Uprisings in the new colonies

Although the purpose of Columbus's second expedition was to establish bases for commerce and agriculture, it did not produce all the expected results. Indeed, Columbus was obliged to acknowledge that famine was devastating the Spanish colony. Greed for gold and internal power struggles hampered the process of colonization. In addition, the indigenous population refused to work for the Spaniards. Columbus

The Columbus brothers

Christopher Columbus had two brothers, Bartholomew and Diego. Records indicate that Bartholomew was with Bartolomeo Dias in the service of the Portuguese crown when Dias discovered the Cape of Good Hope in 1486. Diego came directly from Genoa. Both faithfully served their elder brother during his discoveries and ill-fated administration of the Spanish colonies. They were granted titles, but were later harshly criticized, and accused of cruelty and incompetence. Both ended their days in prison.

Victims of the Orinoco

The great Orinoco River held a strong fascination for explorers and colonizers. From Puerto Rico, Santo Domingo and even Spain, entire fleets came to conquer its shores. Many were forced to abandon their expeditions without realizing their goal, defeated by the savage power of the elements. Juan de Sedeño, Diego de Ordaz, Juan Barrio de Quejo, Jeronimo de Hartal, Pedro Ortiz de Matienza and Alonso de Herrera all lost their lives in attempts to explore the Orinoco.

decided to tax them, demanding the quarterly payment of a certain quantity of gold or cotton. This tribute, which the natives refused to pay, prompted their decision to take flight. At this period in history, the taking of slaves was only considered to be justified if they were prisoners of war. In most cases, however, the peace-loving Indians were goaded into rebellion. Profits from the slave trade helped offset disappointment at the lack of gold.

Columbus had sailed back to Spain with nearly two hundred Spaniards, selected from among the malcontents, as well as more than thirty Indians. During his absence, Columbus's brother Bartholomew founded Santo Domingo, thereby depopulating Isabela. He also built several new forts and sent slaves to Madrid. On his return from an expedition in the region of Isabela, however, he learned that three hundred Spaniards had sickened and died. Not until two Spanish caravels fetched up in the bay announcing a new shipment of food was the colonists' revolt subdued. Not long after, it was the turn of the natives to rebel.

The third expedition

———————●———————

In spite of the serious doubts cast on the administration of the Spanish colony, Columbus succeeded in defending himself against criticism, and won back his sovereign's confidence. He therefore set about preparing

his third voyage. Once his prerogatives had been confirmed, the details of a new system of colonization were drawn up. In addition to colonization itself, objectives of a purely geographical nature were included: Columbus was required to find the passage to the Indian Ocean, thereby enabling him to reach Asia.

The fleet of six caravels set sail from San Lucar, near Cadiz, on 30 May 1498. When it reached the Canary Islands, it split into two groups in order to follow separate routes. The first flotilla headed directly for Hispaniola, where the garrison of Isabela lay, while the second, led by Columbus himself, sailed southwards. At Cape Verde, Columbus's ships turned westward and thereafter set a southwesterly course, and were borne by the currents to Trinidad, off the coast of present-day Venezuela. While exploring the area, Columbus noted an abundance of fresh water, leading him to suspect the presence of rivers and perhaps even the existence of a continent. Columbus guessed that this continent was distinct from Asia, which he situated to the south of *Quersoneso Aureo*.

Columbus in South America

———————●———————

Trinidad—today part of the Republic of Trinidad and Tobago—lies adjacent to, and indeed is practically attached to, the coast of South America; Columbus had thus

In 1506, with the number of voyages to the New World constantly increasing, the Discoverer of America died in a state of total isolation.

unwittingly landed on the American continent. The river that caused the current of fresh water was in fact the Orinoco, and not the river of Paradise on Earth, as suggested by Columbus. The rocky jagged coastline of South America, which Columbus dubbed the Land of Paría, was barely glimpsed during this fleeting reconnaissance. To Columbus, at the time, it seemed no different from any other archipelago of the 'East' Indies. Nothing distinguished it from the lands they had seen elsewhere—save for the parrots. According to Las Casas, 'these birds never talk; they are only interested in being admired; other than that, they are devoid of grace.'

On 11 August, Columbus reversed his course and sailed across the open seas to Hispaniola. Even before he had stepped ashore, he learned that the settlers and soldiers at Santo Domingo had revolted, just as the first colonists had done, and for similar reasons—administrative problems, wounded honour and social injustice. Seething resentment at last exploded into overt violence. Rebellions, desertions and recriminations played havoc with the equitable, peaceful accords previously concluded between the colonists and the Columbus brothers.

The Royal Commissioner

———————●———————

For some time, the Court had been aware that the colonies were poorly run, and there were fears that these rebellions, if unchecked, would spell the end of discoveries and expansion overseas. Ferdinand and Isabella were convinced that any semblance of order remaining on the island was due to the harsh rule imposed by the Columbus brothers. They were furious, however, when they learned that ships had landed in Spain again carrying natives described as 'prisoners of war'. To cap it all, Columbus went so far as to recommend that the unfortunates be sold to the highest bidder so that he could pay off his debts. The king now decided to appoint a Royal Commissioner, Don Francisco de Bobadilla, vested with full powers to conduct an inquiry in the colonies. Later on, and in response to rumours and discouraging letters from Columbus, the Commissioner's functions were extended. He was to act as governor and officer of justice for the islands and the mainland.

On 23 August 1500, the Royal Commissioner descended the gangplank in Santo Domingo. Columbus was not present, and Bobadilla received a frosty welcome. He was obliged to take possession of the fort by force, in the name of the Crown. Columbus, caught off guard by Bobadilla's arrival, refused to recognize his authority and decided to strike back. The new governor responded by ordering the arrest of Columbus and his brothers; they were transported back to Spain imprisoned in the hold of the ship, their legs in irons.

During the six-week voyage, Columbus composed his defence. His address to Isabella and Ferdinand was grandiloquent, but if the sentence is any indication, he does not seem to have entirely succeed in convincing his audience. Although he was set free and his prerogatives reinstated, he was never again to be entrusted with administrative powers. Furthermore, he was forbidden to return to Hispaniola. In 1504 another governor, Don Nicolas de Ovando, was sent to restore calm to the island.

In the wake of Columbus

In Columbus's wake the conquistadores began to compete with each other on the high seas. In February 1499, Alonzo de Hojeda set sail to explore the islands and coastlines that Columbus had recently discovered. Henry VII of England sent an expedition led by John Cabot, which landed in North America in 1497.

In 1499, the Portuguese Pedro Alonso Niño and Crístobal Guerra were granted permission to explore the area Columbus had discovered during his third voyage.

The fourth voyage

With his prerogatives reaffirmed over all the lands he might discover, and with strict instructions to keep out of administrative matters, to treat the local population decently and give up the slave trade, Admiral Columbus embarked on his fourth voyage on 3 April 1502, two months after Ovando's departure. The fleet was made up of four caravels. Southwesterly currents drove the fleet towards Martinique, which it reached on 15 June 1502. A storm blew the ships to Santo Domingo, where the new governor refused Columbus landing rights. He was therefore obliged to continue his journey; he sighted and named several new islands along the way. He followed the coastline of Jamaica and landed on the Islas de la Bahia, some twelve leagues from the mainland of what is now Honduras. He

then sailed down the coasts of Nicaragua, Costa Rica, Panama and Darien. In Honduras, the natives told him of gold mines, and Columbus concluded that they were the mines mentioned by Marco Polo. This encouraged him to continue

Poor and abandoned

The fourth voyage was marked by persistent squalls in the Caribbean and by the equally persistent bad luck that dogged the ailing navigator. Buffeted by one tempest after another, he was forced to abandon two ships broken up by the waves. The other ships were ravaged by shipworm. For months, having just escaped being shipwrecked, Columbus waited for help in a remote bay on the northern coast of Jamaica. One of his officers, Diego Mendez, volunteered to fetch help from Santo Domingo, which he reached after months at sea in a dug-out canoe. Another seven months passed before permission was granted to fit out some caravels and rescue the shipwrecked seafarers.

Columbus landed at last in Spain on 4 November 1504, a few days after the death of Queen Isabella. His own end was not long in coming: Columbus died in poverty on 20 May 1506 in Valladolid, surrounded by his sons, his brother Bartholomew, and a handful of loyal friends.

The coat of arms of the 'Grand Admiral of the Ocean'. Christopher Columbus was extremely attached to the privileges, titles and prerogatives granted to him by Isabella the Catholic.

Captains and crew

Recruitment for sailors to take part in the 'Conquista' aroused keen enthusiasm, as agents of fleet commanders travelled the length and breadth of Spain, preceded by the flourish of fifes and drums. Also enlisted were pilots, helmsmen and cartographers trained at the naval schools of Seville and Lisbon, as well as adventurers and even convicts recruited from their cells. Each and every man received a contract signed in due legal form. All endured the suffering and privations, uncertainty of long and hazardous sea voyages. Some were interested only in adventure on the high seas, and the moment they put in to port would immediately look for another ship. Others, such as topmen and ordinary seamen, often preferred turn their back on the sea, and become soldiers in the new lands, which they helped to conquer and explore.

At the same time as Columbus and later following his lead, other explorers undertook bold maritime expeditions. While the purpose of 'discovery' was to add new territories to the known world and to map them, the aim of the 'conquista' was to take possession of these territories, colonize them, exploit their industrial resources, and subdue the natives before converting them to Christianity.

While exploring the coast of Brazil, Amerigo Vespucci encountered the cannibal practices of the inhabitants.

The conquest of the larger islands

In 1509, Columbus's son Don Diego, himself an admiral, arrived on Hispaniola. At the same time, Juan de Esquivel was occupying Jamaica. The conquest of Puerto Rico, launched by Juan Ponce de Leó (see p. 112), was still in progress, and in 1511, Diego Velasquez de Cuellar landed on Cuba. His lieutenant, Pánfilo de Narváez, was the founder of Havana. Among Velasquez's men was a certain Hernán Cortés.

From the Atlantic Ocean to the South Sea

The geographical theories put forth by Columbus began to be undermined very soon after his first return from the New World. From 1499, many expeditions set out to reconnoitre the coasts of the 'Terra Firma' which the admiral had been first to discover. Their aim was to find a passage to the Indian Ocean, and the much sought-after Spice Islands. Some explorers were convinced that the passage lay behind the great green barrier of the Amazon jungle. The immense coastline stretched from the estuaries of the Amazon River in the south to Cape Honduras in the north, where the conquista was to gain the momentum that would sweep it over the continent. The coasts of Guiana, the mouth of the Orinoco, Venezuela, Colombia and Panama

held out the promise of great riches. It was thought that after two months of danger on the high seas, a sufficiently shrewd and intrepid man could hope to conquer a kingdom. Spurred on by self-interest, the early explorers made superhuman efforts, but no one could locate the famous passage into the Indian Ocean. But increased exploration yielded more accurate geographical knowledge, and far better maps, which smoothed the path for future navigators.

Inventing a continent

Some asserted that the Land of París, the huge continental mass discovered by Columbus, could possibly be Asia, but others stated that it was a different continent altogether. Amerigo Vespucci, a simple trader who was to become the most famous cartographer of his day, attempted to show that Florida and the West Indian archipelagos were part of one and the same continent.

Below the 52nd parallel

In 1500, a Portuguese navigator, Pedro Cabral, was blown by the trade winds across the southern Atlantic to Brazil, which he took to be an island. But it was the Florentine-born Amerigo Vespucci who first realized that the South American coast stretched unbroken from Venezuela to Argentina. Vespucci, formerly a tradesman in the service of Lorenzo de' Medici, set sail on his first Atlantic crossing in 1497; he later made several expeditions, some on behalf of Portugal and some for Spain, always in the hope of finding the passage to the Indian Ocean. During his third voyage,

in 1501, sailing under the Portuguese flag, Vespucci reached Brazil and named one of the bays he found there Rio de Janeiro ('river of January'), before continuing on his voyage southwards. It was then that he crossed the 52nd parallel of southern latitude. He could not find the strait leading to the Indian Ocean, however, and so headed back across the Atlantic, and then followed the coastline of Sierra Leone. He fetched up in Lisbon on 7 September 1502.

Vespucci made another almost identical voyage from May 1503 to June 1504. That same year, he entered the service of Spain once more, and led two expeditions with Juan de la Cosa. Like Columbus, Vespucci wrote letters and accounts of his voyages to correspondents in Europe. In one such letter, addressed to Lorenzo de' Medici, he referred to the territories he had explored as the *Mundus Novus*.

The *Quarta Pars*

Until the early sixteenth century, no navigator had openly challenged the theories put forward by Columbus. But in his letters, Vespucci wrote for the first time of a *Quarta Pars*, and revealed the existence of a new world unknown to the Ancients. 'South of the line of the equinox, where the Ancients affirmed that there was no land, but only a sea called the Atlantic, where, whenever anyone claimed that land existed, the cry went up that any such place was necessarily uninhabited, I have personally discovered extremely temperate and agreeable countries, with a population larger than any we know. This is the *Quarta Pars* (Fourth Part) of the Earth.' No further doubts could be entertained; the new lands were not part of Asia. The line separating the lands Vespucci spoke of from those that lay north of París had not yet been plotted. Just what the

Amerigo Vespucci was well acquainted with navigation in the southern hemisphere, which he had ventured into as early as 1499. Here he is taking bearings from the Southern Cross.

exact contours of this new territory might be was still an open question.

The first map of America

Though no survey existed to support the belief, navigators generally accepted the notion that the lands lying to the north of the Caribbean were islands. Based on knowledge acquired during his many voyages and expeditions, in 1500 Juan de la Cosa had produced a map that established that supposition as fact, although certain key elements were incomplete, missing, or more or less camouflaged. To fill in the unknown regions, the sailor drew pictures of the Holy Spirit and St Christopher, the patron saint of travellers—and discoverers.

Amerigo, Amerige, America

In 1507, the German mapmaker Martin Waldseemüller published his *Cosmographiae Introductio*, based both on the tradi-

tion of Ptolemy and on Vespucci's accounts of his voyages. The German was the very first to name the New World as '*Americi Terra vel América*'. In a way this was only fair, since Vespucci was the first to grasp the geographical reality of the continent, but it was an error nonetheless, for Columbus had been the first to discover it. To repair his blunder, Waldseemüller subsequently inscribed on his maps that the New World had been discovered by Columbus, but it was too late: the name 'America' had stuck!

From Darien to Venezuela

Backed by bankers, trading companies and kings, further naval expeditions were mounted and new colonial outposts founded. Trade with the New World now began in earnest. On 24 April 1500, a Portuguese seafarer named Pedro Alvarez Cabral reached the coast of Brazil at Puerto Seguro (nowadays known as Bahia), while Vicente Yañez Pinzón (Martin Pinzón's brother), and Diego Lepe reached the northeast coast of the continent and the mouth of the

Amazon. Alonso de Hojeda and Juan de la Cosa, former companions of Columbus, explored further. De Hojeda followed the course charted by Columbus on his fourth voyage. In the meantime Juan de la Cosa, who had been present at the discovery of the Bahamas, the Caribbean and the West Indies, completed his training as a geographer on a series of independent voyages.

The two men were fated to become companions in glory and misfortune. Hojeda, under the protection of an influential prelate, obtained a concession and the post of *adelantado* in Maracaibo, Venezuela. His affairs did not prosper, however, until in 1508 he obtained the post of governor of the eastern coast of the Gulf of Darien, in Panama, with Juan de la Cosa as his second in command. But the two conquistadores were plagued by bad luck: Juan de la Cosa was mortally wounded in 1510 by a native's poisoned arrow. Hojeda was not able to hold out for long in the face of the ferocious hostility of the local Indian tribes; he was horribly wounded during the founding of San Sebastian. After a miraculous recovery, Hojeda fled first to Cuba, then to Jamaica. He later expired far from the scene of his former glories, on Hispaniola, the island he had discovered with Columbus.

Golden Castile

The outposts founded on the mainland of Venezuela, known as Golden Castile, proved unsuccessful. Out of a total of seven hundred men who had taken part in Diego de Nicuesa's attempt at colonization, only one hundred had survived to roam the forests. In 1510, a rescue expedition led by Martin Fernandez de Enciso came across the surviving companions of Hojeda in the vicinity of San Sebastian. A conquistador from Hispaniola, Vasco Nuñez de Balboa, took part in the expedition. As someone familiar with the region, Balboa urged the colonizers to give up San Sebastian once and for all, and to found the settlement of Santa María de la Antigua de Darien in a more clement region. At this point, Nicuesa, who had fared even worse than Hojeda at San Sebastian, arrived from Veraguas (present-day Panama). He too was intent on conquering the country and a quarrel broke out between the two leaders. Routed by Balboa, Nicuesa and his men were driven out. They did not get very far, however, for their ships were unseaworthy, and they soon lost their way and disappeared forever beneath the waves.

Threatened by the colonists

Following the failure of their first attempts to grow crops, the colonists of Santa María de la Antigua decided to push inland to conquer the interior. Balboa persecuted the principal caciques (Indian chiefs), hoping to extract information about regions where gold could be found. He created further problems by forcing the Indians to submit to Christian baptism. The only way the natives could rid themselves of Balboa and his men was to mesmerize him with tales of a sea hidden beyond the mountains and rivers 'where you can cast your nets and pull them up full of gold'.

Abandoned by his men

Balboa, who had by now amassed considerable land holdings, resolved to set off in search of the fabulous riches the Indians had described. Prior to his departure, he dispatched to Madrid Nicuesa's former lieutenant, Colomenares, and an Indian, Ponquiaco, son of the chieftan Comogre who had revealed to Balboa the secret of the hidden sea. They were instructed to request from King Ferdinand reinforcements of one thousand men, plus food and supplies. The time spent waiting for an answer was clouded by an atmosphere of hate and rebellion. The gaol of the fort was filled with Spaniards by the time two ships arrived from Hispaniola with reinforcements in June 1513. Balboa was informed that he had been appointed governor of Darien and its adjacent territories two years before, but that this appointment could be revoked without prior notice. He also learned that the king had been apprised of complaints lodged against Balboa by the public prosecutor Enciso, and above all of Balboa's responsibility for the loss of Nicuesa and his men. Balboa was keenly aware that he was in danger of falling from favour; he decided to push on alone with what means he had at his disposal.

The other sea: a divine vision

Without waiting for the help he had requested from the king, Balboa took ship in the estuary of the Rio Darien early in September 1513. With him went 190 men, a two-masted brigantine, ten open boats and a pack of fierce war dogs. Guides and porters were recruited from among the Indians provided by Chima, a chieftain and ally of Balboa. The expedition followed the guides to the narrowest point of the isthmus. And then, leaving a detachment of men in the port which was later to be called Acla, Balboa headed south through the jungle. At Quareca, high in the mountains, he encountered resistance from the tribe of the cacique Torechas. The village and its captive inhabitants were torn to shreds by Balboa's dogs. Balboa continued his march through the green hell. Already, he could see the peaks of the final mountain chain. The party had been on the march for twenty-five days; by this time, more than half the men had given up, exhausted.

On hearing that the sea was in sight, Balboa stepped forward and, alone on a mountain top, brandished his sword. Watching from below, the sixty-seven men who had survived the march saw their leader fall to his knees and recite the Psalms. On the 25 September 1513, a vast new body of water shimmered before their eyes. They called it the 'South Sea' because 'they saw it in this direction when crossing the isthmus [of Panama] which stretched to the west.' No longer a mere supposition, that sea—the Pacific Ocean—was at long last a reality.

The south of the world

Balboa and his men took four days to descend from their lookout post to the gulf, which they named San Miguel in honour of the archangel Michael whose feast day it was. All of them bathed in the salty waters, and claimed the sea in the name of the Spanish crown. From this point, in 1514 and 1523, the first expeditions set out towards the north, led first by Balboa, and later towards the south. All were invariably in quest of gold, and a passage linking the newly discovered sea with the Atlantic.

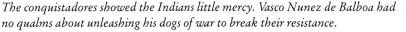

The conquistadores showed the Indians little mercy. Vasco Nunez de Balboa had no qualms about unleashing his dogs of war to break their resistance.

Meanwhile, back in Spain, a court intrigue was mounted against Balboa by Colmenares and Enciso. The king had resolved to transform the colony into a second Castile, and entrusted its administration to Pedro Aria de Avila, otherwise known as Pedrarias, a man of mature years and ferocious temperament.

Death without glory

Pedrarias disembarked at Santa María in June 1514. In December the king learned of the services rendered by Balboa, and raised him to the status of *adelantado* of the South Sea, awarding him the governorship of Panama and Coiba. From that point on, a mortal enmity existed between Pedrarias and Balboa. Several attempts at reconciliation were made: a marriage was arranged between Balboa and the eldest daughter of Pedrarias (the girl was still in Spain), but in the end the conflict exploded with fatal results.

Balboa withdrew to the outpost of Acla where he concentrated his efforts on fitting out ships to explore the South Sea. In 1518, he sailed into the South Sea with two brigantines, and reconnoitred the coast for two months. Balboa's absence provided Pedrarias with an opportunity to withdraw permission to explore the South Sea, and to recall Balboa to Acla; for Pedrarias had decided that the time had come to have done with his son-in-law. Unaware that he was going to his death, Balboa agreed to return, thinking that his presence was required to discuss his expedition. The moment he stepped ashore, Balboa was taken prisoner. Pedrarias rigged a trial in which the explorer was presented as a traitor and usurper of territories. On 13 January 1519 the unfortunate Balboa was beheaded, along with four of his companions, in the public square of Acla.

The way is clear

Two years prior to the ignoble execution of the man who discovered the Pacific, Gonzalo de Badajoz and Luis de Mercado had headed west in hopes of finding the 'land of gold'. Two years later, Gaspar de Espinoza embarked on a series of expeditions that led to the founding of Panama in 1519 and Nata in 1520. Santa María de la Antigua del Darien was abandoned in 1524 on the orders of Pedrarias, who transferred the capital to Panama. Maritime activity gradually passed from the Atlantic to the Pacific seaboard. Henceforth, navigators could choose between two routes, thereby opening the way for new discoveries.

An engraving by Théodore de Bry showing flying fish off the Brazilian coast. Extract from Navigatio in Brasiliam *(1562).*

The magic power of the word 'gold!'

When the Indians realized the power that the word 'gold' held over the Spaniards, they imagined that the syllable somehow contained a message of peace. They began to use the word more and more frequently, just to be agreeable, and in the hope that the Spaniards would cease their acts of cruelty. The Indians also hoped that the magic word might encourage the white men to leave for other lands. The legend of a river where one could 'fish' for gold with nets gave its name to the first Spanish province in continental America: Golden Castile.

An extraordinary personality destined for an unprecedented adventure: Hernán Cortés was to spearhead the exploration and conquest of Mexico—an exploit that combined grandeur with cruelty, courage, tenacity and cunning, and saw much bloodshed on both sides. For the conquistadores this was a glorious episode, but it spelled the end of civilizations that had flourished in these lands for millennia.

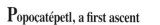

Popocatépetl, a first ascent

The first ascension of the volcano Popocatépetl, located some sixty kilometres from today's Mexico City, in southeastern Anáhuac, was made in 1520, on the orders of Cortés, by Diego de Ordas, accompanied by nine Spanish soldiers and several Indians. With an altitude of 5452 metres, it was the highest mountain climbed to date, a record that stood unbroken until the conquest of the first peaks of the Himalayas.

Extract from the History of the Indies *by Father Diego Duran. Montezuma's envoys offer gifts to Hernán Cortés with the not disinterested aim of winning his good graces.*

First approach

The Yucatán, a land whose existence Columbus had suspected, was discovered by chance by the Spaniards in 1511. Only two men, Aguilar and Guerrero, who were washed ashore after their vessel was shipwrecked, survived this first expedition. They were taken in by the Maya Indians, and one of them, Guerrero, became a cacique, an enemy of his former homeland. The other, Aguilar, was rescued some eight years later by Cortés, who took him into his service.

In 1517, an expedition led by Francisco Fernández de Córdoba, with Antón de Palominos as pilot, landed on the shores of Yucatán. A savage reception awaited them: more than half the Spaniards were massacred by the Indians. The survivors were dazzled by the riches of the civilization. In 1518, captain Juan de Grijalva, accompanied by Palominos, continued the exploration of the Yucatán coastline and the Gulf of Mexico. He discovered the island of Cozumel and made contact with more peace-loving peoples, belonging to the vast Aztec empire which then ruled Mexico.

These two expeditions, commissioned by Diego de Velasquez, the governor of Cuba, were followed by a third, in 1519, led by Hernán Cortés.

The makings of a great epic

The Spanish were disappointed by the West Indies, for the islands did not match their dreams of an America where gold was freely available and virtually for the taking. Furthermore, the Indians under Spanish domination were unfamiliar with the discipline of hard physical labour. Keeping the plantations in good working order was becoming an insurmountable task.

Grijalva's expedition and the revelation of Montezuma's Aztec empire dazzled the Spanish with visions of precious stones, gold, copper, silver, vast quantities of jewellery and magnificent fabrics. There was every indication that the Spaniards had discovered a rich and highly civilized kingdom.

Indeed, when the Spaniards arrived in Mexico, the Aztec Empire was at its apogee. Although heirs to a civilization several thousand years old, the Aztecs of the Anáhuac plateaus were a young nation, only recently emerged from barbarism. Their army was highly organized, and their society structured along theocratic lines. For the very first time, the Spanish were to encounter genuine resistance to their advance, but their boldness would overcome it.

An intrepid individualist

Hernán Cortés, born in Estremadura, abandoned his law studies to become a conquistador. An intrepid individual, he possessed an uncommonly keen intellect; he was the ideal person for carrying out the new conquest and vanquishing the Aztecs. Diego de Velasquez, the governor of Cuba, entrusted the mission to Cortés, his companion in the 1511 conquest of Cuba. Thus began one of the most controversial adventures in Spain's colonial history.

Cortés landed in Yucatán in February 1519. He soon realized that he was faced with an exceptionally demanding situation; in the circumstances, he judged it expedient to free himself from Velasquez's supervision (the governor had accorded Cortés only limited powers); his men acclaimed him Captain General, and Cortés undertook the conquest of Mexico on his own account, and of course, on behalf of the Spanish crown. This second point is attested by an official act, drawn up at the instigation of the future conqueror in order to give his venture legal status. The break between Cortés and Governor Velasquez was complete.

Two decisive encounters

In this part of the world, the Indians were neither timid nor peace-loving: they stood their ground and immediately attacked the Spaniards. But Cortés quickly realized that the natives were divided among themselves, and that some tribes were enemies; moreover, the Aztecs' ascendancy aroused the hatred of the peoples they dominated. Cortés shrewdly turned that situation to his own advantage. He founded Villa Rica de Santa Cruz, the first Spanish town in Mexico, then proceeded to launch his campaign. Ignoring the advice of his terrified men, who sensed their enemy's ferocity and determination, Cortés decided to attack.

Two encounters considerably strengthened his hand. The first was with Jerónimo de Aguilar, a Spaniard who had escaped shipwreck in 1511. After living for eight years among the Indians of the coastal regions, Aguilar was totally familiar with their language and culture. The second was with an Indian woman, one of twenty slaves handed over to the conquerors after a victory in battle. The woman was destined to become famous under the Christian name of Doña Marina. She is believed to have been the daughter of a Mayan dignitary, and had an implacable loathing for the Aztecs.

Aztec human skull with shells and haematites, into which has been inserted a sacrificial knife made of obsidian.

Highly intelligent, she became the faithful companion of Cortés and helped him achieve his aims.

Divide and rule

Cortés advanced into the heartland of the Anáhuac. After forging an alliance with the Totonacs of the coastal region, he defeated the Tlaxcaltecs in battle, and made them his allies as well. Cortés was short on men and weapons, but he was long on cunning. He cleverly fostered and exploited the natives' fear of firearms and the strange beasts called 'horses'; and he took shrewd advantage of weaknesses caused by the Indians' inter-tribal quarrels.

Cortés's amazing campaign took him and his men into the Mexican interior, and onto the high plateaus dominated by the volcano Popocatepetl. On 8 November 1519, he entered Tenochtitlán, the largest and most populous city in Mexico.

A brilliant but terrifying civilization

At the head of four hundred foot soldiers, fifteen cavalry, six pieces of artillery, and with the support of several Tlaxcaltecs, Cortés crossed the drawbridges and gained a foothold in the rich and flourishing lakeside city, while Montezuma tried to decide

how to respond. Cortés profited from the Aztecs' belief—for a time at least—that he and his men were gods whose advent had long been awaited, a situation that was to reoccur in Peru.

The Spaniards were struck with amazement at the sight of so much gold, so many dazzling precious stones and ornaments wrought of gold and silver; and they marvelled at the highly developed urban organization, for Tenochtitlán was as large as Seville. They marvelled at the noble stone temples, paved streets and sewer system. They were filled with admiration and dread at the sight of the great pyramids, whose steps (which many Spaniards were later to climb) led to the realm of the gods and of the human sacrifices performed to honour them. Díaz del Castillo would leave a blood-curdling account of those atrocious ceremonies... Before long, by means of banquets and feigned acts of courtesy, the Spaniards had taken Emperor Montezuma hostage, a prisoner in his own land. Granted, it was a gilded cage, but Cortés nonetheless had Montezuma shackled in irons to attend the public execution of some of his subjects, who had been found guilty of attacking the Spanish base at Veracruz.

Hostilities and rebellions

By now the entire Aztec people was up in arms against the invaders and one of Montezuma's nephews launched a revolt against Cortés. The welcome which they had once

Religion and human sacrifice

To avenge his mother, Cóatlicue, the Earth goddess slain by her brothers (symbolizing the stars) and her sister Coyolxauhqui, the goddess of night and the moon, the sun god Huitzilopochtli beheaded Coyolxauhqui and cast her body from the top of a hill. The ritual human sacrifice performed on the *Templo Mayor* of the Aztecs was a re-enactment of the myth—representing the endless succession of day and night, life and death—and required a constant stream of victims. Once they had been sacrificed, their bodies were thrown down from the temple heights, so that they were torn and battered like the mythical goddess. The Spaniards were horrified by this ritual and it was with a perfectly clear conscience that they fought and annihilated a civilization with such ruthless customs.

extended to the white gods was now transformed into open hostility. Montezuma, although held prisoner by the Spaniards, vacillated and was unable to harness the anger of his people. One moment, he believed that events corresponded to divine will; the next, he changed his mind. He even consented to the capture and punishment of his nephew, who was subsequently replaced by another prince, this time chosen by Cortés.

At this juncture, the situation of Cortés and his men became extremely tricky, for Panfilo de Narváez had arrived, sent by the governor of Cuba to arrest Cortés and take him back in irons, first to Cuba and thence to Spain. Narváez was accompanied by a sizeable armed guard to 'persuade' Cortés to acquiesce. Needless to say, the conquistador had no intention of giving himself up. He harangued his men and intrigued anew with Montezuma, then withdrew from Tenochtitlán and set out to confront Narváez, leaving behind Pedro de Alvarado as lieutenant. Some two hundred men, plus allied natives, accompanied Cortés to meet

the enemy sent by Diego Velasquez. Narváez had set up camp in Cenapoala. Through a cunning and inventive 'psychological strategy', Cortés succeeded in disheartening and corrupting his opponent's forces before the battle took place. Finally, after a daring night raid, he captured Panfilo de Narváez and won over most of his adversary's men to his own side. The year was 1520. On the way back to Tenochtitlán, Cortés learned that the inhabitants of the Aztec capital had risen up in rebellion.

Alvarado's mistakes

With Cortés away fighting Narvárez, Pedro de Alvarado and his companions had taken advantage of his absence to behave like brutes. They burst into the temples of Tenochtitlán, smashing sacred images and creating havoc at a religious ceremony. In their greed for ever larger quantities of gold

and jewellery, they attacked and put to death hundreds of Aztec dignitaries. When Cortés returned, Alvarado was hemmed in on all sides. The Aztecs nevertheless made a gap in the circle when Cortés arrived, allowing the captain to enter freely... only to close the trap even tighter on Cortés and his troops! The conquistador acknowledged that the reasons for the uprising were legitimate, but for the time being he was careful not to say as much, nor did he punish Alvarado and the other culprits. Cortés needed all the men he could muster, for he was now openly at war with the Aztecs.

The 'Noche Triste'

There was no truce in this decisive battle. It was virtually impossible for the Spaniards to leave the city. They urged Montezuma to intercede with his people; the Aztec emperor finally—grudgingly—agreed. Montezuma's address was met with a hail of stones and he fell, mortally wounded by an arrow, most likely fired by an Aztec. Once the controversial monarch had fallen, the Spaniards had nothing but their courage left to oppose a people clamouring for vengance, led by Cuitlahuac.

The situation was desperate; the Spanish invaders were surrounded. And so it was that on 10 July 1520, they resolved to make a daring night raid that was to go down in history as the *Noche Triste*, the 'sad night'. Those who did not die transfixed by arrows, or whose hearts were not cut out with the sacrificial obsidian stone, drowned in the lake, dragged down by the weight of the treasures they obstinately refuse to abandon as they took flight. 'Thus they were killed by their gold, and died rich,' wrote the chronicler Francisco López de Gomara with bitter irony. Spanish losses amounted to 870 soldiers, while their Tlaxcaltec allies lost 1200. But with the help of some friendly Indians who had escaped the massacre, Cortés and the surviving Spanish troops carried the day at a battle at Otumba, a victory which enabled him to regroup his forces.

The Aztecs' pyramidal universe

Like early Greek cosmology, the Aztec view of the universe portrayed the Earth as a disc surrounded by water. According to the Aztecs, the disc was positioned at the centre of the universe, at the junction of the bases of two pyramids. One, upward-pointing, pyramid contained the superior, essentially divine regions of the universe, arranged in tiers. The other one, pointing downwards, held the nether regions, inhabited chiefly by demons; at the very bottom was the kingdom of the dead. The Earth's surface was divided into four horizontal zones, each ruled by one of the gods of the seasons.

The Aztec ritual of human sacrifice consisted in immolating the victim at the top of the temple steps, tearing out his heart, then throwing the corpse down the steps.

Siege and reconquest of Tenochtitlán

Other tribes also lived in the vicinity of Tenochtitlán. With considerable guile, Cortés fanned the fear and hatred that the Indians under Spanish rule felt for the Aztecs, so that these disaffected peoples would join

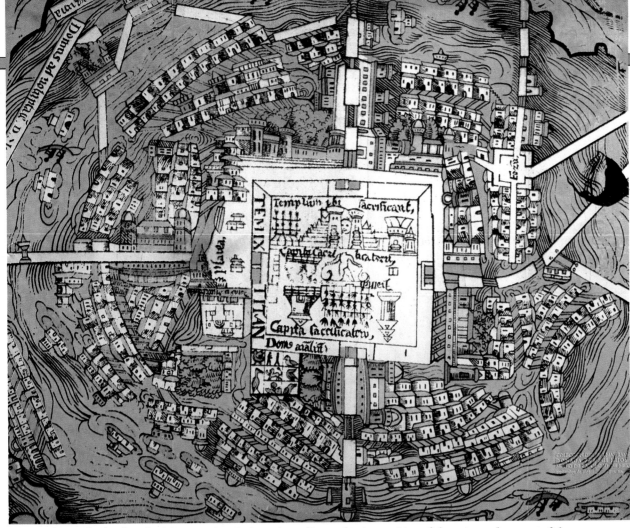

A map of Tenochtitlán based on Cortés's descriptions. According to the Aztec vision of the cosmos, the centre of the terrestrial level was occupied by the templo mayor, the starting point for the four directions of the universe.

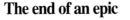

War cries

Even though the Spaniards wrought terror by bursting onto the battlefield with their horses and dogs of war, they were no less terrified themselves by the cries of the attacking Indians. 'They charged ferociously, fighting in a dreadful din of shouts and war cries aimed at frightening the enemy,' notes Solis. According to López de Gomara, 'they uttered cries to whip up their courage when attacking. Some shouted and others whistled in such a way that they struck terror into the hearts of those unfamiliar with such practices.'

his troops; he even won over tribes which had until then remained neutral, thus amassing a quite impressive army. He gradually succeeded in isolating the Aztecs.

The size of the Spanish force was further swelled by the arrival of more Spaniards, for the riches and daring deeds of the Mexican 'campaign' had acquired a fame which attracted new contigents of men. The march on Mexico City looked for all the world like a military parade. Once they arrived at the lakeside, the Spaniards assembled and launched a squadron of brigantines to take out the Aztec positions which neither the infantry nor the artillery could reach.

The siege lasted approximately eighty days, from 30 May to 13 August 1521. Finally, the city of Mexico-Tenochtitlán fell into the hands of the Spaniards and the young chief Cuauhtémoc, Cuitlahuac's successor, was taken prisoner.

Cortés, the new overlord.

Following the fall and sack of the city, Cortés devoted all his efforts to extending the conquered territories. In recognition of his victory and the prestigious war prize which he brought to the Crown, Cortés was appointed governor of New Spain and vested with unlimited powers for the consol-idation and extension of his conquests. The State of Montezuma (in other words the entire Aztec Empire) was to serve as base for ventures towards the south and north, where new lands awaited the conquistadores. Following an unsuccessful and very bloody expedition mounted to prove that the peninsula was in fact an island, the Spaniards managed to annex to New Spain the regions of Honduras and Yucatán.

The end of an epic

During the new governor's frequent absences, Cortés, whose power seemed to many excessive, was inevitably the object of innumerable intrigues and plots. At the same moment, for the very first time in the history of the Conquista, a genuine attempt was being made to establish an administration capable of organizing, managing and exploiting the riches and resources of the conquered territories. For example, in New Spain on 13 December 1527, the first Audience (law court) on American soil was set up: colonization had begun in earnest.

In the prevailing climate of rivalry, Cortés was recalled to Spain to give an account of his activities; he was replaced in his post by a colourless civil servant. Although his signal services were acknowledged, Cortés was in effect stripped of his political power. But the noble title of Marquis of Oaxaca and the riches that went with it were not enough to satisfy the conquistador, who realized that his new rank had seriously narrowed his horizons.

In 1530, Cortés returned to Mexico. In 1536, he took part in an arduous expedition to the Gulf of California, but the meagre results cost Cortés his prestige. Fanning out from New Spain, the first expeditions set out for Central America: Pedro de Alvarado went to Guatemala, while Cristóbal de Olid headed for Honduras; other parties travelled north shortly afterwards. Some took the Caribbean coastal routes, while others went north via inland routes, or along the shores of the Pacific. Among these missions was one led by Francisco de Ulloa, who set out along the Californian coast in search of the seven cities of Cíbola and another, equally illusory place called the Great Ouivire; Niño de Guzmán (1529-30), Alvar Nuñez Cabeza de Vaca (1539-42) and Hernando de Soto (1539) also made arduous journeys towards today's southern United States (see p. 112). But for Cortés the era of glory was over. In 1540, worn out and forgotten, he travelled back to Spain, where he died seven years later. His name lives on, however, immortalized by the vigilance of his chroniclers, among them his old companion from the memorable Mexican campaign, Díaz del Castillo.

Eager to measure himself against the great Cortés, and to achieve comparable glory, another conquistador, Francisco Pizarro, strove ceaselessly to bring another fabled empire—one that he himself had vanquished—to the Spanish crown. The conquest of Peru, like that of Mexico, was marked by heroic exploits, betrayals, massacres—and the eternal lure of gold.

The distribution of the ransom

According to the chronicle written by Francisco López de Gomara, the estimated value of the jewels gathered to pay Atahualpa's ransom before his execution totalled some 52,000 silver marks and 1,326,500 gold pesos. One fifth of this sum was earmarked for the Spanish Crown, in other words nearly 400,000 pesos. Each member of the cavalry was awarded 8900 gold pesos and 370 silver marks, while the infantry received 4450 gold pesos and 180 silver marks. As for the captains, each one carried off 30,000 gold pesos and 40,000 silver pesos. Never had soldiers found fortune so quickly, having risked so little. Some of these lucky men returned home; but others remained in Peru and in the space of a week many had squandered their fortunes at the card table.

A country called Birú

The name Birú had been known since the days of Balboa (see p. 64). In 1522 the captain and historian Pascual de Andagoya explored the coasts lying to the south of the Panama isthmus and reached the Gulf of San Miguel, which he subsequently crossed. Although his voyage had been fraught with danger and punctuated by violent storms, Andagoya managed to make his way back to Spain, bursting with tales of a land called Birú, a country teeming with gold. From then on, the rumour of a great empire in the south was accepted as gospel truth.

Peasant, swineherd and conqueror

When his great Peruvian adventure first began, Pizarro was almost fifty years old. Although of humble origins (he was born in Trujillo in 1475, the son of a country squire and a servant), he held a respected position in society, and while not fabulously wealthy, he was nevertheless comfortably off. He could certainly have lived peacefully on his incomes, after a life of adventure. For Pizarro had been the companion of Vasco Núñez de Balboa on the expedition to the Pacific in 1513 (see p. 64–5). In 1510 Pizarro had also taken part in Alonso de Hojeda's exploration of Columbia. Following his arrival in the New World (probably Hispaniola) in 1504, he had invariably taken part in the most dangerous and exciting missions. But this former peasant from Estremadura who—so the legend goes—had spent his boyhood tending swine, was consumed by a burning ambition to equal Cortés, a distant cousin of his. In 1523 the governor of Panama, Pedrarias, lured by the stories of fabulous riches spun by returning mariners, approved Pizarro's plans for an expedition—in return for a fifty per cent share of the booty.

Two tough conquistadores

To organize and finance the expedition, Pizarro went into partnership with Diego de Almagro and canon Hernando de Luque, the spiritual guarantor of the undertaking. Together, they decided to try their luck in the south, beyond the lands discovered by Andagoya. Twice the mission failed, but finally the Spaniards set foot in the land of Birú in 1526. The conquest of that country proved to be one of the most gruelling episodes in the saga of Spain's colonial adventures.

Francisco Pizarro and Diego de Almagro were men of forceful disposition, courageous and stubborn. They came from similar backgrounds (Almagro was a foundling) and were united by a firm friendship. And yet the singular circumstances and shady political dealings that characterized the Spanish conquest of the New World soon turned the two men into rivals and enemies. Their bitter dissensions inevitably affected the morale of their companions in arms, since each held virtually despotic sway over his men.

Alone with thirteen men

In 1526, following an initial failure in 1524, a second expedition to Peru made evident the real difficulties of carrying out the planned conquest. While navigating the Esmeraldas, the Spaniards got bogged down in marshlands and caught up in mangrove roots, and were forced to backtrack in the face of growing hostility from the coastal Indians. Diego de Almagro sailed back to Panama to gather reinforcements, while Francisco Pizarro waited for him on del Gallo island. Demoralized by hunger and fever, and beset by insects, the soldiers demanded to return home.

Pedrarias, who had learnt of the situation in a secret message, sent a mission to bring the soldiers home. It was at this point, so the story goes, that Pizarro drew his sword and traced a line in the sand: those willing to follow him in the fabulous conquest of the South were to step over the line; the others were free to go back. Thirteen of the hardiest, most courageous men, the *trece de la fama* (the Glorious Thirteen), chose to cast in their lot with Pizarro.

Conflicts and internal wars

Left on their own, Pizarro and the Thirteen (still waiting for the reinforcements promised by Almagro) took refuge on Isla Gorgona, a more welcoming island, which had plenty of game. At last the long-awaited reinforcements arrived. The men took ship aboard a new vessel and reached the Gulf of Guayaquil, where they intervened in conflicts between local Indian tribes. The Spaniards even took part in several battles, choosing sides according to the political needs of the moment.

As in Mexico, the Inca Empire was torn by bloody wars. Atahualpa, an Inca prince and lord of Quito, had risen up against his brother, Huáscar, the legitimate successor to the throne, on the death of their father, Huayna Cǎpac. This fratricidal rivalry would eventually bring about the break-up of the Inca Empire, after two years of bloodshed and Spanish intrigue.

A roomful of gold and silver

One hundred and eighty soldiers and thirty-seven cavalry advanced through Peruvian territory. News of their advance reached Atahualpa, who was with his army in Cajamarca, waging war against his brother Huáscar. Before presenting himself to Atahualpa, Pizarro took the precaution of posting soldiers and horses—cunningly concealed—close by. The Inca monarch awaited Pizarro in the square at Cajamarca, surrounded by his guards. Pizarro sent as ambassador the Dominican monk and interpreter Valverde. The monk, who held a cross in one hand and a Bible in the other, addressed a speech to Atahualpa in which he requested peace and exhorted the ruler to swear obedience to the kings of Castile in the name of the divine will. The Inca, well aware of the atrocities committed by the Spaniards, took the Bible, turned several pages, and hurled it to the ground to show his rejection and rage. Whereupon Pizarro gave the signal to attack. Instantly, the soldiers hidden behind the trees opened fire with their muskets and arquebuses, at the same time letting loose the horses, which galloped towards the Indians. Taken completely off guard, the astonished Indians were easily subdued and Atahualpa was taken prisoner on 16 November 1532.

Although victorious, the Spaniards acknowledged how impressed they were by the dignity and wealth of the Peruvians, and they treated Atahualpa with a certain measure of respect. As for Atahualpa, he quickly realized where the Spaniards' soft spot lay, and offered a rich ransom in exchange for his freedom: he promised to fill the room in which he was imprisoned with gold and silver, to the height of a man.

The death of Atahualpa and Huáscar

While the emissaries of Atahualpa were gathering the ransom to free their leader, the war with his brother Huáscar continued. Atahualpa, suspecting that the Spaniards were plotting with Huáscar, and fearing for his own life, ordered the assassination of his brother. One of Huáscar's sons, who managed to escape the massacre his uncle had orchestrated, reached Cajamarca and related the events to Pizarro. Although they held him prisoner, the Spaniards were alarmed by Atahualpa's power and feared a reunification of Inca forces. A room isn't fil-

When the Spanish arrived in Peru, the country was divided by bloody rivalries. Pizarro's men opened fire on the Incas and captured their monarch, Atahualpa.

led with gold in a day, and the conquistadores were afraid that, because of the delay, they risked losing all the ground gained thus far.

The murder of Huáscar offered the Spaniards a pretext for getting rid of Atahualpa. Pizarro put him on trial, accusing him of murdering his brother and conspiring against the Spaniards, and of practising polygamy and idolatry. Atahualpa was sentenced to be burnt at the stake, but since he agreed to be baptized, the sentence was commuted to strangulation. On the day of Atahualpa's execution, Pizarro donned mourning and seemed profoundly distressed. The date was 29 August 1533.

The end of an empire

Atahualpa's death led to the disintegration of the Inca confederation. But as Pizarro soon discovered, the remaining pockets of resistance, the absence of a leader able to co-ordinate the complex administration of the conquered territories, and the flight of local populations towards other regions

compelled him to seek out an Inca to succeed Atahualpa and to deal with these problems. Since Toparca, the elected successor, had also perished, Pizarro chose Manco, a seasoned warrior belonging to the Huáscar faction. So it was that the crown went to Manco, after he had sworn an oath of obedience to the Spanish Crown. On the same occasion, Pizarro appointed the first mayors and local administrators for the new villages; he also built churches. Thus did colonial life begin to take root in Peru.

Cuzco, a bone of contention

Cuzco, the capital of the Inca Empire, was also its richest city. In the eyes of Incas and Spaniards alike, Cuzco held considerable symbolic value. Throughout Peru's colonial period, the possession or loss of this city was the main cause of wars and revolts waged by the Indians and even the Spaniards themselves. Since Cuzco was far from the sea, the Spaniards founded the city of Lima near the port of Callao on the banks of the River Rimac.

Atahualpa's wives

On the death of Atahualpa, his wives and handmaids set up a great lamentation, wailing and invoking heaven. The favourites rushed to be buried with Atahualpa. When the Spaniards tried to prevent them, some women hanged themselves with ropes or with cords made from their own hair. The monarch's mortal remains were secretly moved by the Indians, either to Cuzco or to Quito (sources differ). The Spaniards, convinced that Atahualpa had been buried with all his riches, hunted for the body, but were never able to find it.

At the time of the Spanish conquest, the Inca empire had some seven or eight million subjects and extended from the Equator to modern-day Chile.

The trial of Diego de Almagro

Anyone who reads the charges brought against Diego de Almagro, on the strength of which the death sentence was pronounced against him, can see clearly that the trial was a travesty of justice. Apart from his responsibility as a leader, all the other accusations could have been levelled at any of the Spanish conquistadores of the period. Almagro was accused of 'entering Cuzco armed; causing the death of a large number of Spaniards; forging alliances with the enemy; attributing and confiscating territories without the Emperor's consent; breaking cease-fires, promises and commitments' and lastly, of 'fighting against the King's justices during the battles of Abancay and Las Salinas'.

The capture of Quito

Following the death of Atahualpa, Cuzco belonged solely to Spain. The only other town of any importance still in the hands of the Incas was Quito. It was there that the Inca Ruminagui, a follower of Huáscar, sought refuge with five thousand warriors on the run from Cajamarca. Exploiting the disgruntlement of the *Cañares*—Incan subjects living in the vicinity of Quito—Pizarro ordered Sebastián de Benalcázar to take the city. At the head of two hundred infantry and eighty calvary of Spanish and Indian origin, Benalcázar gained entry to the city and routed Ruminagui, who abandoned Quito after first setting fire to the city.

The fame of Peru

Drawn by the fame of its riches, large numbers of Spaniards travelled to Peru. Among them was a gentleman named Pedro de Alvarado, the discoverer and colonizer of Guatemala. Almagro and Pizarro rightly suspected that Alvarado had come intent on claiming new territories. Almagro set forth to meet Alvarado. It would have been pointless to fight, since both men knew only too well the intentions of the other. Almagro, on the orders of Pizarro, proposed to purchase Alvarado's fleet and weaponry at a high price; in exchange, Alvarado was to leave Peru for good. Many of his followers decided to stay on, but Alvarado accepted

the offer and used the money to finance an expedition to Cíbola, the fabulous (and mythical) city supposedly located somewhere in the north of New Spain (see p. 113).

The leaders in action

Having entrusted the government of the city of Cuzco to Diego de Almagro, Francisco Pizarro set out on a mission to the north of the country, where he planned to divide up the territories and the Indians. He founded the city of Trujillo, which he named after his native city. Once the northern regions were safely under Spanish control, colonists and conquistadores enjoyed a brief spell of peace and prosperity.

Meanwhile, Almagro had received in Cuzco the envoys of Emperor Charles V (who was also the king of Spain, under the name of Charles I). In 1534, the king had appointed Almagro as Marshal of Peru and governor of all the territories 'at a distance of one hundred leagues from those governed by Francisco Pizarro'. This was great news for Almagro, who had often felt that, compared to Pizarro, he had been given short shrift. Moreover, he had always regarded Cuzco as his personal fief. Now, with the royal appointment firmly in hand, Almagro openly proclaimed himself governor. His new powers enabled him to distribute land to his captains and soldiers, an act that provoked the wrath of Pizarro. The peace between them was at an end.

Seventeen years of civil war

The hostility between Pizarro and Almagro coincided with a major Indian uprising headed by the Inca leader Manco. Their quarrel came to a temporary halt when Pizarro promised Almagro to help him mount an expedition to Chile. But Almagro's expedition was a colossal failure and after two years of fruitless efforts, relations between the two leaders once again soured.

On his return, Almagro resolved to win back the city of Cuzco, the government of which had been taken over by Pizarro's two brothers, Gonzalo and Hernando. A civil war ensued that was to last nearly seventeen years.

Reinforcements from Spain supported first one side, then the other, and there was every reason to believe that the interminable conflict would end only with the death of one or other of the two leaders.

The death of Almagro

In view of the danger posed by the increasingly likely union between Almagro's partisans and the Indians, Pizarro adopted a new tactic. His sense of urgency stemmed from the Almagro faction's siege of Lima in 1538, where four hundred Spaniards had met their death. A meeting between the two leaders was arranged, but they were unable to settle their differences. Shortly afterwards, Almagro was caught in an ambush and, after a bloody battle, was taken prisoner by Pizarro. He was later hanged and decapitated in the public square of Cuzco in 1538. Almagro's son, a potential leader and avenger of his father, was dispatched to Lima to put down a new uprising.

Adventures, intrigues and murders

The conquest of new territories continued in spite of the long period of civil war that ravaged Peru. Since 1534, when Pedro de Mendoza obtained concessions on the banks of the Río de la Plata, settlers continued to discover sites and found townships along the shores of the Pacific. In 1541 Pedro de Valdivia directed the exploration of Chile, while in February 1542 Francisco de Orellana discovered the River Amazon.

Around this time Peru was flooded by an influx of 'licensees', persons invested with special powers conferred by the king, whose duty it was to correct the vices spawned by conquest and colonization. Although the licensees were supposed to be educated, upright individuals, they were in fact no different from common soldiers, once their greedy appetite for riches had been whetted. Furthermore, their scheming sense of intrigue was at least a match for the old campaigners of the conquest. Some of the licensees even went so far as to renounce Spain and declare independence from the king—when the booty they stood to gain warranted such a measure. Far from abating once Almagro was no longer on the scene, the civil wars of Peru went from bad to worse.

In Lima, Almagro el Mozo, the son of Diego de Almagro, plotted against Francisco Pizarro. Ambushed in his own home in the city he had founded, Francisco Pizarro was murdered on the night of 26 June 1541 by Almagro's partisans. A successor stood ready to take up the reins of the Peruvian government: Almagro el Mozo.

Peru the impossible

A long and chaotic period of conflict followed Pizarro's murder. The legal, political, economic, religious and even personal implications of the Spanish conquest were so numerous and diverse that a faction and leader existed to champion virtually every point of view. All factions were at loggerheads with each other, and the city of Lima soon became the scene of endless struggles. In 1542 King Charles dispatched Vaca de Castro, a judicial officer, to restore some semblance of order, but local officials were unresponsive to the legal arguments: war was the only language they understood. The royal troops therefore had no alternative but to combat Almagro el Mozo, who was defeated at Chupas, near Huamanga. He tried to seek refuge in Cuzco, but was taken prisoner and executed; he was buried next to his father. On 20 November that same year, the king of Spain decreed the 'New Laws for the Administration of the Indies', which were vigorously rejected by the settlers. They were unwilling to share what they had earned during years of struggle against the Indians. They refused to accept those who had come to show them how to treat the natives, and were even more adamant in their refusal to pay a tax the Crown was now levying on property they had fought so hard to acquire.

Túpac Amaru, the last of the Incas

Until the eighteenth century, colonists' revolts against the king, the sudden loss or acquisition of territories, uprisings and murders were everyday events in Peru. It is difficult to say exactly when the period of conquest came to an end, if by 'end' is meant the establishment of a new order. The natives had retreated to the region of Vilcabamba in 1537 and founded a kingdom alongside Spain's colonial government. During an offensive launched in 1571, their leader, Túpac Amaru, was captured and brought to Cuzco, where he was put to death the following year. Thus the last of the Incas met his end.

This Portuguese map from 1563 is still very inaccurate. The cities along the Rio das Amazonas represent the wealth that the conquistadors hoped to find in the heart of the equatorial forest.

The true-life story of Garcilaso de la Vega

We owe to Garcilaso de la Vega, otherwise known as 'The Inca', the most immediate and gripping accounts of life among the Inca people at the very moment when that unfortunate nation was about to disappear, the victim of Spanish conquest. Son of Sebastián Garcilaso de la Vega, a companion of Pizarro (whom he backed against Almagro) and of an Inca princess, niece of Huayna Cápac, 'The Inca' was born in Cuzco in 1539. Thanks to him, Inca customs and legends were recorded before they had died out.

73

Born of stories spun by explorers more interested in relating wonders than in recording truth, El Dorado became the symbol of undreamed-of wealth and of a sometimes blood-spattered search for inexhaustible riches. Like many legends, that of El Dorado was based on a historical reality, albeit a rather different one from the fantasies dreamed up by the surprisingly gullible conquistadores.

Salt, the source of civilization

The Chibcha Indians (also known as the Muiscas) enjoyed a fairly high standard of living owing to a source of wealth unsuspected by the Spaniards, which the Indians used to obtain gold and other commodities. This secret currency was salt, more vital to life than precious metals! The Chibchas engaged in a flourishing trade, and their civilization was one of the most advanced in Latin America. The Spanish conquest destroyed virtually every vestige of the Chibcha culture.

According to Chibcha ritual, the chief was covered with oil and gold dust, and then dived from his sacred raft into the lake to offer the precious metal to the gods.

In search of the Gilded One

Long ago, before the Spanish conquest, there lived a tribe in the highlands of Cundinamarca (Columbia) that held an annual ceremony to honour its gods. During the ceremony, the *zipa*, or chief, covered in gold dust, proceeded to Lake Guatavita. There, floating on a raft, the chief threw offerings of gold and precious stones into the lake, before plunging into the water himself to rinse off the gold dust coating his body. Although the practice had died out by the time the Spaniards arrived, Sebastián de Benalcázar heard tell of it during the conquest of Peru. The tale left a deep impression, for only a fabulously wealthy land could indulge in such customs. Time, greed and imagination transformed the legend of the Gilded One into the myth of El Dorado, a term that has since been applied to any

imaginary land of untold riches. El Dorado was thus added to the already considerable list of fantastic lands, such as the Casa del Sol ('House of the Sun') or the mysterious kingdom of the Omaguas, a nation rumoured to be richer even than the Incas. These imaginary countries became the main objective of expeditions to the north of South America, specifically Venezuela and Colombia.

Jiménez de Quesada explores Colombia

In 1536 Pedro Fernandez de Lugo, governor of Santa Marta, a town on the Atlantic coast, sent one of his men to explore New Granada, as Colombia was originally known. The explorer in question was Gon-

zalo Jiménez de Quesada, a magistrate who had come to America with an expedition Fernandez de Lugo had financed. The mission took Jiménez de Quesada up the Río Magdalena and thence, after an arduous eight-month trek through tropical forests, to the Cundinamarca highlands, the territory of the Chibcha Indians led by a *zipa* named Bocatá (a name the Spanish rendered as 'Bogotá'). Once he had defeated Bocatá, in 1538 Jiménez de Quesada founded Santa Fé de Bogotá, in honour of his own birthplace, Santa Fé. He organized the new town and dispatched several reconnaissance missions to search the surrounding countryside for the emerald mines he had heard about. Jiménez de Quesada then returned to Spain to have the King officially appoint him governor of the conquered lands, and to sanction the manner in which the booty had been distributed (the gold and emeralds of New Granada further contributed to the legend of El Dorado). Obtaining the royal sanction had become all the more urgent for Jiménez de Quesada, since two other conquistadores were laying claim to the lands he had explored. One was Sebastián de Benalcázar, a Spaniard who had won fame in Peru; the other was Nikolaus Federmann, a German who had arrived from Venezuela.

Charles V and the Welsers

Five pacts signed in 1528 had turned over the territory of Venezuela to the Welsers, a German banking family. Their powerful support had been influential in the election of Emperor Charles V (also King Charles I of Spain) to the head of the Holy Roman Empire. Since Charles was forever in search of cash and was unable to repay his debts to the bankers, he signed a negotiated settlement, the *Capitulations*. According to the terms of these agreements, the Welsers pledged to organize the colonization of Santo Domingo in collaboration with other Germans, to import four thousand black slaves, and to occupy the lands between Cape De La Vela in northwestern Venezuela, and Maracapana, in the east, with unlimited extension southwards. The land granted to Juan de Ampués, who had founded and settled Coro (northwestern Venezuela) in 1527, was to remain under Spanish rule, and in view of its strategic location a pact was concluded to provide for free passage through that territory. The agreement was signed by Charles and the Welsers' representatives in Spain.

The Germans in South America

From 1531 onwards, as a result of the *Capitulations*, large numbers of German captains streamed into Venezuela. Their aim was not so much to found settlements as to explore the country in search of riches. From this point of view, their expeditions were exemplary; in geographical terms, the Germans made significant progress. Amongst those who launched missions in Venezuela were Ambrosius Ehinger, Georg von Hohermuth (also known as Jorge Spira, since he hailed from Spires, Speyer in German), Philip von Hutten and Nikolaus Federmann. The first explorers, including Ehinger, arrived in Coro in 1530. The Indians were already so terrified by stories they had heard of these bloody campaigns that when Ehinger reached the confluence of the Cesar and Magdalena rivers, they offered no resistance, but plied the German with food and fabulous quantities of gold. Since the booty was much greater than he had dared imagine, Ehinger sent to Coro for reinforcements. However, by the time they arrived, in 1532, Ehinger was already dead of marsh fever.

Ehinger was replaced by Georg von Hohermuth and Nikolaus Federmann. The two men reached Coro in 1534, and Hohermuth immediately set out on an exploratory mission southwards, as far as the River Guaviare. He returned to Coro in 1538, but Federmann was no longer there, having undertaken his own expedition to El Dorado. Hohermuth died two years later.

As for Federmann, after three long years of wandering and on the brink of exhaustion, he found a pass at Suma Paz and was able to cross the mountainous barrier that runs north to south along the edge of the Cundinamarca plateau. In 1539 Federmann

arrived at a spot near Bogotá. At the sight of the pleasant landscape with its warm climate, the band of hungry and ragged men thought they had reached El Dorado. Their illusions were short-lived, however, for Jiménez de Quesada had beaten them to the site quite some time before. Yet faced with the claims made by Federmann and Benalcázar (see above), Jiménez de Quesada was compelled to refer the matter to the authorities in Madrid.

End of the contract

While Jiménez de Quesada was exploring the highlands of Colombia, the German Philip von Hutten, who had settled in Venezuela, obtained permission to set off in his turn on the quest for El Dorado. He travelled by sea from Coro to Bunburata and thence to Barquisimeto. From there he continued on foot across the plains as far as La Fragua, where he spent the winter (the rainy season). However, when von Hutten decided to resume his explorations in the following Spring, his Indian guides abandoned him. Von Hutten spent an entire year in the *llanos*, the plains located between the Orinoco and the Amazon, searching for the celebrated Omaguas and their legendary riches. When at last he came to the end of

his resources, he returned to Coro for reinforcements. But upon his arrival he was arbitrarily accused of treason and put to death without further trial.

Von Hutten was the last of the German conquistadores of Venezuela. Shortly after his death, Spain cancelled the contract signed with the Welser bankers, and the colonization of Venezuela reverted to Spanish control, where it was to remain thereafter.

Tunja and the Temple Sun

The mountain ranges of the Andes protected the various local chieftains and provided ideal boundaries for their territories. The two most powerful chieftains of New Granada were Bogotá (Bocatá) and Tunja. While in the territory of Bogotá, Jiménez de Quesada (who had already amassed a treasure trove of emeralds, thanks to information provided by the Indian chieftain himself) learned of the existence of a sumptuous city where gold plaques hung outside every house, tinkling delightfully in the breeze. It was the village (or *zaque*) of King Tunja. Thanks to a carefully organized strike, Quesada was able to capture Tunja and seize his treasures. The booty was considerable: pure gold, emeralds and silver.

Jimenez de Quesada set out to conquer the high plateaus of Colombia in the hope of finding the legendary El Dorado.

Jiménez de Quesada's campaign to take possession of the Chibchas' treasures did not stop there. He heard that farther to the north lay another town, Sogamoso, the site of the Temple of the Sun. Within the temple the sanctuary of Remichinchaguagua was entirely covered in gold leaf, and the floors with carpets woven of gold thread. The Spanish soldiers arrived at Sogamoso as night was falling, and with lighted torches approached the temple walls the better to view the treasures. Suddenly a spark from the torches set the wood-and-straw structure ablaze; the pillars caught fire, and the flames spread in an instant to the temple's straw roof. According to the chronicler Friar Pedro Aguado, the fire burned for an entire year.

To take revenge on the Spaniards for their cupidity, the Indians made their prisoners swallow molten gold.

With a herd of swine

Sebastián de Benalcázar, a member of Pizarro's forces in Peru, remained behind at Piura as acting governor when Pizarro, after the imprisonment of Atahualpa, left Cajamarca to complete the conquest of the Inca Empire. On his own, Benalcázar decided to march on Quito. But when he got there, he found that it had already been sacked and emptied of its treasures.

In 1534, together with Almagro, Benalcázar founded Santiago de Quito (the Indian city was the seat of the kingdom of Quitú), later renamed Francisco de Quito (the official name of the present capital of Ecuador) in honour of Pizarro; he also organized the city's administration. Like the other conquistadores, Benalcázar had heard tales of El Dorado, and in 1536 he decided to find it. And so he headed north, despite Pizarro's express order to turn back. A long quest ensued. With his men—and a herd of swine to serve as food—Benalcázar crossed the mountains separating the Magdalena and Cauca river valleys. He discovered and explored a densely cultivated and populated region called Popayán. Ever on the look-out for gold, he continued as far as Cali, then headed east, that same year reaching today's Antioquia (a settlement founded in 1541 to prospect for gold in the alluvial deposits of the River Cauca). In 1539, he sighted the Cundinamarca highlands, at virtually the same moment as the German explorer Federmann discovered the Suma Paz pass to the east of the mountain range. At last Benalcázar reached the end of his journey, the land of the Muiscas (or Chibchas), home of the *Hombre Dorado*, the legendary Gilded One. But an unpleasant surprise awaited him, for another Spanish conquistador had got there before him: Gonzalo Jiménez de Quesada, soon to be joined by a third rival, Nikolaus Federmann (see above). By and large, however, the adventure did not end too badly, with Jiménez de Quesada winning credit for the discovery, and the two others receiving sums of gold as their 'consolation prize'.

The beginnings of an amazing saga

Francisco de Orellana, one of the most famous explorers of South America, a veteran of Cortés's campaigns, took part in the expedition led by Gonzalo Pizarro, Francisco Pizarro's half-brother. Starting from Cuzco, the expedition was to cross the Andes in search of the country where cinnamon was known to grow. Indeed, the cinnamon trees that filled certain valleys could generate substantial profits, especially since at the time spices were worth their weight in gold.

In 1539, after a year of meticulous preparation, the expedition set forth. In spite of all the precautions, it was to encounter the same difficulties as other explorers: hostile Indians, an inhospitable natural environment, and an impenetrable jungle, fraught with danger. After months of harrowing and disappointingly unproductive trekking, following obviously false information provided by an Indian chieftain eager to get rid of these unwanted visitors, the expedition struck out on the route to El Dorado, certain that their goal was at hand. The Spaniards knew they had to follow the course of a river eastwards, but they hesitated: should they travel overland, or by water? Since navigation appeared to be the less difficult course, they built a brigantine in which they could safely stow equipment, clothes and the precious booty gleaned here and there in the course of a few forays.

It was decided that Orellana should lead the way with the brigantine and the open boats to El Dorado, and then return with good news (and food) to the camp where Gonzalo Pizarro would wait for him with his men. Gonzalo waited an entire month, in vain.

Four thousand kilometres in a brigantine

In fact, rather than navigate back upstream to rejoin Pizarro, Orellana had decided to build a second brigantine (he broke up the dinghies for wood), in order to seek El Dorado on his own. Later on when Pizarro, saved by a miracle, dragged Orellana into a Spanish court of law, the latter defended his actions, claiming that the current of the River Marañón had pulled him downstream with such force that he had been powerless to turn back.

Orellana and his comrades were attacked by hostile Indian tribes that lived along the river; indeed, if we are to believe the reports of one of the men, a certain Carvajal, the party did battle with the terrible Amazons, fierce female warriors expert in the use of bows and arrows. It was after them that they named the powerful river which carried Orellana and his party, after a voyage of some 4000 kilometres, into open sea on 26 August 1542. No one had ever before sailed such a distance on a river, and no known river had such a wide and majestic estuary. Their expedition had lasted nearly six months. Out of the fifty-seven men who had started out, eleven had died of fever, and three had fallen in combat with Indian tribesmen.

Orellana in his makeshift craft sailed from the mouth of the Amazon over open sea to Cubagna in New Cadiz (Venezuela), whence he embarked for Spain. His aim was to solicit royal sanction for his discovery, and to be granted the governorship of New Andalusia, as he called the land he had explored. King Charles acceded to his request, but refused any financial aid to mount a second expedition, since Spain was feuding over the region with Portugal,

Vespucci observed that the Indians of Brazil wore feather coats for ceremonies but otherwise remained 'quite naked, as Nature made them'.

which claimed that part of the New World as its own. On the strength of the prerogatives accorded by the King, Orellana had assembled an army of five hundred men at his own expense. But he never again set eyes on the Amazon estuary. During the return crossing, not far from the coast, his ship was wrecked by a violent storm and sank without trace.

Diego de Ordas and the exploration of the Orinoco

After Vicente Yáñez Pinzón's discovery of the Orinoco estuary in 1499, years passed before anyone attempted to explore the river. Early in 1531 Diego de Ordas, a veteran of Cortés's Mexican campaigns, set sail from Seville. He departed with three ships,

six hundred infantry and thirty-five cavalry. But the mission was ill-starred from the first, for before he touched the shores of the American continent, Ordas perished (or perhaps was thrown overboard, as the historian Gomara suggests). His men continued, despite their captain's death, but the ships could not keep sight of each other in bad weather, and eventually ran aground. It appears that a handful of survivors made their way into the dense forest somewhere between the Amazon and Orinoco estuaries.

When Francisco de Orellana sailed down the Amazon, he heard Indians tell of all-powerful white men with wavy hair and beards who inhabited that region. Orellana was certain that these men were the survivors of Diego de Ordas's expedition, and that they had stumbled upon the fabled kingdom of the Omaguas, yet another of the wild fancies that for many years kept the legend of El Dorado alive and alluring.

fter the epic conquest of Mexico by Cortés and at the same time as Pizarro's taking of Peru, the exploration of Latin America continued southward—to Chile, Argentina, Patagonia... Vast territories still remained to be discovered, and officers were eager to keep their turbulent troops occupied, to avoid the regrettable incidents that idleness invariably produced. And of course the mirage of El Dorado still fired men's imaginations.

Lope de Aguirre, the mad conquistador

The way Francisco de Orellana told the tale of his adventures on the Amazon River made the viceroy of Peru, the Marquis of Cañete, think that it would be worthwhile to mount another expedition to search for El Dorado and the kingdom of the Omaguas. Moreover, the marquis was happy to find a pretext to rid Peru of some undesirables who had ended up there, and who might one day cause trouble. He put Pedro de Ursúa in charge of the best of these rowdies and ne'er-do-wells. From the first, Ursúa was faced not only with a hostile natural environment, but with the problems

Diego de Almagro led his men into an exhausting and murderous expedition across the Andes.

posed by an undisciplined band of hardened soldiers, among whom was the Basque madman, Lope de Aguirre.

Ursúa departed with this motley crew from Lima in February 1559. Near the River Motilones (as contemporary chroniclers called the present-day Huallaga River) he set up an improvised shipyard to construct boats to take the party down river, but the boats were so badly constructed, and the wood of such poor quality, that they turned out to be unusable. So with just three brigantines, two rafts and a few dinghies the explorers set off down the Motilones towards the Río Bracamoros (the Marañón) and beyond the Cocama (today's Ucayali River) to the Amazon. It is difficult to trace the course of their journey, for according to the contemporary chroniclers Francisco Vasquez and Gonzalo Zúñiga, even the members of the expedition did not know precisely where they were. Indeed, until the seventeenth century geographers could not locate these rivers with absolute certainty.

General dissatisfaction, insubordination, perpetual conflicts among the men and the disturbing presence of women on the journey (including Ursúa's mistress, Doña Inés de Atienza), as well as Aguirre's ceaseless conniving, all came to a climax when the party reached Marchipaso ('very rich and populous lands'), where the men revolted against Pedro de Ursúa. At the urging of Lope de Aguirre, Ursúa was stabbed to death in his cabin in November 1560.

A rebel against the Spanish crown

After this crime Lope de Aguirre solemnly declared his rebellion against Philip II, King of Spain, and proclaimed the inde-

pendent 'kingdom of Peru, Terra Firma and Chile' (*Reino del Péru, Tierra firme y Chile*), and designated as its sovereign Fernando de Gúzman, an ambitious but weak young nobleman who succeeded Ursúa as commander of the expedition. Whether through fear or genuine conviction, all the men followed him, and on 23 March 1561 the royal secretary of the expedition drew up a document that legalized the new dynasty and Aguirre's renunciation of Spanish nationality. But by then Aguirre's madness was ever plainer to see: not a day went by without his sentencing and putting to death those of his companions who had somehow displeased him, or whom he suspected of treason. In spite of this, the party pursued its perilous descent of the Amazon, regardless of hunger and fear and without the faintest trace on the horizon of the kingdoms of the Omaguas or of El Dorado. They crossed the narrow gorge of Obidos and at last reached the mouth of the Amazon (according to the historian Javier Ortiz de la Tabla in his introduction to Vasquez's chronicles, Aguirre did not in fact turn off towards the Orinoco, as has often been suggested). Then, retracing the route taken by Orellana, the party sailed north in the Atlantic. Some forty men had perished owing to Aguirre's bloody fits of madness, including the recently appointed 'king', Fernando de Gúzman.

The party landed on the Isla de Margarita (Venezuela) on 21 July of the same year. From there Aguirre hoped to make his way to Panama and Nombre de Dios to build a fleet that would take him to Peru, where he intended to destroy the king's authority and establish a new dynasty. But one of his men, Pedro de Munguia, deserted and revealed the plan. Before the arrival of forces sent against him from Santo Domingo, Aguirre was defeated by a local army and executed by his own men. But Aguirre managed to commit one final crime: to prevent her falling into the hands of the soldiers, he stabbed his daughter to death.

The exploration of Chile: Diego de Almagro

In 1534 the Spanish Crown instituted three governorships south of the one already granted to Pizarro.

The governorship of Nueva Toledo was accorded to Diego de Almagro (see pp. 70–2). Now rich and influential, the conquistador mounted a large expedition of five hundred men, which left Cuzco in July 1535. Travelling with the Spaniards were some fifteen hundred Indians, among them Pablo Tupac, the brother of Atahualpa, and Villac Umu, a priest from the Temple of the Sun at Cuzco. Almagro's journey was long and arduous. He sent Juan de Saavedra to travel with a hundred men by sea, while he himself undertook a trek across the Altiplano on the shores of Lake Titicaca, and continued south through present-day Argentina. After an eight-month march, Almagro decided to cross the Andes cordillera and head for Chile.

The chronicler López de Gomara reports the hardships, hunger and cold endured by Almagro and his men in those high, snow-covered mountains. Many died, frostbitten and exhausted. Their horses shared the same fate.

To the Río Itata

Seeing the weakness and distress of his men, Almagro resolved to set out with just twenty soldiers and bring back help. It was then, from the summits of the cordillera, that he first looked down upon Chile: the valley of Copiapó was at his feet. South of Copiapóm Almagro went as far as the Maipo valley. On the coast, in the meantime, Captain Juan de Saavedra discovered and named the port of Valparaíso, while Pedro de Alvarado temporarily left off his duties as governor of Guatemala and pushed south to the Itata River, where his way was forcefully blocked by the Araucanian Indians.

His hopes dashed at the sight of the poverty of these newly discovered lands (still no El Dorado!), Almagro made his way back to Peru, eager to learn the ramifications of recent royal decrees and to verify news of a rebellion against Pizarro (see p. 72). In rags and incredibly debilitated, the troops crossed the Atacama desert in August 1536, a trek even more arduous and painful than the crossing of the cordillera: eight hundred treeless, parched kilometres....

According to Inca tradition, two of the four brothers who founded the dynasty were sent to Earth by the Sun, landing in the exact spot of one of the islands on Lake Titicaca.

The saga of Pedro de Valdivia

On the initiative of Francisco Pizarro, the conquest of Chile was attempted once again, three years later, by Pedro de Valdivia, a soldier with a solid reputation. He was a veteran of Flanders and the Battle of Pavia, who had travelled to the New World and joined an expedition exploring the Orinoco. From Venezuela he marched to Peru with a detachment of soldiers sent to restore order after an uprising in Cuzco. There, at the age of thirty-five, he earned Pizarro's favourable notice after he had fought and defeated Almagro's partisans at Las Salinas. Hungry for power and eager to acquire some territory for himself, Valdivia borrowed money and set out from Cuzco in January 1540 with two partners, his mistress, Inés de Suarez, and a troop of 150 Spaniards and a thousand Indians.

What was different about this expedition was that its aim was predominantly to colonize, rather than to conquer. The party included civilians as well as soldiers, among them a considerable number of artisans. They passed through the notorious Atacama desert, dotted with skeletons from Almagro's unfortunate army, and arrived at a native village on the banks of the River Loa, where (thanks to Inés de Suarez) Valdivia escaped assassination. The party camped in the Copiapó valley, and then pushed southward until 12 February 1541, when on the banks of the Mapocho River,

Valdivia founded Santiago de Nueva Extremadura, capital of the kingdom of Chile (New Estremadura was the Spanish name for modern Chile).

The invincible Araucanian Indians

The conquest of Chile was the most difficult episode in the Spanish adeventure in South America. The natives did not enjoy a land rich in resources, and the Spanish invaders themselves lived in isolation and poverty. They discovered precious little gold and encountered the aggressive hostility of the Araucanian Indians. When the conquistadores reached Chile, some of the northern Araucanians, known as the Pincunches, who lived within the Incan sphere of influence, accepted the invader's rule without undue difficulty. But the Mapuches, as the Araucanians of the southern and central zones were known, proved to be ferociously opposed to Spanish colonization. Their fighting spirit and resistance was unprecedented; they managed to hold their ground for over a century and a half; indeed, the Araucanian struggle for independence lasted until 1850. Inevitably, the Spanish responded to the natives' savage defence with merciless repression, thus kindling the undying hatred of a people as proud and courageous as they were ferocious. The fate of Pedro de Valdivia provides a blood-curdling example of their implacable ferocity.

Devoured bit by bit

In 1553, as they pushed farther south beyond the Bío-Bío River into Araucanian territory, Valdivia and his troops were defeated by Lautaro, Valdivia's former servant, who had since become (along with Caupolicán) the chief of the Araucanian resistance. Taken prisoner and sentenced to death, Valdivia was cut into little pieces and eaten alive. This was no isolated incident, for the Araucanians habitually practised cannibalism, as did many other South American peoples at that time.

America's first epic poem

The Araucanians' courage made a deep impression on the Spanish. The first epic poem to celebrate the conquest was dedicated to that fearless Indian tribe. *La Araucana*, composed by the poet-Spanish conquistador Alonso de Ercilla y Zúñiga, commemorated the valour and bravery of chief Caupolicán, brutally assassinated by the Spanish in 1558.

In 1545, the Spanish discovered the silver mines of Cerro Potosi, which they exploited using indigenous labour.

The silver of Potosí

Unlike El Dorado, the celebrated Sierra de la Plata of the 'white king' (the Inca) was not a myth. The silver mine of Cerro Potosí, already known to the Incas, was worked by the Spanish from 1545. The city of Potosí, founded on the same year, was accorded the title of Imperial City by Emperor Charles V. The Potosí mine yielded a vast quantity of silver; the sheer abundance of the precious metal pouring in soon destabilized the economies of Europe.

A river as wide as the sea

Juan Díaz de Solis, a pilot in the service of the Spanish Crown, was dispatched to explore the east coast of South America; he and his backers shared the bold hope that he might find the much-desired passage to China. He set sail late in 1515, and came in sight of the New World in February 1516. De Solis found himself in a broad freshwater estuary, which the natives called Paranaguazu, meaning 'river broad as the sea' or 'great water'. Spotting traces of silver in the sand, de Solis, according to the historians Fernandez de Navarette and López de Gomara, christened it Río de la Plata—the 'river of silver'. He returned to Spain and requested the 'right of conquest and government' over the territories he had discovered. The privilege was granted, but during his second voyage, as they left the ship on a reconnaissance mission, de Solis and his men were captured and devoured by man-eating Indians. Terrified and horror-struck by the scene they witnessed from their ships, the other Spaniards fled those inhospitable shores, and the expedition turned back.

For thirteen years, de Solis's river was forgotten. In 1525 Sebastian Cabot—son of the Genoese John Cabot, a pioneer of North American exploration in the service of the English (see p. 110)—set out with Spanish backing in search of the Spice Islands, following the route discovered by Ferdinand Magellan. But he was diverted from his initial purpose, and suddenly decided to explore South America instead, for Indians had beguiled him with tales of fabulous riches. After three years of aimless exploration, searching for the legendary land of the 'white king' (probably the Inca), Cabot was obliged to admit defeat, for he had found no trace of treasure. Back in Europe, Cabot was taken to task for having abandoned his official mission. He was exiled to Africa, but after two years was granted a pardon and again took up his position as pilot general to the Spanish Crown.

Santa María del Buen Aíre

Not long after, Emperor Charles V ordered the exploration of the Río de la Plata. The mission was instructed to push forward as far as the realm of the 'white king'. Pedro de Mendoza, son of a high-ranking Spanish family, was chosen to head the expedition.

Mendoza set sail from San Lucar in 1535 with two thousand men and eleven ships, a fleet reduced to just seven by the time he reached the Río de la Plata. Two more vessels joined Mendoza in January 1536, when he founded the city of Santa María del Buen Aíre at the mouth of the river, and took up his duties as its governor. The Indians' hostility and the shortage of food caused considerable difficulty. Mendoza resolved to build a route linking his riverside settlement to Peru, to facilitate the transport of supplies. To accomplish this task, he sent out a small party headed by Juan de Ayolas to ascend the Paraná River. Ayolas elected to make Carcaraña his base of operations—the site where years before Sebastian Cabot had built the fort of Espiritu Santo. Ayolas constructed another fort, which he called Corpus Christi. Shortly thereafter, Governor Mendoza changed the name to Fort of Good Hope.

During Ayola's absence, Pedro de Mendoza showed little of the enterprising spirit needed for conquest; his vigour had deserted him, and he felt no inclination to undertake new explorations. In fact, his strange listlessness was attributable to a mortal illness. Mendoza died on 23 June 1537 aboard the ship that carried him back to Spain.

Ayolas, in the meantime, ascended the Paraná and Paraguay rivers, reaching the village of Candelaria in February 1537, where he left behind Domingo Martínez de Irala to defend Spanish interests. Accompanied by the rest of his men and a few native guides, Ayolas penetrated the territory of the Chanos, who showered the Spaniard with great riches. Alas, he never had the chance to enjoy his treasure, for on the way back Ayolas and his party were massacred by the Payaguaes Indians.

Asunción, outpost for conquest

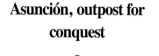

In 1537 Juan de Salazar—sent by Mendoza to search for Ayolas—founded Nuestra Señora Santa María de la Asunción, an outpost destined to become the centre of all the settlements in the la Plata territory. After Mendoza's death, Domingo Martínez de Irala was appointed to succeed him. Irala abandoned the town of Santa María del Buen Aíre, then the colony's principal base of operations, in favour of the recently established town of Asunción (the present-day capital of Paraguay). There he gathered together the few men and supplies at his disposal.

The 'Mountain of Silver'

Around the same time, the king granted the title of *adelantado* and new governor of the territories of la Plata to Alvar Núñez Cabeza de Vaca, one of the early Spanish conquistadores (see p. 112). His arrival at Asunción in 1541 was greeted with suspicion by Irala and the rest of the settlers. Through intrigue and calumny they succeeded in ridding themselves of Cabeza de Vaca, who was sent back to Spain in 1545 as a prisoner (he was eventually cleared).

Once he alone wielded power in the settlement, Irala had a free hand to continue his quest for the Sierra de la Plata (the 'Mountain of Silver'). He organized an expedition, but was surprised to meet resistance from his men, who had apparently grown weary of chasing after mirages and visions. They argued that they preferred colonization to adventure, and trade with Spain to fruitless quests for mythical treasures; they wanted to return to Santa María del Buen Aíre in order to settle and put down roots. But the forceful personality of Martínez de Irala overcame their unwillingness, and in the end they agreed to his scheme. The party set out in January 1548, crossed the cordillera, then reached upper Peru (today's Bolivia). To Irala's amazement he met Spanish-speaking Indians, who must, he surmised, have come from the viceroyalty of Peru. This spurred Irala on to pursue his expedition, which finally took him all the way to Cuzco—not very far, in fact, from the coveted Silver Mountain, the famous mines of Potosí. Although he did not realize it, Irala had accomplished an unprecedented feat: he was the first to cross the cordillera from west to east.

Cabral finds Brazil

The terms of the Treaty of Tordesillas (see pp. 53, 58) seemed to have given Portugal a raw deal in this part of the world, which in 1494 was still unexplored. For what could possibly compare with the fascinating Indies, which Vasco da Gama reached in 1498, or the lands of Africa, explored and exploited from the mid-fifteenth century? For the time being, the Portuguese showed little interest in the unfamiliar, uncharted regions of the South Atlantic. Indeed, it was purely by accident that Pedro Àlvares Cabral, who intended to reach the Indies by following Vasco da Gama's route, hit the coast of Brazil, which he claimed for Portugal in the name of King Manoel I. Cabral

belonged to a noble Portuguese family, long in the service of the Crown. He himself enjoyed the favour of the sovereign, who awarded him the rank of admiral, and entrusted him with the mission of completing Vasco da Gama's exploration of the Indies.

Cabral set sail from Lisbon on 9 March 1500 with a fleet of thirteen ships. Following da Gama's instructions, he charted a south-westerly course to avoid finding himself becalmed in the Gulf of Guinea. Driven on by favourable winds and encountering no difficulty whatsoever, on 22 April he touched present-day Porto Seguro and set foot on the shores of what he believed to be an island. He christened it Island of the Vera Cruz (True Cross); renamed Santa Cruz (Holy Cross) by King Manoel, the land eventually became known as Brazil, after a dye-wood that grows in profusion there.

Cabral spent only ten days in Brazil. He established friendly relations with the apparently peace-loving Indians native to that coast, and after formally laying claim to this 'island' of unsuspected size, he pursued his course towards the Indies, a voyage dogged by misfortune, on which Bartolomeu Díaz, the first man to round the Cape of Good Hope, lost his life (see p. 53).

Vespucci, the first explorer of Brazil

In 1501 an expedition commanded by Nuno Manoel, in which Amerigo Vespucci (see p. 62) took part in the service of Portugal, returned to explore the newly discovered land. Vespucci was the first to realize just how large the landmass was (he had already landed there in June 1499), and he pioneered its exploration. He sailed along the coast, made cartographic surveys, and observed unfamiliar stars and constellations, including the Southern Cross. He also took part in another expedition in May 1503 with Gonzalve Coelho. Once again Vespucci made a noteworthy survey of the coastline, and foresaw the importance of the fine natural harbours, including the famous bay of the future Rio de Janeiro, for eventual colonization. Calendar in hand, he baptized the different points on the coast with the names of the saints of the day. But for several more years Brazil remained unexploited, largely unstudied and a prey to covetous impulses from other quarters—notably from France (see p. 85).

A mysterious etymology

Many theories have been advanced to explain the etymology of the name 'Brazil'. Some sources report that the land was discovered before Cabral by French navigators— perhaps the Norman Jean Cousin— and suggest that the name comes from *Breizh-Il* (Breton island). But the dyewood *pau-brasil*, seen by the traveller Odoric of Pordenone during his wanderings in Asia, is the word's most probable origin.

Forty years after the establishment of a real or provisional settlement, on the mouth of Río de la Plata, the Basque Juan de Garay founded Santa María de Buen Aíre, capital of the future Argentinian republic.

'The natives are quite gentle'

So wrote Amerigo Vespucci. But his statement should be qualified. The Tupinikin—Indians encountered by Pedro Alvares Cabral in April 1500—were indeed a peace-loving people. But those Vespucci met at Cape Sao Roque in August 1501 were much less so. The first volunteers to set foot ashore were immediately massacred and cut to pieces as their horrified comrades watched from the ships. Farther south, tribal customs were less violent, bearing out Vespucci's judgement. It should be remembered, however, that many an explorer was devoured by these 'gentle' cannibals, particularly by the ferocious Topinambous, who were encountered by the French explorers Villegagnon and Jean de Léry as they attempted to establish settlements in Brazil around 1555.

PIRATES AND PRIVATEERS

With the discovery of territories farther south, the Spanish began to neglect their outposts on the islands and coastlines washed by the Caribbean Sea. A new kind of conqueror appeared on the scene, eager to make his fortune and to seek adventure: the privateer. Often backed by one of Spain's numerous enemies, these pirates terrorized communities along the shores of the Caribbean, and established bases there that no one dared disturb.

Piracy and the Reformation

The Reformation and the rise of Protestantism were to have a decisive influence on the spread of piracy. Protestant nations did not recognize the Pope's right to divide up the world and distribute territory. Queen Elizabeth I of England restored England to Protestantism in 1559 and encouraged any initiative that could undermine the power of King Philip II of Spain. She gave privateers her secret support, and in return for her investment in piracy, she saw Spain weakened, while realizing hefty profits for England.

After waging a long war of independence against the Spanish Crown, the Dutch carried the fight into the New World. For twen-

Francis Drake was more than just an unscrupulous privateer. He was also a fine sailor and great strategist.

ty years Pernambuco in Brazil remained under Dutch rule (1630-54). They built a well-planned town where present-day Recife is located.

Francis Drake, 'the Dragon'

The Spanish called Francis Drake 'The Dragon', for they feared his bold, sudden, yet minutely planned and brilliantly executed raids. Drake was the first Englishman to sail the Pacific Ocean in the sixteenth century.

Born on the estate of the earl of Bedford in Devonshire around 1540, Drake was the son of one of Bedford's farmers. He was still very young when he set out to seek his fortune on a merchant ship in the North Sea. It so happened that the young man was related to John Hawkins, England's first African slave trader. Hawkins transported cargoes of 'ebony' (black slaves) from Guinea to Spanish possessions in the Caribbean, a practice the Spanish frowned upon. Hawkins's first voyage, in 1562-3, was so highly profitable that he had no trouble finding backers, including Queen Elizabeth herself, to finance subsequent expeditions. On his third voyage from 1567 to 1569 Hawkins was accompanied by Francis Drake (who by then had already made one trip to the West Indies), who helped him transport slaves to Santo Domingo. On the way, the Englishmen raided the coast of Mexico, and pillaged the port of Veracruz. They carried off a rich prize, but the fleet of viceroy Martin Enriquez counterattacked and routed the English after a violent encounter that ended in death for many of the pirates. It was every man for himself: Hawkins managed to flee at the very last moment, leaving all the captured booty behind, while Drake made his way back to England.

Peruvian gold

Regarded with favour by Queen Elizabeth, Drake—itching to recommence his raids—returned to the Caribbean in 1572, where he mounted a venture of extraordinary boldness that won him a fortune. With his partner, the French Huguenot seaman and cartographer Guillaume Le Testu (who lost his life in the adventure), Drake planned to intercept the convoy of gold and silver that each year sailed from Peru, crossed the Isthmus of Panama, and transported the precious cargo to the port of Nombre de Dios and thence to Spain.

Thanks to excellent intelligence the two partners obtained, the success of their raid was complete, but in a sudden reversal of fortune the English were forced to flee—though this time they did not abandon all their treasure. Drake returned to England (after a detour to the Pacific coast to confuse his pursuers, and a few additional raids), his fortune assured by the Peruvian gold. His return, however, coincided with a truce between Elizabeth and Philip II of Spain. Drake astutely divined that it would be well for him to leave the scene. As it turned out, his absence would last for several years.

Around the world

On 13 December 1577 Drake set off on what would be his most important voyage, one that would take him around the world. His fleet included three large ships and a crew of 166 men, and Queen Elizabeth of England was his principal backer. Drake's initial goal was to sail to the west coast of South America via the Strait of Magellan, discover new territories, conclude treaties with the inhabitants of lands not in the Spanish sphere and perhaps discover the legendary *Terra Australis* rumoured to lie somewhere in the far reaches of the South Pacific.

The expedition set sail from Plymouth and headed towards the coast of Africa; from there, the ships crossed the Atlantic to Brazil, where they landed in the spring of 1578. There Drake ordered the execution of Thomas Doughty, an officer who had stirred up the crew against him. The English pirate had a keen sense of discipline, and given the scope of the mission entrusted to him by his queen, he could not tolerate the slightest sign of disloyalty among his men.

In August 1578 Francis Drake and his crew entered the Strait of Magellan, which they crossed in just two weeks.

With God and the winds against us

———————●———————

This was the second time that Drake had beheld the Pacific, but on this occasion the winds were far from favourable; indeed a storm was blowing hard. It was, Drake wrote, as if 'God himself were against us'. The ships lost sight of each other in the gale, and Drake's vessel, the *Golden Hind*, finally had to go it alone in the vast ocean. As usual Drake preyed on Spanish ports and ships, which he took utterly by surprise, for until then no foreign vessel had ventured into those waters. For Drake, the pickings were rich and plentiful.

In Chile Drake attacked Valparaíso, and in Peru he plundered the ports of Arica and Callao, before putting in to pillage the city of Lima. Heading north, the English looted two ships, one of which was transporting silver from the Potosí mines, before landing, in early summer 1579, on the northern shores of California, which they christened New Albion.

Drake briefly considered continuing his northerly course, in the hope of locating the Northwest Passage into the Atlantic, a discovery he was sure would bring him fame and glory. But the cold prevented his sailing on, and since it was out of the question to pass once more through the Strait of Magellan, his only course was to cross the Pacific.

In sixty-eight days, setting off from present-day Cape Mendocino, Drake reached the Philippines and then the Moluccas where he concluded a treaty with the local ruler allowing the English to trade for spices there in future, rounded the Cape of Good Hope and finally reached England on 26 September 1580. He had been at sea for over two years, and the prizes he brought back were staggering: in addition to the sil-

Predictably, privateering began to develop in the West Indies and along the Brazilian coast, where the treasures carried by the Spanish and Portuguese galleons offered rich pickings.

ver from Potosí, there were 370,000 pesos in gold coins, silk, porcelain, pearls, spices, and more! The queen, mightily pleased with her privateer, knighted him. Henceforth, he would be Sir Francis Drake, the first captain to sail round the world in his own ship.

The height of glory

———————●———————

On two occasions Drake returned to the Spanish Main. In 1585 hostilities broke out again between Spain and England. Sir Francis Drake was instructed by the queen to inflict 'as much damage as possible' on Spanish possessions. In fact, Drake did well to leave England for a while, since his success and hot temper had combined to make him a number of enemies.

After a destructive raid on the Cape Verde islands, Drake attacked Santo Domingo on the island of Hispaniola. He then turned his sights to Cartagena, a fortified town on the Colombian coast, burning it to the ground and demanding a heavy ransom.

On this voyage Drake more than earned his sobriquet 'the Dragon'. His participation in the defeat of the 'invincible' Armada (1588) carried him to the height of glory in his native England. But his next voyage was to be his last. In 1595 Drake sailed once more, accompanied by John Hawkins, with a fleet of twenty-seven ships. His crew fell victim to fevers and Hawkins died on the eve of a planned attack on Puerto Rico. The Puerto Ricans defended their island bravely and successfully. Drake, weakened by dysentery, died on 25 January 1596 at Puerto Bello; his body was committed to the waves in the Gulf of Darien.

Walter Raleigh explores the Orinoco

———————●———————

A fervent Anglican and no less faithful a subject of Her Majesty, Walter Raleigh turned privateer as much from hatred of the Spanish as from any innate taste for adventure. For this man of extravagant tastes, perpetually short of cash, the lure of profit was

Mapping the shores of Guyana

The expedition miraculously escaped the countless hazards of the Orinoco estuary. At this point, the party abandoned the search for gold and adventure, and became instead a bona fide scientific mission. For months Raleigh's ships sailed along the shores of Guiana; the men reconnoitred Georgetown Bay and the mouth of the Surinam River, and discovered Cayenne in 1596. A team of cartographers mapped the coastlines and rivers, and plotted their exact positions. Raleigh himself took copious notes, which he used upon his return to London in 1596 to write *The Discoveries of the Large and Beautiful Empire of Guiana*, a book that met with great success.

In 1603 Elizabeth died and her successor, James I, had little affection for the former courtier. In July of that year Raleigh was accused of plotting against the new king, and was condemned to death. Eventually his sentence was reduced to imprisonment; he was held in the Tower of London until 1616. King James then authorized the former explorer to mount a final expedition, but it was a dismal failure from start to finish. Alhough Sir Walter had a fleet of fourteen ships and a thousand men ready to sail in June 1617, ill winds delayed his departure until August. The fleet fetched up in Trinidad in November. The ailing Raleigh sent his second-in-command, Lawrence Keymis, to explore the Orinoco. On 1 January 1618 the Englishmen engaged battle with a Spanish garrison at Santo Tomãs; Raleigh's son, also named Walter, was killed in the encounter. Keymis took his own life.

Having found no trace of gold, Sir Walter Raleigh sailed back to England late in June. In the meantime, King James had signed an accord with the Spanish, who had protested against the English attack on their garrison. The original sentence pronounced against Sir Walter fifteen years earlier was carried out. He was beheaded on 29 October 1618.

Thomas Cavendish and the third circumnavigation

Inspired by the fabulous treasures that Drake had won for himself and England during his circumnavigation of the globe, the English navigator Thomas Cavendish decided to try his luck in the South Atlantic. With the backing of Queen Elizabeth, he sailed from Plymouth on 21 July 1586 with

Queen Elizabeth's interest in the corsairs was more than purely political: the virgin queen no doubt appreciated their rebellious, daring spirit.

The Church of England: church of state

England's break with Rome was brought about by the refusal of Pope Clement VII to sanction King Henry VIII's divorce from Catherine of Aragon. Henry became the head of the Church in 1532, but remained faithful to Catholic doctrine and persecuted Protestants. After the reigns of Edward VI (who leaned towards Calvinism) and Mary Tudor ('Bloody Mary', a Catholic), the accession of Elizabeth I saw the Anglican Church become the official Church of England, steering a middle path between the continental Reformation and Catholicism.

also important. Born in Devonshire around 1554, Raleigh belonged to one of England's foremost families. His many qualities brought him to the attention of Queen Elizabeth. By 1582, he was the royal favourite. He was thirty years old when he set off on his American venture: between 1584 and 1589 he attempted to found a colony in North America, near Roanoke Island. In honour of the Virgin Queen, Elizabeth I, he named the territory Virginia.

A wit and a poet, Raleigh was the familiar of philosophers and scholars. It was perhaps from them that he heard of the fabulous riches of El Dorado, a land he was sure lay in Guiana, in the New World that had been unjustly and arbitrarily handed over to Spain.

If he could bring back more gold than the Spaniards had found in Peru, he would surely win back the queen's favour (for he had fallen into disgrace when Elizabeth learned of his long-secret marriage to Elizabeth Throckmorton). In February 1595 Raleigh set sail with three ships—one sank

without a trace during the crossing—and, drifting with the current, reached the Antilles and then the island of Trinidad, separated from Venezuela by what is called the 'serpent's mouth'. There the sixteen mouths of the Orinoco fan out in a delta three hundred kilometres wide, a luxuriant and diabolical maze of swamps, rivers, and tropical vegetation teeming with birds, fishes, and other fauna totally unfamiliar to European eyes. Raleigh quickly sized up the strength of the local Spanish forces, then captured the Governor of Trinidad, Antonio de Berrio, who had navigated the Orinoco in search of El Dorado and therefore knew the river well. Raleigh wrung out of him the details he needed to find the upper course of the river. When he arrived at the confluence of the Orinoco and Caroní rivers, Raleigh elected to sail up the latter. It was an arduous journey, for the river had a strong, unpredictable current. In the end, the men found a little gold, but nothing to compare with the fabulous mines they had fancied they would discover.

three ships and a crew of 123 seamen, bound for Brazil. Cavendish sailed down the Brazilian coast, attacking a port here and there; he mapped the shores of Patagonia, then crossed the Strait of Magellan with no difficulty whatsoever, even though the Spanish, on the alert after Drake's destructive forays, kept a garrison posted there. When Cavendish arrived, he found only twenty-three sick and wretched soldiers manning the outpost.

Cavendish sailed back up the Chilean coast, took on supplies on the island of Santa María, and called at Quintero, where his seamen came to blows with Spanish soldiers. He destroyed and terrorized the ports along the coast, sailing still farther north, beyond Mexico. His most memorable feat was the capture of the *Santa Anna* on 14 November 1587, boarded off California as it transported a rich cargo from Peru. Convinced that he could hardly do any better, Cavendish steered back to England by the same route that Drake had taken, thus completing the third circumnavigation of the globe (1588). He returned with just one ship and only half his crew, but his haul was more than impressive. Cavendish died at sea during his second voyage to South America and the Pacific in 1591–2.

support for the Huguenots. In this he did not succeed but managed to pacify the ferocious Topinambous, the earliest inhabitants of that part of Brazil.

The Portuguese looked with suspicion on Frenchmen occupying land that was legally theirs. In February 1560, taking advantage of Villegagnon's absence, the Portuguese attacked Fort Coligny, the colony's stronghold. Yet Antarctic France held on for a few years more, headed by Bois-le-Comte, who ruled the colony until Villegagnon's return. Then in 1567, the French ran out of supplies and were forced to surrender.

End of a century, end of a world

———◆———

By the end of the sixteenth century, many changes had occured: in 1580 Portugal, under duress, concluded an alliance with Spain. The Dutch, long under the yoke of Spain, recovered their independence in 1589. Ten years later, Olivier Van Noort

sailed from Rotterdam for the Indies through the Strait of Magellan. Along the way he massacred some natives, but he also mapped the area, taking careful depth soundings and creating recognizable landmarks by giving names to the countless islands scattered in the strait. He pursued this scientific endeavour along the coast of Chile, occasionally attacking Spanish ships like the good Dutch privateer he was and pillaging the city of Valparaíso. Dutch piracy reached its heights early in the next century, despite the truce signed in 1609 between Spain and Holland.

In 1616 another Dutch seaman, Willem Corneliszoon Schouten, discovered that other lands lay beyond the Strait of Magellan; he sighted the southernmost tip of the world, Cape Horn, which he named after his native city, Hoorn (see pp. 144, 236). The strait between Tierra del Fuego and the Isla de los Estados was christened in honour of his partner, Jakob Le Maire. Schouten was also the first to cross the Drake Passage south of Tierra del Fuego, which links the Atlantic and Pacific Oceans; though it bears his name, Drake never sailed those waters.

(see pp. 144, 236).

The lost land of Paulmier de Gonneville

At a time when navigational instruments were still rudimentary and knowledge of the oceans fragmentary at best, when a captain lost his notes in a shipwreck, there was little likelihood that he could ever again locate the lands he had discovered. Such was the fate of the Norman navigator Paulmier de Gonneville, whose voyage between 1503 and 1505 remained for centuries a geographical puzzle. Where was he coming from when his ship was wrecked off the coast of Jersey? On board was a young Indian, a native of some unknown land. The controversy was brought back to life by his great-grandson, Paulmier de Courtonne, who around 1670 gathered together documents, family papers and the like to provide a coherent account of his ancestor's adventure. Not until the nineteenth century was the mystery finally solved: the ship was doubtless returning from Brazil.

Antarctic France

———◆———

The French took advantage of Portugal's temporary lack of interest in Brazil to organize, early in the sixteenth century, expeditions to the New World. Driven by a number of motives, including a taste for adventure, the lure of profit and the Wars of Religion, French mariners founded settlements in Brazil, mainly in the region of Pernambuco (today's capital is Recife) and in the province of Bahia. The best-known colony was established by Nicolas Durand de Villegagnon in 1555: Antarctic France, as it was known, was situated in a favourable, sheltered location that skilled geographers such as Le Testu (Drake's unlucky associate) had already reconnoitred. The choice was a good one—it was the bay off Rio de Janeiro.

Durand de Villegagnon was a colourful character; a champion of the Catholic cause, he accompanied Mary Stuart to France for her marriage to the Dauphin, and fought Barbary pirates in the Mediterranean. Doubtless a trifle idealistic, he wished to reconcile in this remote province of France intellectual and religious currents that were—at the time—wholly antagonistic. Himself a Catholic, he wished to show

A naval battle between the French and the Portuguese near Buttagar, on the Brazilian coast. The French pirates had no qualms about mutilating their Portuguese prisoners.

U ntil the 18th century South America, a Spanish possession, had remained practically closed to outsiders. Then the pirate, who had been lured by the wealth of the New World, including gold, precious wood and sugar, gave way to the scientist. The borders were opened up to the prestigious world of science and so began one of the great human odysseys.

A pioneer among naturalists

Well before the scientists of the 18th century came along, a Swiss woman, a well-known painter and miniaturist, brought back numerous drawings of the luxuriant riches of the tropical forest. Marie Sybille Merian stayed in Surinam (Dutch Guyana) in 1699, in a colony of Dutch Labadists. Her faith did not stop her from exploring the region, where she observed a large number of insects and plants unknown in Europe. She undertook a 65-kilometre journey on the Surinam River to look for rare essences, before returning to Amsterdam for health reasons.

South America was a land of new adventures, where scientists could observe the natural riches and accumulate specimens of flora and fauna as well as study Andean civilizations.

A scientific debate

When the scientist Charles Marie de La Condamine returned to France in 1732 from a voyage to the Near and Middle East, he found the scientific community in an uproar, hotly debating the size and the shape of the Earth. Partisans of Cassini and Newton were at loggerheads, the first group subscribing to the theory that the Earth was elongated in shape, while the second defended the theory that the Earth was flattened out at its poles. To settle this prickly debate the minister Maurepas decided to send expeditions to Lapland and to Peru under the auspices of the Paris Academy of Sciences, with expenses paid for by the government. The idea was that the scientists would measure from those latitudes the arc of the Earth's meridian, so establishing the planet's shape and thus bringing the dispute to an end.

Yellow fever rages in Peru

The expedition set out from La Rochelle on 18 May 1735 and sailed towards Peru. On board were three scientists, La Condamine, Bouguer and Godin; the naturalist and doctor, Jussieu; a surgeon, Seniergues; and five other scientists, geographers and astronomers. After a long stopover in the West Indies and a stop in Colombia, which was marred by the presence of mosquitoes and scorpions, the scientists finally made it to Guayaquil, travelling mainly by sea. The first signs of dissent began to appear among the team. They would become more and more marked as the days went by. Godin wanted, at any cost, to assert his prerogative as head of the expedition. Finally, more than a year and a half after departing, the expedition established its first triangulation measurements. The geographers Couplet and Verguin made maps of the entire region from Quito to Cuenca. But at this point Couplet caught yellow fever and soon died. Demoralized by their colleague's death, the scientists nonetheless settled down to work, splitting up into two groups: one made up of Godin and Jorge Juan, the other of Bouguer, La Condamine and Ulloa. The two Spanish officers had the duty of watching over the scientists.

Maurepas enjoins the expedition to give up

In 1737, the expedition received a letter from the French government exhorting them to return to France. The mission undertaken by Maupertuis had already returned from Lapland — since it was an easier undertaking — and had published its findings, establishing that the Earth was flat at its poles, thus giving credence to Newton's theory. After the experiment had been hailed as a success, the government saw no further need to send further subsidies to Peru. But the scientists did not see it that way and carried on regardless. They split up into three teams to measure the arc of the

meridian from the north of Quito to the south of Cuenca and undertook the ascent of Mount Pichincha, near Quito, to set up their measuring equipment. A snow storm swept down on them for several days, rendering all work impossible. Godin, already irascible, isolated himself even further from the group and ended up by separating himself completely from the others, refusing to communicate his results to La Condamine and Bouguer. The rift was complete.

Seniergues is assassinated

Shortly after the expedition reached Peru, a smallpox epidemic broke out in Cuenca. The team's surgeon, Seniergues, left his companions to their measurements while he cared for the sick. Given the magnitude of the outbreak, Jussieu, who had up until then spent his time collecting plants in the plateaus of the Andes, wasted no time in joining up with them. The latter had barely arrived when the two scientists had to flee the city as fast as their legs could carry them, as the surgeon had the unfortunate habit of seducing the women of the Spanish bourgeoisie.

By the time the expedition decided to regroup at Cuenca two years later—once the mountain triangulations were finished—no one thought any more about the surgeon's escapades. That is with the exception of Seniergues himself, who took up again with his mistress, Manuela Quesada. During a corrida, the festivities turned to tragedy. The Spanish, irritated by the surgeon's excesses, took advantage of a stir in the crowd to stone him. Fatally wounded, the surgeon died of his injuries. A sham trial was held, but the murderers were soon released.

Cotopaxi awakens

Bouguer reached the Pacific coast to take new measurements at sea level, so as to compare them with those taken in the Andes. At this time La Condamine became interested in vulcanology. He made various geological observations and studied in particular the Chimborazo and the Pichincha volcanoes. While he was exploring the craters and assembling rock specimens, La Condamine witnessed the eruption of Cotopaxi. In the space of a few hours the summit

The pyramids of Quito

As part of his astronomical research La Condamine had two pyramids built to allow for the verification of future calculations. But the two officers who accompanied him, Juan and Ulloa, denounced the inscription affixed to the base of the pyramids as being insulting to the King of Spain. La Condamine found himself once again in legal difficulties with the colonial authorities, who finally acquitted him. The scientist recounted this adventure in his book, *The History of the Pyramids of Quito.*

The development of science in the Age of Enlightenment

The creation of the Royal Society of London and the Académie des Sciences in Paris gave science a more exalted status in the 17th century. But it was the 18th century—the age of the Enlightenment—that would bring a harvest of technological discoveries. The invention of the telescope enabled scientists to probe ever more deeply into the heavens. The barometer, the graphometer and the quadrant joined the ranks of ancient instruments. The octant, the sextant and then the Borda circle facilitated even further the calculations made by scientists exploring the sky, the seas, and the land.

Writing in 1731, the English astronomer Hadley described 'a new instrument for measuring angles' formed by the Sun on the horizon. Below, a wooden octant, made in England in 1750.

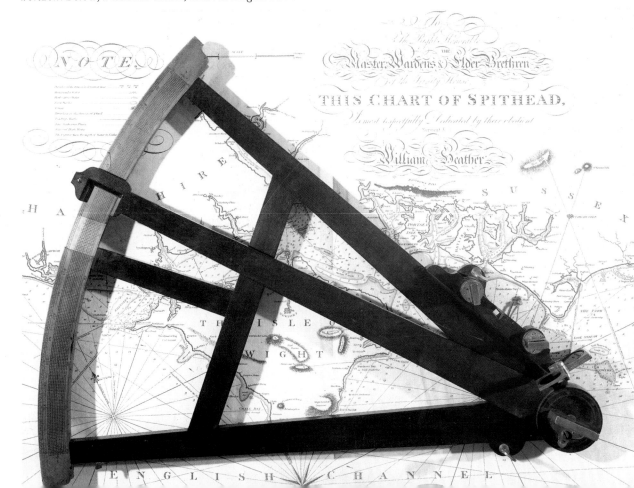

of ice and snow had melted, giving way to a flow of mud spewing out of the awakening volcano.

La Condamine and Bouguer increased their verifications of the measurements of the length of the meridian, calculating its amplitude through the trajectory of the stars. However, by 1743 a conclusion had still not been drawn.

Under an unlucky sign

Jussieu and Bouguer both caught one of the tropical diseases that were running rampant in the region. The latter recovered quickly, and had only one idea in mind: to return to France first, so as to have for himself all the credit for the expedition's findings. To finance his return trip, the geophysicist bartered his scientific instruments. He finally reached Colombia in 1743 and from there he set out for Brest. Upon his arrival, the Académie des Sciences gave him a triumphant welcome.

To meet their needs, Morainville, Hugot and Verguin worked as engineers for the Spanish government. But another tragedy was to mar the expedition. An earthquake struck while Hugot was repairing the great clock of the cathedral of Quito. The scaffolding collapsed, burying the scientist in the ruins.

La Condamine descends the Amazon

Once Bouguer had left, La Condamine pursued his own scientific investigations. He conducted various scientific experiments. Not only did he verify the expedition's observations on the arc of the meridian, but — being a true researcher — he also studied numerous related phenomena. Once his work was done, La Condamine chose as his return route to Europe to follow the river that Orellana had discovered and baptised 'The River of the Amazons'.

As well as the river system and specific features of its basin, the scientist was anxious to study the flora and fauna of this luxuriant region. On 5 June La Condamine and his travelling companions reached the Amazon and decided not to await the arrival of the technician Morainville, who had set off on the journey from Quito. In fact, he completely disappeared and no one ever set eyes on him again.

La Condamine left Tarqui, south of Cuenca, on 11 May 1743, to penetrate Amazonia, beginning an exhausting voyage in the heat of the tropics.

In the heart of the forest

As the days progressed, La Condamine penetrated ever deeper into the heart of the forest. The scientist discovered an unknown plant from which ran a resin with a great future — rubber, 'impermeable to the rain and above all endowed with a remarkable elasticity'. In July he reached a Jesuit mission where he met Omagua Indians known as the Flat Heads. They had the curious custom of flattening the heads of newborn babies by squeezing them between rocks.

While waiting for a boat from Cayenne, La Condamine spent his time observing the native population. He was one of the first to describe the plant Hevea brasiliensis, *the latex of which is collected to make rubber.*

La Condamine continued his journey along the crocodile-infested river, observing pumas and jaguars along its banks, and sloths and parrots in the trees. He encountered unknown native tribes — the Abanes with pierced cheeks and decorated with bird feathers and the more aggressive Xibaros, who hunted with poison-tipped arrows. Finally the scientist reached the mouth of the river. He made it to Cayenne in Guiana, from where he set sail for France in 1744.

From this fantastic adventure La Condamine brought back a map of the Amazon and numerous observations of the flora, the fauna, and the habits and customs of the Indians. He was convinced that the Amazon was linked up with the Orinoco, a theory that was later proved to be correct. The Académie des Sciences gave him a triumphant welcome in Paris.

La Condamine eclipsed Bouguer, who wanted to win all the praise for himself. He thus became the true hero of the Peruvian odyssey.

A miraculous survival in the Amazon

Another participant in the odyssey was Godin des Odonnais, who had gone on the Peruvian mission in the hope of finding his fortune. As his marriage to a wealthy heiress, Isabelle de Grandmaison, a descendant of a French family that had settled in Peru, did not fulfil all his ambitions, he decided to return to Europe. Isabelle told him that she was pregnant, but Godin des Odonnais left alone for Cayenne, Guiana, to prepare for his return to France. In the following year, 1746, Isabelle gave birth to a baby girl, but she gave up the idea of risking the descent of the Amazon and remained in Quito to raise the child.

In 1767, when their daughter fell victim to an epidemic, Isabelle, in her desolation, decided to reunite with her husband. A caravan of nine people left Riobamba in October 1769, bound for Cayenne. Troubles soon began to mount. At the first Indian village the porters left them, frightened by an outbreak of smallpox. Without their guides, the small group plunged into the forest, where they met two Indians who were willing to take them to the nearest mission, but they soon disappeared. A third Indian took over but drowned in the river. The travellers split up. A doctor and a slave left to look for help at the nearest mission, while Isabelle and her companions stayed behind and waited. At the end of a month and with-

The Antilles apricot tree, found in the Caribbean, which multiplies by scattering its seeds.

out word from the two others, they constructed a raft to attempt to reach the mission on their own. But the small craft capsized. Harassed and gnawed by hunger, the group plunged into the jungle. They set up camp in a clearing, but one after another they died — all except Isabelle. Stupefied, the young woman reached the river bank and walked in a daze for nine days. Eventually she was found by Indians who took her back, cared for her, and then led her to the mission. Miraculously saved from this hell, Isabelle des Odonnais finally found her husband in Cayenne.

The couple came to France in 1773, some 40 years after the departure of the scientific expedition for Peru.

The tribulations of Jussieu

In 1745, following Verguin, Godin and Jussieu also prepared to return to France. But an earthquake struck and Jussieu took care

of the injured while Godin, named head engineer, worked on the reconstruction of Lima and Callao. Godin finally left Peru in 1748, but spendthrift as ever, he spent all of his money in Brazil and did not embark for Europe until 1750.

During the entire expedition, Jussieu, naturally melancholic and deeply affected by the death of Seniergues, turned his back on civilization, preferring to dedicate himself to the study of animals and medicinal plants, such as cinchona, the bark of which contains quinine.

After collecting plants in the region around Lake Titicaca, Jussieu settled for nearly four years in Potosi, where he tried to improve the lot of the Indians. The scientist constantly delayed his departure, unable to resist the temptation of increasing his fabulous collection of specimens. He returned to Europe in 1771, tired and ill. The loss of his trunks, crammed with his documents and specimens, obsessed him and soon he lapsed into senility. For some of its participants, the eventful Peruvian odyssey lasted nearly 40 years.

Jesuit missions

The Jesuits established missions in Brazil, Peru, Paraguay and Uruguay where they both converted and protected the Indians. Sick of looking on as spectators, impotent against the massacres committed by the Spanish and the ravages of smallpox, the fathers pleaded with the provincial governors and alerted the Court to the situation. This resulted in their being hated by the colonists, who were desperate for local labour. So the Jesuits organized *reducciones*, small colonies that were off limits to whites, where the tribes were grouped together for their own protection. With the expulsion of the Jesuits from Brazil in 1759 and from all of South America in 1767, a difficult period began for the Indians.

The legendary Amazons

During his journey, La Condamine gathered a great number of stories about the aggressive warriors that Orellana claimed to have fought. An Indian told him that one had to walk for several days through the jungle to reach the land of the 'women without husbands'. The scientist never saw them, but wavering between doubt and eyewitness accounts, he wrote, 'Although today no vestiges of this matriarchal republic can be located, it cannot be said that they never existed. If this world ever had its Amazons, it was in America that they would have lived.'

S *ince Raleigh's expedition, European scientists had argued about the possible existence of a link between the two river basins of the Amazon and the Orinoco. A desire to resolve this question led to the expedition undertaken by the German Alexander von Humboldt between 1799 and 1804. Humboldt's wide range of scientific and cultural interests made him worthy of his nickname 'The Second Discoverer of America'.*

Humboldt (left) and Bonpland's bivouac in the rain forest on the banks of the Orinoco.

Typhus strikes the crew

On 5 June 1799 Humboldt and Bonpland embarked for South America on board the *Pizarro*. After a stopover in the Canary Islands, where Humboldt climbed his first volcano, the Teide peak, the crossing continued. Bonpland took samples of seawater and algae while Humboldt spent his time examining the sky through his telescope. The two scholars had brought with them a large amount of scientific instruments, including sextants, compasses, Borda circles, and barometers. The voyage was not without its dangers. There was the risk of encountering English frigates navigating the same waters, and soon the crew was stricken with typhus. The youngest ship's boy died, and, fearing for his crew, the captain decided to hole up in the nearest port, Cumana, in what is now Venezuela. Here Humboldt and Bonpland were overcome by the beauty of the tropical vegetation. 'What trees...with their monster-sized leaves and perfumed flowers the size of one's hand. And what colours the birds, the fish and even the crayfish possess', Humboldt wrote to his brother. For several months they explored the mountains in the north of Venezuela, acquiring over 1,600 plant specimens and making numerous astronomical observations.

The Orinoco indeed runs into the Amazon

The explorers then turned their attention to the scientific verification of Charles Marie de La Condamine's hypothesis: the existence of a passage between the basins of the Orinoco and Amazon rivers. They travelled across the *llanos* (dry plains) of Calabazo on

Sailing for the King of Spain

Humboldt was born into an aristocratic family and inherited an immense fortune. Throughout his childhood, his dreams were of distant horizons. As he grew older, the idea of an ambitious scientific expedition took form in his mind. He read widely, sought the company of experts in a broad range of disciplines, and built up a collection of precision instruments. A meeting with Forster, the naturalist who accompanied Captain Cook's expedition, further confirmed his plans. Upon his arrival in Paris in 1797, Humboldt made contact with the leading scientists Fourcroy, Cuvier and

Delambre, and met the man who would become his travelling companion — Aimé Bonpland — a young doctor who was passionate about botany and utterly dedicated to scientific research. The two young men had no experience of exploration. Undeterred, they joined a scientific expedition led by Captain Baudin. When this project was aborted the young scientists decided to join Bonaparte's scientific mission to Egypt. But this plan had to be abandoned as well. Humboldt and Bonpland then met Baron von Forell, who in turn introduced them to d'Urquijo — an enlightened minister and patron of the sciences in Spain. D'Urquijo presented them to the king, who gave them permission to undertake an expedition of scientific research in his Central and South American territories.

horseback, but were soon obliged to abandon their mounts because of the dense vegetation. They set out again, this time in a ten-metre open boat, at the back of which they had constructed a platform covered with banana leaves. Measuring equipment, animal cages, and plants that the men had collected were stuffed into the boat, piled precariously one on top of the other. The mugginess and the mosquitoes rendered the atmosphere increasingly difficult to endure.

The small craft had journeyed for 36 days down the Orinoco under an arch of virgin forest before the roaring of the rapids made itself heard.

The Indians fled in terror. Humboldt and Bonpland found other Indians to do the paddling, but their craft, a flimsy dugout, nearly capsized. Following directions given by their rowers, the scientists reached the Pimichin, then the Rio Negro, which flows into the Cassiquiare — a tributary of the Amazon. Humboldt was exultant: the Orinoco did indeed link up with the Amazon.

They had achieved their aim despite enduring considerable hardship during this 10,000-kilometre journey through regions that had barely been explored. Their plant collection had been ruined by the extreme humidity. Bonpland, exhausted by the journey, was struck down by typhus fever. Humboldt nursed him through the worst of the illness and the two scientists set out on the journey back, reaching Cumana in September 1800.

The shame of slavery

After sending numerous cases of specimens to the museum, and having more or less recovered from the fatigue induced by their long journey, Humboldt and Bonpland set out for Cuba. On reaching the island the scholars carried out their usual scientific observations: botanic, zoological, astronomical, meteorological... But when he visited the sugar plantations, Humboldt also observed at close hand the degree of exploitation of the black population. From then on, he dedicated all of his energy to studying their condition. The blacks accounted for 36 per cent of the Cuban population at the time. Over a 30-year period, nearly 225,000 black slaves were imported to Cuba, 85,000 to Jamaica, and a total of nearly 2,130,000 into the British colonies in the West Indies.

Deeply concerned at their death rate — close to 15 per cent each year — Humboldt gathered a number of damning accounts of the brutality of the slave drivers and the colonists. He was to remain an implacable opponent of slavery and an ardent defender of blacks and Indians.

In Cuba Humboldt learned that the Baudin expedition had finally got under way and that it would pass through Lima on its way to the Pacific. He and Bonpland set off in the hope of joining up with it in Peru.

An exhausting trek across Colombia

From Cartagena in Colombia, Humboldt and Bonpland went back up the Rio Magdalena, making precise measurements of the river's flow and studying the local vegetation. After two months' navigation, they found their way blocked by rapids. The explorers loaded their numerous collections and instruments onto mules and continued their journey on foot. They finally made it to Bogota, where they were given a splendid welcome by the archbishop and were invited to a number of receptions. At one of these the scientists met José Celestin Mutis, a doctor with an extensive collection of botanical specimens. Pressed for time, the two explorers left Bogota — not without regrets — to meet up with Baudin. They took with them a month's worth of supplies for the crossing of the uninhabited Andes. The journey was an exhausting and difficult one. The scientists hacked their way through the forests, trudged through mud up to their knees, tore their feet on bamboos, without ever encountering a living soul. When they reached Quito in January 1802, they were in for a disappointment: Captain Baudin had sailed into the Pacific without making a stopover in Peru.

Accompanied by his friend Bonpland, Alexander von Humboldt travelled all over Latin America, leaving a huge body of work that would nourish the developing human sciences.

A revolutionary scientist

In Quito Humboldt and Bonpland had established a close friendship with a young Spanish scientist, Carlos de Montufar. Reckless and courageous, he accompanied them in their ascent of the volcanoes and remained with them until they departed for Mexico. Montufar returned to Spain during Napoleon's invasion and won praise for his bravery during the siege of Saragossa and in the battles of Bailen and Somosierra. On his return to Quito, with the rank of lieutenant-colonel, he embraced the cause of the Peruvian Revolution, his commitment to which was to lead to his execution by firing squad on 31 July 1816.

The undreamt-of wealth of guano

It was in Lima that Humboldt first heard of guano, the dried droppings of sea birds that were deposited in large quantities on the coastal rocks. For centuries, South American peasants had used it as a fertilizer. Intrigued as usual, Humboldt had a shelter built on an island with a dense bird population, and despite the nauseating stench, obtained some samples of excrement. Decades later, ships would circumnavigate Cape Horn to load this precious cargo into their holds. In 1841 a chemist calculated that a ton of Peruvian guano contained the fertilizing properties of thirty-three tons of regular manure.

Assault on Chimborazo

The explorers recovered quickly from their disappointment and set about scaling the volcanoes that surrounded Quito. The Andes at this time remained practically unknown, while the Himalayas were believed to be inaccessible. Having started with an ascent of the volcano Antisana, Alexander von Humboldt, Aimé Bonpland and a young Peruvian scientist, Carlos de Montufar, embarked on the conquest of Chimborazo (6310 metres). This 'porphyry giant' was considered the highest peak in the world. When they reached the snow line, the Indian porters fled, convinced that this was where the kingdom of the Gods began. The three scientists, wearing city clothing and equipped only with long walking sticks, decided to pursue their journey.

They plunged up to their waists in the freshly fallen snow, clearing the crevasses and scratching their hands on the ice. For all their tenacity, the men began to suffer from mountain sickness. With their gums and ears bleeding and their feet frozen, the scientists finally had to give up at 5610 metres. They climbed back down in a terrible storm, buffeted by the wind and hail. Although they failed to reach the summit, the scientists' assault on Chimborazo continued to inspire admiration and curiosity for many years to come.

Water mail

Before returning to the Pacific, the explorers ventured deeper into Peru. Their goal was to observe Mercury passing before the Sun. On reaching the upper basin of the Amazon, they plunged into the steam bath of the equatorial forest. As their path was constantly blocked by waterways, the scientists were obliged to make 27 crossings with their equipment strapped to the backs of mules. Humboldt revised Charles Marie de La Condamine's calculations and observed Jupiter's moons through the telescope. Bonpland collected new plant specimens in a jungle inhabited by sloths, tapirs, crocodiles and jaguars... One day the scientists were taken by surprise by the sight of Indian postmen carrying mail tucked into their turbans, which they delivered by swimming from village to village.

Cajamarca, a vestige of the splendour of the Incas

After a recuperative sojourn in Quito, Humboldt and Bonpland took the Inca Trail, a 2000-kilometre trail linking several provinces of the empire at an altitude of 4000 metres. Thus they reached the well-cultivated valley of Cajamarca, dominated by the ruins of a city where the Inca army was massacred and Atahualpa murdered by Pizarro (see p. 71). Humboldt met Astorpilco, the 17-year-old great-grandson of the Inca, who shared with him his dreams of the treasures buried in the ruins by his people. The scientist was eager to discover all he could about the Inca civilization. He questioned the Indians, searched through archives, re-read the accounts of the conquistadors and concluded that, despite the massacres, the Inca people were far from being threatened with extinction. Contrary to what the Europeans were claiming, the Indians then represented a little less than half of the population of Spain's American empire. The explorers visited the Ataruipe grotto where six hundred skeletons were buried. Humboldt studied funeral rituals, learned the Quechua language, and observed Indian skills in irrigation, cultivation and construction. Horrified once again by the exploitation of the Indians by the white men, Humboldt swore to defend these civilizations that had been so torn apart.

Humboldt's Current

From high in the Andes, Humboldt contemplated the Pacific, recalling the exploits of Vasco Nuñez de Balboa, the first conquistador to reach the South Sea. Although he had decided to return to Europe soon, he was determined to study the climate before he left. From their arrival the travellers had been surprised by the coolness and dryness of the country despite the humidity and ambient mist. They were also intrigued by the large number of birds along the coast. Setting up a position on the coast with their measuring instruments, Humboldt and Bonpland observed—as had the sailors of Pizarro before them (but who were unable to explain the phenomenon)—that a cold current ran along the Peruvian coast, keeping its temperature low. It was the sudden cooling effect of this current that prevented the rain from falling. The current was also home to enormous quantities of algae, explaining the density of the bird population. Having resolved the enigma of this current —which has, since then, borne Humboldt's name—the two men set out from Guayaquil for Mexico.

A raft on the Guayaquil river, after a sketch by Humboldt.

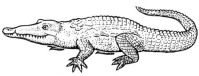

Small Colombian volcanoes letting out nitrogenous gas. Fascinated by volcanic phenomena, Humboldt and Bonpland set out to climb the highest Andean summits and Mexican volcanoes.

A scholar of universal knowledge

Upon his arrival in South America in 1760, the Spanish doctor José Celestin Mutis (whom Humboldt was to meet in Bogota) fell in love with the region, captivated by its wealth of plant species and minerals. He decided to settle in Colombia, which, as a result of his endeavours, became a centre for scholars and scientists. Mutis devoted himself to botany as well as to his personal religious vocation. At the request of Catherine II, he also edited a grammar of the Indian languages of Colombia. His prodigious library, a veritable oasis of knowledge, delighted Humboldt as much as his impressive collection of 20,000 plants enchanted Bonpland. The two explorers cherished treasured memories of their encounter with this remarkable polymath.

From the bottom of the mine to the summit of the volcanoes

On 28 March 1803, the explorers arrived in the port of Acapulco. They proceeded to Mexico, where Humboldt studied the remains of the Aztec and Toltec civilizations. Humboldt and Bonpland were also able to carry out precise cartographical and geological surveys of the area. In Taxco, they visited the mines that produced two-thirds of the world's silver. The mines were worked by Indians—adults and children— who went down into poorly ventilated tunnels, 600 metres below the surface, bringing back the ore on their backs. Contrary to the general situation in South America, the Indians were well paid, in comparison with miners in Europe. Bonpland took advantage of the occasion to collect underground specimens of the local flora. Next the two scientists undertook the ascent of several Mexican volcanoes, including Jorullo, which had recently emerged from the Earth's surface. After an 18-month stay, they set out for Havana. Impressed by the amount of information that Humboldt had accumulated on his country, the Mexican president, Juarez, conferred upon him the title of benefactor of the nation.

A mammoth's tooth for Jefferson

Before leaving for Europe, Humboldt could not resist making a detour to the United States. He wrote to President Thomas Jefferson offering him a mammoth's tooth that he had found in the Andes. Passionate not only about fossils but also about botany, astronomy, and ethnology, Jefferson received him. During a six-week period, the American statesman and the German explorer shared their knowledge and their scientific observations. It was to be their only meeting, but they kept up a regular correspondence with one another.

Humboldt and Bonpland finally headed home with 335 cases filled with specimens, drawings and notes—a rich bounty from their five years of travels in South America.

Two exceptional destinies

The explorers sailed into the port of Bordeaux on 1 August 1804. For the next 25 years Humboldt devoted himself to writing and editing his monumental work, *Travels to the Equinoctial Regions of America*. He classified and inventoried all the observations gathered during this journey to the other side of the world. A brilliant conversationalist and a friend of Chateaubriand and Arago, Humboldt became the darling of Parisian society, which flocked to the *Jardin des Plantes* and to the Museum of Natural History of Paris to admire the specimens brought back by the two scholars.

After his return to Germany, covered with honours, Humboldt became Frederick William III's chamberlain and led several diplomatic missions. But he quickly tired of politics, and in 1829 left for Russia at the invitation of Czar Nicholas I. It was to be his last lengthy journey. After this, Humboldt retired to Berlin, where he dedicated himself to writing his book, *The Cosmos, An Essay on a Physical Description of the World*. He was in constant demand as an authority on scientific matters and developed relationships with the greatest personalities of his age until his death in 1859.

Aimé Bonpland, also honoured and revered, became botanist to the Empress Josephine at Malmaison. After the fall of the Empire, the tireless explorer returned to South America in 1818 and created plantations in Argentina. In Paraguay he was arrested on a charge of spying for the Europeans, and despite his innocence spent 10 years in prison. Bonpland died in 1858 on the continent that had so fascinated him.

The hunt for electric eels

While in the llanos —immense plains that were arid and dry in the summer and became swamps during the rainy season— Humboldt tried to obtain samples of electric eels, the deadly creatures that proliferated there and were capable of killing a man with one sting. To move their herds across the rivers, the peasants would first send in a few horses, which would kick and rear, filled with terror and pain from the stings of the eels. Once the electric charge had dissipated, the herd could safely plunge into the water and the peasants would then catch the eels which had become harmless.

European governments, scientific academies and scholarly societies henceforth pursued a policy of organizing and financing expeditions. The officers in charge of these expeditions were given a scientific education so thorough that some became eminent astronomers or geologists... Every voyage included a team of scientists, and each contributed to the progress of knowledge.

The botanist becomes ethnologist

During the Napoleonic Wars, John VI of Portugal fled to Brazil and transferred his court to Rio de Janeiro. Increasingly, explorers were drawn by the lure of the new kingdom. Auguste de Saint-Hilaire, a former auditor of the Conseil d'Etat turned naturalist, was put in charge of a scientific mission to Brazil by the Paris Academy of Sciences. As the zoologist Delalande had refused to take part in the expedition, Saint-Hilaire himself prepared the insect and bird collections. He arrived in Rio de Janeiro in June 1816, and threw himself not only into geographic observation but also into social and historical research. For four years, Saint-Hilaire covered the states of Parana, Minas Gerais and Sao Paulo, sending cases of animal, plant, and mineral specimens back to the Paris Museum. As his journey progressed, he also developed a particular interest in the customs, cultures and religions of the indigenous peoples of Brazil. He spent time in villages and Jesuit missions, learned various dialects, lived on farmer's *fazendas* and visited the fields. In 1820 Saint-Hilaire left for Paraguay and Uruguay, where, travelling alone in the desert, he was attacked by jaguars and accidentally poisoned himself with toxic honey. Although often on the verge of giving up, he nonetheless managed to make a number of observations and accumulate specimens from these Spanish territories. Finally, after a 12,000-kilometre journey through South America that had lasted six years, this botanist turned ethnologist embarked for France. Having practically lost his voice and his sight, and with his nerves weakened by a trying voyage, Saint-Hilaire retired—universally acclaimed—to Montpellier.

Alone in the tropical forest

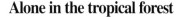

In April 1817, the frigate *Austria* was sailing towards Brazil. On board were the Archduchess of Austria, Marie-Leopoldine—who had left to meet up with her future husband, Dom Pedro—and numerous scientists whose mission it was to explore the unknown regions of Brazil. After an 82-day crossing, the ship berthed at Rio. Two of the scientists, the Germans Spix and Martius, worthy successors to Humboldt, left their Austrian colleagues to head for the Amazon. Accompanied by numerous Indian porters and mules to transport their cases, the explorers plunged into the virgin forest. The convoy passed beneath a canopy of colossal trees whose branches intertwined at dizzying heights, as it headed towards the Amazon River. Until June 1820 the two scientists lived in this tropical universe, tirelessly collecting specimens of exotic plants and animals. Sapped by tropical fevers, Spix had made up his mind to return to Europe, but he died without having had time to classify all of the animal species in his collection. Martius, for his part, dedicated himself to writing botanical works, in particular his *Scientific History of Palm Trees*.

Quechua Indians and mestizos (of mixed Indian and Spanish parentage). An engraving from Journey into Southern America, *by Alcide d'Orbigny.*

Shipwrecked naturalists

After the humiliations of the treaties of 1815, France looked for ways of increasing its international prestige. Accordingly, the government organized an ambitious trans-global scientific expedition. The *Uranus*, captained by Louis de Freycinet (see p. 166) left Toulon on 17 September 1817. After a three-month journey, the ship dropped anchor in the bay of Rio de Janeiro in torrential rain. However, the zoologist Quoy and the botanists Gaimard and Gaud-ichaud-Beaupré profited from the opportunity to explore the hinterland and procure specimens of exotic plants and animals. The specimens they took to France included live sloths and birds.

The expedition then proceeded to Australia, exploring on the way Molucca, the Marianas and Hawaii. In 1820 the *Uranus* was shipwrecked off the Falkland Islands and the naturalists lost a large part of their collections. They returned to Montevideo in an American ship. Freycinet then bought this vessel, naming it the *Physicist*. After a three-month stopover in Rio de Janeiro, the expedition reached France in November 1820.

In Paris a scientific commission examined the material brought back by the naturalists and presented a laudatory report to the Academy, noting that many unknown species had been discovered.

An expedition crowned with success

Buoyed by the interest generated by the latest expedition, France sent a new scientific mission to South America under the leadership of Duperrey. The *Coquille* anchored off the island of Santa Catarina, then in turmoil, in November 1822. Brazil was in the process of establishing its independence from Portugal. Although they were for a while suspected of spying, the naturalists nonetheless pursued their work. The expedition followed the coastline, and in 1823 arrived in Concepcion, in Chile, which was also in the throes of revolution. Duperrey took advantage of the stopover to study the Araucanians — an Indian tribe noted for their warlike exploits — while the zoologists discovered new species indigenous to the coasts, including hitherto unknown types of dolphins, cormorants and terns. When they reached Peru, the scientists found the country in a desperate situation — uncultivated and ruined by successive wars. At Paita,

From the same author, an Aymara ceremony. The zoologist was also an exact observer of Indian traditions.

near the Equator, Duperrey completed his work on the diurnal variation of the magnetic needle and magnetism. After an exploration of the Pacific Islands, the *Coquille* finally returned to France in March 1825, having lost neither men nor material. The Académie des Sciences received the scientists with signal honours. Duperrey presented the findings of his geographical and hydrographical research, while Cuvier presented the life science specimens. The scope of their collection was acknowledged to be without precedent. The first volume of the scientists' account of their voyage appeared in 1825. Crowned with glory, Duperrey succeeded Freycinet at the Académie des Sciences.

Pursued by pirates, Indians, soldiers...

In 1826 Alcide d'Orbigny set out for Rio de Janeiro, sent by the Museum of Natural History at the head of a scientific expedition to South America. From the first his expedition was beset by difficulties and danger. On the way to Uruguay he was nearly shipwrecked. When he arrived in Montevideo

intending to carry out barometric experiments, he was arrested by soldiers and put in prison. Once he had been released, he travelled to Buenos Aires, but found the city under siege by the Brazilians. Having escaped the unwanted attentions of Brazilian guerrillas, he proceeded to Patagonia — an unknown region at this time. Here he was sheltered by the Tobas Indians, but soon found himself obliged to fight for his life as the Tobas were attacked by a hostile neighbouring tribe. At Concepcion, d'Orbigny was forced to flee when pirates set fire to the city. For eight years, he continued to explore South America, travelling from Brazil to Tierra del Fuego, visiting more than 1,600 towns and cities and observing not only the flora, fauna and geological formations of the region, but also the customs, languages and religions of the people.

When he returned to Europe in February 1843, d'Orbigny pleaded tirelessly for the rights of the oppressed indigenous populations of South America. In recognition of his work he was awarded the annual prize given by the Geography Society. D'Orbigny had brought back with him numerous specimens, including 115 reptiles, 860 birds, 5,000 insects and 3,000 plants. For nearly thirteen years, he dedicated himself to writing his book, *Voyages in Southern America*.

'T he voyage of the Beagle *was by far the most important event of my life and determined my entire career', wrote Charles Darwin, on his return from his voyage around the world. From the outset, the 22-year-old English naturalist gained the full support of the crew through his modesty and his amiability. He was nicknamed the 'fly catcher', because of his propensity for collecting everything that flew over the the ship.*

The revelation of nature untamed

Benchunca, **the insect of the pampas**

During his journey into the Andes to meet Mendoza, Darwin was plagued day and night by the *Benchunca*, an enormous black insect: 'Its bite causes no pain, but it is most curious to watch its body fill up with blood; in less than ten minutes, from its flat form, the insect transforms itself into a ball.' After his return from South America, the scientist suffered recurrent bouts of ill-health. When he died in 1882, the doctors had not yet identified the illness from which he was suffering. Darwin had in fact died from a disease transmitted by the Andean insects, which was not identified until 1909.

In December 1831 the *Beagle*, captained by Fitzroy, sailed for South America. Its aim was to carry out a reconnaissance mission around the coasts of Patagonia, Tierra del Fuego, Chile, Peru and the islands of the Pacific. After 63 days of sailing without incident, the expedition entered the Bay of All Saints in Brazil and reached Rio de Janeiro to conduct the first hydrographic tests. Darwin was astonished by the luxuriance of the forests. An Irishman, Lennon, took him to visit his coffee plantation to the north of the city. The men rode through a forest of giant trees whose intertwining branches were alive with the shrill cries of toucans and parrots. Darwin was fascinated by the fauna of the forest, and particularly by the ferocious struggle for existence of spiders, insects and others in this dangerous environment.

He noted how insects would melt into the background of leaves, thorns and flowers to hide themselves from their enemies. Already he was asking himself questions about the interdependence of species—a theme that was to be of central importance in his work. On arriving at the plantation, the scientist was horrified at the harsh treatment inflicted on the black slaves. While the *Beagle* continued its journey of research, Darwin settled at the foot of Corcovado in Rio, where he collected the butterflies, spiders, birds and shells that he would send to his tutor, Henslow, in England.

Darwin finds his vocation

The expedition reached Bahia Blanca in Argentina in September 1832. Darwin's discovery here of fossilized bones in a cliff was to prove one of the most important finds

of his voyage. From then on, the scientist combed the area relentlessly in search of new finds. He extracted from the ground a tusk, claws, a skull and a petrified shell belonging to species then unknown to zoologists and extinct for thousands of years. The bones of these animals resembled existing species but were smaller. A new path of research had opened for Darwin: the history of the mutation of the species. The naturalist had found his vocation.

The failure of civilization

On the way to Tierra del Fuego, the *Beagle* rode out a violent storm through glacial winds. Fitzroy selected three indigenous inhabitants of Tierra del Fuego, and had them educated at his own expense, convinced that these Indians would then spread civilization and religion to their tribe. In Janu-

A studious scene on board the Beagle, *showing some of the specimens collected by the naturalists.*

ary 1833, the returning boats were met by screaming and gesticulating Indians. Fitzroy mollified them with gifts and allowed his three protégés to re-establish links with their people. When Fitzroy returned ten days later, the English missionary Matthews, who had accompanied the three Fuegans, told him that the tribe had taken everything from them and was hostile to all attempts to instil European culture into them. Discouraged, Fitzroy abandoned all hope of converting them. A year later, when the ship dropped anchor near a village, an Indian approached, naked and painted. It was none other than Jemmy, one of the Fuegans educated in England, who had returned to his native state.

A meeting with an Argentine dictator

After a stopover on the Falkland Islands, the *Beagle* sailed back up the mouth of the Rio de la Plata to make maps of the coasts of the Argentine, while Darwin continued his researches near Maldonado. When he returned, the scientist sent more than 1,500 specimens to England.

The expedition then proceeded to the Rio Negro in Patagonia. In August 1833, escorted by a guide and six gauchos, Darwin made the crossing of the vast desert-like plains of the pampas—a journey of more than 1000 kilometres. The group arrived at the camp of General Rosas, an Argentinian commander who was engaged in the systematic annihilation of the Indians to conquer new territory. Despite the revolution that gripped the country, Darwin contrived to accumulate notes and discovered rheas, species of bird similar to ostriches. His energies sapped by fever, the scientist managed with some difficulty to join up again with the crew of the *Beagle* and found them exhausted by the storms that had battered the inhospitable coast of Patagonia for the past year.

Explorations in the mountain ranges

The *Beagle* encountered difficulties as it headed south. By the time it anchored in Valparaiso in Chile, its bridge and rigging were frozen. From Valparaiso Darwin set out on horseback to study the geological formation of the cordillera of the Andes. He discovered sea shells and petrified pines

A cavalryman from the regiment of General Rosas. Rosas was put in charge of Buenos Aires province by the federalists, but was deposed in 1852.

at an altitude of 4000 metres. These were probably vestiges of ancient islands that had surged up from the water as a result of the upward movement of the Earth's crust. Darwin was fortunate to find himself in Chile during a year of massive telluric activity. He was able to observe an earthquake and an eruption of the volcano Osorno. Darwin ascended the cordillera of the Andes, reaching Mendoza in the foothills on the other side of the range within 24 days. In July the *Beagle* left Chile and sailed north to find Peru in a state of anarchy. The expedition conducted some observations in Callao, but as they were not authorized to disembark at Lima, they headed towards the Galápagos Islands.

A stopover in the Galápagos

Initially the expedition explored Chatham Island, formed by black basalt lava and covered with shrivelled trees burnt by the Sun.

In these barren surroundings, Darwin still managed to collect plants and animals. The *Beagle* sailed from island to island, methodically observing the adaptation of the animals to their natural surroundings. Darwin explored every inch of St James Island, which was home to an especially interesting variety of fauna—giant tortoises, sea and land iguanas, and finches. Its mission completed, the expedition sailed across the Pacific to pursue further research in Tahiti, New Zealand and Australia. In the Cocos archipelago, Darwin developed his theory of the formation of coral islands—a theory to be confirmed by deep-sea soundings carried out over a hundred years later. After a final detour to the South American coast, the *Beagle* reached England in October 1836. Fitzroy, embittered by his experiences, was to commit suicide in 1865.

Upon his return, Darwin devoted himself to classifying the enormous collection he had amassed during the voyage, and then to writing a number of books, including *The Origin of the Species by Natural Selection*, his most important work, published in 1859.

The apostle of natural selection

In 1809 the French naturalist Lamarck advanced the first theory of evolution, based on a subject's adaptation to its surroundings. Nearly fifty years later, Darwin advanced his own theory on the natural selection of the species, or, 'the persistence of the most apt to survive, by adapting to the natural surroundings'. On the Galápagos, he identified among the tortoises, iguanas and finches that he found there a great number of species that had evolved from common ancestral forms. These species had undergone mutations and transformations to adapt themselves to their surroundings and so survive. Others had failed to adapt and thus had died out.

A witness to the Earth's power

'We saw in the midst of splendid red flames, black objects spewing incessantly into the air, which then fell down', wrote Darwin. On the night of 19 January 1835, the naturalist witnessed the eruption of the volcano Osorno on the island of Chiloe in southern Chile. Four weeks later, the scientists felt tremors at Valdivia. Darwin travelled to the centre of the quake zone to measure the size of the earthquake. 'Talcahuano and Concepcion present the most terrible of sights, but at the same time the most interesting that I have ever been able to contemplate.' Darwin developed a passion for geology as a result of this experience.

*T*he burgeoning interest in science and a period of relative peace produced an increasing number of ambitious and sometimes risky scientific expeditions. Some were undertaken by individuals, others supported by governments. The study of natural history enjoyed its heyday.

Aristocrats in Amazonia

In 1842 Prince Adalbert of Prussia, accompanied by Count Oriolla and Count Bismarck, headed up one of the tributaries of the Amazon River, the Xingu. Having met up with a young missionary whom they persuaded to join the party, the small group embarked on an energetic exploration of the streams, rivers and waterways of the region. Despite the heavy tropical rains, the voracious ants and piranhas, the four men did not hesitate to venture into dangerous and hostile territories. For several months, the prince carried out a methodical study of the Amazon's currents.

San Pablo lagoon, near Quito. Many of Darwin's numerous followers returned to the sites he had visited.

Victorious over the rapids of Guyana

In 1823 Britain sent an expedition to Guyana—a land the British were keen to colonize— under the leadership of a German, Hermann Schomburg. The expedition was made up of 22 members of the Royal Geographical Society. The venture got off to a bad start, when most of the expedition were struck down with dysentery. Once he had recovered, Schomburg collected samples and made maps of the region, and made several solitary trips to the Corona Falls and to Lake Amucu. In February 1836, the explorers set out to investigate the upper reaches of the Essequibo River. They soon found their way blocked by large cataracts and they had to make up their minds whether or not to turn back. But navigation in either direction was becoming difficult, with the waters swollen by recent heavy rains. At the Etaballly Falls one of their boats was sucked under by a powerful whirlpool, and with it an entire collection of geological and tree specimens.

In September the expedition set out to explore another large river, the Corentyn, but once again gigantic waterfalls impeded its progress. Schomburg, ever tenacious, next turned his attention to the Berbice River. But their Indian guides were resentful, and, terrified by the rapids, abandoned the expedition, which was to be plagued by attacks by thousands of ants and a herd of wild pigs. The luxuriant vegetation slowed them down considerably and their food supplies went bad in the heat. Schomburg, however, had the satisfaction of discovering a passage to the Essequibo. He returned victorious to England in 1840, having gained wide knowledge of the river system and convinced that a colony could be established on the upper Essequibo. The government took his proposals into account and in 1841 put him in charge of establishing a colony in Guyana.

From one misfortune to another...

The Swiss naturalist Johann von Tschudi, decided to follow in Darwin's footsteps. In June 1839, having weathered a storm off the coast of Cape Horn, Tschudi disembarked in Chile. He reached Peru, then at war with its neighbour, and while visiting Lima was captured by the Chileans. After a brief incarceration, he left for the cordillera where a number of mishaps befell him: he succumbed to sunstroke, was bitten by insects, and narrowly escaped plunging into a ravine when the suspension bridge he was crossing with his mule collapsed. He visited Inca sites, observed the condor, and feasted his eyes on untamed nature. Cut off by a blizzard in the Andes he took refuge in a shelter, but woke the next morning to find his mule dead. Tschudi owed his survival to the Indians, who put him on a llama and took him to their village, exhausted and suffering from snow blindness.

Having recovered, Tschudi descended into the virgin forest. He devoted his time to his passion, zoology, studying monkeys, snakes and crocodiles. He met an Indian who claimed to be 141 years old, and who perhaps owed his longevity to the leaves of the coca plant, which he had chewed three times a day since the age of eleven.

Wearied by his adventures, Tschudi returned to Europe, where his work on fauna met with universal acclaim. But he was soon to return to South America.

Down the great rivers of Brazil

It was largely thanks to the influence of the French royal family that King Louis-Philippe put François de Castelnau in charge of a scientific expedition to the Amazon basin. The expedition arrived in Rio de Janeiro in June 1843, and the explorers spent two months 'botanizing' and carrying out geological and magnetic observations. They then set off into the interior—their ultimate goal being the Rio Tocantins in the south. On their journey—which took them through some extraordinary landscapes— the explorers were particularly excited by their friendly encounters with the Chavante and Chamboia tribes. En route they explored the Mato Grosso and discovered the sources of the Paraguay River. While some members of the expedition visited the mines and the Bolivian capital, La Paz, others explored the ruins at Tiahuanaco and Lake Titicaca before heading back towards Peru and the Pacific coast. The entire party enthusiastically set about exploring the whole country. Having crossed innumerable fields of coca, the explorers set off up the dangerous Rio Urubamba.

By now the Indian porters and guides had abandoned the expedition. A worried Castelnau gave d'Osery, a member of the expedition, the responsibility of putting the collections and documents in safe keeping in Lima. But before he could carry out this task, d'Osery was murdered by Indians. The rest of the expedition eventually reached the Amazon, where Castelnau studied in great detail the natural history and tribes of the region. From Belem he reached Cayenne, whence he set sail for England in 1847. The explorers took back with them a considerable amount of information.

An observatory for Chile

Towards the middle of the 19th century, the American government began to take an interest in its neighbours to the south. Congress financed an expedition to Chile whose mission it was to measure the distance between the Earth and the Sun. These measurements were then to be compared with measurements recorded at the same time by the observatory in Washington. The expedition, led by the astronomer James Melville Gilliss, arrived in Valparaiso in July 1849. Its first priority was to find a suitable site for an observatory close to Santiago. The Chi-

lean government found three assistants for the astronomer and within a few months not only had the observatory been constructed and the measurements taken, but the expedition had also gathered a large number of specimens of Chilean flora. Gilliss himself organized an exchange of plants and seeds between the botanical gardens of the Chilean and American capitals. When his mission was accomplished in 1852, the astronomer sold his observatory to the Chilean government. The expedition took back to Washington a large number of scientific observations and many floral specimens. However, in the United States the project that was to have taken astronomical measurements at the same time as the Chilean observatory had ended in failure. But Gilliss's results, far from being useless, were published in an ample, six-volume work.

The naturalists eat monkey

The English naturalists Wallace and Bates, enthralled by Darwin's account of his South American journey, organized on their own an expedition to the Amazon. They financed the venture through the sale of specimens to wealthy collectors. The two friends arrived at Belem in May 1848 and spent more than a year in the virgin forest. They followed the course of the Rio Tocantins, observed crocodiles and multicoloured birds, and collected insects and butterflies. The explorers followed the customs of the region even to the extent of eating monkey. Wallace went up the Amazon as far as Santarem in a craft loaded with provisions and books, where he met the English naturalist Spruce. Bates, meanwhile, explored the island of Marajo, collecting numerous animal specimens. The scientists met up again in Manaus on the Rio Negro. Several weeks of exploration brought them to the mouth of the Rio Cassiquiare.

In Belem Wallace learned of the death of his brother, who had succumbed to yellow fever. Wallace himself was ailing and left for England in 1852, but his ship caught fire and he lost all of his collections. Given aid and comfort by some fellow Englishmen, Wallace settled in Malaysia, where in between attacks of malaria he developed his own theory of natural selection. Meanwhile, Bates continued to explore the Amazon, navigating between Teffe and Santarem. When illness eventually obliged him to return to England in 1859, the naturalist took back with him more than 14,000 animal speci-

A Guianese rock cockrel, from François Levaillant's Natural History of the Birds of Paradise.

A continent in turmoil

Most of the present Latin American republics acquired independence between 1810 and 1824. But the vast surface area of the countries, the difficulty of establishing communication links, economic setbacks caused by incessant war and the inexperience of political leaders, made political stability difficult to achieve. While the states under Portuguese rule quietened down, those that had been under Spanish dominion squabbled over their poorly defined national frontiers for most of the century, at times reverting to armed conflict.

mens, including numerous unknown species of insect and butterfly.

Twenty years in the tropics

The German naturalist Karl Ferdinand Appun left for Venezuela in 1848 armed with references from Humboldt. His first explorations took him along the Rio Yaracuy, beneath the giant bamboo trees of the tropical forest. Leaving the coast, he set off into the interior and headed for the plains of Carabobo and Tocuyito. Here Appun constructed a small shelter from which he observed and drew the surrounding flora. The naturalist then travelled on a boat with an all-black crew to La Ceiba. Battered by a hurricane and devoured by mosquitoes during the journey, Appun arrived at his destination exhausted. After several excursions around Trujillo, a veritable paradise of orchids and tropical fruits, the scientist reached Bolivar City on the Orinoco. With two companions and a stock of jars and crates for his specimens, Appun set out to explore the river. But the wind became so violent that his small craft capsized. Having transferred to a steamboat, the party then ascended the Rio Carani, and discovered a

hitherto unknown waterfall. Appun returned to Bolivar City to send his prodigious collections and numerous drawings of species back to Europe. He was then commissioned by the British authorities in Guyana to conduct scientific explorations of the colony. Appun was to spend a total of twenty years in South America.

Taken in by the adventure of exploration

To resolve the problem of slavery at home, the United States government dreamed up the idea of sending colonists, along with their slaves, to the Amazon. The government dispatched Lieutenant Herndon on an expedition to Brazil. So as not to arouse any suspicions, his official brief was to reconnoitre the region's system of rivers and lakes. Herndon left Peru in May 1851, crossing the Andes and descending into the luxuriant tropical vegetation on the other side. On reaching the confluence of the Chichao and Huallaga rivers, he and his men set out in large boats to travel up the river. He saw many wonders on this journey: Indians fishing with poison-tipped roots and blowing into horns to drive away snakes; a

lemon tree draped with a transparent veil of spider webs. Excited by such scenes, Herndon continued his expeditions with renewed vigour. In Brazil the lieutenant became interested in the rituals and customs of the Indians of the tropical forest. After several months in the Amazon, Herndon returned to the United States without really having explored the possibility of transplanting American slaves to the region. He did, however, return with an enormous amount of information on Brazilian civilizations.

Under fire from the Paraguayans

In 1852 the Argentine Confederation decreed that its borders were open to all foreign countries. The American government seized the opportunity to send a new scientific mission, led by Thomas J. Page, whose brief was to collect samples and also to look into the commercial possibilities offered by the country. The *Water Witch* berthed in Buenos Aires, a city in a state of emergency, the day the new constitution was proclaimed, 25 May 1853. Page travelled up the coast, impressed by the riches of the Argentine, its flora, its woods, its climate, its atmosphere... On the island of Atajo, claimed by the Argentine but still a Paraguayan military base, Carlos Lopez, the future dictator, gave the Americans permission to go as far as Bahia Negra at the border with Brazil, Paraguay and Bolivia. Page captured rare and exotic animals. In Asuncion, the capital of Paraguay, the expedition set out on board a small vessel to ascend the river. But after a disagreement between the American consul and Lopez, the latter forbade them to navigate in Paraguayan waters. Page returned to the Argentine where he visited the property of Aimé Bonpland—now 82. In May 1856 he received orders to leave for the United States. He returned with an impressive amount of information.

On the trail of conquest

In 1862 the Spanish government financed a scientific mission to South America, led by the naturalist Patricio Paz y Membiela.
    In Brazil the scientists studied the flora and fauna of the country and purchased 160 species of bird. The expedition moved on to the Argentine, where Paz prepared to cross the continent overland while the other sci-

The extravagant white king Orélie Antoine Tounens failed to win over the Chilean authorities.

The king of Araucania and Patagonia

Orélie Antoine Tounens, a wealthy solicitor from the Périgord in southern France, was a man in search of a kingdom. In 1861 he had himself proclaimed king of Araucania and Patagonia by the Indians. In exchange he vowed to liberate them from the white man. Crowned King Antoine I, Tounens proclaimed decrees, dispatched envoys, and learned the language of his subjects, but was recognized by no official authority. He declared war on the Chileans, but was betrayed and then arrested. He was sentenced to hard labour and then confined in a lunatic asylum. Araucania was placed under Chilean control in 1871. Tounens was repatriated to France, where he died in 1878.

Away from the main routes and sheltered from political upheaval, a few Indian villages perpetuated their ancestral way of life and social organization.

entists continued their journey by sea. Travelling in a carriage, on horseback and by train, Paz reached Chile and eventually Peru, where he met up with his companions again. He studied Inca sites and local flora and visited a few mines. To avoid being spotted by bandits attracted by its long mule train, the expedition split up, taking different routes. Paz, who had an argument with the captain, returned to Spain.

The expedition continued, but was then ordered to leave the country by the Peruvian authorities. In protest, the Spanish fleet took control of the Chincha islands, a Peruvian possession, and war broke out between the Chileans and the Peruvians. The scientists were for a while suspected of spying, but they were protected by the Chilean scientific community and were able to continue work in Ecuador. They crossed the cordillera and came to the land of the Jivaro, where they observed the customs of the head shrinkers. But the rainy season, combined with the lack of resources and

growing fatigue of the party, made the exploration of the Amazon very difficult.

In December 1865 the scientists met a Spanish minister in Belem who granted them additional funding and congratulated them on the immense amount of work they had accomplished.

The fish of the Amazon

That same year, the American naturalist Louis Agassiz organized an expedition to study the freshwater fish of the Amazon River, financed by the American benefactor Thayer. Agassiz, who had worked with Martius after Spix's death to help him classify the fish in their collections, spent some time gathering specimens in Rio de Janeiro before travelling to the Amazon. Accompanied by a young Brazilian, Talisman, and encouraged by the friendly co-operation of

the natives, the expedition set off in a small craft on the river heading towards Manaus. The scientists collected numerous fish specimens for the American Zoological Museum. They were fortunate to receive as a gift from the Brazilian government a vessel better adapted to their work. Agassiz took the opportunity to increase the scope of the expedition to take in a study of inbreeding among the Indian populations. The scientists took an enormous amount of photographs. With his rich collection of specimens of Brazilian flora and fish from the Xingu, Agassiz was jubilant: 'The Amazon has more fish than the entire Atlantic Ocean', he said. Fossil finds by other members of the expedition were to encourage continued research into Brazil's geological structure. The scientists left the region in July 1866, after a venture that had lasted over a year.

Agassiz was not only one of the foremost biologists of his day but also a teacher who made a great contribution to the study of natural science.

The prisoner of the Patagonians

In 1856 a young French adventurer, Auguste Guinnard, went abroad to make his fortune, travelling throughout Patagonia and the Argentinian pampas. With an Italian companion, he endured the harsh southern winter. Hungry, their feet cut and their compass broken, the two men then got lost in hostile territory. They were attacked by a horde of Indians, who killed the Italian. A terrified Guinnard was tied naked to a horse and led back to the Indian camp. He remained a prisoner of the natives for three years, and was traded from tribe to tribe. The adventurer-turned-slave was subjected to all sorts of punishment. But little by little he learned the language and customs of the Patagonians, and finally managed to escape.

Saved by their firearms

In 1866 the joint commission in charge of establishing the borders between Peru and Brazil was massacred by the Mangeronas Indians. A new commission, directed by Baron de Teffe, ventured into these dangerous parts once again in 1874. They saw two arrows embedded in a tree, an Indian sign indicating a declaration of war. Drums sounded deep in the forest and a group of screaming natives, adorned with red paint and feathers, suddenly appeared in front of the terrified officials; thanks to their Winchester rifles they were able to drive the Indians off.

The massacre of Creveaux's mission in 1882. The French explorer had distinguished himself in Guiana, the upper Orinoco and Amazonia. He was assassinated by Toba Indians on the banks of the Pilcomayo (Paraguay).

The cavalcade of friendship

———————●———————

Chaworth Musters was brought up by an uncle who had served on the *Beagle* and had himself served as an officer on the *Stromboli*, which sailed in South American waters over a three-year period. In 1869 Musters decided to cross Patagonia from the Strait of Magellan to the Rio Negro. To reach Santa Cruz he hired a guide, a Tehuelche Indian who taught him how to hunt and trade pelts in the Indian fashion during the trip. To win the Indians' confidence and to get through the harsh southern winter, Musters spent some time living in an Indian camp. Soon treated as one of them, Musters left for the north with twenty Indians. But the latter had stormy temperaments, and rows—sometimes to the death—occasionally broke out among them. They told the explorer legends of hidden cities, and described to him ancestral customs and celebration rituals. During their long march they crossed vast plains populated with rheas, and stopped alongside lagoons covered with birds. Musters was fascinated by the natural history of Patagonia. A friendship based on mutual respect soon grew up between Musters and the Tehuelches. On their journey they met an-

other group of Indians who joined up with them, forming a troop of nearly two hundred men who eventually reached the port of Carmen de Patagones on the Rio Negro. In this company Musters was able to accumulate an immense number of observations on their rites and customs. The explorers at times turned ethnologist…

The lake trail to the Pacific

———————●———————

The Argentinians, not wishing to stand idly by while their lands were explored by others, organized an expedition of their own in 1878, led by Carlos Maria Moyano. Its goal was to map the lake region of Patagonia. The expedition ascended the Rio Santa Cruz to its source, the Argentino Lake, and then navigated the lakes of San Martin and Viedma, before heading for the Andes. While ascending a summit overlooking the lakes, Moyano saw a huge iceberg, a possible sign of a passage to the Pacific. In 1880, while travelling the same route that Musters had followed along the cordillera and looking for a passage to drive herds through the mountains, the expedition discovered a large lake, Lake Buenos Aires. Moyano noted the topography of the region, which

Musters had not been able to do as the Indians were frightened by his scientific instruments. While crossing some grassland, Moyano spotted a coastal trail with numerous watering holes, ideal for cattle.

In November 1883 the explorer set off on an expedition with twelve men, many horses and measuring instruments, and material for constructing a ship with which they hoped to discover a passage to the Pacific. The party crossed a rich valley, highly suitable for a settlement, but then found the way blocked by an impenetrable forest. On closer investigation Moyano glimpsed the Pacific through a curtain of trees.

In addition to a passage between Patagonia and the Pacific, he studied the region's lakes and explored the possibilities for settling the region.

Massacre in Toba territory

———————●———————

In 1879 Jules Creveaux, a naval doctor posted to Guiana by the French government, ascended the Maroni River to reach the Tumac-Humac mountains, the legendary land of El Dorado. On either side of the water a sombre forest spread out, teeming with garish birds and screaming monkeys.

Continuing his journey towards the Amazon, Creveaux crossed Peru, where he carried out a number of geographic and ethnographic observations. He encountered one tribe after another: the Carijonas, wearing belts made of wooden circles linked by vines, the Coreguajes, whose ears were pierced with feathers from which flowers hung, the Quitotos, whose legs were painted bluish-black and whose eyelids were dyed bright red... The tireless Creveaux led another expedition up the Orinoco to Venezuela, his raft drifting past banks inhabited by jaguars and crocodiles. In 1882, intending to ascend the Rio Paraguay and then descend the Amazon, Creveaux set off up the Rio Pilcomayo. Just as the expedition entered this territory, the Tobas declared war on the Caiza Indians. Creveaux sent one of his scouts, a young Toba, laden with gifts for his tribe. During the meeting ceremony all animosity between the two peoples seemed to have disappeared, but suddenly the Tobas attacked the expedition. Most of the explorers, including Creveaux, were brutally murdered by the Indians. The others were taken prisoner, hardly a more enviable fate.

...all because of a misunderstanding

The French explorer Arthur Thouar, who was then in Chile, was sent by the French government to see if there were any survivors of the Creveaux expedition. Thouar crossed Peru and the Andes, and reached Bolivia in May 1883. There the government granted him an escort of 200 men. At the head of the little troop, Thouar penetrated into Toba territory and discovered the ruins of the boats of the Creveaux expedition. A thousand Indians launched a surprise attack on the party. The battle raged for two days before Thouar was able to negotiate successfully with the Toba chief. The expedition continued along the Rio Pilcomayo, but the heat, the swamps and the mosquitoes made their progress increasingly difficult. The mules died, vermin proliferated, and the men were struck by fever. Thouar himself travelled on to Asuncion to get help. He met the Paraguayan president, Juan Caballero, who sent a boat to rescue them. After these adventures, Thouar returned to France but came back the following year to explore the Pilcomayo region once again. In spite of raids launched by the ever-aggressive Tobas, he carried out a number of observations and mapped the streams, rivers and waterways of the area.

During this expedition he met up with Yalla, Creveaux's young Toba scout, who gave Thouar an account of the tragedy. It appeared that the Indian had told his tribe that the white men had come to take away their fishing rights. The Tobas then reacted by attacking them. Thouar himself only narrowly escaped the arrows of the Indians and returned to France having given up all hope of finding any survivors.

Richly fertile valleys

Towards the end of the century a number of Chilean expeditions sent to establish the borders between Argentina and Chile also contributed to the geographical knowledge of the Andes, and the valleys and the coasts of the region. In 1893, at the request of the Chileans, the German Hans Steffen organized an expedition to the island of Chiloe, to the gulfs of Corcovado and Reloncavi. He

ascended the Rio Palena and headed towards the interior, where he discovered fertile valleys and advanced the theory of a possible passage to the coast, based on the fact that the Rio Palena became navigable at its meeting point with the Rio Claro. But the expedition was stopped by the Argentinians when it inadvertently crossed the border into Argentina. Three years later, authorization in hand, Steffen was able to explore the valleys of the Rio Aisen in Argentina—he listed the lakes, conducted topographical studies and made meteorological observations. Chile called upon his services again in 1896, when he headed an expedition to a little-known region of Patagonia of which the existing maps dated from Fitzroy's 1831 expedition and expeditions undertaken in 1872 and 1888 by Darwin and Chilean scientists respectively. The explorers spread out over the entire region, discovering a river, lakes and richly fertile valleys. After Steffen's explorations, Patagonia, for all practical purposes, was no longer virgin territory.

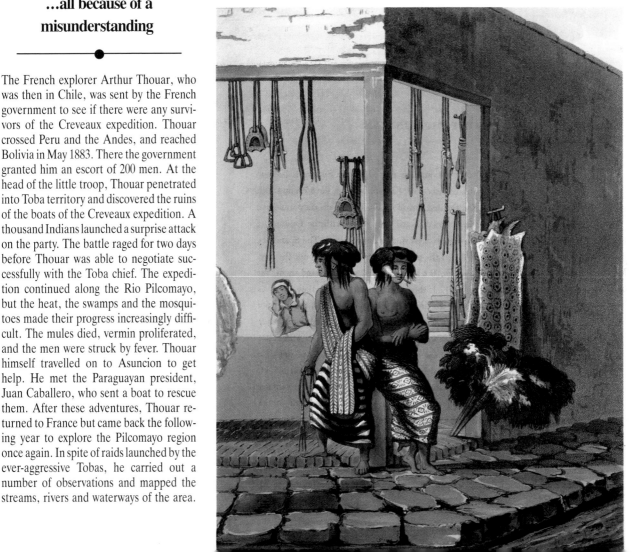

Pampas Indians. At the end of the nineteenth century, only a few gauchos and their herds inhabited the Argentinian plains, which remained virtually unknown.

German ethnologists in the heart of Brazil

From 1884 the German ethnologist Karl von den Steinen explored the banks of the Xingu, a tributary of the Amazon, in search of tribes in the interior of Brazil. With his compatriot Otto Clauss, he penetrated the territories of the Bororos, the Bakairis, the Nahuques and the Kamayuras, and studied their customs. He discovered that a Bororo tribesman can only claim a woman if he can adorn her with the claws of a jaguar that he has killed with a bow and arrow. The two men also studied the sacred animals of the Indians, including tapirs, jaguars and monkeys. Steinen transcribed Indian vocabulary as well as the musical notes of their chants, and accumulated much scientific data relating to the Indians.

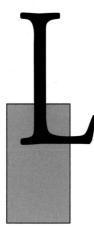

ittle by little, as the centuries went by, the map of South America took shape. After the sailors, the conquistadors, the missionaries and the naturalists came the ethnographers. In the 20th century curiosity, adventure and the quest for knowledge prompted explorers to uncover the last mysteries of the continent and to penetrate the soul of its people.

Cannibals

At the beginning of the twentieth century Hamilton Rice, an American doctor with a passion for travel, undertook a number of expeditions, geographical as well as botanic and ethnographic, to the basins of the Amazon and Orinoco rivers. He was especially interested in studying the diseases afflicting the Indians in these regions. During these expeditions, Rice methodically mapped the river system of the Amazon basin. In 1920, while the expedition was ascending the upper Orinoco in a small craft, it was attacked by the savage Guaharibo tribe. The explorers only narrowly escaped a grisly fate, for the Guaharibos were known to be partial to human flesh. Undeterred by this brush with danger, Dr Rice then explored the Rio Branco, looking for a passage to the Orinoco River. The expedition was equipped with sophisticated modern technology, including a radio system and a hydroplane. Rice collected samples of the local flora and

The epic of the Maufrais

In 1949 the French explorer Raymond Maufrais, ascending the Maroni and then the Ouaqui rivers, set out to explore the Tumuc-Humac mountains along the frontier of Brazil and Guyana. Travelling alone, starving and weakened by fever, the young explorer — wavering between exaltation and discouragement — reached the Tamouri, which he attempted to descend by wading and swimming. He threw himself into his last adventure on 13 January 1950, abandoning his travel diary on the river bank. He was never to be seen again. Thus began another epic — that of Edgar Maufrais, his father. Unable to believe that his son had disappeared, he mounted and led, until 1964, a total of fifteen expeditions to find him, without success...

fauna, and made geological, topographical and anthropological observations. He ascended a tributary of the Rio Branco to its source, the Rio Uraricuera, without discovering a passage to the Orinoco. The detailed mass of information collected by Rice constitutes the most important geographical work done during this century.

A former American president rides the rapids of the Amazon

From the beginning of the century the Brazilian explorer Candido Rondon had crisscrossed the northwest of the Mato Grosso, on the edge of the Amazon, on assignments for his government. Rondon respected and protected the Indians, and was known and liked by them in return. Rondon made a methodical listing of the numerous water-

Latin America continued to inspire scientists and adventurers into the early years of the twentieth century.

ways of the region. In 1913, accompanied by the former American president Theodore Roosevelt, Rondon headed one of the most spectacular expeditions ever sent to the South American continent: the exploration of the Rio da Duvida, discovered by Rondon several years before. Departing from Sao Luis de Caceres, the party set off up the Rio Sepotuba in small craft. When they arrived in Tapirapoan, they sent their collection of specimens back to the American Museum of Natural History. The party then split up, with one group going down the Rio Jiparana and the other following the Rio da Duvida. In spite of mosquitoes and fever, the group of five explorers and thirty porters descending the Jiparana reached the Rio Madeira without difficulty. But the Rio da Duvida party, including Rondon and Roosevelt, which had made an impressive collection of plants and animals, ran into all kinds of setbacks. A succession of rapids forced the men to carry the boats along the banks. When they attempted to negotiate the rapids, their craft were engulfed by the rushing waters. Attacks by vermin increased their discomfort. Soon their food supplies dwindled and some explorers, stricken with fever, grew weak with fatigue. One explorer perished when his boat capsized in a whirlpool. Their morale low and in poor health, the men reached the mouth of the river after two months of navigating. The expedition brought back more than 2500 bird, insect and reptile specimens, as well as a detailed map of an immense river.

In search of lost cities

An Englishman, Colonel P.H. Fawcett, spent nearly thirty years exploring Bolivia, Brazil, Peru and Paraguay for the South American government with the purpose of

Gradually the Latin American republics modernized. The construction of rail networks facilitated communications between towns.

The destruction of the **Amazon rain forest**

If the deforestation of the Amazon continues to accelerate at its present rapid rate, within 70 years the rain forest will have disappeared. While tropical rain forests cover only 7% of the Earth's surface, they harbour nearly 50% of all animal and plant species. The uncontrolled exploitation of the riches of the Amazon—its plant and animal species, precious woods and minerals—with the support of governments and banks, is also destroying the ecological balance of the planet. The Amazon forest is not only the natural habitat of Indian tribes that are dying along with it; it is also a giant regulator of the world's carbon dioxide level.

establishing the boundaries of these countries. During his travels, he discovered various Indian civilizations. In 1925, convinced of the existence of a number of lost cities rich in remains, he organized an expedition to try and find them. In spite of exhortations from all to desist from such a perilous undertaking, Fawcett plunged into the depths of Brazil, accompanied by his son Jack and his son's friend, Raleigh Rimell. At the end of the month of May, a final message sent to a mission announced that they had reached the wild and remote eastern part of the country. No one would ever see them again... A search party sent out in 1928 was told in an Anauquas village that Fawcett and his companions had been massacred by Suyas Indians. However, during the night, a member of the search party overheard the Anauquas chief declaring to the tribe that they should kill this expedition just as they had the last. Awakened by their alert companion, the party managed to escape. Many other expeditions set out in search of these legendary buried cities, but none succeeded in discovering them.

A philosopher in the tropics

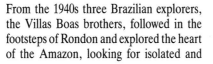

'I hate voyages and explorers...' Fired by an uncompromising and marked scorn for those who pursued personal adventures, the French ethnologist Claude Lévi-Strauss

was one of those who wished to discover the true soul of the peoples of South America. In the first half of the century he undertook a series of voyages to study the Indian tribes of the Mato Grosso in Brazil: the Nambik-waras, the Caduevos, the Bororos, and the Tupis-Kowahibs—survivors of the Stone Age, not all of whom had mastered the use of fire. The ethnologist shared in their daily existence, studied their rituals and customs, and observed their social organization and their relationship with nature. Lévi-Strauss reflected on what civilization and progress meant for these people, whose basic problem was adapting to life in the framework of the economy of the 20th century. Lévi-Strauss observed that for these nomadic tribes the only true social unity lay in the stability of the couple. Lévi-Strauss noted a number of picturesque details of the life styles of these indigenous tribes, which if undeniably primitive, were also carefree and happy. In 1955 the ethnologist published a number of his observations on the region under the title *Tristes Tropiques* (first translated as *A World on the Wane*).

The saviours of the Indians

From the 1940s three Brazilian explorers, the Villas Boas brothers, followed in the footsteps of Rondon and explored the heart of the Amazon, looking for isolated and

often hostile Indian tribes. Establishing communication with the Indians did not always prove to be easy. The explorers would leave gifts, wait patiently until the Indians accepted them, and then attempt to make contact. Sometimes they had to flee, pursued by a hail of arrows. But the three brothers were to devote their lives to saving the Indians. They took part in countless expeditions, built dozens of airfields in the forest, and amassed great quantities of information about the region. Leonardo Villas Boas died in 1961, but Claudio and Orlando pursued their work and in that year obtained national park status for a vast territory within the upper Xingu region. Designed to protect the Indians of the Amazon both physically and psychologically, this reservation remains off limits to whites. To enter it, authorization must be obtained from the government, which grants it only in exceptional circumstances. In the villages of the reservation those Indians who have survived continue to hunt and fish, and have succeeded in returning to their natural state. Driven away by the massive influx of *garimpeiros*—gold diggers and farmers in search of land—decimated by diseases brought by the whites, and sometimes simply massacred, the Indians have been systematically dispossessed of their land. This tragic situation remains the same today, despite some efforts by the Brazilian government. The mixing of races—black, white and Indian—has also contributed to the weakening of Indian culture.

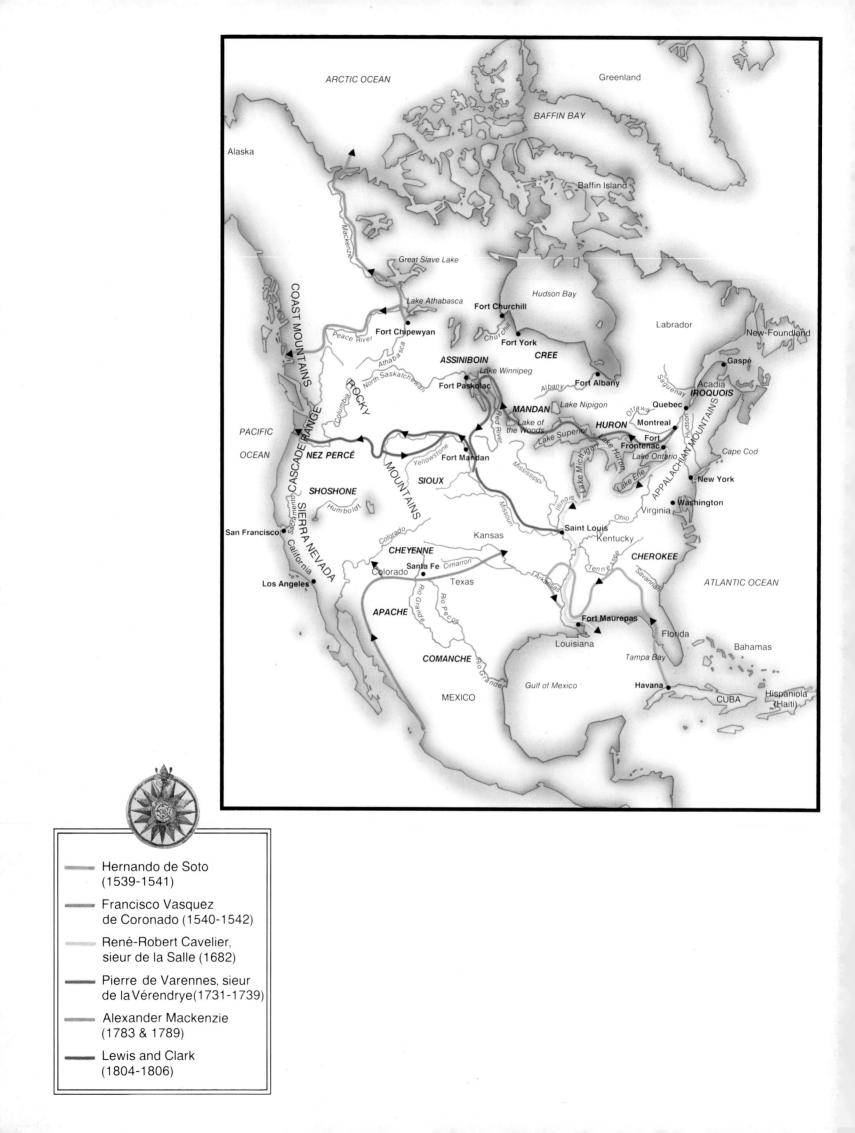

ARCTIC OCEAN

Greenland

BAFFIN BAY

Alaska

Baffin Island

Great Slave Lake

Mackenzie

Hudson Bay

Lake Athabasca

Labrador

New-Foundland

Fort Churchill

Peace River

Fort Chipewyan

Churchill

Fort York

Gaspé

Athabasca

ASSINIBOIN

CREE

COAST MOUNTAINS

North Saskatchewan

Lake Winnipeg

Fort Paskolac

Albany

Fort Albany

Saguenay

Acadia

IROQUOIS

ROCKY

Lake Nipigon

Quebec

MANDAN

Lake of the Woods

Ottawa

HURON

Montreal

Red River

Columbia

PACIFIC

Lake Superior

Fort Frontenac

Hudson

OCEAN

CASCADE RANGE

NEZ PERCÉ

Yellowstone

Fort Mandan

Lake Michigan

Lake Huron

Lake Ontario

Cape Cod

APPALACHIAN MOUNTAINS

MOUNTAINS

Mississippi

Lake Erie

New York

SHOSHONE

SIOUX

Illinois

Washington

Sacramento

Humboldt

Missouri

Virginia

San Francisco

California

SIERRA NEVADA

Colorado

Kansas

Saint Louis

Kentucky

Ohio

CHEYENNE

Cimarron

CHEROKEE

Santa Fe

Tennessee

Savannah

Colorado

Texas

Los Angeles

Rio Grande

Arkansas

ATLANTIC OCEAN

Rio Pecos

APACHE

Fort Maurepas

Florida

Louisiana

Bahamas

COMANCHE

Rio Grande

Tampa Bay

Gulf of Mexico

MEXICO

Havana

CUBA

Hispaniola (Haiti)

Hernando de Soto
(1539-1541)

Francisco Vasquez
de Coronado (1540-1542)

René-Robert Cavelier,
sieur de la Salle (1682)

Pierre de Varennes, sieur
de la Vérendrye (1731-1739)

Alexander Mackenzie
(1783 & 1789)

Lewis and Clark
(1804-1806)

North
America

he question of America's first settlers, and the origins of the earliest Americans, has never been satisfactorily resolved, although it is generally thought that the first settlers were Siberian hunters who crossed the frozen Bering Strait. Thousands of years later, around 1000 AD, the Vikings established short-lived colonies in Labrador, and are supposed to have reached the East Coast of the United States.

According to the sagas of Greenland, Leif Eriksson, the son of Erik the Red, landed on the shores of what is today Labrador, calling it Vinland, or Wine Land, because of the profusion of red berries.

False evidence

British predominance in the colonization of America gave rise, as early as the nineteenth century, to a rash of forgeries, all aiming to prove that Norsemen had preceded Columbus and his crew on American soil. The two most remarkable hoaxes were the affairs of the Kensington Stone and the Vinland Map. In 1957 Yale University acquired the so-called Vinland Map, purchased in Spain for a considerable sum. Experts at the university asserted that the map had been drawn in Basel in 1440, according to accounts by Scandinavian sailors. However, in 1974 an analysis of the ink revealed that the map could not have been drawn before 1920. The Kensington Stone, engraved with what appeared to be Runic characters, was unearthed in Minnesota in 1898, spawning a belief that the Vikings had gone as far as the Great Lakes. To the disappointment of the press, an expert evaluation proved that the stone was a forgery.

The ancestors of the Indians

The names of the first explorers to roam the continent that would later be called America are lost to history. Some forty thousand years before Christ, groups of nomadic Siberian hunters wandered over eastern Siberia, tracking big game. In that glacial period the Bering Strait was in fact a bridge of ice, which the Siberians crossed in search of new hunting grounds. North America was thus populated by a flow of migrations, as archaeological finds have shown. The yel-

low-skinned Mongoloid peoples who swept into North America were the ancestors of the American Indians. Archaeological evidence also indicates the existence of transoceanic relations with the Pacific islands, although the contacts had no great impact on the population. Today, owing to the discovery of prehistoric sites, it is possible to follow the progress of the Palaeo-Indians along the corridor between the Pacific coast and the Rocky Mountains, and trace the spread, at a very early date, of groups into South America. These early cultures have been placed by radiocarbon dating at about 10,000 to 8000 BC.

Before the Spanish conquest

Migratory activity continued until the arrival of Europeans on American soil. Aztec literature tells of the nation's march through hostile lands in what is now the southern United States, to reach a site revealed by an eagle devouring a serpent. The prophecy of their wise men having come to pass, the Aztecs settled in the marshy valley of what is today Mexico City, and set about conquering their neighbours. The Aztecs retained a taste for adventure and exploration; their merchants travelled deep into the tropical forests of Central America, and also established trading links in the Caribbean.

Archaeological findings from the Antilles, and the accounts of Arawak Indians who lived there, prove that the islanders had regular dealings with the Aztecs. The earliest Spanish conquistadors found that the Arawak people had already explored the Caribbean, and were familiar with prevailing currents, winds, and the dangerously changeable climate. The Arawaks also knew of the great continental kingdoms on the mainland, with which they occasionally traded. Like the later explorers of the nineteenth century, Europeans of Columbus's time made good use of the Indians' skills and geographical knowledge in their discovery of America—a continent that had been settled by Indians long before a Genoese captain set foot on Caribbean sands in October 1492.

Legendary voyages

But it appears that Columbus had been preceded by other voyagers, who had reached America via icy northern seas. The earliest of these was Saint Brendan (see p. 28), a sixth-century Irish monk (d. circa 580), who helped to evangelize England, then continued on to Scotland. From there, the saint is said to have sailed northwest, to Iceland and perhaps to Greenland. The only record of these journeys is contained in Brendan's *Peregrinations*, large portions of which are simply stories gleaned here and there from the Scots and the Irish. In the Middle Ages a devotional iconography grew up around the exploits of the saintly Brendan, who braved uncharted seas teeming with monsters and other fearsome beasts. His fame was such that some believed Brendan had brought the Gospel as far as America, though neither the missionary's narrative nor any existing documents confirmed that belief. Also disputed is the account of another Irishman, Bjarni, who according to legend reached the shore of North America around 945.

The Vikings in America

The Viking adventure in North America is related in the Scandinavian epics known as sagas. Recent archaeological findings confirm this oral tradition, which commemorated the exploits of Norse navigators. The

During the 10th and 11th centuries, the Vikings or 'Norsemen' reconnoitred Iceland and possibly North America, before turning their attention towards Europe.

tales from Greenland, and, especially, the saga of Eric the Red, develop in great detail the Vikings' perilous voyages from Greenland to North American shores. For interpreters of the sagas, however, it is not always easy to distinguish actual historical events from the welter of heroic feats, personal histories, more or less true epic tales, and commentaries appended much later by generations of bards. Archaeological digs carried out over the past twenty years on the eastern coast of Labrador have produced the remains of fortifications, natural harbours where the Vikings moored their drakkars, as well as assorted weapons, cauldrons and innumerable arrowheads. The sagas mention the inhabitants of this coast, the Skraelings, described as 'dark, ugly men with shaggy hair. They had large eyes and broad faces'. Several excavation sites show defensive walls bearing traces of fire; what is more, the number of arrowheads and the abandonment of the Viking settlement suggest that relations between the two communities were far from peaceful.

From Eric the Red to Bartholomew Columbus

The reasons for the Viking colonization are not known, but it is clear that around the year 1000 groups of Norwegians consolidated their outposts on the coast of Greenland. From there, Eric the Red, Thorvald Eriksson and Thorhall the Hunter sailed west to Vinland, known today as the Labrador peninsula. Violent conflicts with Indians or epidemics may explain why the Norse settlements did not last. Nonetheless, throughout the Middle Ages the memory of the Vikings' territorial conquests was kept alive by the oral tradition in Britain and Scandinavia. When Bartholomew Columbus, brother of the great explorer, visited Bristol, the largest fishing port in the northern Atlantic, he may well have heard the tales spun by Irish, Scottish, and Icelandic mariners about the 'foggy lands of the West'.

Who were the Ancestors of the American Indians?

Since the discovery of America, the question of the origins of the Indians has perplexed numerous historians. Were they descendants of Adam? If so, from which branch—from Shem, or from another patriarch? Were they related to the Carthaginians, the Spanish, the Irish? What if they were really 'hidden Jews', driven out after the revolts in Judea in 70 and 133? The latter hypothesis was seriously defended in October 1978 when Cyrus Gordon, deciphering a tablet unearthed in Tennessee, read 'for the Land of Judea'. But in fact the Siberian origins of the American Indians is now generally accepted, since it was confirmed by studies of blood types.

In search of the first American

The search for a true native of the United States long beguiled the American mind: such a discovery would mean the spiritual emancipation of the New World from the Old. Since no proof existed, a man finally invented some. In 1869 George Hull, a tobacco farmer from the Syracuse region of New York found buried in his field a giant statue of a man carved into the gypsum. The scientists of the day deduced that America's earliest inhabitants were unusually tall, and had typically European features. A few months later, the hoax was exposed: the statue was a fraud, carved by Hull himself. The 'fossil' is now on view at the Farmer's Museum at Cooperstown, New York.

hen Europeans first arrived in North America, the continent's population numbered only about one million. The inhabitants were spread out over immense territories, and lacked the technology of the Europeans. These mostly nomadic peoples often found that the only way to resist the colonists' inexorable advance was through armed resistance.

The land of codfish

Early in the sixteenth century scores of European fishing boats congregated off the coast of Newfoundland, and each spring Basque, Portuguese, English and French fishermen netted huge hauls of cod from spawning grounds at the confluence of ocean currents off the island's coast. With over one hundred fast days observed each year, Catholic Europe consumed vast quantities of fish.

The discovery of this fishing paradise probably dates from the late fifteenth century, though it may have been known to the Norsemen. The first probable visit that has been documented is that of João Cortereal, a Portuguese captain, in 1472-1474.

Although the ship's log was lost, several years after his voyage the Portuguese appointed Captain Cortereal governor of the Azores, in recognition of his having led the Portuguese to *La Terra do Bacalhau*, the land of codfish.

A Danish source confirms that two Norwegian pilots led a voyage to Greenland at about the same time. Of course, it is also possible that some unknown fishermen discovered the site while following a shoal of fish through British or Icelandic waters. A storm, a captain's sudden decision, or even a sailor's tale overheard in a port town may have led fishermen to the 'the land of codfish'. In any case, by the early sixteenth century the pilots of fishing vessels were remarkably familiar with prevailing winds in the northern Atlantic, and fleets did not hesitate to sail across the ocean.

The Cabots: a route to China?

Had those fishermen any idea that Newfoundland was the threshold of the New World? On the island they met Indians who helped them preserve their catch of cod, traded with them, and offered the fishermen their women. Sometimes boats strayed towards the mainland or the Gulf of St Lawrence, but rarely any farther. These fishing captains were concerned with increasing the size of their catch and keeping up friendly relations with the Indians; there was little to motivate such men to penetrate the dense forests that loomed beyond the coast, or to risk settling for the winter in such a harsh, forbidding land. And even fishermen knew that exploration was an expensive, time-consuming proposition that required a wealthy patron. The Genoese captain John Cabot had both the necessary money and the time. Backed by Bristol merchants, he set out in May 1497 with a crew of twenty, and sailed along the Labrador coast. In the course of a second expedition, however, John Cabot disappeared with cargo and crew. His son, Sebastian, funded by the English king, Henry VII, attempted the same voyage in 1503 with a crew of three hundred men, probably with the intention of founding a colony on the lands his father had glimpsed. His exact

Preserving Cod in the Sixteenth Century

In the days before refrigeration, cod fishermen relied on two different preserving methods, both still used today. In the first method, the freshly caught cod was gutted (the tongue being set aside) on the ship's bridge, thrown into the hold, rubbed with salt, and stacked in tall piles. The second method involved unloading the cod on a Newfoundland beach; they were then salted and dried for several weeks in the brisk sea air. Thus preserved, the cod would keep for many months, and could be sold throughout Europe.

Like his father, John, before him, Sebastian Cabot sailed up the coast of the Americas seeking a passage to India.

route along the North American coastline is not known, but it appears that Cabot sailed up as far as the fifty-eighth parallel. After that voyage Sebastian left England and entered the service of Spain. In fact the Cabots were not so much interested in establishing colonies as in discovering the Northwest Passage, a sea route from Europe to the fabled Indies. Sir Martin Frobisher attempted the same feat in 1576, followed by John Davis in 1587.

The failure of the Portuguese

Envious of Spain's conquests in America, the Portuguese also undertook new expeditions, hoping to discover gold. Gaspar de Cortereal followed the same itinerary as his father João, but veered south after reaching Newfoundland (1500). Gaspar and his brother Miguel probably made landfall on the shores of New England, but the exact site is uncertain, for the pair disappeared in the course of the expedition, from which only a few survived. The discouraged Portuguese turned to the southern regions of America, leaving the north to the English and French.

In the service of the French Crown

Involved in costly wars in Italy, the French Crown had not thought to sponsor expeditions overseas—at least, not until the discoveries of Columbus, and the gold that subsequently poured into Spain's coffers, excited French ambitions. Francis I, eager to check Spain's monopoly in the New World, turned to Giovanni da Verrazano, a Florentine navigator. Verrazano was already well known among the businessmen of Lyons, who looked favourably on voyages of discovery. Merchants in particular were becoming excited by the first amazing descriptions of the strange worlds across the seas. They dreamed of spices, silk, and above all gold, and readily volunteered to finance expeditions to America or the Indies. In Lyons, Rouen and Dieppe, merchants and bankers invested in Verrazano's plan. Francis was more prodigal with encouragement than with funds, but he hoped that the Florentine would bring France glory, if not gold. As for Verrazano himself, his *Relation* of the voyage shows that he was motivated more by curiosity than by a thirst for fame and profit.

Martin Frobisher thought he had discovered the rumoured Northwest Passage when he sighted a 'strait', which was in fact a bay located near Baffin Island.

From Carolina to Nova Scotia

Verrazano set sail for America on 17 January 1524 aboard *La Dauphine*, a vessel lent to him by Francis I. An uneventful crossing brought the ship just short of the Carolina coast. Verrazano decided to steer a northerly course, hugging the coastline in an attempt to find a passage. His very precise account allows us to identify such sites as today's New York and Newport. Verrazano was particularly fascinated by the Indians he encountered on his journey: their blooming health, their gaiety, the warm welcome they gave to strangers astonished him. Verrazano sailed as far as Cape Breton Island, then headed east, along the New-foundland coast. He christened these newly discovered lands 'Francesca', in honour of his adopted country.

Although his voyage was remarkable in many respects, Verrazano did not return with information likely to stimulate the Crown's interest or investment in further explorations.

The Florentine undertook a second expedition in 1526, sponsored by Jean Ango, a shipper from Dieppe. Though he failed to discover a passage to China, Verrazano returned with a rich cargo of furs, which excited hopes for a lucrative trade. During his third voyage —to the Antilles— in 1528, Verrazano was reportedly killed on a beach in a battle with Indians. The memory of the first European to explore America's East Coast lives on in the Verrazano Narrows Bridge, one of the largest in New York.

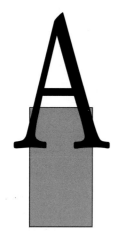

*A*s they had done in Central and South America, the Spanish preceded other European nations in North America. Their voyages of conquest resulted in the establishment of Spanish provinces, which became centres of Latin, Catholic culture. But the expansion of the United States into the West in the nineteenth century put an end to the Spanish presence in North America.

Engraving by Théodore de Bry depicting the village of Secoton, Virginia, and its vegetable garden.

Horses and Indians

It was probably during Coronado's expeditions that some Spanish horses escaped from their camps, and reverted to the wild. Fascinated by these strange animals, the Indians captured and retamed them. Thus in the seventeenth century, the horse spread up North America to the Great Plains, dramatically changing the Indians' way of life.

112

First steps in Florida

In the wake of Columbus's first voyages, pilots of Spanish vessels grew familiar with the courses of the trade winds, and the conquest of the New World began in earnest. In 1507 the conquistadors occupied the Caribbean islands, and within a few years, the last of the Indians' gold reserves had been shipped off to Spain. Certain enterprising adventurers lent an attentive ear to the Indians' tales of fabulously rich kingdoms beyond the seas. While Cortés prepared his expedition to Mexico, another Spanish explorer, Juan Ponce de León, fitted out a ship and sailed north. The course he charted was no accident—he was almost certainly guided by information gleaned from the Arawak Indians, a Caribbean tribe that traded on a regular basis with their American neighbours. In 1513 Ponce de León reached uncharted territory about one hundred kilometres from his starting point in Puerto Rico. He disembarked on 2 April, claiming the land, which he christened 'Florida', for the Spanish Crown. The expedition then sailed along the East Coast, encountered Indians, and turned back. A second mission in 1521 ended tragically. Ponce de León's crew skirmished with Indians, the captain himself was gravely injured, and his men were forced to flee.

Hostile Indians

Yet in spite of this setback, the Spaniards refused to give up. Lucas Vasquez de Ayllon returned in 1521 and sailed part of the way up the East Coast, proving that Florida was not an island, but the peninsula of a much larger landmass. Gold fever kept the Spanish coming. Unperturbed by Indians and other risks, in April 1528 Panfilo de Narvaez and his crew of four hundred arrived in Tampa Bay in western Florida. Narvaez plunged into the interior, sure that fabulous wealth would be his reward. After months of relentless effort, the exhausted Spaniards decided to return to the coast. At Tallahassee, in northwestern Florida, they built five small launches to take them along what is now the Gulf Coast, towards Mexico. They were shipwrecked off Texas, and the few survivors were adopted by local Indians. Many years later, a handful of these Spaniards, including Estevanito—a now famous Arab slave—and Alvar Nuñez Cabeza de Vaca, finally made their way back to Mexico.

The last Spanish foray into Florida took place in 1539, organized by one of Pizarro's comrades, Hernando de Soto. He boarded ship with a crew of five hundred, two hundred horses, and several missionaries. Inspired by the exploits of Cortés and Pizarro, de Soto was convinced that the discovery of unknown lands would win him fame and riches. The Spaniards landed in Tampa Bay, but the Indians did not welcome them with open arms. De Soto contended with guerilla attacks from the Florida tribes as he marched up the peninsula, and later met with more hostile Indians as he pushed west into the interior, towards what the Indians had described as a giant river. The expedition crossed the southern Appalachian Mountains and continued due west, though they lacked supplies. Having crossed the Mississippi, an exhausted de Soto died near the Arkansas River. His successor, Luis de Moscoso, did not dare brave the immense plains that stretched out before him; he turned back to the Gulf Coast, where he ordered ships to be built.

In 1541 three hundred and ten survivors straggled back to Cuba. The failure of the expedition was a terrible blow, after the efforts expended to mount it. With its hostile Indians, inhospitable climate, and not a nugget of gold to be found, Florida seemed unfavourable to colonization, and the Spaniards turned away from it, temporarily leaving the way open for the French.

Spanish Florida stretches West

In 1562 Jean Ribault landed at the mouth of the St Johns River in northern Florida with five hundred French Protestants. Two years

later, a second expedition relieved the first. Led by René de Laudonnière, the French settlers built Fort Caroline and traded with the Timucua Indians. These prudent colonists kept to the coast, and showed little inclination to explore. When news reached Spain of the French presence in Florida, the Spanish king commanded that the Protestant colony be extirpated. On 8 September 1565 Pedro Menendez de Avilés and his men besieged Fort Caroline; the surviving colonists were sent back to Europe. To safeguard against other incursions, the Spanish settled a few of their own colonists on the coast. They were soon joined by Franciscan missionaries dispatched to convert the Indians. In the seventeenth century the Spanish built a fort at Pensacola, near the mouth of the Mississippi. Spanish Florida thus stretched far to the west, and the territory did not fall into British hands until after the Treaty of Paris in 1763.

Another engraving by Theodore de Bry showing a village being attacked at night. The bows and arrows of the Indians proved to be a weak defence against the arquebus carried by the Europeans.

The myth of Cibola

While Spain was making inroads in Florida, a conquistador called Nuño de Guzman advanced into the northern Aztec empire and established New Galicia in the Sierra Madre area, in northern Mexico. The Spanish had reached the outer limits of the Aztecs' dominions, but the vast barren region did not encourage colonization; only the mines at Zacatecas roused the Spaniards' interest. Guzman brought in his wake a number of adventurers ready to go to any lengths to win a share of glory and empire. Back in Spain Cabeza de Vaca had already spread the myth of Cibola, the Seven Cities of Gold, site of the Fountain of Youth and home of the Amazons, a tribe of fierce female warriors. The conquistadors, victims of gold fever since the days of Cortés, readily believed such tales, tallying as they did with stories from the mediaeval oral tradition as well as with ancient Greek and Roman legends. One Spanish expedition, over which something of a mystery hangs, may however have reached the Hopi and Zuni villages of the Arizona plateau. Friar Marcos de Niza, the only man to come back alive, swore he saw the fabled cities of Cibola glittering in the sun.

From the Great Plains to California

Intrigued by the old friar's story, Cortés sent one of his officers, Francisco Vasquez de Coronado, to the north. The captain did not find Cibola. Instead, in 1540 he discovered the mouth of a river he christened the Colorado. For two years, until 1542, Coronado explored a large portion of what is now the American Southwest, battling Indians who fought from fortresses that Coronado called *pueblos*. In his final excursion northward,

Pocahontas, the daughter of Chief Powhatan.

Coronado reached present-day Kansas, beheld the Great Plains with their herds of buffalo, and may even have gone so far as the mouth of the Arkansas River. One of his lieutenants, Hernando de Alvarad, discovered the pueblo Acoma, 'the city of heaven'. None of the territories Coronado and his men explored seemed particularly attractive. These generally arid lands, far from the Spaniards' Mexican base, held only hostile Indians; there was not a gold mine to be found. Vast expanses of southwestern America became part of Spain's Mexican empire, but the area was only settled by a handful of missionaries and a few retired soldiers married to Indian women.

From their base in northern Mexico the Spanish also organized expeditions along the Pacific coast. Navigators explored Baja California, and in 1542 Juan Rodriguez Cabrillo may have pushed as far north as the Monterey peninsula, just south of where San Francisco is today. In 1602 and 1603, the Spanish occupied Monterey Bay, and founded a trading post where ships could call before sailing to the Philippines. A popular belief held that 'California' was the name of an island close to the earthly paradise, and the name first appeared on maps in the late sixteenth century. Already America was the stuff of legend.

The English in Virginia

Besides the Spanish and a few discharged French soldiers, a handful of Englishmen attempted to establish a settlement in the southern reaches of North America. Placed under the control of the Virginia Company of London, an expedition composed of 143 colonists embarked for Virginia late in 1606. Very quickly the personality of Captain John Smith dominated the group. Until August 1609 Smith successfully guided his colony through outbreaks of malaria and typhus, famine and other hardships. Fortunately for the settlement, the Algonquin Indians proved accommodating. Pocahontas, the daughter of the Algonquin chief Powhatan, married a settler named Thomas Rolfe, sealing the friendship between the two peoples. She later accompanied her husband to England. When Smith finally sailed back to London, he left behind a small fort of twenty dwellings called Jamestown, and five hundred settlers who would have to face many more cruel trials.

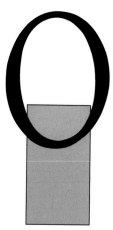

O n 1 September 1557, Jacques Cartier, the first great French explorer of North America, breathed his last in his home port of St Malo at the age of seventy. A founding father of Canada, Jacques Cartier belonged to the generation of great European navigators who in the sixteenth century braved unknown seas, urged on by dreams of discovery.

The king and the seafarer

Little is known of Cartier's private life except that his wife's family belonged to the St Malo bourgeoisie. Jacques Cartier learned the art of piloting the hard way—while at sea. When still very young he sailed out of St Malo to the Newfoundland cod fisheries. His marriage raised Cartier in the social hierarchy, and opened the way to a more illustrious career than that of a fishing-boat captain.

Familiar with Newfoundland's seas, Cartier thought it possible to navigate farther west, and discover, perhaps, a swifter route towards Cathay and its fabled riches. Cartier succeeded in convincing King Francis I that his project was worthwhile, particularly since the other routes were then guarded by Spanish and Portuguese vessels. In the end, the king allocated six thousand pounds for Cartier's expedition to discover the famous Northwest Passage (see p. 225). Cartier encountered considerable difficulty recruiting his crew of sixty, and fitting out two ships. But he set sail on 20 April 1534, the men having heard Mass and duly written their last wills and testaments.

Along the coast of Labrador

A fresh wind blew the ships to Newfoundland in just twenty days. The pilots, sailing familiar seas, knew the route by heart. Once in American waters, ice delayed the fleet. In the first week of June, the French ships skirted the island's northern coast and sailed into unknown waters—the Gulf of St Lawrence. As was the custom, the ships hugged the coastline. But the shores looked so forbidding that Cartier altered his course and sailed instead along the western coast of Newfoundland, a decision his men greeted with a sigh of relief. Indeed, on these exploratory expeditions captains always strove to reassure crews, who panicked easily when navigating in unfamiliar seas. They progressed south without incident, sailing from island to island, when suddenly a cape came into view. 'We named it Cape Hope, for the hope it inspired that we would find a passage there,' wrote Cartier in his log. From the shore, Indians signalled to the ships to land. The next day, Indian canoes surrounded the French vessels 'making us understand that they wanted to trade with us'. The exchanges concluded, Cartier continued his voyage until he reached another bay, where he halted for several days.

The discovery of the St Lawrence River

In the Bay of Gaspé while restocking their water supplies, the Frenchmen met more Indians who had 'come to fish for mackerel'. Ashore, Cartier planted a cross with the words 'Vive le Roi de France' (Long live the King of France). The Indians disapproved: their chief 'gestured at the land all around as if to say that it belonged to him, and that we ought not to place the cross in the ground without his permission'. However, by a ruse, Cartier managed to seize the chief's two sons, who were pressed into service as guides. A few days later, Cartier's vessels fetched up at the mouth of a mighty river. The captain consulted with his men, for the powerful current led him to believe that they had discovered the passage to Cathay. Their mission accomplished, they could sail home. It was now August, and high time to set out on the return voyage if the fleet was to avoid being trapped in the ice. On 5 September 1534, after 137 days at sea, Cartier landed safely in France.

The explorer was welcomed warmly. He presented his sovereign with a map of his voyage. The two Indians played an important role in this scene, for having learned a few words of French from their captors, they made Cartier understand that beyond the passage he had discovered lay 'a land rich with gold'. The imaginations of the French courtiers were immediately fired, and the royal coffers were thrown open to fund an expedition.

Towards the interior

In May 1535, three vessels with a crew of 110 men put to sea from St Malo. Accompanying Cartier were several men of gentle birth who hoped to make their fortune in the New World. By the end of August the fleet sailed into the St Lawrence River, guided by the two Indians. Cartier landed in Stadaconé, the site of present-day Quebec, where the nomadic Indians rejoiced at the Frenchmen's return. The pair of captives declared that they had been well treated. Yet the joyful homecoming was tempered somewhat by Cartier's obstinate insistence that they continue to sail up the river. In fact the Indians feared that the French would ally themselves with neighbouring tribes. The natives resorted to magic to dissuade the French, but Cartier was not to be put off. He set out with one ship on 19 September, and navigated as far as Hochelaga, the site of present-day Montreal. He visited Indian villages, and observed that the natives cultivated a kind of corn, which they stored in corn lofts. Impressed by the Frenchmen's weapons, the Indians attributed magic powers to these strange white men. They even obliged Cartier to lay hands on the sick. But the captain never lost sight of his primary purpose; he asked to be led to the summit of Mont-Royal (from which the modern city derives

An Indian remedy for scurvy

'Our Captain (Jacques Cartier), strolling over the ice, observed a band of men, one of whom had been ill ten days before with [scurvy], for one of his legs about the knee had been swollen to the size of a two-year-old child, his nerves stretched, his teeth rotted and falling out. When the Captain saw him well and happy, he hoped to learn how he had been healed: the Indian replied that he had partaken of the juice and pulp of the leaf of a certain tree, which had healed him. The Indian sent two women to find some of the leaves, and show us how to peel the leaf, boil the pulp, then drink the liquid for two days, and place the pulp on the legs; they called the tree 'ameda' ".

From the *Voyage of Jacques Cartier to the Isles of Canada*

114

its name). The Indians explained the local topography with gestures and sign language, and gave Cartier to understand that other peoples inhabited lands far to the west. Gazing at the wide, wooded horizon, Cartier must have realized what an enormous task it would be to reach the shores of fabled Cathay.

The end of a dream

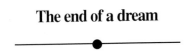

Back in Quebec, Cartier had a small fort built in which he and his men could spend the winter. The river froze over in November, and the Frenchmen's ordeal began in earnest. Enfeebled by weeks of malnutrition, the men fell ill with scurvy, and many died. Cartier himself would have been a victim, had not the Indians treated the survivors with a tea brewed from the leaves of the American white cedar. Throughout the long winter, Cartier conversed with the Indian chiefs, garnering what information he could. But the chiefs were distrustful. Try as he might, Cartier learned very little about a passage to the west.

In July 1536, the fleet reached France. Cartier presented the king with a few gold nuggets, and told him legends he had heard about gold in the Saguenay River. Cartier dreamed of returning there, and founding a 'New France'. But the king was at war, and had more pressing concerns than Canada. It was only in 1540 that Cartier was asked to go on another expedition, to discover gold and establish a settlement. A Protestant nobleman, Jean-François Roberval, was given command of the expedition.

Cartier's third voyage proved a disappointment. He was welcomed warmly by the Indians, but for lack of an interpreter, the navigator's sojourn on Mont-Royal yielded little useful information. He did collect a few diamonds, however, before returning to Quebec. Cartier's account of his travels concludes with his return to the little colony, but we know that he sailed back to France in June 1542. The 'diamonds' he had picked up turned out to be quartz. The king was annoyed at the small return on his investment, and refused to sponsor any more of Cartier's projects. The great captain's disgrace was complete. Cartier and Canada soon sank into oblivion.

In 1535 Jacques Cartier sailed up the Saint Lawrence to Stadoconé, today Quebec, then continued on his route to Hochelaga. There a village was built at the foot of a mountain that Cartier ramed Mont-Royal, or Montreal.

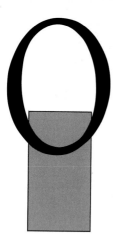

O n 13 April 1608, a small French vessel sailed up the St Lawrence River under the command of Samuel de Champlain. It was the captain's third voyage 'to the land of Canada', and he had resolved to establish a small fur-trading post, and to make forays into the hinterland. At the point where the river narrows, hailed by Kennebec Indians, the French moored their boat and built the town of Quebec.

ABITATION. DE QVEBECQ

In 1608, Samuel de Champlain decided to set up a 'residence' in Quebec, as the site seemed to him to be worth defending as well as settling.

The land of the Algonquins and the Iroquois

In July 1608, when he settled in Quebec, Champlain already possessed a good deal of information about the interior, thanks to the Algonquin Indians with whom the French maintained good trade relations. That summer, the settlers built a small fort. Severe winter weather soon brought all activity to a halt; the French simply hibernated, biding their time. Through the cold months the Algonquins told tales of a powerful nation to the south, the 'vipers' or Iroquois. Champlain resolved to explore these uncharted lands south of the St Lawrence. On 28 June 1609 Champlain and two other Frenchmen accompanied a band of Algonquins on a military expedition. The Indians were pleased to have in their midst these 'bearded men with fire sticks'. On the shores of the lake that now bears his name, Champlain spied several dozen Iroquois braves advancing towards them. The Iroquois insulted the Algonquins, and a battle ensued. The French guns astonished the enemy; leaving one of their chiefs lying dead, the Iroquois took to their heels. Nevertheless, the expedition stopped there, for the Algonquins thought it imprudent to advance further into Iroquois territory. The Iroquois remembered Champlain's gunshots. For a century and a half, the tribe remained mortal enemies of the French.

The following year Champlain determined to organise another expedition on the St Lawrence River, but the mission did not set out until March 1611. The French party sailed down the river, hoping to discover the route to the Orient; the spot where they stopped was christened 'La Chine'—China. Champlain also visited the island of Montreal. But the most important aspect of the voyage, second only to the accurate mapping of the river, was the

The man who mapped New England

Born in Brouage around 1570, and raised during the bitter Wars of Religion, Samuel de Champlain took to sea while still a boy. Brave and ambitious, he sailed on transatlantic voyages, and may have journeyed as far as Brazil. At Honfleur in 1603 Champlain entered the service of Du Pont-Gravé, a Norman entrepreneur in search of commercial opportunities in Canada. In May,

Champlain landed at the little trading post of Tadoussac, ascended the Saguenay River, and traded with the local Indians. The following year another voyage took Champlain to Acadia—the area of what is now New Brunswick and Nova Scotia. There he explored a region that appeared to him less harsh than the shores of the St Lawrence. Staying close to the coast, he ascended the Penobscot River, spent the winter of 1604-1605 among the Indians, and in the spring sailed down as far as Cape Cod. An able geographer, Champlain drew a highly accurate map of what is today New England.

Although they came to explore new lands, the French ended up defending their allies, the Algonquins and the Hurons, from the fearsome Iroquois.

The First *Coureur de Bois*

On 13 June 1611 Champlain met a band of Algonquins. A young brave stepped out from the party. 'I recognized my young man, now dressed like a savage, who praised the way the savages had treated him', Champlain wrote later of the young Frenchman; 'he told me all he had seen during his time with them.' Etienne Brûlé had been left by Champlain to spend the winter with the Indians, as a sign of friendship. Brûlé lived with the Indians for eighteen years. He spoke their language fluently and adopted their way of life. He travelled great distances with the Indians, going as far as the Susquehanna River. He was the first white man to reach Lake Michigan and Lake Superior, in 1621-1622. He was killed by the Hurons, his adopted tribe, who suspected him of establishing relations with their enemy, the Iroquois.

encounter with the Hurons and Algonquins, who became allies of the French. As a sign of confidence, following the Indian tradition, Champlain left a young lad called Etienne Brûlé to winter over with the Algonquins to learn their language and customs. Back in Quebec, Champlain gathered his notes and began to write an account of all he had seen. In January 1613 his travels were published in France. The author gained considerable fame, and the French elite showed growing interest in the adventures of their countrymen's little settlement in the Canadian snows.

The discovery of the Great Lakes

With four experienced explorers and an Indian guide, Champlain set out for Huron country in March 1613. The trip covered hundreds of kilometres of unexplored territory. The party descended the Ottawa River, passing from lakes to rivers, carrying weapons and supplies on their backs. They spent some time with Tessouat, an Algonquin chief. The men were also received with open arms in Huron villages. Champlain believed himself to be on the verge of discovering the river that would take them to the Orient. But what he found was in fact a vast inland sea: the Great Lakes. Champlain questioned the Indians, who told him of a mighty river that flowed towards the south. Upon his return to Quebec, the French captain prepared his final expedition; and the better to understand the Hurons he brought along an interpreter, Etienne Brûlé. In July 1615 Champlain, Brûlé, and two other Frenchmen travelled to Huron country, where they spent the win-

ter. In the summer of 1616, the party marched or navigated with the help of Huron guides. They met other Indians as well: the Tobacco Nation, the Neutrals, and other tribes—but their search for the great river was in vain. Champlain was beginning to have an inkling of North America's vastness. Without men, without money to purchase gifts for the Indians, it would be useless, he decided, to proceed any further.

Champlain returned to Quebec and attempted to establish a colonization programme. He petitioned the Crown for help, but the flow of French immigrants to Canada was slight and the English had no difficulty seizing Quebec for themselves. When in 1632 the colony was returned to France, Champlain journeyed back to Canada. But the explorer was weak and ill. Two years later he died in the land he had done so much to promote.

Frenchmen in the service of England

Champlain's posterity were those children of the forest, the *coureurs de bois*—the trappers. The few immigrants who trickled into Canada were young men who took up the only enticing and lucrative occupation available: fur trading. Small groups of Frenchmen descended the waterways into the interior. They cultivated relations with the Indians, with whom they spent the long winters. Although most were illiterate, these men learned Indian languages, and adapted remarkably well to life in the woods. Few left much more than their names in history books, though the lives of some are better known. Pierre Radisson was just twenty when the Iroquois captured

him. He lived among them for several years. When he finally returned to his colony, he used information gleaned from the Indians to set out with his brother-in-law, Medart Chouart des Groseillers, to explore the Great Lakes. They were the first white men to venture into the region of Lake Superior. The two wintered with the Hurons, who told them of a salt sea to the north: Hudson Bay.

When they returned home, the pair were pursued by the French authorities, who frowned upon individual expeditions of this sort. This strict policy led the pair to enter the service of the English. Chouart des Groseillers accompanied an English vessel to Hudson Bay in 1669. The following year, the English erected a trading post there.

Captured by the Sioux

In those days French trappers roved all over the interior and navigated on the Great Lakes. During the summer of 1680 Daniel Greysolon Duluth settled on the western shore of Lake Superior. As they were marching west, three of his men encountered a band of Sioux transporting salt. The Indians declared that the salt came from a large saltwater lake twenty days' march west. Duluth surmised that he was on the point of discovering the 'Sea of the West'. He and a few men headed southwest and reached the Mississippi. There, they heard that the Sioux were holding some French captives. Duluth changed his plan in order to rescue his compatriots, Father Hennepin and two trappers who were exploring the Mississippi basin with De La Salle (see p. 119). He ultimately abandoned the expedition to the west for fear of the Indians.

The pilgrims of the *Mayflower*

Although they cannot, strictly speaking, be considered explorers, it is impossible, when harking back to the heroic era of America's colonization, not to mention the arrival of the Pilgrim Fathers aboard that celebrated ship, the *Mayflower* on 26 December 1620. Driven out of England by religious persecution, the 102 emigrants, including 41 Puritans, settled on the shore near Cape Cod and there founded Plymouth, the first permanent colony of New England.

117

Around 1660 King Louis XIV resolved to expand France's overseas empire, to magnify his own and his kingdom's grandeur. His dynamic administrator in America, Jean Talon, and Talon's successor, Frontenac, reorganized the young country's economy, attracted thousands of colonists, and pushed French frontiers in the New World as far as the Mississippi.

Explorers among the Indians

From the moment the first Europeans arrived in the New World, they eagerly sought out the continent's native inhabitants, the Indians. Gavriel Sagard, a member of the reformed Franciscan order, lived for many years among the Hurons, as did the Jesuit priest Brebeuf in the years 1635-1648. Both French missionaries learned the Indian tongues, and though obviously prejudiced in their hosts' favour, they left invaluable records of how the Indians lived before the Europeans changed that culture forever. English colonists also left remarkable descriptions, like those of William Penn on the Delaware Indians, or William Bartram's commentaries on the Cherokee. The Frenchman Le Page du Pratz, long a neighbour of the Natchez, was one of the few to witness the rites of their solar religion and to observe their highly organized society. The body of information collected by these 'ethnological explorers' permitted the American author James Adair to write the first history of the Indians in 1775, in which he defended the Indian cause.

Tobacco growing guaranteed rapid prosperity to the English colonies that were springing up along the Atlantic coast. Shown here is William Penn, founder of the Quaker colony in Pennsylvania.

The first expedition to the Mississippi

'The land of the Illinois was first discovered by *coureurs de bois*. They found the climate very pleasant, one of the best they knew. There were many salt springs where wild bulls came, and deer.' The administrator of New France, Talon, disclosed that in the 1670s the French were on the threshold of a new world. The land of the Illinois Indians lay south of the Great Lakes where the forests were less dense, with beautiful clearings where buffalo herds gathered. Indians told trappers tales of a great sea and a river so mighty the natives called it in their tongue 'Father of All Waters'.

Talon's successor, the Comte de Frontenac, was more ambitious. He dreamed of an American empire, of gold mines, and of a passage to the west. In 1672 he entrusted Louis Joliet and Father Marquette with a mission 'to discover the great river that the Indians call Michissipi, which is thought to empty into the sea of California'. The expedition was organized at Michilimackinac, an island in the straits connecting Lake Huron and Lake Michigan, a favourite meeting place for Indians and trappers. Marquette and Joliet set out in May 1673 with a party of *coureurs de bois* and Indians who paddled birch-bark canoes. They journeyed along the far western shore of Lake Michigan, navigated south on the Fox River to the Wisconsin River, then south and west into the Mississippi.

The great plans of the Sieur de La Salle

The descent of the Mississippi began. The party travelled due south, occasionally encountering bands of Indians. When they got as far as the Arkansas River, 'Marquette and Joliet deliberated', fearing that they might 'throw themselves into the grasp of the Spanish in Florida if they advanced any farther'. The return journey was much more difficult, for the party had to travel upstream, against the current. The weeks-long ordeal took its toll on Father Marquette, who died en route. Joliet made his way back to Lake Michigan, and from there to the St Lawrence. Unfortunately Joliet's canoe capsized on the river, and all the expedition's precious papers and maps were lost. Nonetheless, the Mississippi had been discovered and navigated. It was to be left to the Sieur Robert Cavelier de La Salle to complete the exploration begun by Joliet and Marquette.

Joliet's reports confirmed La Salle's ambition to become an explorer. He was familiar with the West, having come to Canada in 1668 after completing his studies at a Jesuit school in his native Rouen. Like most other young colonists, La Salle took up fur trading. He spent several months at Fort

Frontenac on Lake Ontario, where trappers whiled away their time in bad weather. His sojourn at the fort gave La Salle an opportunity to question men accustomed to navigating on the 'inland sea', and he formed many great plans. Although he lacked financial backing to realize these plans, La Salle eventually won the confidence of Frontenac, who introduced him to Colbert—Louis XIV's chief minister—when he returned to France in 1674.

Exploration or trade?

Frontenac presented La Salle as his man in Canada, an individual with interesting projects. He credited La Salle with cleverness and great intelligence, able to undertake 'all expeditions and discoveries with which one might care to entrust him'. For his part, La Salle sought to obtain help from the Crown. He proposed to a royal minister that he, La Salle, would organize exploratory expeditions and maintain Fort Frontenac in exchange for being named master of the outpost and nearby islands. Louis XIV accepted this proposal; he ennobled La Salle on 13 May 1675, bidding him 'to work at the discovery of the western part of our New France'. The young sovereign was ambitious, and the prospect of an immense American empire could only please him. La Salle was given money. The king also asked La Salle to take with him to priests in order to evangelize the Indians. One of them, Father Hennepin, wrote a very lively account of his travels. On 14 July 1678 La Salle returned to Canada, bringing with him thirty men and two officers, and immediately took possession of his new lands.

Before undertaking any explorations, La Salle first filled his coffers by leading several fur-collecting expeditions. In 1679 he had a large, solid ship built, which he christened the *Griffon* in honour of the Frontenac arms. The Indians were astounded at the size of La Salle's 'great canoe'. It was launched on 7 August 1679, with seven cannon and a displacement of forty-five tons. La Salle's plans for the ship were still a mystery. Would the *Griffon* be used for exploration or trade? A few days later, the ship set sail with a cargo of furs. La Salle was never to see the *Griffon* again, for it was wrecked, and later destroyed by Ottawa Indians. To add to his worries, in the winter of 1681, La Salle learned that his possessions had been seized by his creditors. He did not let himself be dispirited by these disasters, and hoped to recoup his losses through new discoveries.

The frontispiece to Father Hennepin's travel book, depicting the trip down the Mississippi.

The Natchez, a theocratic tribe

While journeying along the lower Mississippi, the Sieur de La Salle encountered the Natchez Indians, the only theocratic tribe in North America, ruled by a prince named 'Sun'. Natchez society was strictly hierarchical. The family of Sun was surrounded by nobles called 'Honourables', and by Indians whom the French called 'Puants' (malodorous). The Puants always married a spouse from a higher rank; thus Natchez society was perpetually renewed. But they were wiped out in 1739 when they rebelled violently againt abuses perpetrated by the French.

The Indian pipe, a passport to peace

La Salle formed a party of resolute *coureurs de bois* and Indian guides, which proceeded through the village of Chicagon on the shores of Lake Michigan. The weather was icy and the countryside blanketed with snow. The party dragged their canoes along the snow for dozens of kilometres to the Illinois River, and from there navigated south to the Mississippi. They proceeded warily, for Indians were watching the French party closely. La Salle had taken care to pack his peace pipe, 'which is a sure passport among all the nations allied with the tribe that had bestowed it. The Indians believe great misfortune would befall any who violated the covenant of the peace pipe.' Their descent of the Mississippi was relatively uneventful, marked by the 'glare of the sun's rays, so strong in the countryside they had to cross

that the men were blinded for three whole days, and suffered such pain that they could rest neither by day nor by night'.

One morning La Salle encountered an Indian who was using a horse's leg as a tobacco bag. The Indian declared that he had brought the object back from a land where the men wore long hair and fought with long lances. The Frenchmen surmised that they were nearing Spanish territory. They continued past the village of the Arkansas Indians where Joliet had halted his expedition, and pushed on until they came to Natchez territory. Some days later, the party navigated into a broad delta. They split up into three groups, and on 8 April 1682 a canoe manned by half-starved Frenchmen paddled into the Gulf of Mexico. La Salle claimed the river—which he named after his patron, Colbert—and all the surrounding territory for France. It was christened Louisiana. Thus did a handful of adventurers offer their young sovereign an empire of forests and prairies as vast as Europe.

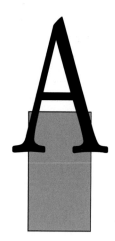

A s late as the eighteenth century, no one suspected how vast the North American continent truly was. European explorers were obsessed with reaching the 'Sea of the West', to open up a new route to Asia and its riches. But no one knew where this sea might lie.

Riding river roads

North America's dense, extensive forests with their innumerable rivers and lakes called for a special means of transportation, adapted to the environment. The Indians of the northeast, the Algonquins in particular, perfected the birchbark canoe. Once peeled from the tree, the bark was sewn with pine roots onto an ashwood frame. Pine tar made the craft watertight. Light to carry around falls and rapids, these canoes drew little water and could navigate the smallest streams. The *coureurs de bois* adopted this remarkable craft as they forged deeper into the West.

The push westward

Early in the eighteenth century the governor of Canada declared that 'the French were after beaver, not the Sea of the West' when they set out to explore beyond Lake Superior. In fact, the two projects were inseparable, for ever since the French had landed in North America, the fur trade had provided the wherewithal for their explorations. Back at the French Court, with the exception of a few enlightened minds, no ministers or courtiers evinced the slightest interest in exploration and discovery. Moreover, in the American provinces of New France and Louisiana, administrators actually feared any further expansion. They did not know how far the territory beyond their borders extended, but it could only be supposed ungovernable, as well as unexploitable, given the trickle of immigrants from France. Exploring the lands west of Lake Superior was left to adventurers, to *coureurs de bois*—trappers—or to a few military officers in quest of fame and fortune.

Before Father Marquette and Cavelier de La Salle decided to explore the southern reaches of the Great Lakes, ultimately to emerge in the Mississippi basin, the *coureurs de bois* kept to the northern shores of Lake Superior in search of furs. Two of these trappers, Pierre Radisson and Médard Chouart des Groseillers (see p. 117), explored the northwestern shore of Lake Superior from 1654 to 1656; they were followed by others, whose names have been lost, and by a few Jesuits. Proof of this French breakthrough came to light with the publication of a map of Lake Superior in a Jesuit volume dating from 1670-1671. The map gave the exact locations of Lake Nipigon and the mouth of the Kaministikwia River, rechristened French River in the eighteenth century.

'Not a single hole in the Wild West was spared from these strapping fellows,' is how George Ruxton expressed his opinion of trappers, the hunters of animal pelts.

Pressure from the English

The arrival of the English in the Hudson Bay in 1670 motivated the French to push even farther into the northwest. Indeed, the *coureurs de bois* settled all along the rivers of the Laurentian Highlands in order to intercept bands of Indian fur-traders taking skins to English forts on the bay. In 1678 Duluth established an outpost at the entrance to Lake Nipigon as a post house for French trappers. With the help of his

brother, Greysolon de La Tourette, Duluth had contacts with the Sioux and perhaps with the Assiniboines as well. And French River gave the *coureurs de bois* access to Lake Winnipeg, where they parleyed with the Cree Indians.

In July 1717 a young French officer, Rubutel de la Noue, was charged with consolidating the outposts on the edge of Lake Superior at the limit of the Canadian Shield. From those outposts the French governor, Vaudreuil, wished to organize an expedition to discover the 'Sea of the West'. However, geography was the least of Vaudreuil's preoccupations. His chief aim was to choke off fur supplies to the English forts on Hudson Bay.

The intrepid La Vérendrye family

The Indians had long spoken of a waterway that flowed from east to west, churned by rising and falling tides. *Coureurs de bois* repeated these tales to the authorities, who believed that the river would lead the French to the Pacific Ocean.

A Canadian, Pierre Gaultier de Varennes de la Vérendrye, offered to lead a party of fifty volunteer soldiers to search for the river. The French authorities granted him a monopoly on all the trading posts he established en route to the 'Sea of the West'. Governor de Beauharnais and the Count de Maurepas, the latter Secretary of the Navy and a fervent supporter of exploration, had full confidence in La Vérendrye. Yet for the La Vérendrye clan, father and sons, the main purpose of the expedition was not discovery, but profit; an objective shared by de Beauharnais, whose only thought was to increase the volume of furs handled by the French, and to ruin the English fur trade.

Vast prairies and plains

On 26 August 1731 Pierre La Vérendrye reached the western shore of Lake Superior. He had no inkling of the immensity of the Canadian wilderness, but he quickly perceived that the environment was harsh indeed. The men of his party, though used to severe conditions, refused to go further, fearing bad weather, early snows, and insufficient game. La Vérendrye resigned himself to spending the winter on the lake shore. The following spring, he pushed onward, building Fort Saint Charles and Fort Saint Pierre along the way. He left men at each site to trade with the Indians. The Indians, as was their custom, demanded gifts, so that much of the Frenchmen's merchandise had to be given away. The party continued onward into the vast prairie; soon they were some four thousand kilometres west of Montreal.

Despite numerous difficulties, the expedition forged ahead, urged on by La Vérendrye and his three sons. Far north on the Winnipeg River, they built Fort Maurepas (1741), and Fort La Reine on the Assiniboine River to the south. Having travelled to the heart of the Laurentian Highlands, the Frenchmen thought they were finally about to reach the Sea of the West. Their push towards the tundra from Lake Winnipeg allowed the French to intercept Indians taking furs to English trading posts, but the party never discovered the great river that was to open the way to the Pacific. The La Vérendrye father ans sons then turned their gaze toward the immense prairie that lay south of the Red River.

Alone against the Indians

The Frenchmen's progress in the Great Plains was far more difficult than in the Laurentian Highlands, where a multitude of lakes and rivers formed a fluvial highway intersected by easily crossed portages. There too the Assiniboine and Cree tribes lived in small, scattered bands that posed no special danger. The Plains, on the other hand, did not offer an extensive network of rivers and streams; and the local Indians proved unfriendly. During the summer of 1736 the Sioux attacked La Vérendrye's eldest son, Jean Baptiste, on an island in Lake of the Woods. They massacred the missionary and twenty trappers in revenge for La Vérendrye *père*'s policy of arming their sworn enemies, the Cree and Assini-

boine tribes. Pierre La Vérendrye and his party were understandably prudent when in 1738-1739 they pushed on to the Missouri River. La Vérendrye left two men with the Mandan tribe as a sign of confidence and friendship, but he was unable to travel beyond the river.

The dream dies in the Great Plains

La Vérendrye's son, Louis Joseph, adopted the same policy in 1742-1743, when he led an expedition into present-day South Dakota. With his younger brother and seven horsemen, the young La Vérendrye ventured forth into the grassy expanses of the Great Plains. He reached the Cheyenne River, and journeyed west for some days, despite the Indians' evident hostility. He halted in the Black Hills, not in the foothills

of the Rocky Mountains as reported in later accounts. Upon his son's return, the elder La Vérendrye returned east. Ill, exhausted, riddled with debt, Pierre La Vérendrye lived out his few remaining years in Montreal. But his sons Louis Joseph and Pierre continued the mission their father had undertaken years before. They consolidated the western forts in 1747, and navigated up the Saskatchewan River. The brothers pushed the frontier of France's American empire to its extreme limit; never had they been closer to the 'Western Sea'. But after their earlier setbacks, and with war breaking out in the east, the pair abandoned all hope of conquering the Great Plains and the towering Rockies, and of ever setting eyes upon the Pacific Ocean.

Located between Lake Ontario and Lake Erie, Niagara Falls was in Iroquois territory, under English protection. The 54 kilometre-long Niagara River currently forms part of the US-Canadian border.

While Samuel de Champlain's French expedition was exploring the shores of the St Lawrence, other Europeans were settling along the East Coast of America. The whole region had been named Virginia in 1584, in honour of Elizabeth I, the Virgin Queen. By the years 1720-1730, the territories had become crowded that the colinists started to look beyond the Appalachians.

Founded by the Dutch in 1626, New Amsterdam was conquered by the British in 1664 and re-named New York after the Duke of York, the future James II.

'Wilderness' and tobacco

After 1650 the notion of 'wilderness' took shape in the imaginations of the English colonists. The very word symbolized both the unorganized space of the forest and the world of the Indians. The settlers distinguished between 'wild' and 'civilized' territory, marked by limits separating the forest from the farmers' orderly planted fields. The strongly religious—often puritanical—character of many immigrants accentuated the aloofness of the colonies. Convinced that demons were everywhere present, the religious leaders encouraged the colonists to be self-sufficient. Finally, unlike the French, the English settlers were farmers, and quickly established trade links with England.

Towards the Appalachians

Commerce was England's major inducement to seek new territories. The demand for furs and, especially, shipbuilding timber, led colonists to plunge ever deeper into the continent's interior. In the 1700s, population growth and increased immigration forced the British colonies to expand as far as the Appalachians, and to envisage founding settlements beyond the mountain range. British explorations resulted from individual initiatives, often taken without consulting the local authorities, in response to local circumstances.

In the northeastern colonies, expansion occurred gradually, the European settlements in Nova Scotia and New England tending to avoid contacts with the Indians. However, the Connecticut River Valley abounded in furs, allowing hardy colonists to make large profits trading beaver skins in Narragansett territory. In 1633 John Old-

A mysterious forest, unpredictable Indians

For a long time the Dutch of New Amsterdam, the English Puritans of New England, and many other colonists, all clustered in settlements close to the seaboard. Unlike the French, who had forged ahead with exploring the new continent, the English colonists showed little interest in such expeditions. There are several explanations for their attitude. The wide estuaries of the East Coast betokened easy access to the interior, although in reality the Appalachians formed a formidable natural barrier. Via Lake Champlain the St Lawrence River could be reached from the Hudson, but the Lachine Rapids and French settlements along those shores discouraged any forays into the northwest. Overland access to the continent's interior was blocked by the Appalachian Mountains. Beyond that ancient range lay splendid waterways like the Ohio River (the Indian name Ohio means 'beautiful river') which flowed into the Mississippi Valley. And although they were not an impenetrable obstacle, the dense eastern forests were peopled with mysterious and (in the colonists' view) unpredictable Indians.

ham ventured into the region, followed by William Pynchon, the founder of Springfield, and later by John Prescott, the first to establish a trading post in Lancaster. The region's mighty forests tempted the colonists; woodmen cut down huge trees and transported the logs to the coast. But as the Puritans advanced in the Connecticut Valley, they encountered serious competition from Dutch settlers from Fort Orange (Albany) and New Amsterdam, and who had been trading furs with the Iroquois since 1616.

The Dutch and the Iroquois

Dutch trappers, called 'bushlopers', were used to venturing into Indian country. The authorities encouraged them to trade with the tribes, but as the English quickly perceived, the virtual absence of new immigrants from Holland put the Dutch in a weak position. They were obliged to put up with English competition. When New Amsterdam was annexed by the English in 1664 and became New York, the Iroquois signed a trade pact with the new masters of the American northeast. New York's governors, Dongan and later Bellomont, continued to rely on the network the Dutch had built up, notably on interpreters like Cornelius and Viele. Many of these men ventured as far as the Ohio River in the late seventeenth century, and attempted to disrupt the Indians' trade with the French, who were firmly implanted south of the Great Lakes. Unable to read or write, the Dutch interpreters left no records, but they gave much detailed information to the New York authorities, and prepared the way for English exploration of the Ohio Valley in the eighteenth century.

First expeditions

Farther south, efforts to explore the interior began in the 1650s with the expedition of Edward Bland and Captain Abraham Wood southwest of the Appomattox River. Accompanied by Indian guides, they reached the site of present-day Roanoke, and discovered an extraordinarily fertile land. Another expedition left Virginia in 1670, heading toward the southwestern Appalachians. The party of twenty colonists and five Indian guides, led by a young German called John Lederer, was the first to explore the Appalachian Piedmont, to record the

customs of the Cherokee people, and to open a trade route for Carolina merchants. In 1670-1671 Henry Woodward, a remarkable individual—a surgeon and adventurer, once compelled to crew aboard a pirate ship—navigated the Savannah River and formed friendly relations with the Creek and Chickasaw Indians.

The French lose ground

Early in the eighteenth century, British colonists realized that the French were expanding into the Mississippi Valley, and recognized the risk this posed for British settlements. English merchants feared French competition, even though better-quality British goods sold well among the Indians. Carolina's governor, James Moore, and merchants like Thomas Nairne pressed for British expansion beyond the Appalachians, and for a face-off with the French. Their aim was achieved through Britain's victory in the Seven Years War. By the 1763 Treaty of Paris, the King of France granted the eastern portion of the Mississippi Valley and Canada to England.

The revolt of the Indians

To mollify the Indians who had sided with France, the English allocated to them all the land west of the Allegheny Mountains. But settlers continued to filter into the Indian territories. The Indians were incensed by the conduct of the colonists who poured into Kentucky and the Ohio Valley. This land had previously been home to backwoodsmen and trappers, who maintained friendly relations with the natives. But in the years 1765-1770 eastern colonists turned envious eyes on these territories, and many families decided to try their luck west of the Appalachians. In Kentucky Daniel Boone blazed trails like the famous Wilderness Road that stretched from southwest Virginia to the southern banks of the Kentucky River through the Cumberland Gap. Boone embodied the settlers' impatience and desire to colonize the continent from sea to sea, a wish that was shared by statesmen like George Washington and Benjamin Franklin. Indeed Franklin believed agriculture would assure the colonies' economic future, a future that depended largely upon the development of the vast territories west of the Blue Ridge range of the Appalachians.

The Cumberland Gap

On behalf of the Loyal Land Company, Thomas Walker set out in search of new sites for immigrants to settle. Around 1748 he came upon a narrow passage in the Cumberland Mountains—part of the great Appalachian range. After 1750 thousands of colonists from Pennsylvania and Carolina funnelled through this pass, known as the Cumberland Gap, to settle on new lands in Kentucky.

Of all the Indian tribes, the Iroquois proved to be the most advanced but also, the cruellest. They were a sedentary farming people, who lived in longhouses.

THE MAN WHO BEHELD TWO OCEANS

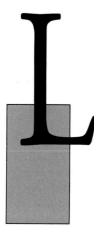

ate in the eighteenth century, by dint of extraordinary courage and tenacity, the Scotsman Alexander Mackenzie conquered the lonely and desolate vastness of the North American continent. He braved the frigid temperatures of the Rockies in winter, then, with the help of Indian guides, discovered the river that led him to the Pacific Ocean.

The *Bois Brûlés*

The *Bois Brûlés*—half-breeds of Indian and French-Canadian ancestry—were so called owing to their swarthy skin. These French-speaking Catholic buffalo hunters and fur traders formed an unusual community that settled west of the Great Lakes in the early nineteenth century. They preserved a nomadic way of life, and maintained good relations with their Indian neighbours. As guides, interpreters, and hunters the *bois brûlés* formed a nation of their own in the nineteenth century. Several bloody revolts, notably one led by Louis Riel in 1885, marked their resistance to English colonization in western Canada. The painter Paul Kane portrayed them in a Romantic light in the late 1840s.

Peter Pond's map

In 1776 Peter Pond, an American working for the Northwest Company, a fur-trading concern that competed directly with the Hudson Bay Company, built a post near Lake Athabasca where he intercepted Crees and Chippewas carrying skins to English trading posts on Hudson Bay. Always in the back of Pond's mind was the age-old dream of discovering the famous Northwest Passage. Pond got on well with the local Indians, who told him about the Arctic region; the trapper came to realize how immense that icy world truly was. The many trading posts that spread north from Lake Athabasca to the Great Slave Lake enjoyed just a few short months of mild weather before being plunged into the long Arctic night, to which the trappers were largely unaccustomed. The information he gleaned from Indians and trappers allowed Pond to map the Northwest Territories in 1787. One feature of this map was a river that flowed west from the Great Slave Lake, and ultimately emptied into the Pacific Ocean. Pond talked about his map with a young employee of the Northwest Company, recently arrived from his native Scotland, Alexander Mackenzie.

The River of Disappointment

Mackenzie spent the winter of 1788-1789 with Pond in a trading post on Lake Attrabasca. The American was certain that 'his' river flowed down into the Pacific, that the Rocky Mountains ended well before that point, and that a week's trek would suffice to complete the exploration. Brimming with energy and ambition, Mackenzie believed that the river would give Britain a new route to Asia. On 3 June 1789 in freezing weather, Mackenzie left for the Great Slave Lake and the descent of the river. The endless Arctic day let the party of five trappers and six Indians paddle their canoes from three o'clock in the morning until ten o'clock at night; they covered from 150 to 200 kilometres daily. In mid-July the expedition found itself bogged down in a swampy delta dotted with islands.

Ice floes

After paddling for several days in this watery maze, Mackenzie finally climbed up some rocks for a wider view. He saw blocks of ice which had broken free of an ice field that extended as far as the eye could see, spotted here and there with blue patches of ocean. But the ocean that stretched before the young explorer was not the warm Pacific, the goal of generations of adventurers who had sought the 'Western Sea'; instead, Mackenzie had opened the route to the glacial waters of the Arctic Ocean. The river he had navigated to reach it, the longest in Canada, would henceforth be known as the Mackenzie.

To return to Fort Chipewyan the explorer had to paddle back on that river for over 3300 kilometres. For two and a half months the party suffered terrible hardship, struggling to cover a mere fifty or sixty kilometres a day. When the men finally reached the fort at Lake Athabasca, the region was already blanketed with snow. Mackenzie harboured a bitter memory of what he called the 'River of Disappointment'.

While going down the river that led him to the Arctic and which today bears his name, Mackenzie confronted rapids, currents and many other natural obstacles.

124

Nonetheless, Mackenzie was widely praised for his achievement. He asked the Northwest Company for a year's leave which he spent in London studying astronomy and learning how to calculate longitude.

The harsh Rocky Mountains

Back at Fort Chipewyan in the autumn of 1792, Mackenzie organized a second expedition. He set off the following spring, heading southwest along the Peace River, with a party of nine volunteers and several dogs. Mackenzie's progress upstream was easy enough at first. But then the river reached the foothills of the Rockies and narrowed dramatically, before flowing along some thirty kilometres through a tight canyon. Unable to navigate the violent rapids, the men were forced to unload all their equipment and skirt round the cascading water. The detour cost them a week. Three weeks into his journey, at the end of May, Mackenzie confronted the harsh environment of the Rockies: unnavigable rapids, storms, cold, and above all, scarce supplies of game. For three weeks Mackenzie navigated up the Parsnip River without meeting a single Indian. Like all trappers, Mackenzie relied heavily on local informants. In their absence, he had to forge ahead blindly. In mid-June the Scot and his party encountered a band of Indians. Mackenzie plied them with gifts, and after some bargaining he obtained precious information and a little drawing, on which was represented 'the great river of the West'. Led by an Indian guide, the expedition reached a lake whose icy waters earned it the name Arctic Lake. Mackenzie did not realize it, but he had reached the division of waters—the watershed of the continent. As a result, when he embarked on a small river he was in fact heading southwest.

Hails of arrows

Treacherous rapids caused the boat to capsize, but by a miracle no one drowned in the chill waters. Morale was by now at a low ebb, but Mackenzie kept to his course. Late in June the party reached the powerful Fraser River, where they were greeted by a hail of arrows from the unfriendly Carrier Indians. Mackenzie mollified them with gifts, and learned after talking with them that the Fraser flowed south, not west as he had thought. But could he trust these Indi-

ans? Mackenzie was worried about running short of supplies in those mountainous regions; he worried too about encountering hostile Indians. Upon reflection, the Scotsman decided to leave the Fraser and pursue the journey on foot.

The first continental crossing

Loaded down with forty-kilo packs on their shoulders, the party headed west, following Indian trails through heavily wooded territory. After a ten-day trek the party reached the eastern slopes of the Coast Mountains. They climbed up to a narrow pass, known today as Mackenzie Pass, where a spectacular landscape of fjords and thuya trees spread out before them. That night Mackenzie discovered a village of Bella Coola Indians. The hospitable Bella Coolas stuffed Mackenzie and his men with fresh salmon. Later the Indians took the party out in their thuya-wood dugouts as far as the Pacific Ocean. Unfortunately, they had little time to bask in the pleasure of their discovery. A rival Indian tribe forced the white men to flee into the interior, and finally to turn back east. In August 1793 Mackenzie was back at Fort Chipewyan. The young Scot had been the first man to cross the entire width of the continent. King George III knighted Mackenzie, who then devoted himself to writing an account of his extraordinary journey: *Voyages from Montreal to the Glacial Ocean and Pacific Ocean*. In the spring of 1803, President Thomas Jefferson advised Captain Meriwether Lewis to read Mackenzie's book before starting out on an expedition of his own.

An Indian woman wearing snowshoes. The tribes living in the heart of the Rocky Mountains were peaceful towards the pioneers.

The fur route

From Montreal to Lake Athabasca the fur route cut a line 4800 kilometres long across a continent of lakes, streams, and dense forest. From Montreal the Ottawa River took travellers to the inland waterways of the Great Lakes. They then reached Fort William on the western shore of Lake Superior. The Great Portage came next: for sixteen kilometres men forded rivers with canoes and cargo on their backs; this was the gateway to the Canadian West. The Great Portage ended at Rainy Lake. From there, following the network of rivers between small lakes and much larger ones—Lake Winnipeg, for example—travellers arrived at the foothills of the Rockies or, at the northernmost reaches of the Canadian Shield, the Great Slave Lake. Throughout the nineteenth century, the forts and trading posts that dotted the route grew into the major cities of the Canadian West.

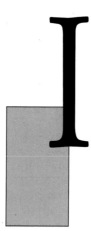

n April 1803 the United States purchased from Napoleon lands extending from the Mississippi River west to the Rocky Mountains, and from Canada south to the Gulf of Mexico. The Louisiana Purchase endowed the young nation with an immense and largely unexplored territory.

A monument: Lewis and Clark's Journal

In the course of their exploration, Lewis and Clark noted precise observations on the plants, animals and Indians they encountered in a journal they kept day to day. The seven volumes of their journal are a mine of information for the historian, the botanist, and the ethnologist. The journal was published to great acclaim. The most complete edition of Lewis and Clark's journal was compiled by Ruben Thwaites at the beginning of this century.

An epic journey

President Thomas Jefferson (1743-1826) decided to send 'an intelligent officer and a party of ten men to explore the territory and push on from there to the Pacific Ocean'. An epic journey was about to begin.

While ambassador to France, Jefferson had read many accounts of travels in the Louisiana territory, and—like Benjamin Franklin—he held great hopes for these virgin lands. When he was elected to the presidency in 1801, Jefferson spoke of a project for an 'exploration detachment' with his secretary, Meriwether Lewis. For long hours the two men secretly planned the expedition that would, when the time came, open a route to the Pacific.

Thirty good men

When the Louisiana Purchase was concluded, Lewis set about recruiting his team and selecting the expedition's equipment. For his second in command, Lewis chose a former army comrade, William Clark, a sturdy, solid Kentucky lad, who enthusiastically accepted the proposition. The recruitment of the rest of the party was a more delicate matter. Volunteers and adventurers of every kind clamoured to join the expedition. Lewis decided to limit the team to thirty men chosen for their talents and experience: hunters, carpenters, blacksmiths and soldiers accustomed to long treks. Of the expedition's thirty members, seventeen were regular soldiers, eleven were civilians—mostly Frenchmen used to navigating in the West—and one Georges Drouillard, a métis of French and Indian parentage, who served as interpreter. Clark was accompanied by York, his black manservant, and Lewis brought along his faithful Newfoundland dog, Scammon. In Pittsburgh Lewis had an eighteen-metre boat built, and he selected several top-notch rifles, including an air rifle for himself. The expedition's largest expense was the purchase of gifts for the Indians: glass jewellery, hachets, iron pots, multicoloured beads, and, for the chiefs, medals bearing President Jefferson's likeness.

Wolves, buffalo, grizzlies...and mosquitoes

The expedition left St Louis on 14 May 1804, and slowly ascended the Missouri River on its heavily loaded barge. In the journals they kept during the voyage, Lewis and Clark both expressed their wonder at the grandeur of the Western landscape. Herds of buffalo grazed along the banks of the Missouri, escorted by packs of wolves; on several occasions members of the expedition barely escaped from the fierce grizzly bears that lumbered along the riverbanks. But the most trying aspect of the trip was the incessant presence of mosquitoes which hung in a cloud about the barge, flying into eyes, noses, ears, and attacking the smallest patch of bare skin. Even Lewis's dog was nearly driven mad by the insects.

The Great Plains Indians, nomads, hunters, warriors, tracked the buffalo which guaranteed them their subsistence. During war dances, they wore magnificent tunics and masks and covered their bodies with bright colours.

Whenever the Americans met bands of Indian hunters, they offered gifts and parleyed with them. Lewis's air gun amazed the natives, who, not finding any trace of powder, were sure it worked by magic. But not all the party's encounters with Indians were friendly. The Sioux demanded that the white men pay tribute for having travelled across their territory in the upper Missouri valley. Yet on the whole, relations with the natives, and with Indian squaws in particular, were most cordial. Sioux and Arikara squaws offered their favours to the explorers, as they had grown accustomed to do with trappers.

Charbonneau and Sacajawea

In November 1804 the party halted near a Mandan village at the mouth of the Knife River to pitch their winter camp. The men built a small fort and cabins, all of which were greatly appreciated when the temperature dropped to forty degrees centigrade below zero.

During their five-month sojourn in the camp, Clark struck up a friendship with the Mandan chief, Big White. Sketching a map in the sand, Big White showed Clark a large river that flowed south to north. Clark thought that it might be the Columbia River, which, he knew, emptied into the Pacific ocean.

For his part, Lewis used gifts to keep up friendly relations with the other Indians. He had the party's blacksmith forge particularly solid hatchets, which pleased the Mandans no end. That winter a French trapper, Toussaint Charbonneau, and his Shoshoni wife, Sacajawea, arrived at the village of the neighbouring Minnetaree tribe. Lewis hired the trapper as an interpreter, and agreed to let his pregnant wife come along. Sacajawea bore a son in February. The expedition struck camp and headed west in April 1805. The men were well rested, but none suspected the hardships that awaited them.

Among the Shoshonis

The expedition continued to ascend the Missouri until they reached a fork in the river. Lewis was uncertain which direction to take. He sent men to explore each branch of the river for some distance, then relied on his intuition and on Sacajawea's advice. In

the end the expedition followed the southern fork. A few days later, they came upon a spectacular sight: the cascading torrents of the Missouri Falls, thirty metres high. To skirt this formidable obstacle the Americans had to undertake a portage of twenty-eight kilometres. They constructed crude carts to haul their boats, but it still took them twenty-four days to transport all their equipment over the rough terrain. Once they reached the high country, Sacajawea recognized the land of her childhood; she guided the expedition up to the continental watershed, close to the Columbia River. Having abandoned the boats, exhausted by their efforts, the Americans were relieved to come upon Sacajawea's tribe, the Shoshonis. Distrustful at first, the Indians were cool to the visitors until a childhood friend recognized Sacajawea and presented her to her brother, a chief. The Indians' welcome then warmed up immediately. The explorers were able to rest and eat their fill before setting out again in late August with fresh horses. Sacajawea accompanied the expedition for several weeks more along the Columbia River.

Waves on a beach

Descending along the western face of the Rockies was no mean feat. The party followed Indian trails, and did their best to cross torrents and gulches without mishap. Scarce game, dead salmon along the banks of the Columbia and mistrustful Indians made the last leg of the expedition an ordeal. Suddenly, on 7 November 1805, the explorers heard a low, rumbling noise coming from the west, a sound that they all instantly recognized: the waves of the Pacific Ocean breaking on a beach. A month later, Lewis had a post built at the mouth of the Columbia River, from which he could signal passing boats.

12,370 kilometres in two and a half years

Lewis's hope was to return East more quickly and easily by sea. All winter the party kept a lookout for the boats that, as they had been informed, travelled among the fur-trading posts on the West Coast. When by spring no boat had been sighted, Lewis and Clark and their men started the long trip back East on 23 March 1806.

Though the men's morale was high, the journey was anything but a pleasure outing.

The six-month return trek was punctuated by bloody skirmishes with Indians. The most serious incident occurred during a clash with the Blackfeet tribe. One Indian was killed and another wounded while attempting to steal a rifle. The Blackfeet thereafter held a terrible grudge against the white man, and many a pioneer or trapper paid with their lives for the explorers' unthinking quickness on the trigger. Meriwether Lewis spent several weeks on a stretcher, wounded by a soldier in a hunting accident. On 23 September 1806, however, the expedition reached Saint Louis, having covered 12,370 kilometres in two and a half years of exploring.

A harvest of vital information

Lewis and Clark's exploit had a considerable impact in the cities of the East Coast. Many Americans had given the explorers up for dead, although a delegation of Osage Indians had preceded them to Washington for a meeting with Jefferson. The party brought back with them a remarkable harvest of information, as well as significant collections of flora and fauna. The West was no longer just a vague blank space on a map. For the first time, Americans had actually crossed the immense continent, and beheld the Pacific Ocean, a dream that had fired the imagination of so many explorers for hundreds of years.

Having left Saint Louis, Lewis and Clarke held council meetings with Indians who gave them information.

Before the conquest of the West became a saga that inspired so many writers and film directors, it began with just a handful of adventurers, trappers and soldiers who ventured forth into unknown lands. They were supported by politicians who were convinced that America's future lay in the West.

Fur traders going down the Missouri.

tenant pushed across Kansas and sojourned for a time in Pawnee villages before heading south in hopes of discovering the sources of the Arkansas and Red rivers. The expedition set out in July 1806 and advanced easily over the Plains, but they ran up against the Colorado plateau in November, just as winter was setting in. Snow had begun to fall; the cold grew intense. Undeterred, Pike was determined to leave his name in the annals of exploration. He considered the high mountain that rose up in the distance, and decided to scale it, the weather notwithstanding. In four days he advanced just sixty kilometers. As they climbed ever upward, the ill-equipped party suffered terribly from the cold and finally gave up; Pike reportedly declared that no human being could reach the summit. Fourteen years later the mountain was climbed by another party, but in recognition of Pike's courage, the peak was named in honour of the man who never made it to the top.

An unlucky explorer

Zebulon Montgomery Pike is one of a long line of unlucky explorers who pursued fame and fortune with great tenacity, yet to whom Fate awarded only the consolation prize of a mountain or river named in their honour. Pike was raised in the military tradition by his father, a veteran of the American War of Independence. The young soldier was just fifteen when he experienced the hardships of life in the forts of the Mississippi Valley. And it was then, in 1805—while Lewis and Clark were exploring the West— that Pike was made head of a mission to discover the headwaters of the Mississippi. He searched through present-day Minnesota without

success. Pike at one point believed he had located the source of Lake Leech, when in fact he had found the source of Lake Itasca. Still, Pike managed to parley with the Sioux before returning to Saint Louis. The following year he was charged with exploring the southern frontier of Louisiana, a region about which the most contradictory information was then circulating.

On the Colorado plateau

To win the favour of the Plains Indians, Pike brought with him fifty-one Osages who had been freed by the Americans. With the Indians and fifteen soldiers, the young lieu-

Prisoner of the Spanish; a literary career

After that failed attempt, Pike turned south and followed the valley of the Rio Grande, which he believed to be the Red River. Early in February, the party was ambushed by a Spanish patrol and led as prisoners to the little town of Santa Fe. Pike and his men were imprisoned, and all the notes concerning the expedition were confiscated. The party returned to Louisiana in June 1807. Back in Saint Louis, without a penny to his name and his reputation tarnished, Pike resigned himself to writing an account of his long journey, which he had published in Philadelphia in 1810. Fortune finally smiled on the explorer. His book was a huge success, with several foreign editions. To top things off, he was awarded a promotion. Brigadier General Zebulon Pike died honourably during the attack on Toronto in April 1813. Although he had not set out to do so, Pike opened the route to the Spanish towns of the Southwest, particularly Santa Fe, whose scenic beauty and riches he described. Numerous Americans attempted the same journey, which is how the Santa Fe Trail was born. It was followed in the 1820s by a regular link between Saint Louis and Santa Fe. The Southwest was thus opened to *gringos* (as white Americans were called), who judged the land on the whole to be arid and unattractive.

Long's bad luck

Some years after Pike's expedition, another soldier reiterated the view that the West was not the paradise that certain politicians had described to credulous voters. Stephen H. Long, who was charged with the same mission as Pike—to explore the sources of the Arkansas and Red rivers—did not have much more luck than his predecessor. Between 1820 and 1824 Long, a topographical engineer, travelled through the vast region that lies between the Mississippi and the Arkansas rivers. His plan to ascend America's greatest river failed, for widespread epidemics decimated the men. Long was no more successful in his exploration of the Great Plains, since his notes were stolen by deserters. A report turned in by another member of the expedition, the physician Edwin James, named the wide strip of land between the Mississippi and the Rockies 'The Great American Desert', a term that actually appeared on maps for almost fifty years. Long wrote that the Great Plains (for that is the land in question) were 'wholly unfit for cultivation, and of course uninhabitable by a people depending upon agriculture for their subsistence'. Long, Washington Irving and other travellers were astonished to note the absence of trees. In those times, people associated the presence of trees with fertile soil, and assumed it would be impossible to cultivate soil in which trees did not grow.

Frémont's good fortune

The saviour of the West belonged to the same 'family' as his predecessors. John Charles Frémont, an officer in the Army Topographical Corps, was acclaimed as a

Following the trail of Jedediah Smith, who discovered the South Pass, Trapper Joe Walker opened up the Rockies (see page 131).

hero by the end of the century. The leader of five expeditions to the West between 1842 and 1854, he surpassed all other explorers in popularity with the public.

Born to a family of modest means, he was a successful student. But his unruly temper and carelessness often got him into trouble. In 1838 fortune smiled on Frémont. He received a second lieutenant's commission and joined an expedition led by the geographer Joseph Nicollet to survey the upper Mississippi. Frémont owed his sudden promotion to Joel Poinsett, a prominent Charles tonian whom the young soldier met in the drawing rooms of South Carolina. Poinsett was an enthusiastic botanist, and an ardent supporter of the Army and of exploration. In the two years he spent with Nicollet, Frémont learned about surveying, and developed a taste for botany and mineralogy. Back in Washington, Frémont was quickly caught up in the social whirl. It was there in 1839 that he met Jessie Benton, daughter of the senator from Missouri, Thomas Hart Benton. After some delicate negotiating, Frémont won Jessie's hand in marriage.

On to the West

Frémont's new father-in-law was a confirmed western expansionist who needed men to advance his political designs. For a dozen years journalists and politicians had been preaching the crusade to open up the West, since boatloads of poor immigrants

were flooding the East. Some politicians even declared that it was America's 'Manifest Destiny' to conquer the continent from sea to sea. Benton helped Frémont obtain the command of an exploratory expedition along the Oregon Trail, then threatened by the British. Frémont's mission was to survey a possible route across the Rockies. He surrounded himself with a highly skilled team, including the German-born cartographer, Charles Preuss, and the famous frontiersman, Kit Carson.

The party set out in June 1842 and easily traversed the Great Plains, territory that Carson knew well. They crossed into Colorado, climbed South Pass at 2500 metres (7550 feet) above sea level, and finally reached the Wind River Range. Frémont, ever the daredevil, resolved to scale what he believed to be the highest peak of the Rockies, today known as Frémont Peak. Climbing ever higher despite severe headaches, the party brought off the feat, a performance Frémont dramatically related in his account of the expedition.

A two-hundred-page report

Frémont's most notable exploit was in fact the two-hundred-page report he wrote upon his return from an uneventful expedition. Presented to Congress in March 1843, the report had the effect of a bombshell. The representatives gave it a standing ovation, and immediately voted a subsidy for the publication of ten thousand copies of the report. The young explorer's romanticism seemed to draw inspiration from his father-in-law's impassioned speeches. The American West was not a desert, but a fertile Garden of Paradise; the Rockies were a wondrous place; the flora, the fauna, the Indians all seemed idyllic, just waiting for the Americans to arrive. The press had a field day with the report, for they had only to copy the text as published, without changing even a comma. Frémont the unknown explorer became Frémont the hero virtually overnight. The following year Frémont headed West once more, but his next two expeditions, notably in California, were less glorious than the first. He proved ineffective as a military commander both during the American campaign in California and later during the Civil War, when President Lincoln was obliged to relieve Frémont of his command. A trapper named Joe Walker had this to say about the hero of the Conquest of the West: 'Fifteen years before Frémont set foot on that unexplored land, I knew more about the subject than he does today.'

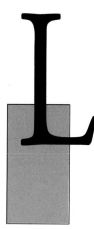

*L*ong *before Lewis and Clark, white men—French and British trappers—had already ventured as far as the foothills of the immense barrier that marked the limit of the Great Plains. The Rocky Mountains glittered on the horizon, hence their early name—the 'Shining Mountains'.*

The powerfully-built mountain men were constantly on the lookout for new beaver-rich rivers.

The mountain men

The Rocky Mountains inspired reverence in the Indians, who considered them a sacred place, where the dead came to rest. The Indians lived on the Plains or in the Great Basin, so that many mountain valleys remained uninhabited. These valleys abounded with wildlife—beavers in particular.

Two centuries of fur trade forced French and British trappers alike to seek new fur sources. In the eighteenth century, they ascended the Missouri River and pushed on to the foothills of the Rockies.

The absence of Indians—and thus of the normal sources for skins—gave rise to a new character on the scene: the Rocky Mountain trapper, or mountain man. Small groups of mountain men would settle for a season in a valley, lay traps in the rivers, then set off in search of other sites rich in game. Their nomadic habits took the mountain men to new valleys and unknown passes as they covered the Rockies in every direction. Most of the men were illiterates who cared little for discoveries and exploration. Their chief concern was to eke out an existence amidst all manner of dangers. Information was exchanged when the groups met in trading posts or at their annual 'rendezvous', the great Rocky Mountain fur fair. Yet some names have been recorded in the annals of exploration; the names of men who were able to make their discoveries known.

The exploits of John Colter

Among the first trappers to work the eastern Rockies was John Colter, a member of the Lewis and Clark expedition. A remarkably strong man, Colter had fought Indians in the East before being recruited by Meriwether Lewis. In 1806 Colter joined the Missouri trappers, working for a fur-trade adventurer called Manuel Lisa. With his knowledge of the Yellowstone and Bighorn rivers, Colter brought Lisa to the foot of the Rockies. Always seeking new horizons, Colter penetrated the Absaroka chain in the winter of 1807-1808, followed the Wind River, then crossed the Tetons and descended the Snake River along the western face of the Rockies. After several narrow escapes from the Blackfeet Indians, in 1810 Colter decided to retire to Saint Louis. There, in the capital of the fur trade, Colter recounted his exploits to a sceptical audience. Forests of giant trees, geysers, hot water gushing from the earth, deserts of glowing mud...why not skeletons of giant monsters too? The good people of Saint Louis wanted nothing to do with these foolish tales, told by a half-wild man with long hair and coppery skin. Only William Clark paid close attention to Colter's stories, and noted the trapper's discoveries on a map. Until his death in 1813, Colter remained a laughing stock with the public, who dubbed the regions he described 'Colter's Hell'.

South Pass

Manuel Lisa established a post at the confluence of the Yellowstone and Bighorn rivers. Another fur-trading entrepreneur, William Ashley, hired a crack team of trappers including Jim Bridger and Tom Fitzpatrick. The latter ascended the Wind River in 1823 and discovered a pass, later christened South Pass, through which he could cross the western slopes of the Rockies. Twenty years later, the flood of pioneers travelling westward to Oregon and California funnelled through South Pass. Mountain men like Bill Sublette and Zenas Leonard explored the Central Rockies and pushed into the Great Basin, while still others— Jedediah Smith and Joe Walker—headed southwest.

Smith and Walker possessed similar qualities: a wide experience of the West, exceptional physical stamina, and the ability to exert authority over trappers with little inclination for taking orders. In the 1830s, beavers were becoming scarce on the eastern slopes of the Rockies. Trappers told tales of new territories to the south, where extensive deserts had discouraged previous attempts at exploration. The trappers feared arid regions, for they could not carry large water reserves.

Towards new territories

In 1826 the mountain man Jedediah Smith joined with Bill Sublette to purchase Ashley's fur company. Smith decided to exploit new territories. He headed south, along the eastern edge of the Great Basin, followed the Colorado River for a time, and finally reached the Mojave Desert. Attempting the impossible, Smith marched straight across the middle of the Mojave, finally reaching the Los Angeles region late in November. In Baja California Smith and his comrades were arrested, but were later freed thanks to the intervention of an American ship's captain. The following year, despite the Mexican authorities' formal prohibition, Smith returned to California. He wintered in the Sacramento Valley, then resolved to march north, to what is now Oregon. But his band of trappers was decimated by an Indian attack. Smith returned to Saint Louis in financial straits, for most of his furs had been lost. In 1830 Smith determined to undertake an expedition to Santa Fe, and set off across the barren lands around the Cimarron River. He and the other trappers were certain that they would find water. Exhausted, they were massacred by Comanches. Jedediah Smith, a man who knew the Rockies better than almost anyone, died at the age of thirty-two.

A dangerous mission

While Smith was a nervous, irritable New Yorker, Joe Walker was a colossus who weighed well over fifteen stone, born to a family of Tennessee pioneers. Walker's two brothers also headed West in search of adventure; one was killed with Davy Crockett

at the Alamo in 1830, and the other worked as a guide for pioneer wagon trains travelling to Oregon. Joe began his career on the Santa Fe Trail where Jedediah Smith had died. In 1832 he met a retired officer turned fur trader, Benjamin Bonneville, who put Walker in command of a team of trappers. Walker asked for volunteers to follow him on a dangerous mission: a march west to the Pacific across the new territories. At a meeting on Green River in the summer of 1833 Walker sought the advice of Zenas Leonard, the most reliable living authority on the Central Rockies. Leonard told him to pack as many supplies as he could carry, and to take extra horses. Unlike most trappers, Walker knew horses, and each trapper was told to bring along three horses, together with ample provisions of dried meat. On 29 August 1833, forty trappers, including Zenas Leonard himself, marched behind Walker towards the setting sun.

The gateway to California

When they reached the Great Salt Lake, Walker questioned local Indians about the route to take across the Great Basin, an

arid, barren region. The party headed due west through the deserts of present-day Nevada, and arrived at the source of the Humboldt River, which they followed southwest. Their progress was impeded by warlike bands of Indians, whose braves had been killed by trappers. After several weeks, the party finally saw the peaks of the Sierra Nevada Range, over 4000 metres high, rise up before them. After three solid weeks of slogging through snow, the efforts of men and horses were rewarded: they were the first to enter the spectacular Yosemite Valley. The trappers reached San Francisco Bay in late November, and they stayed in Monterey for over three months. On the return trip in February 1834, Walker discovered the pass — 1700 metres high — in the Sierra Nevada that now bears his name. The Walker Pass was to be the gateway to California.

After this great success, Walker's fame spread as far as the East Coast. He worked as a guide for Frémont, then returned to settle in Monterey in 1849. He died in California. His grave bears the following epitaph: 'Camped in Yosemite on 13 November 1833.' Colter, Bridger, Smith, Walker: the history of exploration must always commemorate these trappers, who did not follow trails, but blazed them.

The Trappers' Portraitist

In 1837 a British veteran of the Napoleonic Wars, William Drummond Stewart, travelled West to hunt big game. He was accompanied by a young painter from Baltimore, Alfred Jacob Miller, then twenty-seven years old. The artist had recently returned from a tour of Paris and Rome, and had just settled in New Orleans when Stewart proposed that he follow a party of traders heading for the Rocky Mountain trappers' meeting at Green River. Throughout the summer, Miller sketched his strange surroundings, including an astonishing portrait of Joe Walker and his squaw.

The trail to California went through the passes of the Sierra Nevada. Above, a landscape painted by Albert Brerstadt in 1868.

A mong the ranks of explorers, naturalists form a special community of extraordinary individuals, as brave and adventurous as the great discoverers. These naturalists were not simply passive observers or collectors; they contributed to an understanding of Nature's beauty and fragility. But they were often ignored by contemporaries more concerned with transforming forests into wheat fields.

Ecological consequences
of colonization

As early as the 1600s, European colonization of North America radically altered the continent's ecological balance. Colonists cleared and destroyed forests for timber, which they sold to Britain's Royal Navy; they imported new animal species, like the rat and the pig, which quickly multiplied in the new land. In the 1700s, the native American turkey risked extinction, and had to be reintroduced later in the century. Certain species, like the passenger pigeon and prairie chicken, were wiped out to feed growing urban populations. America's sixty to eighty million native buffalos disappeared so quickly that in 1894 Congress passed a law to protect the remaining herds. The creation of the National Parks System saved numerous Western American species from total extinction. But in the East, all wild species are in decline.

A buffalo hunt in snow-covered mountains. In a few decades, millions of the beasts were exterminated by the European colonists.

Catesby in the forests
of Virginia

In 1812, a young Englishman landed in Virginia, eager to discover the natural wonders of America. 'My curiosity was such,' he wrote, 'that I wished to see the animal life and vegetation in their own habitat.' Sponsored by the Royal Society in London, Mark Catesby spent seven years roaming the length and breadth of Virginia's forests. He drew birds, collected specimens, and spent long hours sketching the native fauna and flora. Catesby intrepidly ventured inland, into unknown parts. From 1722 to 1725, supported by Francis Nicholson, the governor of South Carolina, Catesby journeyed along the Savannah River into the Appalachian mountains. There he observed birds in their natural environment, covering his notebooks with remarks and

sketches. Back in London, Catesby laboured for more than twenty years to complete his master work. After learning engraving techniques, he proceeded to cut and colour over two hundred plates; his notes furnished him with enough material for a three-hundred-page volume. Catesby's work profoundly influenced his successors, notably William Bartram and John James Audubon.

Bartram's insatiable
curiosity

Legend has it that John Bartram, the father of William Bartram, one day noticed a daisy growing in the field he was ploughing, south of Philadelphia. Bartram was struck with a sudden thought: 'What a shame we destroy so many flowers and plants about which we

know nothing at all.' John Bartram's interest in botany dated from that moment. He corresponded with an eminent English botanist, Peter Collinson, who encouraged him to continue his studies, and to draw up an inventory of native plants. Bartram gathered specimens all along the frontier to plant in his garden, the better to observe them closely. His passion for discovering plants spurred him and his son William, a skilled draughtsman, to journey as far as the Catskill Mountains and Lake Ontario, describing all the flora and fauna they observed along the way. In 1765 father and son travelled to Georgia and eastern Florida. Insatiably curious, John Bartram proposed to Benjamin Franklin an ambitious exploratory expedition out West, a project that Lewis and Clark would actually accomplish fifty years later.

Thomas Nuttal's passion

Thomas Nuttal holds a pre-eminent place among these largely anonymous naturalist-explorers. The young Englishman who arrived in Philadelphia in 1808 was certainly not cast in the mould of the hardy explorer. Short and slender, Thomas Nuttal appeared weak, but he had a bright gaze and a determined character. At the age of twenty he abandoned the family printing business to devote his life to natural history. In Philadelphia Nuttal met Benjamin Smith Barton, vice-president of the American Philosophical Society, and an eminent botanist. Barton, keen for fame and remarkable discoveries, had advised Meriwether Lewis before his expedition to the Pacific. Taking advantage of Nuttal's enthusiasm and his ignorance of geographic realities and of the American scientific community, Barton offered to hire the young man and pay him a salary if he would agree to undertake an ambitious botanical expedition through the American West. Nuttal, all on his own, was to make a journey of some two thousand kilometres through regions previously only visited by trappers, collecting en route as many specimens as possible. Nuttal had no inkling of the difficulties the journey would entail. He had not even read Lewis and Clark's journal. Yet he was ready and eager to accept Barton's conditions, for it meant he could pursue his passion for botany.

From Sioux villages to Harvard

Nuttal set out from Philadelphia in April 1810. He reached the Mississippi and Saint Louis, gateway to the West, in September. There, while seeking to join a band of trappers going up the Missouri River, Nuttal met a fellow botanist and Englishman, John Bradbury. The two struck up a friendship, and spent weeks together in Sioux, Arikara, and Mandan villages in the Upper Missouri, collecting plants and observing animals. Nuttal did not return to Philadelphia. He embarked for England from New Orleans without sending any specimens to Barton. The latter was vexed because he could not benefit from the knowledge acquired by Nuttal to classify the plants collected by Meriwether Lewis.

Thomas Nuttal returned to America three years later, in 1815. But this time he did not come as a poor immigrant. His work in England had impressed American scientists, and after the publication of his *Genera of North American Plants* (1818), Nuttal was welcomed into the prestigious ranks of Harvard University professors.

A field botanist

But Nuttal was a field botanist. He astonished his honourable colleagues in 1834 by announcing that he was off on a transcontinental expedition organized by an obscure merchant, Nathaniel Wyeth. Nuttal was accompanied by the doctor and ornithologist John Kirk Townsend. The two scientists cared little about Wyeth's commercial disappointments with western trappers. They followed Wyeth as far as Oregon, constantly collecting scientific samples and studying their surroundings. On a Pacific beach, Nuttal discovered an unidentified shellfish, a bivalve that today bears his name. In 1836 he and Townsend boarded a

The naturalist and painter John James Audubon was famous for the precision and the beauty of his engravings of animals. His four-volume Birds of America *contains more than one thousand stunning illustrations.*

brig in San Diego, and sailed back to Boston. Nuttal returned to Harvard, where he spent the rest of his life classifying the specimens he had gathered on the expedition, and passing on to his young botany students a taste for research and adventure.

Scientists and explorers

About the same time that Nuttal was roaming the West, other eminent scientists were setting out on exploratory expeditions. Between 1819 and 1820, the zoologist Thomas Say travelled with Stephen Long, gathering shellfish and insects. In 1849, Congress appointed Lieutenant William Hemsley Emory to produce an accurate map of the frontier regions that the United States had just acquired from Mexico. Emory performed his task remarkably well, not only acquitting himself of his topographical mission, but also evincing interest in the natural resources, plants and animals of the Southwest. From Texas to California, Emory's men collected 2,648 species of mostly unidentified plants and animals. Some were

preserved and sent to museums in the East; others were dissected and studied on the spot. The mission's findings were written up in the three-volume *Lieutenant Emory Reports*, a model of scientific erudition.

Audubon

Thomas Nuttall might have encountered another famous naturalist, John James Audubon. Born in France, Audubon came to America in 1803 and settled in Kentucky. His passion for ornithology took him to the banks of the Mississippi in the 1820s. Back in Kentucky, he showed his drawings to Alexander Wilson, a naturalist, who encouraged Audubon to publish them. Audubon set about finding financial support for the publication of his monumental *Birds of America*. He crisscrossed the continent to capture the rarest species in their native habitat. During the last years of his life, Audubon threw himself into the study of mammals; he transmitted his love of nature to his two sons. The younger, John, completed his father's remarkable undertaking.

fter the exploits of Lewis, Clark and Frémont, accurate maps had still to be drawn, natural resources to be inventoried, samples of rocks and soil to be collected. These tasks were no longer assigned to military personnel, but to civilians. Between 1865 and 1879 a series of important topographical surveys were made of the American West.

The first National Park

●

Ferdinand Hayden, a fervent nature lover, was largely responsible for the establishment of Yellowstone National Park on 1 March 1872. Hayden had spent the summer of 1871 in Yellowstone with the photographer William H. Jackson and a group of natural scientists. Though trained as a physician, Hayden was an excellent geologist and

had travelled widely throughout Kansas and Missouri collecting samples. The Indians called him 'the man who runs and gathers stones'. He had in particular distinguished himself by discovering iron deposits in the area of Fort Laramie, Nebraska. He had also defended the theory of botanist Cyrus Thomas, who declared 'Americans bring the rain with them' into the Great Plains. Thomas believed that 'rain follows the plough', in other words, the aridity of the Plains could be conquered if they were

populated and cultivated. Hayden was one of those incurable optimists who, unlike many members of Congress in the 1870s, viewed the West as the most promising region of the United States. With the help of subsidies from the Department of the Interior, Hayden and his team spent a year, from 1871 to 1872, in Yellowstone, collecting valuable scientific data. From 1873 to 1876, the researchers concentrated their efforts on Colorado, resulting in the publication of a remarkable atlas.

The Yellowstone River has its source in the Rocky Mountains and flows through many steep canyons. It crosses Yellowstone National Park, whose geysers, a natural curiosity, attract numerous visitors.

The way of the transcontinental railways

After graduating from Yale, Clarence King escaped the horrors of the Civil War by heading west, to California. He and Jerry T. Gardner conceived plan to survey the land from the Pacific to the Plains in order to facilitate the construction of a transcontinental railroad. King arrived in Washington in 1867 to gather support for his project, christened 'the geological exploration of the fortieth parallel'. Although he was just twenty-five, King obtained command of the mission, and recruited a team of highly qualified scientists. For the next several years King and Gardner led various research projects in the Rockies, and in 1870 King scaled the crater of Mount Shasta.

A bag full of huge diamonds!

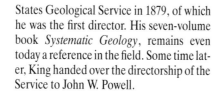

Two years later, King's geological knowledge of the Rockies was put to a severe test. A pair of prospectors, Arnold and Slack, brought a bag full of huge diamonds to a San Francisco banker. The men declared that they had discovered this fabulous treasure in an area that King had studied in depth over a period of years. Gardner and King's honour and scientific credibility were at stake. An expert appraisal by Henry Janin left no doubt about the nature of the stones, especially since Janin, led by Arnold, had himself discovered some specimens on the very spot where the two prospectors had gathered their sparkling harvest. Janin, who had been led to the site blindfold, furnished the geologists with a few clues as to its probable location. After reflecting on the matter, King and Gardner decided to go themselves to a small plateau on the Wyoming-Utah border. Digging among some quartz crystals, King spotted diamonds; they saw rubies winking at them from the openings of anthills. When their first excitement had abated, the geologists began to wonder how and why nature had miraculously scattered out in the open gems normally hidden deep in the earth. King and Gardner uncovered the hoax, and it was learned that Arnold and Slack had acquired the gems in Amsterdam. The two con men fled with 300,000 dollars they had swindled from the San Francisco banker.

Clarence King was then at the pinnacle of his fame. He helped establish the United States Geological Service in 1879, of which he was the first director. His seven-volume book *Systematic Geology*, remains even today a reference in the field. Some time later, King handed over the directorship of the Service to John W. Powell.

A genius for self-promotion

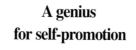

The son of a modest pioneer family from Wisconsin, Powell fought in the Civil War, and lost his right arm. When peace came, he was appointed professor of geology at an Illinois university. But Powell soon had enough of the quiet teaching life, and his thirst for action spurred him to become an explorer. In 1869, with his brother Walter and a small party, Powell descended the rapids of the Green River and the Colorado River, navigating over large stretches of previously unexplored water. In addition to a high degree of intelligence, Powell also possessed a genius for self-promotion. When he returned to civilization, he related his adventures in a series of public lectures. His big-city audiences back East shivered as they listened to the tales of the intrepid explorer. The press quickly latched on to this interesting character, and made Powell a celebrity. Congress, in consequence, easily voted him generous subsidies to undertake a survey of the Colorado plateau (1870-1873).

Following the trail blazed by Frémont, botanists and geographers kept themselves busy by revealing the natural riches of the American continent.

Fascinated by Indians

Powell was not interested only in rocks; he was also fascinated by Indians. Their rich culture, threatened by the advance of pioneers heading West, inspired Powell to establish the American Bureau of Ethnology. The bureau's purpose was to study the Indian world, as well as to preserve it. Powell enjoyed widespread popularity for another reason: he was among the first to voice concern for the damage being done to the environment. As the head of the Geological Service for fourteen years, he tried to increase public awareness of ecological problems.

The end of an era

The last soldier to make a career of exploration was George Wheeler. He did remarkable work, from 1869 to 1879, covering more territory than any of his colleagues or civilian rivals. Civilian explorers—such as Hayden and King—refused to credit a mere lieutenant, a non-specialist, with any competence. They criticized Wheeler ruthlessly. Their manoeuvrings finally won the day in 1879, when Congress voted to halt the Army's surveying activities in the West. Wheeler saw that an era was coming to an end. By 1880 the entire American West had been mapped.

Photography: a Tool for Exploration

In New York in 1851 Robert Vance exhibited daguerrotypes of the still unknown West—pictures of San Francisco, of miners and of Californian Indians. The public greeted this opportunity to discover the 'other America'. Between 1840 and 1850, photographers accompanied many exploratory expeditions to the West. With the invention of lighter equipment, using the wet-plate process, photographers travelled throughout the West in the 1860s. They captured the drama of the Indian wars, and of the pioneers' progress. Many were enchanted by the scenery, and through their pictures introduced the rest of the continent to the wild beauty of the newly discovered West. Thus, thanks to Jackson's photographs, Congress was deeply moved by the splendour of Yellowstone's landscapes, and on 1 March 1872 voted to establish America's first national park, at Yellowstone in the Rockies.

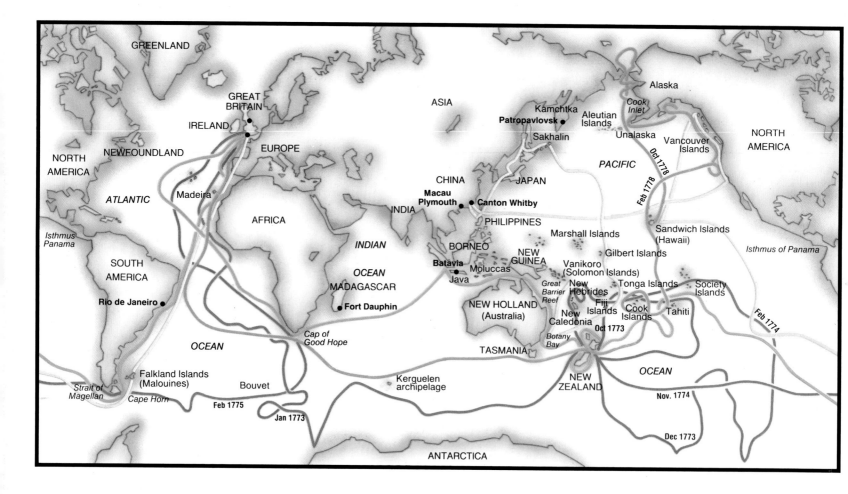

GREENLAND

GREAT BRITAIN

IRELAND

NORTH AMERICA

NEWFOUNDLAND

EUROPE

ATLANTIC

Madeira

Isthmus Panama

SOUTH AMERICA

Rio de Janeiro

OCEAN

Falkland Islands (Malouines)

Strait of Magellan

Cape Horn

Feb 1775

Bouvet

Jan 1773

AFRICA

ASIA

CHINA

INDIA

INDIAN

OCEAN

MADAGASCAR

Fort Dauphin

Cap of Good Hope

Kerguelen archipelage

JAPAN

Macau
Plymouth   ● Canton Whitby

PHILIPPINES

BORNEO

Batavia   ● Moluccas
Java

NEW GUINEA

Great Barrier Reef

NEW HOLLAND (Australia)

TASMANIA

NEW ZEALAND

Nov. 1774

Dec 1773

Kamchtka
Patropavlovsk ●   Aleutian Islands

Sakhalin

Cook Inlet

Alaska

Unalaska   Vancouver Islands

PACIFIC

Oct 1778

Feb 1778

Marshall Islands

Sandwich Islands (Hawaii)

Gilbert Islands

Vanikoro (Solomon Islands)

New Hebrides   Tonga Islands

New Caledonia   Fiji Islands   Cook Islands   Tahiti

Botany Bay   Oct 1773

OCEAN

Feb 1774

NORTH AMERICA

Isthmus of Panama

Society Islands

ANTARCTICA

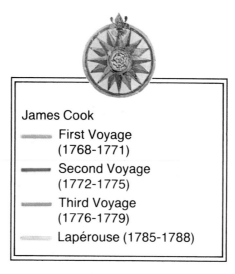

James Cook

━━ First Voyage (1768-1771)

━━ Second Voyage (1772-1775)

━━ Third Voyage (1776-1779)

━━ Lapérouse (1785-1788)

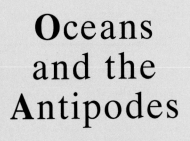

Oceans
and the
Antipodes

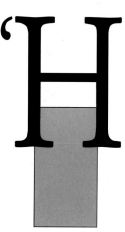

*H*e did not wholly unveil the plan of the voyage he was to undertake, so that his men might not, in amazement and fright, refuse to accompany him on so long a voyage.' But Antonio de Pigafetta, the chronicler of Magellan's expedition, was indeed aware from the start that the voyage was to be the first circumnavigation of the globe and he was one of the lucky few who survived it.

Magellan

Fernão de Magalhães was born around 1480 to a family of provincial gentry in Sabrosa, in mountainous northern Portugal. He sailed to the Indies in 1509 as a subaltern with Viceroy Don Francisco de Almeida, and he took part in the siege and pillage of Malacca. Afflicted with a limp from a wound received in the siege of Azamor in Morocco, Magellan was a proud, prickly character, whose unpredictable temper made him unwelcome at court. A bold officer, Magellan was also a skilled navigator with a keen interest in the maps and globes produced by the great cartographers of the day.

The first man to

circumnavigate the globe

What is usually referred to as 'Magellan's' circumnavigation of the earth was in fact accomplished by El Cano, since the Captain General died during the voyage. In any event, the first man to have actually circled the globe was a Sumatran slave called Henrique, whom Magellan had purchased in the Indies. On 28 March 1521, Henrique spoke in his native tongue with a ruler of one of the Philippine Islands. Overjoyed to return home after so tortuous a voyage, Henrique probably remained ignorant of his unprecedented accomplishment.

Ferdinand Magellan was the first European to sail through the strait that is named after him. His courage in the face of the elements and his natural ability to lead men contributed greatly to the success of his expedition.

The Southern Ocean

By 1510 the Atlantic and Indian Oceans had already become familiar waters for Iberian navigators. Spain had a firm foothold in America, while Portugal was making inroads into the East Indies (modern Indonesia).

When he crossed the Isthmus of Panama in 1513, Vasco Nuñez de Balboa discovered and claimed the Pacific—what he called the Southern Ocean—for Spain. He was followed by scores of explorers seeking a sea passage across America. The Cabots came in the service of England, Corte Real for Portugal, and later the Florentine Verrazano and the Frenchman Jacques Cartier set out in search of a northern passage.

Farther south, the Pinzon brothers among others, and an Italian explorer destined for fame—Amerigo Vespucci—saw in every estuary of the New World's great rivers a potential passage to the vastness of the ocean beyond.

The inaccuracies of the Treaty of Tordesillas

The Treaty of Tordesillas attempted to establish an agreed frontier between Spanish and Portuguese possessions in the Indian Ocean and America (see p. 53). However, because of inaccurate indications of longitude, it failed to resolve the problem of who owned the Spice Islands (in the East Indies), which lay close to the line of demarcation. If the Spanish could find a way to approach this line of demarcation from the west, they would be able to explore the hemisphere attributed to them by the treaty.

Not content to have underestimated Christopher Columbus, who finally turned to Spain for support, thirty years later the Portuguese also allowed Magellan to slip through their fingers. Weary of trying to win support for his plan to pursue the western route to the East Indies, in 1517 the Portuguese subject Fernão de Magalhães became Hernan de Magallanes and entered the service of Spain, along with his compatriot, the visionary cosmographer Ruy Faleiro.

The idea of sailing west was regarded as unorthodox by Magellan's learned contemporaries and by the Church. But Magellan finally succeeded in winning over a former opponent of Columbus's theories, Cardinal Fonseca, bishop of Burgos. He interceded with Charles V, emperor of the Holy Roman Empire, who reigned as Charles I in Spain. On 22 March 1518 Magellan was put in command of a fleet of five ships and instructed to map the boundaries of Spain's sphere of sovereignty in the new ocean. The captain and first mate would be amply rewarded for any important discoveries they made along the way.

Threats of mutiny

Magellan's five ships set sail from Sanlucar, at the mouth of the Guadalquivir River, on 20 September 1519. Magellan himself commanded the expedition aboard the *Trinidad*. His motley crew hailed from every corner of Europe.

The high-born officers of the Spanish nobility baulked at serving under a foreign commander. Haughty, disdainful, conscious of the respect due to his rank, Magellan did not even reveal to his officers the precise aim of their voyage. It may well have been that his reticence was vital to the success of an expedition potentially so dangerous as to provoke the crew to mutiny.

The *Santiago* was lost the following year in Patagonia. On 21 October 1520 a vast strait seemed to open towards the west at a latitude of 52° C, far beyond the Cape of Good Hope. Despite the favourable reports of the advance party, underlying tensions between the fleet's captains and its commander-in-chief flared up: open revolt ensued. The *San Antonio* turned back with most of the supplies.

The captains of the *Concepcion* and the *Victoria*, Gaspar Quesada, and Loys de Mendoza, the fleet's treasurer, paid for the mutiny with their lives: they were drawn and quartered. Juan de Cartegena, as *veedor*, or representative of the king's interests, was pardoned, but abandoned nonetheless on an islet in Patagonia. In an age when violence was common currency, men who led explorations to far-off lands had to impose their authority with iron discipline.

The Pacific Ocean

Magellan's three remaining ships, the *Concepcion*, the *Trinidad* and the *Victoria*, entered the narrow body of water between Patagonia and Tierra del Fuego known since as the Strait of Magellan. They emerged on 28 November 1520 into the open sea, sufficiently calm that day to warrant the name 'Pacific Ocean'.

The fleet made for the Moluccas (in the East Indies). For three months and twenty days, the ships steered west-north-west. Magellan and his pilots used the same navi-

gational instruments as Vasco da Gama and Christopher Columbus. Their marine charts were still largely hypothetical. They were literally sailing into the unknown, across the unexplored expanses of an imprecisely measured globe.

In the vast emptiness of the Pacific, the expedition's supplies dwindled with alarming speed. Famine and scurvy decimated the weakened crews, who were forced to eat marinated leather and wood-shaving soup. Rats were considered a delicacy. Nineteen crew members died of scurvy.

On 6 March 1521 Magellan discovered Guam in the Mariana Islands, which were dubbed the Ladrone ('thief') Islands, since initial contacts between the Spaniards and the natives were hostile and quite violent. The fleet dropped anchor on 16 March at Samar in the Philippines, between Mindanao and Luzon. For the first time Europeans had crossed the great Pacific Ocean. East and West had in some sense met; and the Indies had finally been reached by a western route.

Magellan's glory and misfortune

On 27 April, Magellan was killed in a skirmish with natives on the island of Mactan. The remaining crew burned the *Concepcion* on 3 May, since survivors were too few to man three ships.

The *Trinidad* and the *Victoria* sailed aimlessly between Borneo and Mindanao, searching for the Moluccas under the command of Joao de Carvalho, an adventurer who was quickly deposed and replaced by Juan Sebastian El Cano. On 8 November, the crews finally dropped anchor at Tidora in the Spice Islands. Every square inch of the ships was crammed with precious cargo.

The *Victoria* set sail on 21 December, bearing a king's ransom in cloves. When leaks were discovered on the *Trinidad*, the cargo was unloaded, and the ship heaved onto a beach to carry out repairs. The captain, Gomez de Espinosa, struggled to reach Panama by recrossing the Pacific against the wind. After five agonizing months, twenty-four men (of whom seventeen were close to death) painfully made their way back to Ternate in the Moluccas. All of them, whether able-bodied or at death's door, were taken prisoner by the Portuguese garrison which in the meantime had taken possession of the Spice Islands. There, at the ends of the earth, Spain and Portugal waged a ruthless battle to preserve their share of the treasure of the Indies.

The high cost of exploring the high seas

On 6 September 1522 an unidentified, broken-down vessel pulled into the mouth of the Guadalquivir river. Its arrival was unexpected, to say the least. Two days later, the *Victoria* moored at Seville. Cheers and rejoicing greeted the eighteen men who had miraculously returned from the Pacific. It was as if they had come back from another world. The crew had numbered sixty when they set sail from the Moluccas; forty-two men had perished on the voyage home. Besides the prisoners held by the Portuguese, the three-year circumnavigation — a total of 85,000 kilometres — had cost the lives of 237 men. In the end the Moluccas remained in the hands of the Portuguese.

The date line

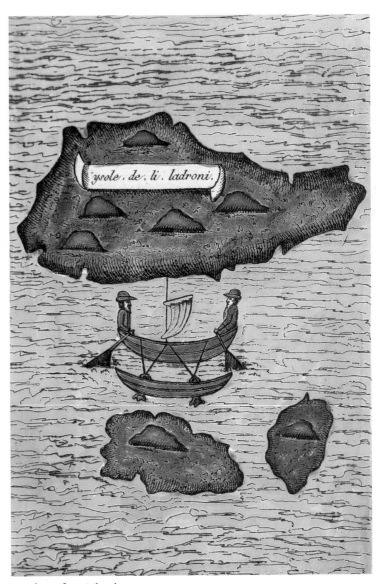

Land was first sighted on 6 March 1521. Magellan christened this island 'Ladrone' (now Guam).

When the Pythagoreans proposed in the fourth century BC that the Earth was shaped like a sphere, estimations of its radius led to the notion of ring-like zones lying parallel to the equator. Early geographers posited the existence of a southern counterearth or 'antichthon' to balance the 'oikoumene' or inhabited world, with a scorched equatorial zone separating the two symmetrical halves of the Earth.

The seaman's plague

The first ocean-going mariners of the great age of discovery were plagued by scurvy. Sailors watched in terror as their hair, then their teeth fell out, while their swollen, bleeding gums made it impossible for them to eat. This dreaded illness was attributed to spoiled food and water, and to the stale air of ships' holds. For centuries the causes of scurvy remained a mystery. We know now that it results from a lack of vitamin C, and appears in the form of weakened blood vessels on the sixty-eighth day of vitamin deprivation. If left untreated, the disease may be fatal after three and a half months.

The Land of the West

In 1570, on a map in his atlas *Theatrum Orbis Terrarum*, the great Belgian cartographer Abraham Ortelius outlined a vast *Terra australis nondum cognita*. He was merely passing on a notion that dated from Antiquity and was accepted as true by most cartographers, of a circumpolar Southern Continent. The discovery of America had strengthened the belief that this as yet unseen land abounded in precious metals, gems, rare woods, spices, and medicinal plants. It was widely thought to be inhabited by unicorns and other strange beasts, perhaps even by exotic—but gentle—human beings. The belief in an unknown but marvellous *Terra Australis* lent zest to dreary reality, much as spices heightened the flavour of insipid foods.

Sarmiento Y Gamboa, a historian in search of a western land with an Inca tradition, set out in 1567 from the Peruvian port of Callao, near Lima, with Alvaro Mendaña. They sailed west and eventually discovered islands which they named after Solomon, the wise king of Israel.

The Manila galleon

Since the dramatic failure of Gomez de Espinosa's *Trinidad*, Spain had sought to establish regular navigational bases throughout the Pacific, the better to exploit waters attributed to Spain by the Treaty of Tordesillas. Emperor Charles V had launched three unsuccessful expeditions from Mexico, commanded by Alvaro de Saavedra in 1528, de Grijalva in 1537, and Ruy Lopez de Villalobos in 1542.

Miguel Lopez de Legaspi and Friar Andres de Urdaneta sailed from Acapulco in 1564 to colonize and convert the Philippines. In the far North Pacific they discovered favourable westerly winds blowing towards America.

This success armed King Philip II with the means to get around the Portuguese monopoly. From 1571 onwards, the Manila galleon provided a regular service from Acapulco across the Pacific. After an overland journey as far as Vera Cruz, the connection continued to Seville or Cadiz via transatlantic fleets sailing out of New Spain.

Papua New Guinea. The island was discovered by the Portuguese explorer Meneses in 1526.

Espiritu Santo

Like all discoveries before the mid-eighteenth century, the exact geographical position of the Solomon Islands was kept secret. Maps were so unreliable that Mendaña, instructed to colonize the islands twenty-seven years later, simply could not find them. He did discover the Marquesas Islands, however, which were named in honour of the Marquise of Mendoza, wife of the governor of Peru, and the Santa Cruz Islands, where Mendaña died.

His pilot, Pedro Fernandez de Quiros, set out again from Callao in 1605 along with Luis Valez de Torres in search of the *Terra Australis*. They sighted the Tuamotu Archipelago, and probably landed in Tahiti and the Society Islands. They made landfall in the Vanuatu Archipelago, where the principal island was christened *Terra Australis del Espiritu Santo*, for de Quiros was certain he had discovered the Southern Continent.

Torres continued the expedition on his own. He ascertained that New Guinea was indeed an island, and crossed—though he did not realize it—the strait which today bears his name. Torres missed Australia though he was no more than a day's sail away from that long sought-after continent.

Bearded round-eyed men

The Portuguese landed in Canton in 1516. Macau was handed over to them in 1533, to thank these bearded, round-eyed men from far-off barbarian lands for having driven off the Chinese, Japanese and Malaysian pirates who terrorized seamen around Canton. Thus did the West discover tea and porcelain. In 1542, three Portuguese adventurers finally reached Japan, the fabled

Cipango evoked by Marco Polo two and a half centuries earlier. They fetched up at Tanega Shima, near the southern island of Kyushu. Though they did not find the hoped-for rivers of gold, the Portuguese did establish a lucrative commercial network between China and Japan, greatly appreciated by the feudal lords of Kyushu—as were the cargoes of Western firearms.

A Portuguese route to the Indies

Heavy merchant vessels called carracks used by the *Carreira da India* replaced the caravels in which Portuguese explorers had plied the seas. The trade route was the same as Vasco da Gama's historic crossing of the Mozambique Canal; commercial shipping followed the seasons, exploiting the prevailing winds, and avoiding recurring storms. A convoy of some ten ships sailed annually from Lisbon to the Indies. The vessels steered for Madeira, then passed the Cape Verde Islands, the Brazilian or Argentine coast, and the Cape of Good Hope. Then they emerged into the Indian Ocean in spring or early summer, so avoiding seasonal storms and catching the monsoon winds.

The voyage to Goa lasted at least three years; but it could stretch out to four, or even eight years. In the best conditions a carrack could make two or three trips to the Indies. But the perils of the sea could easily claim a vessel on its very first time out.

Portuguese secrets in the southern sea

When Portuguese traders got a foothold in China, lines of navigation shifted east. Captains charting a direct course to the Far East sailed to the straits of Sunda or Lombok after they rounded the Cape of Good Hope. While in search of the southeastern trade winds along the eightieth meridian, many vessels narrowly missed wrecking on the southern coast of Australia, though these incidents contributed nothing to knowledge of the region's geography.

It is possible, though not proven, that Cristovào de Mendoça and Gomes de Sequeira landed on the northwestern coast of Australia between 1523 and 1525. Maps of the Dieppoise school, probably copied in the 1530s from Portuguese originals, seem to show that Portuguese seamen were indeed the first Europeans to set foot in Australia. The question of the continent's discovery is moot, for given the inaccuracy of positions charted before the late eighteenth century, 'discovery' meant understanding the significance of a finding and turning it to profit. The Viking Leif Ericsson, for example, who accidentally happened upon the North American continent but paid no attention to it, cannot really be considered the man who 'discovered' America.

From carracks to oil tankers

The carracks used to transport commercial cargo between Europe and the Indies were, in their time, the heaviest merchant vessels ever constructed. Weighing in at one thousand tonnes, the *Garça* was in 1588 the biggest ship of its day. The construction of today's gigantic oil tankers was likewise inspired by the need to make the ocean route around Africa profitable.

During the second half of the 16th century, the Japanese gave the Portuguese permission to establish trade outposts on the island of Nagasaki.

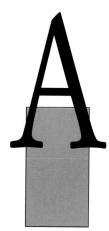

s the sixteenth century came to a close, and with it the era of the conquistadores' glory, a nation of punctilious merchants, guided by pilots accustomed to navigating in narrow, shallow waters, drove the Portuguese from their sumptuous yet fragile commercial empire. In the captains' cabins of India Company vessels, account ledgers lay side by side with route charts.

The price of pepper and tea

A million deaths were recorded in Batavia over a period of twenty-two years. The mortality rate among seamen was such that extra hands had to be hired at the start of a voyage, and replacements found for crews halved by disease by the end of a campaign. Fever, dysentery, the whole gamut of tropical maladies, syphilis on shore and scurvy aboard ship added further to the perils which were the sailor's normal lot: accidents in the rigging or the hold, and the risks that accompany navigation on the open seas.

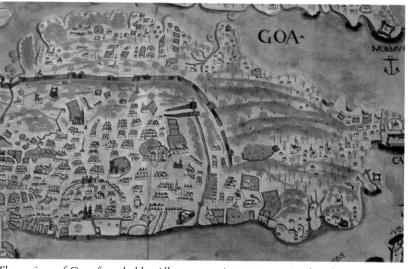

The regions of Goa, founded by Albuquerque in 1510, remained under Portuguese control until 1962, when it was annexed by India.

The end of Portuguese pre-eminence

In the days of Vasco da Gama, Portugal was a nation of one million souls, eight times less populous than Spain, fifteen time less than France. As the wise men of King Manoel's court had feared, Portugal's adventures in India fuelled inflation while the new generations no longer thrilled to heroic tales of discovery and conquest. Managing an empire that extended all the way to Japan overtaxed the Crown's strength.

The Duke of Alba occupied Portugal in 1580 in the name of the King of Spain, then at war with the Seven Provinces (in Holland). Thus Lisbon was closed to the Dutch, who had until then been responsible for coastal trade in the Iberian peninsula. But Amsterdam merchants soon realized that their exclusion from Portuguese warehouses was an opportunity in disguise, for they were obliged to purchase spices and porcelain at source. Indeed, they had already been invited to deal directly with

Eastern suppliers by a learned young Dutchman named Jan Huyghen van Linschoten, secretary to the Archbishop of Goa. Linschoten had had occasion to explore Portuguese possessions in the East Indies, and to analyse the empire's geography and administration. Written at the close of the sixteenth century, his *History of Navigation in the East Indies* was both an economic and commercial handbook and a travel guide to the Indies. The volume was the ideal complement to a previously published marine atlas of the East Indian seas, the twenty-five maps of which had been copied from top-secret Spanish documents. A century of experience was thus revealed to anyone who wished to outfit a commercial expedition to the Indies.

On every sea and every shore

In a famous address to Maria de' Medici, the French queen mother, in 1639, Joost van den Vondel stated in the plainest possible

terms that 'the people of Amsterdam were sailing over every sea on earth for the sheer love of profit'. The Catholic kingdoms of Europe were less inclined to develop lucrative commercial networks, or to encourage intellectual initiatives or exploration. Their religion led them to suspect profit, and to distrust the great unknown spaces, even if the latter offered opportunities to propagate their faith. As of 1578, Amsterdam became a refuge for Protestants and Jews fleeing Spanish rule in the southern provinces, and after 1685 for French Huguenots as well. Thanks to this, Amsterdam had a large population of rich, free-thinking immigrants—an incomparable potential for investments and entrepreneurial ventures.

Strategically located at the nexus of North Sea commerce and promoted since the thirteenth century by the dynamic Hanseatic League, Holland was, so to speak, an amphibious nation. Thanks to the nautical expertise of its sea-faring traders and the acumen of its merchants, in just twenty years Holland was able to give seaborne commerce an entirely new direction.

The difficulties of Dutch explorations

Armed though they were with information and maps, North Sea traders were slow to come to terms with the unfamiliar waters of the East. A fleet of four ships departed from Texel on 2 April 1595 under Admiral Pieter Dirckzoon van Keyser. Nine merchants had banded together under the banner of the Verre Company in the hope of reaping sizeable profits. The Company was headed by Cornelius van Houtman, who, owing to the merchants' efforts, had been freed from a Lisbon prison, where he had been imprisoned for showing too great an interest in Portuguese carracks sailing home from Goa. Houtman was the fleet's *Opper-Koop-*

man, or senior commercial officer. This Dutch expedition heralded a new era in transoceanic trade. For the first time the *Schipper*, or ship's captain, served under the *Koopman*, the merchant responsible for the commercial success of the voyage.

The fleet steered for the East Indies, where the ships docked after fifteen scurvy-plagued months at sea. The Portuguese eyed the Dutch with hostility, and tried to set the natives against the new invaders. Two-thirds of the Dutch crew perished in that first exploratory voyage, which lasted two and a half years and served as an omen of the difficulties and risks to come.

The VOC

Nonetheless, the next six years saw thirteen Dutch fleets set sail for Indonesia. Motivated by misguided nationalism, Hollanders and Zeelanders competed chaotically in the East Indies under the flags of a dozen different companies. A senior government minister, Johan van Oldenbarnevelt, decided in 1602 to create a single company, thus putting an end to independent initiatives. Commercial markets invested in the *Vereenigde Oostindische Compagnie*, the famous VOC (or United East India Company). The markets formed the Company's various chambers. Amsterdam, which held half the shares, was the Great Chamber. A force to be reckoned with, the Committee of Seventeen was formed of merchants and high councillors (the latter were appointed administrators or elected persons of note). The committee coordinated the Company's activities, oversaw accounts, commissioned ships to be built, governed overseas trading posts, decided the make-up of cargoes, and fixed sales quotas for spices so as to keep prices high.

Control of the spice traffic

The ships of the VOC first took over the Moluccas, thus controlling access to the archipelago from Malacca, and later from Sumatra. Conquered in 1612, Jakarta became Batavia, a port for unloading and redistributing cargo, and a powerful maritime arsenal.

In their successful struggle against the English in the East Indies between 1616 and 1663, the Dutch captured Malaysia, Ambon, Ceylon, Cochin, the Malabar Coast and Timor. The Dutch were strategi-

cally positioned at the very source of precious spices—pepper, cloves, cinnamon, nutmeg—and precious stones—diamonds and emeralds from Ceylon.

Portuguese captains had formerly been instructed to Christianize native populations, by fire and the sword if necessary. But Dutch governors placed the interests of the Company over humanitarian concerns, justice, and doubtful questions of individual rights. Cape Town was founded in 1652 in Table Bay (see p. 178), three months out of Batavia and a six-month voyage from Amsterdam.

Trading posts at Formosa and Nagasaki

The Portuguese salvaged Macau from the debacle of their eastern empire. The Dutch abandoned the idea of pushing into China, and settled instead on Formosa, where they built Orange, later renamed Zelandia. From that fortified post, Chinese porcelain was shipped out. In thirty years the Dutch imported three million pieces of *kraakporselein* from the Wan-Li period of the Ming dynasty.

The VOC was first authorized to call at Hirado near Nagasaki, but later received permission to establish an isolated, heavily guarded post in that port on the tiny islet of Deshima.

Concerned more with commerce than spreading the Gospel, the Dutch broke the Portuguese trade monopoly in Japan. In 164... they founded a trading outpost at Deshima. All other ports were closed to European development.

Glory and decline of the VOC

The VOC enjoyed forty years of unparalleled prosperity between 1680 and 1720. In each year of that period, the Company outfitted and sent to the Indies more that twenty *retourschepen*, powerful ships that sailed back to Europe, their holds crammed with cargo gathered by store ships and yachts on station in Chinese and East Indian waters. A single campaign lasted two to three years.

The organization operated on a global scale, and required a cumbersome bureaucracy. Its unbending rigidity was ill suited to deal with the transmission of orders and the execution of campaign schedules. With the discrepancies between colonial currencies and the vast distances separating management centres and trading markets, the Company's inventories and accounts rarely tallied. Thousands of more or less honest directors and agents were responsible for a commercial empire. Operating costs swelled to enormous sums in the latter half of the eighteenth century. The VOC's profits gave way to a growing deficit, which even a radical reorganization could not tame. By the 18th century, it had become a loose territorial organization interested in agricultural produce. The Company was dissolved in 1798 after operating for nearly two hundred years and paying dividends of 186 million florins to its shareholders.

Batavia

An opulent, cosmopolitan city arose upon the insalubrious swamplands near the Tginiwong River. With its canals, gabled houses and mullioned windows, Batavia had a distinctly Dutch look. But a hot, humid, unhealthy climate fostered recurrent epidemics and Batavia's five hospitals were always full of European seafarers. Death and illness were forgotten in the city's perpetual carnival, punctuated by bonfires of spices, intoxicatingly fragrant celebrations which had a practical aspect as well: controlled supplies meant high prices for the commodities on the Amsterdam markets.

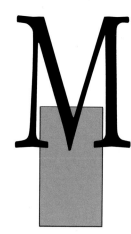

Marine cartography came of age in the last third of the sixteenth century. Its centre shifted from the Mediterranean to the North Sea, owing to the discovery of a new procedure for representing the globe on a flat surface, an increased mass of nautical information, and the development of the printing industry. In the same period, the Terra Australis Incognita *became New Holland.*

The *Mirror of Navigation*

Seaman's charts, or *portolanos*, first appeared in the Mediterranean in the late thirteenth century, an early sign of the new desire to sail the open sea. Rudimentary at first, these early marine maps were useful only in limited areas, such as the Mediterranean or the North Sea. In 1569 the Flemish mathematician and geographer Gerardus Mercator invented the universal projection that now bears his name (which, however, had been conceived some fourteen centuries earlier by Marinus of Tyre). By correcting the variable relation between degrees of latitude and longitude from equator to pole, the Mercator projection allowed cartographers to draw the entire earth on maps intended for navigators. His system is still the basis of today's marine charts.

For seamen navigating in European waters Lucas Waghenaer produced in 1584 a *Mirror of Navigation* (De Spieghel der Zeevaerdt), which for the next hundred years remained the archetype for a new generation of maritime charts.

The VOC employed the best cartographers money could buy, who gathered from the Company's shipmasters the most recent information about a world that was still rather vague, since it lacked one of two vital dimensions—accurately measured longitude. The great Pieter Plancius, Willem Janszoon, Joan Blaeu and Hessel Gerritz laboured to produce a clearer image of the Indian Ocean. In spite of important advances in the transmission of knowledge, maps of East Indian waters, which had once been considered state secrets, remained trade secrets for a very long time. Only in 1743 did the VOC authorize the publication of its maps of the Far East, thereby ending an official policy of secrecy that dated back to the Renaissance and beyond that to the Phoenicians who centuries before had likewise protected their commercial monopoly.

Cape Horn

The extreme climatic conditions that prevailed near the Strait of Magellan led navigators to abandon that arduous route to the Pacific. The prospect of finding open sea south of the strait, near the fabled *Terra Australis*, was worth pursuing. Sir Francis Drake confirmed this hypothesis in 1578 (see p. 82). The new route allowed independent Dutch traders to circumvent the VOC's exclusive right to send ships around the Cape of Good Hope or through the Strait of Magellan.

Jakob Le Maire and Willem Corneliszoon Schouten left Hoorn on the Zuyder Zee on 25 May 1615 for Texel, and from there set sail on 14 June for the Pacific. Their two ships, the *Eendracht* and the store ship *Hoorn*, had been outfitted by the independent Austral Company founded by the navigators' families. The *Hoorn* was destroyed by fire while undergoing repairs on a Patagonian beach. Somehow the crews of both ships managed to squeeze aboard the *Eendracht*, which crossed a strait between the Tierra del Fuego and the Los Estados Islands. The narrow channel, named in honour of Lemaire, opened onto a cape which they rounded on January 29, in fair weather on calm blue waters. They called it Cape Hoorn (Cape Horn).

Sailing past the Tuamotu, Tonga, and Futuna islands, past the Samoas and New Guinea, the delighted Dutch crew joined

Studies of animals made by the expedition led by Gouin de Beauchesne.

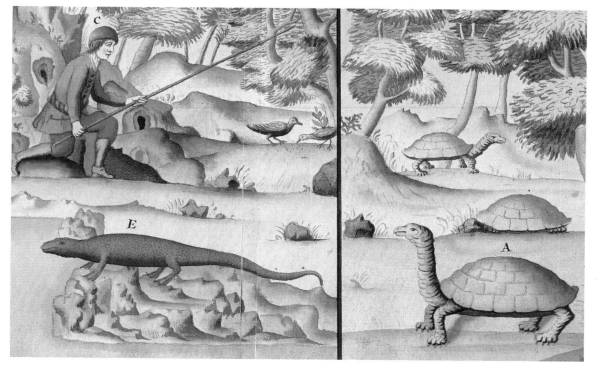

their compatriots at Ternate. But their euphoria was short-lived, for the VOC confiscated the ship which had breached their monopoly. The infant Austral Company was never authorized to exploit its discovery of a new route.

The approach to Australia

From their base in Batavia the Dutch launched several exploratory expeditions into the southern hemisphere. A vessel touched the northern coast of Australia in 1606. Ten years later the *Eendracht* commanded by Dirk Hartog fetched up on the continent's western shore. Many Dutch ships sailed to *Terra Australis* between 1618 and 1623, and fragments of the southern coastline appeared on Dutch maps as Pieter Nuyts' Land (Nuyts Archipelago), discovered around 1626. Ill luck cast other ships taking the direct route to the Orient onto the reefs off the coast of western Australia. On 4 June 1629 the *Batavia* was wrecked on the coastal islands; the passengers were murdered by blood-thirsty mutineers.

New Holland

In August 1642 the Governor General of the Dutch East Indies, Van Diemen, dispatched an exploratory party headed by Captain Abel Jansz Tasman. Tasman had sailed for ten years in the southern hemisphere, and wished to make a systematic exploration of the South Pacific. The expedition's two ships sailed south from Mauritius in October. They skirted Australia without seeing it, owing to the cold, stormy weather. Reaching modern Tasmania, which he christened Van Diemen's Land, Tasman came upon States' Land (New Zealand) on 13 December. In the strait separating the North and South Islands, the body of water dubbed Murderers Bay is a reminder that the Europeans' first contact with the native Maoris was singularly unfriendly.

The Company sent Tasman back two years later to complete his investigations. Although he made no new discoveries, the second voyage allowed him to trace with greater precision the outline of Australia's northern shores in the western Gulf of Carpentaria. It was about this time that *Terra Australis* became known as New Holland. Its western shores were methodically surveyed from 1656. A map by Pieter Goos, drawn in the 1660s, is the first precise depiction of Western Australia.

The native inhabitants of New Guinea were little affected by Western influences and continued to live from hunting, fishing and livestock.

The English around the world

The first English navigators to circumnavigate the globe were untrustworthy explorers, adventurers, freebooters, and even slave traders, encouraged by the Crown to pillage Spanish possessions in the New World. Francis Drake, knighted by Elizabeth I in 1580, accomplished the first British voyage around the globe and returned home laden with booty (see p. 82). From around 1683 another buccaneer, William Dampier, spent twenty years sailing along the west coast of America, with forays into ports as far apart as China and Australia. Dampier's account of his travels awakened British interest in the Pacific Ocean.

Six vessels commanded by Captain George Anson set sail from Spithead on 18 September 1740 with a mission to attack Spanish colonies and lines of navigation in South America. The campaign was a success. Unfortunately the single vessel that returned to London four years later with a glittering cargo of gold was manned by only half of the two thousand original crew members; hundreds had succumbed to scurvy en route.

Bretons sail the South Pacific

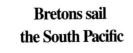

Under the flag of the South Sea Company sponsored by Breton shipowner Noël Danycan, Gouin de Beauchesne led the first French ships through the Strait of Magellan into the Pacific in 1698-1701. During a very trying voyage Beauchesne laid the foundations for French knowledge of navigational and commercial conditions in the eastern Pacific. Upon his return to Saint-Malo, Danycan and other Breton ship-owners launched other missions to Chile and Peru.

The last merchant explorers

As late as the eighteenth century, the mystery of *Terra Australis* had not been wholly resolved, despite the realistic analysis of the French engineer Frézier, a scientific observer sailing aboard the *Saint Joseph* out of Saint-Malo from 1712 to 1715. His hypothesis of an ice-bound southern continent was supported by Vice-Admiral Jacob Roggeveen. The latter was already a man of mature years when, following an old family tradition, he sailed with three ships from Texel in 1721 in search of new lands in the South Pacific. After rounding Cape Horn, he discovered Easter Island on 14 April 1722, then pushed on to Batavia via the Society Islands and the Samoas. The results of Roggeveen's voyage were dismissed by the VOC as uninteresting.

Like their Dutch counterparts, English and French expeditions had little or no scientific scope, at least until the mid-eighteenth century.

The prime motivation for dispatching missions to the South Seas was above all profit. In that age, advances in navigation and in plotting position were regarded merely as a safeguard for overseas investments.

THE AGE OF ENLIGHTENMENT

T*he scientific spirit flourished in the eighteenth century,
and the Pacific became a vast field for exploration. All the nations
of Europe, particularly Britain and France, devoted to that
immense ocean a significant part of the intellectual curiosity that
characterized the Age of Enlightenment.*

The French Encyclopedists

The extraordinary intellectual ferment of Europe in the mid-eighteenth century found an outlet in the remote expanses of the Pacific Ocean. First revealed by an earlier generation of navigators, it was a field for research and exploration vast enough to match the insatiable curiosity of the Age of Enlightenment. Among the many learned societies that sprang up in Europe, the Royal Society in London and the Académie des Sciences in Paris were in a position to gather and exchange new knowledge, and to determine the direction of research. The surge of scientific interest recognized no boundaries, and in an altruistic spirit often ignored the wars that divided nations.

A Tahitian totem etched in a tree trunk.

The first of thirty-five volumes of the monumental *Encyclopédie*, edited by Diderot and others, was published in 1751 at the very moment when Buffon's *Natural History* was changing the way people looked at animal species and nature as a whole.

In 1756 Charles de Brosses, president of the Dijon Parliament, published a general history of navigation in the southern seas (*Histoire des navigations aux terres australes*). Insisting on what he considered the necessary symmetry of continents, he evoked the riches these virgin lands offered to the naturalist. Explorers might investigate the native populations, their cultures and languages, and introduce them to the benefits of science and philosophy. Pleasant, prosperous colonies could be established to provide a fresh start for men whose lives would otherwise be wasted. In England, de Brosses' friend Alexander Dalrymple expounded similar ideas concerning the supposed lands of the Southern Continent and their future uses.

Measuring the world

Great observatories were established all over Europe in the late seventeenth century. Between 1735 and 1743 two missions from the French Académie des Sciences set out to Lapland and Peru to measure the Earth. Yet by 1778 the Académie had recorded only 228 exact geographical points. Astronomical research and advances in mechanics and chronometry promised great progress in techniques for measuring longitude. In the meantime the octant, a navigational instrument presented to the Royal Society by John Hadley on 13 May 1731, represented a modest advance; it was the model for the modern sextant, the prototype of which was invented in 1757 by Captain Campbell.

Salted meat and sea biscuit

Live cattle and poultry were too cumbersome for transport aboard ship. The alternatives were salted meat, which often spoiled, beans, and sea biscuits, which quickly became infested by weevils and tropical insects brought on board in the wood used for fuel.

The sulphates present in spring water reacted with organic matter in the wood of water barrels, producing sulphides. Their putrid odours mingled with the nauseating fumes from the bottom of the hull and the tainted air of damp steerages. It was in these conditions, worse than many gaols, that free-spirited seamen spent years at a time.

146

Yet naval officers were traditionally a conservative lot; they tended to rely on old-fashioned instruments and navigational methods. More enlightened minds in European navies vigorously urged their officers to take a personal interest in navigation, a task often left to pilots. Navigational errors in those days were frequent, and often enormous. The *Saint Denis* spent a year searching for the island of Réunion, while the *Glorieux* was forced to spend winter in Rio de Janeiro in 1750 after missing the Cape Verde Islands. Hourglasses were still used to keep time, and solar time was adjusted daily when the sun was at its zenith.

The Maori triangle

Eighteenth-century scientists who studied the morphology of Polynesians believed that the Maoris were aborigines. In fact, they were descended from explorers who had migrated great distances over the ocean three thousand years ago, driven from the East Indies by southern Chinese peoples fleeing before the Chang invasions. Via Melanesia and the sacred island of Raiatea, successive waves of *pahi*—large double canoes—had reached Tonga and Samoa before the Christian era, then the Marquesas and Society Islands in the ninth century. Easter Island and Hawaii, populated around the millennium, and New Zealand, discovered in the mid-twelfth century, are the three points of the Maori triangle, which marks the boundaries of the small scattered islands occupied by these skilful seafarers. Guided by the stars, the Maoris were quick to discern the smallest atoll far beyond the horizon by observing birds, the sea and the sky.

The disappointment of Commodore Byron

In 1764, by order of the king, George III, the English frigate *Dolphin* and the sloop *Tamar* under John Byron—the poet's grandfather—roved the South Atlantic in a vain search for new commercial opportunities between the Cape of Good Hope and the Strait of Magellan. The commodore had survived the well-known wreck of the *Wager*, a ship that had sailed on Anson's disastrous expedition (see p. 145). Contacts with the Patagonians and Fuegians were not encouraging. With no land in sight south of Cape Horn, Byron took possession of the Falkland Islands, which His Majesty instructed the commodore to reconnoitre. Bougainville had just settled an Acadian colony on the islands, which the French knew as the Malouines (Malvinas). After two months of wandering in the South Pacific, Byron made his way with much difficulty to the Tuamotu Archipelago, which he christened 'Islands of Disappointment'. The expedition called at the Gilbert Islands, put into port at Batavia, and then sailed back to England, bringing the two-year voyage to a close.

The delights of King George's Island

A few months later, on 22 August 1766, the *Dolphin* set out under Samuel Wallis for another exploratory voyage. Philip Carteret, one of Byron's lieutenants, was put in command of a ramshackle old sloop, the *Swallow*, with a promise—never honoured, as it turned out—that it would be replaced with a frigate in the Falklands. But at the Strait of Magellan, the two ships, which had laboriously dragged along together, were separated; the broken-down *Swallow* was no match for the *Dolphin*.

The *Dolphin* sailed into the Tuamotu Archipelago in June 1767, and later reached the Society Islands and Tahiti. After an initial clash with the natives, peace was established. The islanders welcomed the voyagers with remarkable warmth and entranced them with their happy way of life. Wallis, who had fallen ill, was nursed in Queen Oberea's residence. The English took possession of the sunny island in the name of King George, after whom it was named. Tahiti was soon a legend in Europe, the distant paradise sought for so long by feverish, miserable seamen on endless ocean voyages. After a blissful month-long stay, the crew bid the islanders farewell with heavy hearts. Wallis returned via Tinian, south of the Mariana Islands, and Batavia; he had not lost a single man in twenty-one months at sea.

The ordeal of the *Swallow*

Cut loose by the *Dolphin* as soon as the winds steadied on the far side of the Strait of Magellan, the desperately leaky little sloop sailed intrepidly into the Pacific, following its charted course. Carteret had the good fortune to claim Pitcairn Island—which the *Bounty* would one day make famous—and crossed the Solomon Islands after touching Santa Cruz. Carteret then claimed part of the Bismarck Archipelago in Melanesia (islands which he christened New Britain, New Ireland, and New Hanover), and named the Admiralty Islands. The *Swallow* was a floating wreck with a shattered crew when it reached Macassar late in 1767. After four months of repairs in Batavia, the ship continued its voyage, which lasted until late the following year.

Carteret pulled into Spithead on 20 March 1769, four days after Bougainville's return to France. The *Swallow* had been feared lost, and two ships had been sent to search for it. Nearly a year after Wallis, Carteret returned from one of the most remarkable round-the-world voyages in a dilapidated ship, having lost half his crew.

On 12 July 1767 Queen Oberea welcomed Captain Wallis to the island of Tahiti with much pomp and ceremony.

The final victory over scurvy

Dr James Lind's treatise on scurvy appeared in England in 1754. He recommended that lemon juice be distributed along with the sailors' daily rations. The causes of the disease were still unknown, and Lind's proposals were not always followed. It seemed everyone had a different method for dealing with scurvy, some good, some bad. Cook rightly believed that sauerkraut was a remedy, but he also had faith in the virtues of malt juice, which has no anti-scorbutic properties whatsoever. The duration of ocean crossings and the frequency of stopovers were what finally determined the crews' health and fate. Cook lost just one man in three years at sea, while Surville's casualties reached nearly a hundred (see p. 152). From 1800 to 1804 Baudin stubbornly insisted on remaining at sea for long periods, against doctors' advice (see p. 160).

Oberea, Queen of Tahiti

Oberea's island realm was the most pleasant and fertile imaginable. Succulent plants and vegetables grew luxuriantly, the lagoon abounded in fish, domestic animals flourished with little attention. But the exhausted European seamen were irresistibly drawn to the island's sweet, statuesque women, whose feigned reserve would melt when they were offered a nail—to them an article of inestimable worth. Indeed, the *Dolphin* had to be guarded night and day to prevent the crew from taking the ship apart, in their eagerness to please their new sweethearts. Oberea and the ship's commander were naturally drawn together by virtue of their rank; the queen wept inconsolably the day her dashing captain took his leave.

Bougainville's voyage was organized without any specific objectives, and yielded only modest scientific results. Undertaken two years before Cook's first voyage, it nonetheless marked a turning point in the history of discovery. Bougainville's expedition heralded a great wave of scientific voyages which would explore the Pacific and map every landmass of the globe. The merchant's day was over; the hour of the scientific explorer had come.

Maori chieftains tatooed their faces with strange blue spirals.

The grand designs of Colonel Bougainville

It was in Quebec that fate turned a brilliant infantry officer, aide-de-camp of Field Marshal Montcalm, into one of the great French navigators. The fall of Quebec in 1759 left a lasting impression on Louis-Antoine de Bougainville, who took part in negotiating the terms of surrender. From the moment he returned to France, Bougainville worked to resettle the Acadians, victims of the French defeat in Canada.

Bougainville's fame as a mathematician had reached the Royal Society in London; he was acquainted with the most noted explorers and theoreticians of the southern seas, men such as Anson and de Brosses. The Falkland Islands in the southwestern Atlantic, beyond the Strait of Magellan, seemed an ideal site for the displaced Acadians. Moreover, their presence would give France control of the strait and the route to Cape Horn.

Bougainville was promoted to captain. Accompanied by Duclos-Guyot, an officer from the Company of the East Indies familiar with the South Seas, he set out with the Acadians from Saint-Malo on 15 September 1763. The colony was established in the Falklands late in January 1764; more settlers arrived two years later.

The Falklands become the Malvinas

The presence of French colonists in the Falklands naturally irritated the British, who asserted that the islands, discovered by John Davis in the late sixteenth century and claimed for the Crown by Commodore Byron in 1765, belonged to England. But the Anglo-French arguments over the archipelago ended abruptly when Spain claimed that it had a natural right to this dependency of its American colonies. The 1982 Anglo-Argentine conflict over the Falklands was rooted in this eighteenth-century controversy.

Louis XV of France could refuse his Spanish cousins nothing. Bougainville seemed the person best qualified to return the islands to Spain, since he had been the one to draw attention to the Falklands in the first place. The archipelago was thereafter to be known as the Islas Malvinas. To compensate for this task, which nearly broke Bougainville's heart, and to mute the significance of the transfer of power, Bougain-ville was instructed to continue his voyage around the world the moment he had lowered the French flag in the Falklands for the last time.

The first scientific voyage

The frigate *Boudeuse*, a fragile vessel for so long a voyage, was accompanied by the store ship *Etoile*, in keeping with the principle that scientific expeditions required sturdy ships suited to carrying heavy loads of equipment. Duclos-Guyot took part in the voyage as second-in-command of the *Boudeuse*. For the first time, on the advice of Charles de Brosses, Buffon, and the Académie des Sciences, a scientific staff sailed with the mission: Commerson, a noted botanist, doctor and naturalist; Routier de Romainville, an engineer and cartographer; and the astronomer Véron, whose presence would prove particularly valuable for measuring longitude by the new method of lunar distances, a system then under evaluation in a still imperfect form.

Interestingly, the scientists did not sail aboard the flagship, which hosted only one guest of note, the Prince de Nassau-Siegen. As on nearly all subsequent voyages of this type, relations between naval officers and scientists were often chilly and sometimes hostile.

New Cythera

From December 1767 to January 1768, the two ships struggled against snow storms and squalls in the Strait of Magellan, while the scientists got on with their work. Bougain-ville followed a now-classic course; he steered towards the Tuamotu Archipelago, then sailed to the Society Islands. On 6 April the *Etoile* and the *Boudeuse* cast anchor at Hitiaa, on the eastern coast of Tahiti. The disheartening aspect of a dangerous anchorage did not dampen the men's joy and wonder at the naked native beauties who welcomed the scurvy-ridden sailors with open arms.

Ignorant of the violent customs of this warlike people who practised human sacrifice, Bougainville credited the legend of the noble savage. On 12 April he officially claimed the island, which he knew had already been visited by Europeans, and named it New Cythera after the birthplace of Aphrodite, goddess of love. The French ships sailed off two days later, with the crew lamenting their lost loves. Not many days later the first symptoms of syphilis appeared on board.

A rude awakening

Heavy seas made the voyage home an ordeal for the men. Most were still suffering from scurvy, which their brief stay on land had not cured. The Samoas with their reputedly shrewd, savage population, and Lepers' Island made a melancholy contrast with the gentle paradise of New Cythera. The navigators sighted Aoba, in the New Hebrides, and later Louisiade and the Solomon Islands. On 24 August, the first mate died of scurvy, and forty-five crew members were gravely ill with the disease. Bougainville attempted to treat it with lemonade and wine, though the latter was no remedy against scurvy.

Sailing against the monsoon, the ships struggled to the Moluccas, heralded from afar by a sweet tropical breeze which made the seamen forget, if only for a few instants at a time, the putrid odour of rotting supplies. The distribution of these spoiled foodstuffs was, as Bougainville himself admitted, the saddest moment of their dismal days. The Dutch governer of Cayeli, unfriendly at first, was finally moved by the evident distress of these famished, sickly Frenchmen. Via Batavia, a city which impressed Bougainville with its order and efficiency, they travelled to the island of Mauritius, which they reached in November. There the scientific staff disembarked. The *Boudeuse* pulled into Saint-Malo on 16 March 1679; Bougainville was given a hero's welcome in Paris.

Aoturu

The most spectacular of Bougainville's scientific specimens was Aoturu, the son of a Tahitian chief. He had lingered aboard one

The Boudeuse *and the* Etoile *being welcomed by Tahitian pirogues and a crowd of festive natives as they drop anchor at Hitiaa.*

of the strange 'pirogues' from across the sea, and finally made it clear that he intended to remain. On the long voyage home Bougainville was delighted to have the opportunity to study the habits and customs of a tribe he had barely had a chance to glimpse on Tahiti.

Though at first he was the toast of court and the town, Aoturu eventually wore out his welcome. His appearance was unprepossessing (Commerson believed him to be the ugliest man of his race), and his French was simply hopeless. After a year, it was thought time to take Aoturu back home where he could regale his fellows with tales of the French court. He was escorted to Mauritius, and from there Marion-Dufresne undertook to accompany Aoturu to Tahiti. Alas, that noble savage died of smallpox during a stopover in Madagascar. Shortly afterwards Marion-Dufresne was eaten by Maoris in New Zealand, after he had unwittingly felled a sacred tree for firewood.

From the Renaissance through the eighteenth century, the initial wonder felt by civilizations discovering each other for the first time rarely had happy consequences in the long (or even the short) run.

The final assessment

Bougainville's voyage, like that of La Pérouse some years later, consisted of interminable periods at sea interrupted by brief and infrequent stops on land. Not to mention the disastrous effects such a regime had on sailors' health, it tended to yield insignificant scientific results as well. His book, the *Voyage around the World*, published in 1711, was more the tale of drama at sea than a report addressed to scientists and navigators.

Yet Philibert Commerson had gathered a wealth of information in the course of his travels. He died on Mauritius after a particularly exhausting voyage to Madagascar, having published neither his notes nor his fifteen hundred drawings. Buffon and Lacépède put part of Commerson's work to use. The thirty-four crates containing his herbarium held nearly five thousand species, some three thousand of which were unidentified. Among them was the hydrangea and a lovely ornamental plant from South America, which was christened bougainvillea in honour of the chief of the expedition.

Jeanne Barré's trip around the world

Although other anonymous female passengers may have disguised themselves as men and sailed on the first ships to explore the vast Pacific, Jeanne Barré is officially the first woman to have circumnavigated the globe. A sturdy native of Burgundy, she embarked with Commerson, dressed as a valet. Despite close quarters aboard the *Etoile*, no one was the wiser, though a few unsubstantiated rumours seem to have circulated. But Jeanne's true identity was unmasked by the Tahitians, who immediately recognized her as a woman the moment she set foot on the beach at Hitiaa.

A large island of some forty thousand square kilometres, lying just six hundred kilometres off the east coast of Africa between the Cape of Good Hope and Ceylon, naturally attracted the attention of Renaissance navigators in search of the Indies. Madagascar, which formed the eastern boundary of the Mozambique Channel, and the nearby Mascarene Islands offered attractive prospects for establishing ports of call, operational bases and trading posts.

Pirates of the Mozambique Channel

As a major zone for commercial traffic, the Mozambique Channel was a prime target for pirates. Freebooters proliferated there after 1685, and some West Indian pirates had also homed in on this new and profitable maritime route. They had a strong foothold in Madagascar, where they married and were even known to rule as chiefs. The French Royal Navy eliminated the freebooters after 1720. Some French pirates attained fame: Olivier Le Vasseur, called La Buse ('the buzzard'), kidnapped the viceroy of Goa in a harbour on Réunion. More or less respectful of French commercial interests, the pirates sometimes even served the nation's purpose when promised amnesty. They made French the common language in Madagascar. La Buse was hanged in 1735, but he was given a Christian burial. His tombstone, engraved with a skull and crossbones, may still be seen in the St Paul cemetery, in Réunion.

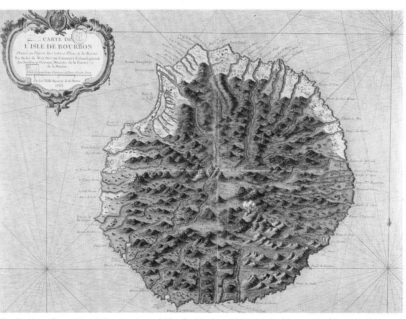

Ile de Bourbon (La Réunion) and Ile de France (Mauritius) were indispensable stopovers on the voyage to India.

The island of St Lawrence

Predictably, it was a Portuguese seaman, Diogo Dias, who first sighted Madagascar on 10 August 1500, the feast of St Lawrence. A fleet commanded by Pedro Alvares Cabral had set out, barely six months after the triumphant return of Vasco da Gama, to conquer the Indian Ocean in the name of King Manoel. Madagascar first appeared on maps of the Indian Ocean in 1502. The Portuguese pursued their reconnaissance of the 'great land' but they did not show particular interest in it. In their wake navigators from all over western Europe set out to see these 'new lands' for themselves. Among them were vessels outfitted by the famous Norman shipper Ango; his *Sacre* and *Pensée* sailed along Madagascar's western coast in July 1529. After put-

ting in there for a time at sites impossible to pinpoint today, the French stopped calling at Madagascar; indeed, they no longer sailed to the Indies at all. But with Henry IV firmly on the throne of France and the long, bloody wars of religion at an end, the French could organize overseas expeditions once again. The example of Holland, then laying the foundations for an unprecedented commercial empire, naturally tempted Breton shippers and sailors to try their luck as well.

The French in Madagascar

In 1602, the storm-tossed *Croissant* and *Corbin*, of the Compagnie de Saint-Malo, Laval and Vitré, made a forced landing in St Augustine Bay on the southwest coast of Madagascar. In similar conditions, the

Ermitage and the *Montmorency* of the first Compagnie des Indes took refuge in the same bay eighteen years later. Augustin de Beaulieu, who commanded the fleet, reported to the Compagnie the advantages of this port of call in an apparently rich land. During the next twenty years many ships out of Dieppe, Rouen, and other Norman ports could be spotted in Madagascan waters engaging in trade, privateering—or piracy. Shunning the perils of the Mozambique Channel, sailors preferred to cast anchor in the spacious bays of the island's east coast, from Sainte-Lucie in the south to Antongil in the north.

The first trading posts sprang up around these anchorages, and were essentially bases for barter with the natives, who furnished the Europeans with cattle and leather. In 1626 a shipper petitioned Richelieu for authorization to occupy the ports of the island of St Lawrence, in order to establish commercial markets. In 1631 Augustin de Beaulieu took up the idea once more, reviving the proposal that the French Crown should claim and colonize Madagascar. In Beaulieu's view, a relay base could be founded there along with a trade centre and an operational base on the route to the Indies. Though he realized the advantages these proposals presented, Richelieu nonetheless hesitated for fear of provoking the Dutch.

Fort Dauphin

In 1642 the French Company of the East Indies was founded upon the initiative of Captain Rigault of the French Royal Navy. He had obtained from Richelieu, in the interest of himself and his friends, exclusive rights to trade in Madagascar and adjacent islands, a privilege confirmed by letters patent from Louis XIII dated 15 February 1642. The fledgling company immediately sent a representative to Madagascar. Jacques Prony caught a ship out of Dieppe, and sailed to the Great Island with instructions to peremptorily enforce the company's rights. Taking possession of the Rodrigues Islands and the Mascarenes (Réunion) on his way, Prony eventually settled in Ste-Lucie and established the precarious headquarters of the company's first trading post. The unhealthy climate and hostile natives stirred up by ousted competitors made Prony reconsider his position. In 1644 he founded Fort Dauphin (Faradofay), a natural harbour on a rocky spur with an airy, wholesome climate.

Unaware that Louis XIV was no longer the dauphin but the king of France, Prony named the new site in his honour as heir to the crown. Disputes over who was in charge of Fort Dauphin quickly divided the settlers into enemy factions. Since the colonists were few in number, malnourished and ill, they soon found themselves in dire straits. The directors finally understood the urgency of taking the colony's affairs in hand and entrusted that task to Etienne de Flacourt. But his efforts were of little avail: prospects for setting up well-run, profitable trading posts in Madagascar remained dim. The island was too remote and too difficult to manage, while the effects of wars, treaties, and domestic politics in France were too unpredictable. Marshal de la Meilleraye, governor of Brittany, showed a glimmer of interest in far-off Madagascar, but he only succeeded in fuelling additional tensions and intrigues.

East France

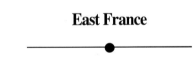

When the new French Company of the East Indies was formed, it seemed opportune to transfer to the Company the rights to Madagascar. The prime minister, Mazarin, had inherited some titles to the island from Marshal de la Meilleraye and was in a position to cede them to the Crown, an act that would automatically entail the withdrawal of the remaining shareholders. Then on 29 May 1664 Louis XIV conceded Madagascar and neighbouring islands to the Company of the East Indies in perpetuity.

A squadron set sail from Brest on 1 March the following year to found a base powerful enough to support French trade in the Indian Ocean. The colonists landed in Fort Dauphin on 10 July with the newly appointed president of the sovereign council of 'East France'. They were dismayed to find that their capital was nothing but a shabby little village built of planks and palm leaves.

Failure of the French colony

In 1669 the Company begged the king to relieve it of the duty of colonizing Madagascar. The island became a royal territory. Convinced that a 'New France' could prosper in southeast Africa, like the French colonies in the West Indies and Canada, Colbert refused to give up. It was only a question, he thought, of seeing things in a wider context than did the Company's agents. A change of location was called for, to more fertile and wholesome regions likely to attract colonists. Blanquet de la Haye was invested with full powers and given the task of finding an appropriate site. His survey led him to propose abandoning Fort Dauphin and developing establishments on Réunion (despite the island's lack of ports) and on Antongil, where a harbour could be created. The Company, in the meantime, simply forbade its captains to land on Madagascar, a miserable land, they said, of famine and troublesome natives. As if to illustrate the wisdom of that judgement, the sixty-three survivors of a murderous attack by Malagasy natives evacuated Fort Dauphin on the evening of 9 September 1674. The dismal result of a half-century of effort was only one example of the difficulties Europeans encountered as they attempted to colonize lands brought to light in the age of discovery.

Mauritius and Réunion

Before receiving the Portuguese name of Mascarenhas, Réunion was called 'mountain of fire' by twelfth-century Arab navigators and 'Santa Apolonia' by the Portuguese seaman Tristan da Cunha early in the sixteenth century. For centuries, it was no more than a volcano assiduously avoided by mariners, uninhabited and unexplored until the 1600s. Claimed by France in 1643, ownership of Ile de Bourbon—Réunion—was confirmed seven years later in the name of Louis XIV. Its fertility and natural beauty lured colonists, the first of whom settled at St Paul in 1663.

Since the island's pioneers had no easy access to the sea, they soon turned their eyes to a nearby island abandoned by the Dutch after a failed attempt at colonization. Guillaume Dufresne took possession of it on 20 September 1715, calling it Ile de France. French sovereignty over Mauritius was reaffirmed in 1721, when it became clear that a seaport was needed there to aid the archipelago's development.

In his pastoral novel Paul et Virginie, *Bernardin de Saint-Pierre's idealized and idyllic view of life on Mauritius heralded Romanticism.*

Mahé de La Bourdonnais

After distinguishing himself in the capture of Mahé on the Malabar coast (southwestern India), Bertrand Mahé de La Bourdonnais was appointed governor-general of Réunion and Mauritius. He landed at Port Louis on 4 June 1735. His instructions were to establish a supply depot in the Mascarenes for Company of the East Indies ships. But he had larger plans in mind. He intended to make the islands under his rule the keystone of the French possessions in the Indian Ocean. In La Bourdonnais's ambitious but neatly conceived project, the natural attractivenss of the Port Louis site destined it to serve both as a naval base and as the capital of the archipelago. Réunion he envisioned as an agricultural satellite of Ile de France, although it was the larger island and had in fact colonized Mauritius.

Despite terrible famines, plagues of locusts, cyclones and rats, under the firm and intelligent leadership of La Bourdonnais, Réunion became a prosperous agricultural province, famed for its coffee, self-sufficient, and able to supply the Company with cattle and grain. Labour was provided by slaves mainly imported from Madagascar. Volcanic basins and mountain forests sheltered bands of black fugitives, who had turned to banditry to survive.

The Ile de Bourbon outlasted the Company of the East Indies, and received its present name—Réunion—from the French revolutionary Convention in 1793. It passed into English hands from 1810 to 1814, before converting, as Mauritius did, to the cultivation of sugar cane in the nineteenth century. Réunion is still a French territory.

The Byenowski affair

The Hungarian Baron Byenowski escaped from a prisoner-of-war camp in Siberia and made his way to Korea, where he embarked on a Company of the East Indies vessel. In the course of his odyssey, Byenowski formed a plan for the conquest of Formosa. The secretary of the French navy proposed that the Hungarian should establish a trading post in Madagascar instead; he travelled there in 1773, and for three years sent back glowing—but utterly fictitious—reports. Dismissed by the French, Byenowski entered the service of the United States, and formed a company for slave trading in Madagascar. He used to say that he had realized a native prophecy by becoming Ampanscabé, or sovereign of the island. Byenowski was killed in 1786, as he was about to be arrested by order of the governor of the Mascarenes.

ince Antiquity, when Greek geographers first wrote of it, the Terra Australis *has been one of the ocean's great mysteries. It has been one of exploration's most persistent myths as well, despite evidence that a rich, welcoming Southern Continent inhabited by gentle natives existed only in the imaginations of philosophers and armchair geographers.*

Bouvet de Lozier's dashed dreams

Two frigates belonging to the French Company of the East Indies, the *Aigle* and the *Marie* sailed due south from Brittany in the summer of 1738. Jean-Baptiste Bouvet de Lozier had convinced the Company that the Southern Continent, which, he assumed, occupied the great space around the South Pole, could no longer remain undiscovered and unexplored. The exploitation of natural resources, trade with economically undeveloped nations, the spread of religion, national glory, scientific progress and the training of a hardy race of navigators were all part of his ambitious programme, which reflected both the noble ideas and the practical aims of the age. Bouvet de Lozier was instructed to find a harbour for Company vessels and to initiate friendly relations with native peoples.

Impeded by exceptionally harsh weather, the French frigates ran into ice fields at a surprisingly low latitude. On 1 January 1739 at the fifty-fourth parallel south, a promontory emerged from the snow and thick fog. The inaccessible cape, which the sailors dubbed Cap de la Circoncision in honour of the day (the Feast of Christ's Circumcision), undoubtedly heralded a barren land. What they found is today called Bouvet Island, one of the rare landmasses of the South Atlantic.

Disappointment greeted the return of the battered party, whose courage and ability at least were worthy of respect. Yet Bouvet de Lozier was denounced as a bungler, and his report condemned as pretentious humbug.

Bouvet Island was rediscovered by a German expedition in 1898, which determined its geographical position but was unable to land. The Norwegian flag was first hoisted over the island in December 1927, and it was annexed to Norway in 1930.

A high price to pay

When Kerguelen arrived in France in September 1774, he was brought before a court-martial. He was accused of transporting a female stowaway and of abandoning the *Gros-ventre*, and was presumed guity of smuggling and of squandering enormous sums. These charges worsened the case against an officer whose principal fault had been to encourage his sponsors' fantasies, and then to smash their dream to pieces. Kerguelen was stripped of his rank and sentenced to six years in a military prison. He was reinstated, however, and promoted to admiral in 1793.

Last glimmers of a dying myth

And yet navigators before Jean-Baptiste Bouvet de Lozier had observed the asymmetry of the climate in the two hemispheres, and the frigid temperatures that prevailed in the most southerly latitudes. In fact Bouvet's report gave the first accurate description of the landscape of Antarctica—the icebergs and ice fields of a desolate, uninhabited world.

One young cartographer did take Bouvet seriously, for he had a similar conception of the world. In 1744 Philippe Buache published his map of the two great oceans which he linked by a glacial arctic sea. Although still imperfect (he divided the continent into two parts), Buache's representation of Antarctica was the first to give it an appropriate scale, relying on a study of earlier navigators' remarks. According to Buache's map, New Holland was the only *Terra Australis* on which life could prosper.

Bouvet de Lozier's failed mission discouraged other voyages to southern waters for some thirty years. *Terra Australis* once more became a subject of controversy and passionate conjecture.

The French *Encyclopédie* and the learned histories of Buffon and de Brosses relaunched—in blatant contradiction of mariners' reports—the age-old myth of the Southern Continent, which they declared was accessible to ships, researchers and merchants.

These affirmations naturally suited the Company of the East Indies—of which president de Brosses was a shareholder—and the scientific academies. It was seen as vital to send men and ships to communicate with the inhabitants of the Antipodes, where several different races ruled—or so de Brosses asserted, astonishing even himself with his own fabrication.

The Odyssey of the *St-Jean-Baptiste*

From the 1770s onwards, a new series of voyages was to confirm the intuition of Philippe Buache, and thus to contain the Southern Continent within the strict confines of the Antarctic Circle. Bougainville had hardly returned from his voyage round the world when Jean-François de Surville set out from the Indies on the *St-Jean-Baptiste*, in search of a fabulously rich island. Its existence was attested to by repeated rumours that a certain Sieur de Gonneville from Honfleur had stopped there early in the sixteenth century. It was not until 1769 that Surville finally found the Solomon Islands, which he christened Land of the Arsacides, and then New Zealand. Nearly half of the 173 crew members perished from scurvy in the course of this voyage, and another twenty-eight seamen deserted.

Tragedy at Waitanoni

When French courtiers grew bored with Aoturu, the Tahitian who had accompanied Bougainville to France (see p. 149), he was packed off to Ile de France (Mauritius) as a first stage in his voyage home. Marc-Joseph Marion-Dufresne, shipmaster of the Company of the East Indies, set sail on 18 October 1771 aboard the store ship *Le Mascarin*, which he had outfitted for slave trading in Madagascar, taking Aoturu with him. The first mate was Julien Crozet. Aoturu succumbed to smallpox on 6 November during a stopover at Fort Dauphin. Marion-Dufresne maintained a southerly course, and was joined by another store ship, the *Marquis de Castries*. In frigid weather—the crew had no warm clothing—the two vessels headed southeast amid thick fog and gusts of snow. A ghostly coastline emerged from the fog on 13 January 1772, which the grateful men christened Land of Hope (present-day Marion Island, in the Prince Edward group). As they steered east along the forty-sixth parallel, other islands appeared, which the navigators supposed to be promontories of the great *Terra Australis*. On 25 January, Crozet disembarked with great difficulty and claimed what appeared to be uninhabitable land for France: it was the Crozet Archipelago. Winter came to the southern hemisphere, bringing heavy seas. After a rest in Van Diemen's Land (Tasmania), the French ships steered towards New Zealand. They cast anchor in Island Bay and were warmly greeted by the Maoris of the Ngatikuri tribe. For two months the Europeans and Maoris enjoyed excellent relations. The ships watered at the Waitanoni waterfall at the Kapowairua anchorage. On 12 June, while collecting fuel, the men unwittingly felled a tree sacred to the Maoris. Nineteen Frenchmen, including Marion-Dufresne, were massacred and eaten. Crozet sailed back to Mauritius with the scurvy-ridden survivors.

Austral France

While Marion-Dufresne led his arduous campaign in the South Seas, a second French expedition was exploring those same waters, with largely the same goal. An officer of the French Royal Navy, versed in hydrography—the mapping of the ocean—with experience on the coasts of Iceland, had convinced Louis XV that it would be worthwhile to take advantage of Aoturu's return to explore the South Seas, search for de Gonneville's fabled island, and claim it for France. Yves-Joseph de Kerguelen de Trémarec was instructed to execute this plan, after investigating a new navigational route proposed by Sublieutenant Grenier between Mauritius and the Indies. His expedition turned out to be one of the most confused and controversial in the annals of the South Seas.

Kerguelen set sail on 16 January 1772 from Mauritius aboard the store ship *Fortune*. The vessel was accompanied by the transport ship *Gros-ventre*, owned by a certain Monsieur de Saint-Allouarn. Heading south, the two ships missed Marion-Dufresne's expedition by only a week. On 12 February a high landmass appeared; its many headlands passed quickly in the squalls that blew gusts of icy sea spray. A landing attempted in these extremely perilous conditions resulted in the loss of the *Fortune*'s dinghy. The *Gros-ventre*'s small

Bouvet de Lozier thought he had discovered the Southern Continent when he sighted a number of icebergs and pack ice. It was simply an approaching island that today bears his name.

craft managed to reach shore with Monsieur de Boisguehenneuc and a frozen landing party, which took possession with little ceremony of what is today known as the Kerguelen Archipelago. In the confusion of the storm, the head of the expedition was not even certain whether the French flag had been planted on the discovery. Struggling for survival, separated by violent winds and blinding snow, the two vessels eventually lost sight of one another. Kerguelen determined to return to Mauritius on his own by the shortest route, and to announce the discovery of Austral France.

A French claim in western Australia

When he realized that his shipmaster had disappeared, Saint-Allouarn resolved to pursue the voyage as planned. The *Gros-ventre* steered towards the western coast of New Holland. On 30 March 1772 a bottle containing an official claim to the territory in the name of Louis XV was buried on the shore of Shark Bay. This claim was never asserted by France. Scurvy once again decimated the *Gros-ventre*'s crew, exhausted by the struggle against the elements in freezing conditions, while the men were clothed in garments fit for the tropics. The poor preparation and equipment of French expeditions in the 1770s was a constant and regrettable factor, which only goes to increase our admiration for the brilliant perspicacity of Captain Cook (see p. 154). Saint-Allouarn died on the voyage.

The bitter truth

Though his reports on a land he had not even visited were scanty, Kerguelen's enthusiasm remained strong. The glowing terms he used to describe his discovery when he returned to France tallied perfectly with the theories of Charles de Brosses and the hopes of the Company of the East Indies. The honours heaped upon Kerguelen, who was promoted to captain and awarded the Cross of St Louis, stirred jealousy and harsh criticism of his decision to abandon the *Gros-ventre* in wild seas.

On 26 May 1773 the *Roland* and the frigate *Oiseau* sailed out of Brest with a mission to establish a base in Austral France. Colonists and soldiers took part in the voyage, but scientists were limited to an astronomer and a naturalist. The two vessels were in a pitiful state when they put into Mauritius, after battling through a terrible storm off the Cape of Good Hope. A corvette, the *Dauphine*, joined the party as it made its way south towards the fiftieth parallel. Harsh weather prevailed throughout the voyage; the passengers and crew were riddled with scurvy. Land was sighted on 14 December. But for a whole month the ships lay at anchor, unable to land, suffering the repeated assaults of sub-polar low-pressure troughs in near-zero temperatures. On 18 January the captains' council resolved to head back to Mauritius. Returning to France via Capetown, Kerguelen had to admit in a letter written to the minister on 17 June 1774 that Austral France was nothing more than a desolate island.

The roaring forties

The pioneers of the southern seas were astonished to discover the 'roaring forties'. The seas of the fortieth parallel in the southern hemisphere are blanketed with fog and snow, and swept by nearly continuous westerly gales. The heavy seas whipped up by strings of sub-polar depressions in the southern winter is dangerous even for the most modern ships. The courage and endurance of eighteenth-century navigators who endured these conditions deserve admiration and respect.

James Cook holds a special place in the history of exploration. His fame rests partly on the scope of his navigations, which took him from the Bering Strait to the Antarctic Circle; to this a certain piquancy is added by the dramatic circumstances of his death. However, the true foundation of Cook's reputation is surely his outstandingly rigorous professionalism—pursued in an age of often makeshift schemes.

The heroes of exploration

In forty years of exploring the oceans, some five hundred men lost their lives, including four astronomers, five draughtsmen, two physicists, six naturalists, two engineers, and four horticulturists. Among the ships' captains, Surville, St-Allouarn, Clerke, La Pérouse, Baudin, Huon de Kermadec, d'Entrecasteaux and d'Auribeau died of disease or accidents at sea. Cook, Fleuriot de Langle and Marion-Dufresne were massacred and probably eaten by cannibals. La Pérouse wrote that all these men shared in the quest to complete the knowledge of man's history, and to increase the islanders' happiness.

A self-made man

Cook certainly earned his fame and reputation, for this energetic individual was literally the author of his own life. Born to a poor Yorkshire family in 1728, apprenticed as a boy to a grocer, he soon deserted the shop to seek his fortune as a sailor. The nearby port of Whitby was at once a temptation and a source of fascination for a brave, resolute lad like Cook. His prospects were modest—the fourteen-year-old was engaged as a cabin boy aboard a coaler. He would remember this experience later in life. While the ship was laid up in winter, young James concentrated on his mathematical studies. Promoted to the rank of second captain at the age of twenty-three, he joined the British Royal Navy when the Seven Years' War broke out between England and France in 1756. He passed his pilot's exam in 1757 and embarked for Canada, where he charted the mouth of the St Lawrence River. Skilled enough to become a hydrographic engineer, in 1763 Cook was charged by his patron, Admiral Hugh Palliser, with surveying the Newfoundland coast. Three years later, an article Cook wrote on a solar eclipse observed in the course of his mission attracted the attention of the Royal Society.

James Cook's rise in society determined his destiny, but the coal ship out of Whitby counted as much as the solar eclipse in Newfoundland among the sources of his future success.

British contributions to navigational science

Since the early eighteenth century England had been in the forefront of research on scientific navigation. In 1675 John Flamsteed had been appointed to head the Royal Observatory at Greenwich. His task was to devise astronomical tables to facilitate applications of a theory for calculating longitude by measuring the position of the moon. In 1713 Isaac Newton published a theory of the moon. The following year the Board of Longitude announced a competition to encourage the development of a clock that could keep the time of the port of departure while at sea, so that longitude could be deduced from local time.

Since 1731 English inventors had worked at perfecting the sea octant, devised by John Hadley. In 1757 Captain Campbell proposed the more efficient sextant, following experiments to measure lunar distances by means of a circle. English workshops produced large numbers of high-quality instruments. Jesse Ramsden was a great and forward-looking engineer, considered an equal by the scientists of his day. He belonged to the Royal Society, and his workshop employed some fifty technicians, ten times more than the best French *ateliers*.

With his *Treaty on Scurvy* published in 1754, Doctor James Lind also contributed to Britain's pre-eminence at sea.

As stated in Cook's orders, Britain was ready to 'contribute directly to the advance of commerce and navigation'.

Dalrymple, the Southern Continent, and the transit of Venus

Alexander Dalrymple shared the views of his friend Charles de Brosses (see p. 152), and was in a position to impose his interpretation of the southern hemisphere. As a shareholder in the East India Company, a gifted cartographer and marine surveyor, a historian of discovery, and a member of the Royal Society, Dalrymple was naturally

Cook succeeded in establishing some relations with the fierce Maoris. Below, a chieftain offers him a rock lobster.

considered an authority, and his description of the Southern Continent carried considerable weight.

A rare astronomical phenomenon was due to appear in the sky of the southern hemisphere on the night of 3 to 4 June 1769: the transit of Venus in front of the sun. Wallis (see p.147) had just returned, wonderstruck, from King George's Island (Tahiti) when the Royal Society proposed to launch an expedition to install a temporary observatory on the island. The Society of course proposed that Dalrymple be placed in command of the mission. Haughty and swollen with self-importance, the theoretician of the Southern Continent demanded that he be given the rank of captain. The First Lord of the Admiralty was staggered by Dalrymple's presumption. Admiral Sir Hugh Palliser then suggested Cook as a candidate to lead the mission to Tahiti. The choice of Cook was a turning point in the history of transoceanic exploration.

Methodical preparations for a voyage round the world

Lieutenant Cook quickly proved to be an innovator, starting with his choice of ship. He selected a twenty-nine-metre coaler, which was stout, solid and spacious, and capable of transporting a scientific expedition in comfort; at the same time it could resist bad weather, shipworm and the diverse perils of an ocean voyage. The *Endeavour* was refitted to carry one hundred crew members and scientists, their equipment, fifteen months' worth of supplies, the specimens the naturalists would collect, and the maps and instruments of marine surveyors. Cook carefully selected dependable, experienced men for his staff, most of them officers who had sailed with Byron or Wallis. The scientific team was made up of international specialists. Cook himself was director of astronomical observations, assisted by Charles Green of the Greenwich Royal Observatory. Two draughtsmen, Sydney Parkinson and Alexander Buchan, a Swedish naturalist named Daniel Solander, and a German scientist, Hermann Spöring, were directed by a remarkable supervisor: Joseph Banks. This wealthy son of a prominent family, fatuous and arrogant in the manner of aristocratic young Britons, was the real sponsor of the expedition. Banks found the prospect of a Continental tour such as his contemporaries undertook too tame for him, so he set out on a voyage round the world, accompanied by four valets and two greyhounds. But at 25 Banks

was also a genuinely learned individual whose fame would soon spread over the globe. Cook and Banks had nothing in common, yet they got along famously.

To the Society Islands

On 26 August 1768 the *Endeavour* set sail from Plymouth, bound for Tahiti. The expedition followed a classic itinerary, travelling via Madeira, Rio and Cape Horn, and reached the Tuamotus in April 1769; on 13 May the vessel dropped anchor in the Bay of Matavai in Tahiti. A three-month sojourn gave the scientists their first chance to observe the local flora and fauna, as well as the customs and daily lives of the natives. The passengers and crew adapted quickly to the free-and-easy relations that prevailed between men and women on Tahiti, yet this unrestricted freedom did not interfere with the expedition's order and discipline, nor with the work that had to be completed. As if the goddess of love who reigned over Tahiti had arranged matters herself, the transit of Venus was duly observed thanks to a break in an otherwise stormy sky.

The *Endeavour* put back out to sea in mid-July. In an ironic twist for men who had worshipped Venus so assiduously with Tahitian maidens, half the expedition found that they had contracted venereal disease. The party sailed on to Huahine, then Bora-Bora. Cook named the archipelago in honour of the Royal Society, then steered due south.

Secret instructions

Secret instructions, to be opened only after the expedition had left Tahiti, ordered Cook to reconnoitre farther south, down to the fortieth parallel, in search of the Southern Continent which Dalrymple and others so firmly believed in. No land was sighted until early October when the *Endeavour* touched New Zealand. For six months Cook and his men explored the North and South Islands, making a nearly complete survey of the coastlines. By then, no member of the party continued to credit the existence of a Southern Continent. With winter approaching, Cook was obliged to plan the return voyage. To travel to Cape Horn along a high latitude would definitively solve the mystery of the mythical *Terra Australis*. But the ship's condition ruled out that difficult route. After due deliberation the council decided to return via New Holland (Australia), New Guinea and the Cape of

Cook's was demonstrated both in the way he dispelled the myth of a hospitable Southern Continent and that there was no easily navigable Northwest Passage between the Atlantic and the Pacific.

Good Hope; the sailing date was fixed for 31 March 1770. Four weeks later the *Endeavour* dropped anchor off the eastern coast of New Holland. In contrast to the aggressive, cannibalistic Maoris, the natives seemed wretchedly backward but happy and peaceful. The naturalists marvelled at the innumerable unidentified species they collected near their anchorage. A little farther north Cook discovered a second deep bay, which he did not explore but christened Port Jackson.

Death in Batavia

As the *Endeavour* navigated gingerly within the Great Barrier Reef that runs parallel to the coast of eastern Australia, it rammed an outcrop of coral on the night of 11 June. Showing great presence of mind, Cook managed to save the vessel, which took a month to repair. Cook sailed along the Australian coast up to Cape York, which he claimed for England before crossing the reef-strewn Torres Strait. New Guinea natives greeted the Europeans with a hail of assegais—sharp wooden spears. Cook just had time to note that the island was indeed separate from Australia. Because the *Endeavour* had sprung some alarming leaks,

Cook's method

Ever vigilant and imperturbable in the face of danger; quick-tempered but just; stern and, if necessary, unbending, yet attentive to his men's welfare: Cook possessed to an extraordinary degree the qualities needed to win a crew's utter confidence. He saved men's lives with his ceaseless (if not always successful) battle against scurvy: sauerkraut, fresh vegetables, and frequent rest stops were his weapons. On matters of discipline, hygiene and cleanliness, Cook was unyielding. Incredibly, he was the first to supply his crews with warm clothing for Antarctic expeditions and to provide dry garments for men exposed to rain and heavy seas.

Botany Bay

On 29 April 1770 dinghies launched from the *Endeavour* landed on the southern shore of a sheltered bay. The Europeans were greeted coolly by the natives—naked, dark-skinned, smooth-haired people. Unimpressed by the small gifts left on the beach to appease them, they quickly disappeared from sight. The expedition's naturalists found so great an abundance of plants there that Cook dubbed the site 'Botany Bay'. It was there on 26 January 1788 that the French explorer La Pérouse chanced upon the fleet of Commodore Phillip, charged with implanting British settlers at Port Jackson in what was still New Holland. Such was the beginning of Sydney and the British colony of Australia.

On 14 February 1779, during a minor incident between Hawaiians and his crew, Cook was mortally wounded.

Cook decided to put into Batavia as quickly as possible.

He pulled into the capital of Dutch East Indian trade on 10 October, unaware that he was entering a deadly trap. Through sound seamanship and hygienic principles, Cook had managed to preserve the health of his men. And yet, though they were rested and free of scurvy, the English explorers could not tolerate the heavy, corrupt air of Batavia's trading posts. After two months in Java the *Endeavour* was seaworthy once more, but fully a third of the crew had succumbed to malaria and raging dysentery. Among the victims were the ship's surgeon, the astronomer Charles Green, and the draughtsman Sydney Parkinson, who survived only briefly his colleague Alexander Buchan, who had died in Tahiti. Hermann Spöring was the final victim of the contagion that felled every member of the scientific staff save the naturalists Joseph Banks and Daniel Solander.

Results of Cook's first voyage and preparations for the second

The *Endeavour*'s return on 13 July 1771 unleashed a wave of enthusiasm that swept through England. The scientific harvest was of enormous significance, ranging from observations of Venus to hundreds of specimens, many previously unidentified, of flora and fauna; from maps of New Zealand and the eastern coast of Australia to objects and artifacts that revealed how the peoples of the South Pacific lived. Yet while the theory of the Southern Continent had been dealt a serious blow, the expedition had not absolutely disproved its existence.

A second voyage was deemed necessary to resolve the matter once and for all. Cook himself was eager to sail around the world again, and already had an itinerary in mind. He also had greater means at his command and improved methods for safeguarding the health of his crew.

It was strategically important for England to block French initiatives in the South Pacific. The loss of Canada and the disastrous toll taken by the Seven Years' War were bound to spur France to develop colonial interests in that part of the world. The expeditions of Marion-Dufresne and Kerguelen to seek the Southern Continent were an indication of France's revived interest in exploration, after a hiatus of some thirty years.

Cook's second voyage

The Admiralty gave young Commander Cook two new vessels, identical to the valiant but worn-out *Endeavour*. The *Resolution* and *Adventure* were minutely outfitted at Plymouth. Rescue craft, soldiers, more powerful weapons, provisions that would ward off scurvy—sauerkraut in particular—were all calculated to safeguard the lives and well-being of the crews.

The scientific detachment did not include Banks, whose schemes for taking along colleagues, servants and equipment far exceeded the ships' capacity. A naturalist called Foster and his son were selected instead, as well as the astronomers Wales and Bayly, and the painter William Hodges, who would bring back from the Pacific the first portraits of those happy isles. For the first time a precision instrument was to be used to determine longitude, using local time as a point of comparison. The horologist John Harrison had developed a marine chronometer that kept the time of the port of departure. A copy of Harrison's model number four was, as Cook later wrote, 'the unfailing guide' of the *Resolution*.

Towards Antarctica

On 11 July 1772, the two ships left Plymouth, headed for the South Pacific. Cook sailed to Madeira, then made for the Cape of Good Hope. He intended to reach Antarctica by the shortest route, then sail from west to east at the highest possible latitude. He would thus make best use of prevailing winds and currents, and would head into the South Pacific during the southern summer. Just two weeks after putting out from the Cape, the *Resolution* and the *Adventure* reached the sixtieth parallel. Navigating through fog and pack ice, on 17 January 1773 the ships became the first in history known to have crossed the Antarctic Circle; they pushed on to 67° 15' south.

Noting the ever-thicker barrier of ice, Cook decided to steer north towards the islands which Kerguelen had reported (see p. 153); but he did not find them. Cook's two ships lost sight of each other and sailed separately to New Zealand, the *Resolution* holding steady along the sixtieth parallel.

From heaven to hell in the Pacific

The two ships eventually rendezvoused and began their exploration of the Pacific, covering a vast triangular area via Tahiti and the Tonga Islands before sailing back to New Zealand, where a storm separated the *Resolution* and the *Adventure* for good. Commodore Furneaux, at the helm of the *Adventure*, decided to return to England by the shortest route, after a terrible episode: ten men sent to gather edible plants had been savagely massacred by Maoris. Furneaux's ship pulled into Spithead on 14 July 1773; like Bougainville before him, the commodore had brought back a Tahitian called Omaï.

Cook also concluded, with a certain sadness, that nothing was to be gained from the Maoris, who seemed impervious to any civilized exchange. The *Resolution* headed south once again. On 30 January 1774 it reached 71° 11', the highest southern latitude ever recorded, where the ship was turned back by a seemingly infinite ice field.

The end of a myth

Cook could easily have returned home to England after so fruitful a voyage. Yet he decided to winter in the tropics and then continue his explorations. He visited numerous islands, all of which afforded a rich harvest of information for the expedition's scientists. In March 1774 Cook sailed to Easter Island, to the Marquesas in April, to Tahiti again, then to the Tonga group, to

Malakula in the New Hebrides, to the eastern coast of New Caledonia, and to the Isle of Pines, so named because of the remarkable *Araucaria columnaris*, veritable pillars of wood. These were the ports of call on Cook's methodical investigation of what were by then familiar waters, which would one day belong to Britain's colonial empire. The *Resolution* fetched up once more in New Zealand. From there Cook resolved to head straight for the Tierra del Fuego. He had proved conclusively that no Southern Continent existed, unless it lay within the inexplorable—and unexploitable—polar circle. When he cast anchor at Spithead on 30 July 1775 after three years of roving the southern seas, Cook had lost just four men; scurvy had not claimed a single victim.

Fame, glory, and more unanswered questions

Cook's second voyage was an unqualified success. The bounty gathered by the naturalists, the drawings, maps and ethnographical collections—all blazed new paths in every field of natural and human science. The marine chronometer had enabled navigators to locate the archipelagos they had explored with minute precision. Cook had been the first man to sail the Antarctic Ocean. With his wide experience at sea he could settle the long-standing argument about the nature and extent of the Southern Continent. Thanks to Cook's efforts, the English Crown could boast pre-eminence in the South Pacific. He was promoted to captain in recognition of his diligence and talent. Cook was also favoured with a royal audience and election to the Royal Society. The Lords of the Admiralty believed they were rewarding his tireless endeavours by offering him an honorific post at the disabled soldiers' hospital of Greenwich.

Cook had hardly taken up his new position when the Admiralty noticed that a large problem still remained to be solved. Since the discovery that North America blocked the direct route to the Indies, it had been thought that a maritime passage might exist to the north. Repeated failures to find the Northwest Passage provoked passionate argument among geographers. Disputes about the boundaries of the North Pole had revived. It seemed a good idea to attempt to determine them from the Pacific, particularly since Omaï the Tahitian had in any case to be escorted home. No one dared suggest that Cook should lead a third expedition, but in the end he requested the honour himself and immediately set to work.

The flora and fauna of New Holland (Australia) offered English naturalists a multitude of curiosities. Amongst these were strange jumping animals, such as wallabies.

The third expedition

The stout ships *Resolution* and *Discovery* were outfitted for a long campaign. Cook's scaled-down scientific staff included the landscape artist John Webber. At His Majesty's behest, tools, domestic animals, and seed for crops were to be offered to natives encountered on the voyage. After sailing to familiar island groups in the western Pacific, the expedition's general programme defined a new zone for exploration in the North Pacific Ocean. Just as the ships were about to set sail, the American colonies declared their independence. France rallied to the insurgents' cause. Yet Louis XVI, who considered Cook a benefactor of humankind, instructed his fleet to treat Cook's ships as neutral if they were encountered at sea. Captain Cook's final expedition put out from Plymouth on 12 July 1776.

In accordance with his instructions, Cook sailed to the South Pacific islands, then headed for the Kerguelen Islands, where he took on fresh fruit and vegetables. From Tasmania, the expedition sailed for New Zealand, discovered the Cook Islands, and then spent three months feasting in the Tongas, where the men were received like old friends. From August to December 1777 the expedition cruised the Society Islands, before heading north to begin work on its scientific programme.

Murder of a god

The Sandwich Islands (Hawaii) were discovered on 20 January 1778. The ships then travelled to the western coast of Canada, which Cook investigated from Vancouver Island up to the Aleutians. The party sailed into the Bering Strait in July and reconnoitred Siberia and Alaska. Hemmed in by pack ice, the ships were forced to turn back at a latitude of 70° 44' North. If the famous Northwest Passage did indeed exist, it was not negotiable in the conditions then prevailing. Cook led the party back to winter in the Sandwich Islands. The natives greeted Cook with an almost mystical fervour, taking him for a god. On 14 February 1779 a series of minor incidents led to a violent explosion: Cook was mortally wounded as he tried to restore calm. In a kind of collective exorcism, the captain's body was ripped limb from limb. Hawaiians venerated Cook's remains until nineteenth-century American missionaries suppressed native taboos.

Longitude

In the late eighteenth century two different methods of calculating longitude were available to navigators. From around 1714 researchers sought to perfect a chronometer that could keep accurate time; the English produced such an instrument in 1761, the French some ten years later. Because marine chronometers were so costly, ships were not routinely equipped with them until the mid-nineteenth century. Astronomical tables—necessary for measuring lunar distances, the second method for calculating longitude—were published in England in 1766.

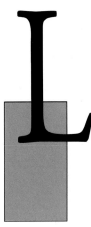

ate in May 1785 the store ships Autruche *and* Portefaix *lying in the port of Brest were rechristened the* Astrolabe *and* Boussole. *Crossing the narrows of the harbour at daybreak on 1 August 1785 to shouts of 'Vive le roi! Long live the king!', the two ships sailed into the annals of great sea adventures. No one imagined at that joyful moment that nothing would be heard of the vessels for nearly half a century.*

The Golden Age of the French Navy

The Seven Years' War had confirmed English mastery of the seas. But Choiseul, promoted Minister of the Navy by Louis XV, reorganized the French fleet. His efforts bore fruit: the American War of Independence took Europe by surprise. From Ouessant to the West Indies, from Cape Verde to Trincomalee, d'Estaing, d'Orvilliers, de Grasse, Suffren, and many younger officers had bravely resisted the English. For seven of the most brilliant years in the history of the French Royal Navy, its fleet wielded enormous influence over the course of world events. Beyond the theatre of war, England and France also competed with each other in the scientific sphere.

Royal intentions

In ten years of exploration, James Cook had amassed a vast amount of information about the Pacific, coming to a true understanding of that immense ocean and opening the way for colonization and trade. The French Navy, in the first flush of its new-found glory, was to complete the great work that England had brought so far. A French expedition was organized, based on Cook's plan to establish a fur trade between North America and China. Louis XVI added a broad humanitarian purpose to the mission, but as an enthusiastic amateur geographer fascinated with remote islands and far-off oceans, France's sovereign also gave the expedition a specific geographical objective: to complete the mapping of the globe.

La Pérouse had seen combat in the American War of Independence as commander of the *Amazon* and later of the

Astrée. Aboard the *Sceptre* he fought the British in Hudson Bay. His seamanship and humanity during that campaign had attracted the king's notice. La Pérouse was placed in command of the great French expedition around the globe. Upon his suggestion Fleuriot de Langle, La Pérouse's second-in-command in Canada, was given charge of the *Astrolabe*.

Programme for an expedition

The itinerary was specifically planned to allow the mission to complete the systematic survey of the Pacific's circumference. Those portions of the ocean which had remained unexplored after Cook's tragic demise were to be reconnoitred and mapped, particularly the coasts of North America, China, Siberia, Mongolia, Korea and Japan.

The officers, astronomers and engineers were duly to guarantee the accuracy of the scientific results. Expert geographers helped to plan the voyage, under the direction of Marshal de Castries and Claret de Fleurieu, director of ports and arsenals, and guided by the wishes of Louis XVI, who took a close interest in the mission. French academies proposed research topics in all fields of physical science, both natural and human. Their most valuable instruments were made available to the expedition, which was in truth the most carefully prepared and most scientifically sophisticated ever to sail for the southern seas.

Crowded aboard two small vessels 41 metres long were 250 seamen and scientists, including the astronomers Monge and Lepaute d'Agelet, the physicist Lamanon, the naturalist Dufresne, the botanist La Martinière, and the draughtsmen Prevosts and Duché de Vancy. Collignon, a horticultu-

rist, oversaw 150 bushels of seeds as well as 60 food-producing trees and shrubs entrusted to them by Thouin, head horticulturist of the Botanical Gardens in Paris.

Outfitting in Brest

Like Cook before him, La Pérouse chose to sail with solid, spacious store ships of 550 tonnes in preference to other more prestigious vessels. After their hulls had been protected with wide nails against shipworm, the ships put into Brest for loading. Livestock—steers, forty sheep and two hundred fowl—were herded aboard to supply the crew with fresh food and animals to raise on far-off islands. Spare masts, rigging, anchors and disassembled dinghies were stowed away as well, to make the expedition self-sufficient during the long voyage far from convenient ports of call.

The voyage

After nineteen days lying at anchor, waiting for favourable winds, the *Astrolabe* and *Boussole* sailed out of Brest on 1 August 1785. They halted at Madeira and Tenerife that same month; in November they reached Santa Caterina Island in Brazil, then rounded Cape Horn in January 1786 in fine weather. The expedition stopped over at the Chilean port of Concepcion in February before reaching Easter Island in April and Maui (in the Sandwich Islands) in May.

La Pérouse crossed to North America from June to September and sailed along the continent's northwestern coast, from Alaska south to California. During a stopover in Port-des-Français (Alaska), twenty-one seamen drowned on 13 July 1786 in a terrible accident.

Ferdinand Berthoud's marine chronometers

La Pérouse took five marine chronometers crafted by Ferdinand Berthoud to guide him on his voyage around the globe. Since 1735 the French Navy had followed English experiments with such devices, and in 1766 ordered two longitudinal chronometers from the Swiss-born Berthoud, who was in fierce competition with rival Pierre Le Roy, a brilliant theoretician of precision chronometry. Berthoud was able to make the instruments operational, accurate, reliable, relatively compact and inexpensive. From 1764 they were tested aboard the *Hirondelle*, the *Isis* and the *Flore*, until Berthoud perfected in 1771 his marine chronometer number eight, which in a year lost only one and a half seconds. His invention won Berthoud the enviable sinecure of Watchmaker to the King and the Navy.

La Pérouse recrossed the Pacific from east to west and sailed into Macau in January 1787. Two months later he fetched up in Cavite southwest of Manila, then headed northward to the Kamchatka peninsula, investigating the coast as far as the Bay of Avatchine (Petropavlovsk), where he cast anchor in September.

The final days of the expedition

A long sail due south took the *Astrolabe* and the *Boussole* to Navigators' Island (Tutuila, in the Samoas). There a second dreadful misfortune befell the ill-fated expedition: thirteen seamen and scientists, including Captain Fleuriot de Langle, commander of the *Astrolabe*, and the physicist Lamanon, were massacred by native Samoans on the island of Apia while the rest of the crew were taking on fresh water supplies. La Pérouse put in at the Tonga Islands in December, and called at Botany Bay in New Holland on 26 January 1788. There he encountered the fleet of Commodore Philipps, who had come to Port Jackson with gangs of English convicts to establish the first British colony in what is today Australia.

The two ships under La Pérouse's command weighed anchor in March. The captain had made his course known: they were to go to Mauritius in December 1788, and thence to Brest in July of the following year. Yet after the expedition sailed out of Australian waters, it was never heard from again.

Vanikolo

Peter Dillon, a captain of the British East India Company, was the first to shed light on the fate of La Pérouse and his party — thirty-nine years after the expedition's disappearance. Guided by a silver sword hilt he had discovered on the island of Tikopia, he sailed to Vanikolo, an unexplored island also in the Solomon archipelago. In 1827 Dillon, and a year later Dumont d'Urville, learned from stories that the islanders had passed down over the years that two shipwrecked sailors were still living on Vanikolo when d'Entrecasteaux had sailed thereabouts in his vain search for La Pérouse in 1791-1793 (see p. 160). The latter's two frigates, the story went, had been wrecked one night during a fierce storm. According to the islanders, the survivors had built a large boat and then set out to sea, leaving two of their party behind.

No trace was ever found of those last survivors of the La Pérouse expedition.

The last witness of the La Pérouse expedition

The notes, maps and journal of La Pérouse were forwarded to France from Macau and Manila. The final dispatch was entrusted to Barthélémy de Lesseps, a young vice-consul, brought along as an interpreter. He left the expedition in Petropavlovsk on 29 September 1787; his perilous return journey across the Kamchatka peninsula and the Russian Empire lasted for an entire year. Lesseps was stationed in Lisbon when he received instructions to return to Paris to identify remains brought back from Vanikolo. Ferdinand de Lesseps, who would gain celebrity for building the Suez Canal, accompanied his uncle on that sad errand.

Captain Cook's and La Pérouse's 'Table of Discoveries' represents the diverse ethnic groups of the Pacific as they were imagined at the beginning of the 19th century. Contrary to what the philosophers were saying, La Pérouse contradicted the existence of the noble savage.

n the early years of the nineteenth century navigators sailed all the way round New Holland, as Australia was then called, yet many questions about its coastal geography remained unsolved. Some believed the landmass might actually be two enormous islands. The resources of this vast territory had still to be investigated. As late as the middle of the century, explorers lost their lives in attempts to penetrate the mysterious Australian interior.

Maori dwellings are decorated with sculpted figurines representing spirits that protect the home.

The ordeal of Rear-Admiral d'Entrecasteaux

The La Pérouse expedition vanished in the South Pacific late in 1788. Despite political upheavals in France, the plight of the missing men was not forgotten. On 22 January 1791 the Natural History Society petitioned the Constituent Assembly, which officially requested that Louis XVI send a rescue party to search for La Pérouse.

The mission was coupled with a programme for scientific exploration and entrusted to Rear-Admiral Bruny d'Entrecasteaux, a navigator with experience in the China Sea and the Indian Ocean. He sailed out of Brest on 22 September 1791 with the *Recherche* and the *Espérance*. But the expedition was doomed from the first: undermined by bad morale and unclear objectives, and then becalmed in the damp, unwholesome intertropical zone, the mission turned into a disaster in which the admiral and the two commandants lost their lives. The legacies of this courageous but ill-starred undertaking were the marine maps of Beautemps-Beaupré, father of modern hydrography, and the data from the first scientific and hydrographic exploration of the coasts of Van Diemen's Land (Tasmania).

The mission of Captain Baudin

In the latter half of the eighteenth century France and England stood at a critical juncture, where they could either consolidate or lose their modern colonial empires. Both nations were excluded from America, but they were competitors in the southern hemisphere. Cook had presented England with the better opportunity by exploring New Zealand and the eastern coast of Australia—the largest and most promising territories in the Pacific. France did not officially lay claim to the western coast of Australia, reconnoitred by Saint-Allouarn in 1772 (see p. 153), nor to Van Diemen's Land, explored by d'Entrecasteaux. Yet paradoxically, Australia held considerable interest for the French. Though he wished to counter English settlements with colonies of his own, First Consul Bonaparte gave Captain Baudin purely scientific objectives for his expedition to Australia. Baudin was familiar with those far-off seas; his first goal was to investigate the lesser-known coasts of Australia, from the Gulf of Carpentaria west to Van Diemen's Land.

The scientific staff of twenty-four experts assembled at Napoleon's behest was truly exceptional. The aptly named ships, the *Géographe* and *Naturaliste*, set sail from Le Havre on 29 October 1800.

The arithmetic of scurvy

The expedition was duly prepared to spend many months at sea. Devices for making sea water drinkable, abundant supplies of fresh food, explicit instructions on matters of hygiene and health, the presence of three doctors and a pharmacist—all efforts were made to keep the crew in good condition. Baudin had already sailed eleven times around the Cape of Good Hope, enough to recognize the dangers inherent in such long periods at sea. Via Tenerife the voyage to Mauritius took five months. The ships were virtually becalmed in the equatorial doldrums off Africa. The expected supply ship did not arrive. Men deserted, and a dozen officers and scientists refused to continue under Baudin's command. By forcing his ships to sail too far too fast, by ignoring the advice of the ships' doctors, Baudin was responsible for three successive attacks of scurvy. Scurvy occurs after 68 days of deprivation of vitamin C; on four occasions the *Géographe* and the *Naturaliste* remained at sea for periods of 110 and 120 days without fresh food, before they finally reached Port Jackson. A stopover in Timor from August to November 1801 eased the scurvy, but brought on attacks of dysentery. In Australia Baudin spent five months studying and reflecting upon the English method and finally recognized his errors. But his change of heart came too late to save his prematurely aged men. Baudin himself was fated to die of exhaustion on Mauritius on 16 September 1803.

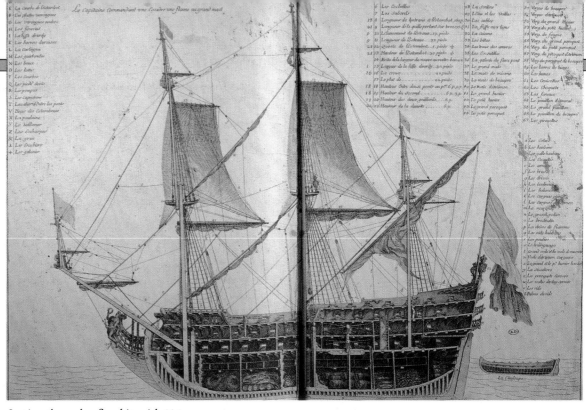

Section through a flagship with 104 cannons.

Apparent failure, real success

Baudin's mission seemed doomed to failure. Desertions, mutinous grumblings, unsanitary conditions, the two ships' repeated separations—all indicated the men's abhorrence of the captain and his brutality. In November 1802 the *Naturaliste* was ordered back to France with its diseased crew and the scientific data already gathered. The *Géographe* would continue alone, and finish mapping the southern and western coasts of Australia. When he resolved to sail back to Mauritius in August 1803, Baudin had turned his ship into a floating zoo and botanical garden.

The *Naturaliste* put into Le Havre on 7 June 1803. Rumours of the expedition's failure were immediately silenced by the wealth of scientific material produced by zoologist François Péron and draughtsman Charles Alexandre Lesueur. The Académie des Sciences applauded their collection of over one hundred thousand specimens, more than 2500 of which were previously unidentified. The specimens were accompanied by a remarkable study of the animals' habits and characteristics. Never before, declared Georges Cuvier, the most celebrated naturalist of his day, had such a collection been amassed. The botanical samples were equally impressive. The Paris Botanical Garden and the Tropical Garden at Malmaison were endowed with new species. The eucalyptus thrived in southern France and was introduced into North Africa as well. Péron was heaped with honours, but did not live to complete the *Voyage aux terres australes*, on which he collaborated with Lesueur; he died peacefully seven years after his return, at the age of thirty-five.

England's riposte: Matthew Flinders in Australia

Baudin's mission had just sailed from Le Havre when the corvette *Investigator* put out of Spithead for the same destination under Matthew Flinders. Flinders was no stranger to the Pacific and Australia; he had sailed under the notorious Captain Bligh on his second attempt to transplant Tahitian breadfruit trees into the Antilles. The governor of New South Wales (which with Queensland to the north occupies the eastern portion of Australia) had requested the exploration of the coastal regions of Tasmania and his own territory, a mission in which Flinders enthusiastically took part from 1796 to 1800. Back in England, Flinders contacted Joseph Banks, sponsor of all Britain's scientific voyages. He had no trouble convincing Cook's brilliant collaborator of the value of surveying Australia's coastal regions. The Admiralty was quick to see the project's potential profit and supported the expedition. Banks's young protégé, Robert Brown, was appointed to serve as the mission's naturalist. An astronomer, a mineralogist, two horticulturists, and two painters made up the scientific team that left Spithead on 18 July 1801. The *Investigator* sailed to Madeira, then rounded the Cape of Good Hope and steered towards Cape Leeuwin on the southwest tip of Australia. As he sailed close along the continent's south coast, Flinders met the *Géographe* on 8 April, and then the *Naturaliste* on 9 May as he cast anchor in Port Jackson.

Pitfalls in Australian waters

Joined by the brig *Lady Nelson*, Flinders—on board the *Investigator*—sailed out of Port Jackson in July 1802 to explore Australia's northeast coasts as far as the Gulf of Carpentaria. Caught in the Great Barrier, the two ships laboriously picked their way through the coral reefs. The *Lady Nelson* lost her keel and was forced to turn back. Though its condition was anything but seaworthy, the *Investigator* pursued its course through Torres Strait, pausing for hasty repairs in the Gulf of Carpentaria. After calling at Timor, the ramshackle ship and ragged crew sailed back to Port Jackson in June 1803. Seven men were dead or dying.

Two months later the survivors returned to Europe, squeezed aboard three small vessels offered to them by the governor of New South Wales. A week after they set sail, the *Porpoise*, with Flinders aboard, and the *Cato* both ran onto a reef. The shipwrecked seamen made camp on a coral islet, watching in disbelief as the *Bridgwater* shamelessly continued its course towards Batavia. But misfortune awaited that vessel which vanished without trace in the Indian Ocean.

Glory and woe: the explorer's lot

Flinders made his way back to Port Jackson in an open boat rigged with a sail. He came back to Wreck Reef aboard the schooner *Cumberland*, with two other ships to rescue his unfortunate companions. He then sailed back to England. Flinders wisely decided not to take his dilapidated ship around the Cape of Good Hope. Instead he put into Port Louis on the French island of Mauritius. Flinders possessed a French passport, presented in recognition of the English document graciously given to Baudin. Yet in spite of this safe-conduct and all his explanations, Governor Decaen threw Flinders into prison as a spy; there he languished for six years. In 1810 Flinders was allowed to return to England, where he died four years later after completing an account of his voyage. He was forty.

The naturalists who had stayed behind in 1802 to pursue their research did not travel back to England until 1805, when they returned aboard the much-repaired *Investigator*. With them they brought 1700 new species out of the 3900 they had collected.

The transaustralian passage

Baudin had been instructed to study the feasibility of building a canal across Australia, from the Gulf of Carpentaria in the north to Spencer Gulf, a deep indentation in the continent's southern coast. Flinders had a similar idea in mind when he made his detailed survey of the same gulf. Ever since the Renaissance men had clung tenaciously to the dream of maritime passages across Africa, the Americas, and the Southern Continent. Australia too incited such imaginings, for in the days of sailing ships navigators naturally longed to shorten their interminable ocean voyages.

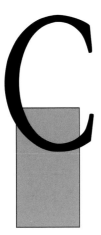

ook's Pacific expeditions laid the foundations for British colonies in New South Wales. Australia's nineteenth-century settlers were eager to find land suited for cattle-raising and farming. These pioneers became the explorers of the still-unknown continent. Braving a harsh land and hostile climate, with their blood and sweat they forged the epic of the Australian nation.

Aborigine massacres

When white colonists settled in Australia, the indigenous population numbered about 350,000, made up of over 680 tribes that spoke some 500 dialects. Decimated by massacres and epidemics (which were sometimes deliberately introduced), the aborigines barely escaped total extermination. What saved them was the immense size and aridity of their land. In recent years laws protecting aborigines have helped their numbers increase. Some live on reservations and continue to live the nomadic life of their ancestors, hunting and gathering food; others work on cattle ranches or have put down new roots in the cities.

The Australian gold rush

When Hargraves struck gold in the Bathurst Plain in 1851, gold fever infected Australia. The news unleashed a frantic rush that virtually emptied the towns. In a matter of weeks twelve thousand men wielded picks in the dry bed of the Forrest River in a mad hunt for nuggets. Adventurers came from America and Europe to get their share of the gold. The government needed the help of a British regiment to restore order. Gold created wealth and attracted the new immigrants Australia badly needed. In just ten years, the country's population tripled.

A colony of convicts in Sydney

America's independence deprived England of a colony for its convicts, who could no longer be packed off to Virginia. The Crown therefore turned to Australia as a likely site for a penitentiary colony. The first shiploads of 752 men and women prisoners under Captain Phillip, governor of New South Wales, fetched up in Botany Bay on 18 January 1788. At Port Jackson Phillip established a colony and raised the British flag over what would later become Sydney. The convicts broke rocks, cleared land, planted crops, and built the town. But they soon grew restive and showed signs of resisting the tasks they had been set to; officers quarrelled amongst themselves and provisions grew short. The English government, absorbed by troubles in Europe, gave little thought to sending supplies to the infant colony. Yet in Port Jackson famine loomed. Convoy after convoy poured new prisoners and voluntary immigrants into the new land. Then gradually, despite enormous difficulties, New South Wales saw the first fruits of its labour. Convicts who had served their sentences settled down to farm. With the arrival of Governor Maquarie in 1809, order and hard work prevailed in the young colony. Along with the cities of Perth, Albany and Fremantle, the population of Sydney grew, and so did demand for arable land. The colonists became explorers.

2500 kilometres on foot

The discovery of pasture land and rivers beyond the abrupt cliffs of the Blue Mountains spurred explorers to push ever deeper into the Australian interior. John Eyre was one such pioneer, who in 1840 attempted to cross the unexplored regions to the north. He found only impassable salt lakes—central Australia did not appear to offer brilliant prospects for the future. But then it had not yet occurred to anyone that sheep could thrive on the region's scrubby saltbush. Eyre turned around and decided to

Captain Phillip takes possession of Australia.

explore Australia's south coast. He set out west from Adelaide accompanied by a man called Baxter, three aborigines, some horses, and a flock of sheep. As watering holes grew rarer, the expedition's progress slowed; tensions simmered between the whites and the aborigines. In the end Baxter was murdered, and Eyre was left with one aborigine, Wylie, in the middle of the desert with no water and no horse. For months the starving, thirsting pair marched on until they were finally rescued by a French whaling ship. When Eyre reached Albany on 14 June 1841, he had journeyed over 2500 kilometres on foot.

Journey to an imaginary sea

Steadfast in the belief that an inland sea lay somewhere in the Australian hinterland, Charles Sturt organized an impressive, government-backed expedition of sixty well-equipped men, a herd of cattle, sheep, and dogs. On 10 August 1844, the caravan headed north from Adelaide into the unknown. By following the course of the Murray River the convoy hoped to avoid the salt lakes which had stymied Eyre's continental crossing. After making his way through a harsh, drought-ridden region, Sturt reached a pleasant area rich in game and fresh water. But before long the terrain turned hostile once more; the party gazed out over an immense stretch of sand and stone. Prostrated by the heat, the men dug underground shelters to protect themselves from the blazing sun. While the caravan rested, Sturt set off with three men to reconnoitre. Day after day they saw nothing but endless desert. The men found no water, and turned back to rejoin the caravan. But when Sturt and his party reached the site, the caravan had disappeared. By dint of superhuman efforts the four men eventually caught up with the expedition. The

162

exhausted rag-tag crew reached Adelaide after a journey of seventeen months. Sturt had not reached central Australia, but he had pushed back the frontiers of unexplored territory. He sailed back to England, having lost his eyesight. He died shortly after his return.

Leichhardt vanishes

The Australian government gamely continued to offer considerable sums to explorers willing to open up rivers or overland routes across the continent to new pasture lands. In 1845 Ludwig Leichhardt, a German explorer, set out from Brisbane on Australia's east coast, and eventually made his way to Port Darwin in the north. Along this five-thousand-kilometre journey he discovered several rivers. Two years later Leichhardt attempted an even more ambitious east-to-west crossing with a German companion and a herd of steers, goats and horses. He vanished without trace.

A sole survivor

In 1860 the Royal Society of Victoria financed a transcontinental expedition from southern Australia to the Gulf of Carpentaria. Equipped with camels on which they planned to cross the desert, a caravan led by Robert O'Hara Burke left Melbourne on 20 August, applauded and cheered by well-wishers. Under a scorching sun the expedition crossed the Torowoto swamps and the rocky desert plains before reaching the Cooper's Creek oasis on 11 November. After a month's rest Burke split the caravan in two: Brahe remained at the oasis with supplies, while Burke headed north with three men. They eventually reached the verdant landscapes of Queensland, where they gathered specimens of flora and fauna. Burke noted amused observations of the aborigines in his journal. On the evening of 10 February the men beheld the Gulf of Carpentaria. They were the first to have travelled the entire length of the continent. Burke and his companions started back to rejoin the supporting party, but by now they were sickening and desperately short of supplies. In mid-April Gray succumbed. Burke, Wills, and King painfully made their way to the depot at Cooper's Creek. They arrived on 21 April, but found no trace of Brahe and the others. That very morning, weary of waiting and ill with scurvy, the troop had broken camp and headed back

south. Burke unearthed the supplies Brahe had buried at the oasis, but he and Wills were too weak to survive. Months later a rescue party found King, the sole survivor, living with a tribe of aborigines.

The struggle to reach the ocean

John MacDonall Stuart was an experienced explorer, having participated in Charles Sturt's expedition. In 1860 he set out from Adelaide; his destination was Port Darwin. Four months later repeated attacks by aborigines forced Stuart to retreat. When he learned that Burke was also attempting a transcontinental crossing, Stuart hurriedly organized another expedition funded by the townspeople of Adelaide. He set off in January 1861 and successfully crossed three-quarters of Australia, making studies of animal and plant life along the way. But

Stuart was defeated by the impenetrably dense bush and was forced to turn back. In Adelaide everyone was talking about the tragic end of Burke's expedition. More determined than ever to conquer the continent, Stuart started out for a third time in October 1861. Armed with information gleaned from his previous expeditions, Stuart adjusted his itinerary by a few degrees to the west in order to skirt the bush. He reached the shores of Port Darwin on 25 July 1862. Stuart raised the British flag and buried an account of his journey at the site, then set off to return to civilization. Worn out, weary, and nearly blind, the explorer arrived in Adelaide in December, where he was greeted by a cheering crowd. But his adventures had severely sapped his strength; he died not long after his triumphant return. The trail he blazed was adopted by the telegraph company, thus linking Australia's two farthest points. In the wake of these pioneers, Australians pushed their sheep ever deeper into the interior.

An Australian Robin Hood

Disgusted by the tyranny of 'squatters', as wealthy proprietors were called, Ned Kelly and his gang launched cattle raids from their forest hideout, braving the police and causing much glee among the poorer classes. In 1880, as they were preparing an ambush against a police convoy, the Kelly gang was betrayed. The men barricaded themselves with forty-six hostages in the Glenrowan Hotel while the police fired on them relentlessly. Two of the bandits were shot, a third killed himself, and Ned was wounded and taken prisoner. He was tried and hanged in Melbourne.

One of the early explorers of Australia, Thomas Paines, made a number of sketches, including this kangaroo seen near De Camp, in 1856.

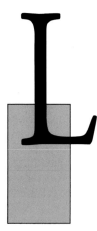

ate in the seventeenth century Czar Peter I of Russia — Peter the Great — gave the Russian Empire access to the Black Sea and an opening onto the Baltic. The czar was naturally interested by rumours that the Cossacks had reached America by water. Since the mid-1500s navigators had sought the Northeast Passage, a maritime route among ice fields and Arctic wastes that would open European ports to the Orient.

A remarkable achievement

English navigator George Vancouver (1757-1798) produced an accurate marine map of North America's northwest coastline. Between 1792 and 1794, placed in charge of British efforts to counter French and Spanish advances in the fur trade, Vancouver charted the coast from the island that now bears his name north to the Aleutian Islands. Vancouver had previously taken part in Cook's second and third voyages, and had also explored the western coast of South America.

Extract from the book Picturesque Voyage Around the World, *by Kotzebue, showing the temple of the king of the Sandwich Islands (Hawaii).*

The legacy of Peter the Great

One of Peter the Great's last acts before he died in 1725 was to appoint a Dane, Vitus Bering of the Russian Navy, to explore the area between Siberia and Alaska (see p. 192). Bering left Kamchatka in 1728 and crossed the strait that bears his name, but dreadful weather conditions prevented him from measuring the strait's width. From 1733, in the course of a wide-ranging exploration and map-making campaign in Siberia, Bering directed the surveying of the Kuril Islands and the Kamchatka Peninsula (where the town of Petropavlovsk was founded), before he discovered the Aleutian Islands in 1740 and Alaska in 1741. The latter remained Russian territory until its sale to the United States in 1867. Bering himself died of scurvy during this expedition.

A lucrative fur trade between Alaska and China had developed in a haphazard way before a merchant named Chelikov created the America Company and set up fortified trading posts in the Aleutians.

The Krusenstern expedition

Commandant von Krusenstern had been a navigator aboard an English ship in the Indian Ocean and the China Sea. He fully understood how direct relations between Alaska and China could improve the otter-fur trade, which at that time was carried on very slowly through Okhotsk. His report to Count Romanzov, Russia's enlightened minister of trade, met with Czar Alexander I's enthusiastic approval. So pleased indeed was the czar that Krusenstern, who was preparing to return to his family home, was named ship's captain in 1802 and placed in command of an expedition to the Orient.

His ship, the *Nadjedjeda*, sailed out of Kronstadt on 7 August 1803 with Captain Lissianskoy's *Neva*. The scientific objectives of the expedition were entrusted to German experts: the astronomer Horner, and the naturalists Baron von Langsdorff and Doctor von Tilenau.

Krusenstern was instructed to examine the possibilities of direct commercial relations between the America Company and China, but he also had on board a mission to Japan led by Resanov, the czar's chamberlain. He was charged with confirming and extending if possible the authorization given in 1792 for a Russian merchant ship to stop over in Nagasaki.

A brilliant campaign, but a diplomatic failure

During the crossing of the Atlantic towards Brazil, naturalists displayed growing interest in the infant discipline of marine biology. In March 1804, Krusenstern's two ships rounded Cape Horn with great difficulty. Bad weather caused the two ships to lose sight of each other, but they met up according to plan at the island of Nuku Hiva in the Marquesas. The Russians admired the natives' customs, marvelling at their tattoos. Sailing through the Hawaiian Islands, Krusenstern set a course towards Petropavlovsk, while the *Neva* went on to Alaska. Hindered by unfavourable weather and shifting monsoon winds, the *Nadjedjeda* set sail from Kamchatka in September and steered towards Japan. It arrived in Nagasaki the following month. Since 1641 the Dutch had been granted the privilege of a harbour concession, the tiny and closely guarded islet of Deshima. The Russian expedition was badly treated. The crew was confined aboard ship, and the ambassador placed under house arrest — he never actually met the emperor. Five months later he learned that the czar's gifts had been refused and that no Russian ship would be welcome in Japan thereafter.

Krusenstern decided to return to Petropavlovsk via the western Japanese islands, Sakhalin and the Kuril Islands, a route previously travelled by La Pérouse. An inquiry into the functioning of the America Company and a survey of the northern coast of Sakhalin occupied Krusenstern until late August 1805; he then set sail for China, where the *Nadjedjeda* and the *Neva* arrived in December. Thorny commercial negotiations lasted for two months, after which the Russian ships set out from Canton on 6 February 1806, barely escaping the seizure ordered by the emperor.

Krusenstern put into Kronstadt in August after a three-year voyage. His crew was safe and healthy, and the scientific results of interest. The confirmation that direct relations between America and China were possible established Russia's supremacy in these remote waters, even though their ships and scientific collaborators were mostly imported from abroad.

Captain von Kotzebue's voyage round the world

The Napoleonic Wars put a temporary halt to explorations. But in 1815 Romanzov, who had since become Foreign Secretary, requested that Krusenstern organize another expedition. Krusenstern proposed that one of his former officers, Otto von Kotzebue, lead the mission.

Kotzebue's father, an influential German courtier, had arranged for his son to go to sea as a cadet, and the young man had served as secretary during Krusenstern's voyage. Now promoted to lieutenant-commander, he took command of the specially constructed Estonian brig *Kurik*. One of the naturalists aboard was a celebrated Prussian writer, Adelbert von Chamisso.

The expedition sailed out of Kronstadt for the Pacific in late July 1815. The ship called in Brazil, Chile, Easter Island, the Marshall Islands and the Gilbert Islands. The naturalists showed a great interest in marine biology, observing jellyfish in particular. Yet relations aboard ship between scientists and officers were chilly at best. Perhaps this was not so surprising, considering that the forty members of the expedition lived in uncomfortably close quarters on a small, 180-tonne ship. Their arrival in Petropavlovsk in June 1816 met with a warm, friendly welcome.

From the Bering Strait to a tropical paradise

In Kamchatka, the party prepared for their exploration of the Bering Strait. Kotzebue's intention was to take advantage of the summer season to seek out a home base for future missions. The *Rurik* plunged into the Bering Strait late in July 1816. Hopes of finding a passage east were dashed when the party reached a deep bay, today known as Kotzebue Sound, that proved to be the same dead-end that had fooled Captain Cook in August 1778. The expedition

explored the coast of the Chukotski Peninsula and put in at Unalaska, the America Company's base in the Aleutian Islands, where they left instructions for the mission planned for summer 1817. Kotzebue then headed for California, and afterwards to the tropics for the winter. After a few weeks of rest in San Francisco's missions, Kotzebue and Chamisso began to deplore the shabbiness of the villages and the negligence of the Spanish Franciscans, whose religious zeal was of little material aid to the miserable, dwindling populations in their charge. La Pérouse had also lamented the Spanish missionaries' indifference to the earthly needs of their American flocks.

On 1 November the *Rurik* set sail for Hawaii and the Marshall Islands, which the crew were eager to revisit. The discovery of new islands and the Russians' friendly exchanges with the natives completed the reconnaissance of the archipelago. Too soon it was time to return to the wintry north. The expedition sailed into Unalaska on 24 April 1817. The instructions left by Kotzebue had been executed, and several Aleuts were ready to board with their kayaks. But the unfortunate Kotzebue, not yet recovered from a chest infection that dated from a violent storm a few weeks earlier, collapsed in mid-July, as a result of the vast ice fields and freezing temperatures of the Bering Strait. The party sailed back to Unalaska, then returned to Hawaii, the Marshalls yet again, Guam in the Marianas,

Manila, and the Cape of Good Hope, before casting anchor on 3 August 1818 in St Petersburg.

The voyage of the *Predpriarte*

Despite his turning back in the summer of 1817, which the imperial court found less blameworthy than did the crew and passengers of the *Rurik*, Kotzebue was given command of yet another expedition round the world.

The name of Captain Kotzebue's ship—*Predpriarte* or 'Enterprise'—was inspired by Cook's glorious *Endeavour*. From 1823 to 1826 the vessel sailed the Pacific from Polynesia through Micronesia, calling at the Tuamotu Archipelago, the Society Islands and the Marshalls, where the Russians were well-liked and had been welcomed as friends since 1816. The expedition's programme naturally included a sojourn in Kamchatka and in Alaska. It was a mission with both scientific and political objectives. In any case it was a routine trip for the Russian Navy, which over twenty years had amply demonstrated its ability to conduct long and arduous expeditions at sea. Their ability also showed the originality and cleverness of enlightened minds, which set great store by Russia's participation in world exploration and the affirmation of its presence in the northern Pacific.

Kotzebue demonstrated a special interest in the archipelagos of the North Pacific. Below, inhabitants of the Gulf of Kotzebue on the Kamtchatka peninsula.

The Northeast Passage

The search for a direct route to the Far East north of America or Europe was an obsession among navigators from the sixteenth century onwards. Sir Hugh Willoughby vanished with two ships in 1533. Chancellor, his pilot, made his way alone into the White Sea by means of a route familiar to the Russians since the late fifteenth century. In a dramatic contest across the Land of the White Death, Barents was one of the most celebrated victims of the search for a Northeast Passage at the close of the sixteenth century (see p. 225). The passage—or at any rate a possible commercial route running along the coast of Siberia—was opened in 1878-9, an unusually mild year, by the *Vega* sailing under a Swede named Nordenskjöld.

The fur trade

In spite of its exotic aura, the commerce in furs that the Russians organized between Alaska and China attracted attention in Europe. Cook gave a hint of the potential profit to be made, stating that 100,000 pounds worth of merchandise for barter—fabrics and metal implements—could be exchanged for 2500 otter skins, and generate a profit six times greater when sold in China. This potentially lucrative trade was one motive for La Pérouse's voyage. He was given specific instructions, annotated in the king's own hand, to determine the best site for establishing such a trade on the northwest coast of America and to verify market conditions for the furs in Canton and Nagasaki.

E xploration of the Pacific continued until the mid-nineteenth century. And a new contestant had entered the stakes: the United States backed expeditions as well, to compete with Europeans over this disputed terrain. Colonial expansion, trade, Protestant missionaries—all marked the end of the scientifically minded Enlightenement and the return to the profit motive that had characterized Rennaissance exploration.

French Oceania

France's disputes with the British minister and consul in Tahiti—who supported the royal Pomaré family against the Catholics—came to be known as the Pritchard Affair, a diplomatic fray that deepened the frostiness of Anglo-French relations. French Captain Dupetit-Thouars set out in December 1836 aboard the *Vénus* to enforce French territorial claims in the Pacific. Promoted to rear–admiral and commander of the Pacific naval station based in Valparaiso, Dupetit-Thouars took possession of the Marquesas on 1 May 1842, and on 9 September obliged Tahiti's Queen Pomaré to accept the French protectorate of her island. New Caledonia was annexed in 1853, the Gambier and Tuamotu islands in 1880-81. Wallis and Futuna became French protectorates in 1886.

French presence affirmed in the South Pacific

On 15 July 1815 Napoleon surrendered to the British and quit France forever aboard the *Bellerophon*. The Treaty of Paris redrew French borders as they had been at the Revolution, and took away Mauritius and the Seychelles. The French Navy lost fifty vessels. Yet as early as 1816 the Navy presented the government with a plan for exploration in far-off waters. Between 1817 and 1840 France sponsored nine great voyages in the South Pacific. The expeditions to Australia and Melanesia in particular contributed to every branch of natural history. But apart from their scientific goals, these voyages also kept the French flag flying from the Indian Ocean to the shores of South America, thus affirming French influence in Oceania.

From 1820, explorers studied mostly fauna, flora, and architecture. Below, a bridge at Manado, Celebes (Sulawesi).

Pont sur un Torrent à Manado.

Adventures of the *Uranie*

Commander Freycinet proposed the first of these scientific missions. After the disappearance of Baudin and the naturalist Péron's slow death from exhaustion in 1810, Freycinet was one of the few officers of that expedition to have escaped not only with his life but without undergoing hospitalization in Mauritius (see p. 160). Thus it was he who submitted the scientific findings from the voyage of the *Naturaliste* and the *Géographe*. The project had introduced Freycinet into scientific circles and given him the stature necessary to propose a second expedition. His programme encompassed not only the natural sciences but also a study of the earth's magnetic field, gravity, the atmosphere, oceanography, and the shape of the Earth. The corvette *Uranie* sailed from Toulon in September 1817. Along with 126 crew members, the expedition included the botanist Gaudichaud-Beaupré, two naturalists, the surgeons Quoy and Gaimard, and Arago, a draughtsman; all were experienced naval officers—civilians, it seemed, quickly became unbearable at sea. Yet there was one astonishing exception to the rule of 'seamen only': the captain's wife, Rose de Freycinet, was not exactly a stowaway, but she did board ship surreptitiously. She quickly made herself useful, and was soon accepted by one and all. The *Uranie* meandered from Australia to Hawaii. Returning to France via Cape Horn, the ship was damaged in a violent storm. The vessel hit a rock while attempting to find shelter in the Falklands, and was beached and ultimately sank. The shipwrecked party shivered in the cold for two months before they sighted a ship and could signal for help. They salvaged precious few of the many specimens they had collected during the voyage. The Frenchmen purchased the American ship that carried them to Montevideo; rechristened the *Physicienne*, it put into Le Havre in November 1820.

Despite the mishaps and losses, the scientific data brought back by Freycinet was impressive indeed. Sifting through, classifying, and cataloguing the material took over twenty years.

Birds of paradise lost

In 1822 the corvette *La Coquille* set out from Toulon on a similar voyage under the command of Lieutenant Duperrey, who had served as an officer on the *Uranie*. His mission was to complete the work begun by Freycinet. The staff was made up of learned, enlightened officers, including a pharmacist, Lesson, who was destined to become a brilliant naturalist, and a rising young lieutenant named Dumont d'Urville.

The expedition stopped off in Brazil, the Falklands, Chile and Peru; the *Coquille* then sailed to the Tuamotu and Society islands. The men were naturally eager to visit New Cythera—but they were immensely disappointed by that fabled isle. English missionaries had 'civilized' the natives' warmth and joviality into cold, formal stiffness. Experiments on magnetism were carried out, and the expedition amassed an exceptional range of specimens along an itinerary that took them through the Tongas, Melanesia, the Moluccas, Sydney, New Zealand, New Guinea and Java. Rocks, coral, seaweed and ferns, reptiles, fish and birds made up the six thousand specimens collected, including five hundred previously unknown samples. Duperrey's expedition yielded the first scientific description of the magnificently coloured birds of paradise, which until then no European had observed in flight.

The *Coquille* returned to Marseilles in March 1825, with every crew member safe, after a voyage that had lasted nearly three years.

Beginnings of an illustrious career

It was—more than his limited experience at sea—intelligence, curiosity and erudition that destined Dumont d'Urville for a life of adventure and exploration. In April 1820 the marine surveying vessel *Chevrette* had cast anchor at Milo in the Cyclades, where a fascinating statue of Venus had just been brought to light. Dumont d'Urville, then a young naval officer, was greatly excited by the discovery. He convinced the French ambassador in Constantinople to buy the sculpture in the name of his government. Called to Paris the next year, Dumont d'Urville read a report on the excavations to the Académie des Sciences, explaining how the statue was discovered and acquired by France. The ambitious young officer was promoted and decorated. Absorbed by the study of Provençal flowers and plants, Dumont d'Urville spent much of his time at the Museum of Natural History in Paris. So knowledgeable was he in the field of natural history that he was appointed to advise Quoy and Gaimard in their preparations for the voyage of the *Uranie*. Later Dumont d'Urville was the effective—if frustrated—second-in-command to his friend Duperrey aboard the *Coquille*. Immediately upon his return from that voyage, he proposed yet another expedition, to be limited for efficiency's sake to New Guinea and the Lou-

The stopover at Timor from 9 to 23 October 1818 marked the beginning of the most difficult part of the Uranie's *journey. Above, Louis and Rose de Freycinet being received at Dili in northern Timor.*

isiade Archipelago, which were then unfamiliar territory. He was given commander's rank and command of the *Coquille* with an ambitious mission to fulfil. The corvette was rechristened *Astrolabe* in honour of La Pérouse. Rumours fed a frail hope that traces of that expedition, which had vanished thirty-seven years earlier, might have been discovered.

An eventful voyage from Toulon to Tasmania

Dumont d'Urville set sail from Toulon on 25 April 1826. The course he charted took the expedition to southern Australia, New Zealand, the Tonga Islands, Fiji, the Loyalty Islands, New Ireland, and New Guinea. On 19 December 1827 the *Astrolabe* put into the port of Hobart, Tasmania. The voyage so far had yielded excellent results, and a wealth of dramatic incidents. Pertinent new observations were made of the flora and fauna of New South Wales, on the English settlement of Port Jackson, and on the aborigines; over sixty new specimens were discovered in New Zealand. A thorough survey of the Fiji Islands was completed, and hundreds of islands were accurately charted. But the voyage had seen

adventure as well: for three dramatic days the *Astrolabe* teetered on the brink of shipwreck, after a violent gale caught the vessel lying at a risky mooring off Tongatapu and ripped off its three main anchors. When the crew manning one of the launches was kidnapped, the French had to fight the natives to rescue their comrades. A number of sailors had jumped ship in the Tongas and at Port Jackson; and one seaman was seriously wounded when the crew were attacked by Papuans.

A mystery solved

On 26 February 1828 the *Astrolabe*'s largest launch was guided to the wreck of one of La Pérouse's ships. Dumont d'Urville had become convinced while on Tongatapu that the ill-starred expedition had called in the Tongas as planned after sailing out of Botany Bay forty years earlier. But it was during the stopover in Hobart that Dumont d'Urville learned that Peter Dillon had discovered La Pérouse's trail on Tikopia Island, between the New Hebrides and the Solomons. This information was not much more credible than the rumour that an American captain had seen a Cross of St Louis somewhere in Melanesia, which had spurred the

Origin of Species

With his exceptionally rich fund of material from Punta Alta, Tierra del Fuego and the Galápagos Islands, Darwin was able to reflect upon Jean-Baptiste de Lamarck's persuasive theories, and to elaborate a theory of evolution of life forms from a common ancestor. Natural selection, or the 'survival of the fittest', postulates that those individuals that are better suited to life in a particular environment are more likely to survive and so pass on their beneficial characteristics to the next generation. Thus, over the vast expanse of geological time, species become increasingly well adapted to a given way of life—or become extinct. Not even man can escape this inexorable logic. *On the Origin of Species by Means of Natural Selection* was published in 1859, and immediately fell under violent attack by religious authorities.

Mutiny on the *Bounty*

The *Bounty* had been dispatched on
a peaceful mission when it set sail in
1787 under Lieutenant William
Bligh: the ship was to take on
breadfruit trees in Tahiti for
transplanting in the West Indies. An
idyllic stopover in Tahiti made the
commander's discipline, severe to
the point of brutality, all the more
unbearable to his men. An officer of
the *Bounty*, Fletcher Christian, led a
mutiny. Bligh and the sailors who
remained faithful to him were put
out to sea in a dinghy, and eventually
reached Timor (in Indonesia). Most
of the mutineers settled on Tahiti.
The *Pandora* was sent to arrest them
and bring them to justice, but the
vessel ran aground on the Great
Barrier Reef in August 1791. The
rest of the *Bounty*'s crew founded a
prosperous little colony on Pitcairn
Island.

French Secretary of the Navy and the Colonies to add a special note to his instructions. In fact the mystery had been cleared up. Told to go to Vanikolo, Dumont d'Urville landed there five months after Peter Dillon's *Research*, which was then taking back to France proof that the La Pérouse expedition had been wrecked.

After two weeks in one of the most unwholesome islands in the tropics, the *Astrolabe*'s crew was so weak that they were barely able to set their sails to the wind and start off. Dumont d'Urville had not even the strength to attend the unveiling of a cenotaph in honour of La Pérouse and his comrades.

The long voyage home

The *Astrolabe* sailed directly to Guam, in the Mariana Islands, where the party remained for two months of rest and recovery. Forty of the crew were ill enough to be hospitalized. During the voyage to Ambon dysentery replaced malaria as the men's main affliction. Dumont d'Urville sailed to Mauritius via Java for another six weeks' rest. Fourteen seamen ill with scurvy left the ship at Réunion. After three eventful years at sea the *Astrolabe* put into Marseilles on 25 March 1829, and Toulon on 2 April. The death toll was ten crew members; and there had been thirteen desertions. The Academy solemnly congratulated the explorers on an exceptionally productive campaign: their notes and collections of specimens surpassed all expectations and included new species for science to identify. The body of the expedition's scientific data and maps together with Dumont d'Urville's report filled nineteen volumes and an atlas. The voyage resulted in an extensive revision of charts of South Sea waters.

Dumont d'Urville was promoted to captain, but he was not elected to the Académie des Sciences, a slight that wounded him deeply.

Missed rendezvous in the Arctic Ocean

While Dumont d'Urville sailed around the world, an English ship was exploring the North Pacific. The expedition of the frigate *Blossom* under Captain Beechey was the first in a series that kept the English in those freezing waters almost continuously from 1825 to 1842. Polar expeditions in search of

the Northwest Passage had turned back one after the other at the entrance to Baffin Bay (see p. 226). Ross, Parry, Franklin—none had crossed the Melville Strait, situated approximately in the middle of Canada's Arctic rim. Two unconventional expeditions were launched in 1825. Captain Franklin (see pp. 96-7) was to explore by land and by boat the Canadian coastal strip west of the Mackenzie River (near the present-day Alaskan frontier). The *Blossom*, sailing for the North Pacific, would cross the Bering Strait and attempt to rendezvous with Franklin.

The two parties missed each other, but not by much. Franklin turned back in August 1826 less than three hundred kilometres from the *Blossom*'s dinghy, which had reached Cape Barrow, the extreme eastern point of its voyage.

Descendants of the *Bounty*

Beechey had been instructed to land at Pitcairn Island, where some mutineers of the notorious *Bounty* had founded a colony. He set out from Spithead on 19 May 1825, steering for Pitcairn via Brazil, Cape Horn, Chile and Easter Island. The *Blossom*'s launches landed with great difficulty on a steep shore pounded by huge waves. The last of the mutineers, Alexander Smith alias John Adams, was the leader of a happy, healthy colony descended from the followers of Fletcher Christian, instigator of the mutiny, and the eighteen Tahitian men and women kidnapped forty years before. The island's tortuous topography seemed to guarantee a safe refuge for the *Bounty* crew. The British government no longer considered the mutineers criminals. They welcomed the *Blossom*'s crew to their island, and Beechey later submitted a glowing report on the Pitcairn colony. The *Blossom* passed on to the Gambier Islands, the Tuamotus, Tahiti and Hawaii before sailing into the Bering Strait. Although Beechey missed his encounter with Franklin, stops in Macau, Petropavlovsk, San Francisco and Monterey provided an abundance of data, drawings and samples to further scientific and geographical knowledge.

Naturalist aboard the *Beagle*

The expedition that set out from Devonport aboard the *Beagle* on 27 December 1831 is famous not for its leader, Lieutenant Fitz-

roy, son of a celebrated exploring family, but for its naturalist, Charles Darwin. Though afflicted with incurable sea-sickness Darwin was chosen to replace his mentor, Professor Henslow, prevented at the last moment from embarking; nothing foreshadowed the impact Darwin was to have on natural science as a result of this apparently routine world voyage. Indeed, Henslow had proposed as his replacement a seemingly ordinary young theology student blessed with a rigorous intellect and a passion for natural history. When Darwin returned in 1836 at the age of twenty-seven from the longest of all scientific voyages, the Cambridge student was to shatter traditional scientific and Christian interpretations of the origin of species.

Five years spent in Brazilian forests, on Argentine pampas, observing earthquakes and volcanic eruptions in Chile and coral reefs in the Indian Ocean, transformed the earnest, enthusiastic student into a seasoned naturalist. More especially, his discovery of prehistoric fossil deposits in Punta Alta near Bahia Blanca in Argentina, his observations on the Fuegians' primitive culture, and his minute study of tortoises, iguanas and chaffinches in the Galápagos were so many catalysts in the process that brought Charles Darwin to the world's attention.

Darwin was not only a serious scientist, he was also adventurous. He rode with the gauchos in Argentina, joined shooting expeditions and seemed to relish danger.

Misfortune and fame

When an account of the voyage was published in 1839, Darwin's report on his findings overshadowed all else. Fitzroy, the captain of the *Beagle*, was embittered by Darwin's fame. His subsequent appointment to the governorship of New Zealand and a belated promotion did little to assuage his resentment, and in 1865 he slit his throat. Six years earlier the publication of *Origin of Species* had assured Darwin's lasting reputation. Weak and ill, Darwin had given up personally defending his 'heretical' theory before the Church. Darwin had contracted a disease while in the Andes (cordillera) for which no treatment was known in Europe. He died in 1882, a belated victim of the curse that had struck down so many explorers, since the malediction of Adamastor, guardian of the Cape of Storms, in the famous epic poem *The Lusiads* written by the Portuguese Camoëns in 1572.

Mapping the western coast of the Americas

———●———

The ambitious mission entrusted to Captain Beechey in 1835 took nearly seven years to execute. The former commander of the *Blossom* set out with the *Sulphur* and the little *Starling* to complete and verify the mapping and marine survey of North and South America's Pacific coasts. After a year at sea Beechey was relieved of duty in Valparaiso because of illness. He was replaced by his former second-in-command, Captain Belcher, who gathered the flotilla together in Panama the following year.

Between 1836 and late 1839 the expedition surveyed the American coastline from Valparaiso to Port Etches (near present-day Anchorage, Alaska). Belcher returned to England across the Pacific, mapping all of New Guinea and briefly taking part in the Opium Wars that would eventually make Hong Kong a British Crown colony.

Last shores for adventure: Antarctica

———●———

After Cook's investigations within the Antarctic Circle in 1773 and 1774, the next voyage to Antarctica was led by a Russian, Fabian von Bellingshausen, who sailed out of Kronstadt aboard the *Vostok* in 1820. He discovered Alexander I Island off the Antarctic peninsula, which juts out towards Cape Horn. First sighted by an American, Captain Palmer, the territory today bears his name. English whalers and seal hunters had sailed these antipodal seas since the late eighteenth century, and had sometimes pushed beyond the polar circle. One such was Weddell, who ventured beyond the seventy-fourth parallel into the sea named in his honour.

The Adélie Coast

———●———

Captain Dumont d'Urville completed the account of his memorable voyage in 1835. Life's disappointments and difficulties—the death of two young children in a cholera epidemic, the gout that made every movement painful—had cast a cloud over him. He was expecting nothing more of his career when the navy offered him the command of an exploratory expedition to the South Pacific, a proposal he accepted with alacrity.

The *Astrolabe* set out from Toulon on 7 September 1837 accompanied by the *Zélée* under Captain Jacquinot, with instructions to complete the survey of Oceania and to search for land in the southern polar regions. Dumont d'Urville sailed due south from Tierra del Fuego. The ships struggled in pack ice from January to March 1838. They could not cross the sixty-fourth parallel; from afar the expedition sighted and named Louis-Philippe and Joinville Islands, which lay off the Palmer Peninsula. The *Astrolabe* and *Zélée* then called in the Marquesas, Tahiti, Samoa, the Tongas, Vanikolo, the Solomon Islands, and the Moluccas before landing in northern Australia in March 1839. Rested and refreshed, the expedition explored Melanesia and the great Asian archipelago via Java, Sumatra and Borneo. When the French ships arrived in Tasmania late in 1839 from Western Australia, the men were suffering from severe dysentery. Dumont d'Urville lost nearly a third of his men to disease or desertion.

On 1 January 1840 the corvettes sailed out of Hobart, heading for Antarctica. By the 19th they were nearly within the polar circle, at longitude 140° East; they sighted land, which Dumont d'Urville claimed for France and named after his wife, Adélie. The expedition put into Toulon on 6 November 1840 with an abundance of new scientific data. After surviving every peril of the sea, Rear-Admiral Dumont d'Urville met his end one Sunday afternoon in May 1842. Returning to Paris from an outing at Versailles, the intrepid adventurer was killed when his train was derailed.

The last three-masters in Antarctica

———●———

While sailing within the polar circle Dumont d'Urville encountered ships under the command of Lieutenant Wilkes of the United States Navy. The Wilkes expedition was following a course similar to that of the French mission. In addition to carrying out certain scientific objectives, Wilkes had been instructed to enforce American claims in Antarctica. He discovered Wilkes Land, west of the Adélie Coast. Only three of six American vessels, heavily damaged by ice, returned to New York from the southern polar regions in 1842.

Captain James Clark Ross led the first great English expedition to Antarctica, from 1839 to 1843 (see p. 237). The *Erebus* and the *Terror* crossed the Antarctic Circle on 1 January 1841 and navigated for three months in the Ross Sea. They discovered Victoria Land and a mighty volcano, which they christened Erebus. The Ross Ice Shelf halted their progress at 78° 4' South. Beyond stretched ice fields and the South Polar Plateau. But the stubborn explorers returned to those frigid wastes early in 1842; a year later they spent three more months in the Weddell Sea before sailing back to Folkestone.

Cook, Bellingshausen, Dumont d'Urville, Wilkes and Ross sailed their three-masters to the earth's farthest limits. When steamships made their debut on the oceans shortly after, nothing was left for them to discover.

The British Empire in the South Pacific

By sheer accident, on 26 January 1788 La Pérouse was present at the founding of New South Wales in eastern Australia. When he cast anchor in Island Bay, off North Island, New Zealand, after completing his Antarctic campaign, Dumont d'Urville learned that contrary to repeated affirmations, Britain had annexed the archipelago on 6 February 1840, making the territory a dependency of New South Wales. The tiny French colony of Akaroa, founded at the same time in the southern island by the Compagnie Nanto-Bordelaise with the support of the French Navy, struck colours two years later, but preferred to remain in New Zealand.

As indicated by the French, English and American flags on board the Uranie, *the Sandwich Islands (Hawaii) were controlled by three nations. Here, a Hawaiian notable is being baptized.*

ARCTIC OCEAN

Alaska

Bering Sea

Alentian Islands

Barents Sea

Kara Sea

Ust'-Kamcatask

Petropavlovsk

• Saint Petersburg

Okhotsk

Sea of Okhotsk

Kamtchatka

Kiev •

• Moscow

Lena

Sakhalin

RUSSIA

Kouriles

Tobolsk

Tomsk

Siberia

Tunguska

Khabarovsk

Hokkaido

Kazan

Volga

ASIA

Lake Baikal

Amur

Black Sea

Astrakhan

Ural

STEPPES

Irtysh

Jenisejsk

Angara

Nercinsk

Vladivostok

Tokyo

Trebizond •

Caucusus

Omsk

MONGOLIA

Ulan Bature

Manchuria

JAPAN

Caspienne Sea

Aral Sea

Karakorum

Gobi Desert

KOREA

Nagasaki

Baku

Tabriz

Tartary

Peking

Yellow Sea

Baghdad

Teheran

Perse

AFGHANISTAN

Tien Shan

Kagoshima

Isbahan

Hindu Kush

Kabul

KARAKORAM RANGE

Huang

Hormuz

Kandahar

Lahore

HIMALAYAS

Plateau of Tibet

Yangtze

CHINA

PACIFIC OCEAN

Indus

Pendjab

TIBET

Lhasa

Shigatse

Karachi

Thar Desert

Delhi

Agra

NEPAL

BHUTAN

Canton

Macau

HONG KONG

Ganges

Brahmaputra

Yunnam

Hanoi

Surat

Bengal

Chandernagore

BURMA

Bombay

INDIA

Calcutta

Irrawaddy

Siam

Da-Nang

PHILIPPINES

Golconda

Goa

Deccan

Machilipatnam

Bangkok

Mekong

Calicut

Pondicherry

Phnom Penh

Saigon

INDIAN OCEAN

CEYLON (Sri Lanka)

Singapore

SUMATRA

INDONESIA

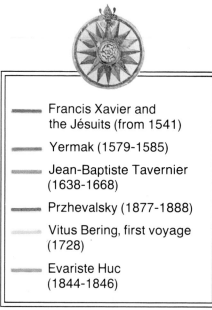

	Francis Xavier and the Jésuits (from 1541)
	Yermak (1579-1585)
	Jean-Baptiste Tavernier (1638-1668)
	Przhevalsky (1877-1888)
	Vitus Bering, first voyage (1728)
	Evariste Huc (1844-1846)

Asia

In ancient Roman times, rare and precious commodities reached the empire from the Far East. When Islam gained control of the great caravan routes, merchants journeyed instead to Aleppo, Damascus, and—especially—Esfahan in search of valuable merchandise; thus did Europe discover the marvels of Persia.

A city of sages

Chardin lodged in the former residence of a celebrated courtesan and frequented the best circles of Esfahan society. He was particularly charmed to find that 'the Persians care for and respect learned men and diligent students so much that one could say that their principal trait is esteem for knowledge, which they tirelessly seek. Even peasants and artisans read books on doctrine and seek earnestly to understand them. They send their children to school and cultivate in them a love for literature, at least so far as their means permit.'

'The beauty of Esfahan', wrote Jean Chardin in his Travels in Persia, 'lies especially in its large number of magnificient palaces, gay and cheerful homes, spacious caravanserais, and very beautiful bazaars...'

Inspired by maps

Jean-Baptiste Tavernier reached Esfahan—then the capital of the Persian empire—in May 1639. He was the first great explorer to familiarize Europe with Persian geography, and to excite the imagination of European writers.

The young Parisian had grown up surrounded by navigation charts and atlases printed by his father, a cartographer: 'If education is a second nature, I can affirm that I came into the world with a desire to travel. The conversations that learned men daily held with my father concerning questions of geography, a discipline my father knew well, inspired me early in life to visit the lands shown to me on maps.'

The pearl route

In the course of his first whirlwind tour of Persia in 1632, Tavernier abandoned his studies as an apprentice cartographer to become a trader in pearls and gems. By the time he set out on his second voyage in 1638, Tavernier was already an established and prosperous merchant. He was accompanied this time by his young nephew, his physician, and a painter. Thereafter he travelled the 'pearl route' along the Persian and Indian coasts many times, a journey that took him beyond Esfahan to India. Yet Tavernier never forgot his youthful enthusiasms. Abbé Prévost, an eighteenth-century popularizer of travel literature, wrote of Tavernier in 1752: 'Few travellers have better

served the geography of this vast region, owing to his accurate renderings of roads and distances.'

Tavernier's 'ghost'

During a stay in Paris in 1668 Tavernier set about writing an account of his travels, intending to present the volume to King Louis XIV. Unfortunately, he was utterly lacking in literary talent. Tavernier spoke German, Italian, Turkish and Persian, yet his written French was execrable. He therefore compelled a certain Chapuzeau, a professional writer who happened to be in his debt, to transcribe into proper French the memoirs that he would dictate. The long-suffering Chapuzeau complained later of having been 'mortified, not to say tortured for the year and more that this miserable task lasted, both by the husband's brusqueness and the wife's foolishness'. The book, *Les Six Voyages de Jean-Baptiste Tavernier*, was published in 1676 in Paris. Everyone who was anyone read it eagerly—a pirated edition even appeared in Amsterdam.

The ambassador and the Jesuit

In 1653, La Boullaye-le-Gouz, a gentleman from Anjou, published an account of his travels in Persia and India, but his work met with less success than Tavernier's. La Boullaye-le-Gouz had stayed in Esfahan in 1647, and upon his return to France Louis XIV had entrusted him with an embassy to the Mogul emperor, Shah Jahan. The Frenchman assumed the Turkish name of Ibrahim Beg. In 1648, en route to Hormuz, where he was to embark for India, La Boullaye-le-Gouz encountered a Jesuit, Alexandre de Rhodes, who was travelling back to France from China. As the Jesuit later recounted: 'After several days of walking to Shiraz, I had a chance meeting for which I have since thanked God a thousand times. I was on foot, saying my prayers, a little apart from my companions. I saw on the road a man of exceedingly pleasant mien, mounted on a fine horse, in Persian dress, wearing a turban, jacket, scimitar, and a long, squared-off beard. I took him to be a Persian or Armenian nobleman. From my hat and black robe he saw that I was a European priest. He greeted me most civilly in Latin; by his pronunciation I perceived that he was French. I answered him immediately in our common tongue, and he was so overjoyed that he dismounted, we embraced, and conversed for half an hour so agreeably that in a very short time we formed a friendship which I shall cherish the rest of my life.' And indeed, the friends met later in Rome, then in Paris whence they returned together to Esfahan. La Boullaye-le-Gouz died in that city soon after and the Jesuit did not long survive him: death united these firm friends in their Persian graves.

The complete traveller

Persia was hard on weary travellers. A few years later, in 1667, Jean Thévenot was another to die there, near Shiraz. His companion brought Thévenot's travel diary back with him to Paris; like Tavernier, he em-

Shah Abbas II's despotic reign over Persia lasted from 1642 to 1667. Chardin denounced the damaging effects of his absolutism.

ployed a ghostwriter to put the diary in readable form and published it in 1669. Son of a Parisian bookseller specializing in travel literature, travel was Thévenot's sole passion. He wrote, 'travel has always been quite natural to man, but it seems to me that never has that passion pressed men so strongly as it does in the present day'.

Thévenot reached Esfahan on 1 October 1664; he described the town as a 'caravanserai that serves as a conduit for money going from Europe and Turkey to the Indies; and for the cloth and spices that come from the Indies to Turkey and Europe'. After five months of closely observing Persian habits and customs, Thévenot joined the opulent caravan led by the ageing Tavernier. The latter's great wealth had made him so disagreeable that Thévenot left the group before it reached Hormuz, where the party was to embark for India. Instead, Thévenot took ship on an Armenian vessel at Basra; he explored India, then returned to Shiraz.

The celebrated Chardin

Esfahan played host to other French visitors over the years. In 1665, the city's fabled riches attracted the son of a great Parisian jeweller. Jean Chardin had left the French capital in disgust, incensed by the Crown's policies against Protestants. He spent ten years in Persia and in so doing amassed a huge fortune. Chardin returned to Europe after a long journey through India. He settled in London, where his wealth procured him a knighthood and the means to engage a high-level ghostwriter, a member of the Académie Française named Charpentier. In 1711 the complete account of his travels was published in London under the title *Journal of the Travels of the Cavalier Chardin*—a work that launched a literary genre. Montesquieu borrowed from Chardin's work to lend his *Persian Letters* authentic local colour.

The land of the *Thousand and One Nights*

Even more than the works of Chardin and Montesquieu, the *Thousand and One Nights*, published in 1704 by the French diplomat Antoine Galland, filled the French imagination with visions of Persian harems and sultanas. 'Born of poor but honest parents', Galland's facility for Oriental languages led him to Constantinople and the Levant. Upon his return to Europe in 1780, Galland's talents brought him into the sphere of the French Royal Library. His translation of the *Thousand and One Nights* made Persia so fashionable that Montesquieu used the popular Persians to mirror the follies and foibles of contemporary Frenchmen in his mordant *Persian Letters*. The *Thousand and One Nights* was translated into English first by the Arabist Edward Lane and then by the famous explorer Sir Richard Burton (see p. 214). The latter's 16-volume edition of the *Arabian Nights* was published between 1885 and 1888.

173

F or a century the Portuguese ruled the maritime routes to the riches of the East. Their commercial empire stretched from Goa, Ceylon, Malacco to Indonesia, the Moluccas and the Celebes. Early in the seventeenth century that monopoly slipped through their fingers, to the profit of the Dutch, the French and the English.

Vasco da Gama's fleet of four ships at the end of the year 1497.

Rounding Africa

Inaccurate maps played a nasty trick on Christopher Columbus. Even after several voyages to the Caribbean (see p. 56), he still believed that he had discovered the Great Indies—China and Japan—when in fact all he had discovered was America. Columbus was the agent of Spain, which coveted control of international seaborne trade. Portugal had similar ambitions, but set about re-

alizing them in a more scientific manner. Portuguese navigators first prospected the western coast of Africa, pressing ever farther south. Their findings were carefully recorded at the royal headquarters in Sagres (see p. 146), and kept absolutely secret from other European powers. According to the maps used by Columbus, it was impossible to sail around the African continent by a southerly route. But the Portuguese cartographers at Sagres were by then persuaded that such a passage did indeed exist. In December 1488 a Portuguese navigator, Bartholomeu Dias, fetched up in Lisbon with revolutionary news: his two small caravels had rounded Africa and sailed up its eastern coast for more than five hundred kilometres. According to the information he had gathered, he could have reached India, had his crew not been on the brink of mutiny. Nonetheless, a southern passage to the spice route had been opened.

Dividing up the world

The news did not discourage Columbus, who persuaded King Ferdinand of Spain not only that a western route to the Indies existed but that it was probably shorter than the southern route. He was duly dispatched to discover it. In March 1493 he returned triumphant from his first voyage. He had—or so he believed—sailed to China. The rivalry between Portugal and Spain grew ever more fierce.

To forestall threats of war between these two Christian kingdoms, Pope Alexander VI persuaded them to sign a most unusual treaty at Tordesillas (Spain) in June 1494 (see p. 53). The pope drew an imaginary line of demarcation 370 leagues west of the Cape Verde Islands, thereby dividing the world into two spheres of influence. Territories discovered west of this meridian were to belong to Spain, while those to the east

would fall to Portugal. Both countries were honour-bound to convert the populations of any new-found lands to Christianity.

Vasco da Gama's mission

In 1497, Portugal mounted an expedition to reach India via the route Dias had discovered. The expedition was led by Vasco da Gama, a shrewd seaman known for his lack of scruples. In July 1497 da Gama sailed with 170 men and four ships (including one caravel), three years' worth of supplies, and a handful of condemned criminals who were to be employed on especially dangerous missions. The small fleet reached the waters of the Cape of Good Hope after ninety-three days of bold navigation. Their course followed a wide curve that took them far out into the Atlantic, well beyond any coastline. The pilots were equipped with the latest navigational instruments, perfected by the experts at Sagres, and were guided by the most up-to-date maps. Da Gama had even brought along milestones engraved with the arms of Portugal (*padraos*), to proclaim that nation's primacy on any territories he might discover.

Da Gama placed one milestone on the Cape, and another in Natal, named in honour of the day he landed there: Christmas, 1497. Steering a northerly course, da Gama entered the Muslim sphere of influence. The sultan of Mozambique and later the sultan of Mombasa both greeted the Portuguese ships with a hail of cannonballs. Finally, at Malindi, on the Kenyan coast, da Gama managed to land and take on supplies. He hired two Hindu pilots who informed him of the monsoons, and explained how they changed direction with the seasons. On 20 May 1498 he dropped anchor off Calcutta, south of Goa. Da Gama had reached the coveted coast of India.

A strange sort of Christian

Vasco da Gama sent two of the condemned criminals to reconnoitre on shore. When they reached the port, they were addressed sharply in Spanish by a Tunisian Muslim. The Portuguese brought the Muslim back to their ship, where he was questioned closely. The port they had reached was Calicut, ruled by the samorin, a monarch whose name means 'king of the seas'. The local warehouses were crammed with spices: pepper, ginger, cinnamon from Ceylon, and even cloves from the Moluccas. Da Gama was delighted and requested an audience with the great king.

After waiting for three months, always expecting the worst, da Gama made an exchange of hostages and was finally permitted to leave his ship with just thirty men. On his way to the palace da Gama stopped at a Hindu temple, believing it to be a church; he also mistook the statue of a goddess and her son in the sanctuary for the Virgin and Child. He could not understand a word of the prayers recited by the faithful; and the local rites of worship astonished him. Yet he knelt, and like a good Christian said his prayers.

Once inside the palace da Gama was led into the presence of the samorin, who lay on a ceremonial bed, half-naked but adorned with many costly jewels. Da Gama's credentials were accepted, and he was dismissed and told to attend an audience at a later date, when he would be expected to present his gifts. Alas, the Portuguese offerings did not meet with royal approval. Da Gama was sent back to his ship and ordered to clear off immediately. If he wanted spices, he would have to pay for them with gold! Furious at the rebuff, da Gama set sail for Europe. As he steered off the coast of Goa, he sent a party on shore in a dinghy to set a Portuguese milestone on the beach.

The return voyage to Lisbon was agony. Only fifty-five survivors disembarked with da Gama in September 1499. He was promoted to admiral, and sent out again in 1502 with a new expedition.

Muslim curry

The second mission was not exploratory—its aims were vengeance and conquest. Vasco da Gama set out with a veritable armada. As he drew into the coastal waters of India, he encountered a vessel transporting pilgrims home from Mecca. He pillaged the ship and burned the passengers with gunpowder. Da Gama put in at Calicut and

The admiral of India, Vasco da Gama, at the height of his glory.

ordered the samorin to drive out all the Arabs. Angered by the monarch's stalling tactics, he had several hundred fishermen and shopkeepers rounded up. These unfortunates were then hanged from the ship's yards, and their heads, hands and feet were lopped off and sent to the samorin, so that he could make himself a curry! With that, da Gama sailed back to Lisbon to relate the good tidings to his king, leaving part of his fleet behind with orders to clear all Muslims from the Indian Ocean. In 1504 one of the officers, Almeida, sacked Mozambique and Mombasa, massacred the inhabitants, and built fortresses on the sites. In 1506 da Cunha exterminated the population of Socotra. A year later Albuquerque destroyed an Arab fleet off Hormuz and exacted a heavy tribute from the sultan of the city. In 1509 Almeida's massacre of Muslims at Diu (off the Gujarat coast) surpassed all others in ferocity. And in 1510 Albuquerque landed on Goa and put the entire Muslim population to the sword. Goa became the capital of Portugal's new Indian Empire.

Beggars of the sea

Despite their willingness to make any sacrifice to acquire the riches of the Orient, the Portuguese simply did not have a knack for commerce. Stored in Lisbon's warehouses,

the treasures of India were distributed throughout Europe by thousands of small Dutch shippers. The proud Iberians scornfully dubbed them 'the beggars of the sea'. In 1594 Lisbon came under the dominion of His Most Catholic Majesty, the King of Spain, who refused the Protestant Dutch shippers access to stockpiles of Oriental merchandise. The 'beggars of the sea' were therefore obliged to find a way to purchase the goods at source. The Protestant Reformation thus resulted in the decline of Portugal's eastern empire.

Commercial espionage

In those days Holland boasted the greatest number of experienced seamen of any European country. Amsterdam's cartographers were producing the finest and most accurate maps in the world. In 1593 a young Dutchman, Jan Huyghen van Linschoten, who had travelled to Goa as the archbishop's secretary, returned to his native city to write an *Itinerario*, a detailed description of Portuguese sea routes to Goa. The long-kept secrets of Sagres were finally revealed. Another Dutchman, Cornelius van Houtman, was engaged as a pilot aboard a Portuguese carrack, an ideal post for a spy to discover the sea route from Lisbon to Goa.

Thus when in 1595 nine Amsterdam merchants founded what would later become

Goa, city of the pure

Portugal made Goa the capital of its eastern empire. There the Portuguese amassed immense wealth, thanks to their control of the spice trade. But in 1580 Spain conquered Lisbon, causing Portugal's Indian empire to decline. The Portuguese were the first Europeans to reside long enough in India to discover its civilization. For instance, it was they who named the caste system: the Portuguese word 'casta' at first designated pure-bred Portuguese born in Goa. The term was later used for Hindu communities, which were just as concerned with racial purity as their European conquerers.

An Indian 'Joan of Arc'

For several centuries Goa had been a vital centre of Brahmanic culture. After he had cleared the island of its inhabitants, Albuquerque resolved to destroy its temples, particularly the most important one, dedicated to the goddess Shanta Durga or Bhagavati. In 1649 the French traveller La Boullaye-le-Gouz (see p. 173) described her in these terms: 'Bagoti is a saint whose strength was great enough to combat and vanquish the Giants; she was, as I see it, another Maid of Orleans, who fought victoriously out of zeal for her Religion and for the liberty of her Country.' On the same site, with the same stones, the Portuguese built a cathedral dedicated to St Catherine, who became the patroness of Catholic Goa, as Bhagavati had been of Hindu Goa. Yet the goddess's name survived the destruction of her temple, and lives on in the word 'pagoda'.

175

the United East India Company (VOC, see p. 142), they were able to send a ship to Java that same year. In 1602 the Dutch established a post in Melaka (Malaya), and in 1616 they expelled the Portuguese from the fortress they had founded there in 1511. In 1612 the Dutch occupied Jakarta, which they rechristened Batavia and made into the capital of their new eastern empire (see p. 149). Nevertheless, since Amsterdam was a six- or seven-month voyage across the oceans, the Dutch needed to establish a string of secure ports of call along the way.

French Huguenots to the Cape

In 1652 the surgeon Jan van Riebeeck founded the Dutch city of Cape Town (then De Kaap) with a handful of men and some slaves imported from Mozambique. The colony stagnated until 1685, when Governor van der Stel, with a stroke of genius, invited one hundred and sixty Huguenots expelled from France after the revocation of the Edict of Nantes. These men and women developed the colony, planting vineyards and raising cattle and horses, to supply the Dutch Company ships that called at the Cape.

The fabulous mines of Golconda

The thirty-eight principal diamond-bearing sites of this region, which in Tavernier's estimation resembled the forest of Fontainebleau, are situated between the Godavari and Krishna rivers. Golconda, the capital of the ruling dynasty of Qutb Shahis from 1500 to 1686, was the market where precious stones were sold under the watchful eye of royal inspectors. The most famous gem found in this region was the Kohinoor diamond, mined around 1656 and presented to the Great Mogul. The stone was stolen in 1739 by the sultan of Kabul, and recovered in 1813 by Ranjit Singh, Sikh king of the Punjab. His son was deposed by the British in 1849, and the Kohinoor diamond was sent to Queen Victoria. It is now part of the British crown jewels.

Facing page:
the flagship Zeelandia.

The 'liberators' of Cochin

It took Holland less than half a century to wrest control of the spice trade from Portugal. In 1603 the Dutch bombarded Goa, but did not risk an attempt to capture the formidable citadel. For while they were seamen to be reckoned with, the Dutch were poor fighters. In 1606 they established fortified trading posts on the eastern coast of India, in Pulicat, north of Madras—well known for the red handkerchiefs woven there—and in Chinsura on the Hooghly River south of Chandernagore. The Dutch, with their haughty airs, were universally unpopular and Batavia, their capital, was built along strict apartheid lines. In India they were bent upon eliminating every last Portuguese: they captured Nagappatinam in 1658 and massacred the entire population; in 1662 the same fate befell Cranganor further south, and in 1663 Cochin on the Malabar coast, where the Dutch were solidly entrenched. Four years later they expunged every vestige of Portuguese presence from the Moluccas, Timor, Ternate and Ceram in Indonesia.

Canny traders

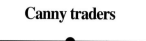

Once they gained control of the spice trade, the Dutch intended to wring every florin from that lucrative commerce. When the Portuguese controlled the pepper supply, they flooded European markets with the spice, causing prices to fall by seventy-five percent. The Dutch, on the other hand, kept prices high by destroying pepper trees; and each year Batavia celebrated its own peculiar festival, which culminated in a bonfire of spices. The Dutch piled the surplus spice crops in an enormous heap—one hundred feet long and twenty-five feet wide, according to one traveller—and set it on fire. Batavians then feasted and danced 'in an atmosphere made fragrant by a strong, very sweet odour'.

Competition from France

While the nine merchants of Amsterdam were establishing a company to corner the clove market in the Moluccas, three Frenchmen—Sieur Frotet, a burger of Saint-Malo; François Martin, an apothecary from Vitré; and Monsieur Pyrard, a merchant from Laval—founded a rival trading company. On 18 May 1601 they embarked with two ships, the *Croissant* and the *Corbin*. The latter vessel was lost in the Maldive Islands. Pyrard survived the shipwreck, and after five years reached Goa. There he was thrown into gaol by the Portuguese Inquisition and sent back to France in 1611.

Martin had better luck—to begin with, at any rate. After a difficult crossing that lasted fifteen months, he landed in Sumatra. Although neither the Portuguese nor the Dutch would sell him spices, he managed to put together a cargo in Achem in the north of Sumatra. But on his return voyage Martin was attacked off the Spanish coast by a Dutch ship. The pirates seized his spices but spared his life. Martin made his way back to his native city in 1603.

The tale of the Frenchmen's adventures spurred Admiral de Montmorency to outfit a fleet. Commanded by a Dutch captain, the vessel brought in an abundant harvest of spices at Bantam on the island of Java. The shareholders realized a windfall profit of four hundred percent. Montmorency was obviously buoyed up by this coup, and created the Compagnie des Indes. Unfortunately, the next voyage was an utter fiasco, and the company was dissolved.

Colbert's India Company

In 1664 Jean-Baptiste Colbert (Louis XIV's leading minister) launched a new Compagnie des Indes, modelled on the successful Dutch enterprise.

While war between France and Holland was brewing in Europe, Colbert outfitted the *Flotte de Perse* under the command of Admiral de la Haye. The ship fetched up in Surat in November 1671. In January 1672 the French fleet undertook a survey of all the ports on India's western coast, still unfamiliar territory for France. That mission accomplished, the Frenchmen sailed north along the east coast of India. On the way they reconnoitred San Tomé, which for some obscure reason the admiral attacked and occupied on 25 July 1672. The city's Mogul governor appealed to the Dutch for help. The French vessels were destroyed, and de la Haye was obliged to surrender on 23 September 1674. During the siege he had sent young Bellanger de Lespinay to seek supplies around Pondicherry. Instead, Lespinay sought permission from the governor of Gingi to settle in Pondicherry. The defeated admiral set sail for France on two vessels lent to him by the Dutch, but he left behind the representative of the Compagnie des Indes Orientales, François Martin, who bought some land for France and set up the Compagnie's headquarters in 1701. The French town of Pondicherry was born.

French exploration of India

Meanwhile, Surat had become a centre for long-distance travellers. Dr Bernier, physician to the Great Mogul, stopped there in 1659 on his way to the imperial court of Agra by the Malwa road. Tavernier (see p. 172) crossed the region four times between 1645 and 1666. His unvarying aim was to discover the diamond mines of Golconda, but he also made his way as far north as Agra. There he met Bernier and followed the physician to Benares. Back in Surat, Tavernier encountered Thévenot, who had just travelled the length and breadth of the Deccan. In 1669 Dr Dellon landed at Surat and headed south, crossing the lands of the great Shivaji, rajah of the Marathi. Dellon became the rajah's first European biographer.

Since these travellers published accounts of their adventures in India, Europeans of the late seventeenth century were becoming ever more familiar with the land of the Great Mogul and Shivaji.

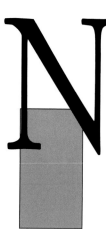

Nothing predisposed the British to found an empire in the Indian subcontinent. Indeed, of all European powers Britain seemed least likely to harbour such ambitions. Britain's armies were not so experienced under fire as the French; its navy was not so large as Portugal's; and British bankers wielded considerably less power than their counterparts in Amsterdam.

The porcelain monopoly

From the early seventeenth century the Dutch played an active role in the porcelain trade. In 1614 Holland imported some 350,000 pieces. At first they shipped authentically Chinese 'blue and white' articles, but before long the Dutch sent Chinese artists designs of their own and wooden models of beer steins. Thus did tulips (Holland's national flower since 1587) bloom among Chinese blossoms, and bourgeois coats of arms and humorous scenes from Dutch life appear on Oriental porcelain pieces. By the end of the century, British competition had put an end to the Dutch monopoly.

The 'blue and white' porcelain of China met with great success and became very fashionable in 17th-century Europe.

Seafaring bandits

London bankers grew envious, it seems, of the fabulous prizes that English freebooters were bringing home. Indeed, in view of the Portuguese and (later) the Dutch monopolies on the spice trade, piracy was the only means to obtain these precious commodities for Britain—to such an extent that Queen Elizabeth I encouraged it. In 1587 Francis Drake attacked the royal Spanish carrack the *San Felipe*, a vessel so crammed with gold that the English queen rewarded the bold corsair with a knighthood. In 1592 William Burrough captured the *Madre de Dios* and sold the precious cargo of spices

and silks in London for a quarter of a million pounds sterling. More valuable still were the marine charts obtained with each capture. The spice route soon held no secrets for English cartographers.

A cautious 'Old Lady'

In 1600 James Lancaster outfitted three ships, two of which were subsequently lost along with their cargoes and crew. Despite these inauspicious beginnings, two hundred and eighteen London merchants founded the English East India Company, immediately dubbed the 'Old Lady'. Queen Elizabeth signed the company's charter in 1601 with considerable misgivings. That same year the director of the infant company, Thomas Smith, sent Lancaster with Sir Francis Drake and four ships to Java and the Moluccas. They returned, to great acclaim, laden with over a million pounds' worth of spices and lac. Over the next twenty years eighty-six ships made similar voyages, of which only nine were lost. In 1621 the profits realized on the initial investment were in the order of 138 percent.

First footholds in India

In 1612 Captain Best, abetted by a handful of ruffians, ousted the Portuguese from their post in Surat and settled there himself. In 1615 Sir Thomas Roe, in great state and with all the trappings of an ambassador, journeyed from Surat to the Great Mogul's court at Ajmer, and obtained permission to retain the trading post. He was surely sincere when he assured the Mogul that Britain harboured no territorial ambitions in India: 'anyone seeking profit should stay at sea

and conduct his trade peaceably; to encumber oneself frivolously with garrisons and expeditions would be pure folly'. That statement long remained the guiding principle of the Company's London directors.

To reinforce their control of the Indian Ocean, in 1622 the English drove the Portuguese out of the strategic port of Hormuz, the key to the Persian Gulf, thereby gaining the port themselves. But a year later the British warehouse at Ambon in the Moluccas was attacked by the Dutch; there were no survivors. Britain was thus compelled to confine its trade to India, and textiles, particularly Indian calicos, replaced spices as Britain's foremost commercial interest. Gradually British posts mushroomed along the coasts of the subcontinent. For a pittance merchants leased from local princes tracts of what was often unwholesome, uninhabited land, such as the Madras swamps, leased in 1640, the Hooghly swamps in Bengal, in 1651, and Calcutta, in 1690.

A dowry fit for a king

In 1662 King Charles II of England wed Catherine of Braganza. Portugal enriched the princess's dowry with the island of Bombay, a territory that held little interest for them but which the English of Surat had long coveted for their headquarters. The concession took effect in 1665. Bombay was Britain's first Indian territory and remained its sole possession for many years. The English Company was granted permission to raise a private army (Charter of 1661), and not long thereafter declared war on local princes (Charter of 1683). Fortresses went up in Bombay, Madras and Calcutta. The Company became a quasi-military organization, and its local directors in India were the next thing to proconsuls.

The French example

The French had taken a considerable lead over England in the exploration of India's interior. La Boullaye-le-Gouz, Thévenot, Tavernier, and even Dr Bernier (see p. 173) had roamed the length and breadth of the Indian subcontinent virtually on their own; the British, meanwhile, had limited their explorations to the coast. Thomas Roe, on his official visit, did not venture outside the precincts of the Great Mogul's court, and Henry Lord, author of *Religion of the Banyans* (which Voltaire studied most attentively), hardly ever left the Surat post where he was chaplain.

In the meantime, the French post at Pondicherry was prospering. Young François Martin (see p. 176), who had been abandoned on the beach with a handful of sailors in 1674 by Admiral de la Haye after a failed mission, proved to be a most efficient manager. The ruins he occupied became a settlement, and later a proper town. In 1689 he obtained permission to fortify the site and recruit mercenaries to defend it. By the time of his death in 1706, ships arrived at Pondicherry direct from France, and returned to Europe with cargoes of cloth. But it was the appointment of Joseph-François Dupleix as governor-general of all French establishments in India in 1742 that gave new shape to European ambitions in India.

French nawabs

Dupleix's father, a director of the French East India Company, sent him on a voyage to India in 1715, at the age of eighteen. He was appointed to the superior council of Pondicherry in 1720. Ten years later he became manager of the trading station in Chandernagore. Owing to this experience, and thanks especially to his wife, a Goanese Indian, Dupleix was uncommonly knowledgeable about India's political system. In 1729 he resolved to become part of it, obtaining from the Great Mogul himself the official status of nawab. As governor of Pondicherry from 1742, Dupleix acted as a local deputy of the Great Mogul, on the same legal footing as other petty nawabs and local rajahs. For twelve years, with his young lieutenant Bussy (also named nawab over broad territories north of Madras), Dupleix made France a major power in southern India. After Dupleix was recalled to France in 1754, no French governor was bold enough to pursue his policy.

The 1686 Blaeu Atlas shows that there were still some uncertainties over the outline of Asia's coast.

Clive: a gifted disciple of Dupleix

A young English merchant-soldier called Robert Clive had ample time to study Dupleix's ideas. He had fought the Frenchman with varying degrees of success between Pondicherry and Madras. When he was called to Bengal to recapture Calcutta, from which the English had been expelled by the local nawab, Clive put Dupleix's lessons to work. He bribed the enemy generals, who deserted at the crucial battle of Plassey in 1757.

Clive then had the defeated nawab assassinated, and put his own man in charge. In 1765 Clive purchased from the Great Mogul the office of *diwan*, which placed him at the head of the administrative and financial affairs of the entire Bengal province. Clive was nominally at least a civil servant of the Mogul. Thereafter it was in the name of the Great Mogul that Clive conceived a plan to conquer India for Britain.

Exploring the Indian interior

Clive's project required precise knowledge of the Mogul Empire's various provinces, a knowledge the British did not then possess. They therefore hired French-speaking cartographers to draw maps: Polier for Bengal, Claude Martin for the Avadh Plains, Wendel and Tieffenthaler for the Agra region—provinces that were the first objectives of British expansion towards Delhi. In an effort to counter this threat, Indian princes also took Frenchmen into their armies and administrations. Thanks to them, by the late eighteenth century the map of the Indian interior was virtually complete. Gentil in the North, Perron, de Boigne and Dudrenec in central India, Raymond and Piron for the region of Hyderabad, and Legoux de Flaix for the sultan of Mysore, surveyed India from north to south. And the foremost French Orientalist of the day, Anquetil Duperron, made an extraordinary journey, unescorted and on horseback, from Chandernagore to Surat, passing around Cape Comorin. He produced the first map of India's modern languages.

The new Great Mogul

Like the French, the British Company was in fact reluctant to embark on a conquest of India. Yet though Dupleix had been unable to convince his superiors of the wisdom of conquest, Clive and his successors—Warren Hastings (1772-1785) and Richard Colley Wellesley (1798-1805)—used bribery, intrigue and the promise of vast fortunes to be made in India to persuade the Company's directors in London to give them a free hand. However, when he returned to England Clive was accused and convicted of misappropriation of funds, and committed suicide. Hastings, accused in his turn, stalled proceedings against himself for so long that he was finally able to buy off his judges.

By 1805 Wellesley had destroyed the three great powers obstinately opposed to British ambitions: the French, the Marathas, and the sultan of Mysore. In 1818 British hegemony in India was nearly complete. After 1827 the British Company no longer claimed to act in the name of the Great Mogul; it had become the Great Mogul.

Commerce, contraband and piracy

From the time of Vasco da Gama, security on Asian sea routes was a major worry for European shippers, since by far the greatest proportion of merchandise was transported by sea. In the sixteenth century, Portuguese and Dutch traders waged a bitter war. The triumphant Dutch captured every trading post, save that of Macau, a notorious centre for opium traffic and piracy. The Dutch destroyed traditional commercial routes and used piracy for their own ends, especially on the Malabar coast of India. The Portuguese paid privateers to hijack cargoes of spices. Pirates trafficked not only in contraband goods but also in slaves; they were known to hold high-ranking personages and even entire towns for ransom.

s masters of India, the British strove to turn their conquest to profit. For while the capture of India had filled the purses of the new English nawabs, it had all but emptied the Company's coffers. However, in the long run, the introduction and development of cash crops disrupted the economy and ecology of the Indian subcontinent.

The advent of landownership

The introduction of landownership in 1793 had far-reaching implications for India's village societies and economies. Land in India had never before been owned, in the Western sense of the word. Rather, a community of people held certain rights to the land; these included the farmer, the artisans who forged farm tools, and the prince who claimed a portion of the revenue produced by the land. The prince's share of every crop was harvested by his local representatives, the zamindars. But in 1793 the zamindars were recognized by British administrators as the land's legal owners and were taxed annually by the government. This reform made farmers hostage to the new master, who exploited them ruthlessly. The farming class soon fell into abject poverty.

The British conquest of India benefited from the complete support of English staff officers who commanded an army of sepoys.

Indians serving Britain: the sepoys

To consolidate its rule over India, England used three institutions: sepoy troops, maharajahs, and a centralized tax system. The Portuguese had already employed sepoys—Indian mercenary soldiers of every caste, trained according to European methods by European officers. In the navy, these native fighters were called lascars (both sepoy and lascar are words of Persian origin). Dupleix and Bussy had created and refined this system; but it was Boigne, in the service of the Marathi prince Shinde, who turned the sepoys into an elite fighting corps. His brigades were so famous for their prowess that the British themselves did not dare cross swords with them. Clive also employed sepoys, but only in auxiliary positions.

Later, with the enormous expansion of British dominance, sepoy units multiplied, allowing Britain to emerge victorious from many battles in which a minimum of British blood was spilt.

The maharajahs

Maharajahs were a British institution. Small Indian kingdoms were traditionally ruled by dynasties that had emerged from all the castes, including the lowest. India's real aristocrats were the Brahmin civil servants who oversaw the continuity of the administration through frequent dynastic changes. But the great majority of the population, generally thriving in villages highly organized according to the caste system, was largely unaffected by such changes.

The English retained the main outlines of this traditional system but modified its content. Having assumed the role of Great Mogul, the Company wished to keep the rajahs and nawabs on a tight rein. Those who refused to sign over their independence were eliminated and the administration of their territories taken over by the Company. Those who consented to the new arrangement and collaborated with the British were permitted to maintain their titles. But they were compelled to accept the presence of an official English resident and a garrison of sepoys, and to cover all their expenses. Thus the rajahs were transformed into richly pensioned idlers, whose position depended on their docility to British rule. The Company could dismiss them, and when a rajah died, the Company appointed his successor from among the more biddable scions of the dynasty. Consigned to the role of puppet princes with very little to do, most of the new maharajahs built vast, ornate palaces where they lived out their days in luxurious leisure, much to the amusement of nineteenth-century travellers and journalists from the West.

The Sepoy Rebellion

In 1842 a British force made up chiefly of sepoys attempted to conquer Afghanistan. The army was cut to pieces. Between 1845 and 1848 another army, dispatched to capture the Sikh kingdom of Punjab, suffered many bloody reverses before finally achieving its objective. The British army's reputation for invincibility was gravely compromised. Thus when in 1856 the Company resolved to depose the Muslim nawab of Lucknow and the Hindu rajah of Nagpur and to annex their lands, it sparked off a revolt among its own—mostly Muslim and Hindu—sepoy troops.

The English (left) attend a night festival in northern India.

The sepoys believed that 1857, date of the hundredth anniversary of the Battle of Plassey (see p. 179) could well mark the end of British rule in India. They rose up in Meerut, took Delhi, and proclaimed the last descendant of the Great Moguls, Bahadur Shah, the one true emperor. The revolt spread like wildfire throughout northern India. The queen of Jhansi and the troops of Gwalior rallied to the rebellion, as did the last descendant of the peshwas, Tatya Topé, imprisoned by the English at Kanpur, and the begum of Lucknow. But the other rajahs, in the pay of the British, did nothing. A ruthless suppression followed. The mutineers were massacred, and the queen of Jhansi murdered.

Birth of the Raj

The Sepoy Rebellion shook British public opinion. Parliament voted to close down the Company and transfer responsibility for governing India directly to the Crown. Queen Victoria became Empress of India, and named a viceroy to represent her authority over the new empire, the British Raj. The army was reformed, the proportion of sepoys to European soldiers cut sharply; Muslim sepoys in particular were dismissed and replaced by Hindu sepoys, Sikhs, Jats, Rajputs and Gurkhas, whose princes had remained faithful to Britain. The fidelity of such princes was rewarded with increased autonomy, particularly in the choice of their successors. In addition, tax collection was organized more coherently and entrusted to a corps of civil servants whose honesty could be verified.

Salvation from sugar, tea and opium

The British strove to reorientate the economy from food production to more profitable crops. They leased fallow farmlands to European planters who hired (at slave wages) local farmers ruined by the land reform of 1793 (see facing page). They planted indigo first, followed by sugar cane for export to Europe. Legoux de Flaix wrote in 1807: 'For some ten years now perhaps half of Europe's sugar has come from Bengal and other lands on the Coromandel Coast under British administration.' For the European and, especially, the Chinese market, plantations of tea and opium were expanded apace.

International drug traffic

With or without sugar, England was a nation of tea drinkers. While waiting for India's tea plantations to supply most of its needs, Britain had to buy tea from China, in exchange for opium. The best opium in the world was grown in the region of Patna (just south of Nepal), but Indians used the drug with moderation. Warren Hastings, as soon as he had taken Bihar, compelled local farmers to plant poppies on the lands where they had formerly grown their food. Enormous quantities of opium were thus produced for the Chinese market. But since the Chinese authorities forbade the importation of the drug, a clandestine network smuggled it into China. The Chinese government took stringent measures to prevent the illegal trade on its territory. The British and other European nations involved in the traffic—the Dutch and especially the French—sent gunboats to force China to accept the drug: such were the Opium Wars of 1840-2.

The new nawabs

High- and middle-ranking members of the British administration in India became progressively Indianized. Often of modest birth, they enthusiastically adopted the lifestyle of former nawabs of the Mogul empire. They built comfortable bungalows and surrounded themselves with Indian staff and platoons of domestic servants, who did most of their masters' work. They took up smoking hookahs, invited nautch girls to dance for their entertainment, and even set up harems for their private enjoyment.

The fishing fleet

To counter the Indianization of its employees, the Company organized what was wryly dubbed 'the fishing fleet'. Its quarry was not fish at all, but marriageable European girls, especially Italians, who could be enticed by the prospect of an advantageous match in India. The moment they arrived, often before they had left the quays of Madras or Calcutta, the maidens found eager suitors, bachelors and widowers, who quickly chose their bride and wed her on the spot. Such marriages did not always last. A young Florentine girl tired of her elderly husband, James Hull, within a year and she fled her new household to seek her fortune in the courts of India. She surrounded herself with a squadron of daring young girls and entered the service of the nizam of Hyderabad, and later of the Marathi peshwa of Poona, where she gained fame under the name of Jamal Sardar.

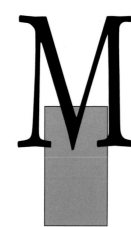

arco Polo's explorations had opened the silk route for the West. His Book Concerning the Kingdoms and Marvels of the East *had set all of Europe dreaming of the riches of the Great Khan's empire. But the Mongol heirs of Genghis Khan were ousted in 1368 by the Chinese Ming dynasty. The silk route was abandoned. Travel to China had become an impossible dream.*

Ming porcelain

In the Ming period (1368-1644) Chinese porcelain diversified considerably. In addition to a large production of whites in the kilns of Te-hua in the province of Fukien, a taste developed for 'blue and white' porcelain, which was reproduced in Japan, Persia and Delft. More characteristic of the Ming period, however, are 'three-colour' enamels, which used new tints (violet, turquoise, aubergine) and 'five-colour' (enamelled white porcelain), with foliage motifs. To satisfy foreign demand, certain workshops produced two grades of the same object; articles of lesser quality were exported, while the finest pieces were reserved for the imperial court, which sometimes commissioned dinner services numbering thousands of pieces.

Francis Xavier preaching to the Japanese.

Through India to China

In 1557 the Portuguese ended their eastward push when they settled Macau. The Chinese had requested Portugal's aid in driving pirates—mostly Japanese, with some Chinese and Portuguese—out of the China Sea. The Portuguese executed the task swiftly and ruthlessly. In return, the Chinese leased the territory of Macau to the Portuguese for 22,000 escudos per year; Portugal turned it into a flourishing trading post, fortified against attack by the Dutch. Prosperous Macau became the gateway for European trade with China.

The Ming dynasty had by this time fallen into decline. Mandarins and corrupt eunuchs tyrannized Beijing and the puppet emperors. Since Europeans could no longer journey to China by overland routes, they travelled by sea; Goa became an indispensable port of call on the long ocean voyage. A consequence of this is that certain common Chinese words have Indian roots: Chinese public officials were called 'mandarins', from the Portuguese corruption of *mantrin*, which in Sanskrit means 'councillor' or 'minister'. And 'pagoda' comes from the Portuguese adaptation of 'bagoti', their name for Hindu temples.

The Jesuits' great dream

In 1542 Francis Xavier (see p. 196) landed at Goa. One of the seven founder-members of the Society of Jesus, he had been sent to India by the pope and the king of Portugal to reform the colony's dissolute morals. What the Jesuit witnessed there was indeed so shocking that he felt himself unequal to the task, and requested that the Inquisition take over.

Francis Xavier then spent several years catechizing fishermen in Malaya and the Moluccas. In 1549 he travelled to Kagoshima in Japan, where he found the civilization and standards of behaviour more to his liking. He baptized a few converts to Christianity, but soon understood that all the finest and most noble aspects of Japanese culture were rooted in China. He resolved to travel there and to convert the emperor. On 13 November 1552 he landed on the little island of Sancian, a nest of pirates and smugglers lying off the coast from the city of Canton (Guangzhou). There Francis, waiting for authorization to enter the country, fell ill and died on 3 December 1552. The visionary Jesuit was no more, but a great Jesuit dream was born: if the emperor of China could be converted, the entire Far East might be won over for Christianity.

The magic of a clock

In 1577 that dream inflamed the spirit of a fiery young Roman Jesuit, Matteo Ricci. Ricci was born in 1552 of a noble family in Macerata, in central Italy. There he entered the school opened by the Jesuits. In 1571 he requested permission to join the order. He arrived in Goa in 1578, ready to learn everything about the Orient. He studied with fierce determination, and in 1582 was dispatched to Macau, where he devoted his efforts to mastering Chinese. Before long he was preaching to the natives in their own tongue; he settled on the outskirts of Canton with a fellow Jesuit, Father Ruggieri, and there he spent seven years. But the cruelty and arrogance of Macau's rulers turned the Chinese against the two Italian priests, whom they took to be Portuguese, and the pair was expelled from Canton. They pushed deeper into the Chinese interior, and made their way as far as Beijing, where the Emperor Wan-Li lived sequestered in his forbidden palace. The Jesuits were arrested just outside the city and thrown into prison and their belongings were confiscated.

Among the priests' possessions were two clocks, one operated by weights, the other with a spring mechanism. The mandarin in charge of the gaol took the timepieces and presented them as his gift to the delighted emperor. But when the weights had run down, the first clock no longer chimed on the hour. Furious, the emperor ordered his chief eunuch to give the two Jesuits three days to repair the clock, on pain of death. Ricci explained the mechanism to four imperial mathematicians, who were able to make the clock chime once more. The emperor was beside himself with joy; he summoned the prisoners and named them mandarins of the imperial clocks. The Jesuits thus became important personages at court. Francis Xavier's dream was coming true, with the help of a clock.

A Jesuit mandarin

As Ricci's Chinese grew ever more fluent, he began to think in Chinese as well. When he adopted the mandarin's way of dress, it was not as a disguise or a trick. Ricci found that Confucian philosophy was entirely compatible with Christian dogma. He preached a Christianity that the Chinese found acceptable; and the integrity of Ricci's personal life impressed those around

him. Soon a growing community of Chinese Christians formed in Beijing. When Ricci died in 1610, he was surrounded by fellow Jesuits, all astronomers or mathematicians and all dressed in mandarin's robes. The emperor had such great confidence in the Jesuits that he entrusted to them the construction of artillery for repelling Manchu invasions. Jesuit ordnance was excellent, but the Manchu were stronger still. The Ming dynasty was overthrown and replaced by the Ch'ing in 1644. The new emperors adopted the Jesuits, particularly the young K'ang-hsi, who in 1692 published a famous edict of toleration, which guaranteed religious freedom for all Chinese Christians. Seven years earlier in France Louis XIV had revoked the tolerant Edict of Nantes. In 1688 the French sovereign sent six Jesuits to China on a mission that combined both political and scientific aims.

Jesuits map China

Ricci had in his possession the most recent maps of the world. At that time China was poorly represented on those maps, occupying only a tiny corner of the whole. Ricci's idea was to place China in the centre of the paper on which the map was drawn, a plan that pleased everyone and enhanced his reputation as a great geographer—and an able courtier. But the map of inner China remained in many respects a work of fiction.

The generations of Jesuits who arrived in Beijing throughout the seventeenth century were all skilled geometers. Father Verbiest, a Fleming, was named President of the Mathematical Tribunal of Beijing, as well as mandarin of the second class. A talented astronomer, he specialized in calendar reforms and in drawing maps with a zero meridian that passed through Beijing. The Jesuit Adam Schall, a first-class mandarin and a confirmed disciple of Galileo and Copernicus, built telescopes for the emperor which improved the accuracy of the imperial army's artillery.

The French Jesuits sent by Louis XIV were authorized to travel throughout the empire, which enabled them to produce accurate maps that proved to be a revelation to European geographers. The Jesuits were received at the imperial court on 21 March 1688. 'After the visit,' wrote Father de Fontenay, 'Father Le Comte, Father de Visdelou and I thought only of dividing the provinces amongst us, and of setting about converting the heathen. But before leaving Beijing, we were very happy to visit the most curious sights of that famous city.'

Detail from a Ming ceramic vase depicting women weaving silk.

The end of a dream

In 1709 Emperor K'ang-hsi entrusted to the Jesuits the task of producing a new map of the empire, a mission completed only in 1718 after numerous expeditions to the Russian and Tibetan borders. But that enlightened ruler died in 1722, and his successor proved less tolerant. The storm finally broke in 1724.

In 1715 Pope Clement XI issued a bull forbidding missionaries in China to adopt local customs and dress. Two Dominican priests living in a mainland city facing Formosa followed the pope's directives, but in doing so drew the hostility of the provincial governor, who complained to Beijing. In 1724, the emperor decreed that all missionaries in every province of the empire were to be expelled to Macau. Exempt from banishment were those missionaries living in Beijing whose presence was useful to the empire. The decree marked the end of the Jesuit dream for the Far East; barely fifty years later, in 1773, the Society of Jesus was disbanded by order of the pope.

A Jesuit painter at the court of Ch'ien-lung

Among the Jesuits authorized to remain in Beijing after 1724 was the Milanese coadjutor, Castiglione, who was also a painter of considerable talent. The emperor named him artistic adviser, and he supervised the decoration and layout of the many edifices the emperor commissioned for his capital. Those palaces have since disappeared, but evidence of Castiglione's talent remains in some beautiful silk rolls, such as the famous *Mulan Hunts*, which combine Western technique and Chinese subject matter in wonderful harmony. The Jesuit dream in some sense survived the age of intolerance.

*T*he relentless expansion of Russia preoccupied China's last Ming emperors. In 1689, under the Ch'ing dynasty, the two nations signed a peace treaty negotiated by the Jesuits, but Moscow continued to send explorers all over Central Asia. But were they really explorers? Or were they spies?

Navigating an automobile over mule trails in the mountains of Mongolia did not seem to frighten European explorers too much.

A nation of conquerors

'Now a warlike yet civilized nation has spread itself along the fifty-fifth parallel; from these high latitudes it threatens both China and India, the two great axes of trade with Europe. Through Zuruchaitu the Russians penetrate into the native land of the present masters of China. From the Caspian Sea the Russians push into the region that produced Mahmud of Ghazni, the mogul Grabu, and all the other conquerors who for eight centuries have dominated India. What Russia needs is not more Asian conquests, but a powerful means of influence which would compel seaborne trade to take to overland routes instead.' The author of these lines was Count Potocki, writing to Czar Alexander I from Irkutsk in 1806.

Ethnologist and novelist

The man who dreamed of replacing the maritime spice route by the ancient silk route—a road that stretched over the entire breadth of Asia (see p. 21)—was a most remarkable character. When he wrote this letter to the czar, he was forty-six years old, with a long career already behind him. Member of a famous Polish family, he had devoted himself to the study of the Slavs. While writing a novel, *The Manuscript Found in Saragossa*, which would bring him considerable posthumous fame, Potocki was seeking a stable post in Moscow as director of Asiatic affairs. He was sent to China with a group of experts to accompany Count Golovkin's embassy to the Chinese emperor at Beijing. The party never got farther than Mongolia, however, for the absurd reason that Golovkin adamantly refused to perform the low bows required by Chinese protocol. Nevertheless, Potocki put his stay to good use, sending cartographer-spies to survey the Sino-Russian border.

A French spy for Catherine the Great

Catherine II had long contemplated the possibility of Russia's expansion towards India and the southern seas. It has been said that the Russians sent the Count de Boigne on a mission in 1775 to explore the route to India via Kashmir and Tartary. He did travel to Calcutta and sail up the Ganges, but when he reached Delhi, de Boigne entered the service of the Maratha Mahaji Shinde, rising to the rank of general in his army. No mention was ever subsequently made of his Russian mission.

The dazzling Lake Koko Nor

The positive consequence of Russia's ultimately fruitless dreams was the scientific exploration of Central Asia by Russian experts. One such was Nikolay Przhevalsky, who between 1871 and 1888 made four trips in the Tarim Basin, on the silk route. On his first trip he marvelled at the beauty of Lake Koko Nor (Qing Hai) in western China: 'Its salt waters are a gorgeous dark-blue colour; now, in October, the surrounding mountains are covered with snow, making a dazzlingly white setting for the lake.' Przhevalsky twice tried to reach Lhasa. The first time he was forced to cut short his journey for lack of funds. His second attempt, in 1879, was foiled by Tibetan authorities, who refused him entry. So downcast was he by his failure to repeat the exploit of Abbé Huc, who had made the journey twenty years earlier (see p. 187), that he even questioned the veracity of the French cleric's account of his Tibetan sojourn. Years later, academic circles long refused to credit Alexandra David-Néel's report of her travels in Tibet (see p. 187).

Hunting big game with the Prince of Orléans

Prince Henri of Orléans had no greater aim in life than to spend a pleasant holiday shooting exotic big game. In 1889 he and the veteran explorer P.G. Bonvalot organized an ambitious hunting expedition that took them all over Central Asia, from Siberia to Tonkin. It was the era when Britain and France were at the height of their colonial power and considered the entire world their hunting ground; and wherever they went, Britons and French alike were certain to bring their creature comforts with them. The impedimenta of the Bonvalot— Orléans hunting party included 1600 pounds of small bread rolls, 320 pounds of the best flour, 280 pounds of mutton fat, 80 pounds of salt, 80 pounds of sesame oil, packets of tobacco for the gentlemen, and six tonnes of barley for the horses.

The Prince cast doubt on Przhevalsky's criticisms of Abbé Huc, as he followed the same itinerary as the abbé had described and found Huc's book to be a faithful guide. 'We led the life of Abbé Huc. We endured the same privations; we lived amidst the same populations, here drinking a cup of milk under a black tent at Si Fan, there conversing with a *kalun* (minister of Lhasa), elsewhere using a Mogul lama as an interpreter. Always and everywhere we were astonished by the accuracy of the French missionary's account.'

Geographers and archaeologists

Since Russian explorations invariably heralded the arrival of occupying troops, local populations were rarely cordial to visiting teams of Russian scientists. No one minded the Hungarians or the Swedes, however. The Swedish explorer Sven Hedin made a great advance in the scientific knowledge of the Tarim Valley when he surveyed the area with a large team of geophysicists and geologists. From 1893 to 1897 Hedin crossed the

Ethnologist and novelist Count Jan Potocki encouraged the Russian expansion into Central Asia.

southern branch of the silk route near Lake Koko Nor. From 1905 to 1908 he roamed the Trans-Himalayas in the southern part of Tibet and accurately described the source of the Indus. Later in 1927/8, the intrepid Swede took part in a joint expedition with the Chinese through western China.

In 1906 and 1915, the Hungarian Aurel Stein retraced the same itinerary as Hedin. On his first journey he set out from Kashgar, reaching the Lop Nor via Yarkand, Khotan and Keriya. His second time out, Stein started from the Gobi Desert and made his way to Samarkand, passing through Hami, Turfan, Aqsu and Pamir: the ancient silk route, once travelled by Marco Polo. By this time, however, caravaneers no longer transported rich silks along that arduous route.

The intentions of French geographers were probably less innocent than those of their Hungarian colleagues. Napoleon III imposed French rule on Annam (Central

Vietnam) in 1858, and later on Cambodia and Cochin China; Tonkin was occupied in 1885 (see p. 199). Ten years later Charles Bonin made an epic journey around China, Tonkin and the Gobi Desert, passing through Tibet. In 1907 Jacques Bacot explored the high valleys of the Yangtze, Mekong and Irrawaddy rivers. The following year Paul Pelliot set out on an important archaeological mission that took him all along the ancient silk route. Excavations were made at Tashkent, Kashgar, Kucha and Urumchi. Near the last of these towns the team discovered the famed caves of Tuen-Huang, also called the 'Thousand Buddhas'. There Pelliot unearthed a cache of Chinese and Tibetan manuscripts dating from the seventh to ninth centuries, the basis of a landmark study in 1924. Pelliot was a noted Chinese scholar, and owed much of his success to his excellent relations with local mandarins.

Caterpillars on the silk route

In 1931 the modern era dawned on the silk road with the thunder of machinery. The French industrialist André Citroën launched fourteen vehicles on caterpillar treads along the road travelled by the peaceful caravans of yesteryear, as well as by more recent scientific missions. It was one of history's first great publicity campaigns. What seemed to be the most insurmountable obstacles could not stop the newfangled vehicles. Occasionally the trail had to be improved for the half-tracks, progress, or bridges built. No advances in geographic knowledge resulted from this expedition, for the trails had already been carefully marked by scientific missions.

For this *Croisère Jaune*, which was intended to symbolize the unstoppable march of progress, the leaders of the automobile industry were joined by a consultant who also happened to be the most admired Jesuit of his day: Pierre Teilhard de Chardin. A palaeontologist fascinated by the problems of man's origins, Teilhard had supervised excavations in the Gobi Desert and on the steppes of the Ordos Desert in search of the sinanthropus, one of man's primitive apelike ancestors.

ibet has always held a peculiar fascination for seekers after truth. Catholic priests were the first to reveal the existence on the 'roof of the world' of a community of strange monks who resembled Christian hermits and who were known as 'lamas'. The dialogue between Rome and Lhasa started as early as the seventeenth century.

Were lamas Christian?

The 'roof of the world' was not an easy place to reach, and few travellers made the effort.

In 1661 the Jesuit fathers Grueber and d'Orville passed through Lhasa on their overland return to Europe from China. Back in Rome they joyfully announced that the inhabitants of Tibet already possessed the true faith. As Grueber put it: 'Though they have had no contact with Europeans, there is complete concord on all essential points between their religion and the faith of Rome. They celebrate a sacrifice with bread and wine. They have monasteries and convents for women; they sing in their temples like Christian monks.'

Rome was profoundly affected by the news. In 1714 two more Jesuits, Fathers Freyre and Ippolito de Desideri, were dispatched to verify the earlier reports and to initiate a dialogue with the lamas. They set out together for India. From Agra they climbed to Kashmir, and then followed the valley of the Leh with a caravan transporting woollen shawls to China. They constructed wobbly 'monkey' bridges to cross the chasms that often blocked their progress: 'From one edge to the other were stretched two stout cables woven of willow twigs about four feet apart; the cables were held together by shorter ropes knotted across them at eighteen-inch intervals. To make one's way across, one had to slide one's arms quickly along the larger parallel cables, while catching at the rope rungs with one's feet, hoping all the while that one would arrive safely on the other side. With each step the bridge swayed back and forth; meanwhile waterfalls crashed down on every side, blinding us and stunning us with their terrific noise.' Finally on 18 March 1716 the exhausted party reached Lhasa. Desideri spent five years there and wrote

The Rome of Tibet

Disguised as a Buddhist nun and accompanied as ever by her faithful lama Yongden (whom she later adopted), Alexandra David-Néel reached Lhasa in 1924. She exulted in her triumph, but discreetly—for she feared discovery. 'I shall go about for two months in the Rome of Tibet', she rejoiced, 'I shall wander through its temples and go for walks on the highest terraces of the Potala, and no one will suspect that for the first time since the beginning of the world, a foreign woman has beheld the forbidden city.' What this intrepid traveller saw and so vividly described in her books will never be seen again by anyone; for the Rome of Tibet, like the other Rome, was razed to the ground by barbarians.

Portrait of Abbé Huc, dressed in Chinese clothing.

the first important study of Tibetan Lamaism. Father Horace de La Penna, along with some Capuchin friars, succeeded him, and confirmed Grueber's opinion. The lamas of Tibet 'take vows of poverty, chastity, and obedience, among several others. They have confessors chosen by their superiors, and receive their power from the lama, as from a bishop, lacking which power they can neither hear confessions, nor impose penances. The structure of their hierarchy is not so different from that of Rome.'

A land that fosters philosophers

In November 1761 a certain Chevalier, agent of the French East India Company, set out on a wide-ranging search for markets and trade in Tibet. He crossed the same swaying, dizzying monkey bridges, which

frightened him even more than they had Desideri. He was horrified by the slovenliness of Tibetan women: 'They never bathe; they do not wash their mouths, nor their hands, and even less, I suspect, certain other portions of their anatomy. In a word, they smell like animals. But no one seems to mind, and in any case no one is in a position to reproach his neighbour. The women are otherwise lively, gay, pleasure-loving—not to say wanton! They openly tease strangers, in plain sight of their husbands, who are not so foolish as to be jealous.' But the grandeur of the situation and the scenery made travellers to Tibet willingly bear the hardships of the journey: 'A philosopher curious to climb to the clouds, and hear thunder rumble below his feet, would often enjoy such spectacles in Tibet. He could also satisfy his taste for natural history with the profusion of plants, herbs, birds, and quadrupeds he would encounter, and with the abundance of minerals and gums whose properties he would discover.'

Temptations for the collector

In 1773 Captain Claude Martin, a Lyonnais soldier of fortune in service with the British, invaded Bhutan at the head of a small group of sepoys. Another adventurer, the Count of Modave, described the expedition three years later in these terms: 'He easily defeated those mountain men, inexperienced as they were with firearms... After much killing, bloodshed, fires, and the like, he obliged the inhabitants of that valley in Bhutan to beg for peace... He showed me several rare objects to which he had helped himself while pillaging Bhutan's temples. He even gave me several manuscripts which he had found in the hollows of statues. I sent them to the Académie des Inscriptions.'

Two strange 'long noses'

In January 1846 the inhabitants of Lhasa watched in astonishment as two weary lamas came into the city, accompanied only by a female camel, a white horse, and a young Mongol. The lamas' long noses betrayed their foreign origin. Fathers Evariste Huc and Joseph Gabet, both French Vincentian priests, had come from an extraordinary journey in Mongolia. They proceeded to win the Tibetans' friendship, and, as protégés of the lama regent, thought that they might establish a little mission in the forbidden capital of Tibet. But in fact the priests remained in Lhasa for only six weeks, for they had not reckoned on the pressure of the Chinese, who had them expelled—albeit with a thousand polite phrases. China had its own designs on Tibet, intending to profit from the vacancy of the Dalai Lama's seat to dominate its smaller neighbour and to reduce it to a state of vassalage. The Chinese ambassador at Lhasa dismissed the French clerics, because, he said, they were foreigners. Huc tried to reason with him.

What is a foreigner?

'"Yes, we are foreigners, but we know that the laws of Tibet are not the same as the laws of China. The *Pebun*, the *Katchi*, the Mongols are foreigners just as we are, yet they are allowed to live in peace—no one torments them. What then is meant by this arbitrary decision to exclude Frenchmen from a country open to all people? If foreigners must leave Lhasa, why indeed do you remain? Does not your title of ambassador show clearly that you are nothing more than a foreigner here?" At these words the ambassador leaped from his crimson cushion: "I, a foreigner!" he cried, "a foreigner! I who represent the power of the great emperor!" ... He dismissed us curtly, telling us that he would see we left Tibet.'

The yellow goat has no country

Throughout their travels the good fathers had benefited from the veneration that Tibetans feel for their lamas. According to the Buddhist maxim, 'the yellow goat has no country, the lama has no family'. A monk, in other words, is by nature cosmo-

Disguised as a Tibetan, Alexandra David-Néel was the first European woman to penetrate Lhasa. Her accounts and translations contributed greatly to the understanding of the Himalayas.

politan. In Tibetan lamaseries, the moment a man shaves his head and puts on the religious habit, he renounces his former name and takes another. If he is asked where he comes from, he answers 'I have no country'. The Chinese, however, did not share the Tibetans' mystical bent, and they escorted the two Vincentian priests as far as Macau.

A *Parisienne* in Lhasa

Abbé Huc's *Travels in Tartary, Thibet, and China*, published in 1850, was the first classic work of travel literature on Tibet. The second did not appear until 1928. It was Alexandra David-Néel's *Travels of a Parisian Lady in Lhasa*. Nearly eighty years separate the works, but they have in common their palpable authenticity, an essential characteristic that books on Tibet have often lacked.

When Alexandra David-Néel finally reached Lhasa in 1924, she was elated thus

to avenge herself on those who had for fourteen years tried to discourage her every attempt to travel to Tibet. In 1912, for example, her route was barred not by the Tibetans, nor even by the Chinese, but by the British! Indeed, she could not have chosen a more inopportune moment to arrive on the scene. In 1903 Lord Curzon, viceroy of India, had sent a political mission to Lhasa led by Sir Francis Younghusband. His objective was to force the Dalai Lama to sign an inequitable treaty, of the kind that had allowed Britain to dominate India. After a terrible struggle, Tibet acquiesced, and the British left troops at Gyangtse. According to the terms of the treaty, the Tibetans promised to bar any non-British foreigner from entering the country. David-Néel, a Parisian, was one of the treaty's first victims, as were the mountain people who had helped her. 'This behaviour, unworthy of civilized people, awakened in me a desire for vengeance, but of a clever sort, befitting the native spirit of Paris, where I was born. Yet I was obliged to bide my time', she wrote later.

Arrogant ambassadors

The Dalai Lama, who was at war with Bhutan, was much pleased with Claude Martin's punitive expedition, and had him request in Calcutta the dispatch of an ambassador to Lhasa. In 1774 Calcutta sent George Bogle on an official embassy. He was the first Englishman to visit much of Bhutan, but he never actually reached Lhasa. After a journey of fifteen months, Bogle returned to Bengal. Samuel Turner was sent next in 1783. He struck the Tibetans as so arrogant that he was expelled less than a year after his arrival. For more than a century Lhasa received no more European ambassadors.

The characters created by Rudyard Kipling in his famous novel Kim *were not purely fictional. In fact, from the 1810s, the Himalayan region was mapped by spies working for the four great world powers of the day which sought to dominate the region: France, England, Russia and China.*

The Caucasians took up arms to resist Russian domination until the middle of the 19th century. The fiercest among them, mountain-dwelling Muslims, emigrated in large numbers to the Ottoman Empire.

Moorcroft's double death

While in Lhasa, Abbé Huc heard tales of a strange affair. He learned that from 1826 to 1838 a British spy called Moorcroft had lived in the capital, disguised as a Kashmiri horse dealer. He spoke Persian so fluently that no one, not even his Ladakhi servant, suspected his true identity. He owned herds of goats and cattle which his Tibetan shepherds led to pasture in the mountains nearby. Under cover of visiting his herds, he was able to draw detailed maps of all the roads leading to Lhasa. Moorcroft's true identity was revealed only after his death. As he journeyed back to Ladakh, he was assassinated by bandits, who were later arrested by the Tibetan police. It was then that the spy's papers and maps were discovered. Now according to declarations filed by the British secret service, Moorcroft was supposed to have died in Afghanistan in 1825 on the road from Herat to Balkh. It was Moorcroft's companion, a man called Tribeck, who announced his disappearance to the head of the secret service in Ludhiana. The only thing that is clear in this murky tale, Huc states, is that the date of Moorcroft's death in Afghanistan coincides exactly with his reappearance in Kashmir as a horse dealer travelling to Lhasa.

The clue of the Russian lapdogs

Moorcroft's taste for espionage was revealed in Tibet, where he had been posted in 1810 as a veterinary officer, with orders to round up a contingent of small Tibetan horses, sought after for their adaptability to all climates and all sorts of tasks, and to explore, if possible, the region of Lake Manasarowar and Mount Kailas, both sacred to the Hindus. Moorcroft and his companion, Hearsey, disguised themselves as Hindu pilgrims and accomplished their reconnaissance mission. They then disguised themselves as horse dealers in order to purchase the desired Tibetan stock. While haggling with the mountain people, they were surprised to see some tiny lapdogs frolicking about the village. The dogs could only have come from the court of some Russian prince. The two Britons concluded that the Russians had reached Tibet before them. To return to India they had to cross Nepal, which they had already traversed in their pilgrim garb. But with their new disguise, they looked for all the world like successful horse traders, their remounts trotting behind them. The pair were attacked by Gurkhas and taken prisoner. In Calcutta the British paid the ransom demanded for the men and their horses; Moorcroft and Hearsey were finally handed over on 1 November 1812. By then Moorcroft had been bitten by the espionage bug, and he became one of the most active agents in Central Asia.

A major player retires

One of Napoleon I's great ambitions was to end British rule in India, and so to deprive his enemy of the resources needed to finance their European wars. As the maritime route was closed to him, Napoleon planned an invasion of British India via Persia and Afghanistan. In 1805 he sent one of his aides-de-camp, the Count of Gardane, to Tehran with a team of experts and geographers. The ambassador was to obtain permission from the shah for French troops to cross his territory; the geographers were instructed to produce detailed maps of all possible approaches to India. Fabvier was sent on a reconnaissance mission to Turkestan, Trezel was dispatched to Afghanistan, and Truhlier mapped out the itinerary from Tehran to Herat via Meshed.

Persia willingly accepted the French, but was much afraid of the Russians. Napoleon signed a treaty with the czar at Tilsit in 1807, which provided for a joint action against the British in India. The Russians, chiefly interested in the Caucasus—they had annexed Georgia in 1803—opened hostilities against Persia in 1809. The shah then solicited French aid from Gardane, who refused to intervene and was expelled from Tehran in February 1809. Napoleon, otherwise occupied in Europe, never went back to his Indian project; in that territory the Russians and the British were left to face each other alone.

Official missions, secret explorations

The British administrators in India made public their alarm over the Franco-Russian pact. For some time many of them had considered Afghanistan, if not India's natural frontier, at least its private yard. But the threat posed by the new allies made a strong argument for annexing Afghanistan, hence the increase in secret explorations carried out in the guise of official missions. In 1808, Mountstuart Elphinstone, a diplomat destined for a great career, was sent to the Emir of Kabul to obtain an alliance against a possible French invasion. He reached Peshawar on 7 February 1809. Barely a week later, more than a thousand kilometres away, the Gardane embassy was expelled from Tehran, marking the end of French designs on India. The British mission thus lost its raison d'être, but the envoy remained in Peshawar until 16 June. He spent his leisure admiring the landscape and meeting all the quarrelling chiefs in the emir's entourage. But beforehand, Elphinstone reconnoitred the approach to the Khyber Pass beyond Peshawar. It was this route that was to be taken thirty years later by a British army intent on restoring to the throne the same emir who had been deposed just days before Elphinstone's departure. Out of 16,000 British soldiers, only one was to return across the Khyber Pass alive.

The ambassador's invisible entourage

In 1809, after the expulsion of Gardane, the English ambassador John Malcolm arrived in Tehran with an impressively large staff, which included scholars and geographers, such as James Morier, who was to carry out a detailed study of Persia. But two members of the ambassador's staff had slipped off unnoticed. Christie and Pottinger, disguised as horse traders—a role so frequently adopted by spies that Kipling used it in his novel *Kim*—crossed Sind and Baluchistan. Pottinger halted in Kalat and took copious notes on the Baluchis and the Brahuis. Christie, disguised as a Hindu pilgrim, continued north towards Herat across territories no European had ever travelled. When the two met up again in Tehran, Christie had covered 2250 miles to Pottinger's 2412.

The triangulation of the empire

All these 'walkabouts' were part of a highly ambitious project begun in 1802 by the Survey of India, a bureau charged with the systematic geographical survey (by means of triangulation) of all British territory in India and neighbouring states. So it was in 1807 that officers Webb, Raper and Hearsey set out from Haridwar to explore the high valley of the Ganges as far as its source. Beyond Uttakashi Webb lost his way and was nearly killed as he crossed a torrent over one of the dangerous monkey bridges described earlier (see p. 186). The men finally reached the source of the Ganges, and discovered that it flowed from a rock, and not from Lake Manasarowar, as they had been told. 'A great rock, with water flowing from both its sides, presented a vague resemblance to the body and head of a cow. The rock is called Gangotri, or the mouth of the cow, which according to popular belief, spews out the water of the sacred river.'

While the promoters of the great triangulation project—George Lambton and George Everest—were sending geographers up every peak and pass, the Russians were carrying out a similar project on their side of the 'roof of the world'. Farther west Heinrich Klaproth, a German Orientalist who in his younger days had accompanied Count Potocki to Mongolia (see p. 185), took advantage of Russia's annexation of Georgia to make an extensive exploration of the region, and to publish a magnificent book entitled *Travels in the Caucasus*, which he presented to the czar.

The conquest of Everest

George Everest (see p. 251) did not attempt to scale the summit that now bears his name. He was long dead in 1921 when Colonel Howard-Bury made the first try (he turned back at an altitude of 7000 metres). The following year General Bruce reached 8292 metres. Two years later he pushed his way to 8500 metres, losing two of his companions in the attempt. After many more tries, the summit—8840 metres high—was attained in 1953 by Tensing, a Nepalese, and the New Zealander Edmund Hillary (see p. 250).

Britain's three attempts to conquer Afghanistan in the 19th century all ended in failure. Below, the Afghan-Russian border post at Bala Murghab, painted by Sir Thomas Hungerford (1843-1929).

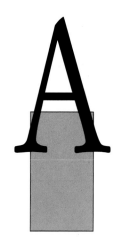

*A*fter living for centuries under Mongol rule, in 1579 Russia launched the conquest of its eastern reaches, a campaign that closely resembled the American colonists' gradual winning of the Far West. Russian fur trappers and traders and Cossack explorers were at the vanguard of this movement.

Rise and development of an ogre nation

In 1547 Ivan the Terrible, then a lad of seventeen, rose to the rank of czar—a title invented by the metropolitan Makary, as a Russianized form of the Latin 'Caesar.' Ivan set about building himself an empire centred in Moscow. In 1552 he destroyed the

A shaman priestess of the Krasnojarsk region. Shamanism brought together the worship of nature and magical practices.

Mongol capital of Kazan and reached the banks of the Volga; in 1556 he pushed farther south and annexed Astrakhan on the Caspian Sea; in 1558 he turned towards the Baltic, capturing Livonia and Estonia; in 1581 Ivan dispatched his Cossacks from the Don—which he had just annexed as a vassal state—to conquer Siberia; Tobolsk was founded in 1587, Tomsk in 1604. The appetite for conquest of Ivan's 'Ogre Nation' was apparently insatiable. To the west, Ivan tried to expand as well! For example, he tried to marry the sister of the king of Poland and to negotiate a Polish-Muscovite political union.

The beauties of Tobolsk

A famous French traveller, Abbé Chappe (see p. 193), spent June 1761 in Tobolsk to observe the transit of Venus across the disc of the Sun. It had been decided by the Paris Académie des Sciences that this phenomenon should be observed from vantage points all over the world. Upon his return, Chappe published a much-acclaimed record of his travels. 'The women of Tobolsk', he wrote, 'are generally beautiful. Their skin is very white, their features are gentle and pleasant; their dark, langorous eyes are always lowered. They never dare to look a man in the face... Most of them boast fine figures, at least until they are about eighteen or twenty; but their legs are invariably thick, and they have large feet. Nature seems thereby to betoken the stout figure these women acquire with age, which demands uncommonly sturdy supports. The baths they take twice a week further deform their figures, for they cause a general slackening of the body. Thus by the time they are thirty, their looks are nearly gone.'

Trappers and fur traders

In Chappe's day western Siberia had been Russianized for almost two centuries. Trappers and fur traders had gradually advanced along the coasts of the White Sea and the Kara Sea, establishing normally peaceful trade relations with the natives. At the same time, explorers sent by the St Petersburg Academy had produced maps of the region's coastlines. Cossacks finally imposed Russian domination by massacring earlier settlers; they established a string of fortresses that progressively stretched eastward: from Tobolsk on the Ob to Tomsk, thence to Krasnoyarsk on the Yenisey, and then to Irkutsk on Lake Baikal. In a final push they founded Yakutsk on the Lena, and in 1639 reached Okhotsk on the Pacific coast. From these towns they followed the rivers north to the Arctic Ocean and southward to the mountains of Mongolia and China. Thus from Yakutsk the Cossacks led by Poyarkov were able in 1645 to reach the Amur River and the Chinese border, while in 1649 Dejnef and his Cossacks made their way to the (then unnamed) Bering Strait.

The Muscovy Company

Danes, Germans, and even the British battled for shares of the rich fur market. As early as the dawn of the sixteenth century, the German Siegmund von Herberstein purchased pelts from the Voguls and Ugrians of the lower Ob River and from Ostiaks who inhabited territories near the White Sea. Likewise, the Englishman Richard Chancellor prospected the region of Arkhangelsk, where he established trading posts. He travelled to Moscow at the invitation of Ivan the Terrible. Their first meeting led to the creation of the Muscovy Company. Chancellor's successor, Anthony Jenkinson, even considered seeking a new overland route to China from Arkhangelsk. He journeyed to Moscow in 1557, and in the course of exhausting orgies with Ivan the Terrible finally obtained permission to cross the entire Russian territory.

Jenkinson set out in 1558 for Kazan, Volgograd and Astrakhan. He followed the northern coast of the Caspian eastward, observing on his journey the mouth of the Ural River. He then pushed south, along the coast of the Aral Sea, and with the greatest difficulty crossed the Urgench Desert on horses obtained from the Turkomans. Late in 1558 Jenkinson was received with great pomp by the sultan of Bukhara; he was convinced that he had managed to establish a more direct connection with the silk route. But the sultan was at war with the rival city of Samarkand, and Jenkinson left Bukhara hastily in April 1559, taking back with him to Moscow some Russian slaves purchased from the sultan.

The czar welcomed the Englishman with signal honours, and carefully noted Jenkinson's topographical data with a view to an eventual invasion. The Englishman returned to London, where in 1562 he published an account of his travels, which enchanted British cartographers. But the Muscovy Company set aside its dreams of a direct route to China via Moscow, for Jenkinson's reports made it seem far too hazardous.

The Hindus of Astrakhan

Count Potocki (see p. 185), who stayed in Astrakhan in June 1797, discovered to his astonishment that there was a Hindu community in the city: 'The Hindus settled in Astrakhan are chiefly from Multan, and are Afghan subjects. Their colony currently numbers seventy-five. They live here with their Brahmins, penitents, a supply of water from the Ganges, all things holy to their religion. I attended their evening prayers; they are addressed to Vishnu in the form of Salagrama. Their cult is duly magnificent, at least so far as the premises permit. One is struck with a genuinely religious sentiment when one hears the harmony of their chant and the sound of their drums, but particularly when one sees their look of perfect confidence in the power of the little statues that adorn their altar.'

During the reign of Ivan the Terrible, the Russian empire stretched from the Caspian Sea to the banks of the Ob River. But already Cossacks and fur traders were heading even further east.

The Parsis of Baku

Astrakhan's Hindus were not the only incongruous community swallowed up by the Russian Ogre as he annexed territories to the east and south. When Peter the Great extended his rule over the Caucasus in 1722, he discovered a tiny Zoroastrian community established in Baku. The Zoroastrians had made the region a holy place. In 1858 Alexandre Dumas (père) described the sect in picturesque terms: 'Today the two principal homes of the unfortunate Parsis are Bombay, where they live under the British protectorate, and Baku, where they are under Russian rule. They claim to have maintained the true tradition of Mithra's cult, sanctioned and perfected by Zoroaster, and to possess the real Zend-Avesta, written in the hand of their founder, and to warm themselves with the self-same fire as the one that warmed Zoroaster. It is obvious that no religion is more innocent than theirs. And few men, consequently, are more gentle and humble than the Parsis. We visited these poor souls in their holy place, the sanctuary of fire at Artech-Gah.'

Falcons for furs

Not all communities were swallowed up so easily as the Hindus or the Parsis. The Cossacks were forced to inflict terrible massacres on the Kamchadales (or Itelmen) of far-eastern Siberia in order to implant their own fur trappers there. The Tartars in particular long resisted Russian rule. In 1557 the Tartar khan of Sibir on the Irtysh sent the czar the paltry tribute of 1100 sable pelts, practically an insult. But eventually, in 1571, they signed a treaty with the Russians. The czar's conditions included the return of Russian prisoners taken as slaves by the khan, and at least one sable pelt per inhabitant of Tartary. The khan, in exchange, demanded guns and, especially, falcons trained for the hunt, for falconry was a favourite pastime of Tartar princes. In 1581 a Cossack expedition some 1600 strong attacked Sibir and defeated the Tartar hordes, who pulled back for good to the territory of the Kalmuks on Lake Saisan. However, the Tartar nobility preserved its civil and military leadership into Russian times, until the Russian Revolution.

The Cossacks

The Cossacks were the pioneers of Russian expansion to the east and south. Rebellious peasants who refused the lowly rank of serf, they organized themselves into independent bands and elected war chiefs, who formed confederations like those of the Sikhs in India, who at that time were fighting to free themselves from Mongol domination. When Ivan the Terrible resolved to push the frontiers of his empire beyond the Ural river, he sought the aid of the Don Cossacks, mercenary soldiers under the leadership of the great chief Yermak. The Cossacks captured the Tartar capital of Sibir on the Irtysh river, and built Tobolsk, a fortress on the Ob, to enforce their control over the entire length of the river, which had already been explored by trappers.

ussia's expansion eastward was decisively advanced under Peter the Great (1694-1725) and Catherine the Great (1762-96). At its most vigorous, this eastward push aimed as far as Alaska and northeastern China. In 1725, an expedition led by Vitus Bering left Moscow. It was finally to prove that there is no land passage between Asia and America.

The long road of exile

To populate and till lands that scientists had declared suitable for agriculture, Catherine the Great deported literally millions of serfs. This practice lasted long after her death. On 22 August 1839, before he arrived at Nizhni-Novgorod, the Marquis of Custine witnessed the pathetic spectacle of a troop of armed Cossacks escorting exiles to Siberia: 'And so it is not a dream, it is not a fable invented for gazettes; I see here truly wretched souls, actual deportees, marching forward to the land where they must spend the rest of their days, forgotten by the rest of the world... They are not criminals, on the contrary, they are Poles, heroes of misfortune and devotion... There is something vaguely poetic about this distant exile, which haloes the law's severity with all the power of the imagination.'

Travellers and explorers brought back vivid accounts and colourful drawings of their trips to the land of the czars. Above, a boat transporting coal.

A czar in a hurry

Peter the Great dreamed of building Russia into one of the world's great military powers. But he lacked the up-to-date weaponry which other European armies had in their arsenals. He therefore invited to Russia the European experts and technicians who could help him modernize his armed forces. In 1703 Peter resolved to establish his capital on the sea, at St Petersburg. He created a base, Kronstadt, on a nearby island to defend his capital and house his arsenal. Bernardin de Saint-Pierre, who visited the city in 1762, observed: 'Peter the Great was blamed for situating the centre of his empire in the swamp-lands of the Neva; but in order to open his country to the arts of Europe, he could choose no other position than the far reaches of the Gulf of Kronstadt, for at the time Livonia and Finland were not in his possession.'

The arts of Europe

Europe's technological contribution allowed Peter the Great to achieve his goals with stunning swiftness. In 1709 he defeated the Swedes, stripping them of their supremacy in the Baltic. In 1721 he annexed Latvia, Estonia and Karelia, and in 1723 took possession of the Caspian's western shore. For a time he even occupied the port of Azov on the Black Sea. Having conquered seaports to the north and to the south, Peter could then devote himself to his grand scheme of expanding his empire east to the Pacific—and beyond. In 1724 he founded the St Petersburg Academy of Science, and gathered about him the world's most noted scholars, surveyors and geographers. Peter sent a Danish officer, Vitus Bering (see p. 227), to explore Siberia along with an international team of experts, which included among others two Frenchmen, the Delisle brothers (one a surveyor, the other an astronomer), the German naturalists Steller and Gmelin, the historian Gerhard Müller and the Swedes Tabbert and Renot.

The first expedition of Vitus Bering

Scholars of the day still debated whether a land link existed between Asia and America. The Danish officer Vitus Bering was given the task of solving the mystery and at the same time establishing Russia's future rights to Alaska. An immense caravan set out from Moscow in 1725 for the Trans-Siberian trail, a route that cut across Siberia from west to east, via Tobolsk, Yeniseyskiy and Yakutsk. Along the way, the expedition's geographers and botanists often halted to make notes and observations, a practice that considerably slowed the party's progress. Bering did not reach the Pacific until 1728. He settled in the little port of Okhostk, founded nine years earlier by Russian officers who had been ordered to map the Kamchatka Peninsula and the Kuril Islands.

More months went by as the men constructed a small ship, of the type used by Russian coastal navigators in the White Sea. Bering was not ready to sail before July. The death of the czar in 1725 apparently did not affect the course of the expedition. Bering steered north along the Gulf of Anadyr; to starboard he observed a large landmass, which he christened St Lawrence Island. He continued his northerly course in the freezing waters, amidst thick fogs. Bering then went about and followed a more easterly course; he did not, however, catch sight of the Alaskan coast. The existence of a strait between Asia and North America was virtually proven.

Bering's second expedition

The rich harvest of scientific data brought in by Bering's first expedition determined the St Petersburg Academy to organize a second, this time on an unprecedented scale. The princely sum of 360,000 rubles was appropriated for the undertaking. Hundreds of officers, soldiers and sailors were sent along the Trans-Siberian trail to Okhotsk. When Bering arrived there in 1741, a new harbour had been dug and two brand-new ships awaited him. He embarked on the *St Peter* in the spring of 1741. His orders were to establish the topography of the Siberian and Alaskan coasts.

Navigating along the string of archipelagos that form the Aleutian Islands, Bering reached the foot of Mount St Elias, south of Anchorage, Alaska. He dropped anchor in the shelter of Kayak Island and sent a small party ashore to bring on fresh water. The naturalist Steller accompanied the group, furious at having only ten hours to explore the New World: 'By every conceivable means I was prevented from carrying out my task; after ten years of preparation, a mere ten hours were allotted to visiting the New World. Scurvy, the lateness of the season, and the stubbornness of the ship's officers all contributed to this unfortunate result.'

Science versus man

In fact Bering was in such a hurry because he wished to spare his men's lives. The *St Peter* had been damaged by the bad weather and the icebergs. Yet it managed to continue for a time, south along the Alaskan coast, putting in here and there to make contact with the scattered Eskimo populations. Steller was even able to observe a sea cow, an animal now extinct, which was named in honour of the naturalist: *Rhytina stelleri*. The ship beached on a little island off the Kamchatka Peninsula. Bering decided to winter there, and built a large

boat to send teams of scientists to the mainland. As for Bering himself, wasted with scurvy, he died on the island with thirty of his comrades. The patched-up *St Peter* landed in Petropavlovsk on 27 August 1742; it had been presumed lost.

The human cost of mapping Siberia

While Bering hovered near death on the island, his lieutenant, Chirikov, aboard the expedition's second vessel, the *St Paul*, explored the Aleutians and the southern coast of Alaska, which thereafter formed part of Russia's southern sphere of influence. Steller remained in Kamchatka for several months, studying the flora, fauna and human population. But he was destined never to see Moscow again: he perished on the return journey, in 1746, at the age of thirty-seven. The French astronomer Delisle also lost his life on that perilous expedition. The human cost of mapping Siberia had been heavy indeed.

Muraviev and Paulov explored the Arctic Ocean from a base in Arkhangelsk in 1735, but pack ice forced them to turn back. In 1736, Malygin and Suratov were more fortunate—they succeeded in mapping the entire coastline of the Kara Sea. The same year Prontischev, setting out from the mouth of the Lena River, pushed north towards the Pole and reached ice fields at 77°29'N. He had brought along his young wife. Unfortunately their ship was blocked by pack ice and they died. Their record would remain unbeaten until Nordenskjöld surpassed it in 1901 (see p. 232). Another of Bering's assistants had his ship broken up by ice, but he turned the misfortune into an opportunity, and completed the mapping of what is now the Bering Sea.

Tobolsk revisited by Venus

Catherine the Great pursued the policy of annexation initiated by Czar Peter I. In 1768, she acquired the northern shore of the Black Sea; in 1783, Crimea; in 1791, Moldavia. In 1792, part of Poland and the Ukraine, Byelorussia, and Lithuania were conquered in their turn. To the east, there was nothing left for Catherine to annex, but much still to discover and explore. The Trans-Siberian route was already dotted with military outposts and trading posts, but the vast territories to the north and south of that great caravan trail remained

unexplored. Catherine decided to mount an ambitious scientific expedition. She summoned Peter-Simon Pallas, a Berlin physician with a passion for natural history. Pallas set out from Moscow on 30 April 1768 with a party that included five naturalists, seven astronomers, and several physicians.

Since he had a year to reach Tobolsk, where he wished to observe the transit of Venus on 3 June 1769, as Abbé Chappe (see p. 190) had done eight years before, Pallas first took the time to explore the land of the Bashkirs of the Caspian. After his astronomical mission had been completed, he followed the caravan route to the Manchurian border. His team gathered a wealth of data in natural and human sciences. Fossils of mammoths, rhinoceroses and prehistoric horses were discovered—a rich treasure for European palaeontologists. Pallas furthered the geographical knowledge of vast tracts of land previously left blank on maps. What is more, Pallas raised the study of climates to an exact science. When he returned to St Petersburg in July 1774, at the age of just twenty-seven, he was a passionate supporter—and practitioner—of long-distance exploration.

From the Pacific to the Baltic

Siberia, the largest region of the Soviet Union, covers an area of 12,700,000 square kilometres. As a land of passage, its cultural importance was considerable at certain epochs, particularly in prehistoric and protohistoric times. From the Pacific to the Baltic, its long rivers and its mountainous valleys have fostered contacts between civilizations. Siberia was one of the itineraries of the famous silk route during the first millennium.

Penetrating into eastern Siberia, where temperatures frequently drop below −45°C in January, proved to be costly in human lives.

he Trans-Siberian trail brought furs — sable in particular — to Moscow, where the pelts were highly prized. Starting out from that caravan route, Russian trappers navigated up rivers and roamed the lands of Tartary, where sables were abundant. That is when they clashed with Chinese trappers, their rivals...

The Black Dragon treaty

In 1689, on the banks of the upper Amur river, which the Chinese called the Black Dragon, a truly international conference was convened: the Russian representative was a Dane, Isbrandt Ides, who was accompanied by the Dutch painter Cornelis de Bruyn; interpreting for the Chinese were the French Jesuit Gerbillon and the Portuguese Pereira. A treaty was signed at Nerchinsk, a place the Chinese called Nipchu, and for a time the Russian penetration of China was halted.

In 1703 Father Fontaney communicated to Father de La Chaise, confessor to Louis XIV, the circumstances of the treaty, for which the Jesuits were rewarded by China's ruler with an edict of toleration for Christians (see p. 183): 'The eastern Tartars, subjects of the emperor [of China], who occupy this vast stretch of territory between the Great Wall and the Black Dragon River, were astounded to see Moscovites arrive to fight over sables hunted in a region which they — the Russians — claimed they controlled, and build forts to capture those territories. They believed that they should oppose the action, which is what obliged them to take Yacsa on two occasions; the Muscovites were determined to conserve that fort... On both sides, it was proposed that the limits of the two empires be defined.'

Cossacks on the rampage

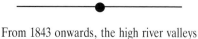

A long, uneasy peace settled over Tartary, but the Russians were only waiting for a chance to push farther into China. When the Middle Kingdom had been weakened by the Opium Wars (1840-2), the Russians launched Muraviev and his Cossacks on a raid on Tartary and Manchuria. In 1854 they descended from the upper Amur to the Pacific, destroying everything in their path. The death and havoc wreaked on Manchurian and Chinese populations was staggering. The entire coastal region was conquered and Vladivostok was founded in 1860. The Imperial Geographic Society of St Petersburg then set about exploring the region. An important mission directed by Schwartz with the noted geologist Schmidt and the naturalists Glend and Radde yielded significant scientific results. In 1854 Prince Kropotkin explored and annexed the huge island of Sakhalin, which Staritsky mapped in 1871. The Trans-Siberian route was prolonged to Vladivostok by a trail that cut straight across Manchuria. One of the first to profit from the new road was a French gold-digger named Martin, who prospected between Irkutsk and Vladivostok in 1875.

Explorers on the waterways

From 1843 onwards, the high river valleys that cross Siberia from south to north were nearly overrun with explorers. That year Alexander von Middendorf explored the Yenisey and the Katanga rivers; he then set out from Irkutsk to reconnoitre the Amur river. In 1865 Lopatine travelled north to the source of the Yenisey, and produced a geological map of the region. In 1873, Chekanovsky studied the geology of the Lena and the Tunguska. In 1877 Khandatchevsky followed the course of the Ob and Irtysh rivers. In 1891 the entire region of Lake Baikal was scientifically explored by Chersky. He travelled up the Selenge to the Yablonoi mountains, before dying of exhaustion as he beheld the majestic scenery of Lake Baikal.

Indiamen in Japan

The conquest of upper Tartary and the sources of the Amur gave Russia a virtual monopoly on sable pelts. Henceforth, Russia strove to extend its control to other types

A Tartar hunter. Engraving taken from Costumes russes, *published in Paris in 1815.*

of fur. Czar Alexander I (1777–1825), vanquished by Napoleon at Austerlitz (in 1805), decided in 1802 to rationalize the fur trade: Russia's occupation of Alaska and the unbridled activity of trappers furnished the czar with pelts in abundance, but at the cost of excessive waste. He appointed Adam-Johann Krusenstern to direct a wide-ranging operation in Alaskan waters (see p. 164). A seasoned sailor, the Russian had served in the British navy and had visited Bombay and Calcutta. In London Krusenstern purchased two Indiamen—large merchant ships—which he rechristened the *Nadjedjeda* and the *Neva*, and provided himself with the most modern navigational instruments, such as Arnold's and Pennington's chronometers. He set out from Kronstadt on 7 August 1803 with an elite team of scientists and a Russian ambassador, whom he was to escort to Japan. Krusenstern made for Brazil, Cape Horn, the Marquesas Islands, and Hawaii. At Nagasaki, the Japanese refused to allow the ambassador to come ashore.

A rich source of furs

On 10 May 1805 Krusenstern called at Hokkaido and had every square inch of the island explored. The expedition's heat-sensitive sounding line allowed the scientists to discover a cold current flowing south from the Kuril Islands. The naturalist and ethnologist Gottlieb Telesius studied the habits and customs of Hokkaido's inhabitants, the Ainu, and brought back to Europe the first portraits of that singular race. The party's next stop was Petropavlovsk, where the disappointed ambassador was finally put ashore. The second ship, the *Neva*, commanded by Lisiansky, sailed north to Kodiak Island off Alaska, where a few years earlier Chelikov had created an enormous warehouse to store furs obtained from the Eskimos. The Eskimos, in fact, were then besieging the trading post—the Russians had earned the natives' hatred with their brutal methods. Lisiansky relieved his countrymen and filled his ship with precious pelts, which he sold in Canton. The huge profit more than covered the expenses of Krusenstern's entire campaign. But this was the first and last success of the short-lived Russo-American Company, which Krusenstern had founded in Moscow, modelled on the English East India Company (see p. 178). On 7 August 1806 the two ships made a triumphant entry into the harbour of Kronstadt. He later wrote a book entitled *Voyage Round the World*.

Following its discovery in 1725, the Bering Strait served as a point of departure for the exploration of new shores. The aim was mainly to extend hunting territories.

Prestigious visitors

Petropavlovsk, founded in 1735 as a base for Bering's second voyage, grew rapidly owing to the lucrative Alaskan fur trade. All the long-distance travellers who circulated between the Kamchatka peninsula and Alaska halted there for supplies. In 1779 the survivors of Cook's third expedition deposited at Petropavlovsk the papers of Clerke, the officer who had succeeded Captain Cook after the latter's tragic death (see p. 157); Clerke, in his turn, had succumbed to tuberculosis while in the Bering Strait. Krusenstern brought the precious documents back to Europe in 1806, along with the papers of Delisle, the French astronomer who had died in 1741 during Bering's second voyage. In 1787 La Pérouse called at Petropavlovsk, where Frenchmen and Russians fraternized to the strumming of balalaikas. De Lesseps (see p. 159) docked at Petropavlovsk in order to return to France via the Trans-Siberian trail, so as to reach his superiors as quickly as possible with his observations on the Alaskan fur trade. He arrived at Paris just one year later.

The governor's ball

La Pérouse wrote a description dated 10 September 1787 of a ball given in Petropavlovsk by the Russians in honour of the French: 'They began with Russian dances; the melodies are very pretty and much like the *cosaque* popular in Paris some years ago. Next came the Kamchadal dances, which can only be compared to the movements of the convulsionaries of the famous tomb of St Medard. The dancers in this part of Asia move only their arms, their shoulders—their legs hardly at all... The women tire themselves out so thoroughly in these dances that at the end they are dripping with sweat, and lie exhausted on the floor, lacking the strength to stand up. The abundant exhalations that emanate from their bodies fill the room with the scent of fish oil, an odour too unfamiliar to be appreciated by European noses.'

When first reported in 1697, the Kamchadal, or Itelmen, were still technologically in the Stone Age. Their pattern of life was based on the annual salmon run. They also hunted and made extensive use of wild plants.

A walking tour of Siberia

Between 1805 and 1809 an English eccentric named John Dundas Cochrane made a walking tour of Siberia. The trek was part of a grand plan to walk around the world. When Cochrane arrived in the land of the Chukchis in eastern Siberia, he fell in love with the daughter of a sacristan. Convinced that he had found the ideal companion, he married the girl. This was not the end of his walking career, however. We find Cochrane later in Colombia, where death finally put an end to his wanderlust. It is not known whether his Chukchi sweetheart was still walking by his side in South America.

B y the mid-nineteenth century, the entire inhabited world had been explored, with one exception: Japan. When travellers from far-off lands approached Japanese waters, they always gave the island nation a wide berth, for uninvited visitors were cruelly treated there. However, from 1868 the emperor Meiji opened his country and launched Japan on the course of westernization.

A young lady 'explorer'

In 1875 Japan, at the start of the Meiji era, was undergoing a profound transformation. Clara Whitney, a fourteen-year-old American girl, arrived in Japan, where her parents had just founded a business school. She was to live there for twenty-five years, and from the very first kept a journal of her experiences, a daily 'exploration' of the customs of a land slowly emerging from centuries of isolation. 'Thursday 7 October [1875]; last night we lived through our first earthquake... The entire house shook on its foundations, the roof creaked and everything swayed like a baby's cradle. I truly believed that Judgement Day had arrived... Wednesday 1 December; I have begun to learn Japanese, and I like it very much. Of course at first it is a bit difficult to reproduce the written characters exactly... Mr Ono says that each social class in Japan has its own spoken language, or dialect; the daimyo, the Samurai, the great merchants, the lesser merchants, the artisans, mechanics, peasants, coolies, and jinrikishas, etc. Ladies also have a language of their own.'

Barbarians from the south

On 22 October 1543 'a ship docked at Tanega Shima. The crew, about two hundred in all, had a singular appearance; the strangers' language was unintelligible; their homeland was, like them, unfamiliar to us. Aboard was a Chinese, named Gohu, who could read; we learned from him that this ship was a *nan-man* vessel, that is, it belonged to barbarians from the south.' Thus did the governor of Tanega, an island in the Gulf of Kagoshima at Japan's southernmost point, inform the emperor Konara of the arrival of a Portuguese ship under Antonio Mota. Adverse winds had pushed the vessel onto these unknown shores. The Portuguese were so warmly welcomed that some remained in Japan and wed Japanese women. A tiny Christian community sprang up. The Portuguese also passed on the art of musket construction.

The dream of Francis Xavier

Discouraged by the dissolute morals of the Portuguese in Goa, which made the spread of the faith in India problematical, the Spanish Jesuit Francisco de Jaso—Francis Xavier—set sail for Japan (see p. 182). He landed in Kagoshima in 1549. He was soon won over by the Japanese way of life, and set about learning the language of these 'people of great honour', whose curiosity about all that came from abroad assisted the spread of Christianity. The Spanish hidalgo felt very much at home in the land of the samurai, poor but heroically proud noblemen. And for the first time since leaving Paris, the former Sorbonne student encountered exquisitely cultivated intellectuals eager to discuss new ideas.

Saint Francis Xavier bringing back to life the daughter of an inhabitant of Cangoxima in Japan, *painted by Nicolas Poussin.*

Francis Xavier conceived the missionary strategy that would be widely adopted by the Jesuits: to touch the heart of a nation, one must first appeal to its head. He baptized some princes and princesses of high birth, and even some Buddhist priests. The latter informed Xavier that their supreme doctrinal authority was a Beijing university presided over by the emperor of China himself. As a good Christian soldier, Xavier resolved to convert the emperor. He set out with a smuggler, who put him ashore on Sancian, a pirate-ridden island across the bay from Canton. But there Xavier contracted a debilitating fever, which carried him off on 3 December 1552. He was probably the first European to have travelled through and described Japan...and he was virtually the last, for a long time to come.

The dangers of politics

Japan was governed in the Indian manner by a puppet emperor, the mikado, who was dominated by the shogun, an all-powerful prime minister. The shogun Taiko, often compared to Richelieu, reigned until 1598. He protected Japan's rapidly growing Christian community. At his death, a savage war brought into conflict his son and the father of his daughter-in-law, who both coveted the office of shogun. Japan's Christians supported the son, whom the Jesuits hoped to convert, but in 1615 the father-in-law finally proved the stronger. The new shogun outlawed Christianity and had all foreigners expelled. A fearful persecution followed. Japan's last Christians cloistered themselves in the fortress of Shimabara, on the tip of the Nagasaki peninsula.

The war of religion

The Christian fortress stood on nearly inaccessible rocks, so the new shogun appealed for help to a Dutch ship then anchored in the bay. The Dutch eagerly seized the opportunity to torment a colony of Catholics and proceeded to bombard Shimabara. The fortress surrendered on 12 April 1638, and the last Japanese Catholics were massacred. However, this notorious deed did not earn the Dutch the recognition they had counted on. In 1611 the shogun had indeed granted them permission to establish an outpost on Firato to offset Portugal's post at Kagoshima, but after Christianity had been wiped out, access to Japan was forbidden to all foreigners. To honour the letter if not the spirit of the shogun's oath, the Dutch were forced to destroy the Firato post and settle instead on the island of Deshima, under close surveillance. The Dutch officer in charge of the forced transfer in 1640 was none other than François Caron, later hired by Colbert to found the French Company of the East Indies (see p. 176).

An ill-fated embassy

After 1640 Japanese ports were off limits to foreigners. Only the Dutch were authorized to go ashore on Deshima, but before long business dried up, and Holland's only gain in Japan was a certain prestige. The Portuguese of Macau did not willingly give up their outpost in Japan, for they had made enormous profits there. They sent a seventy-one-member embassy to Nagasaki, of which every single one was executed. All had suffered sadistic tortures witnessed by their servants, who were spared and sent back to Macau with the message: 'In future let no one, so long as the Sun shines on the earth, sail to Japan even as an ambassador... The Christian God Himself would be treated like anyone else were he to contravene this order, indeed, he would encounter even greater cruelty.'

American ships serve the Dutch

The closing of Japanese ports was observed with scrupulous discipline by local authorities. Ships in distress were provided with wood and water, but crews were forbidden to land or to communicate with the Japanese, who in their turn were absolutely forbidden to leave Japan. This isolationism benefited local industry, which set about producing everything which had previously been imported or smuggled from abroad. But soon the rare Dutch ships that continued to dock in Deshima's harbours were forced to confront English buccaneers of the East India Company, which was seeking to replace the Dutch Company. The authorities in Batavia therefore chartered American ships for the voyage from Batavia to Deshima.

Russian ventures

In 1792 Adam Laxmann, a Russian captain, put some Japanese seamen he had saved from shipwreck ashore at Matsmai, south of Hokkaido. He was politely thanked for his humanity, but was not allowed to land. In 1804 Krusenstern attempted in his turn to put ashore at Nagasaki a Russian embassy led by Count Resanov (see p. 195). The ambassador was closely guarded in a fish-market while the negotiations were carried on; in the end, the would-be ambassador was invited to return to Russia, empty-handed. The Russians were infuriated by this affront, and in 1806 sent a punitive expedition to the Kuril Islands, which their troops proceeded to ravage.

In 1810 two Russian officers, Golownin and Ricord, on an exploratory mission around the Kurils, successfully landed on the island of Kunashiri. The pair were tied up by the natives and taken to Matsmai, where the prince held them prisoner for two years. The Japanese learned Russian from the explorers, and picked up information about technical progress in European industry. The Russians were released only when their country conveyed formal apologies to the shogun for the massacre of 1806. Russia was politely but very firmly warned not to renew its attempts to conclude a trade pact with Japan.

British ventures

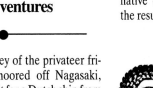

In 1808 Captain Pelley of the privateer frigate the *Phaeton* moored off Nagasaki, intending to lie in wait for a Dutch ship from Batavia which he planned to attack. But that year the ship did not come. The Japanese authorities sent out a boat with two Dutchmen aboard to warn Pelley not to attempt to enter the port, but Pelley took the pair prisoner and sailed into the bay. He sent one of the Dutchmen ashore with orders to demand fresh water and food in exchange for the hostages. The Japanese governor, determined to attack the frigate the moment he had mustered sufficient troops, sent back the messenger with a few skins of water and some provisions. But the British corsairs, convinced that an attack was in the offing, hastily took the supplies, rid themselves of the Dutch hostages, and set sail. The Japanese governor, mortally ashamed to have let his victims escape so easily, gathered his council around him to commit collective hara-kiri (suicide). Henceforth, the British blockaded the Nagasaki harbour.

The Opium Wars (1840-2) confirmed the Japanese belief that they had acted wisely in preventing foreign traders from gaining a foothold in their country. The situation remained the same until 1853, when an American fleet under Commodore Perry aimed its cannons at Japan and obliged the authorities to open the ports. This action fuelled a political crisis. Mikado Komei dismissed his shogun, and his son, Mutsu-Hito, transferred his capital from Kyoto to Tokyo in 1867. This was the dawn of the Meiji 'enlightened' era. European explorers were not needed in Japan, however, for native experts transmitted to Westerners the results of their own studies.

Americans in disguise

In 1797 the *Eliza* fetched up in Nagasaki flying the American flag, under Commander Stewart. He and his crew spoke only English, a fact that aroused the local authorities' suspicions (the outpost was only open to Dutch traders). They demanded an explanation from the Dutch governor of the Deshima trading post, who replied that the sailors were simply second-rate Englishmen working for the Dutch. Stewart was permitted to unload his cargo and sail back to Batavia. But when in 1803 he returned to Nagasaki on his own account, he was not allowed to go ashore or to unload merchandise there.

Upon arriving in Japan, the American fleet led by Perry compelled the Empire of the Rising Sun to open up to the West.

THE SIAMESE SISTERS

he maritime trade routes for spices, tea, opium and porcelain skirted round Southeast Asia, with no scheduled stops. Western explorers and geographers habitually neglected this part of the globe. The first maps of the region were drawn by missionaries, who sailed there in search not of spices or silks but of new converts to Christianity.

Upon their arrival in Siam, the French ambassadors were invited to board ceremonial boats that were to take them to their palace on piles.

The mysterious Mekong

The Mekong flows for 4200 kilometres, the longest river in Southeast Asia, and one of the biggest in the world. Its source lies on a Tibetan plateau more than 5000 metres above sea level. For over 2000 kilometres the Mekong flows through virgin forest, interrupted by deep, wild gorges, waterfalls and rapids. Until the mid-nineteenth century the upper reaches of the Mekong remained one of the world's great geographical (and ethnographical) mysteries, for virtually nothing was known of the local populations.

If not Japan, then Southeast Asia

Driven out of Japan, the Jesuits took refuge in Macau, and from there sought other fields for their evangelical labours. In 1615 Fathers Buzonni, a Neapolitan, and Carvalho, a Portuguese, landed at Da Nang in Vietnam, and won the favour of the local prince. In 1625 six other Jesuits who had stopped in Macau on their way to Japan were re-routed and sent to Da Nang. The priests began a systematic conversion of Annam. One of the Jesuits, Alexander de Rhodes, from Avignon, learned enough Vietnamese in just six months to enable him to preach; he then covered the entire province between the coast and the Annamite mountain range. The map he drew of the region does not emphasize rivers and mountains so much as sites where he managed to baptize some 'heathens'. De Rhodes admired the Vietnamese method of admin-

istering justice: 'No one ever pays to defend his right; thus there are no formalities, no briefs to drain the parties dry with their costs and chicanery; such proceedings are unknown to these pagans, whom we call savages; I shall let you imagine what they think of us!' In 1627 Alexander de Rhodes was sent to the kingdom of Tonkin, where he remained for three years, carrying on his explorations in his own unscientific fashion. From 1640 to 1645 he spent nearly five more years in Vietnam, but the justice he had praised so highly condemned the priest to death—though his sentence was eventually commuted to expulsion. He returned to Europe via Persia. His travel memoirs, published in Paris in 1653, aimed more to edify readers with reports on the progress of Christianity than to inform them about the geography and ethnology of Vietnam.

The Vulture and the Falcon

Louis XIV reacted immediately to Alexander de Rhodes's book. In 1658 he sent Bishops Pallu and Lambert to Siam, whose sovereign was more ready to accept Christians than the ruler of Vietnam. The king of Siam's Greek prime minister, Constance Phaulkon (nicknamed 'the Falcon'), welcomed the bishops most warmly. Before long, Christian communities had grown up on the banks of the Me Nam and Mekong rivers. Eager to magnify the importance of his prince, the Falcon dispatched an embassy to France on the *Vautour* ('Vulture'), which, however, sank without trace off the Cape of Good Hope. Not to be discouraged, he sent a second mission in 1684. The embassy arrived in Versailles on 6 November. Voltaire observed that 'Louis XIV had a marked taste for splendour, which was flattered to the highest degree by the embassy sent from Siam, a land where until most recently the very existence of

France had been unknown'. An impressive French embassy was dispatched to Siam the following year, which included the Jesuit Tachard as its official geographer. In 1687 an expeditionary force of six hundred French troops landed in Siam to construct fortresses on the coast. Yet two years later a coup d'état overthrew the Falcon, who was assassinated shortly afterwards. The French survivors took refuge at Pondicherry, for Siam was then closed to European explorers and remained so for many years.

A civilizing bishop

In 1775 the French Bishop Pigneau de Béhaine arrived at the court of Gia Long, pretender to the throne of Vietnam. The bishop became the young prince's friend and adviser, and shared all his many tribulations. Gia Long had been stripped of his crown by a coup d'état, and obliged to flee first to Cambodia, and later to the island of Phon-Qok. Pigneau de Béhaine and his retinue of priests and seminarians followed Gia Long into exile, along with many Vietnamese Christians who chose to remain faithful to the legitimate ruler. They all took refuge in Bangkok with the king of Siam, a general who had just seized power. But the king unexpectedly fell in love with Gia Long's sister, and declared his intention to marry her. Gia Long and his followers managed to escape, and returned to their island refuge. Pigneau then suggested that they seek help from France. He set out with the king's son, his pupil, whom he hoped to convert, and was received at Versailles in 1787. A treaty promising French support for the exiled king was signed. But when the party stopped in Pondicherry on the return voyage, Governor Conway refused to give assistance. Nevertheless, Pigneau engaged some fifteen engineers as well as artillery and naval officers.

In the meantime Gia Long had begun his successful reconquest of Vietnam. In 1790 he rebuilt Saigon, where French technicians constructed an arsenal and reorganized his small army. A terrible repression punished the usurpers of the throne and their supporters. Men, women and children were ruthlessly massacred. Pigneau died in 1799, but the reunification of Vietnam continued: Hue fell in 1801, Tonkin a year later. The reunited nation enjoyed a period of spectacular recovery. Missions sprang up everywhere, and Vietnamese Christians became the king's most loyal partisans. After Gia Long's death in 1819, his son Minh Mangh, disturbed by the missionaries' influence, launched a fearful persecution. Vietnam was subsequently sealed off from any European influence.

Exploration and colonization

Minh Mangh's successors continued to persecute Christians. In 1847 news reached France that Bishop Lefebvre was being prosecuted in Hue, and threatened with death. France was at that time seeking to build a colonial empire in Asia, after its successes in the Opium Wars. The government sent the corvette *La Victorieuse* to Da Nang to demand the liberation of the bishop, who had in fact already fled to Java. The port was bombarded and the Vietnamese fleet destroyed as it rested at anchor in the harbour.

In 1857 an Anglo-French fleet inflicted the same fate on the Chinese port of Canton, to avenge the presumed murder of an English missionary. The French Admiral Rigault de Genouilly sailed south along the Chinese coast to chart its topographical features. In 1858, to punish Vietnamese persecution of Christians, the admiral attacked Da Nang and captured Hue; a year later, he took Saigon. Such were the beginnings of French colonial exploration of Indochina.

Angkor and the ascent of the Mekong

The exploration—and conquest—began with the ascent of the Mekong. In the 1850s Father Bouillevaux, in the course of semi-clandestine travels to bring the gospel to Southeast Asia, had discovered the ruins of Angkor. The discovery was confirmed in 1861 by the naturalist Mouhot. In 1866 an expedition led by Doudart de Lagrée, assisted by Lieutenant Francis Garnier, was instructed to ascend the river as far as possible towards its source. The party halted at Phnom-Penh, and began talks with the king of Cambodia before beginning a scientific study of Angkor. The explorers set out again to the north, reaching Kratie, Stung Treng and Bassac. At Ubon Garnier was sent overland to explore the region of Siem-Reap. At Luang Prabang he rejoined the boats and pursued the ascent of the river to the point where mighty waterfalls made further passage impossible. Doudart, who had fallen ill, allowed Garnier to continue on foot to China; he arrived in 1867. Furthermore he discovered that the river route to China from the south was not the Mekong River but the Red River, which flows into the Gulf of Tonkin. Garnier pressed on to the Yangtze before returning to Saigon by sea.

Dupuis and the ascent of the Red River

The conquest of Tonkin was sparked off by a French arms dealer, Jean Dupuis. In 1872 he took a convoy into China via the Red River, then sailed back down that waterway loaded with valuable cargo. But before he could return to Europe with his merchandise, he was arrested by the Vietnamese authorities in Hanoi. Dupuis appealed to the admiral-governor of Saigon, who considerably exceeded the orders given to him by the French government and dispatched the warship *D'Estrées* with a detachment of marines under Francis Garnier. In November 1873 Garnier gave the Hanoi authorities an ultimatum, put his troops ashore, and occupied the delta. Anarchy spread throughout the region: it was 'every man for himself.' A guerilla group called the 'Black Flags' approached to pillage the city. Garnier rushed forth to meet the guerillas and fell into an ambush at a place called 'Paper-Bridge.' He was beheaded, in the Tonkinese fashion. French public opinion made Garnier a hero, a myth that facilitated France's annexation of Tonkin in 1885. Some French inhabitants of Tonkin set out not to conquer a territory or to win a market, but, like Auguste Pavie, a telegraph agent and ethnologist fascinated by the Tonkinese, to conquer the inhabitants' hearts and minds.

The golden idols of Mergui

In 1690, the French naval officer Robert Challe fetched up off the Siamese coast with a large fleet to rescue the survivors of the coup d'état in Siam. In his memoirs he wrote 'Let me come back for a little to the subject of Mergui, where we are said to be going; everyone on board ardently hopes so, not only to avenge the Frenchmen who were so badly treated there, but also to restore the honour of our nation, and to pillage their temples or pagodas.... In France it had been said that their idols were of pure gold. That was only a manner of speaking however, and a flattering one at that. In fact they are simply encrusted or covered with an uneven layer of gold, which at its heaviest is no thicker than a thirty-sou coin, or than a four-sou piece at its thinnest. Their talapoins, or priests, are cowardly and effeminate; they are unlikely to resist us. Indeed, the Siamese in general are a base, faint-hearted lot.'

Annamese Mandarin and their wives going back up the Mekong. Doudart de Lagrée and Francis Garnier had maintained that the river could not be navigated into China.

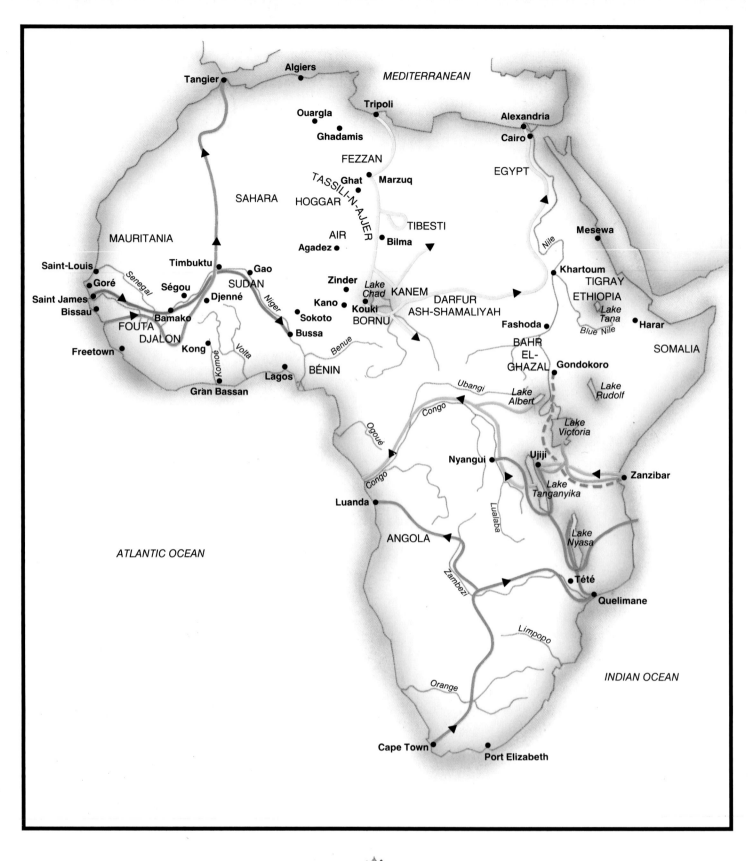

MEDITERRANEAN

Tangier • Algiers

Tripoli

Ouargla
Ghadamis

Alexandria
Cairo

FEZZAN

EGYPT

SAHARA

TASSILI-N-AJJER
Ghat • Marzuq

HOGGAR

TIBESTI

Mesewa

AIR
Agadez • Bilma

Nile

MAURITANIA

Saint-Louis
Goré
Saint James
Bissau

Timbuktu • Gao

Senegal

Ségou

Djenné

Niger

SUDAN

Zinder
Kano
Sokoto
Bussa

Lake
Chad

KANEM

Kouki
BORNU

DARFUR
ASH-SHAMALIYAH

Khartoum

TIGRAY
ETHIOPIA
Lake
Tana
Blue Nile

Harar

Fashoda

BAHR
EL-
GHAZAL

SOMALIA

FOUTA
DJALON
Bamako
Kong
Freetown

Benue

BÉNIN

Gondokoro

Lagos
Gran Bassan

Komoe
Volta

Ubangi

Lake
Albert

Lake
Rudolf

Ogoué

Congo

Lake
Victoria

Nyangui

Ujiji
Zanzibar

ATLANTIC OCEAN

Congo

Luanda

ANGOLA

Lualaba

Lake
Tanganyika

Lake
Nyasa

Zambezi

Tété
Quelimane

Limpopo

INDIAN OCEAN

Orange

Cape Town
Port Elizabeth

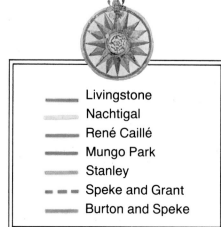

——	Livingstone
——	Nachtigal
——	René Caillé
——	Mungo Park
——	Stanley
- - -	Speke and Grant
——	Burton and Speke

Africa

While Europeans actively explored America and Asia, Africa remained largely unknown territory, and indeed elicited very little interest. Ptolemy's maps and the works of Leo Africanus gave geographers just enough information to elaborate some rather fanciful theories about the 'Dark Continent'. The Niger, for example, was declared to be a tributary of the Nile, and the continent was said to be the home of cannibal kingdoms.

In the port of Sao Tomé

The African captives were first thrown into prison, then exposed, naked, in the public square, both men and women together, before being examined and sorted. The sick and the crippled, called *macrons*, were put aside. Those who were fit were branded with the arms or name of the company that purchased them. Women sold for one-quarter or one-fifth less than men. The slaves then returned to prison and were fed bread and water until the moment they were hustled aboard ship. The passage across the sea was horrible indeed; the mortality rate was so high that some slave-trading companies were forced to declare bankruptcy.

Pioneers of African exploration

The Portuguese were the first to establish contacts with coastal Africa and to make limited forays inland (see pp. 52-3). In 1434 Gil Eanes rounded the feared Cape Bojador and sailed along the coasts of Senegal and Gambia in the service of Prince Henry the Navigator; the Italian Ca' da Mosto ascended the Senegal River in 1455, and the following year pinpointed the exact position of the Cape Verde Islands. In 1483 Diogo Cam explored the mouth of the Congo River. In 1487 Bartholomeu Dias rounded the Cape of Storms, which was rechristened by King John II the Cape of Good Hope.

In time friendly relations were established with the conquered peoples. The rich nations of Guinea owed their wealth to the majestic Niger, which gave them access to the interior. They traded pepper, ivory, resins and slaves to the Europeans in return for weapons and copper. On the eastern coast, where Islam was deeply entrenched, the Portuguese set up trading posts and sailed up the Zambezi River to the fabled gold-mining regions of Monomotapa (present-day Zimbabwe). In the seventeenth century, certain commodities were identified with the regions from which they were shipped; thus the coastal region of Guinea was known for centuries as the Grain Coast (after the pepper that was traded there); other types of merchandise gave their names to the Ivory Coast, the Gold Coast and the Slave Coast.

The conversion of the Congo's royal family

In the Congo the Portuguese discovered a rich nation, a harmonious civilization that lived off the fruits of the land: the Congolese cultivated millet, bananas, yams, raised cattle, goats, pigs and sheep, and manufactured iron. In 1491 the Congo's royal family finally gave in to the zealous proselytism of European missionaries and converted to Christianity. Contemporary accounts attest to the extraordinary piety of the young King Alfonso I. Unfortunately, his good relations with the Portuguese were threatened by slave dealers who had settled on the island of Sao Tomé. By the time of Alfonso's death in 1543, the slave trade had spread almost as quickly as the Gospel. Its destructive effects eventually undermined Portugal's earlier efforts to win the hearts and minds of the Congolese. In the following century the Portuguese lost interest in the kingdom, turning their attention instead to Dongo (present-day Angola), where they held political sway and could with impunity raid villages for prospective slaves.

The Dutch at the Cape of Good Hope

The decline of Portugal's African empire began with the conquest of Brazil and India, whose sugar and spices brought in enormous profits. The Portuguese then regarded Africa as little more than a source of slaves. This weakening of Portugal's position in Africa ultimately served the enemies of Spain, which took control of Portugal in 1580. The Dutch occupied the Moluccas early in the seventeenth century, and made their appearance on the coasts of Senegal and Angola around 1620. But Holland's great success was the settlement of a European community at the Cape of Good Hope, which proved to be a vital port of call for the vessels of the Dutch East India Company. Jan Van Riebeck landed at the Cape in April 1652, in Table Bay. He erected a fort and a hospital, and then introduced agriculture into neighbouring territories. Trade relations were slowly initiated with the Hottentots. In 1688, when the colony numbered some six hundred, one hundred and fifty French Huguenots, driven out of France as a result of the revocation of the Edict of Nantes, landed in Capetown. The new French settlers would contribute significantly to the colony's development.

First French contacts with Senegal

Two centuries after the conquest of the Canary Islands by Jean de Béthencourt, explorers from Normandy and La Rochelle, encouraged by Cardinal Richelieu, navigated along the West African coast. The first French settlement, St-Louis, was founded in 1638 at the mouth of the Senegal River by Thomas Lambert. In 1643 Jannequin de Rochefort ascended the river to Podor. Since settlements in Guinea yielded disappointing results, the French concentrated their efforts on Senegal instead. André Brue, appointed governor in 1687, travelled throughout the Galam, along the coast, where he built Fort St-Joseph; he also gathered considerable information on western Sudan. In his wake, explorers and prospectors scoured the region's interior. Control over the coasts of Senegal alternated between France and Britain during the 18th century. During the French Revolution and the Napoleonic wars, the European interest in the colony subsided temporarily.

From exploration to slave-trading

As sworn enemies of Catholic Spain, the British intervened on the African coast during the second half of the sixteenth century. In 1551 Thomas Windham travelled to Morocco, and two years later visited the

royal court of Benin. These early contacts resulted in Africa's becoming one of England's major sources of gold—witness the British minting of a new gold coin: the guinea.

In 1664 Fort James was permanently settled at the mouth of the Gambia River. King Charles II founded the Royal African Company in 1672. Trading posts were implanted farther south as well. The largest, Ouidah, was located in Benin. But British activity in Africa focused principally on the slave trade. Eighteenth-century Liverpool held the dubious distinction of being the largest slave-trading port in Europe.

The business of slavery

Slave-trading started in the Cape Verde Islands and Sao Tomé. From 1510 onwards, Spain needed cheap labour for its American colonies; Portugal also required a supply of slaves from 1550. At first the 'ebony' trade, as it was euphemistically termed, was merely tolerated, but the practice became

official under Emperor Charles V of Spain in 1517. The slave trade expanded considerably in the seventeenth century, when the Portuguese kingdom regained its independence and wished to people its colonies. Black Africans were rounded up by Portuguese dealers who travelled to Senegal and Sierra Leone; British traders soon joined them around the mouth of the Gambia River, exchanging slaves for firearms and spices.

In the eighteenth century every European nation with American colonies engaged in slave-trading. Cities such as Nantes and Bordeaux, or Bristol and Liverpool, grew prosperous as 'middlemen' in the slave business. In Africa, Guinea's ports developed rapidly owing to the exceptionally dense population of its hinterland. Slave raiders, called *pombeiros*—men of mixed blood, or slaves themselves—swooped down on villages of the African interior in search of victims. It has been estimated that one hundred thousand Africans were transported to America each year. To that figure must be added the lives of the Africans who died in transit—about fifteen per cent.

As they penetrated ever deeper into what is now Nigeria, the Portuguese discovered a flourishing civilization on the brink of urbanization. The kingdom of Benin was then a centralized state, chiefly agricultural, with an artistic tradition of elaborate ivory and metal carving. These native craftsmen produced some materpieces admired worldwide. They practised their art at the royal court, and their carvings were devoted to glorifying the ruling family. Sometimes realistic, sometimes symbolic, their art displays remarkable creative freedom; the carvings depict warriors' exploits, court scenes, portraits of dignitaries on horseback, busts, and horn players.

This head is typical of the beauty and elegance of the art of the Benin sculptors (18th century).

In the latter half of the eighteenth century, Africa kindled the curiosity of European intellectuals. For these cultured, often well-to-do individuals, exploring the African continent offered not only the obvious commercial rewards, but also the opportunity to broaden their horizons. Moreover, the myth of the 'noble savage' made black Africans seem more worthy of consideration.

The anti-slavery movement

In the eighteenth century a current of humanist, egalitarian thought swept through Europe. In France the protests of philosophers like Montesquieu, Diderot and the Abbé Raynal laid the groundwork for the abolitionist movement. In 1794, following the French Revolution, the French Convention abolished slavery. The practise was restored, however, a few years later.
An anti-slavery trend had also been present in British thought since the time of John Locke in the 17th century. In 1760 the accelerating growth of England's black population led the government to impose limits on the slave trade, and later to attempt to prohibit it entirely. But the war then raging between Britain and France (1756-1763) made social reforms a low priority, and the project was abandoned. However, Britain made the slave trade illegal in 1807, and abolished slavery in all the British territories in 1834. France followed suit in 1848.

The African Society, formed in 1788, initiated many of the great explorations of Africa. In 1859 it was absorbed by the Royal Geographical Society.

James Bruce in Ethiopia

James Bruce was one of the most remarkable adventurers of his day. Born in 1730, this giant of a man (nearly two metres, or six and a half feet tall) left his native Scotland to travel throughout North Africa, and later to Crete and Syria, to indulge his passion for archaeology. From Lebanon he journeyed to Alexandria and the coast of the Red Sea, accompanied by a young Italian called Balugani. The pair sailed to Ethiopia, landing at Massawa. They visited the ruins of ancient Aksum before arriving on 15 February 1770 in Gondar, the capital of the Emperors. No European had ventured into

Gondar since the Frenchman Charles Poncet, some seventy years before. Bruce remained in Gondar for two years; the region was then in the throes of anarchy.
Following his original plan to visit the source of the Blue Nile, in November 1770 Bruce finally laid eyes on what he called 'the modest springs'. He then headed north through Sudan, paused in Khartoum at the junction of the Blue Nile and the White Nile, then travelled due north through the Nubian Desert to Aswan. Having fallen seriously ill, Bruce docked in Cairo aboard a felucca. Back in London, Bruce's arrogant temperament irritated his countrymen; his exploits never brought him the acclaim he had hoped. He retired to Scotland, a disappointed man. Fifteen years

later, Bruce wrote an account of his travels; these memoirs paint a unique and colourful picture of Ethiopian society at the close of the eighteenth century.

The land of the Hottentots

The French explorer François le Vaillant brought a scientific approach to his expeditions in the land of the Hottentots. Since childhood, le Vaillant had felt drawn to the beauty of the equatorial regions. His vocation as a zoologist was born when he read Buffon's *Natural History*. In 1778, he set sail for the Cape of Good Hope to study plant and animal life in the virtually unexplored South African hinterland. Bearing trinkets and tobacco, and armed with pistols, he set out from the colony in 1781, certain that he would discover the Hottentots, those 'noble savages.'
The good-natured le Vaillant indeed succeeded in making himself welcome among local tribesmen before he ventured into the territory of the Xhosa — a notoriously hostile tribe. Yet le Vaillant found certain 'gentle' qualities even in them — a judgement the European colonists greeted with some suspicion.
Le Vaillant's first journey lasted nearly sixteen months, and took him over 3,000 kilometres. A second expedition in 1784 led him into the land of the Bushmen. As an eye-witness to the battles between the Bushmen and Hottentots (or Khoikhoins), le Vaillant was forced to admit that they were a bloodthirsty lot. He returned to the Cape, where he hastily boarded ship, along with the precious objects he had collected. Le Vaillant reached Paris in January of 1786. His *Natural History of Birds*, published between 1796 and 1812, was enthusiastically received by the scientific community.

The African Society of London

The credit for initiating an African exploration society in London goes to Sir Joseph Banks, an eminent example of the wealthy men who supported scientific endeavours in the eighteenth century. A member of the aristocracy and a personal friend of the king, at 35 Banks was elected president of the Royal Society. He was an ardent proponent of exploration, and as a naturalist had accompanied Cook on his first expedition around the world.

In 1774, Banks met James Bruce upon the latter's return from Ethiopia. That encounter marked the beginning of Banks's interest in the African continent. In June 1788 he and other members of his club founded an 'association to prepare expeditions to explore the African interior', which was to become the African Society. In 1791, the Society numbered one hundred members, and its financial resources were sufficient to plan exploratory expeditions to Africa.

Mungo Park: the Niger

The African Society conferred on Mungo Park, a 23-year-old doctor, the honour of being the first to navigate the length of the Niger river. In 1795 the young Scot, accompanied by two interpreters and bearing gifts for the natives, plunged into the African jungle. At one point captured by Moors, later welcomed with open arms by black tribesmen, Park managed with considerable difficulty to reach Bambara, a kingdom of astonishing splendour on the banks of the Niger. Later, he lived among the Mandingos, of whose customs and beliefs he wrote a highly picturesque description. They were rich in gold and ivory, and practised slavery. With the help of some hospitable caravanners, Park journeyed to the Gambia and from there returned to England, where he was hailed as a celebrity. In 1805 Park returned to the banks of the Niger river, with an official mission to establish an English presence in the region. But hardly had they started down the Falémé river than the troop of 35 soldiers accompanying Park was decimated by disease. The last news of Park was sent from Sansanding (north of Ségou), where the explorers were to begin their ill-fated descent of the Niger river. Witnesses report that the expedition reached Djenné, then Timbuktu, with no difficulty. The men then crossed into Hausa

territory, where they were apparently murdered, to a man, in a surprise attack. No one survived to contradict the armchair geographers who continued imperturbably — and wrongly — to insist that the Niger flowed due east.

Mollien at the source of the Senegal river

Gaspard Mollien's adventures began with the wreck of *The Medusa*, one of two French frigates sent to Senegal to recapture the colony from the British. After his lucky escape from the *Medusa*'s ill-fated raft, Mollien stayed on for a time in Dakar. He returned to France to seek support for an expedition to discover the sources of the Senegal, Gambia and Niger rivers. On 28 January 1818, Mollien set out from Saint-

Louis in Senegal with just a marabou stork, a horse, a donkey and a few trinkets. He crossed Ouolof territory and the Ferlo desert, and very nearly reached the source of the Senegal river — however, he did not realize how close he was, as he was misled by incorrectly drawn maps. Mollien then headed south. Sometimes welcomed by friendly tribesmen, sometimes exploited, Mollien finally reached his goal: the neighbouring sources of the Rio Grande (now the Corubal), Gambia and Falémé rivers. A few days later, on 26 April 1819, he discovered the source of the Senegal river as well. Near exhaustion, Mollien nevertheless reached a remote Portuguese outpost, and then Bissau. Mollien was a gifted writer and shrewd observer, equally interested in geology, ethnology and native traditions. Wanderlust soon got the better of him, and he visited Colombia, Haiti, the United States, India and China, always returning with detailed descriptions of every place he visited.

Adanson discovers the baobab tree

Naturalists — rather than geographers — were the real pioneers in Europe's discovery of Africa. The French botanist Michel Adanson, a friend of Bernard de Jussieu, was the first European to describe the baobab, which he identified while exploring the Senegal river in 1749. The discovery of this broad-trunked giant of the African grasslands caused great excitement in scientific circles. During the four years he spent in Senegal and the Gambia, Adanson pursued his studies of local plant species.

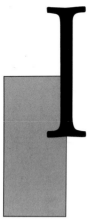

I n September 1769 the defeat of the Ottoman Empire by
the Russian armies of Catherine the Great marked the beginning
of Western interest in Egypt. In France, intellectuals showed a
lively curiosity about the land of the Pharoahs. As the Mamelukes
who ruled over Egypt were threatening French commercial
interests, France's government decided to entrust the conquest of
Egypt to the fiery young general Napoleon Bonaparte.

*Travelling with archaeologists, painters were enthralled by the magic of Egyptian landscapes. Above, the Sphinx at Giza
engraved by Luigi Mayer in 1803-54.*

Hieroglyphs

Hieroglyphic writing first appeared
around 3100 BC. This highly
complex system remained in use
until the fourth century AD: the last
known inscription dates from 24
August 394. Hieroglyphs were
inscribed on all monuments and
nearly all objects that have come
down to us from the Egyptian
Empire. Hieroglyphs are not letters
but pictures of birds, men, animals,
plants and everyday objects, which
together make up a complete,
detailed catalogue of social life in
ancient Egypt. In 1822 the French
archaeologist Champollion
deciphered the meaning of
hieroglyphs, using the Rosetta Stone,
which was engraved with a Greek
text along with hieroglyphic and
demotic translations.

Archaeological pioneers

Before archaeology had attained a truly scientific status, some individuals had already
travelled to Egypt to carry out what could
only be termed archaeological research. In
the eighteenth century Philippe d'Orléans
dispatched Father Siccard to make a precise
survey of ancient Egyptian monuments; he
was the first Frenchman to sail up the Nile to
Aswan. Travel to the Middle East remained,
however, a relatively novel undertaking at a
time when the most learned orientalist
scholars, such as Sylvestre de Sacy, had
never set foot in the countries on which they
were focusing their studies.

The mysterious journey of Monsieur Volney

The motives for Constantin-François Chasseboeuf's journey to the Middle East were,
officially at least, scientific. Indeed, it was
natural that a young religious historian
should travel to the birthplace of Christianity. But his diary reveals valuable information on Mameluke war strategy and methods, and on Syrian populations. As a French
traveller, Volney — as Chasseboeuf became
known — was received by consular authorities, but official correspondence contains
no trace of his passage. He was introduced
to Egyptian life when he arrived in Cairo in

1783; he then journeyed to the pyramids at
Giza. In Suez Volney studied, as others had
before him, the feasibility of connecting the
Mediterranean and the Red Sea. In September, he set sail for Syria, Libya and
Lebanon. In Gaza, Volney shared the daily
life of the Bedouins. He concluded his journey at Acre, and after a brief halt in Alexandria returned to France. Volney, an intellectual nurtured on the liberal ideas of the
French Encyclopédistes, brought back a
wealth of information on the peoples,
places, and beliefs he had minutely observed on his travels. This information
turned out to be of great use in the preparation of the French expedition to Egypt. Although General Bonaparte consulted him
on matters concerning the Middle East,

Egypt, 'Gift of the Nile'

The Ancients considered the Nile to be the mightiest river in the world. It had been Egypt's life-giver since prehistoric times and Herodotus very aptly described Egypt as the 'gift of the Nile'. The river links the 'two lands', as the Ancients designated Upper and Lower Egypt, depositing a fertile layer of silt each year at flood time. That silt, combined with a favourably sunny climate, made the Nile Valley the richest land of the ancient Middle East.

A camp by the Nile in 1816. A characteristic sight in the Egyptian landscape, the felucca is still in use today.

Volney persistently opposed French intervention in a land with a culture and religion so different from those of Europe.

A lightning campaign

Bonaparte's campaign in Egypt, authorized on 5 March 1798 by the French government, was to win the Corsican fame and glory. Bonaparte landed in Egypt on 2 July at the head of an army of twenty-four thousand. France at first portrayed itself as the protector of Islam and ally of the Egyptian people, but war soon proved inevitable. French troops had no difficulty capturing Alexandria. The Battle of the Pyramids, on 21 July, ended in a defeat for the Mamelukes. The French then entered Cairo where Turkish resistance was soon broken. On 1 August their British allies, under the command of Rear-admiral Nelson, destroyed the French fleet at Abùkir. Yet in the interior the French won battle after battle: generals Desaix and Davout in Upper Egypt, Donzelot on the Red Sea, among them. In Syria Gaza, Jaffa, and later Nazareth fell to Bonaparte's troops.

A sudden return

After the brilliant victory at Abùkir over English troops (25 July 1799), which effaced the memory of the preceding year's naval disaster, French forces had a lengthy respite. News from home was not encouraging, and Bonaparte decided to return to France. He turned over his command to Kléber, who did not like the look of the situation. Kléber signed an agreement with the British general Sidney Smith at El-Arich, stipulating the withdrawal of French troops. But Admiral Keith refused to recognize the agreement, and hostilities broke out once again. The assassination of Kléber on 14 June 1800 brought General Menou to power. Crushed by the Anglo-Turkish coalition, he was forced to surrender in Alexandria on 2 September 1801.

Scholars turn explorers

Three years of French occupation in Egypt left a significant scientific legacy. For the first time, respected scholars revealed the splendours of the nation's past. No fewer than 143 French *savants* carried out research in Egypt. On 22 August, Bonaparte, who wished to emphasize the 'civilizing' purpose of his mission in the Middle East, created the Egyptian Institute. In Lower Egypt, General Andréossy submitted a report on the presumed deviations of the course of the Nile while Berthollet studied the process of silt formation in lakes. In Upper Egypt, others worked on the problem of rising river levels. From Alexandria Bonaparte conducted an expedition to Suez. With him were a mathematician, a chemist and a draughtsman. The sum of their work was published in a nine-volume opus which describes ancient Egypt, modern Egypt, and the natural history of the region. This extraordinary scholarly achievement was an important contribution to the modernization of Egypt.

Cailliaud and Letorzec in Nubia

The geologist and archaeologist Frédéric Cailliaud was, with Jean-François Champollion, the most brilliant Egyptologist of the first half of the nineteenth century. His first trip to Egypt in 1815 took him to Nubia, in search of the ancient emerald mines mentioned by writers of the Ptolemean era. In the service of the viceroy Muhammad 'Ali−, he subsequently visited many oases and studied the temple of Abù Simbel (near Aswan). From September 1819 to late 1822, accompanied by Letorzec, a young naval officer, Cailliaud pushed far southward into Upper Nubia, where he identified numerous ruins buried in drifting sands. He discovered and revealed the ancient splendour of the Meroe civilization.

Cailliaud and Letorzec continued on to the White Nile, taking copious notes on the local flora, fauna, climate and monuments. In January 1822 the party journeyed on foot to the Ethiopian highlands. Back in France, Cailliaud published the acclaimed *Journey to Meroe*; in opposition to the views of James Bruce (see p. 204), Cailliaud had the acumen to assert that the White Nile was longer than the Blue Nile.

Thebes, 24 November 1828...

'I was finally on my way to the palace, or rather the city of monuments at Karnak. There I beheld all the magnificence of the pharaohs, the most grandiose scene imagined and created by man ... No other people, ancient or modern, has ever conceived architectural art on a more sublime scale than the Egyptians of old; they imagined a man one hundred feet tall, though most men measure no more than five feet eight inches. Our imagination which, in Europe, soars high above our porticoes, halts and falls in abject impotence at the foot of the one hundred and forty columns of Karnak's pillared temple...'
Excerpt from a letter written by Champollion to his brother.

T he sands of the northern part of Africa form a natural barrier that isolates the region. Conquered by the Arabs in the eighth century, the Sahelo-Sudanese strip, where the great medieval empires of Ghana, Mali and Songhai sprang up, contrasted starkly with the western and eastern parts of the Sudan. To the west, small rival nations lived by trading gold and spices. To the east, Bornu was the centre of a flourishing slave trade.

The legacy of Leo Africanus

An Andalusian Arab born in Grenada in 1483, a scholar and geographer, El Hassan ibn Muhammad el Wazza el Fasi, known as Leo Africanus, was the author of *The History and Description of Africa*, which was for many years the sole reference on the subject, and was frequently copied and cited by others who wrote of the Dark Continent. In 1518 Leo was captured by a Sicilian pirate and taken to the court of Pope Leo X, where he was converted to Christianity. There too Leo shared the store of knowledge he had accumulated while travelling through North Africa and ania Minor. He later reverted to the faith of his fathers and returned to the Maghreb. He died in Tunis in 1554.

A road to unexplored lands

During the 18th century, the British made numerous incursions into West Africa, but their progress was impeded by the hostile climate and perpetual tribal wars, which exacted a high toll in human life. When the political situation of the central states of the Sudan got more stable, they made use of their foothold to launch expeditions to the Mediterranean coast. The caravan route linking Tripoli and Chad via Libya's arid Fezzan and the Bilma oasis took on great importance in Britain's estimation, since that much-used commercial artery led directly into unexplored lands.

In addition to their commercial and political schemes, the British also had the laudable philanthropic objective of halting the slave trade. Such was the aim of the Anti-Slavery Society, an association that enjoyed energetic support in influential religious circles. The British were the first to grasp the importance of the Saharan route. French and German explorers soon followed their lead and made significant contributions to the discovery of new lands and new African itineraries.

Clapperton on the shores of Lake Chad

The Clapperton expedition set out from Tripoli in 1822. The members of the party were the Scot Hugh Clapperton, Dr Walter Oudney, and Major Dixon Denham; their objective was to explore Lake Chad, the course of the Niger, and the fabled cities of the Sudan. After a long and arduous trek across Fezzan, the party finally espied the green and populated region around Lake Chad. On 4 February the three men beheld the shores of the lake itself, a sight very few Europeans had seen; they immediately set about taking notes and making a minute survey of their surroundings. Two weeks later they reached Kukawa, the capital of Bornu (southeast of Lake Chad), where they were greeted with great pomp. While Denham carried out explorations on his own south of the lake, Oudney (who was to die shortly after) headed west with Clapperton into Fulani territory. When Clapperton arrived at Sokoto, he convinced Sultan Muhammad Bello to enter into commercial and diplomatic relations with Britain. His mission accomplished, Clapperton rejoined Denham on 8 July. Together they retraced their path across the desert, reaching Tripoli and then England in 1825.

The first man to cross the Sahara

For his second expedition Clapperton was accompanied by a young servant, Richard Lander, who soon became the veteran explorer's protégé. Clapperton intended to reach the route to Sokoto via the West African coast. Setting out from Benin in 1825, the pair advanced inland to the Niger at Bussa, penetrating into Fulani territory, where to their delight they encountered Muhammad Bello. They witnessed an assault on a city by sixty thousand warriors armed with sabres, arrows—and forty guns. The explorers then continued on their way to Sokoto.

In the course of two expeditions Clapperton crossed Africa from north to west. Exhausted and wracked by dysentery, he died on 13 April 1827. Lander preserved his patron's journal and papers; thanks to Clapperton's notes, numerous new itineraries across the eastern Sahara, Lake Chad and the eastern Sudan were mapped.

Unveiling the secret of the Niger

The mouth of the river Niger, which Mungo Park (see p. 205) had been seeking at the time of his death, remained a mystery. Richard Lander, whose explorations with Clapperton had given him a taste for adventure, persuaded his younger brother John to accompany him on an expedition to the mouth of the river. They started from Badagry in Dahomey and crossed Yoruba territory on their way to Bussa on the banks of the Niger. As they could not push farther north, the pair decided to sail along the river. The brothers miraculously escaped treacherous currents, hostile natives and surprise attacks; eventually they reached the sea.

The discovery the Landers made—one of the most important of their time—brought them neither fame nor glory. But it gladdened the hearts of Liverpool merchants, who saw the profits that would come from a new route to central Africa.

The mirage of Timbuktu

Since the Middle Ages the mysterious city of Timbuktu had fascinated explorers. Leo Africanus had described its princely palaces, wealthy merchants, renowned scholars, innumerable slaves, and the fabulous shipments of gold that passed through the valley of the Niger. After its conquest by Morocco in 1591, the city had fallen into decline.

In 1825 the British dispatched Gordon Laing, a dashing young major, from Tripoli to Timbuktu. Despite an attack by blood-thirsty Tuaregs, Laing arrived safe and sound at the city's gates on 18 April 1826. He was cordially welcomed at first, and was

The oasis in Bahir Mandia as Denham, Clapperton (author of this drawing) and Oudney found it while exploring Western Africa from 1822 to 1824, travelling through the Fezzan desert towards Lake Chad.

even allowed to map Timbuktu and study the course of the Niger. But the situation deteriorated when the new chieftains of Sheikh Amadou, full of fanatical zeal, urged that the European be driven out. Laing was taken prisoner, and then murdered in his sleep; his notes were destroyed.

René Caillié's exploit

———◆———

Caillié was a self-made man of modest origins. At the age of sixteen he embarked for Senegal, landing in St-Louis in 1816. Several expeditions inland familiarized the young novice with the hardship and adventure that were the explorer's lot. It was eight years, however, before the governor of Senegal gave Caillié permission to visit the Brakna Moors to learn Arabic and the basic tenets of Islam. But the Frenchman's foremost ambition was to travel to Timbuktu. His plan was rejected first by the French, and later by the English in Sierra Leone, who did not wish to see Laing stripped of his glory as the discoverer of Timbuktu. But on 19 April 1827 Caillié set out on his own, clad in a burnouse and accompanied by a party

of Mandingos, passing himself off as an Arab sherif. He published the story of his trip in 1830.

When he reached Djenné, Caillié knew he was on the threshold of his dream. He wrote a vivid description of Djenné, an ancient commercial metropolis on the banks of the Niger, where millet, butter, dried fish, dates and calabashes were traded for cloth and hardware from England, and where Muslims exchanged salt for gold, ivory and slaves. On 20 April 1828 Caillié finally reached the city he had yearned to behold. But the sight that met his eyes was one of utter desolation: rising alone out of desert sands, Timbuktu was a huge disappointment for the country boy from Saintonge. No one paid the least attention to him, and unlike Laing, he did not seek out the company of the city's educated natives. Free to move about, he got to know the city, studying its mosques, the three thousand towers that crowned its heights, and its traditional dried-brick dwellings.

Two weeks later, Caillié turned around and headed back north. Exhausted and prematurely aged, he reached Tangier after an arduous 1200-kilometre trek across the desert. Back home in France, Caillié won the acclaim that his courage deserved.

Heinrich Barth in the heart of the Sudan

———◆———

Heinrich Barth, a native of Hamburg, was already familiar with the African desert and the Arab tongue when James Richardson, an active member of the Anti-Slavery Society in the Maghreb, sent him to explore the Sahara and the Sudan with a view to basing Christian missionaries there. Barth set out from Tripoli on 24 March 1850 with Adolf Overweg, a German geologist. They trekked through the previously unexplored Aïr mountain range. Barth then continued alone to Kano, a city visited earlier by Clapperton, before heading to Bornu across lands laid waste by pillaging Tuaregs, and to Lake Chad. From Sokoto Barth pushed into the Nigerian Sudan towards Timbuktu. Posing as a Syrian sherif, he won the natives' respect. From Timbuktu Barth brought back detailed notes on peoples, trade, and caravan routes. His return journey was hampered by the worsening political situation in the surrounding states: a coup d'état in Bornu and war in the Aïr mountains. On 28 August 1855 Barth reached Tripoli, and on 6 September he arrived in London.

The incomparably rich harvest of scientific and ethnographic data that Barth had gathered during his journey filled five volumes and included many highly detailed maps. A man of many parts and great learning, Barth had proved himself one of the most accomplished explorers of his day.

The peoples of Senegal

When the French landed in Senegal, they discovered a mosaic of native tribes. The most important were the Wolofs, who occupied territories extending from Cape Verde to the mouth of the Senegal river. These tall, thin people lived by farming and rearing cattle. Farther inland is the land of the Fulanis, who also live in the Macina and the Sudan. They originally inhabited the most barren regions, where they mixed with the Wolofs. But from the seventeenth century on, the Fulanis gradually emigrated south towards the Futa Jallon range; in the eighteenth century, they gained their freedom by converting to Islam. A hundred years later they dominated Sokoto, Macina, Nigeria and Bambara. Northern Senegal is home to the Toucouleurs, and in the Gambia river valley live the Mandingos, originally from Mali.

Two Germans in the Ahaggar and Tibesti mountains

The scientific forays of Barth and Overweg introduced a new style of exploration, which inspired two of their compatriots to make a similar journey a few years later. Gerhard Rohlfs, a wealthy adventurer who had served in the French Foreign Legion, knew the western Sahara well, for he had trekked over its sandy wastes in 1861, posing as a Muslim. The following year, he set out from Tripoli through Fezzan, reached Bornu, and then headed south from Kuka and embarked on the river Benue, which flows into the Niger. Rohlfs sailed upriver from one British post to another, and reached Lagos in 1867, having made the first direct crossing of Africa from Tripoli to the Bight of Benin. In Tripoli Rohlfs had met Gustav Nachtigal, who had come to

North Africa for his health. Rohlfs persuaded him to take a gift from the King of Prussia to the Sheikh of Bornu. Although he did not realize it, Nachtigal had agreed to undertake an epic journey that would last from 1869 to 1874. While in the desert he explored the Tibesti massif, where no European had previously set foot.

After more than a year in the Sahara, Nachtigal joyfully reached the fertile lands surrounding Lake Chad. Living in the Arab fashion and making forays into neighbouring territories, he remained in Kuka for three years. He studied the Bornu language and supplemented Barth's observations on the history of ancient Karem. In 1873 Nachtigal set out eastward through Wadai and Darfur, and from there reached the Nile and Egypt.

Upon his return, Nachtigal's travel notes won deserved success.

Duveyrier among the Tuaregs

As a boy, Henri Duveyrier was raised in the belief that humanitarian socialism and the steady progress of science would set the pattern of the future; it is not surprising, then, that from an early age he showed an interest in geography, science and languages. When

he first travelled to Algeria in 1857 to perfect his Arabic, he was entranced by the beauty of the desert. Back in Algiers two years later, Duveyrier headed south: Biskra, Ghardaïa and El Goléa were the principal stops on his first expedition, cut short by threats from the Chaambas. He then went north to Touggourt and visited southern Tunisia: Ouargla, the salt lake of el Djerid and the Gabès oasis, before heading for the Ghadames oasis in Libya.

Duveyrier's first reports to France drew attention to the young explorer, who was rewarded with a government subsidy. In 1861 he set out for the Tassili n'Ajjer plateau, and Ghat, where he was pursued by hostile Tuaregs. He prudently withdrew to Murzuk, before heading back to Tripoli through Fezzan. In view of the natives' unfriendliness, Duveyrier felt he should warn French military authorities of the dangers that threatened further attempts to penetrate these territories.

Back in France, much weakened and afflicted with bouts of amnesia, Duveyrier handed over his notes to Dr Warnier, who published *The Tuaregs of the North* in 1864. Duveyrier was wrongly accused of having contributed to the failure of French expansionist aims in the Sahara, because of his inaccurate description of the Tuaregs. The bitterness of his disappointment led him to take his own life in 1892.

The tragic end of the Flatters mission

Paul Flatters, a young French army officer fresh from the St-Cyr military academy, first travelled to Algeria in 1853. At that time, the French conquest of the Maghreb was far from complete. Flatters went on to become a specialist in Muslim affairs, and was a natural choice to head a mission to study the feasibility of building a railroad across the desert. On 6 March 1880 a small French column marched into the desert towards the mountainous Ajjer region, visited by Duveyrier nearly twenty years earlier. But when he reached the foot of the rocky mountain range, Flatters had a sudden fear of ambush, and ordered his troops back.

A second mission took Flatters into the Ahaggar, where he was to be the first to raise the French flag. But this patriotic hope led the officer to act imprudently. The Tuaregs, it was known, were generally well-disposed towards the French, but no distinction had been made between the truly peace-loving Ajjers and the Ahaggars. And so brushing aside threats from the Ahaggar

In September 1853 the German Heinrich Barth arrived in Timbuktu. Like René Caillié, he pretended to be an Arab.

chieftain, the French mission set forth in October 1880. On 16 February the men were attacked by a party of Tuaregs. Flatters and the higher-ranking officers were massacred. The remains of the column retreated in appalling conditions: to survive, the men were forced to eat their comrades' corpses. Barely a dozen soldiers made it back alive to Ouargla. The failure of the Flatters mission brought Saharan exploration to a halt.

Explorers of the late nineteenth century

●

While most exploratory missions were carried out by soldiers as a preliminary to colonial expansion, some adventurous individuals still struck out on their own. The journey made by the German explorer Oskar Lenz resembled that of René Caillié, but it proceeded in the opposite direction. Lenz arrived on 1 July 1880 in Timbuktu, a city that Heinrich Barth had described in detail; Lenz noted that the rich cloth of Sansanding had been replaced by 'the most wretched quality goods from England'. Eighteen days later, he continued his trek west, passing through large fortified cities, until he reached St-Louis on the Senegalese coast on 22 November 1881. Lenz's journey was one of the century's last scientific and essentially altruistic explorations.

In 1880 Paul Soleillet also travelled to Timbuktu, dispatched by the French government's Ministry of Public Works. Opposed to expansionism, he proposed to strengthen the unity of French possessions in the Maghreb and the Sudan by constructing a railway from Algiers to St-Louis via Timbuktu. But the bloody fate of Flatters's mission thwarted the project.

Two more French officers made separate attempts to push farther into the Sahara; neither was ever heard from again. Marcel Palat was apparently murdered in 1886 in the Tidikelt, west of Aïn-Salah. Twenty-five-year-old Camille Doubs, on a journey across the desert to Timbuktu in 1889, was strangled in his sleep.

White Fathers and Protestant missionaries

●

The Sahara attracted not only soldiers and scholars, but missionaries as well. In the middle of the century the missionary movement gained new impetus from the Vatican's condemnation of slavery and the selling of black Africans, and from the promulgation of the Catholic missionary doctrine. From Algiers Cardinal Lavigerie undertook a far-reaching evangelization programme in the Sudan. In spite of one unfortunate initiative, which ended when three 'White Fathers'—Paulmier, Ménoret and Bouchand,—were murdered by their Tuareg guides, Father Richard was sent to establish a mission at Ghadames in Libya, in 1878. From that base he roamed about the eastern part of the Ahaggar range, an area believed to be less dangerous, and initiated friendly relations with the Tuaregs. The year after the massacre of the Flatters expedition, Father Richard set out for Ghat but was murdered along with Fathers Morat and Pouplard. This unmistakable evidence of the Tuaregs' implacable hostility towards the White Fathers led to the withdrawal of Catholic priests from the North Saharan missions.

Some Protestant missionaries made heroic efforts to pacify the native populations. Coming in the wake of colonial expansion, these missions contributed significantly to the development of literacy and to the improvement of sanitary conditions.

The Tuaregs, whom Arab travellers named the 'people with veils', treated the first European explorers with hostility. Left, a Tuareg warrior in 1843.

Tuaregs, the lords of the desert

In the early days of French colonial expansion, the Tuaregs were the undisputed masters of the Sahelo-Sudanese territory. Their society was organized according to a strict hierarchy. At the top of the social pyramid are the nobles, who wage war, pillage, and live by rearing camels and collecting 'fees' from the people they protect. Next in rank are the 'lettered' classes, Arabs instructed in religious matters who often act as teachers and judges. Below them are the livestock herders, who rear goats, sheep and a few camels. Four confederations of small tribes shared the Sahara among themselves: the Ajjers to the north, the Ahaggars in the central desert region, the Iforas to the southwest, and the Kelouis in the Aïr mountains.

I n 1880 only a few limited regions of Africa were under direct European domination. In the main, the continent was divided into kingdoms of varying types and sizes, governed by tribal chiefs. But in the course of the following thirty years a veritable upheaval drastically altered the situation. All the great powers of Europe adopted policies of swift annexation, which were usually backed up by military force.

The Sudan opens its doors

A policy of commercial and political expansion had already been put into practice in Senegal when Louis Faidherbe, a brilliant military officer and engineer, was named governor of St-Louis in 1854. By force of arms, he strengthened and consolidated the French presence in Senegal. Despite limited means, which should have confined his activities to Senegal, from 1859 Faidherbe mounted a series of explorations and reconnaissance expeditions into neighbouring countries. He dispatched three officers as well as to Mauritania, a party to the south. But the most important mission was entrusted to Ensign Mage, who in 1863 was instructed to initiate friendly relations with Ahmadou, the Sultan of Ségou. Held in semi-captivity until 1866, Mage ultimately obtained a vaguely worded trade pact and brought back to Senegal a wealth of information on the powerful Fulani empire. Thanks to his efforts, the western Sudan opened its doors to France. By 1864, by which time Faidherbe had left Senegal, all the necessary military, scientific and administrative infrastructures that would facilitate French colonization in West Africa were in place.

Brazza wins the Congo for France

French naval officers had first attempted to penetrate the great equatorial forest in 1862, ascending the Ogooué River to Lambaréné in Gabon. However, France soon found that she was not alone in her desire to gain a foothold there. Britain and Germany were interested in the region too. It was at this point that Savorgnan de Brazza entered the scene.

Son of a noble Italian family and a former student at the French naval academy, Brazza was fascinated by tales of exploration. He persuaded the French Secretary of the Navy and the Colonies to sponsor an expedition on the Ogooué, which, Brazza claimed, was a tributary of the Congo. In the spring of 1875 he set out in a pirogue from Gabon and navigated upstream. The party reached a small eastward-flowing river, the Alima; then, threatened by natives, they were forced to turn back, just short of the River Congo. Twenty-three months of effort and hardship resulted in nothing but bitter disappointment.

In 1879 Brazza overtook Stanley (see p. 217), and set out to conquer the Congo. He won the confidence of the natives, and on 10 September 1880 signed a treaty by which King Makoko solemnly entrusted his country to France. On 7 November Stanley and Brazza met : relations were chilly, to say the least. In February 1881 Brazza was back in Paris. He had surveyed 4000 kilometres of itineraries, studied ways to reach the interior, and brought France a new colony.

Germans in Togo and Cameroon

The German flag was already flying over Cameroon and Togo thanks to Nachtigal (see p.210), when Captain Kund and Lieutenant Tappenbeck advanced eastward and founded Yaoundé in 1888. The following year Lieutenant Morgan began a series of exploratory expeditions that took him to the kingdom of Tibati in Douala, via the Benue and Niger rivers. Dr Adolf Krause had earlier set out to cross the Volta savannah from what is now Ghana, while Kurt von François followed the course of the Volta and Ludwig Wolf progressed towards the Niger across Bariba territory to found Bismarcksburg.

Pierre Savorgnan de Brazza, painting by Thadeus (1886).

Binger discovers the Volta territories

To counter the strong British presence on the Gold Coast, the French government reinforced its posts at Grand-Bassam and Assinie—even today called the French Gold Coast—and signed numerous new treaties with the natives. The French merchant Treich-Laplène, a resident of Assinie, advanced inland as far as Kong, and won for France the allegiance of several native kingdoms. In February 1889 he was joined by Lieutenant Binger, who had set out from Bamako in 1887 to explore Upper Volta. A military officer and topographical engineer, Binger was also a protégé of Faidherbe; he had received instructions from the Secretary of the Navy to explore the lands south of the bend in the Niger. With a single companion Binger had just completed a two-year campaign in the major cities of the Sudan. From Kong the two men sailed down the Komoé River through the forest to Grand-Bassam. They established the first direct link between the Sudan and the southern coast of Africa. Binger's fluency in Mande, his knowledge of Fulani, and his indefatigable curiosity allowed him to amass a huge store of geographical, botanical, zoological and ethnological documents, which put to rest the legend of the Kong mountains: 'The countryside around Kong has been bled dry by centuries of cultivation. Not even the barest brow of a ridge breaks the horizon: the Kong Mountain range has never existed anywhere but in the imagination of a few badly informed travellers', he wrote in 1887.

In 1893 Binger became the Ivory Coast's first French governor; he was later appointed director of African Affairs at the Ministry of the Colonies, and was involved, notably, in preparing the Marchand mission to Fashoda (see below).

The race for Chad

In 1899 a plan to join the three parts of France's colonial empire—Algeria, West Africa and the Congo—involved the dispatch of three missions, which were ordered to rendezvous in Chad. The Central African Mission from St-Louis was headed by Captains Voulet and Chanoine; the Saharan Mission from Algiers was placed under the command of Foureau, seconded by Commandant Lamy; and the Shari Mission from the Congo was led by Emile Gentil.

The Marchand mission carrying the dismantled barge Faidherbe *along the Nile.*

Voulet had made a name for himself in Upper Volta, where he had defeated the tribal chief Samory (a formidable adversary, and the last founder of a black empire), and outmanoeuvred the British and Germans, who were trying to gain ground in Mossi territory. Yet very quickly the expedition, which included herds, slaves and womenfolk, degenerated into a pillaging band of extortionists that earned the hatred of the indigenous populations and worried the military authorities. A relief troop led by Klobb and Meynier was sent after the first mission. Following the execution of the officers responsible for the disturbances, Joalland and Meynier restored order, defeated the troops of the sultan of Zinder, and occupied the city; they then marched on Chad unhindered. The mission skirted the lake's eastern shore and arrived at the village of Goulfei, the appointed meeting place of the three expeditions.

Breaking the hold of the slave lord

In October 1898 Foureau and Lamy plunged into the Sahara at the head of a thousand-camel caravan. Late in July of the next year, when they reached Agadez, only two of the animals were still alive. The reformed column crossed Zinder, and in January 1900 joined up with Joalland near Fort-Archambault.

On 21 April the three columns met up on the left bank of the Shari River. Together they fought to break the powerful hold of

Rabah, the slave trader who tyrannized Bornu and had imposed his bloody rule over the Sudan for some twenty years. On 22 April 1900 Lamy was killed, but the 'Rabistes' were pursued and defeated at Koussri (now Fort-Foureau). By this victory France captured the territory that was the keystone of her African empire.

Marchand's odyssey to Fashoda

In 1894 Jean-Baptiste Marchand had succeeded brilliantly in crossing the Baoulé savannah (south of Bamako) to Kong, thus establishing the first overland route between the Sudan and Ivory Coast. Two years later he was given command of a political mission whose aim was to thwart Anglo-Egyptian designs on the Upper Nile basin and the region of Bahr el Ghazal. The expedition arrived in Brazzaville on 10 January 1897, then ascended the Ubangi River to the Mbomou rapids. Marchand then had the little steamer *Faidherbe* dismantled, and porters carried it on their backs through the brush. In September the party reached the Congo-Nile watershed, and in June 1898 the steamer was reassembled in order to cross the marshy maze of Bahr el Ghazal. For days the men marched through a mosquito-infested labyrinth of reeds six metres tall. Marchand and his companions finally reached the White Nile, and Fashoda on 10 July. Despite this courageous exploit, France did not succeed in imposing her rule in the Upper Nile.

Hostains and d'Ollone in the heart of darkness

Excerpt from d'Ollone's journal; with Jean Hostains he crossed the great equatorial forest in 1899 near the border of Liberia and the Ivory Coast: 'In the narrow path one sees nothing but low-hanging branches that whip one's face, treacherous vines that tangle around one's feet, and enormous tree trunks that have fallen across the path... The track twists and turns so that one cannot even enjoy the clearing that has been opened up: we go forward like burrowing animals, never seeing anything. Not an ape, not a bird, not even a snake: like all the other beasts, they are quiet and hidden. You go forth in silence, and in darkness. How can I express the horror of this silent forest, where not even a murmur is heard...?

F or Europeans of the mid–nineteenth century Africa was becoming an object of increasingly intense curiosity. Among its most intriguing mysteries was the location of the sources of the Nile. Eratosthenes and Ptolemy had already advanced the hypothesis that the Nile flowed from one of Africa's great lakes. Exploring them would require an ambitious expedition, a project that roused the enthusiasm of London's African Society.

The Bakers shared a passion for African adventure.

Elephants, lions, panthers...

Africa's lake region is famous for its stupendous wildlife, especially large mammals such as elephants, rhinoceroses, zebra, antelope, hippopotamuses, lions and panthers. Speke and Grant were great big-game hunters. They made gifts of their prizes to local princelings in exchange for valuable information about their kingdoms. The fertile land and gentle climate also impressed European explorers.

Burton and Speke in quest of the Nile

The race to locate the Nile's sources began in earnest with the Burton and Speke expedition in 1857. Richard Francis Burton, a colourful, fanciful, and indomitable Irishman, was already a veteran adventurer and explorer. He had made a pilgrimage to Mecca and Medina in 1853, and was highly knowledgeable about Islam. He penetrated deep into Abyssinia along with Captain John Speke, like him an officer who had served in the British Army of India. On his own Burton visited the forbidden city of Harar, capital of Somaliland.

In 1857 Burton and Speke joined up again on Zanzibar, an island off the East African coast ruled by an Arab sultan. It was a flourishing commercial centre under British influence, where slaves, ivory and cloves were traded. The explorers' departure for the inland lakes was carefully prepared. Their expedition—a caravan composed of porters, Indian soldiers, servants and a treasure trove of presents for native chiefs—left Bagamoyo, in present-day Tanzania, on 25 June on the slave—and ivory—trade route, heading towards the great Lake Tanganyika, the explorers' first objective.

The efforts required to cross the savannah and the often arid plateaus took their toll. On 13 February 1858 Speke and Burton reached the lake's edge at Ujiji, where an exuberant crowd welcomed them. But they were so weak that they abandoned the notion of pushing on or any farther. While in Ujiji Burton learned of the existence of a river to the north; it could not, however, be the Nile, for it flowed into—not out of—Lake Tanganyika.

A controversial discovery

Burton thought it preferable to turn back, but Speke set out northward and finally reached the edge of a vast expanse of water, which he christened Lake Victoria. Convinced that he had completed his mission and found the source of the Nile, he declared: 'I no longer felt any doubt that the lake at my feet gave birth to that interesting river'.

In February 1859 Burton and Speke were back on Zanzibar; they then split up in Aden. Speke reached London first to announce his discovery to the president of the African Society. Burton, who did not credit his comrade's reports, covered him with sarcasm in his scathing *Voyage to the Great Lakes of Equatorial Africa*.

Speke set off on a second expedition to furnish positive proof of his discovery. He asked his former comrade-in-arms, Captain James Grant, to accompany him. Shortly after their departure, another traveller, Samuel Baker, celebrated in England for his epic big-game hunts in Ceylon, resolved to join Speke in the Nile Valley. Baker travelled in company with his young and intrepid Hungarian wife, Florence.

Speke dies amidst controversy

Speke and Grant decided to take the northern route, skirting Lake Victoria's western shore. When Grant fell ill, Speke travelled alone to the kingdom of Uganda. Cordially received by King Mutesa (who was in fact a bloodthirsty despot), Speke stayed on long enough to observe the opulent royal court and to take part in some big-game hunting. On 26 May Grant joined his friend, but was unable to accompany him to the banks of the Nile. On 21 July 1862 Speke, alone again, reached the banks of the river: the luxuriant beauty of the scenery left him speechless. He was absolutely convinced of the truth of his discovery.

Speke and Grant crossed the kingdom of Unyoro, followed the course of the Mountain Nile to the Karouma Falls, north of Lake Albert, and then left the river and pushed north into the jungle. They encountered their friend Samuel Baker at Gondokoro.

Speke returned to a triumphal welcome in London in June 1863. The French Emperor Napoleon III offered to sponsor another expedition to dispel any lingering doubts about Speke's findings. But Speke's enemies rekindled the polemic, despite the publication of the *Journal of the Discovery of the Sources of the Nile*. Upon the very day he was to debate publicly with Burton in Bath, Speke died in a hunting accident. Livingstone, who was to be present at the debate, made no secret of his scepticism concerning Speke's claims. The explorer's death aroused much emotion, but did not silence his critics.

The Bakers take up the quest

Samuel Baker and his wife took up Speke's quest. The latter had confided to them that another great lake, the Luta Nzige, which (according to the natives) emptied into the Nile after emerging from Lake Victoria, was situated a little farther west. On 22 January 1864 the couple arrived at the Karouma Falls. The only way they could continue their journey south was to conclude a pact with slave raiders, a bitter pill for the Bakers to swallow, since one of their aims had been to put a halt to slave traffic. Having overcome countless difficulties, they finally stood on the shore of the lake on 14 March: 'England had won the sources of the Nile...' wrote Baker later. 'In undying memory of a man [Prince Albert] whose recent death was mourned by our gracious queen and by all of England, I christened this great lake Albert Nyasa. Lakes Victoria and Albert are the two sources of the Nile.'

Yet one point remained unclear. No one could affirm with certainty from which of the two lakes the Nile flowed. It was not until Livingstone and Stanley's expeditions in 1889 that Speke's intuitions were confirmed: Lake Victoria was indeed the source of the White Nile.

In the swamps of Bahr el Ghazal

The explorations of Burton, Speke, Grant and the Bakers in equatorial Africa were followed by a few individual expeditions. The most important of these, in 1869, took the German scholar and botanist Georg Schweinfurth into particularly hostile, unexplored territory, which was ravaged by tribal warfare and raids by slave traders. In 1869, after two years in Egypt, Schweinfurth resolved to ascend the Nile from Khartoum. He set out from Fashoda in February, and journeyed ever deeper into the Bahr el Ghazal, to observe how the natives of those swampy marshlands lived. Passing through the land of the fearsome Dinka warriors to the lands of the more peaceful Bongos, who lived by raising chickens and goats, the naturalist pursued his explorations into the land of the Nyam-Nyam. From there he reached the banks of the Uele river (he mistakenly believed it to be the upper course of the Shari, which empties into the Chad). In February 1870 Schweinfurth came into contact with the Azandés and the Akkas; the latter were a pygmy tribe related to the Bushmen of South Africa, who had taken refuge in the forbidding lands of the Congo basin. He returned via a slightly different route, and reached Khartoum on 21 July 1871.

Schweinfurth soon recovered from the strains of his uncommonly arduous journey, and, like Livingstone, campaigned vigorously against the deplorable effects on the natives of the African slave trade.

The basin of the Upper Nile

Thanks to discoveries made by British explorers and supplemented by the Italians Miani, Gessi and Piaggia, we now know that the Nile rises in present-day Burundi on the slopes of Moufoumbiron, at a latitude of four degrees south. In those regions it is called first the Kasumo, then the Kagera, before it empties into Lake Victoria at 1134 metres above sea level. The Nile is the principal stream to emerge from Lake Victoria; it then flows into Lake Kyoga and Lake Albert, at 619 metres above sea level. North of Lake Albert the river is called Bahr el Jebel, the 'river of the mountain'. It flows swiftly down from the high plateaus of Uganda towards the Sudanese plain; on the relatively flat terrain, the course of the Nile slows considerably.

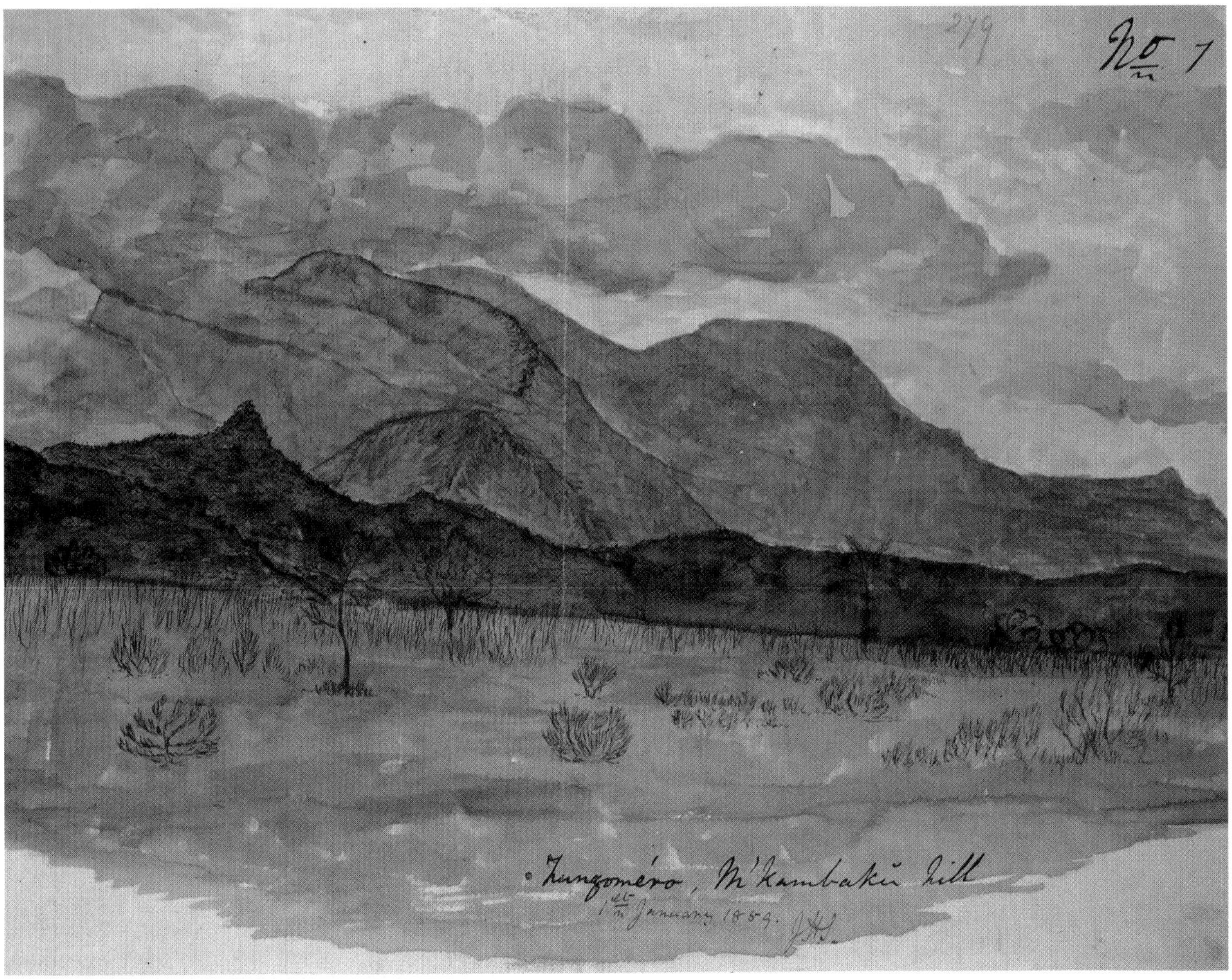

Landscape of hills and steppe painted by Speke on his way back to Zanzibar in 1859.

A lady explorer in search of the Nile

At a time when female explorers were an exceedingly rare breed, the Dutchwoman Alexandrine Tinné (1835-69) earned an enviable reputation for courage—and eccentricity. She made her first attempt to find the headwaters of the Nile in 1861; on this occasion she was accompanied by her mother and her aunt. Tinné reached Gondokoro, then changed direction and made her way to Bahr el Ghazal to explore the Nile basin near Lake Chad. After a second expedition in 1863, Tinné was murdered by Tuaregs as she crossed the Libyan desert.

A legendary figure in the annals of discovery, Dr David Livingstone was a great explorer, but also a spirited defender of black Africans against the depredations of slave traders. His travels led Livingstone to the southern reaches of the continent. He discovered Lake Nyasa (now Lake Malawi) and the Victoria Falls, and explored the lake country of East Africa. He located the courses of the Zambezi, Shire, and Lualaba rivers.

The meeting of Stanley and Livingstone is one of the high points of African exploration.

Stanley negotiates rapids on the River Congo.

A medical missionary

Born in 1813 to a poor but proud Scottish family, young David laboured in a cotton factory from the age of ten. He never went to school, but he was an intelligent lad, studious and determined to better himself. As a young man he felt a growing vocation to spread the Gospel among African populations; to fulfil this calling, Livingstone studied medicine as well as geology and botany. In 1840, his medical diploma in hand, he was sent by the Missionary Society of London to Cape Colony, and thence to present-day Botswana, to evangelize Africans and combat the local slave dealers.

After 1849 Livingstone's missionary activities were coupled with explorations. He firmly believed that commerce 'destroys the spirit of isolation that paganism engenders, and leads the tribes to feel interdependent, and useful to each other'. Despite his excellent intentions and perfect good faith, Livingstone set in motion a downward spiral of destabilization from which black Africa took many years to recover.

From the Zambezi to the Victoria Falls

Livingstone's first exploration, in 1849, in some ways resembled a family excursion, since he travelled with his wife, their three children, and a handful of friends. With great difficulty the little troop made their way across the Kalahari Desert, encountering Bushmen as they went. They trekked north to the shores of Lake Ngami, which very few Europeans had ever seen. Having sent his family safely back to Scotland, Livingstone made his first important discovery late in June 1851 when he located the course of the upper Zambezi. His progress was slow and, despite the hospitality of his friends from the Makololo tribe, the explorer was plagued with fever. He headed west, and came to the great seaport of St Paul de Loanda (present-day Luanda) on the Angolan coast. The Portuguese received the Scot amicably and he was able to regain his health.

In September 1855 he set out once more to follow the Zambezi downstream, and beheld 'the most incredible spectacle that I have yet witnessed in Africa', the Mosi-oa-Tunya, or 'Smoke that Thunders', which he named the Victoria Falls. Continuing his route along a fertile valley, he reached Tete, a Portuguese outpost, then journeyed to Quelimane on the Indian Ocean. Livingstone was thus the first European to cross southern Africa from west to east.

An expedition clouded by death

Livingstone returned to Africa in 1858, amply funded and equipped. From Quelimane he pushed inland into Mozambique, accompanied by his family, his brother, a physician, and a geologist. At the head of a veritable caravan so unwieldy that it considerably slowed his progress, he ascended the Zambezi with the intention of exploring its tributary, the Shire. On 16 September the explorer discovered Lake Nyasa, source of the Shire river, and took copious notes on the fauna, flora and inhabitants of the neighbouring regions.

The second phase of his expedition was clouded by the deaths of his wife and of his friend, the chief of the Makololo. Livingstone was further depressed by the conviction that his explorations were making little headway. At this point, the British government suspended his mission and recalled the explorer to give an account of his findings. Though he had but little time, he wrote a *Relation of the Exploration of the Zambezi and its Affluents*, the first comprehensive work on the mighty river that flows across southern Africa.

Searching for Livingstone

In 1866 the intrepid Livingstone returned once more to Africa. He set out from Zanzibar for Lake Nyasa. He reached the northern shores of Lake Tanganyika, and succeeded in defining the watershed between the two lakes. But during this journey his health took a sharp turn for the worse. He received little help from the natives, who were under the thumb of Zanzibari slave merchants. But in spite of these hardships, Livingstone pursued his explorations: he discovered Lake Mweru and Lake Bangweulu, crossed the Lualaba River (which he briefly mistook for the Nile), and then returned to Lake Tanganyika. Sick and exhausted, he was taken to Ujiji in October 1871.

In the meantime, the most alarming stories about Livingstone had spread through London, where the public eagerly devoured news of his discoveries. Indeed, he was believed dead. Expeditions were organized to search for the great explorer: Grandy went west, Cameron went east, and the fortunate Stanley, who ultimately found Livingstone, followed his predecessor's itinerary from Zanzibar. Henry Morton Stanley had never before set foot in Africa. He was dispatched as a reporter for the *New York Herald*, which funded his search most generously. On 28 October he was able to address his quarry with the now-famous phrase: 'Doctor Livingstone, I presume?' Stanley became Livingstone's spiritual heir, and continued his work after Livingstone's death.

Livingstone's last expedition

The two men struck up a friendship and together undertook in 1872 what was to be Livingstone's last exploration, north of Lake Tanganyika, in search of the Nile. They were forced to admit that the river Rusizi could not be one and the same as the Nile, for it emptied into the lake. After four months Stanley was obliged to leave his friend, but Livingstone, driven by his obsession with exploration, set off again. On 1 May 1873 he died, exhausted and wracked with dysentery, in Chitambo, on the marshy shores of Lake Tanganyika. His faithful

Before becoming the great explorer of Central Africa, Stanley - whose real name was John Rowlands - had led a roving life.

black servants carried Livingstone's embalmed body to Zanzibar, where it was sent back to England. Deemed to be a benefactor of mankind, Livingstone now rests in Westminster Abbey, amongst the heroes of British history.

On the Congo rapids

Henry Stanley was thirty-three in 1874 when he undertook one of the longest and most ambitious overland expeditions ever attempted in Africa. The *Daily Telegraph* and the *New York Herald* sponsored the project, putting at his disposal a squadron of porters and a boat, the *Lady Alice*, which could be dismantled and carried when convenient. In February 1875 Stanley reached Lake Victoria. His good relations with the Ugandan king, Mutesa, gave him free access to Lakes Edward and Albert. From Lake Tanganyika he headed—like Livingstone—to the river Lualaba, which he was eager to explore. Skirting rapids that were later christened Stanley Falls, amidst attacks by cannibals, Stanley and his men found to their surprise and delight that they were on the banks of the mighty Congo. After an arduous trek the party reached Boma on 9 August 1877, where a group of Euro-

peans came to their aid. The journey had lasted 999 days and had cost the lives of 114 men.

The last British explorations in Africa

From 1879 to 1884 Stanley ascended the Congo in the service of the Belgian sovereign Leopold II, who dreamed of a colonial empire and of 'civilizing' the 'backward' populations of Africa. All along his route Stanley established study bases, and dynamited jungle vegetation in order to open up a trail. He pursued his explorations as far as Lake Leopold. In 1880 Stanley met Brazza (see p. 212), who was then exploring the opposite bank of the river for France.

By the time Stanley returned to England, the European powers were firmly implanted in the Congo region; the economic and commercial hopes of King Leopold II had been amply confirmed.

The river explorations of the Englishman Grenfell and the Belgian Delcommune, the overland expeditions of the Portuguese Capello and Ivens, and of the Germans Pogge and von Wissmann, completed the work of Brazza and Stanley.

(see p. 212)

Livingstone and the slave trade

In this excerpt from his last journal, Livingstone describes his relations with a tribal chief of the Lake Nyasa region: 'I thought that a visit to Makate would make a good impression. He is one of those who, urged on by the Arabs, continue to hunt for slaves among the Mauganyas. I had a long discussion with Makate. The evils that greeted our sight, the skulls, the corpses, the ruins of villages, the countless men who perish from here to the coast, the mass murders—Makate tried to make light of it. We can do very little, but at least we sow in their hearts a seed of protest which, with time, will germinate.'

Cameron's exploits in southern Africa

British naval officer Verney Lowett Cameron was sent to southern Africa by the Geographic Society of London to assist David Livingstone. But on his way, he met the party carrying the explorer's remains to Zanzibar. Cameron then decided to continue on his journey, and to complete the celebrated missionary's work. After investigating the shores of Lake Tanganyika, in 1874 he began his march west, and eventually reached the Lualaba. But instead of descending the river towards the Congo, he headed south to reach the West African coast. Weakened by illness, Cameron nevertheless came in sight of the ocean in April 1876 after three years and four months of trekking across Africa.

ETHIOPIA, LAND OF ADVENTURE

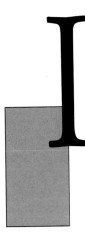

I n the nineteenth century, after three hundred years of isolation, torn by royal rivalries, divided and virtually in ruins, Ethiopia, the land of the Negus, opened its borders to foreign travellers. This mysterious 'Tibet of Africa' fired the Romantic imagination, and expeditions to Ethiopia increased in frequency around 1840. From 1869, with the opening of the Suez Canal, the European powers saw Ethiopia as a particularly tempting prize.

'A deposit of *Australopithecus'*

In 1932 and 1933 Camille Arambourg studied several deposits of vertebrate skeletons discovered near the shores of Lake Rudolf in the Omo valley. Excavations carried out in 1967 unearthed more than fifty tonnes of fossils, including nearly three hundred partial skeletons of *Australopithecus* (one of man's ancestors), from one to four million years old. An international team of scientists is currently conducting research at the site.

In the hands of the Jesuits

Ethiopia was a land of legends, but also the cradle of one of humanity's oldest civilizations, fruit of the fabled romance of King Solomon and the Queen of Sheba. Abyssinia (the name 'Ethiopia' became official only in 1974) closed its borders to outsiders in 1634, after a clumsy attempt by the Jesuits to win over the Abyssinians to the faith and authority of Rome.

Two Spanish Jesuits had settled in Abyssinia early in the sixteenth century. Their Portuguese neighbours took up their mission in 1544. The ruins of the cathedral of Sousenios, built in 1621 by Father Pedro Paez, attest to the importance and far-reaching influence the Jesuits enjoyed until they were expelled in 1634.

A French physician at the court of Gondar

In the eighteenth century a few individual travellers ventured alone onto the Ethiopian plateau. The most famous was the French physician Charles Jacques Poncet, who visited Abyssinia around 1700. He brought back to Europe much valuable information on the court of Gondar, enabling France to take the first steps towards a reconciliation with the emperor. Invited to be the guest of the emperor Iyassou, whose ambassador he had treated and cured in Cairo, Poncet sailed to Ethiopia on the Nile in June 1698, crossed Nubia, and spent three months at Sennar waiting for his Ethiopian escort. Poncet wrote a vivid description of Gondar—its castles, its hundred churches, its ceremonies and religions. He visited Sousenios, Aksum, Adowa and Debarwa, stayed at the monastery of St Catherine at Mount Sinai, and then returned to Cairo, not through the desert but via the Red Sea. His journey lasted three years and ten days.

In Poncet's wake a French embassy headed by Lenoir du Roule was dispatched to Gondar in the hope of establishing direct relations between France and Ethiopia. The mission was aborted at Sennar where, owing to a tragic series of circumstances, the men were massacred on 25 November 1705. All relations with France ceased immediately; and in the aftermath of Emperor Iyassou's death, Ethiopia fell prey once more to anarchy.

On the trail of James Bruce

The Abyssinian odyssey of James Bruce (see p. 204) and Bonaparte's Egyptian campaign combined to awaken British interest in Abyssinia, a country about which little was yet known. King George III was the first English sovereign to send emissaries to Gondar. The Salt mission yielded negligible results, but an embassy headed by Sir Cornwallis W. Harris in the 1840s led to the signing of a friendship and trade treaty with Sahle Selassie, the ruler of the Shawa province. The British thus stole the thunder of a

During the 19th century, far-off Abyssinia fuelled the imagination of the Europeans. Many painters, writers and fortune-seekers travelled there.

French mission led by Rochet d'Héricourt (see below). Another success was the appointment in 1848 of Walter Plowden as consul to the Ra'is Ali, who ruled over Dabra Tabor, a neighbouring province.

Richard Burton was the most illustrious British subject to travel to Ethiopia. The intrepid adventurer visited Harar, at the very centre of dangerous Galla territory, in 1853. At the time the city was still off limits to foreigners, so Burton was obliged to disguise himself as an Arab merchant. He was wounded, however, and returned to England where he published *First Footsteps in East Africa*.

French explorers on the Ethiopian plateau

French explorers made a significant contribution to knowledge of Ethiopia. The expedition led by Edmond Combes and Maurice Tamisier in 1836 marked a new beginning for relations between France and Ethiopia, after a long interruption. The two young gentlemen made their way with considerable difficulty across the Tigré states, Amhara and Gojam, skirted Lake Tana, and stayed at Gondar; a year later the pair reached Massawa and Jiddah.

In 1837 the French Navy dispatched Charlemagne Théophile Lefebvre on an exploratory mission. Accompanied by Petit, a zoologist, and the botanist Quartin-Dillon, he made several visits to Ethiopia, travelling through the territories of Tigré, Shawa and Gojam, and around Lake Tana and Gondar. He amassed a vast store of geographical, sociological, archaeological and linguistic data. Two brothers, Antoine and Arnaud d'Abbadie, also pioneered French exploration of Ethiopia. But unlike their predecessors, they focused their efforts on the country's virtually unexplored southern reaches, where they hoped to find the headwaters of the White Nile (they mistakenly put their faith in faulty information from James Bruce). In fact, what Antoine d'Abbadi discovered was the upper course of the Omo river.

Pledges of friendship and trade

Another adventurer, Charles Rochet d'Héricourt, was more interested in encouraging trade and human relations. He formed a long and fruitful friendship with Sahle Selassie, the ruler of Shawa. Rochet advocated the creation of a direct road from Shawa to the Gulf of Aden via the navigable Awash river, and in 1843 signed a treaty with Sahle Selassie giving France trading privileges. Successive expeditions took him into Galla territory, to Dabra Tabor (kingdom of the Ra'is Ali), and to the shores of Lake Tana. But Rochet's efforts did not immediately yield the results he had foreseen: the construction of the Shawa road was undertaken some thirty years later, in 1874, by the French engineer Pierre Arnoux, by which time Ethiopia's political situation had been clarified.

The massacre of the Bottego expedition

The opening of the Suez Canal in 1869 and the new economic perspectives it opened up rekindled European interest in Ethiopia. French, Italian, Swiss and British missions visited the African nation in turn. One of these, the Bottego mission, took particular interest in the Omo river valley. While the Italian army suffered a terrible defeat at Adowa at the hands of Menelik's forces, in 1896 the Italian Geographical Society was considering questions raised by the recent discovery of the Omo by the d'Abbadie brothers. The Society sent a large escort to the site under Captain Bottego. He crossed Somali territory, which he had already visited in 1892, then continued along the pleasant shores of Lake Pagadé, before reaching the Omo basin. Bottego quickly discovered that the river emptied into Lake Rudolf, and was therefore not a tributary of the Nile. It was up on the plateaus separating the basins of Lake Rudolf and the Nile that the mission—decimated after many deaths—was attacked by Gallas and massacred nearly to a man. Only a few survivors were taken before Menelik, who showed little interest in them. Menelik, from that point on, was the sole master of Abyssinia. By pursuing a policy of conquest, this great strategist would finally rescue his country from anarchy and repel foreign schemes for annexation.

After the liberation of Ethiopia in 1896, the emperor Menelik II strove for the modernization of his country, developing education and setting up a Franco-Ethiopian railway company.

t the dawn of the twentieth century West Africa belonged—at least in theory—to Europe. The era of great explorations was drawing to a close. Geographical problems had been resolved, and explained in numerous scientific publications. Yet some centres of native resistance still remained, particularly in the Sahara, which had just been ceded to France by the terms of an Anglo-French agreement signed in 1890.

The exploration and pacification of the Western Sahara started up again in 1890. It stopped in the thirties.

The Sahara Desert

The Sahara is not just an immense stretch of sand, nor is it a vast and monotonous plain; on the contrary, it displays an extremely wide variety of topographical features. A majestic massif of great antiquity, the Ahaggar (2500 metres) is a portion of the ancient rocky Precambrian platform that extends south of the Tropic of Cancer, bordered by the sandstone and schistose formations of the Tassili. The Ahaggar is prolonged to the southwest by the Adrar des Iforas and to the southeast by the Aïr range, while to the east it is linked to the Tibesti Massif (2700 metres), which is continued to the southeast by the Ennedi plateau.

Military missions and adventures

By the end of the nineteenth century, exploratory missions in Africa were mostly assigned to the military.

In 1890 Lieutenant Colonel Monteil, accompanied by Senegalese infantrymen, established a direct route between St-Louis and Tripoli, via Sokoto, Hausa, Bornu and Fezzan. Without firing a shot, Monteil covered more than 7000 kilometres and succeeded in linking the itineraries marked out by Barth and Binger (see p. 209). In 1896 a French navy lieutenant called Hourst de-

scended the Niger below Timbuktu, a feat no one had tried to achieve since Mungo Park had died in the attempt. Hourst had a lightweight aluminium barge constructed, to which he joined two wooden barges. Posing as the nephew of Barth, Hourst easily won the friendship of the Tuareg chieftain. He spent the winter at Say, then descended the river to the sea. His mission yielded the first detailed maps of the Niger from source to mouth.

In 1903 Captain Lenfant led an expedition from the Niger basin to the Chad basin. Accompanied by Lieutenants Anthoine and de Peyronnet, Lenfant ascended the Niger and its tributory, the Benue, to Garoua. The men then carried their boat

upstream through marshes and swampland. Three months later the party reached a river that flowed into the Logone, in the Chad basin. The mission was thus able to demonstrate that the two basins were in fact connected.

From 1912 to 1917 Commandant Tilho supervised the mapping of every topographical detail of the Tibesti range and Ennedi plateau; he also revealed the existence of the high Jebel 'Uweinat mountain, which stands 1435 metres above sea level in the middle of the Libyan desert. Tilho's precision and scientific rigour earned him a place in the French Academy of Science.

The conquest of Mauritania

The Western Sahara, which had long been closed to European penetration, mounted a determined resistance to French colonization. After René Caillié, Panet, and Lenz, French missions in the region steadily increased, and advanced ever deeper, going after nomadic bands. The Erg Iguidi, Trarza, Brakna, Tagant and Adrar were successively occupied. The city of Smara in the Saguia el Hamra fell in 1913. In 1920 the first liaison was established between Mauritania and southern Algeria.

The 'land of fear'

The conquest of the Tanezrouft in the heart of the Western Sahara was a remarkable exploit. This rocky desert of over 150,000 square kilometres was literally virgin territory. Not a single trace of life broke the sinister monotony of this 'land of fear'. Captain Cortier was the first to cross the Tanezrouft from north to south in 1913: nine days of privation and solitude, with not a soul—enemy or otherwise—in view. Twenty-three years later, the scientist Théodore Monod repeated the exploit, walking for twelve hours a day. After crossing 450 kilometres of desert, the little caravan of three natives and one soldier went back on their tracks to complete their exploration.

Laperrine, the great 'Saharan'

Every French regiment served a common cause, but their separate victories would not have caused such a stir, had they not been exploited by an exceptional individual. General François Laperrine was the great peacemaker of the Sahara. During his years of service in the Sudan and the Tuat, he acquired an intimate knowledge of the desert and its peoples. In 1901 Laperrine was named commander of the oases, and he created the Saharan Companies, elite forces that performed military miracles in the desert. Always on the alert and ready for action, these companies were made up of volunteers. Laperrine's officers were all men of character, with rare leadership abilities and independent minds. The troops were mainly *méharistes*, soldiers mounted on swift camels, recruited from among the Chamba tribesmen, who were traditional enemies of the Tuaregs. Using force and diplomacy, Laperrine subjugated virtually the entire Sahara in just a few years.

In March 1920 Laperrine met his death in an air raid between Algiers and the Sudan. His Tuareg and *méhariste* comrades paid their last respects to this extraordinary officer at his funeral in Tamanrasset.

The mystical adventure of Charles de Foucauld

Charles de Foucauld was born on 15 September 1858 in Strasbourg. Orphaned at the age of six, he was raised by his maternal grandfather. His rebellious character kept Charles out of the *Ecole Polytechnique*; he went instead to the military academy of St-Cyr, and later to Saumur, where he led a boisterous student life.

In 1882 Foucauld left the army to arrange a trip to Morocco, a land then still largely unknown. On the advice of the geographer Oscar MacCarthy, the young man disguised himself as a Jewish merchant. He carried with him all sorts of scientific equipment and was able to make highly important geographical surveys, as well as astronomical

The half-tracks of Citroën's Croisière noire *had to cross the Sahel bush, the desert and the marshy rivers of the Chad.*

and hydrographical observations. These studies are all the more remarkable in view of the obstacles he had to surmount—a climate of suspicion surrounded him wherever he went. Foucauld ventured much farther into Morocco's mountainous interior than had his predecessors. In the course of a second trip in 1885, Foucauld visited the principal oases of southern Algeria and Tunisia. He struck up a friendship with some Saharan officers, and got back in touch with his former schoolmate from St-Cyr, Laperrine. A mystical revelation impelled Foucauld to embrace once again the religious faith he had abandoned as an adolescent. He entered the Trappist order in 1890 and was ordained in 1901.

Laperrine suggested to Foucauld that he settle in the recently pacified Ahaggar. Together they took part in a mission among the Tuareg tribesmen, in which Foucauld's experience as an explorer proved an asset. In 1905 a second mission took them to Tamanrasset. Foucauld established his first hermitage there, followed by another, set in an even more isolated spot in the assekrem highlands, 2900 metres above sea level. Ten years later, in 1916, Foucauld was murdered by pillaging Senusis.

The *Croisiere Noire*

Automobile magnate André Citroën organized what would later be called the *Croisière noire* ('black cruise'), after the documentary film that recorded the first

long-distance run in Africa. Citroën's aim was to open up a driveable road between Algeria and the French colonies of West Africa. His project was enthusiastically approved by the Secretaries of War, of the Colonies, and of Foreign Affairs, as well as by the Museum of Natural History. Vehicles mounted on caterpillar tracks had already been tested in a rally from Toggourt to Timbuktu in 1923.

On 28 October 1924 eight teams set out from Colomb-Béchar for Chad, where they were to pair off to make four teams. One would then head for Djibouti, another for the Cape of Good Hope, while the third and fourth would set out for Dar es Salaam, one via Kenya, the other via Tanganyika.

Braving the terrible Tanezrouft desert, suffering extreme heat by day and cold by night, the expedition pulled up on the banks of the Niger on 18 November, before reaching Zinder and the neighbourhood of Lake Chad. The muddy ground and dense vegetation of the lake shore gave way to grassy savannahs and black African populations. Everywhere the drivers were welcomed with cheers and applause. After a long halt in the Ubangi-Shari region, in January 1926 the vehicles set forth once more, destination Kampala. The teams separated on 19 April, each following its predetermined route.

Despite adventures, accidents and incidents involving both vehicles and drivers, the contestants all reached the rallying point of Tananarive, the capital of Madagascar. The *Croisière noire* still figures among the greatest exploits in the history of Saharan rallies.

A tireless traveller: Mary Henrietta Kingsley

In 1892, at the age of thirty, Mary Kingsley, a stout-hearted Englishwoman, decided to set out for West Africa to study African religions and laws, in order to complete a book her uncle, the pastor Charles Kingsley, had left unfinished at his death. From the moment she arrived on African soil, she crisscrossed the continent tirelessly. Between 1893 and 1894 she travelled to Angola, Nigeria and the Fernando Po Islands (now Equatorial Guinea). The artifacts she gathered on her journeys enriched the natural history collections of the British Museum. Miss Kingsley also visited the Congo and penetrated into previously unexplored regions of Gabon. Her legacy consists of prolific writings; many of the texts express her deep affection for the peoples of black Africa.

Pictures of the Sahara

Before the Sahara became the world's largest desert, various human communities settled on its vast expanses over three millennia, from 5000 to 2000 BC. They left behind them cave paintings and carvings of considerable artistry, in which men and animals are rendered with impressive skill. Scenes of war, hunting, pastoral life, vignettes of everyday activities that show huts where these early humans ate and slept—all provide clues as to how our prehistoric ancestors lived. The most important groupings originated in the area south of Oran, in Fezzan, and the Ahaggar, Tibesti and Tassili n' Ajer highlands.

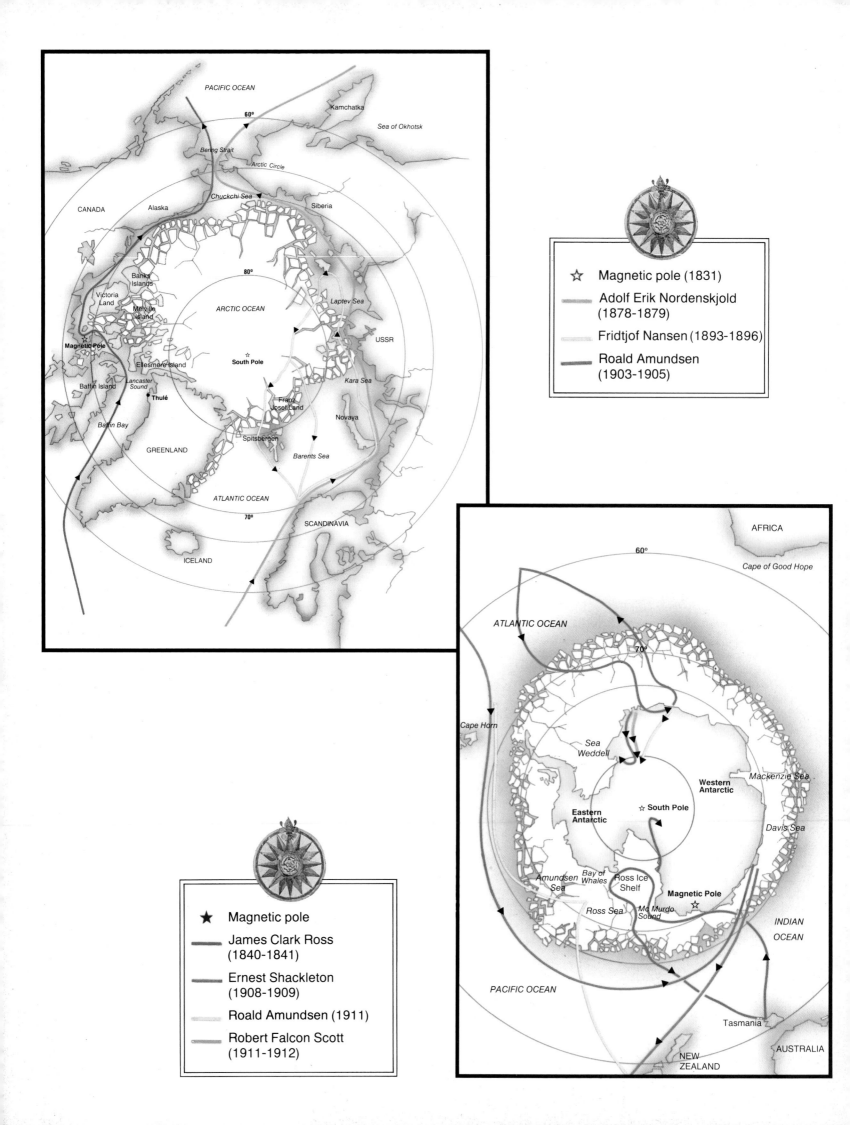

PACIFIC OCEAN

60°

Kamchatka

Sea of Okhotsk

Bering Strait

Arctic Circle

Chuckchi Sea

CANADA

Alaska

Siberia

Banks
Islands

80°

ARCTIC OCEAN

Laptev Sea

Victoria
Land

Melville
Island

USSR

Magnetic Pole

South Pole

Ellesmere Island

Kara Sea

Baffin Island

Lancaster
Sound

Thulé

Franz
Josef Land

Novaya

Baffin Bay

Spitsbergen

GREENLAND

Barents Sea

ATLANTIC OCEAN

70°

SCANDINAVIA

ICELAND

☆ Magnetic pole (1831)

Adolf Erik Nordenskjold
(1878-1879)

Fridtjof Nansen (1893-1896)

Roald Amundsen
(1903-1905)

AFRICA

60°

Cape of Good Hope

ATLANTIC OCEAN

70°

Cape Horn

Sea
Weddell

Mackenzie Sea

Western
Antarctic

Eastern
Antarctic

☆ South Pole

Davis Sea

Amundsen
Sea

Bay of
Whales

Ross Ice
Shelf

Magnetic Pole

INDIAN
OCEAN

Ross Sea

Mc Murdo
Sound

PACIFIC OCEAN

Tasmania

AUSTRALIA

NEW
ZEALAND

★ Magnetic pole

James Clark Ross
(1840-1841)

Ernest Shackleton
(1908-1909)

Roald Amundsen (1911)

Robert Falcon Scott
(1911-1912)

The Poles

Not in the interest of science, nor for the sheer thrill of discovery did sixteenth-century merchant-adventurers brave the rigours of the Arctic. The notion of exploring for personal fame or national glory had not yet emerged, and the pretext of bringing the Gospel to new lands could be invoked only if there existed heathen populations to convert! No, what drew the first explorers to the frigid polar wastes was, quite simply, the lure of profit.

On the north coast of Novaya Zemlya, Barents and his crew built a shelter in the Dutch style in which they spent the winter of 1596.

When the Bering Strait was a bridge of ice...

Pushed by other peoples coming from the south, the ancient populations of northern Siberia and Lapland probably crossed into North America and Greenland via the frozen Bering Strait. Tribes accustomed to the cold remained in the polar regions. Relatively few in number, they migrated over ice and land, following herds of caribou and musk ox. Their hunting and fishing methods were quite sophisticated, considering the limited materials available to them: walrus tusks, whale teeth, bone, leather, driftwood, horn and reindeer antlers. Over the centuries few changes have come to alter the convivial, communal way of life that helps these peoples to face the long winter months.

Towards the great Northwest

Pioneers of polar exploration were pressed by the need to find a new route to the spices and silks of Cathay (China), so eloquently described by Marco Polo (see p. 34). What they sought was a shorter route, free of ferocious Arabs and well away from the Portuguese sea route around Africa and from Spain's American colonies. At the same time, those hardy seamen were on the lookout for new territories to conquer, populations to subdue, and for fresh hunting and fishing grounds to exploit.

Sixteenth-century mariners were not the first to sail the waters of the far North. Pytheas, a Phoenician sailor from Marseilles, probably reached Iceland in the fourth century BC, and left a bizarre description of the formation of ice floes. But very little is known of that early voyage (see p. 15). A thousand years later, according to the legend of St Brendan, Irish monks navigated those same seas in leather-covered wicker boats called coracles. Between the ninth and twelfth centuries, owing to a slight climatic warming, Vikings from Norway and from present-day Denmark colonized Iceland and raised livestock on the southern coast of Greenland. Some pushed farther west or were blown by high winds to Newfoundland and territories near the mouth of the St Lawrence (see p. 109). The Vikings, however, were not interested in a passage to China. The notion of a round Earth, like other philosophical and scientific speculations of the Ancients, had been forgotten.

Ever onward...

Five more centuries passed before the theory that the Earth was round was revived in the Renaissance. Thanks to Mercator (see p. 52), great strides had been made in cartography, and navigational astronomy had progressed as well. Exploration and discovery gained momentum: thirty-two years after Columbus's accidental landing in the 'western Indies', in 1524—the year Vasco da Gama died while circumnavigating the globe—the French monarch Francis I hired Giovanni Verrazano to seek a northern passage to China. What the Florentine actually found was the mouth of the Hudson, and an island which the Dutch later purchased for a pittance from the local Indians. Ten years later the French explorer Jacques Cartier sailed up the St Lawrence and discovered Canada (see p. 114). In the second half of the sixteenth century, British navigators advanced still farther: they searched both for a northeast and for a northwest passage.

In the service of merchants and princes

After serving the Spanish Crown, Sebastian Cabot, a native Venetian and naturalized Englishman, returned to London in 1520 (he was the son of Giovanni Caboto, who rediscovered Newfoundland and explored both Greenland and the Labrador coast). He convinced King Edward VI that England should take its share of the rapidly expanding, highly profitable seaborne trade. Cabot put together a cartel—the Governor and Company of Merchants of London Trading into the East Indies—that financed the first expeditions to search for a northern passage. Although European rulers were eager to acquire new territory, they also wanted gold. The merchants who banded together to fund explorations were engaging in what modern businessmen would call 'high-risk investment'. If the passage were discovered, they would recoup their investment and far more besides, as some lucky sponsors did. The company financed Sir Hugh Willoughby, who in 1553 landed on the large island of Novaya Zemlya, where he died while wintering over. One of his ships, under Richard Chancellor's command, crossed the White Sea and reached Arkhangelsk in Russia (see p. 191).

Elizabeth I of England hired Martin Frobisher, a notorious pirate and skilled navigator, who in the course of three voyages from 1576 to 1578 pushed as far north as 60° N. He sailed round Labrador, discovered what is now Baffin Island, and mistook the entrance to the Hudson Strait for the famous Northwest Passage. Frobisher searched for gold ore, but in vain; in 1577 he was the first white man to encounter Eskimos. Their small stature and Mongoloid features fed European hopes that China lay only a short distance farther in the same direction.

John Davis: right place, wrong time

Seven years later, a different company of merchant-adventurers financed three expeditions led by John Davis, from 1585 to 1587. A marine surveyor and cartographer, as well as an able navigator and inventor of the quadrant (a navigational instrument, ancestor of the sextant), Davis mapped the western coast of Greenland and the eastern seaboard of the Canadian archipelago up to 72° N. His progress was ultimately halted by bad weather and the pack ice that still blocked the waters in June. Davis did not realize that he had indeed located the long-sought entrance to the Northwest Passage. But his sponsors, discouraged by the apparent lack of success, did not give him the funds to mount a fourth expedition.

More hunters than explorers

The Dutch, in the meantime, ever eager to turn a profit, had launched an intensive whaling industry in the teeming Arctic waters, rich in plankton, fish and whales. Slightly farther south, in Canada, a lucrative fur trade flourished, and soon the ani-

mals of the frozen North—seals, walruses, polar bears—were mercilessly tracked down for their valuable skins. Though European hunters and fishermen kept secret the exact location of their rich new sources of skins and fish, and though their knowledge of geography was strictly empirical, as time passed more and more seamen sailed the seas of the Far North. They grew accustomed to the region's hostile climate, and soon learned that the small, round, manoeuvrable craft preferred by Dutch mariners were best suited to navigating in frigid northern seas.

From Novaya Zemlya to New Amsterdam

In 1594 Willem Barents searched for a northeast passage by sailing around the northern coast of Novaya Zemlya, but the route was obstructed by dense pack ice. Cornelius Nay found the Kara Sea ice-free, but he didn't have time to profit from his discovery because of the lateness of the season. Two years later, in 1596, Barents sighted Spitsbergen, and again tried to round the northern end of Novaya Zemlya. His ship was frozen in, and the crew was obliged to winter at 76° N. When the weather improved, they set out in open boats. After three months at sea, they reached the Kola Peninsula. Barents died on the voyage, but the fact that twelve men survived the ordeal

proved that it was possible to winter in those far-northern latitudes and to complete a voyage in two stages—no one ever made the trip in one stretch.

In 1607 the Muscovy Company of London fitted out the Englishman Henry Hudson with a small boat that reached 80° 22 N but could not progress farther because of pack ice. In 1609 he repeated the voyage in the service of the Dutch East India Company. Thwarted again by frozen seas, Hudson resolved to sail for America. He rediscovered the island where Verrazano had landed, at the mouth of the future Hudson river, and claimed it for the Dutch. Holland purchased the island from the natives for a symbolic sum, and in 1626 founded New Amsterdam, which the English, who won the island in 1664, rechristened New York.

A tragic winter in Hudson Bay

Hudson was determined to find the Northwest Passage. In 1610 he outfitted the *Discovery* and sailed west, intending to round Labrador and take things up where Sir Martin Frobisher had left off. This turned out to be an unwise choice. Had Hudson, a veteran of far-northern latitudes with a stout ship, continued Davis's course, Hudson Bay might have remained unexplored for a time, but the Northwest Passage might well have been conquered. The crew could

Icebergs, floes and ice fields

Icebergs made a great impression on the first men who ventured into the polar regions. Some fishermen even exaggerated their frightening appearance in order to discourage competition. Frobisher was the first to surmise that the largest icebergs were not frozen seawater but enormous masses of ice detached from glaciers. Sea ice first forms floes—relatively thin, floating ice sheets—and then pack ice—a large area formed by ice pieces driven together by wind and currents. Steamships with reinforced stems could sometimes free themselves from pack ice. Ice fields, the largest type of floating ice, can be several metres thick, and form icecaps.

Together with his son and a few faithful companions, Hudson was thrown into a rowing boat by the mutineers of the Discovery *and left with only a few hunks of meat to survive on.*

surely have wintered in a region where Eskimos find adequate supplies of seal meat even in the coldest months. Instead, Hudson endured a terrible winter at the southern end of the bay. His crew, unused to such cruel conditions, could not hunt enough game to fill out their dwindling supplies. Half the men mutinied when Hudson declared his intention to continue his explorations. The mutineers set Hudson, his sixteen-year-old son, and seven loyal crewmen adrift in an open boat. The following year, Thomas Button's expedition found no trace of the Hudsons but completed the exploration of the bay's western coastline.

Endangered species

So long as harpoons were thrown by hand from whaling ships manned by crews of six or eight, whales could reproduce quickly enough to keep their population levels steady. But with the advent of motorized whaling boats, factory-ships, cannon-powered exploding harpoons, and sonar detection, many of the world's largest mammals moved onto the threshold of extinction. Some species of whale are already extinct, others may not be able to reproduce fast enough to ensure their survival if whaling continues at its present level.

The price of clemency

The mutinous crew sailed the *Discovery* back to England, falsely claiming that the instigators of the mutiny against Hudson had all perished en route. The authorities pretended to accept these dubious explanations, to avoid the necessity of hanging men who possessed valuable information. Robert Bylot, one of the mutineers, was named ship's captain, but he was not sent out on his own: the person really in charge of the 1615 expedition to Hudson Bay was William Baffin, an able pilot, mathematician and astronomer. The merchants who put up cap-

ital for the expedition were hopeful about trade prospects. They chartered a new company and outfitted a small commercial fleet, to make what profits they could while the seamen sought the famous Northwest Passage. In time the Hudson's Bay Company, successors of the London merchant-adventurers who had set out in quest of the Northwest Passage, would make a fortune trading furs and bartering with the natives.

A missed opportunity

While Hudson and Frobisher had mistaken the vast bay for the long-sought northern passage, Bylot and Baffin, aboard the still-seaworthy *Discovery* in 1615 and 1616, mistook the straits they discovered for bays and failed to explore them. They sailed up the Greenland coast to 78° N, even farther than Davis had done, and as they followed the archipelago to the west, they sighted Smith Sound, Jones Sound, and on 12 July 1616 Lancaster Sound (the names commemorated the expedition's backers). They did not, however, realize that Lancaster Sound was in fact the entrance to a route leading to the Pacific. They returned from their voyage convinced that the passage did not exist and that an eastern route should be sought instead.

The Dutch continued to earn handsome profits from trapping and fishing. The English prospered by maritime trade and established colonies in North America, thereby adding to their empire and prestige. The French taught the Hurons their language, and made New France a flourishing land—a handsome war prize that the English would carry off a century later.

Apart from a few observational expeditions, like the one led by Captain Moore and the geographer Ellis in 1746, or voyages involving the exploitation of their North American possessions, the English abandoned the quest for the Northwest Passage. A northeastern route was sought instead along the Arctic coast of Siberia.

The northwest route abandoned

The Northwest was virtually abandoned for two centuries, save for rare scientific voyages. Whalers and fishermen occasionally provided information, but on the whole the myth of a northern passage now rested upon hopes to sail north around Eurasia. To navigate along the Siberian coast, cross the Bering Strait (then unknown, as was Alaska), and then steer south—that was the new challenge set for intrepid mariners. What

For a century and a half, the Dutch and the English went in for intensive whale hunting. They were helped by specialist Basque harpooners.

the Europeans did not know was that Russia had long navigated those northern waters, at times and in places where ice was not a hindrance. Few attempts were made to explore those upper latitudes, however, for the seventeenth century witnessed the decline of Spain and Portugal, giving the British, Dutch and French access to the southern sea route around the Cape of Good Hope to India and China. With that motivation removed, they left to the Russians the task of forcing a path through the Arctic ice.

An encouraging error

Their sketchy knowledge of Eurasia's northern reaches allowed sixteenth-century Europeans to believe that the route to the East was shorter than it actually is. No one suspected that the Siberian coast embraced nearly half the circumference of the seventieth parallel. Unlike the northern coasts of North America, which remained mostly virgin territory, the Russian Empire gradually occupied the Siberian coast. Cossacks made frequent incursions, but they were more interested in conquest, hunting and pillage than in exploration (see p. 190).

In 1553 Sir Hugh Willoughby headed an English expedition of three ships. Two of them, including Willoughby's, were lost, but the exploration continued under the leadership of its pilot, Richard Chancellor (see p. 191), who managed to open a sea route to Arkhangelsk.

This success led to the creation of a company of merchant-adventurers that traded with Russia in the era of Ivan the Terrible. Willem Barents's three voyages from 1594 to 1596 ended tragically, but they fuelled navigators' hopes of crossing the Arctic to the east and brought home the fact that men could indeed winter in latitudes as far north as 76° N. Barents's explorations also opened new hunting grounds for whalers and, curiously enough, provided absolute proof that a passage did exist. For whales harpooned off Spitsberg, but which escaped capture, were occasionally killed between the Kamchatka Peninsula and Japan, with the harpoons of the first hunters found plunged into their blubber.

Russians conquer the East

From the early sixteenth century bands of Cossacks rode ever farther eastward. These illiterate raiders made no systematic obser-

A people of eastern Siberia with an ancient civilization similar to that of the Eskimos, the Tchouktches live from hunting, fishing and rearing reindeer.

vations; all they brought back were reports of what they had seen, along with the booty obtained by barter or pillage from local populations. The existence of a maritime route to the East held no interest for the hard-riding Cossacks. And yet—as happened later for the Northwest passage—the exploration of coastal land made it possible to explore the seas, which were blocked with ice for most of the year.

Russian seamen frequently sailed in the Barents Sea, west of Novaya Zemlya. When the ice was thin or broken up, they crossed the Kara Sea (east of Novaya Zemlya), covering roughly half the distance of the Northeast passage. The Russians had designed suitable ships, called *kochis*, which were not too large and were heavily reinforced below the waterline. These versatile craft could be operated either with sails or oars, and could be hauled along a canal or dragged over ice. In short, Russian *kochis* were light and easy to handle, unlike the heavy, cumbersome vessels that Europeans used in these hostile waters. Much later, the steamboat would overcome most of these handicaps.

In the seventeenth century Russian hunters and adventurers pushed still farther east into Yakut country, then part of Mongolia. Under the command of Semyon

Dezhnyov, in 1648, on foot and by *kochi*, sixty men reached the mouth of the Anadyr River in the farthest reaches of northeast Siberia. They had seen what would one day be called the Bering Sea. But Dezhnyov's reports were buried for a century in the archives at Yakutsk, so the discovery was not known until after Vitus Bering and others had explored the sea.

The testament of Peter the Great

In 1724, shortly before his death, Czar Peter I funded an expedition led by the Dane Vitus Bering, who attempted to reach North America from the Kamchatka Peninsula, aboard a ship built for him on the spot (see p. 193). Bering gave his name to the strait, sighted in 1728, that separates Cape Dezhnev from Alaska. He did not sail far enough to land in Alaska, though he did call in at some of the Aleutian Islands. During his second voyage, in 1741, he touched Alaska's southern shore; his discovery whetted Russia's appetite for new colonies, although the vast Russian empire was al-

Ancient peoples of the North

Nomadic hunters or herders, Onikilons (recently died out), Chukchis, Koriaks, and, to a lesser extent, Samoyedes, Ostiaks, and ancient Lapps are or were the last survivors of prehistoric times—civilizations that hunted, then domesticated the reindeer. Their techniques for surviving for so many centuries in a frozen world—in conditions that prevailed throughout the Northern Hemisphere in the last glacial epoch—are an extraordinary example of man's ability to adapt to a hostile environment.

Eskimos

Eskimos boast the most northerly human habitat on the planet. Their racial characteristics are of the Mongoloid type, but are distinct from those of the Amerinds of northern Canada. Traditionally, Eskimos neither grew nor gathered their food, but lived chiefly on meat, fat, and fish. Today, their culture is disappearing under pressure from Western civilization.

John Ross recorded his encounters with the inhabitants of Prince Regent Bay after he put into port there in 1829. Above, portrait of an Eskimo.

ready far-flung and nearly unmanageable. Bering died at the age of sixty in 1741, as he was on the point of completing his third voyage (see p. 193).

Catherine II also granted generous subsidies to explorers, continuing Peter the Great's enterprise. The aim of the Great Northern Expedition (1733-42) was to carry out surveys in Siberia, in the hope of discovering a maritime passage to the East somewhere along its extensive coastline. A thousand men, divided into five teams, explored some 5000 kilometres either by dogsledge or aboard *kochis*. Khariton and Dmitry Laptev are remembered in the annals of exploration for their epic journeys from the mouth of the Lena in 1741-2; the first brother headed west, the second east, but despite their courage and perseverance, they were foiled by impenetrable ice. The brothers' explorations were completed by Chelyuskin, Khariton Laptev's lieutenant, who travelled overland by dogsledge to the continent's northernmost tip, a cape that now bears his name.

An impassable sea route

Eighteenth-century Arctic explorers regretfully concluded that, though a Northeast Passage indeed existed—since whales frequently made the trip—the route was impracticable for ships, unless they were prepared to winter repeatedly in those frigid latitudes. A century later, in 1867, the czar decided that he would never make a profit from Alaska's one million square kilometres and sold the territory to the United States for 7.2 million dollars. Meanwhile, inland Siberia had been thoroughly explored. Sannikov investigated the islands off its coast in 1806, and Kotzebue reconnoitred the Alaskan coast (see p. 165). Nevertheless, 2500 kilometres of Siberia's northernmost coastline remained largely uninvestigated until Ferdinand Petrovitch Wrangel led three expeditions to that harsh land between 1821 and 1823. Equipped with dogsledges, he searched in vain for the mythical land or ice bridge leading to a great

land, a feature of many Chukchi legends. Paradoxically, he was always stopped by a sea free of ice.

The English in the Far North

In the years that followed the Congress of Vienna (1819-20), the world enjoyed a short period of peace. Britain's First Lord of the Admiralty, Sir John Barrow, an ardent apostle of Arctic exploration, gave his officers the means to win considerable prestige for the Crown. On the strength of information provided by a whaling captain, William Scoresby, in 1817, John Ross set out the following year with two ships, the *Isabella* and the *Alexander*, to conquer the Northwest Passage. Ross failed, but on a subsequent mission Ross's former second-in-command, Edward Parry, at the helm of the *Hecla* and the *Griper*, sailed as far west as Melville Island at the 110th meridian in September 1819, an exploit that won him a reward of £5000. He also succeeded in mapping 1000 kilometres of Arctic coastline.

Another naval officer, John Franklin, was dispatched on an overland polar expedition, aided and abetted by the Hudson's Bay Company. In the course of two expeditions (1819-22 and 1825-27), Franklin gathered information which, when combined with Parry's data, defined the location of the passage. Yet no sailing ship could hope to pass through it, owing to the dense pack ice. Since the British did not follow Eskimo survival techniques in their Arctic adventures, these expeditions took heavy tolls in human life. But Franklin himself made it back to England alive, where he won fame and a knighthood. These rewards only made him more determined to be the first to cross the impossible passage.

Amassing information

During the same period Parry undertook a second, and then a third voyage. He improved methods for wintering in the Arctic, learned about the Eskimos and their dogsledges, and then set out for the North Pole in 1821 with James Clark Ross—nephew of John Ross and future explorer of Antarctica—and Francis Crozier. When they arrived north of Spitsbergen, the men were forced to abandon the *Hecla*. They continued north over the icefield, without realizing that the ice was drifting south. The exhausted party pushed on to 82° 45' N, a record that would stand for half a century.

In his journal, Ross tells how, with the Victory *and the* Isabella *stuck in the ice, their interpreter, John Sacheuse, 'set off as a messenger, carrying a small white flag and a few gifts'.*

John Ross spent the years 1829-33 in the far northwest. He successfully weathered repeated Arctic winters and systematically accumulated a wealth of scientific data relating to meteorological and magnetic phenomena. In 1831 his nephew James Clark located the north magnetic pole. The following year, John Ross's ship, the *Victory*—the first steamship used in the Arctic—was crushed in the ice. John Ross and his men were rescued by a whaler in August 1833 at Lancaster Sound, after a terrible trek south.

The lost expedition

John Franklin ought to have paid closer attention to his compatriots' experiences in the Arctic. He certainly underestimated the difficulties of polar navigation and the fearsome hardships of Arctic winters. In 1845, at the age of fifty-nine, he set off on an ill-fated polar expedition at the helm of the *Erebus*. He died two years later, on 11 June 1847, with his own ship and the *Terror*, under Francis Crozier, stranded in the ice. Never had a disappearance so stirred the public imagination. Rich rewards were of-

fered for information leading to the discovery of Franklin, his crew, and his ships. Throughout the following decade, more than forty expeditions set out to seek the lost Arctic explorers.

After Franklin's death, the 105 surviving crew members agreed that they could not withstand a third polar winter. Abandoning the marooned ships, the men trekked south, hauling lifeboats behind them. But to no avail; all eventually perished on the way. It was not until 1854 that the world learned the fate of the expedition, thanks to evidence gathered from Eskimos and a written message left behind by the survivors before they set out on their ill-starred march south.

Lady Jane

The explorer's wife, Lady Jane, made every effort to obtain help from the British Admiralty, from the United States, and from the Czar of Russia. The numerous search parties launched to rescue Franklin failed to save Sir John and his crew, but they were not fruitless. A generation of explorers gained valuable experience in the Arctic. They

learned to rely on sledges rather than ships to travel over polar ice. Fifty years passed before another attempt was made to cross the murderous Northwest Passage. But other Arctic expeditions investigated the northeast and the northern reaches of Greenland; men also travelled to Antarctica in search of the South Pole.

A turning point in history

In 1870, the year of Wrangel's death, the great northern passage had yet to be discovered. Cook, the most famous explorer of the preceding century, had cast doubt on the very existence of such a passage. Yet the late nineteenth century had a different perspective on virgin territories—no less covetous, certainly, but more orientated towards scientific and economic interests. The new stakes of exploration were scientific prestige and personal or national glory. Before fifty years had passed, the Northeast and Northwest Passages would be conquered; explorers would plant their flags at the poles; and many lives would be lost in attempts to accomplish these exploits.

Sea monsters

Legendary accounts of terrifying sea monsters were supported by fanciful descriptions of 'spouting' aquatic mammals which bumped into ships and sometimes threatened to capsize them. These inoffensive Leviathans, which did not seem to fear men, were found to be a rich source of oil, ivory (whale teeth, walrus tusks), and other valuable products. The hunting of whales and walruses grew so intense that certain species became nearly extinct in less than two centuries.

DEFEATS AND VICTORIES

Crossing the Northeast Passage, proving that it could be done—this feat was accomplished by Baron Nordenskjöld in 1879. As for the Northwest Passage, the early nineteenth century witnessed repeated attempts to make that historic voyage, attempts that exacted a heavy toll in human life. And soon the desire to be first at the North Pole obsessed explorers who travelled to Greenland. Success was not, however, just around the corner.

Captain Sverdrup and his huskies on board the Fram, *during a later voyage to Greenland (1898-1902, see p. 235).*

230

Discovery of the Northeast Passage

———————●———————

The explorers who had paved the way left the glory of actually crossing the Northeast Passage to the Swedish scientist and historian Nils Adolf Erik Nordenskjöld. A number of earlier expeditions had infected him with the 'exploration bug'. He was determined to force his way through the Northeast Passage, and that determination helped him to obtain the means to achieve his ambition.

Aboard the steam-powered *Vega*, accompanied by the *Lena* to the mouth of the river of the same name, Nordenskjöld started out on his epic voyage in July 1878. His theory was based on a recurrent observation noted by earlier explorers, namely that the Arctic Ocean was warmed by the waters of several large rivers that emptied into it from various points on the north Siberian coast. This warming influence made the north Asian portion of the Arctic slower to freeze than one would expect at those latitudes. It should thus be possible, Nordenskjöld reasoned, to navigate in those waters in the autumn, so giving him enough time to make the passage. And indeed this reasoning proved correct, though the Swede was obliged to winter—for 294 days!—a few hundred miles from the Bering Strait. The *Vega*'s scientific staff used the respite to confirm previous observations and to establish contacts with the Chukchis. On 20 July 1879 the *Vega* fired its cannon in triumph to salute the long-awaited crossing. Two days later, Nordenskjöld reached Port clarence, on the Alaskan coast.

Nordenskjöld's return voyage took him around Asia and through the Suez Canal. He was then forty-seven years old. Created baron by King Oskar of Sweden, he was the first to savour an unalloyed victory in the Far North.

Polar fever

———————●———————

The heroic era of polar exploration dawned in the mid-nineteenth century and continued into the early years of the twentieth. In 1853 an American named E.K. Kane set out in search of the Franklin expedition and eventually fetched up in Greenland. His brig, the *Advance*, was frozen in, so the crew made numerous overland treks to find a channel to open water. They explored a vast area before embarking in three large open boats to escape a third winter season. Upon their return, the men spoke with certainty of the existence of open sea at the North Pole.

Isaac I. Hayes, who had travelled with Kane, set out in 1860 aboard the *United States*, a small sailing vessel, intending to reach that 'mythical' open sea. When his boat was marooned in the ice, he covered 2000 kilometres on a dogsledge. Hayes returned convinced that the sea in question was situated not far from the highest latitude which had then been reached, 81° 35' N.

Another American, Captain Charles Francis Hall, attempted to sail as close as possible to the North Pole. His propeller-driven steamship *Polaris*, rigged as a schooner, reinforced and equipped with an icebreaker, was designed to fight its way free to open sea. But the vessel was blocked by the ice-pack and spent the winter imprisoned in its grip. Hall sledged to 83° N but died suddenly on the return trip. The expedition ended in a terrible ordeal for some crew members who had left the ship during the debacle. They drifted on an ice floe for six months between October 1872 and April 1873, and the survivors owed their lives to the hunting prowess of two Eskimos in the party. When the ice raft grew too small to hold them, the men climbed into their small lifeboat and were eventually rescued by a seal hunter. The other seamen of the *Polaris* wintered over; their ship was lost, but fortu-

Having left for the North Pole with Johanssen on 14 March 1895, Nansen dealt with the harsh winter like a true Eskimo: killing bears, dressing in their pelts and building himself a stone hut.

Polar rations

In the Far North no edible plants grow wild, no lemons can be brought aboard ship at ports of call: raw seal meat is the daily ration. One advantage of polar exploration is that food conservation poses no problem. At temperatures of - 40° C, meat stays fresh. Indeed, it becomes so hard that a hungry man should be sure that he has the means to reheat it, or else eat the meat on the spot, the moment it is killed. An old Amerindian staple was frequently used by Arctic and Antarctic explorers: pemmican. Pemmican is a nourishing dried paste of meat, fat and vegetables, which keeps for long periods without danger of spoilage.

Inlandsis

Unlike the polar icecap that covers part of the frigid Arctic Ocean—a flattish layer of frozen seawater several metres thick—*inlandsis*, or 'Inland Ice Sheet', as the immense glacier that blankets Greenland's interior is called, is formed of fresh water and can measure several kilometres in thickness. Composed of layer upon layer of compressed snow, the very thickest glaciers are thousands of years old.

nately the crew was picked up in Melville Bay in July 1873.

What is the Pole?

Is the North Pole land, open sea, or an icecap? In 1880 the answer to this question was still unknown, and many believed that it would be sufficient simply to go and see. The *Jeannette*, a small American ship powered by sail and steam, fitted out by the press magnate James Gordon Bennett, and commanded by George Washington De Long, set out from San Francisco for the Bering Strait, with the intention of pushing as far north as possible. But the ship was soon trapped in ice. After drifting, frozen, for two winters, it was ultimately crushed. The crew abandoned the vessel during the second winter, and a small number managed to reach the coast of Siberia in lifeboats. The *Jeannette*'s unfortunate end is notable in the history of Arctic exploration because of the clue it gave to Fridtjof Nansen, a Norwegian doctor with a lively interest in polar expeditions. In 1884 he learned that portions of De Long's wrecked ship had turned up on the northwestern coast of Greenland, and from this he reasoned that the ice field must drift. Whether it was an icecap or a frozen crown around an open polar sea, if the ice moved, a ship could drift with it, provided that it was uncrushable. With architect Colin Archer, Nansen designed the famous *Fram*, the first ship with a specially conceived hull that rose when squeezed by ice.

Just 400 kilometres from the Pole!

Having found financial backers and a crew, Nansen weighed anchor on 24 June 1893 from Bergen. He steered through the Northeast Passage and was frozen in north

The true conqueror of the Pole: the Eskimo

Inventor of the kayak, the igloo and perhaps of the snowshoe as well; earliest trainer of the sledge dogs that roam the Arctic wastes—the Eskimo gave Arctic explorers the help they needed to succeed, or even merely to survive. But the white man had first to humble himself and accept the Eskimo's lessons. Modern equipment has conquered the poles, but in 1900 only Eskimo techniques allowed Peary, Nansen, and others to carry out their projects. Survival tactics learned in the Arctic were naturally applied at the South Pole too.

The *Fram*

The *Fram* was the first true polar ship, designed by Norwegian architect Colin Archer to Fridtjof Nansen's specifications. After thirty years of service in the Arctic and Antarctic, the vessel was conserved by the Norwegian government, and remains a monument to polar navigation. The three-masted steam-powered schooner, thirty-nine metres long and eleven metres wide, pulled out of Oslo in October 1892. Designed to resist the assaults of polar ice, the *Fram* boasted a hull eighty centimetres thick, armoured with steel plates. The ship's stem could rise up onto portions of the ice field that were not yet frozen solid, break up the ice under its own weight, and thus clear a path. The *Fram* also possessed the most modern electrical equipment then available (a windpump took over from the steam engine when the ship wintered over), a retractable propeller, and a raiseable rudder. It was a mobile polar base.

'The star-spangled banner has been raised over the North Pole'. Peary's famous words inspired countless artists.

of the Lena in eastern Siberia at a latitude of 77° 14' N. Nansen speculated that the drift of the pack ice would carry the *Fram* past the Pole. In fact, he was wrong, but nothing daunted, he resolved to complete the trip on foot. He set out with a single companion, Lieutenant Johanssen, three sledges, thirty dogs, and two kayaks, determined to trek straight ahead to the Pole, and thence to Franz Josef Land. Thanks to their phenomenal courage and resourcefulness—they transformed the kayaks into catamarans to cross open water—and despite a forced wintering, they reached a latitude of 86° 14' N, just four hundred kilometres short of their goal. The two men struggled back to land and a ship gave them passage to Vardö. Meanwhile the *Fram*, under Otto Sverdrup, finally broke free of ice after passing 85° 55' N, and sailed back to Tromsö.

Amundsen makes the Northwest Passage

Before the discovery of the North Pole, the Northwest Passage was finally conquered by the Norwegian explorer Roald Amundsen, who would one day win the race to the South Pole (see p. 241). An Irish explorer, Cmdr. Robert McClure, had proved in 1853 that the passage was continuous, since he travelled it from west to east, from the Bering Strait to Lancaster Sound. But he had a ship on either side of the critical central zone, between Victoria Island and King William Island, and completed the trip by dogsledge. Amundsen was the first to make the passage exclusively by sea.

In 1901 Amundsen (a great admirer of Nansen) decided to try his luck. He purchased a forty-seven-tonne sloop, the *Gjöa*, and fitted it with a fourteen-horsepower engine. He then set out with a crew of six experienced Arctic sailors and enough supplies to last five years. The expedition spent two years at Gjöa Haven, just off the Canadian mainland. The men established excellent relations with the Eskimos and made scientific studies of their surroundings. They purchased extra dogs in the hope of reaching the magnetic pole, but the project was abandoned for lack of time.

In spring 1905 Amundsen was determined to push forward and make the crossing. He had wisely chosen a small ship, for some parts of the passage were exceedingly shallow and a light vessel proved far easier to manoeuvre around the ice floes. On 26 August Amundsen rounded Banks Island, the last island in the northwest archipelago. The bay to the south was thereafter called Amundsen Gulf. It took the party a year to reach the Bering Strait, but the Northwest Passage had finally been conquered. The victory was dedicated to the memory of Sir John Franklin.

To the Pole in a balloon

Around the same time, the Swede Salomon Andrée launched another serious attempt to reach the North Pole—in a balloon. A student of aeronautics, Andrée planned to sail a hot-air balloon from Spitsbergen to the North Pole. Balloon travel, he reckoned, would eliminate many of the difficul-

ties of polar expeditions: heavy sledges, dogs, food supplies, slow progress, and the inevitable hardships of surviving in the ice and snow; with a favourable wind, he hoped that he could make a quick trip of it. Sponsored by Alfred Nobel, King Oskar of Sweden and other wealthy patrons, Andrée made a first attempt in 1896, but was forced to give up for lack of wind. He had another try in 1897: having prepared his base camp and supply drops, he waited for the south wind to rise early in July. After being inflated with hydrogen on the spot, the *Oern* took off, but could not maintain altitude as the atmosphere grew colder. After several short jumps the balloon crashed and Andrée and his two companions decided to head back. But they had not reckoned with the southwesterly drift of the ice field, which caused them to miss the closest landmass. In mid-September they reached White Island and improvised a winter camp. Alas, Andrée was dead by early October, and the others did not long survive him. Their camp site was not found until 1930. At about the same time, in 1895 and 1898, the American Walter Wellmann made two attempts to reach the Pole. He failed, but at least he lived to tell the tale. In 1900, aboard the *Stella Polare*, the Duke of Abruzzi, Prince of Savoy, and Captain Cagni headed north to Franz Josef Land. In the manner of mountaineers, the expedition proceeded in several stages, with intermediate bases set up in between. When the duke's frostbitten fingers had to be amputated, he yielded his place as the head of the group to Cagni, who led them to 86° 34' N, thus beating the record set by Nansen. The party struggled back to the ship with great difficulty.

The race to the North Pole

Peary against Cook: the two men raced each other to reach the North Pole in 1909, just as Amundsen and Scott would later compete to be first at the South Pole. Twenty years of methodical training, of acclimatization, of imitating survival techniques learned from the Eskimos of northern Greenland—these gave the American explorer Robert Peary invaluable experience for his conquest of the icy Arctic wastes. This unique experience counterbalanced Peary's relatively advanced age (he was born in 1856) at the time of his final—and victorious—effort to reach the Pole.

In 1897, after the creation of the 'Peary Arctic Club', which was organized to collect funds to support the expedition and to pro-

Frederick Cook set out for the North Pole in 1907, on an expedition which only he and two of his Eskimo companions would survive. When they returned in April 1909, Cook contested Peary's victory, claiming to have reached the Pole on 21 April 1908.

233

mote the explorer's achievement upon his return, Peary was convinced that his mission in life was to raise the star-spangled banner at the North Pole. Each preliminary expedition took him farther north and taught him how to improve his methods for the next trip. Throughout, Peary was accompanied by Matthew Henson, a black American who was highly accomplished in the disciplines vital for Arctic survival (dog driving, orientation, the use of skis and snowshoes), and whose friendship for Peary was equalled only by his remarkable stamina and endurance.

Ever closer to the Pole

Unlike earlier explorers, who had tried to approach the Pole by sailing throughout the summer, Peary, who had chosen to travel over the ice, used to set out in early spring to have a better trail and, above all, sufficient time to return before the break-up of the ice field. He arrived at his base before winter set in. He and his men hunted and stored up food at numerous supply points, before undergoing the terrible rigours and hardships of the polar winter. Having worn out his first ship, the *Windward*, Peary had the *Theodore Roosevelt* built, a three-masted schooner equipped with a one-thousand-horsepower engine and a strongly reinforced, double-framed hull capable of weathering several polar winters. With his new ship, Peary decided in 1906 to push north of Ellesmere Island as far as 82° N, which would be his point of departure for the Pole. But once again Peary fell short of his goal: he merely beat Cagni's record for reaching the highest northern latitude (Peary reached 87° 6' N). But he would surely have perished without the support of his Eskimo companions, and had he not decided to travel quickly to Greenland rather than try to reach his ship, which was still stranded in the pack ice. In Greenland the men regained their strength before setting off again to find the ship.

In 1909 Peary made a last push for the Pole, aware that at his age he would have no more chances. But this final attempt was successful, despite the competition of Frederick A. Cook, an American veteran of the Arctic who had crossed Greenland with Peary. He had set out a year earlier 'to steal his Pole' from Peary, and returned just days before the elder man to dispute his victory and to claim for himself the distinction of having been the first man on the 'roof of the world'. The matter went all the way to court, and though some may have harboured doubts about the exact time of Peary's arrival at the geographical pole, most were sure that Cook had cheated at least a little, or was deluded by his own ambition.

Peary had once more organized his trek with impressive thoroughness. Seventeen men, including a dozen Eskimos, marched towards their goal with 133 dogs and twelve sledges. Only six—four Eskimos, Matt Henson, and Peary—would have the privilege of actually standing at the top of the world. On 6 April they arrived, exhausted, and remained at the North Pole for thirty hours to savour their triumph before the relatively short but excruciating ordeal of their return.

During this time Cook did his utmost to discredit Peary. While in the end Cook was generally believed to have lied, it seems that Peary's allegations against Cook were not totally justified.

Who conquered the Pole?

Despite the controversy—still not entirely over—stirred up by Cook's objections and accusations, experts on the question award the (moral) victory to Peary, although he lacked the means to take an absolute reading of his position. At the conclusion of an in-depth study of Peary's notes, the Navigation Foundation, sponsored by the National Geographic Society, determined that his final position was in fact five miles from the exact geographical pole. Cook, who had set out a year before Peary and asserted that he had reached the Pole first, put forward dubious claims and questionable surveys. Verifications made possible by modern instruments have corroborated Peary's observations: in particular, his estimation of the depth of the Arctic Ocean at the Pole has been confirmed. The expedition led by the Englishman Wally Herbert in 1969 was the only one to reproduce Peary's exploit with dogsledges.

Greenland: hell frozen over

In 1869 Bismarck dispatched two German ships, the *Hansa* and the *Germania*, to explore the eastern coast of Greenland. The mission was beset by difficulties. The *Hansa* was lost early on, crushed by ice. A fearsome winter followed, and an arduous return: the crew were forced to pilot small lifeboats along the frigid coast. The men of the *Germania* made several treks north by sledge, and found camps of Eskimos living as humans must have done in the Stone Age.

In 1875 two British vessels, the *Alert* and the *Discovery*, reached the northernmost point ever attained by ship (82° 24' N) or by sledge (83° 7' N, and later 83° 20'23'' N; in other words, just 740 kilometres from the Pole). Having reached that latitude, the leader of the sledge party, Captain Albert Hastings Markham, was obliged to abandon any notion of pushing further, for they were on the brink of utter exhaustion. Their ships wintered over for eleven months before sailing back to Portsmouth on 2 November 1876. The leader of the expedition, George Nares, was knighted for his courage.

In 1881 an American mission conducted by Lieutenant Greely was instructed to establish a polar base in Robeson Strait on the coast of Ellesmere Island. A ship, the *Proteus*, put the men ashore with dogs, a steam-powered sloop, and some rowing boats. The following summer, having failed to sight the *Proteus*, Greely determined to head back south. It was a tragic journey: only six of the twenty-four men survived; the coffins sent back home held partially devoured corpses...

Alone in the Northwest

In 1977 Willy de Roos of the Netherlands re-enacted Roald Amundsen's crossing of the Northwest Passage in a light boat. At the age of fifty-three, he made most of the voyage alone aboard a thirteen-metre steel ketch (the Dutchman's prickly character quickly discouraged his sole shipmate, who took the first opportunity to go ashore). Willy de Roos had prepared for the expedition with meticulous care, and completed the voyage in just three months, thus escaping the Arctic winter. He was helped by favourable weather and excellent meteorological information, but de Roos's chief aid was his own will, apparently forged of the same metal as his ketch, the *Williwaw*.

The ethnologist Paul-Emile Victor was the instigator of the French polar expeditions. From 1947 onwards, he organized a large number of scientific missions to Greenland and Adélie Land.

In 1875, the commander of the Alert, *George Nares, dispatched a group of officers and seamen to make their way to the North Pole. Here, the exhausted expedition makes camp before finally reaching 83° 20' 23" North.*

The discovery of frozen wastes

———●———

The men who explored Greenland's interior journeyed over the glacier on snowshoes and skis, behind sledges pulled by dogs, in the Eskimo fashion. Dogs alone could take men over long distances: suited to the climate and bred for endurance, they were fed on game hunted from day to day, or else they were killed in their turn and fed to their yokemates as the sledge's load grew lighter. In 1888, before embarking on his famous expedition aboard the *Fram*, Nansen crossed Greenland on skis from east to west, before it was known that Greenland was an island. From 1898 to 1902, Otto Sverdrup, aboard the same ship, explored completely the northern part of the Arctic archipelago. In the last decade of the nineteenth century, Otto Nordenskjöld, the nephew of the hero of the Northeast Passage, studied greenland's interior.

The Danish-Eskimo Knud Rasmussen completed that exploration, and founded the Thule outpost in 1910. In the course of numerous treks by dogsledge, he demonstrated the soundness of the Eskimos' survival tactics. Rasmussen preceded another famous explorer, Paul-Emile Victor, who spent several winters in 1934-7 among the Angmassalik and later in Lapland, before his appointment (1947-76) as director of French Polar Expeditions in Greenland and Antarctica.

An aristocratic cruise

———●———

The Belgian nobleman Count Adrien de Gerlache, owner of the polar ship *Belgica* built especially for Arctic navigation, had already completed one successful voyage from 1877 to 1879. Duke Philippe d'Orléans, better known as a world-class big-game hunter than as a scholar or explorer, brought de Gerlache back into action in 1905, accompanied by a cosmopolitan crew, for a cruise between Spitsbergen and Greenland. In addition to a few geographic and climatological observations (much to the party's credit), the duke returned from his travels with an impressive hunting tally of seals, walruses, narwhals and birds, not to mention twelve bear skins and two captive cubs...

Killed for an impossible cause

———●———

Tragedy marked the final stage of the exploration of Greenland. Denmark, which had ruled the island since 1814, sent out a mission in 1906/7 to reconnoitre the northeastern coast. The aim was to prove that Peary Land was not an island, and that it was attached to Danish territory and thus fell under Denmark's dominion.

Despite infinite precautions—the preparation of supply drops, the creation of several independent teams, the use of dogs, —the expedition's head group led by Mylius Erichsen, with instructions to push as far north as possible, exhausted itself trekking round fjords in order to map the coastline. As the ice melted in the Arctic summer, it turned into free-flowing channels that made the return journey a fatal nightmare from which the exhausted, starving men never awoke.

235

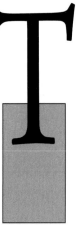

he ancient Greeks suspected the existence of a frozen continent, called it anti-arktos, *or 'opposite (the northern constellation of) the Bear'. But it was not until the eighteenth and nineteenth centuries that the island outposts of Antarctica were discovered. Sailors, sealers and whalers from many nations believed that these lands might be a new El Dorado, perhaps even a new, easy route to the East...*

Residents of Antarctica

Except for a small number of human beings (the first of whom wandered there lost and horror-struck, the most recent of them on exploratory or scientific missions) the only warm-blooded inhabitants of the desolate Antarctic wastes are marine mammals — whales, dolphins, seals and sea lions — and a few birds, including the extraordinary penguin. Walruses, seals and penguins live in large colonies, feeding on marine life, and occupying the narrow seaboard during the Antarctic spring and summer.

Geographical symmetry

Among the first navigators to approach the South Pole was Francis Drake, who in 1579 was caught in a gale off Tierra del Fuego and came into view of the scattered islets off the Antarctic peninsula. Other early visitors included Dirck Gherritz, blown off course to 64° S in 1599, as he tried to cross the Strait of Magellan, and Le Maire, who discovered Cape Horn in 1615. Pierre Paulmier de Gonneville claimed to have discovered in these latitudes an 'island of parrots', which fired many a navigator's imagination, until such an island was found at a more northerly position, far from eternal ice and emperor penguins.

A century and a half later navigators again showed interest in the legendary southern continent, the counterpart to Europe and Asia in the northern hemisphere. Eighteenth-century seamen confirmed the existence of uninhabitable lands, but it was not until the twentieth century that anyone risked staying in so hostile an environment.

The search for Terra Australis

In the meantime, most of the navigators who had ventured into these waters, spurred either by curiosity or by dreams of conquest, had been repelled by the fearsome roaring winds that prevail in the latitudes between 40° and 60° S — by storms, snow, sleet, wind and fog, to say nothing of waves that licked the upper reaches of a ship's rigging.

In 1738 Jean-Baptiste Bouvet de Lozier was cruising in waters south of the Cape of Good Hope. Around 55° S he sighted a landmass, which he christened Circumcision Cape, in honour of the day's liturgical feast. Today his discovery is known as Bouvet Island, which is situated some thousand miles from Antarctica. In 1772, south of New Zealand, Marion-Dufresne sighted a volcanic archipelago inhabited by penguins, but before he could explore it, the unfortunate navigator was devoured by Maoris along with his lieutenant, Crozet, and fifteen of his men (see p. 163). Captain James Cook later named two of the group's larger islets in honour of these unfortunate French officers. Cook's wide-ranging explorations in the South Pacific convinced him that no southern continent existed in the zone between 40° and 50° S, and that if a continent indeed lay farther south than 71° S, where pack ice had halted his progress, it would be covered with ice.

Kerguelen's error

In 1772 Yves de Kerguelen-Trémarec, commander of the *Fortune* and *Gros-ventre*, believed that he had made an important discovery when he reached the islands that today bear his name (see p. 153). Upon his return to France Kerguelen claimed that he had found the long-sought Terra Australis, and quickly raised the capital needed for another voyage. Yet he came back from the expedition empty-handed. He was accused and found guilty of deception, but was later pardoned, since the Kerguelen Archipelago was undeniably a useful port of call and the region abounded in fish.

James Cook, first Antarctic navigator

From 1772 to 1775, aboard the *Resolution* and accompanied by the *Adventure*, James Cook voyaged south from the Cape of Good Hope to Tierra del Fuego. He went a few hundred miles more to the south, reaching South Georgia, beyond the Falkland Islands. Cook was convinced that only inhospitable lands lay farther south, and that it was pointless to dream of an El Dorado in those high latitudes. From his voyage in the far South Pacific, he gathered important information about populations of mammals such as whales, walruses, seals and sea lions. For the time being, it was concluded that — with the exception of whalers and sealers — navigators would be foolish to risk life, limb and property amongst the icebergs of a hypothetical continent that obviously offered neither the spices that merchants hoped for, nor the 'noble savages' that philosophers longed to find on the supposed Terra Australis Incognita.

Whalers were for many years the only seamen willing to make incursions into the Far South; in so doing, they paved the way for later explorations.

Pioneers of the Antarctic

A century later, in 1819 and 1820, Fabian von Bellingshausen, a German baron from the Baltic in the service of Czar Alexander I, brilliantly circumnavigated Antarctica with the *Vostok* and the *Mirny*. He discovered Peter Island, named after Czar Peter the Great, and the larger Alexander Island, christened in honour of his patron. At a latitude of 69° 25' S, in January 1820 — at the height of the southern summer — Bellingshausen sighted the Antarctic continent, but did not recognize it. In fact, the first to set foot on the extreme north of Antarctica were the Englishmen William Smith, who took possession of the South Shetland Islands for the British Crown in 1820, and Edward Bransfield, who gave his name to a peak he sighted. A few months later the American whaler Nathaniel Palmer reached Antarctica and claimed to have been the first to discover a continent more immense than anyone had yet imagined.

In 1822-4, James Weddell, aboard a British sealer, descended to very high latitudes—he reached 74° 15' S, quite close to the magnetic pole—and sailed through the open waters of the sea that bears his name. The weather conditions there are such that oceanographic exploration of the Weddell sea could not start before the twentieth century and are still under way. At the southern end of that sea, scientists have discovered a perpetually frozen bay, with an area comparable to that of France, bordered by the Filchner Ice Shelf, a sheer cliff of solid ice one hundred metres high, with a frontage of eight hundred kilometres. The American sealer John Biscoe was also a pioneer of Antarctic surveying; he gave his name to an island. Professional explorers did not begin to write the history of the frozen continent until the 1830s.

For France and his lady

In 1837 the Frenchman Jules Dumont d'Urville, sponsored by several learned societies, obtained from King Louis-Philippe the warships *Astrolabe* and *Zélée*, together with orders for an ambitious mission in the Far South. He was to explore Antarctic waters, attempt to approach the south magnetic pole, and carry out a variety of geographical observations in the Pacific (see p. 169). Dumont d'Urville embarked in 1838. He was the first to set foot on the actual continent of Antarctica, after sailing along and studying the peninsula which earlier parties had already explored. Navigating due south from Australia, in January 1840 at 66° 30' S Dumont d'Urville came upon the land he christened Adélie, in honour of his wife.

A Franco-American encounter

Backed by American President John Quincy Adams and spurred on by pressure from the whaling industry, naval officer Charles Wilkes put together an expedition composed of a motley flotilla of five ships, two of which were utterly unsuited to polar navigation. He set out in 1838, planning to explore the Weddell Sea, but was forced to turn back, reduce his party, and target a new objective: the very same one that the

During Dumont d'Urville's expedition to Adélie Land (1838-9), the Astrolabe *and the* Zélée *are caught in the pack ice.*

French were seeking. Wilkes overtook Dumont d'Urville's expedition, but his imagination must have got the better of him when he 'sighted' a landmass that was later proven to lie three hundred miles farther south; Wilkes may simply have wished to report a sighting before his French rival. The French and American ships passed within signalling distance of each other, but the messages were misinterpreted on both sides. Some time later, Wilkes did find ice-covered land, now called Wilkes Land, west of Adélie Land. He also surveyed more than two thousand kilometres of Antarctic coastline, confirming the existence of a vast polar continent. Many crew members deserted in the course of the excruciating voyage. Those who were found were brought before a court martial, but were later reinstated. Wilkes himself was promoted to the rank of admiral.

Scientific contributions

James Clark Ross, nephew of John, was no newcomer to polar exploration. He had accompanied his uncle to the Arctic, and had reached the north magnetic pole; he had also taken part in several of Parry's expeditions to verify German theories of terrestrial magnetism. Physicist Karl Gauss and geographer F.H. von Humboldt had produced models for variations in the intensity and localization of the planet's magnetic fields, and expressed the hypothesis that there is a separation between the location of the dipole poles (of the terrestrial magnetic field) and the geomagnetic poles.

In 1840, astonished to learn that French and American teams had beaten him to the zone he had announced his wish to explore, Ross took note of their observations and set

Penguins

Penguins do not fly—they waddle along on land, while in the sea they swim and dive with remarkable agility and speed. Unlike seals and sea lions, which in freezing temperatures plunge into the relatively warm sea (around O °C), penguins have an especially efficient mechanism that regulates their body temperature by transforming fat (stored in their tissues during periods of intense feeding) into heat. When they return from these gorging sessions, literally stuffed with fish, the penguins are so fat that oil accounts for nearly twenty-five percent of their body weight (a far higher proportion than seals or whales). That kind of yield naturally attracted hunters...

In 1902 the German five-master Preussen *was the biggest in the class of long-distance sailing ships whose voyages took them round Cape Horn.*

Erebus and Terror

Two volcanoes—one active, the other dormant—stand nearly 3800 metres high over the fantastic landscape of Ross Island, the landmass that borders McMurdo Sound, west of the great Ross Ice Shelf. They were a daunting sight for the crews of the *Erebus* and the *Terror*, commanded by James Ross Clark, after which the volcanoes were named.

out from Tasmania on an easterly course for New Zealand, and thence due south to Antarctica. Ross himself commanded the triple-masted *Erebus*, while the second ship, the *Terror*, sailed under Captain Crozier. Both were stout vessels, capable of pushing through pack ice, and were manned by experienced crews. Ross penetrated without undue difficulty into the continent's second deep indentation, now known as the Ross Sea. On turning southwest, he sighted the mountainous landscape of Victoria Land in January 1841 and reached a latitude of 77° 10' S, beating all previous records.

The Ross Ice Shelf

McMurdo Sound, named after the first mate of the *Terror*, served both as an entry point for many an Antarctic expedition and as a site for scientific observation bases. Like the Weddell Sea, the end of the sound is covered by an immense glacier, the face of which is a high cliff called the Ross Ice Shelf. Dominating the site are two volcanoes—an impressive presence in an all-white world; Ross named them Mt Erebus and Mt Terror in honour of his two ships. He headed back to Australia, only to set out again the following year, determined to sail around the ice shelf. Although he was finally obliged to admit defeat, Ross pushed farther south

than his predecessors, to a latitude of 78° 9' S.

When Ross sailed from the Falklands for his third campaign, intending to continue Weddell's route along the coast of Graham Land on the Antarctic Peninsula, he was checked by the early arrival of winter. He abandoned his project in 1843, having failed to achieve his dream of being the first man to reach both the north and the south magnetic poles. Nevertheless, together with Dumont d'Urville and Wilkes, in his five years of exploration in the Antarctic Ross had contributed immeasurably to knowledge of nearly half the circumference of what had up until that time been terra incognita. But for the next fifty years, international interest in Antarctica waned, while interest in the North Pole grew stronger.

Whalers and explorers

Whale oil, seal oil, even penguin oil, skins, a little ivory (walrus tusks, whale teeth)—in the late nineteenth century the prospect of this bloody but profitable booty continued to lure rare, intrepid souls to the freezing waters of the Antarctic. Some whaling captains even showed an inclination for environmental studies: they took careful surveys of the waters they sailed, and passed the information on to governments and colleagues. The Norwegian Carl A. Larsen,

captain of the whaler *Jason*, returned from the Far South with rocks containing fossils of conifers and ferns, which proved that the Antarctic climate had varied in the course of geological time. Lars Christensen, aboard the *Antarctic*, demonstrated that the ice field could be circumnavigated, provided that a vessel managed to hug the coastline closely.

Before any expedition could hope to reach the South Pole, suitable winter quarters had to be found, which would offer ships and men some protection from the elements. As ever, successive 'failed' campaigns provided essential information and paved the way for future triumphs.

A Belgian, a Swede...

The Belgian aristocrat Adrien de Gerlache was no novice, though he was not a professional explorer. He offered to take part in a Scandinavian expedition and to spend the winter in the Antarctic. When no invitation ensued, de Gerlache launched a sponsorship campaign, found patrons, and fitted out his own three-master, the *Belgica*, for a polar expedition. He set sail in August 1897 for the Antarctic Peninsula with a small team of scientists. As fate would have it, his second lieutenant was Roald Amundsen, and his ship's surgeon Frederick Cook. The mission was to make numerous meteorological, zoological and hydrographic observations; it was also the first to winter over in a ship in the Graham Land ice field, from March 1898 to March 1899.

Otto Nordenskjöld, nephew of Baron Nordensjköld, author of the Northeast Passage exploit, set sail in 1902 aboard the *Antarctic* under the command of whaling captain C.A. Larsen. The expedition had a double objective: Nordenskjöld and his five companions would travel and winter over on land (in a shelter they carried with them to assemble on site), then journey south by dogsledge; Larsen's brief was to sail north and search for additional inland waterways. But the vessel was trapped and crushed in the ice of the Weddell Sea in February 1903. The crew abandoned ship and established improvised winter quarters on Paulet Island, but could not keep the rendezvous with Nordenskjöld's team. In November 1903, by an extraordinary chance, all were rescued by an Argentine vessel. As it pulled into the port of Buenos Aires a month later, a little three-masted schooner dubbed the *Français* was about to carry Jean-Baptiste Charcot to the same lands from which they had—only just—escaped.

The British, the Germans...

Around the same time, an ambitious, heavily equipped British expedition embarked aboard the *Discovery*, a ship designed especially for polar exploration, under Captain Robert Falcon Scott. In the course of the campaign, techniques would be perfected that Scott would use later on his tragic expedition to the South Pole. He refused to employ the technique of dog-sledging whereby the weaker animals were killed and fed to the stronger—he preferred manpower for his sledges. He also used anchored balloons to mark routes and topographical features. Scott carefully prepared food depots before advancing far inland onto a high plateau, beyond the Ross Barrier to 82° 17' S, some eight hundred kilometres from the Pole. He was accompanied by Ernest Henry Shackleton, who would later go down in the annals of Antarctic exploration (see p. 240). On this occasion Scott remained in Antarctica for three years, from 1901 to 1904.

In 1902 a German expedition led by Erich Drygalski aboard the *Gauss*, a polar ship modelled on the *Fram*, travelled due south from the Kerguelen Islands to raise Kaiser Wilhelm's colours over the portion of Antarctica that abuts the Indian Ocean.

Charcot for France

Charcot's first expedition to the Far South from 1903 to 1905 aboard the *Français* drew amiably condescending comments from hardened explorers like Scott. In truth, Charcot's cruise along the western coast of Graham Land (including nine months spent in winter quarters and a near-shipwreck) produced more accurate maps for some five hundred kilometres of coastline, and gave crew members experience in the fearsome conditions of Antarctic exploration. Charcot set out a second time in 1908 aboard the *Pourquoi Pas?*, a legendary polar ship that gave nearly thirty years of service in the worst possible cold and winds, until the day in September 1936 when that doughty vessel sank in the North Atlantic with its captain (then seventy years old) and crew. The solid-oak ship cost a small fortune to build, but Charcot had little difficulty enlisting sponsors after his first voyage, which had gratified French national honour. A three-master with a five-hundred-horsepower engine constructed at the Gautier shipyard in St-Malo, the forty-metre vessel had a highly reinforced stem and waterline,

double-planked on both sides of the frame. It was swift, manoeuvrable, and could be managed by a small crew; it also boasted modern amenities and the most sophisticated instruments available. The *Pourquoi Pas?* long remained the model for polar ships intended for exploring in open water or zones of thin ice.

The last great reconnaissance missions

By December 1908 Charcot was back at the point where he had interrupted his previous expedition. In the course of two campaigns, he explored new coastal zones, amassed significant scientific data, and gave his name to a newly discovered island. With the exception of Wilhelm Filchner's 1911-13 odyssey into the unknown reaches of the Weddell Sea, Charcot's was the last of the great reconnaissance missions in Antarctica before the Great War. Antarctica had yet to be declared neutral territory—the property of all mankind, a privileged site for scientific study and a major ecological asset.

A frozen hell

In contrast to the Arctic, which is essentially a frozen ocean, the Antarctic Ocean forms an icy belt that surrounds a platform of palaeozoic rock interspersed with mountainous folds of Tertiary rock and large volcanic massifs; it measures fourteen million square kilometres, double the area of Australia. Because of the difficulties caused by icebergs, pack ice, and recurrent debacles (of ice), only in the last few decades has it been possible to probe and analyse satellite pictures, draw conclusions from recent research on the geological structure of rock slabs, and produce precise maps of the continent. Antarctica is covered by a glacier, parts of which are up to four thousand metres thick, but the average elevation of the land above sea level is far lower.

On the high plateau the climate is incredibly harsh. Temperatures vary between −25 and −70 °C in July and August, and between −10 and −35 °C in the high-summer month of January. A glacial wind—which can reach 300 km/h—sweeps the plateau, occasionally reaching speeds of three hundred kilometres per hour.

Jean Charcot (centre) and Paul-Emile Victor (left) on board the Pourquoi Pas? *in 1936. Later that year the ship sank, killing his captain and crew.*

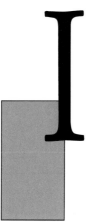

n 1911 the Norwegian Roald Amundsen reached the South Pole. From the middle years of this century, ever more well-equipped, amply funded scientific expeditions have set out for Antarctica. Several nations have claimed territories in the continent. By the terms of the Antarctic Treaty signed in 1959, these nations pledge mutually to promote research in the south polar regions.

A last-minute rescue

In 1901, during his first Antarctic expedition, Captain Robert Falcon Scott sent Ernest Shackleton home to England for health reasons. The latter swore he would have his revenge, and be the first man at the South Pole. Backed by an industrialist called Beardmore, whose name is forever commemorated by a gigantic Antarctic glacier, Shackleton embarked in 1907 aboard the *Nimrod*, a stout old sealer.

To avoid the cruel necessity of having to kill sledge dogs en route, Shackleton decided to use Siberian ponies to haul men and supplies. But although ponies can pull heavy loads and eat less than dogs in proportion to their weight, they require plants in their diet and cannot feed on their dead fellows. Nor can ponies withstand blizzards, since they are incapable of curling up in the snow like dogs. In short, ponies are fragile animals, and Shackleton's decision to use them was most unwise; inexplicably, Scott made the same ill-considered choice in 1911. Shackleton set out with a dual aim. During the climb up the glacier to the Ross

plateau, the leading group travelled with the second team, which included Australian scientist Edgeworth David and Douglas Mawson. But once upon the plateau, they were to split, the leading group making for the geographical pole and the other party for the magnetic pole. The second group completed their mission successfully.

Scott refused Shackleton access to his base at McMurdo Sound. The latter then decided to build his own base in the Bay of Whales, but it was still frozen in January 1908 and the *Nimrod* could not get close to the land. So they finally landed close to Scott's base. Situated east of the Ross Ice Shelf, the Bay of Whales was closer to his destination, a fact that Amundsen would later keep in mind. After an exhausting trek, which had brought them to 88° 23' S by 9 January 1909, Shackleton had the courage to renounce his aim and turn back, though he was just ninety-seven miles from the Pole. He did this to give himself and his worn-out men a chance, however slim, to keep their rendezvous with the *Nimrod*, and thus avoid certain death. The ship was scheduled to set sail on 1 March at the very latest, to escape being frozen in, leaving Shackleton's group very little time to reach it. Indeed the ship had already withdrawn, though not very far, when someone aboard spotted smoke from a hut that the desperate Shackleton, with no other means to signal his position, had set on fire. For all his efforts, his sole personal accomplishment was to have beaten the standing record for reaching the highest southern latitude.

Amundsen conquered the South Pole in 1911. He died at the North Pole in 1928 while attempting to rescue the Italian explorer Nobile.

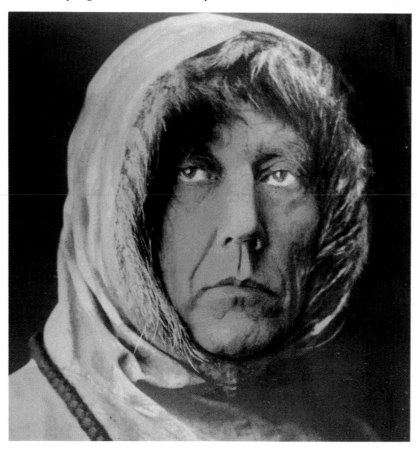

A detour through the southern hemisphere

Around the same time, Roald Amundsen was preparing to set sail aboard Nansen's *Fram* with the intention of reaching the

North Pole by drifting with the ice field. But considering Peary's successful journey and Cook's allegations, the Norwegian discreetly changed his plans and headed south instead. He would in any case have to sail around South America to reach the Bering Strait (the Panama Canal did not yet exist); and after all, he could change his course as he liked, for he was sole master of the *Fram*. Amundsen advised Scott of his intentions with a brief message during a stop-over, by which time it was unlikely that anyone would attempt to dissuade him. He acquired a number of sledge dogs, and planned his expedition in minute and rigorous detail (he had learned much about polar survival from the Eskimos of the Canadian Arctic). In January 1911 Amundsen set up winter quarters near the Bay of Whales, at Framheim east of the Ross Ice Shelf. Scott, who had rushed ahead, had just pitched camp at McMurdo.

Throughout the month of March, Amundsen established large supply depots at 80°, 81°, and 82° S. He set out for his destination with four comrades and forty-two dogs to haul three sledges.

The victors

Amundsen's group left their base on 20 October 1911 after a false start in September, which had barely missed ending in catastrophe. In November, the explorers had made their way to 85° S and were only six hundred miles from their goal. They made steady, regular progress; their major difficulty was to scale the crevassed, windy Axel Heiberg glacier to a plateau 3200 metres above sea level. The Norwegians advanced, with infinite precaution, keeping one another in view or roping themselves together. On 7 December they reached a higher latitude than Shackleton had done, and arrived at the South Pole a week later. Having taken and verified all the necessary astronomical readings, and raised the Norwegian flag, the men savoured their success. Jubilant, they photographed each other, and pitched a tent which they dubbed 'Polheim'—Pole House. Inside they placed letters for Scott and for the King of Norway, as well as copies of their notes, in case misfortune should befall them on the return journey. Their burden far lighter (they left much of their equipment behind), the Norwegians reached Framheim and the waiting *Fram* in just forty-one days. They soon sailed homeward, their place in history assured. By the time they fetched up in Tasmania, Scott's polar nightmare was coming to a tragic end.

In 1910 Scott embarked his men, ponies, dogs and equipment on the Terra Nova. *He himself joined the expedition in South Africa.*

Unwise choices

From the moment that Scott—a man dogged by a history of near-successes, wounds to his pride, and financial disasters—received the telegram apprising him of Amundsen's intention to reach the Pole, he speeded up his own preparations. First off the mark aboard the whaler *Terra Nova* and convinced that his scientifically ambitious expedition to the South Pole would go down in history, Scott began his journey in earnest on 7 January 1911. He organized his teams of observers (including geophysicists, naturalists and meteorologists) and carefully prepared the details of his trek.

Less realistic than his Norwegian rival, Scott failed to draw the proper conclusions from previous experiences in Antarctica. Shackleton's ponies had not withstood polar conditions, where dogs were in their element. Scott decided to employ a combination of snow tractors, dogs and ponies, reserving the latter for use by the leading group. In the end the ponies died and men were obliged to haul the sledges, a task that fatally sapped their strength. Although the best technique for making steady progress was to follow a route marked out with food supplies and aid stations, Scott preferred the caravan system, in which teams were sent back as they weakened or proved no longer useful. He failed to take into account the one hundred extra miles added to the journey by setting out from McMurdo. For that additional distance he ought to have planned on more supplies and more time, increased fatigue, and greater risk—even without possible blizzards. For all these reasons, Scott's mission met its gruesome end, a cruel human and scientific failure.

The Pole's first victims

On 1 November 1911 Scott's convoy moved forward: in quick succession tractors broke down and the ten ponies failed. A month later, the long pull up the Beardmore glacier commenced. It is 160 kilometres long, a daunting distance to cross for men hauling sledges. For on 12 December Scott sent back the two dogsledge teams, followed by two more teams and more sledges, so that

Warming alert

Studies of the upper atmosphere have revealed that the ozone layer, a buffer that protects the Earth from ultraviolet radiation harmful to life on the planet, has thinned above the North and South Poles. At these points, it appears to be more drastically depleted than in other regions. Chlorofluorocarbons (CFCs) have been implicated and most industrialized countries have forbidden their production.

The progressive warming of the Earth's atmosphere attributed to the build-up of 'greenhouse' gases (especially carbon dioxide) also threatens to disturb the delicate balance between the melting and refreezing of Antarctica's vast inland glacier; such a shift would certainly alter the extent and volume of the ice pack. It is now known that evaporation in warmer zones would not compensate for the melting of polar ice, since water always flows to the sea; a one-metre rise in the ocean level would pose a critical threat to low-lying coastal regions.

The faces of Scott (standing, centre) and his men are tense and serious as they pose for the last time before beginning their tragic return journey. Scott has just found the letters left behind for him in a tent by Amundsen.

International Years

In order to gather together the knowledge of the Poles acquired over the preceding fifty years, the second International Polar Year was declared from August 1932 to August 1933. Nations organized synchronized observations at their northern and southern polar stations, working on common projects (studies of the atmosphere, magnetism, solar radiation, meteorology) and comparing their results in a spirit of international cooperation.

The International Geophysical Year, declared in 1957-8, also produced an extraordinary wealth of information and helped the world scientific community to establish closer contacts. The Year concluded with the signing of the Antarctic Treaty, which has so far preserved the southern continent for peaceful scientific research.

by 4 January 1912 there remained but one sledge, Scott, and four comrades, Dr. Wilson, lieutenant H.R. Bowers, lieutenant L.E.G. Oates and Edgar Evans. Their trek quickly degenerated into a nightmare, but they pushed on, grimly determined to raise Britain's flag at the Pole. The men already knew that they would not be the first team at the site, for they were following a track marked out by their victorious Norwegian rivals.

Scott's return from the Pole was a gruesome journey indeed. On 18 January he saw with his own eyes positive proof of his defeat—the testimony left by Amundsen's party was a crushing blow. Worse, the Englishmen's supplies were short and their spirits at a very low ebb. Two of the five perished in quick succession. Scott and two companions carried on for a time, but finally they too succumbed to starvation and cold. The following November Robert Falcon Scott's comrades from the McMurdo base discovered the frozen corpses of the three explorers less than twenty kilometres from a large food depot they had set out for them. They also found Scott's journal, the last entry dated 29 March 1912, in which he explained his failure by a run of uncommonly bad luck...

Odyssey in an open boat

In 1914 Ernest Shackleton set forth to cross Antarctica via the South Pole, from the Weddell Sea to the Ross Sea, a daring exploit destined to redeem Britain's honour and make up for the tragedy of Scott's disastrous mission. No aspect of the expedition turned out as planned, but Shackleton acquitted himself honourably, without losing a single man, after a staggering odyssey in an open boat.

On 16 January 1915 Shackleton's ship, the *Endurance*, was caught in early-forming pack ice. He had no choice but to make improvised winter quarters, and hunt for food. The party drifted slowly westward. During the debacle the ship was crushed, and sank; three open boats, some equipment, and supplies were saved. The party of twenty-eight men hoped to reach Paulet Island, first by hauling the craft behind them, then by drifting on polar ice, and finally by rowing or sailing. However, they eventually landed on Elephant Island. Shackleton did not wish to subject his men to the risks of wintering and famine. He

therefore embarked alone in the largest boat (a 6.70-metre launch) in a courageous attempt to reach a whaling base in South Georgia, eight hundred miles distant. He fetched up there on 20 May 1916. There he chartered four boats and finally rescued his comrades with the help of a Chilean tug, on 25 August, in the very heart of the austral winter.

Except for the 1912-13 voyage of the Australian explorer Douglas Mawson to George V Land near the Adélie Coast, an adventure that concluded with Mawson's heroic return and the deaths of his two companions, the era of perilous polar expeditions had come to a close, yielding to an age of scientific and technical exploits.

On the subject of pre-World War I competition for the exploration and appropriation of virgin land, the geologist Raymond Priestly, a personal acquaintance of the three great heroes of Antarctic exploration, had this to say: 'To head a scientific expedition, take Scott; for a fast, efficient polar trek, take Amundsen; but in adversity, in a desperate situation, pray that they send you Shackleton.' His words are as eloquent for what they leave unstated as for what they actually say.

Scientific exploration

The last heroic explorations of Antarctica, if one excludes contemporary treks, such as the recent Transantarctica of Jean-Louis Etienne, were made in the air over the South Pole. The earliest aeroplanes used at the Pole were built in the 1920s. They were fitted with runners and capable of carrying equipment and a technician to make repairs. The pilots' objective was not simply to fly over the Pole, but rather to make scientific observations, geographical surveys, and systematic photographic records.

Given the hostile Antarctic environment, aeroplanes and (later) satellites have proved to be the most efficient means of reconnoitring the continent's icy wastes.

The first men over the South Pole in a plane were the Alaskan bush pilot C.B. Eielson and the Australian pilot Hubert Wilkins, in November 1928—a mission of little scientific interest. Around the same time, the American pilot Richard Byrd, the first man to fly over the North Pole, established a permanent station in the Bay of Whales, which he christened 'Little America'. Five expeditions made use of the station from 1928 to 1956.

In 1929 Byrd decided to follow Amundsen's trail aboard his hulking Ford trimotor, the *Floyd Bennett*—the name of the recently deceased pilot whith whom he had flown over the North Pole. In the meantime, three smaller aircraft engaged in systematic reconnaissance of the terrain. Their task was not an easy one: violent winds, high mountain ranges, flight compasses rendered inaccurate by the pull of the south magnetic pole, the absence of refuelling stations—all these factors complicated the undertaking.

On 25 and 26 November Byrd and the pilot Bernt Balchen made the historic flight over the South Pole, pushing their machine to the limits of its capacities. Byrd flew several more missions in the 1930s and 1940s, including the famous 'Operation High Jump' in 1946. Its aim, he stated, was to 'clarify our knowledge of the planet's last unexplored frontiers'. Byrd ended his military career with the rank of admiral.

Dangers of airborne exploration

Between 1933 and 1936 the American millionaire Lincoln Ellsworth, who had already financed and taken part in a flight over the North Pole aboard the dirigible *Norge*, resolved to duplicate his exploit over Antarctica. His first attempt failed, but he persevered and finally succeeded—just. After several landings and take-offs that wasted precious fuel, the aircraft crashed on the Ross Ice Shelf. The crew members barely escaped with their lives, and completed their crossing with an eight-day trek to Little America. There the pilot and his flight crew spent several weeks, in precarious conditions, until a search party came to their rescue.

The challenge of the Antarctic

Today huge Hercules aircraft fly regularly between national airports and the permanent stations that dot the frozen continent. The planes fly in food supplies, fuel, and relief teams, unhampered by the pack ice that plagued supply ships in the past. Nonetheless, landings in Antarctica are hazardous in bad weather. Aircraft departing from Tasmania or South America depend on accurate weather reporting, for once they reach the point of no return, they must land on the frozen continent no matter what the ground conditions may be.

The work of the various SCAR (Special Committee on Antarctic Research) groups relates mostly to amospheric physics, geology, geomagnetism and biology. Study of the ozone hole is continuing, as well as examination of its effect on life in Antarctica. At the moment, destruction of fauna and flora seems unlikely. A more probable effect would be a change in the marine population.

The Antarctic Treaty, signed in 1959 for a period of thirty years (1961-91), forbids territorial claims (despite pressure by nations that would like to establish stations on the continent) and military activities. It also prohibits industrial or mining activity, which could upset the ecological balance and development of Antarctic fauna. The 39 treaty adherents are discussing the possibility to enlarge the list of prohibitions.

The continent is the planet's climatic pole—an immense water reservoir which, if disturbed, could spell catastrophe for the entire world. It is also an observation laboratory for earth sciences (500,000 years of climatic memory are preserved in the Antarctic ice) and for the study of space. It is essential, therefore, that Antarctica remains free of industrial pollution and protected from conflicts of interest.

The Transantarctica

In August 1989 Jean-Louis Etienne of France and Will Steger of the United States organized a spectacular trek with a cosmopolitan team that hailed from England, China, Japan and the USSR, and included forty-two dogs and three sledges. The 6300-kilometre itinerary crossed Antarctica from King George Island off the northern tip of the continent's peninsula, to William II Land, via the South Pole. Although the expedition was well supplied and equipped (there were food depots set out along the entire route, by aircraft or by tractor, surveillance by Argos beacon, and constant radio contact with the expedition's ship), the journey was an arduous one, made more difficult by violent winds, unfavourable ground conditions, and bouts of exhaustion. The trek lasted seven months and the expedition reached its goal without once requiring the aid of a rescue team.

During his treks in 1907 and 1914, Ernest Shackleton acquired detailed knowledge of the polar regions. Shown here is a painting of a frozen grotto based on the explorer's descriptions.

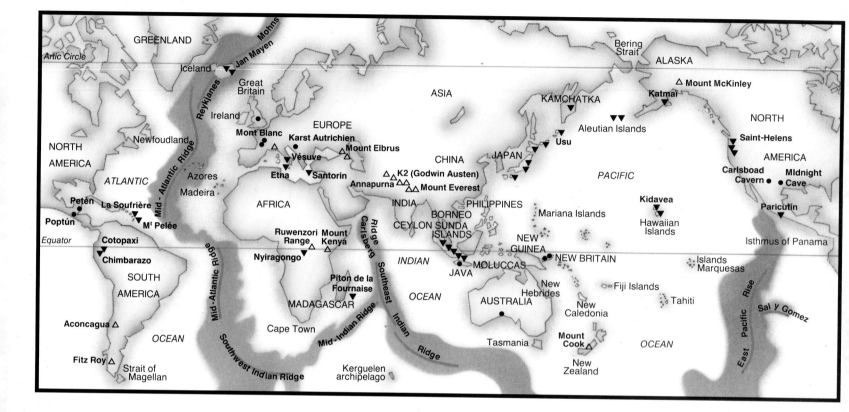

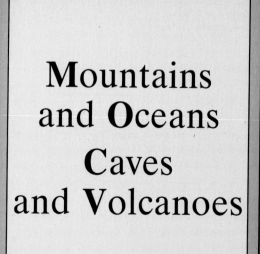

Mountains
and Oceans
Caves
and Volcanoes

CONQUERING THE SUMMITS

Safe from the hunger for conquest that pushed European nations over land and sea in search of new territory, the world's mountain summits remained unexplored. The road to the mountain tops was not yet considered a path to glory, and mountains still inspired more terror than fascination. Not until the mid-eighteenth century did the fathers of mountaineering launch the first assaults on the Alps, the birthplace of alpinism.

Poles and ladders

In the early days of alpinism, climbers used only the most rudimentary equipment: alpenstocks (long, cumbersome staffs with iron points), hob-nailed boots, and eight-spike crampons. The axe used to hew steps in the ice resembled an ordinary hatchet. Climbers crawled over crevasses on ladders laid across the abyss. The Alpine Club, organized in London in 1857, set forth highly detailed guidelines that aimed to improve equipment and techniques. It was from that date that the practice of roping climbers together was systematically employed.

Mont Blanc's fiancée

The fist woman to ascend Mont Blanc was Marie Paradis, a villager from Chamonix, who was carried by her companions to the summit in 1808. Thirty years later another woman, Henriette d'Angeville of Geneva, resolved to reach the summit. Her family did its best to discourage her, but the young woman methodically organized her expedition, down to the details of her costume: a cross between zouave trousers and thick skirts. Obsessed with the mountain, which she called her 'icy lover', Mlle d'Angeville reached the summit on 4 September 1838. Her remarkable exploit inspired other women to scale the 'accursed mountain', including Isabella Stratton, who was the first woman to climb Mont Blanc in winter.

The accursed mountain

From time immemorial the residents of Alpine valleys, awed by their enormous size, by glaciers, icefalls and rockfalls, believed that mountains were wild, mysterious places inhabited by demons, mischievous gnomes, witches, or monstrous dragons. As they sat by the fireside through long evenings, villagers spun tales of the devils who reigned over the mountains, hurling flocks into the abyss, setting off avalanches, and toppling huge ice blocks. The residents of Chamonix, terrorized by the great icy dome of Mont Blanc, nicknamed it the '*montagne maudite*', or 'accursed mountain', the symbol of the hostile nature that surrounded them.

Saussure's explorations started a veritable craze for mountaineering.

The fathers of mountaineering

Ancestral fears notwithstanding, the boldest—and most enterprising—Alpine residents ventured above the snowline in search of crystals and precious stones, or to hunt ibex and chamois. Their familiarity with steep mountain paths made these hunters and crystal-seekers the first guides to introduce travellers to Alpine regions. On 26 June 1492 the French courtier Antoine de Ville, upon the orders of King Charles VIII, made history's first recorded climb, up Mont Aiguille in the Alps, a steep, forbidding rock peak 2097 metres high, which he and his party ascended with the aid of lad-

ders. Almost three centuries after that isolated attempt, in June 1741, a party led by the Englishmen William Windham and Richard Pococke, climbed up to Montenvers, a shoulder beneath the Chamonix Aiguilles in the Mont Blanc range. They discovered the Mer de Glace ('sea of ice'), the vast glacier that cuts down through the range. Their highly publicized expedition heralded the dawn of an era; the lure of mountaineering began to be felt.

Saussure invents alpinism

In 1760 a young Genevan, Horace-Benedict de Saussure, arrived in the valley of Chamonix. Since his early youth Saussure had been dazzled by the beauty of the mountains, and he yearned to climb to the summits. On his first journey to the Alps, Saussure explored the Taconna and Bossons glaciers. The better to study Mont Blanc, the highest summit of the Alps, de Saussure climbed the Brévent, a lower peak across the valley. Dumbfounded with admiration at the mountain's majesty, he then and there conceived a plan to scale the *montagne maudite*. Back home de Saussure published in all the parishes of the surrounding valley the promise of a handsome reward to anyone who discovered a practicable way to the summit. In the meantime, he and his faithful guide, Pierre Simond, tirelessly roamed the region's caves, gorges, and the Mer de Glace. De Saussure made scientific observation his pretext for indulging in his passion, for thinkers of the eighteenth-century Enlightenment regarded mountains chiefly as objects of study.

But de Saussure was not the only man to heed the mountain's call. Around this time, a stubborn amateur climber called de Bourrit also devoted his energies to scaling Mont Blanc—though without much success.

Victory on Mont Blanc

Twenty-six years had passed since de Saussure had offered his reward. In June 1786, crystal-seeker Jacques Balmat joined an expedition to scale the 'accursed mountain'. The climbers failed to achieve their goal, but the myth of the mountain's impregnability was beginning to crack. Balmat had spent a night on the glacier. Doctor Michel-Gabriel Paccard, an eminent citizen of Chamonix, was impressed by Balmat's exploit, and engaged him as a guide in hopes of finally conquering the *montagne maudite*. At four o'clock in the morning on 8 August 1786, the two men set out from their camp on the Montagne de la Côte. To perform scientific experiments they took with them a barometer, a compass, and a thermometer. They approached the Grands Mulets, advancing slowly and with great difficulty through drifts of new-fallen snow. Fatigue, frigid temperatures, dwindling oxygen all began to tell on the mountaineers. After a brief halt at the Petits Mulets, they still had 120 metres to climb. At 6.23 pm they reached the summit: 4807 metres above sea level. Though Paccard was suffering from snow-blindness and frostbite, the two men were jubilant. The crystal-seeker collected the reward, and even received a title from the King of Sardinia. From that day on he was known as 'Jacques Balmat, called "Mont Blanc"'. The exploit of Balmat and Paccard drew worldwide attention. De Saussure, who had instigated the climb, would make it himself in August 1787. And so dawned the first golden age of alpinism.

The tragic conquest of the Matterhorn

Climbers began to set their sights on other Alpine summits. By around 1850 a hundred peaks had been scaled, including the Jungfrau (4158 metres) in Switzerland, and the Zugspitze (2963 metres), the highest peak in Germany. A wave of British climbers invaded the Alps; one of the most brilliant was Edward Whymper, who launched an attack on the Matterhorn (4477 metres), a seemingly impregnable pyramid of rock and ice above Zermatt in Switzerland. After numerous attempts, on 14 July 1865 Whymper's expedition climbed to the summit from the Swiss side, via the Hörnli Ridge. Whymper reached the top three days before Jean-Antoine Carrel, a guide who had left him in order to try his luck on

Armed with the indispensable alpenstock and equipped with ladders, Saussure sets off to climb Mont Blanc with his servant and guides.

the Italian side. But during the descent one of the less experienced climbers in Whymper's party slipped, dragging three of his comrades with him in his fall, including the guide Michel Croz. Croz's death left Whymper shattered, for the Englishman had made many daring first ascents in his company, notably the western summit of the Grandes Jorasses (4200 metres). The tragedy overshadowed the impressive achievement in the same season of the British team of Mathews, Moore and Walker, who with the guides Jakob and Melchior Anderegg successfully climbed Mont Blanc by the Brenva Spur, a steep ice ridge on the Italian side. It was a significant feat in the history of mountaineering, since from that time the route chosen to make an ascent has been as important as the actual conquest of the summit.

The ascent of the Meije

The last of the big Alpine peaks to be climbed was the Meije (3983 metres), a formidably rocky peak in the French Dauphiné Alps that had repelled numerous attempts. In 1875 two Frenchmen—Henri Duhamel and Henri Emmanuel Boileau, Baron of Castelnau—set out to best their numerous British rivals and take the Meije. The next year Duhamel successfully scaled the Carré glacier at the foot of the western peak. Boileau de Castelnau, with his guides Pierre Gaspard and his son, retraced Duhamel's route and reached the Pyramide Duhamel, at that time the farthest point yet attained. The men struggled to within six metres of the summit, then found themselves stopped by a seemingly impassable shelf. For a time

they considered giving up. But one of the guides kept on and worked his way round to the northern side of the peak. Finally on 16 August 1877 the party scrambled to the summit where they left a cairn as a memorial to their victory.

Mummery, 'king of the rock'

In 1878 the guide Alexander Burgener successfully ascended the Grand Dru (3754 metres) in the Mont Blanc range. The following year Jean Charlet made his way to the top of the neighbouring Petit Dru (3733 metres), an even more impressive rock spire, for the first time making systematic use of abseils. This marked the birth of serious rock-climbing on Alpine peaks, an approach best embodied in the exploits of the English climber A. F. Mummery. When quite young he met Burgener, and with him achieved some of the most remarkable climbing feats of the day on the Grands Charmoz and the Aiguille Verte. In 1881 the same party took on the Grépon (3482 metres), which although not the highest, is certainly one of the most spectacular summits. They worked their way up to the northern ridge, and thanks to various contortions, leg-ups on hands and shoulders, and their trusty ice axes, they conquered the sheer faces and jagged peaks of the Grépon. Mummery left his ice axe on the summit, as the 'signature' of his achievement. The 'king of the rock' made no pretense of accomplishing a scientific—or poetic—exploit. For Mummery, rock-climbing was pure sport, a conception of mountaineering that has remained influential through the years.

Mont Blanc buries its first victims

In 1820, despite his guides' urgings and manifestly unfavourable snow conditions, a certain Doctor Hamel stubbornly insisted on leading an expedition to the summit of Mont Blanc. As the party was setting off from the Grands Mulets, a violent avalanche swept three guides into a crevasse: thus did the *montagne maudite* engulf its first victims. Their remains were given up forty-one years later by the Bossons glacier. Many more deaths punctuate the mountain's history. In 1870 eleven persons disappeared in a storm. In the winter of 1956 two experienced alpinists, Henry and Vincendon, after an exhausting climb over the Brenva Spur, waited for help for six days at temperatures of -30°C—only to watch in horror as the rescue helicopter crashed. The mountaineers finally succumbed to cold and exhaustion. Five years later, a strong party of Italian and French climbers set out to make the first ascent of the Central Pillar of Freney, on of the hardest rockclimbs in the region, high up on the inaccessible south face of Mont Blanc. Not far from the top a terrible blizzard descended. There then began a terrible retreat in which, one by one, four of the climbers died, leaving only two survivors. Every year, Mont Blanc still claims several lives.

he Alps were the first mountains to be explored by climbers, but soon no virgin peaks remained to spur mountaineers on to new exploits. Climbers looked to other lands for inspiration. No land was too remote if it boasted summits that could challenge their courage, strength, and ingenuity. British climbers were especially ambitious, launching expeditions beyond Europe that heralded the epic feats achieved in the twentieth century.

The mysterious Caucasus

When in 1868 the British climber Douglas William Freshfield visited the Caucasus, a range that stretches from the Caspian to the Black Sea, those mountains were still surrounded by mystery. With two friends and a guide, Freshfield climbed the lower eastern summit of Elbrus (5593 metres), the highest peak in the range, and Kazbek (5030 metres). Freshfield's reputation rests on the fine mountain topography he left behind. And, thanks to his efforts, mountaineering was recognized as a genuine form of exploration.

In 1874 Walker, Grove and Gardiner conquered the western peak of Elbrus

In 1906, the expedition led by the Duke of Abruzzi reached the summit of Margherita Peak, in the Ruwenzori Mountains of Africa.

(5629 metres), which Freshfield had failed to see, as it had been swathed in clouds. But the summit that all alpinists yearned to climb was the twin-headed fang of Ushba (4698 metres), the 'Matterhorn of the Caucasus'. A German team attempted an ascent of the (higher) southern summit in 1903 but the guide, Schulze, had a terrible fall. Back on his feet again, he set out once more with a German-Swiss expedition that included Helbing, Reichert, and Weber. On 26 July they arrived at the summit, and pitched camp in a storm at 4600 metres. The Great War and, especially, the October Revolution interrupted exploration in the Caucasus. The range was thereafter largely the private domain of Soviet climbers, who scaled the remaining virgin peaks.

New Zealanders beat the English

On the other side of the world from the Alps, Mount Cook, surrounded by giant glaciers, rises majestically over New Zealand (3765 metres). In 1882 the Reverend W.S. Green and his two Swiss guides confronted the mountain's daunting snow ridges and seracs. The party reached the dome of the glacier, where the men discovered a way to the top. But battered by a violent storm they were forced to abandon their climb just sixty metres from the summit. Deep snow resulting from the area's heavy precipitation thwarted all attempts to conquer the peak. Racing against the English climber Edward FitzGerald and his Swiss guide, Matthias Zurbriggen, a party of New Zealanders including Tom Fyfe, George Graham, and Jack Clarke arrived first upon the central summit of Mount Cook (3712 metres) on 20 December 1894. Encouraged by their success, the men decided to push on, and five days later scram-

bled to the top of the northern summit, the highest of all. FitzGerald bowed before his rivals' achievement and abandoned his attempt. But Zurbriggen went on alone to accomplish the second ascent of Mount Cook. Early in the twentieth century New Zealanders grew expert at climbing difficult glaciers and ice ridges and conquered most of their island's highest peaks.

The icy wastes of Alaska

From Alaska to Mexico the Rocky Mountains stretch along the North American continent. At its northern extremity, the range boasts some of the world's largest glaciers outside Antartica and Greenland, and climbing expeditions to the area have to be almost polar in style. In 1897 Luigi di Amedeo di Savoia, Duke of Abruzzi, mounted the largest alpine expedition attempted to date. After 154 days the expedition guided by Joseph Petigax and X. Maquignaz reached the summit of Mount St Elias (5495 metres) on 31 July.

One of mountaineering's more colourful exploits occured in 1910, when, in order to win a bet, four American prospectors (or 'sourdoughs') set out to scale Mount McKinley (6240 metres). Although they had no climbing experience to speak of, the men were inured to hard living by years in Alaska's hostile climate. They finally won their wager when two of the party planted the 'Star-Spangled Banner' on the mountain's northern summit on 10 April. The southern summit—the highest in North America—was climbed in 1913 by Archdeacon Hudson Stuck and three companions. The frozen wastes then fell back into silence until 1925 when Mount Logan (6052 metres)—the highest peak in Canada—was conquered. After a six-week trek over the glaciers, pulled by dogsledge in fearsome weather conditions, A.H. MacCarthy led his team to victory. Since that time, climbing in Alaska and the Rockies has been marked by boldness, with many hard routes being achieved in very remote settings.

The Duke of Abruzzi on the Mountains of the Moon

Africa boasts relatively few high mountains, and so attracted few alpinists. Kilimanjaro (5894 metres) was climbed in 1889 by the German geographer Hans Meyer with his Austrian guide, Ludwig Purtscheller. The much harder Mount Kenya (5199 metres) succumbed to Sir Halford Mackinder in 1899, who succeeded after an arduous climb up the mountain's rocky walls. Only the peaks of the Ruwenzori, a heavily glaciated chain, continued to resist conquest. Stanley's 1888 expedition failed, as did Freshfield's in 1905. Both were foiled by rain, fog and dense virgin forest. In 1906 the ubiquitous Duke of Abruzzi led a huge expedition (four hundred men, including doctors, geologists, botanists, and photographers). The best alpine guides accompanied the party, along with two hundred porters and an entire tribe of Askaris, who were charged with escorting the enormous caravan. Among the expedition's many achievements were the conquest of Margherita Peak (5119 metres), the highest summit in the range, Alexandra Peak (5098 metres), and Savoia Peak (5005 metres). The Duke brought back from his epic journey a vast collection of maps, photographs and scientific observations. Exploration of Africa's mountains proceeded at a slow pace, and it was not until 1973 that the Diamond Couloir of Mount Kenya—a very steep ice route—was eventually climbed.

Zurbriggen braves Aconcagua

Edward Whymper, the first man to scale the Matterhorn, had since dedicated all his efforts to the methodical exploration of Chimborazo (6310 metres), one of the highest points of the Andes range. After Humboldt and La Condamine's attempts to climb that giant mountain (see p. 92), then believed to be the world's highest, in 1880 Whymper made a successful ascent with Louis Carrel, a guide who had once been his rival. Together they made several other notable first ascents in the *Cordillera*

On 4 January 1880, accompanied by Jean-Antoine Carel, his rival in the conquest of the Matterhorn, Edward Whymper reached the summit of Chimborazo, in the Ecuadorian Andes.

Blanca. But the one peak that all climbers then dreamed of scaling was Aconcagua (6959 metres), an Argentine peak on the Chilean frontier, which proudly resisted all attempts. In 1897 the British team of FitzGerald and Vines, guided by Mathias Zurbriggen, set out to climb the northern face of Aconcagua. The *viento blanco* ('white wind') blew up to 250 kilometres per hour, and sudden storms hampered upward progress. After a prolonged siege, the party eventually neared the summit, but suffering from altitude sickness (see p. 251) and painful chilblains, Zurbriggen's companions were forced to descend. Alone, the guide continued his ascent and on 14 January stood on the top of the Andes' highest summit. FitzGerald made another try a few days later, but was once again struck down by altitude sickness. The second highest mountain in the Andes, Huascaran (6768 metres) in Peru, almost fell in 1908 to an American climber, Annie Peck, who made the first ascent of the slightly lower north peak. Shortly after this exploit, Miss Peck left a 'Votes for Women' banner on a lower summit of Coropuna, another Peruvian giant.

Windy Patagonia

During the twentieth century the pace of Andean exploration quickened, and by the early 1950s nearly all the 6000-metre summits had been conquered. Only the Patagonian cordillera remained largely unknown. Although little higher than 3000 metres, the spires of Patagonia demand rock-climbing of the highest standards, and to make matters worse, the area is subjected to almost continuous storms. One of the most spectacular spires is Cerro Fitzroy (3325 metres), and in 1952 the French alpinist Lionel Terray took up the challenge. Terray's party solved the problem of their tents being destroyed by the wind by digging ice caves, and after a month of hard climbing, their obstinacy paid off. Even more needle-like than Fitzroy is its neighbour, Cerro Torre (3133 metres), which Cesare Maestri and Toni Egger set out to climb in 1959. On the descent Egger was killed, and Maestri's summit claim was disputed. In 1970 Maestri returned, drilling a line of bolts all the way to the summit—a tactic wich was widely condemned as unethical.

The all-important guide

Wealthy young Englishmen who travelled to the Alps in the nineteenth century needed guides to conduct them through the mountains. And so local men who had begun life as shoemakers or carpenters became professional mountain guides, sometimes accompanying the young climbers for a season at a time. The best guides were in great demand among alpinists. Their selfless devotion and fearlessness in the face of danger contributed not a little to the fame of certain climbing teams, such as Whymper and Carrel, Mummery and Burgener, Freshfield and Devouassoud, and Fitzgerald and Zurbriggen. Indeed the guides planned and led the actual climbs.

THE GIANTS OF THE HIMALAYA

Twentieth-century mountaineers set their sights on the exploration of the Himalaya, a range that stretches over 2500 kilometres from the loop of the Indus to the bend in the Brahmaputra. The opening of Nepal's borders in 1950 brought climbers to the region, eager to pit their skill against the 8000-metre peaks. Expedition followed upon expedition, and within fourteen years the conquest of the world's highest summits was complete.

Sherpas

Their personal traits and physical aptitudes, and their intimate knowledge of high-mountain terrain made the Sherpas much-sought-after high-altitude porters for Himalayan expeditions. Sherpas belong to a Tibetan ethnic group that emigrated to the Sola Khumbu and Walungchung areas of Nepal. Tenzing Norgay, the most famous of them all, accompanied Edmund Hillary to the summit of Mount Everest in 1953. Since then, several Sherpas have been to the summit of Everest, although now many prefer the less dangerous business of working for trekking companies.

For only a few rupees, the Sherpas undertook to carry equipment for the parties setting out to climb the Himalaya. On the horizon, Dhaulagiri.

The inaccessible 'roof of the world'

After the war mountaineers returned to the greater ranges, conquering several 6000- and 7000-metre peaks in the Himalaya and the Karakoram. The greatest challenge remained the fourteen 8000-metre giants, the tallest peaks on earth. The fact that these challenging summits were concentrated in the British sphere of influence gave British climbers a clear advantage. The Dalai Lama granted the British exclusive right-of-way through Tibet to attempt the highest summit of all, Mount Everest (8863 metres). In 1921 a possible route to the top was discovered and the following year a height of 8225 metres was achieved without the use of oxygen. The 1924 expedition had to contend with violent storms but, on 3 June E.F. Norton and Howard Somervell reached 8500 metres. Exhausted and snow-blind, they were unable to go on. George Mallory and Andrew Irvine replaced them as the assault party, and brought a supply of oxygen along. On 8 June, in spite of clouds and fog, Noel Odell, another member of the team, spotted the two men on the ridge leading to the summit. The storm grew ever more fierce, and the next day no trace could be found of Mallory and Irvine, who were never seen again. Some still think that Mallory and Irvine might just have reached the summit. The Dalai Lama, fearing divine displeasure, forbade further climbs until 1933.

Annapurna, the first 8000-metre peak

Political upheaval brought considerable changes to the Himalaya, divided in 1947

Pioneers of the Himalaya

From the middle of the nineteenth century, Indian emissaries called 'Pandits' secretly took note of the summits and paths of the unexplored mountain range. Engineers from the the Survey of India eventually replaced them, and their presence heralded the arrival of mountain climbers. The first serious expedition was that led by Martin Conway to the Karakoram range in 1892. The party included Lieutenant Charles Bruce, a young officer of the British Army in India, and the celebrated Swiss guide, Matthias Zurbriggen (see p. 249). The expedition discovered the Baltoro Glacier,

and scaled numerous peaks between 5000 and 7000 metres. Three years later, A.F. Mummery, hero of many Alpine triumphs, perished during an attempt on Nanga Parbat (8125 metres) above the upper Indus valley. On 12 June 1907 Tom Longstaff and his Italian guides reached the summit of Trisul (7120 metres). The Duke of Abruzzi made an unsuccessful attempt to scale K2, one of the chain's 8000-metre-plus giants, but he reached 7500 metres on Chogolisa (7654 metres), setting a record for altitude. More expeditions set forth to explore the Karakoram, Garwhal and Sikkim ranges, but the Great War sent climbers from struggling with mountain peaks to struggling with enemies on the field.

between India and Pakistan. Tibet sealed off its borders, while Nepal opened its frontiers. A wave of mountaineers surged into the region, which boasts eight of the world's fourteen 8000-plus-metre peaks (the rest are in the adjoining Karakoram range). Many a climber dreamed of conquering one of those giants—Dhaulagiri, for example, or Annapurna. In 1950 a French expedition led by Maurice Herzog, with two hundred porters carrying many tonnes of equipment, pitched camp at the foot of the Dhaulagiri (8172 metres). A thorough reconnaissance was made of possible routes to the top. Time passed, and the monsoon season inexorably approached, increasing the danger of avalanches. On 23 May Herzog decided to attack Annapurna (8091 metres). Teams took it in turns to lead the way up the mountain and set up camps. As they pushed further up into the snow, the wind-whipped climbers progressed slowly across crevasses and around seracs. On 3 June the first rope, Herzog and Louis Lachenal, started out on the final summit assault. The wind whistled and the air grew ever thinner. But the men persevered, and finally stood triumphant on the summit. Then began the harrowing descent in a violent storm. When the mountaineers returned to civilization, cruelly mutilated by frostbite, a triumphant welcome awaited them. They had looked death in the face, but their victory held valuable lessons for their successors on how to organize a Himalayan expedition.

The British on Everest

With the coming of Indian independence, the British lost their traditional prerogative on the 'roof of the world'. Nepal obliged the many nations eager to be first on top of Mount Everest to send expeditions one at a time. The British expedition in 1953 was organized down to the least detail—nothing was left to chance. Drawing conclusions from earlier failures, Colonel John Hunt, the expedition's leader, adapted his plan of ascent to the terrain and climate. The team first spent a month climbing several 6000-metre peaks, growing acclimatized to the altitude. Thus trained, the parties of climbers progressively set up camps on the mountain. For days porters and climbers ferried many tonnes of equipment up the mountain. The wind and cold slowed their progress; climbers and Sherpas alike suffered from the altitude. On 28 May, the New Zealander Edmund Hillary and the Sherpa Tenzing Norgay spent a bitterly cold night at Camp IX, at 8500 metres. The next day,

The French ascent of Annapurna exacted a high cost. Herzog lost his gloves and had to have his fingers partially amputated on the way down.

indefatigably hacking steps into the ice, and equipped with bottled oxygen, the men crept slowly upward. At half-past eleven that morning Hillary and Tenzing stood on the summit. The photograph of Tenzing holding his ice axe aloft, with the flags of the United Nations, India, Nepal, and Britain, was seen around the world. Not a single life was lost on the expedition, making its victory complete.

Alone on Nanga Parbat

Christened the 'mountain of thirty-one dead men', Nanga Parbat (8125 metres), long resisted attempts (launched mostly by Germans) to conquer its lofty heights. Although he had no previous experience in the Himalaya, Karl Herrligkoffer organized an expedition in 1953 with the support of the Pakistani government. With the considerable help of Hunza porters, the climbers pitched several high-altitude camps. Then heavy cloud and snow settled in. Fearing the early arrival of the monsoon season, the expedition's leader ordered the men to withdraw. But an Austrian climber, Hermann Buhl, refused to obey. He and his rope-mate, Otto Kempter, were determined to climb to victory. They reached Camp V at 6900 metres. At dawn on 3 July, though now abandoned by Kempter as well, Buhl forged on. He climbed 1200 metres in

seventeen hours, climbing alone over six kilometres of ridges and icy cornices. On all fours, practically hypnotized, Buhl crawled the last few metres separating him from the summit. The solitary Austrian thus avenged the victims of Nanga Parbat. The first climber to have conquered two 8000-metre peaks, Buhl disappeared four years later during the ascent of Chogolisa.

The Italians conquer K2

In 1954 an expedition led by Professor Ardito Desio followed in the footsteps of their compatriot, the Duke of Abruzzi (see p. 248) to K2 (8611 metres). The expedition fixed ropes along the Abruzzi ridge in order to bring up supplies and equipment and on 30 July the lead rope, Achille Compagnoni and Lino Lacedelli, pitched Camp IX at 8060 metres. Walter Bonatti and Pino Galloti supplied the summit party with the oxygen needed for the final assault. Making slow and painful progress Compagnoni and Lacedelli set foot on the summit of K2 at six that evening. The operation's military-style discipline, the solidarity that reigned among the climbers and Desio's sense of organization all contributed to the expedition's success. The era of the 'eight-thousanders' thus continued until the last 8000-metre peak, Shisha Pangma, was conquered by a Chinese expedition in 1964.

(see p. 68)

Mountain sickness

When Cortés (see p. 68) scaled Popocatepetl in 1519 his men complained of sluggishness and an insurmountable desire to sleep. They believed they were bewitched, when in fact they were simply victims of mountain sickness. Metabolic disturbances brought on by inadequate oxygen supply may cause dizziness, anxiety, cramps, and even hallucinations. High up on the Jungfrau in the Swiss Alps researchers were seized with sudden fits of laughter, another symptom common in those altitudes. Today, climbers overcome mountain sickness by giving themselves ample time to become acclimatized to high altitudes.

The abominable snowman

The Nepalese and Tibetans claim that the Yeti, an anthropoid with a human face, a sly being with a whimsical sense of humour, inhabits the highest reaches of the Himalaya. His enormous footprints embedded in the snow and his wild whistlings terrorize villagers. The Yeti keeps himself hidden from the eyes of strangers, but John Hunt, Edmund Hillary and Eric Shipton all collected considerable evidence of his existence. Even today the legend of the giant of the snowy summits persists....

T he era of conquering the world's highest mountain peaks was drawing to a close. Heavily equipped, highly organized expeditions had accomplished miracles in the Himalaya, reaching the most inaccessible summits, overcoming the perils of high altitudes. But a new kind of mountaineering was about to burst on the scene: climbers began to concentrate on the style in which they attempted climbs of greater and greater technical difficulty.

Like the first mountaineers, Boivin used ladders during his expedition to Everest.

One man against the Dru

Walter Bonatti, a member of the expedition that had conquered K2, returned to the Alps looking for an even greater challenge. He decided to match himself against a gigantic vertical pillar on the Southwest Face of the Petit Dru. On 17 August 1955, alone, with a huge pack of pitons, karabiners and ropes, Bonatti made his way up the

Charpoua Glacier. Trapped when his rope got caught in a crack, he was forced to spend his first night squatting on a ledge carved out of the ice. For four days Bonatti slowly continued his ascent, his hands swollen with constant contact with the tough granite. Stymied by an impassable crack, he flung his rope around a spike above and to the side and swung out over the void. When he came to a standstill, Bonatti shinned up his rope until he got onto climbable rock, and went on with his ascent. On the sixth day, leaving behind part of his equipment to lighten his load, Bonatti forced his way up the final fifty metres. At 4.37 pm, he stood at the top of what was then one of the hardest routes in the Alps, which would from then on be known as the Bonatti Pillar, conquered by a lone climber in six days.

Climbing Jannu

The Himalayan peak of Jannu (7710 metres), a gigantic tower with sheer sides and numerous monstrous seracs, is the embodiment of the type of summit that lured the best climbers of the day. The Sherpas regarded the mountain with a kind of religious awe. Despite two failed attempts in 1957 and 1959, the Nepalese government granted permission for a French expedition led by Pollet-Villard to try again in 1962. Early in April Camp III was established at 6000 metres. On 23 April the climbers, with ice axes and hammers at the ready, began to cover the mountain with fixed ropes before commencing the final assault. Imprudently, they had left their oxygen bottles behind to lighten their burden. As a result, the altitude took its toll and, exhausted, they were forced to give up. Clouds and snow thwarted their attempts until 27 April, when the team of Robert Paragot and René Desmaison launched a final assault on the moun-

tain. They made rapid progress thanks to their oxygen inhalers, and quickly ascended the packed snow. The weather was bitterly cold but clear as they climbed onto Jannu's summit. The next day, the other ropes repeated the exploit. For the first time eleven climbers from the same expedition made it to the top of a Himalayan peak, by one of the hardest routes then achieved at altitude.

The South Face of Annapurna

High-risk mountaineering crossed a new threshold of difficulty in 1970. A British expedition led by Chris Bonington resolved to try the South Face of Annapurna (8078 metres), an awesomely steep rock and ice face 2500 metres high, strewn with innumerable obstacles—snow crests, seracs and rocky walls.

With quasi-military tactics and logistics, Bonington established his high-altitude camps. The head rope blazed the trail, fixing ropes, while the other climbers and Sherpas progressively hauled up supplies and equipment to the camps. Their efforts to scale the main rock barrier in a blizzard exhausted the climbers, and the altitude also began to take its toll. On 27 May, in spite of the ever more violent storm, the leading rope of Don Whillans and Dougal Haston forged ahead into the swirling snows, pushing upwards 750 metres in a single day. Though they did not at first realize it, for they were banked in cloud cover, they reached the summit. Their victory was greeted with great acclaim, not only for the difficulties they had overcome, but also for the expedition's superb organization. Using a similar strategy, a French team succeeded the following year in ascending the West Pillar of Makalu (8841 metres).

Straight upward

El Capitan is one of the world's highest and steepest cliffs, 900 metres of sheer granite standing at the entrance to Yosemite Valley in California. Although several extremely hard multi-day routes had been climbed on El Capitan, The Wall of Early Morning Light, an immense vertical expanse of granite, had not yet been climbed when American mountaineers Warren Harding and Dean Caldwell launched their assault, keeping television viewers glued to their screens. They photographed and studied every fragment of their route for two years before setting out on 23 October 1970, hoisting behind them a great sack packed with 180 kilogrammes of equipment. Making very slow progress, by 27 October the climbers had scaled only 230 metres. Stopped by a blizzard from 4 to 10 November, their situation looked grim. Journalists lobbied for a rescue mission and twenty-one rescue workers landed by helicopter on El Capitan's summit. The two climbers angrily refused help. The snowstorm abated and they recommenced their slow climb, reaching their goal at noon on 18 November—after a record 27 days living and sleeping in hammocks on the rock face. The route was the final culmination of the big wall aid routes of the 1950s and 1960s; thereafter climbers turned far more to free climbing.

The 'roof of the world' without oxygen

Like the Alps at the turn of the century, the Himalaya in time became a favourite area for climbers to test their mettle. The goal of an Austrian expedition in 1978 was to bring every member of the party to the summit of Mount Everest. Two climbers, Peter Habeler and Reinhold Messner (the latter from the Italian Tyrol), resolved to reach the top without using any oxygen. On 3 May one rope made it to Everest's summit using oxygen. Five days later, Messner and Habeler set out on their summit bid without the bottled gas. Struggling and halting often to gasp for air, the pair forged on. At one point Messner lay down in the snow, and Habeler abandoned some gear. They moved slowly, like automatons, as they climbed past the southern summit and finally reached the mountain's higher northern summit. They descended to a hero's welcome, Habeler limping, and Messner suffering from snow-

blindness. But they had achieved their objective, and won their wager. Messner had already climbed three 8000-metre peaks in the Himalaya, and went on to climb the remaining ten—the first man to do so.

Faster, more perilous climbs

While a very few years ago even the best climbers took several days on the harder Alpine routes, the present generation of mountaineers has invented 'climbing games' such as climbing in series. In a single day climbers scale the greatest possible number of routes on adjoining mountains, or ascend a single rock face via several itineraries. Jean-Marc Boivin, a French guide, achieved a record by climbing four of the most dangerous north faces of the Mont Blanc range in just seventeen hours using a hang-glider to descend from one summit to the foot of the next. Christophe Profit, another French alpinist, launched a solo assault on the 900-metre West Face of the Petit Dru entirely without artificial aids, completing his ascent in just three hours.

Everest has been climbed solo in under twenty-four hours from base camp, and in 1990 the huge and very steep South Face of Lhotse (8 501 metres)—which had repelled several strong attempts—eventually fell to the phenomenal Yugoslav climber, Toni Cesen, who made his ascent solo. Cesen's feat must rank as one of the greatest in mountaineering history.

Twentieth-century alpinists have penetrated the last unexplored mountain kingdoms. The summits have lost some of their mystery, but the thrill of adventure and the challenge of turning in a record-breaking performance remain powerful stimulants for the imagination. 'Firsts' made in winter, alone, without oxygen, by a woman, or by ever harder routes all push back indefinitely the frontiers of the possible.

The technical resources now available mean that the new generation of climbers are able to take on new kinds of challenge. Here, Christophe Profit is let down by helicopter.

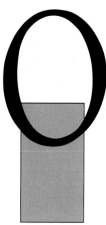

*Over more than thirty centuries, from the days of the early
Egyptians to the late nineteenth century, mankind knew
surprisingly little about what lay beneath the sea. And yet men
fished and sailed the sea, and fought battles on the waves....
Putting superstitions fears aside, the first divers daringly began to
penetrate the ocean's secrets, tempted by the unfathomable depths,
dreaming of machines that could take them ever deeper.*

A recent development

The history of underwater exploration is
inextricably linked to that of the machines
that made it possible for divers to go
beneath the ocean's surface, and to remain
there safely for an extended time.

Though for countless centuries human
beings have known how to swim and sail,
and though they have long made timid
attempts to investigate below the water's
surface, the undersea world has remained a
mystery until relatively recently. In contrast
to many other scientific disciplines, knowledge of the sea long consisted of rudimentary facts learned through experience,

*The Renaissance saw a proliferation of designs for diving machines. This
is a sketch for the construction of a wooden submarine.*

combined with a vast store of legend and
myth. But much of what had been taken as
truth was shown to be either insufficient or
false by the sciences of physics, chemistry
and physiology, which progressed enormously between the late eighteenth century
and the beginning of our own. Myths about
the ocean received an even more decisive
blow when technological advances produced equipment that made it possible for
divers to venture into the watery depths.

Why do divers take the plunge?

In the first place, there is curiosity, which
incites philosophers to explain the world
around them; then there are the superstitions or fears that emerge in reaction to
inevitable accidents; and finally there is the
desire of the boldest individuals to explore
the unknown. For the sea is a source of
food, of treasures, perhaps of wonders.
How could man secure these riches? He
could catch fish with a line or net or har-
poon; but to obtain sponges, coral, pearl or
mother-of-pearl, he had to dive, taking
great risks for a relatively small profit.
Among the first recorded motives for
underwater exploration were the demands
of war. Accounts from Greek and Roman
Antiquity, from Arab chronicles and from
ancient Oriental texts tell of divers who
boldly cut the mooring ropes of enemy
fleets, or destroyed the underwater
defences of a besieged town, or who transported supplies by water when overland travel was impossible. Early divers also
attempted to recover cargoes—arms, gold
or coins—from wrecked ships. Experienced
pearl- or sponge-divers were employed for
these tasks, divers who sometimes owned
special equipment that enabled them to
remain under water. But they did not, stric-

tly speaking, 'explore' the underwater
world. Without goggles or masks, early
divers probably could not see very well, nor
did their rudimentary equipment allow
them to stay below for very long.

An enigmatic world

Greek philosophers such as Plato and especially Aristotle, and the Roman author
Pliny the Elder (an admiral and naturalist,
who died in the eruption of Vesuvius as he
endeavoured both to rescue victims and to
observe the phenomenon) explained as best
they could the tangible aspects of the sea
around them: currents and tides, salinity,
the opacity of deep water, marine fauna and
flora, and so on. Until the Renaissance their
opinons were considered authoritative by
Western scholars. And to give the Ancients
their due, they did observe carefully and
took meticulous notes of their findings,
although they did not understand all they
saw. But over the next thousand years—the
Dark Ages, explanations that were fantasti-
cal (tides were attributed to the contortions
of an enormous beast far down in the sea-
depths), or metaphysical (underwater
abysses were believed to be the lairs of fabulous beasts exiled there by God or his
angels), or terrifying (the oceans had no
bottom since the depths could not be fa-
thomed), could be contradicted neither by
scientific verification—particularly where
questions of religious dogma were involved—nor by experience, since the means
were lacking. And mariners, traditionally
superstitious and often uneducated or gullible, set great store by the tales of monsters, maelstroms and hellish phenomena
witnessed at sea.

Not until the fifteenth and sixteenth centuries were men motivated once more to
investigate what lay below the sea, pressed

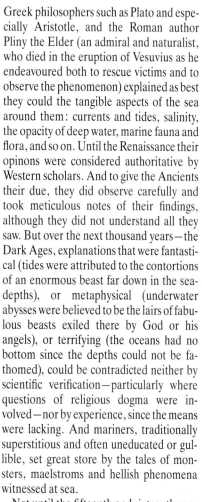

In 1784, the inventor Fréminet imagined a 'hydrostatergatic' machine for exploring the depths and 'securing lost effects'.

Ancient theories of the deep

Although the Roman author Pliny the Elder lacked the tools of modern physics, he had a wide-ranging knowledge and an interest in the sea, and was further aided by the table of concordances developed by Posidonius a century earlier. Pliny affirmed that there was a connection between the phases of the moon, its position with respect to the sun, and the tides: *'Verum causa in sole lunaque'*, he wrote: 'The sun and the moon are the real cause [of the tides]…'. Although he did not — could not — explain the phenomenon, Pliny anticipated Newton's discoveries by seventeen centuries.

by the need for more accurate navigational techniques, for better charts, and for more effective military strategems (could it be possible, for example, to approach enemy ships underwater and pierce their hulls unseen?). Over the next four centuries various types of heavy, cumbersome diving suit were developed, the first submarines appeared, and the science of oceanography was born.

The first diving suits

Lung capacity limits the time divers can hold their breath when swimming, exploring, or performing other tasks under water. At some date a diver reasoned that by breathing through a tube that extended above the surface of the water he could remain beneath the surface for a longer time; but water pressure makes this system impractical at depths below two metres. Yet many designs of 'diving costume' proposed over the centuries were based on the erroneous assumption that one could breathe through a tube, a pitfall even Leonardo da Vinci did not escape. Leonardo did, however, come up with the idea of webbed gloves, a notion later adapted in the flippers worn by scuba divers. Before rubber came into use, no impermeable material was avai-

lable to divers. Greased leather was not fully waterproof, and tightly tied knots were needed at the wrists if the diver wished to use his hands. The day that someone had the idea of sending air down to the diver, research was heading in the right direction. But the only type of air pump known in those days was the bellows; what was lacking was an air inlet valve to allow the diver to return to the surface. Early diving suits constructed on this model were thus functional for only a brief span at shallow depths.

Diving bells

The only other solution was for divers to bring their air supply with them. Inflated skins were tried, but they did not hold sufficient quantities of air, and tended to float up to the surface, obliging the diver to take on more ballast. Later experiments focused on large, rigid, hermetically closed chambers, like a barrel fitted with a porthole that allowed the diver to observe the sea bottom. Another device looked more like a bell which the diver entered and in which he could breathe while carrying on his underwater activity: this is the principle of the diving bell. Legend has it that Alexander the Great descended far beneath the seas in

a glass barrel. If that exploit actually took place, it is doubtful that it lasted very long, for it is reported that Alexander took with him two oil lamps, which would have rapidly used up his oxygen. The idea of a bell was a development of a technique used by divers in Antiquity, who let down large upturned vessels that kept air within them, and so allowed the divers to take several breaths.

From the sixteenth century onwards, true diving bells came into use. Fashioned from metal and totally waterproof, their only real disadvantage was their immobility. Divers using bells recovered treasure from many sunken ships. In the seventeenth century, inventors sought ways to replace or regenerate the stale air in the bells, but they had little success until the advent of pumps able to overcome water pressure (about one kilo per square centimetre for every ten metres of depth) which were based on a principle put forward by Pascal and Torricelli, a disciple of Galileo. Before this principle could be applied, early in the eighteenth century Sir Edmund Halley had changed the air in a diving bell by lowering barrels of fresh air to it; and John Lethbridge invented and used a prototype of the rigid diving suit, the outer layer of which compensated for the surrounding water pressure. The most significant result of this technique was to allow divers to draw air from the diving bell — at the same pressure as in the diving suit — by means of a pipe.

The task of the oceanographer

Classic oceanographic research involves a multitude of tasks: taking samples and soundings, performing geological and chemical analyses of samples from the seafloor (plant life, sediments, and so on), capturing and studying marine organisms living at different depths, making topographical readings of the ocean floor and mapping the continental plateau, observing and studying water displacement (tides, waves, currents, etc.), recording temperatures, observing meteorological conditions, keeping watch over migrating fish to guide fishing boats….

Submersibles

At the same time, some far-sighted inventors examined with interest projects for submarines. The Dutch physicist, Cornelius Drebbel (1572-1633), tutor to the children of James I, was responsible for the designing of the first submarine. In 1624, Drebbel had an egg-shaped, wooden submarine built which was propelled by twelve oarsmen in addition to the crew. Trials took place on the Thames between Westminster and Greenwich, much to the amazement of the general public. Other early models were less convincing: for instance, a craft powered by a paddle wheel, presented by the Frenchman De Son in 1653; and a wooden submarine with air reserves in leather bags and powered by articulated webbed oars, which was invented by the Italian G.A. Borelli in 1680. The first successful submarine actually built was the work of the American David Bushnell. In 1776 he constructed the *Turtle*, a small, egg-shaped wooden submersible large enough for one man, which was equipped with ballast to dive and a pump to drain off water and was powered by a hand-turned propeller. The craft was designed to attach explosives to the hulls of enemy ships.

In 1800 the American inventor Robert Fulton, who in 1797 built a working steamboat, was commissioned by Napoleon to design a submarine. Made of copper and equipped with ballast and supplies of compressed air, the craft could dive to a depth of seven metres manned by a crew of three, who operated the screw-propeller. Fulton had provided the submarine with nearly every essential (even a name, the *Nautilus*)—the only thing lacking was a motor. For that, it would be necessary to wait until the end of the century.

Paul Bert: breathing under pressure

Paul Bert (1833-1886), a French physiologist and politician, discovered the causes of caisson disease (decompression sickness or 'the bends'), so called because of the watertight, pressurized chambers or 'caissons' used for underwater construction and other tasks. Bert's observations also applied to symptoms that afflicted undersea divers. He demonstrated the toxicity of oxygen when it is breathed under pressure greater than 1.7 kilos per square centimetre—that is, at depths of over seven metres. Bert also showed that the release into the blood and tissues of gases that make up compressed air (nitrogen, in particular) causes a condition that can be safely reversed only if the diver returns to the surface progressively. John Haldane later established the rule that for a long dive at depths of more than ten metres, decompression in stages is absolutely essential. Otherwise, nitrogen bubbles are released into the bloodstream, causing cerebral embolism, paralysis, and severe damage to the joints.

The first modern diving gear

An early diving suit designed by the German K.H. Kleingert in 1796 was a cross between a suit of armour and a barrel. It was improved upon in 1829 by the Englishman Augustus Siebe, who reduced it to a rigid helmet—a small-scale diving bell, in fact—fitted with an air inlet valve and joined to a flexible and relatively water-tight suit into which air was pumped from the surface through a tube. The French inventor Paulin improved upon this system, which was further refined in 1855 by Cabirol, who added a thick rubber diving dress, which made him the first diver to use a truly modern diving suit. In 1860 the French naval officers Benoit Rouquayrol and Auguste Denayrousse created an air regulator, which allowed air to be delivered from a surface pump or from a compressed-air tank at approximately ambient pressure. In 1867 a combination of Cabirol's system and the features designed by Rouquayrol and Denayrousse produced the first self-contained diving apparatus. Around the same time, the British were developing closed-circuit systems using pure oxygen; they were lighter and more convenient, but dangerous to use at depths greater than ten metres.

Modest results

Nineteenth-century technical and metallurgical advances led to the first functional solutions to the problems of underwater exploration. Yet it was still unclear why divers were often violently ill or paralysed, and sometimes even died when they returned to the surface after long sessions deep under water. In 1878 the findings of Paul Bert (see feature) prepared the way for the work of John Haldane, a British physiologist who in 1905 produced decompression tables that made diving far safer. As for submersible ships used in war, they could dive only a few metres, and even those fitted with Gramme's electric motor (1873) were not wholly satisfactory. They were more likely to sink themselves than to wreck an enemy ship—unless it happened to be lying at anchor.

The oceans remained a mystery. There was no knowledge of underwater flora and fauna beyond what fishing nets had brought up from the deep. And little was understood about the motion of the sea, its currents, or variations of temperature. Yet in the seventeenth century the connection had been made between tides and the lunar

In addition to submarine exploration, deep-sea diving also opened the way to 'treasure-hunting' and underwater archaeology.

cycle, and the principle was understood when in 1665 Newton published his law of gravitation.

The incredible cruise of the *Challenger*

———————•———————

HMS *Challenger* was entrusted with a mission to sound the three main oceans, analyse samples of water and matter dredged up from the sea bottom, to note temperatures at various depths, and to observe marine plants and animal life. From December 1872 to May 1876 the mission covered nearly 70,000 miles and crossed the Equator six times, ushering in the era of oceanographic studies.

Leading the expedition was Charles Wyville Thomson, a respected professor and naturalist. Since 1868, with William Carpenter and in cooperation with the Royal Navy, he had conducted two campaigns aboard the *Lightning* and the *Porcupine*. In laying the foundations of what would emerge as the science of oceanography, these men were following precedents set by François Péron, a researcher financed by Napoleon between 1800 and 1804, and by the polar pioneers John and James Clarke Ross. The Rosses habitually made careful depth soundings, and measured currents and temperatures during their polar navigations (see p. 228 and p. 237). But Thomson and his colleagues aboard the *Challenger* carried out the first systematic study of deeper ocean waters, finding answers to some of the most basic questions: the ocean floor, they discovered, is neither flat nor featureless, but presents the same diversity as surface terrain—there are even underwater volcanoes. Life, they observed, exists far beneath the ocean's surface, and water forms masses and layers. They also determined the seven major constituents of sea water. The seventy-three scientists instructed to interpret the data and draw conclusions from the operation spent nearly twenty-five years producing the fifty volumes of the *Challenger Reports*—oceanography's bible and the departure point for research that has been carried out for over a century.

'Classical' oceanography

———————•———————

The discipline of oceanography encompasses the measurement, observation, and study of all aspects of the planet's oceans

Prince Albert I of Monaco was a great patron of oceanography. Here he poses for the camera beside a whale brought back by a trawler.

and seas; the research is usually performed aboard ship. Between 1870 and 1930 advances in the means of investigation, as well as in the theoretical tools that determine the scope of study and in the techniques used to carry out research projects, allowed scientists to lay the foundations of a discipline; but oceanography was seriously hampered by scientists' inability to explore the very object of their study. But thanks to financial support from public and private sources, the new discipline eventually earned the recognition of the scientific community, and awakened considerable public interest and curiosity.

After Thomson, whose work was continued by his collaborator John Murray and by William B. Carpenter, who continued to carry out on-site research, Alexandre Agassiz, a Swiss emigré to the United States, was the most active practising oceanographer of his day. Backed by considerable financial support, in 1877 Agassiz procured a ship (the *Blake*), and later an eighty-metre laboratory vessel, the *Albatross*; he led several campaigns, concentrating chiefly on warmer waters, where he tirelessly dredged marine life and sediments for observation. Although he was not aware of his discovery, he brought up the polymetallic nodules, which are now known to be a very important resource.

Royal patronage and national interests

———————•———————

From 1885 to 1931 Prince Albert I of Monaco, a generous supporter of oceanography, fitted out his yachts as increasingly sophisticated research vessels. He made a significant contribution to our knowledge of seafloors and of fish migration.

Germany sent out ships and organized expeditions, mainly in the Indian Ocean. The Russians also launched oceanographical campaigns. The most famous was Stepan Osipovitch Makarov's voyage aboard the *Vitiaz*, which demonstrated that in all deep oceans layers of water of different temperatures or different levels of salinity circulate without mixing. Makarov later investigated Arctic waters, and established the basic principle for ice-breaking ships; he designed and built the icebreaker *Ermak*. Nansen, aboard the famous *Fram*, engaged in oceanographical research as well (see p. 231). By the twentieth century the 'mystery of the deep' had not yet been elucidated, but scientists were beginning to conceive of how to represent theoretically what they did not yet know. Even today much remains to be learned in this field, and research is slow, costly and perilous.

(see p. 228 and p. 237)

(see p. 231)

A prince of oceanography

Born in 1848, the young man who would become Prince Albert I of Monaco began his career as a naval officer. His first yacht, a fine English schooner which he christened the *Hirondelle*, sailed the seas for eleven years merely as a pleasure craft. But the prince's encounter with Alphonse Milne-Edwards, son of a courageous diving pioneer, stimulated his interest in the new science of oceanography. He took part in several expeditions that fuelled his interest further. The prince's yacht was not adequately equipped for research, so Albert had other, larger ships built and fitted out for oceanographical missions: the *Princesse Alice II* saw service from 1898 to 1910, and the *Hirondelle II* was used in research expeditions until the prince's death in 1922. Though they still resembled yachts in appearance, the vessels were equipped as veritable floating laboratories, able to fish, dredge and take samples and soundings. Prince Albert's scientific contribution and his generous funding of research were vital to the development of oceanography in France.

For the past fifty years scuba divers have been able to move freely beneath the ocean's surface; they have seen (and filmed so that we too can see) the underwater world, a world with which they have grown increasingly familiar. Bathyscaphes have taken divers down to the greatest depths. Manned or robot-operated submersibles have explored the intermediate underwater zones, where researchers have successfully stayed and worked.

Current undersea research

Oceanology may one day reveal all the secrets of the underwater world. It encompasses the study of marine biology (it is now known that life exists even in the deepest abysses of the ocean), geology (rocks and sediments), and the observation of marine ecology and the effects of undersea volcanoes. It further involves archaeological research and the excavation of sunken ships, and the gathering of mineral samples. The possibilities brought into play by this young discipline have opened up an unforeseen field for the study of our planet. This technological revolution has progressed from the use of sounding leads greased with mutton fat to the latest multidirectional sonic depth finder, coupled with a device for extracting core samples of sediment. Geologists can 'read' such samples like history books, as they contain traces of volcanic eruptions dating back to Antiquity. They also make use of direct scanning, via video camera, or recording buoys placed on the seafloor. The results yielded by such devices are then interpreted by computers.

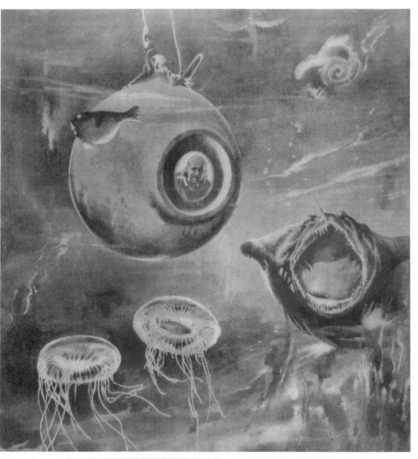

The bathysphere invented by the American scientist Beebe was the first machine capable of reaching the depths. Beebe was struck by the darkness he found there.

may explore, film, or study the undersea world. Underwater archaeology has in its turn added a chapter to human history, by interpreting the artefacts given up by sunken ships.

Underwater businesses

Very quickly new difficulties emerged, which underline the limits of human physiology: narcosis, or 'depth sickness', excessively long decompression time, and other physical and psychological problems connected with changing pressure. The oil industry, in particular, has pushed back the frontiers in the field. Thus experimental undersea dwellings have been developed in France (Aquabulle, Galathée). In the United States medium-depth underwater laboratories (Sealab, Hydralab) have been constructed, and deep-sea stations (for use at 300 to 350 metres), which are supplied with nitrogen-free mixtures and a controlled oxygen input, have gradually led to permanent underwater installations.

Nowadays, hydreliox (a mixture of helium, hydrogen and oxygen) allows man to descend to depths of over 500 metres with no respiratory discomfort or psychological side effects. Undersea laboratories for growing plant or animal life or for producing energy—underwater mines and 'factories' —will probably not be a reality until the next century; the first attempts to descend beyond 500 metres in 1988 and simulated descents in diving chambers beyond 600 metres have shown that new technology will be necessary to make further progress. Since human beings are designed to live in atmospheric pressure, they can only hope to reach and explore the farthest depths of the oceans in some sort of rigid diving apparatus. As for spending long periods at such depths, that is another matter altogether.

The first self-contained diving apparatus

For diving in shallow waters—under 100 metres in most conditions—the invention of scuba apparatus was a major breakthrough. It was first developed by the Frenchman Yves Le Prieur in 1933. Far from perfect, his system did, however, allow divers to come into direct contact with the underwater world—to observe it at first hand, and to

move about unencumbered. It was the first step towards virtually danger-free exploration of the underwater zone that is illuminated by sunlight (forty to sixty metres in clear water). Diving for sport or as a profession was still a long way off. But both activities were eventually made possible by the experience gained by military divers during the Second World War and by the invention of the aqualung by Jacques-Yves Cousteau and E. Gagnan. So long as they follow the rules (and are in reasonably good physical condition), after a period of training divers

Bathyspheres and bathyscaphes

———•———

In 1930 William Beebe, an American naturalist interested in undersea life, tried out the diving bell he had invented with engineer Otis Barton: it was a steel shell thirty-eight millimetres thick with portholes of molten quartz. Suspended from a cable running out from a ship and linked to the ship by telephone, the bell descended into the water. After several attempts, each time going down a little deeper, in 1934 the men reached 906 metres off the coast of Bermuda. The bathysphere thus opened the way for deep-sea exploration. Around the same time, the Galeazzi submersible went down to 210 metres; improved some thirty years later, it could descend to 900 metres. And in 1949 Barton invented the benthoscope, which reached the limits of the capacity of suspended apparatus, diving to 1370 metres. Beyond that point it risked breaking its cable, because of the vibrations caused by its swaying back and forth.

Depths never reached

———•———

A significant contribution was made by Auguste Piccard of Switzerland, inventor of the bathyscaphe. Piccard already had to his credit the design of a stratospheric balloon, the *FNRS*, and had reached an altitude of 17,000 metres in 1932. After the Second World War, in 1948, he obtained funding to test the first bathyscaphe, which consisted of a buoyancy chamber filled with gasoline, supporting a sealed steel sphere in which two passengers could breathe at normal atmospheric pressure. For ballast, the system used iron filings held up by an electromagnet, which could be released to allow the bathyscaphe to surface; Piccard called his invention the *FNRS II*. Several failed trials and disagreements between Piccard and the French Navy, which was involved in the undertaking, led, as of 1953, to two simultaneous series of experiments with two bathyscaphes. The first, the *FNRS III*, a Franco-Belgian craft commanded by G. S. Houot, reached 4050 metres the following year and saw service until 1961, though it never went deeper than 6000 metres. Another bathyscaphe, the *Trieste*, built by Piccard and his son Jacques in conjunction with the Italian navy, could not go deeper than the French craft. With American financial aid, Jacques Piccard took the *Trieste* to the Pacific after fitting it with a

more robust sphere. He reached 5500 metres late in 1959, 7000 metres in January 1960, then attempted the dive of the century, in the Mariana trench, the deepest known. On 23 January 1960, Jacques Piccard and an American, Don Walsh, touched bottom at 10,916 metres. The water pressure gauge registered 1156 bars (one bar equals atmospheric pressure, or 1.17 tonnes per square centimetre). Since that time, the French have developed *Archimède*, an apparatus supposed to be capable of descending to 11,300 metres.

Plate tectonics

———•———

Plate tectonics is a scientific concept that seeks to explain the changes in the earth's crust due to movements of continental or undersea plates. Structural alterations in the rock of which the plates are made, resulting from exceedingly slow but continuous movements that force the rocks together, compressing them or causing folds or overlaps, are now better understood thanks to oceanographers' increasingly precise observation techniques, which have revealed the existence of oceanic ridges, and provided clues to how they were formed.

Over the past forty years sophisticated equipment—multidirectional echo-sounding instruments, magnetometres, seismometres—has revealed that a single undersea mountain chain some 65,000 kilometres long snakes over the world's ocean floor. Deep clefts have been discovered comparable to the rift of the eastern Horn of Africa. Observations have been made of intense tectonic activity, which gradually renews the ocean floor. Immense abysses have also been discovered where, in all probability, the edges of huge blocks (or plates) of the earth's crust are pushed into the magma. Alfred Wegener's theory of continental drift (brilliant in principle but flawed in its elaboration), which postulated the fragmentation of a single continent—a theory that was generally mocked early in this century—has received scientific confirmation: the bottom of the sea does indeed give birth to the land.

The 'Epaulard' is an entirely autonomous, unmanned submarine capable of reaching a depth of 6000 metres.

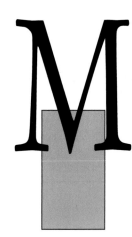

an has roamed the globe and sailed the seas, explored mountain chains, and sounded the depths of the sea. On the planet's surface, the era of great explorations has ended, but the subterranean world still conceals mysterious labyrinths and secrets that have only begun to be studied. The first cave explorers brought back evidence of long-lost ancestors, giving rise to a new science: speleology.

Cave-dwelling animals

Biospeleologists have identified many creatures who dwell exclusively in caves. All of these insects, amphibians and fish share certain characteristics, including the partial or total atrophy of their sense of sight, and loss of skin colour—both phenomena due to their living in perpetual darkness. Other species divide their time between the darkness of caves and daylight: foxes, bears, and bats for example. Bats hibernate in caves, packed close together, hanging upside down. Some 100,000 bats cohabit in this way in a single chamber of the Carlsbad Cave in the United States.

The colour of water

To trace the course of subterranean streams speleologists dye the water, then keep a close watch on the spots where the water is most likely to reappear. By dumping fluorescein into the chasm of the Trou du Toro on the south side of the Pyrenees, Casteret was able to identify the source of the Garonne River when he saw the orange-red waters reappear on the northern side of the range. By locating rivers' sources it is possible to combat contamination of subterranean streams polluted by waste or decaying animal carcasses.

The first cave explorers

Caves served as refuges for human beings during periods of glaciation in the Pleistocene epoch (1.6 million to 10,000 years ago). In the Upper Palaeolithic period, soon after 16,000 BC, wall painting appeared, and this early art has survived in caves such as Lascaux in France and Altamira in Spain. In the Ancient World, caves were places to hide from invading armies, as well as to worship or to bury the dead. Centuries later, tempted by legendary riches or in pursuit of prey, hunters and treasure-seekers penetrated into unexplored caves. By sheer chance, a trapper named Hutchins discovered in 1809 the Mammoth Cave in the United States, Bonnemaison uncovered the Grotte d'Aurignac in the Upper Garonne in 1842, and an American cowboy, Jim White, found the Carlsbad caves in 1901. Others in search of saltpetre or crystals contributed to the mapping of caves, which were often deliberately hidden. Outcasts, brigands and hermits sometimes sought refuge in these secret sites deep in the earth. Scientists soon followed in their footsteps.

Descent to the bottom of the cenote at Bolonchen, in Yucatan (Mexico).

Scholars go underground

In the Middle Ages, the force of superstition kept people away from caves, which they assumed were populated by demons. Yet authenticated inscriptions dating from the thirteenth century prove that the Adelsberg Cave on Austria's limestone plateau had been explored during this period. It was there, five centuries later, that the first scientific research on caves was begun. In 1748 the Emperor of Austria sent an engineer named Nagel to study the caves of the limestone plateau or *karst*. Nagel ventured the hypothesis that the caves led to underground rivers. In 1770 a Briton named Lloyd explored Eldon Hole in England. In 1774 a German zoologist proved that the bones found in certain natural caves belonged to animal species no longer in existence. In 1781 Laurenti first described the olm (Proteus anguinus), an eel-like salamander discovered in the caves of Carniole in Italy. Half a century later, the German archaeologist Schmerling studied human remains and artefacts from the Palaeolithic period and confirmed that the people then had dwelt in caves. In 1857 Charles Lespès discovered cave-dwelling insects, and in 1901 the prehistorian Rivière reported on the wall carvings of La Mouthe in the Combarelles area of France. Palaeontologists, archaeologists and prehistorians were all fascinated by these holes in the earth, which were soon to become objects of scientific study.

The 'father' of speleology

The attraction that caves held for the jurist Edouard-Alfred Martel led him at a very early age to scour every cranny of the Causses, a region of limestone plateaux in south-central France. The magistrate spent intense hours exploring the region's caves and underground rivers. With only rudimentary techniques at his disposal—rope ladders, a windlass, and folding boats to explore the rivers—and accompanied by his faithful comrade Louis Armand, from 1888 to 1899 Martel led a double life, split between the bright lights of the law courts and the shadows of underground caves. He explored the Bramabiau cave, and followed from end to end the underground river that crosses the Causses, before, in 1889, investigating the Padirac chasm, a vast network of lakes and galleries, the largest known at the time. Martel also devoted a portion of his energies to fitting out the chasm so that it could be opened to the public. The speleologist proved how mechanical erosion worked, and created and developed the discipline of hydrogeology. His renown spread beyond his native France, and foreign governments also called upon him to solve hydrological problems. In 1897 he reconnoitred the Armand sinkhole, which his colleague had discovered, and found a veritable virgin forest of stalactites. Martel founded a learned journal, and pushed for the passage of a law in 1902 protecting cave environments. A true pioneer, Martel revolutionized knowledge of the underground world with his research and observations.

Bisons in a cave

Martel opened up an entire world to explore. An Italian team set a world record when they descended 450 metres below the surface in the Bertarelli chasm. In 1922 a young Frenchman, Norbert Casteret, alone and with no special equipment, made his way across two sumps (water-filled passages) into the Montespan cave, where he discovered sculpted clay figurines of bison and wall carvings dating from the Magdalenian period (which ended around 10,000 years ago). In 1926 Casteret and his wife, Elisabeth, explored the icy caves of the Spanish Pyrenees, a phantasmagoria of frozen lakes and waterfalls, crystals and frozen stalagmites. The couple carried out a geological and hydrographical study of the Monts Maudits, and identified the source of the Garonne River. In Ariège the Casterets discovered in 1932 the Cigalère cave, filled with gypsum crystals; two years later they found France's deepest chasm, a vertiginous chain of vertical wells set one over the other. They christened it the Martel chasm, in honour of speleology's pioneer. The death of Elisabeth Casteret, and the advent of war, put an end to the expeditions.

Crystal palm trees

Unlike Norbert Casteret, who often set out into the unknown with only the most rudimentary means, Robert de Joly worked to improve caving equipment. He introduced ladders made of light materials, hard hats equipped with acetylene lamps and inflatable dinghies. In 1929 he set up the first underground camp, and systematically prospected the chasms of the Causse Noir, which Martel had been unable to explore. In 1935, accompanied by Abbé Glory, a photographer, and three boy scouts, Joly came upon the Orgnac sinkhole in the Ardèche. At forty-nine metres below the surface, perched on a pile of bones at the very bottom of the hole, the party stood frozen with awe in the silent darkness at the sight of a thirty-metre chamber filled with magnificent limestone concretions and crystal 'palm trees'. One hundred metres farther down, they discovered a canyon created by an underground river; and at 181 metres, an imposing stalagmite rose up before them: according to their estimations, its volume was 500 cubic metres, and it had needed 300,000 years to get to that size. Their adventure marked the end of amateur explorations.

Journeys into darkness

The exploration of the Henne-Morte chasm in the Pyrenees, interrupted by World War II, was resumed in 1946 by Félix Trombe and his team.

With the support of the French Army, Trombe pitched an underground camp of insulated tents at 250 metres below the surface for his party of twelve speleologists. Trombe had designed a cockpit to protect the men from waterfalls as they descended ever deeper. The lead team reached 446 metres, a French record soon beaten by Chevalier, who went down as far as 603 metres in the Glaz hole. Between 1948 and 1949, a forty-man expedition equipped with eighteen boats resumed the exploration of the Padirac chasm, beyond the farthest point reached by Martel. In 1953 the world record for subterranean exploration was broken in the Pierre St-Martin chasm by speleologists who descended to 700 metres; three years later an international team reached the final sump of the Berger gorge in the Vercors—1,100 metres down. French speleologists were recognized as the best in the world, for their scientific precision and the scope of their investigations deep in the earth.

The formation of caves

Virtually all the world's big caves are in limestone, a sedimentary rock that forms at the bottom of oceans. Over time, the movement of earth's continental plates has pushed up many limestone areas high above sea level, spectacularly twisting the rock to form cracks and faults. All these fissures drain and absorb water, which over the centuries dissolves and erodes the limestone, enlarging the cracks into the passages and chambers that form cave systems. This process takes many millions of years, and in several more millions of years, the same processes will lead to the disappearance of the cave.

The famous wall paintings of Lascaux were made seventeen thousand years ago by artists of the Magdalenian era. They were discovered by chance during World War II.

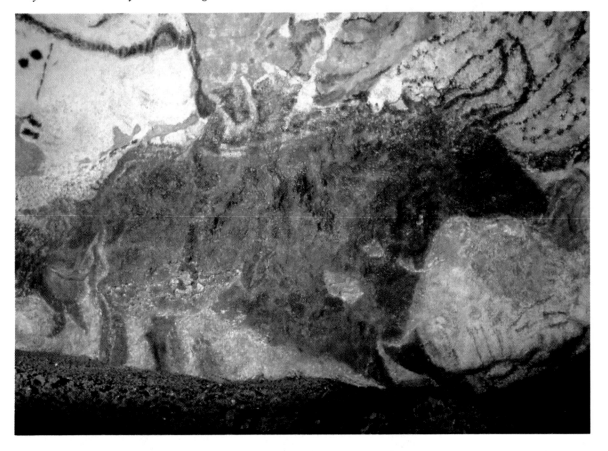

fter World War II, interest in underground exploration grew enormously. Speleologists ventured ever deeper into the bowels of the earth; at first considered a sport, speleology earned a place among the earth sciences. Fascination with the subterranean world, which still conceals thousands of unexplored caverns, has spread worldwide.

The technical progress of the 1960s has made it possible to get beyond flooded areas such as sumps in underground galleries.

An adventure outside time

The 1961 expedition to the Scarasson chasm (not far from Nice, in the South-east of France) resulted in the discovery, at a depth of one hundred metres, of a glacier thirty metres thick. Michel Siffre, an experienced young speleologist, went underground for two months to study the phenomenon—probably unique—of the subterranean glacier. His experience 'outside time' also furthered knowledge of human physiological reactions to isolation in utter darkness and silence, with no way of telling time. One tonne of equipment was taken below the surface to set up Siffre's camp. On 16 July 1962 Siffre began his voyage underground; in just three days he had lost all notion of time. Suffering from dizziness and profound depression, he nearly abandoned his project. He spent much of his time lying down. Finally, on 14 September, the surface team announced to Siffre that the experiment was completed—much to Siffre's surprise, for he believed that it was only 20 August. Bringing the exhausted speleologist back to the surface turned out to be a rescue mission. But the experiment was deemed a success, and drew an enthusiastic response from physicians specializing in aerospatial medicine.

Other volunteers repeated Siffre's exploit. Josie Laurès, the first woman to attempt the 'journey outside time' spent three months underground in 1965, and in 1966 Jean-Pierre Mairetet shattered an American record by remaining beneath the surface for six months.

Volunteers in the abyss

Experiments in solitary survival underground fascinated many speleologists. On 14 February 1972 Siffre entered Midnight Cave in the United States for a seven-month stay. The cave fitted out for Siffre resembled a chamber for simulating isolation in space. Throughout the experiment Siffre underwent regular psychological and physiological tests to evaluate the evolution of the physical and intellectual faculties of a human being existing outside time. Electrodes placed on his face recorded brain waves during his sleep, and measured his heartbeat. Despite the dampness and all-enveloping silence of the cave, Siffre withstood his isolation for sixty days. After that time, he was invaded by doubts and discouragement. He stopped making scientific observations. His only comfort was the food supplied to him by NASA. Finally, on 10 August, the above-ground team alerted Siffre that the end of the experiment was at hand. Siffre emerged to a triumphant welcome, but he suffered from impaired vision, and was in so depressed a state that he could not immediately resume a normal life. Milutin of Yugoslavia spent 463 days in a Serbian cave, but he was not entirely alone: he had a cat, a dog, two chickens, and a pair of ducks for company.

Traces of ancient civilizations

British and American speleologists in the meantime were quite active, exploring karsts—areas of limestone formations characterized by sinks, ravines, and underground streams—from Mexico to India. Siffre, by then the foremost French speleologist, resumed more conventional modes of subterranean exploration. In 1975 along with Gérard Cappa, a guide, and two porters, he followed the course of the Rio Panuelo o Cante, systematically investigating the caves of the Poptun region in Guatemala. The team carried out hydrological analyses, locating many underground streams, although the earth's surface in that region was dried out by the sun. They also found the remains of ancient burial grounds, shards of Mayan pottery, wall carvings, and footprints preserved in clay. In the following years the same party investigated the Petén caves on the Belize border, where they discovered clay figurines, pottery, and a dozen sculpted heads that dated back to the pre-Columbian Olmec civilization (circa 1000 BC). Successive expeditions turned up archaeological treasures, but the discovery of the Nar Tunich cave, a Mayan sanctuary, was the most significant discovery of all.

Hacking with machetes in the chasms of New Britain

After numerous discoveries made by British explorers in New Guinea, the French organized a far-ranging exploration campaign on the nearby island of New Britain. In 1980 a team of eleven speleologists led by Jean-François Pernette descended 459 metres into the Kavakuna cave. At the bottom they found a river, which the men followed for about a kilometre before an impassable sump blocked their way. The expedition also investigated the Lusé sinkhole, the largest chasm then known, measuring 750 metres in diameter—in fact the interest it held for speleologists was chiefly its colossal size. The team then set out for the Grand Vuvu. The descent was difficult, for the men had to hack their way with machetes through the dense vegetation that covered the rock face. They finally touched bottom at 414 metres, where they discovered a labyrinth of different levels and vaults. The exploration of the Petit Vuvu revealed 6200 metres of underground

galleries which no human had ever beheld, full of sparkling crystals and petrified waterfalls. The explorers recorded a large fund of hydrological observations concerning the chasms of New Britain, which may not be the world's deepest, but are surely the largest.

The largest cave known was discovered in 1980 by the Anglo-Malayan team Mulu, in the Gunung Mulu National Park (Malaya).

Diving beneath the earth's surface

In 1981, after eighteen years of explorations in the Jean-Bernard chasm, a vast underground network in Savoy, a French expedition broke the world record for descending deepest into the earth. The venture's logistics were meticulously planned. Thirty speleologists made forty-two descents to transport diving and filming equipment and medical supplies to the subterranean camps. At last on 27 February 1981 divers Patrick Penez and Fred Vergier plunged into the underground river. After a six-hour dive during which they crossed two sumps (sections of subterranean galleries lying under water), they came up with their topographical surveys. Their calculations in the Jean-Bernard chasm revealed that it was 1455 metres deep. Helped by ever more sophisticated equipment speleologists penetrated deeper still, overcoming the dangers posed by sumps. In 1982 an Australian team made it past a sump 2500 metres long, travelling some seven kilometres under water. Today, thanks to relays (not unlike the technique used by mountaineers in the Himalayas), divers in the lead team replace their used air bottles with full ones set out for them on preliminary dives. Considering the problems of adequate air reserves and the risks of decompression, subterranean diving remains a particularly daring aspect of speleological research.

A victim of timelessness

On 18 August 1988 Véronique Le Guen went down into the Valat-Nègre cave on France's Causse Noir, for an experiment in 'atemporality' similar to those attempted in preceding decades. She volunteered to live utterly alone beneath the surface for one hundred days, with no means of telling time. Le Guen descended into a specially fitted-out cave situated eighty metres below the surface. The temperature was a

Two specialists in travelling outside time, Véronique le Guen and Michel Siffre, in a sinkhole at Aven Armand (Lozère, southern France).

constant 9°C, and the humidity steady at about 90 percent. Totally in control of her activities, she was linked to an aboveground team by telephone, which she could employ at will, as well as by electrodes that measured her biorhythms. Owing to her menstrual cycle, Le Guen was able to remain more closely in touch with reality than previous pioneers in this sort of experiment. Intense periods of activity lasting nearly forty-eight hours alternated with long stretches of sleep, illustrating human beings' rapid adaptation to a 'bicircadian' rhythm, which differs from the habitual 'circadian' cycle that follows the alternation of day and night. Day after day, Le Guen underwent tests, took measurements and scientific notes, and devoted the rest of her time to reading. At last on 29 November she returned to the surface, triumphant after 110 days underground. But after such an experience the human organism faces a difficult period of readaptation to life above ground, as the generally depressed state of those who return from the depths attests. A few months after her experiment with atemporality, Véronique Le Guen committed suicide.

Underground landscapes

For thousands of years raindrops and running and stagnant waters have produced the concretions of carbonates, limestone, calcite, or aragonite that compose the strange world of underground caves. Transparent stalactites that fall from tall vaults, or stalagmites that grow from the cave floors, spindly or twisted columns that form crowns, petals, or lace, translucid or coloured curtains, gypsum crystals or beads are some of the subterranean formations that tell the story and reveal the age of a cavern.

VOLCANIC FIRES

he cataclyms caused by volcanic eruptions inspired innumerable superstitions that combined irrational fears and extravagant hypotheses. At the dawn of the twentieth century, pioneering explorers of the smoking monsters no longer limited their efforts to describing the eruption—they actually measured and interpreted volcanic activity. Thus a new earth science was born: volcanology.

The first fruits of volcanology

The Latin poet Virgil attributed the eruptions of Mount Etna to the desperate efforts of the Titan Enceladus to escape from the prison where Zeus had thrown him. Other Romans said that volcanoes were Vulcan's workshop, where he forged arrows for Apollo. Early philosophers were the first to approach volcanoes scientifically. Empedocles tried to pierce the mystery of Mount Etna by climbing up to the crater, but he perished for his pains. Plato affirmed that volcanoes were born of subterranean rivers of fire, and Seneca held that molten matter from the depths of the earth sometimes rose to the surface, causing volcanic eruptions. Pliny the Younger's detailed account of the eruption of Vesuvius in 79 AD made him history's first volcanologist. He described the tremors, the falling ash, the red clouds and pillars of fire of the cataclysm that destroyed Pompeii, and which buried in molten lava those who tried to flee. In the Middle Ages volcanoes were believed to be the vents of hell. Only in the Renaissance was scientific observation of volcanoes resumed. In the Enlightenment of the eighteenth century James Hutton, Sir William Hamilton and Georges Buffon all contributed to the knowledge of volcanic phenomena. And in order to study volcanoes more closely, some scientists decided to explore them.

In the smoke of volcanoes

Early in the nineteenth century Alexander von Humboldt (see p. 90) explored several cones of active volcanoes in the volcanic ranges of the Cordilleras of the Andes and Mexico, in order to learn about the geological stratifications of the New World. On 23 June 1802 the explorer and his comrades reached 4500 metres above sea level on Chimborazo, a now-extinct volcano which dominates the Andes of Ecuador. The porters, terrified by the mountain, which they believed to be inhabited by demons, abandoned the expedition. One member of the party, suffering from altitude sickness, fainted. The mountain's steep sides were covered with ice and snow, and crevasses increased the difficulty of the climb to the summit, from which sulphurous vapours steamed. Having reached an altitude of 5610 metres the expedition decided not to climb farther, but the men had gathered much valuable data. Humboldt established that volcanoes are clustered along faults in the earth's surface, and showed the relationship between earthquakes and volcanic eruptions. In the course of his explorations he counted 407 volcanoes, 225 of them active; he thus produced the very first report on the world's volcanic activity.

Desolation from Mount Pelée

On 8 May 1902 a nuée ardente (a burning cloud of volcanic fragments and poisonous

The eruption of Vesuvius, which destroyed Pompeii in 79 AD, as seen by a painter of the nineteenth century. Since then, the region has been shaken by other, albeit smaller eruptions.

The pioneer of volcanology, Alexander von Humboldt, explored several volcanic chains in the Andes and in Mexico, counting one hundred and twenty volcanoes.

The Valley of Ten Thousand Smokes

Violent explosions shook the region of Katmai, in Alaska, on 1 June 1912. The local Eskimo population fled. On the following days, more explosions tore the air. Enormous plumes of ash rose into the sky, and hails of pumice fell as far away as Kodiak, a village 160 kilometres distant. In 1916 the geologists Griggs and Folson, visiting the deserted site of the eruption, were astonished to discover an immense orange-tinted valley buried beneath the ash, from which thousands upon thousands of plumes of smoke rose to heights of one to three hundred metres.

gases) hurtled down the slopes of Mont Pelée on the West Indian island of Martinique, tearing up trees, setting fire to the town, razing houses, and sinking boats in the bay.

In just a few minutes the volcano's fury destroyed St Pierre, the capital, and all but two of its 28,000 inhabitants. American President Theodore Roosevelt commissioned an expedition to study the eruption. The *Dixie* touched land on 21 May, carrying Thomas Jaggar and Alfred Lacroix of France, who were destined to become experts in volcanology, then only a minor branch of geology. Struck by the scope of the destruction, the scientists sifted through the ruins. They estimated the temperature of the nuée ardente to have been as high as 700 to 1000 °C, and concluded that the victims had died of suffocation.

Helping the inhabitants

When in 1929 clouds of smoke, gas and ash were seen issuing from Mont Pelée, foreshadowing another eruption, the population—still haunted by the memory of the previous cataclysm—prepared to evacuate the region. It was then that an American engineer, Frank Alvord Perret, travelled to Martinique. He calculated the curve of the eruptive cycle, and, persuaded that the molten lava would flow over the same course it had followed before, an area unin-

habited ever since, he concluded that no danger was present. The eruption proved him right. Only the volcanologist's observatory, situated on the path of the nuée ardente, was destroyed. Volcanology became a science in its own right, producing theories that explained how and why volcanoes erupt.

Jaggar keeps watch on Kilauea

A geologist turned volcanologist, Thomas Jaggar roamed the world in search of erupting volcanoes. At the time only one permanent observatory existed, built in 1845 on Vesuvius. Jaggar grew weary of reproducing volcanological characteristics in a laboratory; he wrung funds from every possible source, and in 1912 was able at last to construct the American observatory on Kilauea in Hawaii, on the edge of a crater 120 metres deep. Jaggar installed seismographs, measured temperatures in the fissures of the volcano, and perfected a method for gathering volcanic gases; he recorded vast quantities of data, and kept a close watch on the volcano's activity.

In 1924 after the eruption of a neighbouring volcano, Mauna Loa, a flow of lava threatened to bury the town of Hilo. Jaggar attempted to divert the flow by bombing the lip of the crater with explosives. The bombs blew holes in the crater, which caused the

temperature to drop, and the lava to become less liquid. In 1933 Jaggar had walls built to deflect the lava flow. Not only did Jaggar introduce the practice of keeping constant watch on active volcanoes, he was also the first to counteract the destructive violence of volcanic eruptions.

Birth of a volcano

On 20 February 1943 a Mexican peasant named Dionisio Pulido heard rumblings from under the earth; he saw the trees tremble and the ground swell. The next day, he was stupefied to discover in his maize field a twenty-four-metre crevasse that spouted ash and stones. His little patch of land had disappeared; a similar fate awaited the neighbouring village of Paricutin. Geologists swarmed to the site to witness the birth of a volcano. In a week's time the volcano had risen to 165 metres, and was spewing out incandescent lava that destroyed all the surrounding terrain. Its growth gradually slowed, and finally stopped nine years later; the volcano measured 2808 metres. In the meantime it had spewed out some 3500 million tonnes of ash and lava, and had razed 6000 dwellings in Paricutin and San Juan Parangaricutiro. Then the volcano, christened Paricutin after the town it had buried, fell silent. In 1943 Showa-Shinzan in Japan, and in 1948 Kituro in Zaïre were formed in a similar fashion.

Rafting on a lava flow

During the 1938 eruption of a cone of the Klyuchevskaya volcano on the Kamchatka Peninsula, Soviet volcanologists Popkov and Ivanov leapt on to a block of solidified lava in the incandescent sea that surrounded them, and started measuring temperatures and taking gas samples. Their raft drifted along on a flow of molten rock, heated to 870 °C. They navigated in that fashion for over an hour, covering two kilometres borne on the wave of lava. Though they were wearing asbestos boots they felt the heat of their improvised raft, which mounted to 300°C, heated by the intensely hot lava.

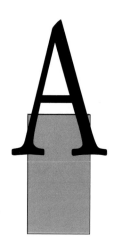

*A*dvances made in twentieth-century volcanology showed that it is possible to resist, and even to counter the devastating effects of an unchained natural monster. Volcanologists now regularly listen to the rumblings at the earth's core the better to predict the awakening of dormant volcanoes, and to prevent heavy loss of human life.

The rescue of Sapunza

In March 1983 the Sicilian town of Sapunza was threatened by an eruption of Mount Etna, Europe's largest active volcano. Lava had already buried hotels and villas on the volcano's southern flank. Volcanologists proposed to divert the flow from inhabited areas. A gigantic earthen dike was built, 500 metres long, 20 metres high, and 40 metres wide. At the same time a breach was dynamited into the lava channel 2200 metres up the mountainside, to force the flow into the channel built for the detour. After weeks of frantic efforts against the lava flow, Sapunza was ultimately saved.

A lake at the bottom of Nyiragongo

During a 1948 expedition in Zaïre, French geologist Haroun Tazieff explored the Nyiragongo volcano. He climbed down into the crater, where he discovered a boiling lava lake, some 200 metres below the crater rim. He resolved to study the phenomenon, and though the authorities refused to grant him permission, in 1953 Tazieff organized a clandestine expedition to explore the bottom of the crater. But the men needed a windlass to go down into the chimney and Tazieff was obliged to abandon this attempt. He tried again in 1958. He had become a recognized volcanologist, and went back once more to study the volcano with an organizational plan as meticulously drawn up as those for Himalayan expeditions. The team pitched camps on two banks at different levels in the crater and set in place a windlass to take them down to the viscous, burning lake. Wearing masks to protect them against acidic fumes, the scientists measured temperatures and took seismographic records. Buoyed by their success, in 1959 the expedition attempted to gather samples of volcanic gases at temperatures above 1000°C. All that was then known of these gases was based on information acquired from samples taken thirty years earlier on Kilauea in Hawaii by Jaggar, Shepherd, and Day. There, the quantity and type of gas released from magma varies from one zone to another. The level of the Nyiragongo lava lake lowered, uncovering a third terrace. Using skills that would have done credit to a mountain-climbing team, the volcanologists descended to a mass of cooled lava that overhung the lake, and enclosed the valuable samples in a thermocouple. The analysis of the gases' composition turned out to be vital to the understanding of volcanic eruptions.

266

The terrifying magic lake

In 1973 an expedition started out for the smoking chasm of Nyiragongo. Equipped with fireproof suits, gas masks and climbing gear, Maurice and Katia Krafft of France set out to spend a week on the shore of the 400-metre-long lava lake that bubbled and boiled at the bottom of the crater. Once they had pitched camp on the rim of the crater, they studied the crater's structure, the petrography of the rocks, and the variations in temperature of the magma that bubbled beneath their feet. Gases smelling strongly of sulphur burst at the surface and dripped back down the sides of the crater. Four years later what had been a fiery but harmless spectacle exploded. Lava burst through the volcano's walls, escaping from every fissure; a tidal wave of molten rock heated to 1000°C swept down over villages and fields, burying all in its wake. The Kraffts rushed to the site of the catastrophe, and discovered in the crater a smoking hole 1200 metres in diameter, 800 metres deep, filled with fallen rocks and drained of the lava lake which they had studied earlier. In June 1982 a 200-metre-long fissure split the volcano's bottom, and a fresh flood of lava escaped. The new lake grew until it rose to within 400 metres of the crater's lip., and once again the Kraffts were there to study the lake's formation.

Mount Erebus, volcano of the frozen South

In 1974 Tazieff led a team of scientists from France and New Zealand to Mount Erebus (3794 metres), a perpetually erupting volcano in Antarctica first climbed by Shackleton in 1908. From the American base at McMurdo Sound, an airlift transported men and equipment to the acclimatation camp at 3000 metres above sea level, and thence to a base camp at 3700 metres, where the team could carry out their research on Mount Erebus. From the moment they arrived at camp, the men were buffeted by a polar blizzard and temperatures that dropped as low as −60°C. They descended the frozen walls of the crater to an active vent in which they saw a lake of lava. The volcanologists used a windlass to position their equipment for taking samples of eruptive gases that escaped from the seething magma. But the risks of the operation were multiplied by constant explosions, and by projectiles that shot out suddenly from the dense smoke. The scientists made seismographic investigations, studied the fumaroles (emissions of hot gases and steam) outside the crater, and took geological samples. After two weeks of taking measurements, the team was still unable to approach the lava lake owing to the number and force of explosions within the crater. Tazieff had to abandon his project, but he returned to Mount Erebus in 1978. On that expedition the volcanologists did not attempt to descend into the crater. Instead they used newly developed techniques to gather samples that would allow them to isolate the minor and major components of the volcano's eruptive gases.

The explosion of Mount St Helens

In 1980 volcanologists observed signs of the impending explosion of Mount St Helens (2950 metres), the most active volcano in the Cascade range of the northwestern United States. Steam and ash plumes rising above the crater made residents evacuate the area. On 18 May the mountain was shaken by a tremor that measured five on

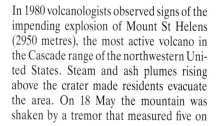

the Richter scale. In a matter of seconds a gigantic avalanche of rocks and ice swept down the mountainside to Spirit Lake. The lake's water level rose by some sixty metres. With no cap to hold back the pressure, the magma exploded. A gust of gases and ash heated to 300°C surged from the crater and buried everything that lay up to thirty kilometres north of the volcano. The catastrophe destroyed nearly 600 kilometres of forest, and killed sixty persons including the American volcanologist David Johnston, who had hurried to the site to study the eruption. Many other scientists, among them Maurice and Katia Krafft, rushed to the United States. On the evening of the eruption, Mount St Helens was shorter by 430 metres, but had gained a crater 700 metres deep. Two months later, a second eruption shattered the dome of unset lava measuring 200 metres in diameter, which was swelling in the bottom of the crater. The Kraffts explored the smoking hole and waded up to their knees in clouds of volcanic dust in order to measure temperatures and to take gas samples. Since the eruption, American volcanologists have studied Mount St Helens closely, and can now predict eruptions several days in advance.

Nevado del Ruiz awakes from a long sleep

———————●———————

In the last weeks of 1984 a few small tremors shook Nevado del Ruiz, a volcano in Colombia. The glacier was melting, covered with grey dust spewed forth by explosions of steam in the volcano's crater, the Arenas. Colombian and foreign volcanologists alerted the authorities, recommending that the town of Armero be evacuated. According to their calculations an eruption had a sixty-seven per cent chance of triggering destructive mudslides. Nevado del Ruiz threw out blocks of lava and ash over a period of ten months. The mayor of Armero urged the townspeople to flee, but his warnings went unheeded. On 13 November 1985 the volcano erupted, burying 22,000 inhabitants in a torrent of mud, tree trunks and rocks that flowed down the mountainside at thirty-five kilometres per hour. The deluge swept all before it: first cold, then progressively hotter, it scalded the survivors. The next day Armero was covered by a grey layer five to eight metres thick. Only a few hills poked above the muddy tide to the north and to the east. Survivors clung to floating debris, waiting to be rescued. Helicopters saved some victims who were sinking in the mud. Tens of thousands of dead or injured, thousands of head of cattle lost, a town buried, and acres of crops destroyed made this eruption one of history's most dramatic volcanic disasters. Now, since its eruption, Nevada del Ruiz smokes peacefully, and the Colombian government has declared Armero a sanctuary and place of prayer.

The birth of volcanoes

Volcanoes are temporary or permanent openings in the earth's crust; what we see of them is their craters, cones and domes. Hidden underground is the magma, which circulates unseen and becomes lava when it is spewed forth from a volcano. This reservoir is buried beneath the surface, sometimes hundreds of kilometres deep. More than a thousand volcanoes are currently active. Strewn from Iceland to Indonesia, Africa, Japan, Hawaii, the Aleutian and Kuril Islands and the Americas, all regions studded with volcanoes, they are constantly watched by teams of specialists.

'Waves of molten rocks spilled out from the twisted crater like a torrential river, tearing out huge chunks from the edges of the blowhole. Enormous, rugged scoriae... are carried on the river of lava, in a sea of fire.' (The Conquest of the Volcanoes, *by Katia and Maurice Krafft.*)

Space

F rom the dawn of time, it seems, the heavens have been imagined as the home of the gods. Yet in his unrelenting quest for new horizons, man inevitably looked towards the skies and began to regard them as virgin territory to be explored. The first step in the long conquest of space occurred when people began to scrutinize the firmament, searching for signs, a language, an underlying meaning.

Science-fiction films

Ever since the *Improbable Flight of a Group of Scientists of the Incoherent Geographical Society* by French film pioneer Georges Méliès in 1902, the cinema has conjured up a vast number of imaginary journeys. Perhaps the most famous is Stanley Kubrick's *2001: A Space Odyssey*. Since then, *Star Wars*, *E.T.*, *The Planet of the Apes*, and *Close Encounters of the Third Kind* have portrayed fascinating fictional worlds. However, what all these films have in common is their treatment of very down-to-Earth problems transposed into fantasy settings where anything is possible. Thus they differ greatly from real-life explorations.

The Greeks and the heavens

———————●———————

'When we had progressed farther into the land of the Moon, we were captured by Hippogryphs. They were men mounted on triple-headed winged griffons...' That is how, around 180 AD, the Greek satirist Lucian of Samosata recounted in his *True History* man's first battle with creatures from space. Not long after, Lucian published the *Icaromenippus*, the story of another space traveller who, thanks to the vulture's wing affixed to his right arm and the eagle's wing to his left, could fly about where he wished. After Lucian's humorous flights of fancy, the notion of space travel disappeared from literature for centuries. The astronomical theories propounded by Aristotle and Ptolemy and later imposed by the Church dominated—and severely limited—knowledge of the universe. Through observation the Greek astronomer Thales of Miletus was able to predict the solar eclipse of 585 BC; as early as the sixth century BC the Pythagoreans maintained that the Earth is a sphere that revolves around a central fire; while in the third century BC Aristarchus of Samos propounded his heliocentric theory: the Earth rotates on its axis and like the other planets revolves around the Sun. Yet it was Ptolemy's erroneous system that ultimately prevailed. His assertion that the Earth—and therefore man—was at the centre of the universe represented a huge step backwards for science.

Return to reason

———————●———————

In 1507 Nicolaus Copernicus rediscovered Aristarchus's theory of heliocentrism. After him, Johannes Kepler of Germany calculated the elliptical orbits of the planets and the distances that separate them from the Sun. In the *Somnium*, published posthumously in 1634, four years after his death, Kepler gives a minute description of the Moon, a veritable compendium of the astronomical knowledge of the age. In places the work even reads like a science-fiction novel, telling of the problems that would arise in the course of a space journey—the thinning of the atmosphere at high altitudes, the phenomenon of weightlessness...

The invention of the telescope by Galileo in 1609, particularly after it had been improved by Isaac Newton in 1672, allowed closer observation of the Moon and the planets; scientists began to surmise the infinite dimensions of the universe. Two seventeenth-century English clergymen, John Wilkins and Francis Godwin, published accounts of travel to the Moon. Wilkins's *Discovery of a World in the Moon* of 1638 describes the possibilities of life in space with appealing naivety. In contrast, Godwin's *The Man in the Moone* is far more realistic. The protagonist builds his own space machine, and launches his expedition from Tenerife, an island that lies, by an odd coincidence, at the same latitude as Cape Canaveral, the site of so many modern-day blast-offs. Godwin then relates with astonishing precision the entry of the vehicle into orbit, the phenomenon of weightlessness, and the appearance of Earth viewed from space. On the Moon the hero encounters fabulous beasts and an ore which he is certain will put a permanent end to energy problems.

The power of imagination

———————●———————

Cyrano de Bergerac was a colourful character: a noted gambler and brawler, he was also sickly, syphilitic, bald, short-sighted, and chronically lacking in funds. Yet his vivid imagination made him a pioneer in the art of science fiction. His best-known work, *A Voyage to the Moon: with some account of the Solar World*, which dates from 1649, is a masterpiece of inventiveness. To fly through space, Cyrano's protagonists use diverse means, always the products of serious 'scientific' reflection. One voyager surrounds himself with 'flasks filled with dew', which are drawn up by the Sun; another invents a reactor powered by solar rays that pulls him up into the heavens. Cyrano was the first to imagine multi-stage rockets to break through the Earth's gravitational field. His fertile imagination produced idyllic extraterrestrial landscapes: he describes the Moon as a paradise where one could while away a pleasant life of leisure. The nations and empires of the Sun are models of social organization, and the Sun itself is the home that welcomes all philosophers after their death.

After Cyrano, however, space travel disappeared as a literary theme. Only Voltaire, in his *Micromégas*, created an extraterrestrial protagonist—an inhabitant of Sirius—who visits Earth with a companion from Saturn. Not until the nineteenth century did space fiction re-emerge as a popular genre.

Jules Verne

———————●———————

With the coming of the Industrial Revolution, science returned to the forefront, creating a rich new landscape for the imagination. A widespread taste for science fiction and tales of space travel soon developed, a vein exploited with unparalleled success by Jules Verne, whose work is now synonymous with nineteenth-century science fiction. Verne's passion for technology and his precision and attention to detail make his writings a veritable encyclopedia (albeit in

What Jules Verne wrote may have been fiction, but it nevertheless anticipated reality. In From the Earth to the Moon *he sends a spacecraft into the infinite cosmos.*

novel form) of the scientific knowledge of his day. Blessed with an imagination that fairly teemed with ideas, Verne always made painstaking efforts to back up his literary inventions with scientific information. Thus in *From the Earth to the Moon* the author's space vehicle, an artillery projectile fired by a gigantic cannon, is launched from Florida 'so that the Moon would sometimes be directly overhead, a position possible only in the tropics'. His calculations of speeds and travel times are amazingly close to those actually achieved by modern spacecraft. Of course Jules Verne had no notion of the effects of acceleration on the passengers of his spaceship, who in real life would have been crushed by the increased pressure. And naturally Verne was unaware of the resistance of the lower layers of the atmosphere, which would have immediately destroyed his craft. Yet Jules Verne has the distinction of being the first to state that the only way to pull clear of the Earth's gravitational force is to attain sufficiently high velocity.

Bluffs and hoaxes

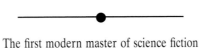

In 1835 the *New York Sun* published what remains to this day one of the biggest hoaxes in the history of space exploration.

Journalist Richard Locke dreamed up a newspaper article on discoveries made by the astronomer Sir John Frederick Herschel (Sir William's son) with a giant telescope set up in South Africa. From his station on Earth the scientist peering at the Moon could see dense vegetation and abundant animal life. To add a final touch to his clever deception, Locke invented the Selenites, flying creatures with bat-like wings who inhabit the Moon. The hoax succeeded beyond Locke's wildest imaginings. Sales of the *New York Sun* reached record heights. The existence of extraterrestrials seemed so natural to the public that even scientists began actively to search for them. A huge reward was offered to anyone who produced proof of their existence. Extravagant schemes were put forward. By the time the hoax was discovered, Locke had disappeared. He was never heard of again.

On 30 October 1938 Orson Welles threw New York into uproar with his Hallowe'en radio dramatization of H.G. Wells's *War of the Worlds*, a broadcast so frighteningly realistic that New Yorkers ran out of their homes into the streets, convinced that their city was being invaded by Martians.

Science fiction

The first modern master of science fiction

was the English writer H.G. Wells (1866-1946). His two masterpieces in the genre are the famous *War of the Worlds* (1898) and *The First Men on the Moon* (1901). Wells did not share Jules Verne's concern for scientific accuracy. His imagination alone guided the construction of his plots. In 1869 the American novelist Edward Everett Hale, in *The Brick Moon*, dreamed up the first artificial satellite sent into orbit around the Earth, powered by a high-speed revolving wheel.

In the twentieth century science fiction has grown into a major popular genre, marketed by major publishing houses. Masters of 'sci-fi' – Alfred Elton Van Vogt, Isaac Asimov, Ray Bradbury, Philippe Curval – have each created a distinctive universe of extraterrestrial civilizations, involving interplanetary travel and intergalactic rivalries. Most often the inhabitants of different systems are mortal enemies (extraterrestrials are almost invariably presented as warlike peoples). Broadly speaking, it was not until American film maker Steven Spielberg's *Close Encounters of the Third Kind* that positive relations with creatures from space were presented as possible. But even the hero of Spielberg's film *E.T.* remains a victim of 'racism' against extraterrestrials: only children can communicate with him; adult 'earthlings' remain walled up in their prejudices. In Ridley Scott's *Blade Runner*, however, the hero falls in love with a beautiful android.

*W*hat sort of machine could explore the cosmos? How would it be powered? What sort of fuel would it use? While aviation was still in its infancy, some visionaries were already thinking ahead to space travel. The road from dream to reality is often more difficult than originally envisaged. As it turned out, the route to the stars was opened not only by human genius and courage but also by the imperatives of war.

Rocket launchers with shafts for directional guidance (1610).

The Chinese invent gunpowder

Gunpowder was invented by the Chinese, and at first was used in the manufacture of fireworks. Instructions for preparing the explosive mixture of potassium nitrate (saltpetre), charcoal and sulphur are found in a work dated 1050. In 1258 'Cathay arrows' caused a sensation when the Mongols captured Baghdad, devastating the Arab army with their fire-powered rockets. The Mongols had simply adopted the weapons from the Chinese, who had defeated them in 1232 at the siege of Kai-feng-Fu with their own rockets. In 1792 Indians employed rocket weapons to defend themselves against the British army at the Battle of Seringapatam. The British in their turn made such weapons part of their arsenal in 1799, but abandoned them at the end of the nineteenth century in favour of artillery, which could fire heavier shells to greater distances.

Rockets had peaceful uses as well, principally in the hugely successful art of fireworks. During the Renaissance no festivity worthy of the name lacked a display of coloured flames, Catherine wheels, and Roman candles. These pyrotechnic extravaganzas sometimes caused accidents, as at the 1748 Spring Festival in Paris, when fireworks killed forty people and wounded three hundred others.

Adventures of an extraordinary chemist

The weather in Paris was not fine on the morning of 24 August 1804. At ten o'clock hopes for a clear sky were slim. But in the garden of the Conservatory of Arts and Crafts, Jean-Baptiste Biot and Joseph-Louis Gay-Lussac decided that they could delay their experiment no longer. They gave the order to free the balloon in which they had taken their places. For the first time in history, Science left the ground for the air. The experiment had a twofold objective: to measure variations in the Earth's magnetic field at high altitudes, and to gather air samples to see if the composition of the upper atmosphere differed from air closer to the ground. Back on terra firma, the scientists had to admit that their results were unremarkable. They immediately began to plan a second ascent. Thus it was that on 16 September 1804, at 9.40 am, Gay-Lussac (alone this time) ascended to what remained until his death in 1850 the record altitude of 7016 metres above sea level. In fact the scientific value of these two ascents was limited. At most, they established that the composition of air does not vary at different altitudes, and that its temperature and humidity drop as altitude increases.

Gay-Lussac later won a reputation as a great chemist, but his youthful adventures in a balloon kept their symbolic value as the first scientific conquest of space.

The scientific prophet

In Kaluga, a city in the central Soviet Union, a little wooden house stands next to the modern buildings that house the Soviet Space Museum. In that house the man who is now regarded as the prophet of space flight lived and died. Konstantin Eduardovich Tsiolkovsky, a tactiturn, solitary country school teacher, had one consuming passion: space travel. In 1903 he published his first thoughts on the subject in an article entitled 'Exploring Cosmic Space with Reaction Engines'.

Tsiolkovsky provided solutions for just about every aspect of space exploration. He devised a multi-stage spacecraft, space suits, special seats to withstand the thrust of take-off, and rocket fuel composed of liquefied hydrogen and oxygen. He also foresaw the problems of walking in space and the need for protection against wide variations in temperature. His writings contain formulae for calculating weightlessness, a design for an artificial satellite, and plans for an interplanetary spaceship. Tsiolkovsky readily acknowledged the influence of Jules Verne, and declared that Verne's imagination alone had spurred him to such elaborate projects and calculations.

In the Leningrad Gas Dynamics laboratory in 1931 the first engine was built according to Tsiolkovsky's specifications. When he died at the age of seventy-six, the inventor was promoted to the rank of hero of Soviet science.

The unlucky inventor

When in 1960 the United States government was ordered to pay the sum of one million dollars to the widow of Robert Hutchings Goddard for unlawful use of her husband's patents, it was a belated compensation for the work of a man who had devoted his entire life to developing a high-altitude rocket. A professor of physics at Princeton University, Goddard had surmised before almost anyone else that rockets were the only means of flying at high altitudes, above the Earth's atmosphere. It seemed obvious to him that only liquid fuel could compensate for the thinning of the oxygen needed for combustion. In 1919 Goddard published a paper entitled 'A Method of Reaching Extreme Altitudes' in which he discussed the possibility of sending a rocket to crash-land on the moon. To many the project seemed sacrilegious, and the press reacted with a hostility that was to last throughout Goddard's life. Yet on 16 March 1926 he experimented with his first liquid-propellant rocket, which in just two and a half seconds reached the unheard-of cruising speed of 95 kilometres per hour. A second rocket reached an altitude of 2300 metres, coming very close to the speed of sound.

Goddard then settled on a farm in New Mexico where with four assistants he worked on perfecting his liquid-fuelled rockets. Before long he had registered over two hundred patents. World War II put an end to his efforts, but by then Goddard had designed the essential components of a rocket capable of reaching very high altitudes.

Installation of an experimental V2 rocket at the launching site at Kalbshafen, Germany (1942).

Blind passion

The father of European astronautics was Hermann Oberth, a German born in 1894 in Transylvania (in present-day Romania). At the age of thirty he published his doctoral thesis, *The Rocket Into Interplanetary Space*. Like Konstantin Eduardovich Tsiolkovsky and Goddard, he set forth the decisive advantages of liquid fuel, and discussed orbital flights and space stations as stops on the way to very distant destinations.

The impact of Oberth's book was so great that it led to the founding of a German space flight society. Wernher von Braun joined the group when he was just eighteen. In 1933, after launching several rockets under the society's auspices, the government proposed that he complete his doctoral dissertation in the army, though with civilian status. Four years later the Nazis showed that they understood the military value of von Braun's research, and established a centre at Peenemünde, on the Baltic coast, where before long the young engineer was directing some twelve thousand workers. Von Braun worked with a military physicist, Captain Walter Dornberger, to perfect the first long-range missile, the A-4, later rechristened the V-2, which Hitler started putting to military use in June 1944. Weighing thirteen tonnes and with a range of three hundred kilometres, some four thousand V-2 missiles were fired between June 1944 and May 1945, most of them aimed at London and Antwerp. After 1942 von Braun worked on a different project, the rocket A-9/A-10, which the Americans took over—along with the German engineer—at the end of the war.

Missiles for military use

Thanks to constant tinkering and steady improvement, the rocket was to become an accurate weapon used by the British in all their conflicts, notably in two important engagements against the United States in the War of 1812. It was to that weapon that the American national anthem alludes: '...and the rockets' red glare, the bombs bursting in air...' William Congreve, an English colonel, introduced the rocket into the British army in 1799. He perfected the principle of the weapon, and created an incendiary rocket that weighed 14.5 kilograms, with a range of three thousand metres. The rocket made an explosive entrance onto the military scene when the British attacked Boulogne in 1806 and Copenhagen in 1807. In 1867 rockets designed by another Englishman, William Hale, replaced Congreve's version. In World War I France was the only major power to use rockets, notably on Nieuport-Delage biplanes, where they were positioned under the wings, like today's rockets.

Lindbergh helps Goddard

Goddard had no funds to continue his research. It was the American aviator Charles Lindbergh, fresh from his successful crossing of the North Atlantic in 1927 and convinced of the importance of Goddard's work, who persevered in the search for financial backing. Lindbergh finally persuaded millionaire Daniel Guggenheim to award Goddard an annual grant of 25,000 dollars.

Working for the Americans

At the close of World War II von Braun and most of his aides surrendered to the Americans. The V-2 launching base was transported to the United States with a hundred or so captured missiles. The first rockets launched from New Mexico reached altitudes of 112 kilometres and later of 400 kilometres. Von Braun's team developed a new launcher, the Atlas rocket, inaugurated in December 1957.

*T*he greatest adventure of modern times began in October 1957. In retrospect, Sputnik 1 can be regarded as the herald of a new age. From the moment it was launched, electronics and the search for new materials became the all-important factors in the race for space. Considering the place that those technologies now occupy in our everyday lives, we may well conclude that the conquest of space determined the development of Western society.

The Atlas rocket

The Americans' slow start in the construction of rocket launchers explains Soviet supremacy in the field. Not until the Atlas rocket was perfected in 1962 could the United States send payloads heavier than one tonne into orbit. A monkey called Goliath perished on 10 November 1961 when an unstable Atlas rocket self-destructed. Another, named Skatback, had better luck, and a third, Enos, made three orbits around the Earth three months before John Glenn performed the same exploit.

On 12 April 1961 Yuri Gagarin, the first man in space, completed a full orbit of the Earth at an altitude of 327 kilometres.

Beep-beep Beep-beep

On 4 October 1957 the world learned that the USSR had just launched the first artificial satellite. The Moon was no longer the only body to orbit the Earth, and since that day it has never been alone. The reaction was one of amazement. The technical implications of the achievement were immense. Who would have dared imagine that the Soviet Union could take the lead in the race for space? Yet at an altitude that varied from 229 to 946 kilometres, and at a speed of 28,800 kilometres per hour, Sputnik 1 took just 92.6 minutes to orbit the Earth. Although the 'fellow traveller' (for that is what Sputnik means in Russian) did not weigh very much (83.460 kilogram, with a diameter of fifty-eight centimetres), it weighed heavily in the balance of history.

American scientists had been foiled in their attempt to be first in space. Only a few months earlier they had made an unsuccessful launch. Sputnik 1 proved to the world that the USSR had acquired an unexpected advantage in rocket technology, which enabled them to build engines capable of reaching any spot on the globe.

The man behind this exploit, as the West was later to learn, was Sergei Pavlovitch Korolev, the 'great draughtsman', who had been working since 1930 on the design of space launchers. In 1933 he ignited the first Soviet liquid-fuelled rocket. In 1945 he launched an A-4 missile, recovered from von Braun's factory in Peenemünde, to an altitude of 300 kilometres.

One month after Sputnik 1, the Soviets launched Sputnik 2; aboard was the first living creature to reach outer space, a dog named Laika.

Early American successes

Although the Soviets held an undeniable advantage after the launchings of Sputnik 1 and 2, the Americans overcame their momentary discouragement and resolved to take up the challenge. On 31 January 1958 the Jupiter-C rocket, launched from Cape Canaveral in Florida, put into orbit Explorer 1, a satellite that weighed just eight kilos. NASA (the National Aeronautics and Space Administration), created on 29 July 1958, chose from the start to regard the conquest of space as a purely utilitarian matter. The first satellites were scientific devices, crammed with electronic equipment. Explorer 6 (41 kilos), sent into orbit on 7 August 1959, transmitted the first pictures of Earth seen from space. Tiros 1 (128 kilos), launched on 1 April 1960, was the first meteorological satellite put into orbit. Gradually, as one successful launch followed another, the United States proved its superiority in high technology.

A programme of manned space flights was initiated on 26 December 1958. Recruitment of future astronauts began in January 1959, and in April seven fighter pilots—Scott Carpenter, Gordon Cooper, John Glenn, Virgil I. Grissom, Walter Schirra, Alan B. Shepard, and Donald Slayton—made up NASA's first crew. The Mercury programme was officially off the ground. Yet a launcher had not yet been designed, nor had a space capsule been constructed that could successfully carry a man into space and bring him back to Earth.

Getting ready

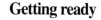

The immediate goal of the first satellite launchings was of course to send a man into space as soon as possible. On 15 May 1960

the Soviets sent Sputnik 4 into orbit. It weighed 4.5 tonnes and included a 2.5-tonne pressurized cabin in which a life-size dummy had been placed. Because of an error in the calculation of the trajectory, the satellite bounced back off the upper atmosphere instead of re-entering it and orbited the Earth for five months before burning up. On 19 August Sputnik 5 was launched with a dummy, some plants, and two dogs named Bielka and Strelka. After eighteen revolutions around the Earth, the satellite returned safe and sound. But on 10 December Sputnik 6 encountered problems upon re-entry, and the capsule was lost along with its canine passengers.

On their side the Americans were putting the finishing touches to the Mercury capsule. The need to build it in a hurry forced the designers to make the vehicle simple and light. In fact it weighed just 1 360 kilos, making Mercury the smallest space capsule ever built. Monkeys were used to test the craft, and the first, Sam, made a ballistic flight of 150 kilometres on 4 December 1960, propelled by a Redstone rocket. On 31 January 1961 his colleague Ham reached an altitude of 250 kilometres. By this time, both sides were ready. The Soviet rocket was much larger than its US counterpart: Vostok 1 weighed 4 500 kilos, three times more than Mercury. On 25 March 1961 both the Soviets and the Americans made a final test. The Americans wished to make it the actual launch date, but von Braun insisted that the flight be regarded as a test.

The first man in space

The announcement of this test did not have the same impact as the flight of Sputnik 1. Repeated test flights on both sides made it obvious that the 'real' flight was imminent. On 12 April 1961 at 6 am GMT, an official Soviet communiqué announced to the world that Colonel Yuri Gagarin, aboard the spacecraft Vostok, had just been launched into an elliptical orbit around the Earth. For safety reasons, the flight, which had been scheduled to make six complete revolutions, was shortened to just one. The low trajectory was calculated to allow the craft to re-enter the atmosphere unaided in a few days, if the retrorockets were to fail. When he landed, after a flight of 108 minutes, Gagarin refused to eject, as Sergei Pavlovitch Korolev had advised him, fearing that the impact would be too violent.

Born on 9 March 1934, Yuri Gagarin was a carpenter's son. As a boy during World War II, he decided to become a pilot. In 1955 he began pilot training school, and later entered the airforce. On 12 April 1961 Gagarin earned his place in history as the first man in space. The psychological impact of the exploit, which came off without a hitch, resounded all over the world.

Wherever Gagarin went—Britain, India, Japan, the United States, France—he received a hero's welcome. The cosmonaut died at the age of 34 on 27 March 1968, in an aeroplane accident. He is buried in the Kremlin beside Sergei Korolev, who died two years later.

The challenge

The United States felt the urgency of meeting the Soviet challenge. John F. Kennedy had just been inaugurated as president, on 20 January 1961. After the shock of the Soviet triumph on 12 April, exacerbated by the American fiasco at the Bay of Pigs in Cuba five days later, Kennedy called his principal advisers together to find a way to beat the Soviets to the Moon. How could it be done? What resources would be needed?

On 5 May Alan B. Shepard reached an altitude of 186 kilometres during a ballistic flight of 15 minutes and 22 seconds aboard a Mercury capsule propelled by a Redstone rocket. It was not an exploit to compare with Gagarin's orbit of the Earth, but one aspect of the flight made it technically very interesting. In the Mercury capsule the passenger actually piloted the craft, while in the Vostok the controls were all automatic. Shepard was thus the first 'active' man in space. After considering the report submitted by his advisers, President Kennedy made an historic speech before Congress on 25 May 1961 in which he stated this challenge: 'Our nation must resolve to put a man on the Moon, and to bring him back safely to Earth before the end of this decade.' That day marked a drastic change in the organization of NASA. On 21 July Virgil Grissom repeated Shepard's exploit. Then on 20 February 1962, once the reliability of the Atlas rocket was beyond doubt, the United States sent their first astronaut, John Glenn, into space; he made three orbits around the Earth in a mission that lasted 4 hours and 55 minutes.

The Soviet Vostok programme involved six expeditions in space. Yuri Gagarin was aboard Vostok 1 and Valentina Tereshkova on Vostok 6, the last in the series.

he 1960s were surely the golden age of space exploration. Virtually every month brought a harvest of new results and discoveries. The backdrop to all this feverish activity was the prospect of a lunar mission. These years of intense effort culminated in the most exciting adventure of all: man's landing on the Moon.

Automatic vehicles

Reaching the Moon was the ultimate objective, and it was clear that information gathered by observing the Moon from Earth would be insufficient to prepare for a landing. For this reason exploratory satellites were sent to relay data on the Earth's natural satellite.

Inability to reach or maintain sufficient velocity was responsible for the destruction of three Pioneer satellites launched by the Americans in January 1959. The Russians responded with Luna 1, which had no trouble attaining the required speed but which missed the Moon by 6000 kilometres; it thus became the Sun's first artificial satellite. On 12 September Luna 2 crash-landed on the Moon at the edge of the Jupiter crater. On 4 October, the anniversary of the Sputnik 1 launch, Luna 3 headed for the dark side of the Moon, from which it transmitted photographic images back to Earth. In 1964 and 1965 Rangers 7, 8 and 9 sent back some 17,200 photographs. And finally on 4 February 1966, Luna 9 made a perfect landing on the Moon and transmitted pictures taken from the lunar surface. Luna 10, 11 and 12, launched respectively on 31 March, 24 August and 22 October 1966, slipped easily into orbit around the Moon.

On the American side, Surveyor 1 landed on 30 May 1966 with no difficulty, and a series of Pioneer-Orbiter and Lunar-Orbiter satellites tested various orbit patterns from less than one hundred kilometres from the Moon's surface. The five Lunar-Orbiter missions launched from 10 August 1966 to 1 August 1967 would allow NASA to choose the best sites for a lunar landing.

The tragedy of Apollo 1

The first Apollo mission, scheduled for 21 February 1967, was to be flown by Virgil ('Gus') Grissom and Edward H. White, both experienced astronauts, and novice astronaut Roger B. Chaffee. On 27 January a run-through of the final countdown was scheduled, and the capsule was hoisted onto the Saturn I-B rocket. The astronauts took their places at 1 pm, but upon entering the capsule Grissom detected a strange smell. After a thorough check, everything seemed in order. The procedure continued. But on that particular day nothing went off as planned: the pressurization of the capsule took longer than usual; radio links proved to be defective. The countdown was interrupted again. Suddenly the biological sensors placed on White's body registered an abrupt acceleration of his heartbeat. Ten seconds later—it was 6.31 pm—came the shout: 'Fire!' The capsule was an inferno. The flames were fed by the concentrated oxygen in the cabin. In moments the temperature reached 2500 ºC; thirteen seconds later, it was all over. The fire subsided; the three men were burnt beyond recognition.

In April of the same year, the spacecraft Soyuz 1 was also to meet a tragic fate, with Vladimir Komarov, the oldest of the Soviet cosmonauts, aboard. Sent on what was probably intended to be a long mission, the capsule had stability problems from the moment it was sent into orbit. The authorities resolved to bring the craft back immediately, but the parachute recovery system apparently failed and the capsule crashed to Earth.

The triumph of Apollo 8

The American strategy for winning the race to the Moon was based on a spacecraft composed of three modules: the service module, containing the supplies needed by the crew, the command module or Apollo capsule, and the lunar module, bolted to the nose cone of the capsule. Since construction of the lunar module had been delayed, Apollo 8 was unfinished, yet it was nonetheless expected to carry out the difficult mission of taking the first manned capsule into lunar orbit. The mission began on 21 December 1968. A Saturn V launch vehicle was to send the Apollo spacecraft 400,000 kilometres from the Earth. After completing one orbit around the Earth, the engines of the third module were fired and it went onto a translunar trajectory at a speed of 39,000 kilometres per hour. On 24 December the spacecraft entered a circular orbit around the Moon; the radius of the orbit was 112 kilometres.

On that Christmas Eve of 1968 Frank Borman, James Lowell and William Anders completed ten orbits around the Moon. It was the first time in human history that men had lived in the gravitational field of a celestial body other than the Earth. And then with a low rumbling sound, the craft's service motor ignited. With a thrust that lasted less than three and a half minutes, Apollo 8 headed back to Earth.

The complete success of Apollo 8 dashed Soviet hopes to be first on the Moon.

21 July 1969

With the exception of the Chinese, then in the throes of the Cultural Revolution, on 21 July 1969 everyone was glued to a television set. In Great Britain, despite the late hour, everyone heard the latest bulletins from Houston predicting that Neil Armstrong would step onto the lunar surface at 2 am. It was a supremely historic moment. The flight of Apollo 11 had gone off without a hitch. Yet just as the spacecraft was about to land on the Moon, irregularities in the terrain forced the lunar module *Eagle* to hover for a few seconds, in order to locate a

Mascons

Irregularities in lunar gravity were observed when the first satellites were placed in orbit around the Moon. It was a disturbing discovery. Further study revealed that at certain points on the lunar surface meteorites called 'mascons' (short for 'mass concentration') had so much matter that they had a stronger power of attraction than the rest of the Moon. This phenomenon explained why it was so difficult for spacecraft to maintain regular orbits around the Moon.

favourable landing site, while every light on the instrument panel signalled that fuel was dangerously low and that the astronauts should take off again without landing. In their tiny cabin the pilots followed point by point the 184 pages of instructions they had been given. At last, at 2 am GMT the door of the *Eagle* opened. It took Neil Armstrong another half hour to extricate himself from the module, arrange on the platform the tools he would use on the Moon, and set out the camera that would record man's very first Moonwalk. He finally started down the ladder, and the dazzling white mass of the Moon appeared on television screens. A few centimetres, a few seconds later: 'That's one small step for a man, a giant leap for mankind.'

Lunar missions

American lunar missions came to an end in December 1972 with Apollo 17. Only Apollo 13 failed to achieve its objective. Damaged by an explosion, it was brought back to Earth, its crew safe and sound, thanks to an ingenious salvage procedure. In 1969 very little was known about the Moon. Today, though its origins remain a mystery, the Moon's age, the composition of its soil, and its geological evolution are becoming clearer. Not all of the scientific data accumulated by the instruments put into place during six Apollo missions have been completely analysed. Of the 365 kilos of rocks gathered, only a quarter has been examined by scientists. The remainder awaits improved techniques for analysis, which will doubtless be developed before long. Seismographic results are still kept for processing at a later date. But it is already known that the lunar surface 'shivers' as a result of tides on Earth, and that at the Moon's centre a core with a radius of 700 kilometres has a temperature of 1500 °C. Scientists are now also familiar with the hidden face of the Moon, on which the Earth exerts but little influence. The range of different types of rock is much smaller on the Moon than on Earth. Mechanical and chemical erosion do not occur, so the Moon's geological history is much simpler than ours. After a long active phase, volcanic activity seems to have stopped on the Moon some three billion years ago. And finally, as samples prove, the Moon is at least 4.4 billion years old, more likely 4.6 billion years, like the Earth itself. These calculations provide one more clue to the age of the solar system, which only fifty years ago was known only by conjecture.

The end of Apollo

After the exploration of the Moon, many ideas for the continuation of the Apollo programme were put forward. But the tightening of federal budgets put an end to these dreams, and only the Skylab project was developed. The third stage of one of the four remaining Atlas rockets was transformed into an immense space laboratory, thirty-nine metres long and weighing some ninety tonnes. Launched on 14 March 1973, Skylab was immediately plagued with problems. A solar panel was ripped off as the vehicle left the atmosphere, and another was damaged. A repair crew was sent out, and after four weeks of strenuous efforts the space station was functional once more. In July the first scientific team moved into Skylab. But the astronauts had to deal with problems that had plagued Apollo capsules, for two of the motors were leaking oil.

The final mission lasted twelve weeks, from 16 November 1973 to 8 February 1974, and gave astronauts an opportunity to work with the many instruments Skylab had transported into space. Thanks to the ATM telescope, they were able to observe the Sun, the comet Kohoutek and numerous stars. The astronauts carried out teledetection observations of Earth, performed medical experiments, and produced various industrial materials under conditions of zero gravity. Skylab was never again employed; the space station crashed prematurely into the Indian Ocean on 11 July 1979 after 39,980 orbits.

The final Apollo mission featured an international space rendezvous with Soyuz 19 on 17 July 1975. Soviet cosmonauts Leonov and Kubassov welcomed American astronauts Slayton and Stafford into their capsule, while Brand piloted the link-up from the Apollo spacecraft.

The Soviet programme

Although they were forced to abandon the goal of putting the first men on the Moon, from 1968 the Soviets devoted their energies to two other programmes: the development of remote-controlled vehicles and the construction of a permanently manned orbiting space station. On 20 September 1968 Luna 16 soft-landed in the Sea of Fertility, where it gathered one hundred grams of soil from the Moon's surface and brought the core sample back to Earth. Two months later, Luna 17 landed Lunokhod, a lunar vehicle operated from Earth by remote control. Over eleven months the ve-

Gravity on the Moon is one sixth of that on Earth. Armstrong and Aldrin moved about its surface by giant bounds when they landed there in 1969.

hicle covered 10.5 kilometres and took some twenty thousand pictures. In February 1972 Luna 20 repeated the Luna 16 mission on bumpy terrain, confirming that it was possible to send these vehicles to explore the most inhospitable planets. Lunokhod 2 was set in place in January 1973. This series of lunar missions came to a close in August 1976 with Luna 24, which took rock samples from two metres below the Moon's surface.

Salyut 1, the first orbiting space station, was launched on 19 April 1971. In June the three Soviet cosmonauts Dobrovolski, Patsaiev and Volkov, taken to the station by Soyuz 11, spent 569 hours there, but a technical malfunction of the door seal occurred as the cosmonauts were returning to Earth, causing their cabin suddenly to lose pressure. All three died.

The first permanent space station, Salyut 6, launched on 29 September 1977, set several duration records. Salyut 7, put into orbit on 19 April 1981, was visited by Svetlana Savitskaya, the second woman in space, in August 1982. Berezovoi and Lebedev spent 211 days in the space station. Since then, Mir, an advanced orbiting facility, has made long missions in space relatively commonplace.

Two and a half years on the Moon

Apollo 12, launched on 12 November 1969, landed on the Moon's Sea of Storms, a few hundred metres from the spot where the space probe Surveyor 3 had landed two and a half years earlier. The astronauts brought back with them the probe's camera and digging arm. Scientists subsequently discovered on the camera certain terrestrial microorganisms which had survived in the lunar environment.

oday even the most modest work on astronomy is illustrated with magnificent photographs of Saturn, Jupiter and their moons. We owe this archive of astonishingly detailed pictures to the most ambitious interplanetary adventure of all time: the missions of interplanetary space probes, particularly the two Voyager probes. Before these explorations, next to nothing was known about the giant planets of the outer solar system.

Amazing Miranda

Uranus's moon Miranda is one of the most surprising bodies in the solar system. Geologists expected Voyager to find desolate terrain covered with impact craters, but instead the pictures showed deep scars, canyons, and valleys sixteen kilometres deep, mountains that soar to a height of twenty-four kilometres, basins, and curious chevron patterns that have yet to be explained. Such a variety of violent geological activity continues to baffle scientists.

The inferno of Venus

Hidden under a thick layer of sulphuric clouds, the surface of Venus had long remained a mystery for astronomers. Some scientists even imagined that Venus resembled Earth in its prehistoric period, covered with hot, humid jungles and inhabited by dinosaurs. On 14 December 1962 the American probe Mariner 2 got within 35,000 kilometres of Venus, and detected a very high surface temperature. But the systematic exploration of Venus did not begin in earnest until 1967. In October of that year two space vehicles were launched: Venera 4, a Soviet probe, and the US Mariner 5. Venera 4 released a capsule into the Venusian atmosphere. It established that the atmosphere was largely composed of carbon dioxide (more than 36 percent) and nitrogen (about 3.5 percent) and exerted a much higher pressure than Earth's atmosphere—indeed, the pressure was so great that the space probe was crushed. Venera 7, built of stronger materials, made a successful landing on 15 December 1970. Measurements revealed that the surface pressure is one hundred times greater than that of Earth. The surface temperature of 475 °C was high enough to heat rocks red-hot.

In February 1974 Mariner 10 swung past Venus en route to Mars and confirmed that its cloud cover was composed of droplets of concentrated sulphuric acid. The first photographs of the surface transmitted by Venera 9 and 10 in October 1975 showed rough terrain with sharp-edged basaltic rocks. In 1978 and 1979 Pioneer-Venus 1 and 2 produced the first accurate maps of the surface, locating the contours of the terrain, impact craters, and a giant, active volcano. They also detected a series of very rapid flashes.

Venus is one of the three planets in the solor system known to be subject to active volcanism.

Mercury

Exploration of Mercury by the Mariner 10 space probe in 1974 offered no surprising revelations. The planet is indeed as scientists had imagined it—with virtually no atmosphere and a surface comparable to that of the Moon, pitted with craters from innumerable meteorites. The only feature breaking this monotony is the Caloris Basin, a low-lying plain 1400 kilometres long.

Mariner's photographs allowed scientists to complete the map of Mercury, and the data transmitted by the space probe confirmed information obtained by radar. For a long time astronomers had believed that Mercury completed a rotation on its axis in eighty-eight Earth days, the time it took to revolve around the Sun. But closer observation revealed that the planet rotated in fifty-nine days, two-thirds of its orbital time. Thus on Mercury the time span from sunrise to sunset is in fact 176 Earth days, during which time the planet turns three times around the Sun and three times on its axis.

Looking for Martians

Ever since Giovanni Schiaparelli from his Milan observatory noted in 1877 the existence of numerous canals on Mars, which the public immediately assumed were irrigation canals, the notion that Mars was inhabited took root in the popular imagination. But alas, Mariner 4, launched on 28 November 1964, transmitted twenty-one pictures of the planet that showed neither canals, nor signs of intelligent life, nor water—just a surface discouragingly similar to that of the Moon. In May 1971 the Soviets, who already had three fruitless

attempts to their credit in 1960 and 1962, sent Mars 2 and 3 into orbit. By the end of the month the Americans had launched Mariner 9. Mars 2 and 3 released capsules which made successful landings but were immediately destroyed by the violent dust storms then raging over the surface of Mars. The Soviets then decided to put a halt, temporarily, to their exploration of Mars. In the meantime, the American probe Mariner 9, then in orbit around Mars, transmitted pictures taken by television camera, revealing the impressive volcano called Olympus, twenty-seven kilometres high, and obvious traces of fluvial erosion, which proved that water had once flowed on Mars.

In 1975 Viking 1 was launched with a precise mission: to land on Mars and to determine whether or not life existed or had ever existed there. The probe's equivocal answer was 'Yes and No'. Yet a close analysis of the results led scientists to think that the various reactions observed were purely chemical, not biological. Doubts on the subject have yet to be definitively dispelled!

Mars will surely be the next step in humanity's conquest of the solar system. It is now a certainty that the Soviets are actively preparing a manned flight to the red planet. Long-duration flights in the Mir space station are believed to be preliminary steps to a longer mission, which is expected to last at least four years.

The amazing adventure of Voyager 2

The idea of sending a spacecraft to explore the far reaches of the solar system took shape in the 1960s. To reduce costs, NASA scientists devised a plan for a long-term mission flown by two probes, which would use each planet's gravity to speed them onwards to the following stage of their trajectory.

The great adventure began on 20 August 1977 with the launching of Voyager 2, followed on 5 September by Voyager 1. The latter travelled faster and was scheduled to reach Jupiter first. But Voyager 2 was destined to make the grand tour out to Uranus and Neptune, which it reached in 1989. The voyage was not trouble-free. Indeed, throughout their missions, the two probes suffered numerous breakdowns, obliging the scientists and engineers at Pasadena's Jet Propulsion Laboratory to accomplish unprecedented technological feats to keep them in operation. On 23 February 1978 the scan platform of Voyager 1 got stuck. On 5 April the radio receiver of Voyager 2 died. After a week of frantic efforts, contact was re-established; engineers made hasty repairs, which they later consolidated, exploiting technological advances made after the launch of the Voyager mission. On 25 August 1981, after Voyager 2 had made a spectacular crossing of Saturn's rings, its scan platform froze up and stuck. Scientists decided to wait to make repairs, for the probe was already en route to Uranus.

The gaseous giants

Voyager 1 made a systematic survey of Jupiter, beginning on 6 January 1979. On 1 March the probe was 4.8 million kilometres from the giant planet and began its observation of Jupiter's moons. Four days later Voyager made its closest approach to Jupiter: 780,000 kilometres. On 7 March the existence of a gaseous ring around the planet was detected and confirmed. Two days after that, geologists studying pictures of the moon Io discovered eight active volcanoes. At last it was ascertained that Jupiter's Great Red Spot is a violent windstorm three times larger than Earth. On 9 July Voyager 2 made its approach to Jupiter and observed other Jovian moons: Ganymede; Europa, with its astonishing surface, smooth as a billiard ball; and tiny Amalthea. As Voyager 2 continued on its course, it discovered three still smaller moons. In October 1980 Voyager 1 was 50 million kilometres from Saturn; Voyager 2 began to transmit data on Saturn from 5 June 1981. The planet's famous rings were at last examined at close range, and were even crossed by Voyager. The scientists at the Jet Propulsion Laboratory were astounded by the number (about a thousand) and structure of the rings, composed of icy particles ranging in diameter from microns to kilometres. Observation of Saturn's largest Moon, Titan, studied from a distance of 4000 kilometres, revealed the existence of organic molecules in slow activ-

Colour images of Mars obtained by American probes have revealed the presence of numerous meteoric impact craters.

ity in that environment of frozen methane.

Voyager 1 then flew away from Saturn, its mission completed, or nearly so—for the probe would carry into interstellar space a message for any intelligent extraterrestrial civilization that might discover it. Voyager 2 travelled away from Saturn on 25 August 1981 after soaring past the planet at a distance of 100,000 kilometres, to regain speed for its trip out to Uranus.

The outer limits of the solar system

On 24 January 1986, 3.2 billion kilometres from Earth, at the appointed hour, Voyager 2 came within 29,000 kilometres of Miranda, the smallest moon of Uranus. Ever since its discovery in 1781 by William Herschel, the planet Uranus has intrigued astronomers. Because it is so far from Earth, little was known of it, except that it rotated on an axis tilted towards the Sun; five of its moons had been discovered. Voyager 2 relayed a veritable avalanche of infor-

mation concerning its previously unknown magnetic field, ten additional satellites, a surface temperature that remained stable day and night (a period which on Uranus lasts for forty-two Earth years), and an atmosphere rich in hydrogen, which revolves more slowly at the planet's equator than at its poles. Moreover, Uranus did indeed possess the ten rings spotted from Earth by French astronomer André Brahic in 1977. The harvest of data would keep astronomers busy for several years.

After a three-year journey to the outer limits of the solar system, on 25 August 1989 Voyager 2 reached the planet currently farthest from the Sun: Neptune. The first data transmitted to Earth seemed to show that Neptune was a world still in formation, a desolate planet swept by ceaseless, violent winds. At such an enormous distance from the Sun, the planet's formation will doubtless continue for a very long time. On Triton, the largest of Neptune's moons, there are erupting ice volcanoes, an indication of considerable internal activity. Were the temperature of Triton not so low (−200 °C), life could conceivably exist there, for the other conditions are favourable.

The exploration goes on

Two projects are currently under way to continue the exploration of the solar system. Galileo, launched on 18 October 1989, will drop a probe by parachute into Jupiter's atmosphere. Ulysses, launched a year later, was sent on a remarkable mission to explore the poles of the Sun in order to enlarge our understanding of how a star functions and how the Sun influences our own planet.

279

INDEX

Design

Isabelle Martin, Stéphane Danilowiez and Judith Chahine

Picture Research

Colombe de Meurin

Picture credits

Bibliothèque Nationale: 133; Bridgeman Art Library Ltd: 21, 71, 88, 111, 125, 130, 134, 146, 148, 154, 160, 162, 163, 189, 195, 215, 217, 235, 241, 243. Citroën: 221. Dagli Orti: 12, 15, 17, 19, 29, 39, 44, 47, 48, 49, 52, 53, 54, 55, 56, 57, 60, 61, 65, 66, 67, 68, 69, 72, 73, 74, 75, 77, 79, 81, 83, 84, 85, 87, 89, 91, 93, 94, 95, 97, 98, 102, 103, 104, 105, 112, 113, 121, 122, 123, 135, 138, 139, 140, 143, 144, 147, 159, 161, 164, 165, 166, 167, 169, 174, 175, 177, 178, 179, 181 183, 186, 188, 192, 196, 202, 203, 206, 207, 209, 210, 211, 212, 213, 218 226, 227, 228, 229, 231, 233, 248, 254, 260, 264, 265. Dorka: 25, 28, 32, 34, 38 42, 43, 62, 64, 76, 78, 80, 86, 90, 92, 96, 100, 109, 110, 113, 116, 117, 118, 119, 120, 124, 127, 129, 155, 156, 157, 172, 173, 180, 184, 204, 214, 216, 219, 224, 225, 230, 232, 240. D.R.: 11, 23, 51, 99, 107, 137, 171, 201, 220, 223, 245, 246, 247, 269, 271, 272, 273. Édimages: 149 (Jourdes). Explorer: 132, 255; 150, 151, 190 191, 197, 198, 199, 256, 257 (Charmet); 194 (Devaux); 267 (Krafft); 249, 258 (Mary Evans Picture Library). Finley-Holyday Films: 277, 279. Fondation Alexandra David-Néel: 187. Gamma: 14 (Maklakis); 193 (Novosti). Gamma-Sport: 252 (Boivin); 250 (Buu); 251 (Desjardin); 253 (Profit). Ifremer: 259. Jacana: 205 (Varin). Josse Hubert: 20, 24, 26, 27, 30, 31, 33, 35, 36, 37, 45, 46, 59, 63, 82, 115, 126, 128, 131, 141, 142, 145, 153, 182, 185, 237, 238. Kon-Tiki Muséum: 16 (Mittet). Magnum: 13, 18 (Lessing). Musée de l'Homme: 101 (Arhex). Nasjonalgalleriet/Oslo: 108. Roger-Viollet: 234, 239, 242. Sygma: 263; 262 (IFS); 261 (Vauthey). Agence Tass: 274, 275.

Maps

Béatrice Couderc